ARCHAEOLOGICAL INSTITUTE OF AMERICA
Monographs New Series, Number 4

EXTERNAL RELATIONS OF EARLY IRON AGE CRETE, 1100–600 B.C.

Donald W. Jones

ARCHAEOLOGICAL INSTITUTE OF AMERICA
Monographs New Series, Number 4

EXTERNAL RELATIONS OF EARLY IRON AGE CRETE, 1100–600 B.C.

Donald W. Jones

Published for
Archaeological Institute of America
Boston, MA, 2000

by
THE UNIVERSITY MUSEUM
University of Pennsylvania
Philadelphia, PA, 2000

KENDALL/HUNT PUBLISHING COMPANY
4050 Westmark Drive   Dubuque, Iowa 52002

Design and production
University Museum Publications
University of Pennsylvania of Archaeology and Anthropology
Philadelphia, PA

CONTENTS

LIST OF ILLUSTRATIONS

MAPS

TABLES

PREFACE

The centerpiece of this study is a catalogue of foreign artifacts found at thirty-three sites in Crete and Cretan artifacts found at overseas sites. How these artifacts should be interpreted requires studied consideration, however, and I attempt to review the possibilities thoroughly. I offer a short guide to my argumentation to help the reader maintain orientation and stamina. The first chapter, "Scope and Method," lays out my interpretation of the problem: What tangible evidence of foreign influences exists? I introduce the current concerns about the selective character of the artifactual remains and the degrees of freedom that selectivity gives to interpretations of the artifacts' methods of transportation. The second chapter, "Summary of Foreign Artifacts Found in Crete," identifies the Cretan sites and summarizes the artifacts from the catalogue.

The third chapter, "Elements in, and Mechanisms for, Transmitting External Influences in Dark Age Greece," examines the possible roles that foreign commercial intercourse—trade—might have played in transporting the foreign artifacts from this period. There are substantial differences of opinion regarding the existence, character, volume, and role of foreign trade in the Greek Dark Age. Any interpretation of foreign artifacts in Crete, or of Cretan artifacts found overseas, must address these ideas. The first section considers the archaeological evidence for the suitability of shipping during this period. Suitable shipping probably existed. The following section considers the same questions for harbors and finds mixed

archaeological evidence for harbors; but extensive harbor installations may not have been necessary for much of the shipping. Next, piracy must be assessed: Could it have been such a pestilence as to have reduced international shipping to a trickle, then turning to land targets? Piracy is an intricate predator-prey problem, and although its seriousness is not in doubt, neither is its long-run dependence on shipping. The next section reviews evidence for foreign trade in the eastern Mediterranean and the Aegean during the Late Bronze Age. The purpose of this turn to the Bronze Age is to establish a rough beginning point of a trajectory for which later evidence is scanty at best; around the eighth to seventh century, evidence on trade becomes more abundant, if not crystal clear. Some understanding of what was happening around the beginning and terminal points of the Dark Age may help interpret the scant evidence between those points. This section also collects and reviews the hypotheses of prominent scholars, both archaeologists and ancient historians, regarding trade during parts or the whole of the Dark Age. Having introduced foreign trade explicitly as a possible primary mechanism for transporting the artifacts found, I turn in the next section, "Further Evidence on Characteristics of Dark Age Trade," to literary and archaeological evidence for specific characteristics of overseas shipping during the Dark Age. In some instances, I have relied on post-Dark Age literary and historical evidence, which there is reason to believe may also apply to earlier periods. The following section considers personal travel as a mechanism for transporting artifacts, primarily itinerant craftsmen's movements and religious travel. The physical and social conditions surrounding personal travel during the period restrict its scope as a transportation mechanism for archaeological remains.

The fourth chapter, "Analysis of Crete's External Relations in the Early Iron Age," presents the catalogue material from the various sites on Crete as well as overseas. After a series of sections reporting material from the sites, four sections synthesize the material bearing on Cretan relations with mainland Greece, mainly Attica and Corinth; with Cyprus; with the elusive Phoenicians; and with the peoples to the West. The section on Cretan-Phoenician relations brings in the mainland Asian background of Phoenician activities—Assyria, Neo-Hittite North Syria, and Egypt—on the rationale that events affecting potential Cretan trading partners must affect Cretan trade. It is difficult to tie the events in these areas tightly to the Cretan archaeological evidence, but review of events in these areas identifies major parameters of the eastern orientation of Crete's external relations: Who was, or could have been, prosperous at what times, and who was preoccupied with warfare? The final section addresses the natural question of how important commercial intercourse might have been in the Greek Dark Age, particularly to Crete.

The final chapter, "Taking Stock," reviews the Cretan evidence in light of the sections that examined the limits of interpretation of evidence from the Dark Age. Crete's external contacts are early, diverse, and continuous throughout the Dark Age. The relative scarcity of Cretan artifacts found at overseas sites points more to a prosperous Cretan agricultural trade and to its role as a stopover on shipping routes than to any imbalance of material flows.

I include three textual appendices. The first appendix discusses measures of agricultural risk and illustrates the possibilities for comparative production advantages of Crete and several other regions of Greece with twentieth century A.C. data. The second explores the possible magnitudes of effects on an economy like that of Dark Age Crete initiated by various changes in external economic relations, as well as by several changes in domestic economic circumstances. The third contains the catalogue of artifacts.

At this point, I would like to acknowledge my debts to Geraldine Gesell and David Tandy of the Department of Classics at the University of Tennessee for reading earlier drafts of this study, and for their advice and assistance at various points. I also owe debts of gratitude for reading and commenting on portions of earlier drafts of the study, for information supplied, for field demonstrations, and in general for encouragement to John Boardman, William Coulson, Leslie Day, Gail Hoffman, Hartmut Matthäus, Robert Merrillees, Ian Morris, Iannis Sakellarakis, Joseph Shaw, Anthony Snodgrass, Elizabeth Lyding Will, and the reviewers for the Monograph Series. The indexing was provided by the Archaeological Institute of America. I thank Sherry Wert for her excellent editing of the manuscript. I cheerfully accept full responsibility for all shortcomings of the work.

Donald W. Jones
Department of Classics
University of Tennessee-Knoxville
and
Energy Division
Oak Ridge National Laboratory
Summer 1999

I

SCOPE AND METHOD

Considerations of the external relations of Early Iron Age Crete, as well as of other prehistoric Greek communities, have focused predominately on cultural diffusion, the transmission of artistic ideas and styles, technological know-how, language, religious ideas, etc. We want to know what groups of people influenced which other groups of people, and in the absence of literary evidence (and sometimes in the presence of it as well), we must rely on the existence of apparently exotic artifacts in datable contexts for information on one group's activity and influence in another group's territory. Even obviously locally made artifacts may betray some kind of foreign influence in their shapes and decorations. Because of the scarcity and muteness of the evidence, the ways in which these foreign influences were felt, even the ways in which the foreign-made artifacts reached their final resting places, are difficult to assess.[1] Often there are several different stories consistent with the physical evidence that can explain how an artifact ended up in the place where it was found. Indeed, frequently there are more reasonable stories than there are stories that the evidence rejects outright. Consequently, a certain vagueness often remains about "transmission."

One specific transmission mechanism that has been suggested in several instances is population movement, often of refugees from the political turmoil of the Early Iron Age in the eastern Mediterranean, sometimes in the context of adventurous or religious travel. The other major category of transmission mechanism in problems of external relations is movement of physical goods. For Early Iron Age Crete, I have assembled some eight hundred published artifacts that fit this latter category. These goods raise two major related questions of interpretation, however. First, how did they get to their excavation locations–via trade, personal travel, gift exchange, or some other means? Second, are they the indestructible tip of an otherwise vanished iceberg of foreign goods? Varieties of affirmative answers to the second question, indicating the existence of foreign goods now lost, probably will involve trade of some kind, but they will also raise further questions, such as what might have been the composition of such lost goods and what were the characteristics of the exchanges that brought them; they also, despite stressing trade, still will leave questions about other transportation mechanisms, such as migration and gift exchange, under the first question. A negative answer to the second question would largely terminate efforts in that direction, but it also would leave a considerable range of issues for examination under the first question, about how the goods moved.

Artistic influences as evidence of external relations—for example, the relations between the Nimrud ivories and ivories from the Idaean Cave, and Urartian or North Syrian influences in the Idaean shields—have been discussed widely and thoroughly, but certainly not finally. The questions I ask of the foreign artifacts I report

---

[1] Sherratt and Sherratt 1991:351: "The facts do not speak for themselves."

take me more into matters of social organization; on the one hand, there is even less artifactual evidence for these, but on the other hand, theories and some literary evidence are available to a limited extent. A number of the theories to which I refer are essentially stories about how different social institutions operated in Dark Age Greece. Others are simple economic models that I think fit the circumstances of that period. My strategy for addressing the two questions identified in the previous paragraph is to search for evidence that would bear on the possibility of trade during the Dark Ages, but not with exclusive reference to Crete. This examination brings up for comparison other competing and complementary mechanisms for getting foreign objects into Dark Age Greek communities. I examine evidence on ships, harbors, and piracy in the Dark Age because they are important components of trade, then turn direct attention to evidence on, and stories about, Dark Age trade itself. I subsequently address other transmission mechanisms, including individual travel for various reasons, population movement, and gift exchange. The goal of this examination is to develop justifiable interpretations of the Cretan artifacts.

I begin by introducing the array of artifacts reflecting Crete's external relations during the Early Iron Age. I discuss the organization of the catalogues and the tables summarizing them and offer a brief, descriptive overview: spatial-temporal patterns of sources of foreign objects and of overseas locations of Cretan products, types of artifact, salient differences at different Cretan sites. I then present the more general discussion described in the previous paragraph. Thereafter, equipped with as much circumspection as the general evidence on trade and other sources of product movement can offer, I return to a more detailed examination of the corpus of the Cretan artifacts.

The artifactual remains of foreign contact are predominantly painted pottery, whole or sherds, and metal objects, often artistic rather than utilitarian. Considerable caution has been urged regarding the use of these artifacts as evidence of trade of one form or another.[2] Snodgrass has pointed to difficulties in establishing provenances of painted pottery and the reassignment of provenances since the 1930s, particularly stressing modern atomic techniques.[3] Cook has estimated the small size of the Athenian ceramic industry's employment in the fifth century and has warned that although pottery made up a part of Greek trade, it was "presumably a minor and inconstant part, so that the total value of trade cannot be estimated from pottery." He has also suggested that the "more universally admired wares," such as the pots of Corinth and Attica, may have traveled indirectly to their final resting sites.[4] Additionally, Cook states that frequencies of foreign artifacts are much more important than simple reports of artifact finds, without reference to how prominent they appear to have been in the articles of the site: "An isolated find is of very little importance."[5] Boardman has reiterated the view that a high proportion of foreign artifacts in an assemblage is more significant than "stray finds."[6] Humphreys includes the importance of frequency information for artifacts as one element in the contextual information needed to interpret foreign artifacts found in graves: comparison of each tomb's grave offerings with those in other tombs, the number of other tombs excavated, apparent occupants of graves, etc.[7] Watrous has offered several cogent reservations about using pottery as evidence of foreign relations, particularly for inferring traded items rather than for simply indicating foreign contacts: pottery generally was a peripheral trade item that may not accurately characterize the range of traded goods; the absence or relative

---

[2] Austin and Vidal-Naquet (1977: 27 n. 49) point to some of the literature that has analyzed potential pitfalls in applying archaeological information in historical study, particularly in using those data to study ancient external relations.

[3] Snodgrass 1980:127—29.

[4] Cook 1972: 276. On the profitability and contemporary significance of the pottery trade, and the interpretability of its remains, the discussion between Boardman and Johnston on the one hand and Gill on the other produces some useful clarifications of terminology and context: Boardman 1988a: 27—33; 1988b: 371—73; A. Johnston 1991: 403—9; Gill 1988a: 1—12; 1988b: 369—70. Boardman and Johnston (as cited above) offer evidence for bounds on both profitability and the overall role in trade or share in shipments.

[5] Cook 1972: 276.

[6] J. Boardman, personal communication, October 28, 1992.

[7] Humphreys 1967: 386.

scarcity of pottery from particular places may be unrelated to the degree of contact between those areas; the contents of imported jars usually are unknown; and characteristics of the interactions, such as the identities of the carriers, the owners of the goods, and many elements of planning and intent, are invisible.[8] In keeping with Cook's concern for magnitude of presence, Clairmont rightly warns that a few pottery finds may not mean trade, that the artifacts may have reached their find sites by other means. He gives the example of Cretan workmen involved in the construction of the pyramid of Hawara, who could have received supplies of their native wine in ceramic containers. He wisely recommends that "confusion could be avoided if the kind of [external] relationship would be specified," although such specificity often may be difficult to clarify, conceptually as much as artifactually.[9] Boardman has pointed to potentially more serious inferential problems stemming from the vagaries of publishing, independent of the fortuitous process of selecting sites for excavation.[10]

Each of these cautionary notes is cogent, but may be excessively pessimistic. Together, they effectively serve a strategy of preserving reasonable doubt rather than introducing reasonable suspicion. Establishing provenance of pottery by visual inspection is intricate, and misassignments have been made, although subsequent reassignments have been made on the same basis, but with greater collective experience. The laboratory alternatives are too expensive to be used except on a very judicious basis. Even locally made copies yield interesting information about some kind of interchange, but they often are detectable by inspection of decoration, fabric, or both. The painted-pottery industry certainly was small, but recognizing pottery, fineware and coarseware, as a major container industry that carried the products of other industries as well widens its interest somewhat. Cook's warning that quantitative estimates of trade volumes cannot be derived from the ceramic artifacts is cor-

rect, but qualitative information may be derived from it. Some of the ceramic artifacts, and certainly some of the metal ones, may have had intermediate stops before their interment in Crete. That may be important if one is interested in tracing face-to-face cultural exchanges, but in an analysis of resource transfers and allocations, indirectness is of secondary importance.

The concept of relative presence that frequency distributions embody is important and is, or should be, one of the principal goals of an examination of external influences, but these statistics harbor dangers for the initiated and uninitiated alike. We usually work with small samples, whose properties are subject to radical change with new finds. Statistical significance is but one issue; instability of the samples can make it a minor one. I refer to some frequency statistics myself, but I am reluctant to go much beyond judgments of small, medium, and large on the basis of them, and sometimes I stick simply with distinctions of small and large. The scatter of sites and small number of artifacts involved generally did not seem to justify either the effort of calculating frequencies or the daring of using them as sharp instruments. Isolated finds are not unimportant, although their informational content may be ambiguous. Alone, such finds serve as boundaries to hypotheses or as general alarms, and additional information—contextual, historical, or theoretical—may clarify their informational content. However, each secure, foreign artifact unambiguously represents its own physical transportation to its find site and demands an answer about implied return flows. The context of all artifacts, not only foreign ones, is important, but judgment must determine how much is enough.

Garlan points to several egregious applications of archaeological data to historical questions,[11] and it is clear that something was lacking in each case, but it is not equally clear that widening contextual boundaries would solve each problem. Watrous, fortunately, does not let

---

[8] Watrous 1992: 169–70.

[9] Clairmont 1955: 90 n. 1.

[10] Boardman (1990a: 171–72) discusses the scanty publication of Greek pottery from Woolley's excavation of Al Mina. The Greek pottery was scattered among museums and private collections shortly after excavation, and only a misleadingly small proportion of it was ever published. In personal communication (October 28, 1992), Boardman has reiterated the potential biases deriving from nonidentification, nonpublication, and selective publication.

[11] Garlan 1983: 27–30.

his warnings about imported pottery impede his own analysis of the external relations of Late Minoan III Kommos, but rather uses those constraints to sharpen his assessments, subject, of course, to the usual remaining uncertainties.

Some of the issues that are most resistant to enlightenment, either with further excavation, physical analysis, indirect information, or social reasoning, are probably the least important: for example, the flags [sic] of the ships and the owners of the goods. In the present study, the archaeological information alone has been insufficiently informative, and I have resorted to applications of historical and literary information, all of it filtered, of course, through twentieth century A.C. theoretical constructs. One person's high theory may be another's rank speculation, but I have endeavored to constrain raw speculation, as I would call it, with a combination of explicit social theory and empirical referents. I may devote more space than I should to developing a background to support specific mechanisms of external contact; to help maintain the flow of the story, I have kept most, but not all, of this discussion in footnotes and three appendices.[12]

The arbitrariness of publication operates similarly to the selectivity of excavation, yet this problem retains the status of the *argumentum ex silentio* and has its greatest force when artifact frequencies are low. The admonitions of this literature are sobering, but not intimidating.

A final pair of philosophical notes before embarking. First, I occasionally use social-science models in what follows, but I am concerned not with formulating laws about socioeconomic processes, but rather with illuminating certain categories of archaeological evidence on Crete in the first half of the first millennium B.C.[13] Nevertheless, some may find my results "ahistorical," whatever that may mean to different readers. Still, the period under study is for the most part prehistoric in Greece, and I find the proposal of particular events difficult to defend—even catastrophic events have been elusive for this period. I find the prospect of identifying processes that operated over particular periods more practical than naming specific events that occurred as parts of those processes. I try to achieve a useful balance between deriving results that are general or encompassing enough not to be certainly wrong, and specific enough to be interesting and applicable to the time and place under study.[14] Second, on skepticism toward evidence: opinions vary on what can be known with the evidence that ever will be available for this period, but I am inclined to view all the evidence available as resources for developing understanding rather than to "wait ... for *all* the evidence before formulating models." Models affect evidence as well as vice versa. I am not sympathetic, however, to romantic historicizing.[15]

---

[12] Using footnotes, relegating material to appendices, putting all material in the text, or simply omitting material that may address some, but not all, readers' questions—all of these approaches entail costs in terms of distraction to readers. It is impossible to minimize the sum of all these costs to each reader, but I have striven at least to make the tracks of my reasoning transparent while maintaining a coherent story line throughout the text.

[13] I have found the remarks of B. G. Trigger (1978: ch. 2, esp. 33—35; originally in "Aims in Prehistoric Archaeology," *Antiquity* 44 [1970]: 26–37) particularly aligned with my own research goals. Snodgrass (1983: 73–86) reflects on the tensions between, and complementarities among, the alternative emphases on processes and events in the Greek Early Iron Age.

[14] Cf. Chapter 3, note 319; Chapter 4, notes 17 and 325.

[15] Hallo 1990: 190–93, quotation from 192. Hallo describes the instability of the middle ground on this issue as spuriously revolving around gullibility, which is eschewed by all. Nonetheless, he characterizes a knife's edge between reservation and nihilism, which exists in attitudes to the evidence left by ancient societies. Again, I concur with Trigger's distaste for romanticism: Trigger 1978: 28–29.

II

FOREIGN ARTIFACTS FOUND IN CRETE

The only pieces of tangible evidence for external relations in the prehistoric period are the surviving artifacts, which are restricted to a few ceramics and metals, some ivory, and an occasional wooden item. These can encourage seriously misleading interpretations. The patterns of geographical and cultural contact that these artifacts reveal are interesting in themselves, but I wish to push them a bit further to see if they yield additional information that may extend beyond the prehistoric international art trade. I have in mind as such information further, reasoned hypotheses, directions for subsequent dialogue and investigation, rather than a series of "answers" that merit reflexive defense.

The artifactual evidence on which the study of Crete is based is presented in some detail in Appendix C, which contains two catalogues and several tables. Maps 1 through 7 identify a number of sites and areas to which reference is made throughout the remainder of the text. Sites in Crete are identified in Map 8, near the beginning of Chapter 4.

In addition to four groups of sites in the Knossos area—Fortetsa, the North Cemetery, the town, and a miscellaneous group—foreign artifacts are reported in northern and eastern Crete at Amnisos, Avlí, Gouves, Aghios Georghios, Anavlochos, Arkades, Rhiza, Olous, Dreros, Vrokastro, Kavousi, Mochlos, Sitea, Karphi, the Lasithi Plain, the Trapeza Cave, Liliano, the Diktaean Cave, Patéla, Praesos, Palaikastro, and Zakro; in southern and central Crete at Tylissos, Aghia Triada, Phaistos, Priansos, Prinias, Kommos, Kourtes, Gortyn, the Idaean Cave, Lasaia, Kato Syme, and Inatos; and in western

Crete at Eleutherna, Chania, Kissamo, the Cave of Hermes Kronaios near Patso, and Tarra on the south coast. Knossos, Kommos, and the Idaean Cave have the largest numbers of foreign artifacts. In this discussion of the patterns of artifacts found at the sites, I will approach the objects as a corpus rather than deal with each individually. When I return to the more detailed discussion of the Cretan material after the intervening development of a perspective on Dark Age trade and exchange, I will deal with more specifics.

The four sites or groups of sites from the Knossos area have different patterns of overseas sources for their foreign artifacts. The Cyclades and Cyprus account for thirty-nine of eighty-two foreign artifacts at Fortetsa. The Cycladic imports, all pottery, tend to be earlier, although there is substantial chronological overlap between Cycladic and Cypriot products, the latter of which are earlier metal items and all ceramics from the eighth century. Fortetsa produces three secure Attic artifacts in the tenth century, several possible Attico-Boeotian fibulae later, and a single vase fragment in the first half of the eighth century. Corinthian pottery is modestly represented, all save one piece from after c. 750. The eastern sources—Egypt, Phoenicia, Syria, Cyprus, and Rhodes—have scattered representation, but if aggregated have over twice as many artifacts as Attica and Corinth together. The foreign artifacts published to date from the North Cemetery are predominantly Attic, which cease prior to the appearance of two Corinthian pots and six East Greek items, and Cypriot, which occur from the mid-ninth century into the seventh. Half of the foreign artifacts from Knossos town are

Corinthian, and they begin a half-century to a century earlier than at Fortetsa. Together, Attic and Cycladic artifacts from the town amount to somewhat over half of the Corinthian, but the Attic artifacts are earlier, and the Cycladic appear just after the middle of the period. The only easterly item from the town is a Rhodian ceramic fragment, and it is still Greek rather than Near Eastern. The remaining Knossos sites together generate a more diverse pattern of sources for their foreign objects. Attica and Corinth are the most heavily represented, but together account for slightly less than one-half of the foreign items. The Attic items again halt completely by the end of the eighth century, but the Cypriot items continue from the earliest period through the seventh century. As among the Fortetsa finds, the early Cypriot articles are metal products, and the later ones are all ceramic. In the aggregate, the eastern sources, excluding Cyprus and East Greek areas, account for somewhat less than half as many foreign artifacts as do Attica and Cyprus together, and they appear from the earliest to the latest periods. Corinth accounts for a little under twenty percent of the foreign artifacts, and they have nearly a century of overlap with the Attic artifacts.

Foreign artifacts appear later at Kommos than they do at Knossos, and compared with Knossos, Kommos has a remarkably strong eastern orientation. Nineteen of sixty foreign artifacts (some of the "artifacts" are groups of sherds probably belonging to different vessels) come from eastern sites, excluding Cyprus and East Greece. The East Greek and Rhodian presence is strongest, accounting for twenty-four of sixty reported objects. Attic, Cycladic, and Cypriot representation is very weak, and the Attic is much later than it appears at Knossos. Corinthian artifacts account for fifteen percent of the reported foreign artifacts, beginning somewhat later than at Knossos. The Egyptian and Phoenician presences are strong, the Egyptian artifacts all being cult items, transport amphora fragments accounting for a large proportion of the Phoenician (many described as Levantine, possibly Phoenician) artifacts. The artifacts from Kommos have come from in and around temples and from a commercial building rather than from graves, which are contexts strikingly different from those at most of the other sites, the cave sanctuaries excepted. The Kommos finds have a commercial air not present in the predominantly funereal contexts from other sites.

The sites in northern and eastern Crete also demonstrate a strong relative orientation toward the east, nearly as strong as their orientation toward the Aegean. Sixty-eight of 173 foreign artifacts from twenty-three Cretan sites come from eastern regions, and seventy-seven come from mainland Greece and the Cyclades. The most frequent proposed origin is Corinth, followed by Egypt. These artifacts appear in all periods, from the earliest to the latest.

Some scattered foreign artifacts are found in the earliest periods at southern and central sites, but consistent appearance begins in the ninth century, again with an orientation that is as much eastern as Aegean. Of the 201 foreign artifacts from this region, 110 have been found at the Idaean Cave, and three-fifths of all the objects from this group of sites are eastern (eighty-two of these 151 come from the Idaean Cave). The other sites in this region are much more oriented toward other Greek sites outside of Crete. Only a handful of possible Cypriot items appear, and one of these is judged more likely Argive, another possibly Phoenician.

A small number of foreign artifacts has been found at sites in western Crete. Some part of the scantiness of reported finds must be attributable to less extensive excavation at western sites, but many of the western sites that have been excavated have yielded few, if any, foreign artifacts between the end of LM III and the beginning of the sixth century. Eleutherna has produced a scattering of overseas artifacts, however; though small, this group possesses the same array of provenances as the artifacts from sites in other parts of Crete. Interaction with other parts of Greece, however, appears to begin only in the ninth century, whereas evidence for eastern and Cypriot contacts goes back to the eleventh century.

Metal objects, with the exception of some fibulae, come to Crete almost exclusively from the east and Cyprus, but the eastern products include a small proportion of fine pottery (although some of the fineware is not of particularly high quality). The Egyptian products are nearly all faience pieces, with a few metal items. The Greek products, including those of East Greece, are almost exclusively pottery, with the exception of a few small, personal items like fibulae.

Just 153 Cretan artifacts have been found at overseas sites—far fewer than the overseas artifacts found in Crete. The earliest Cretan artifacts found overseas are in Cyprus and Italy—Latium and Etruria—although the early Italian artifacts may represent movements of populations, either community migrations or artisan movements, rather than of artifacts, since the finds themselves raise suspicions of influence more than they indicate actual imports. The finds in Cyprus date from the eleventh century, although some have been found in later deposits. The later finds at Italian and Sicilian sites suggest some Cretan presence, possibly in a sustained manner from the last third of the eighth century through the seventh century. Considering the Attic and Cycladic ceramics appearing at Cretan sites from early in the period, there is remarkably little Cretan work in either Attica or the Cyclades, and those items appear to postdate the majority of the inward flows from the north. The same is true of any apparent reverse flow of goods to Corinth, although the single report of a Cretan product at Corinth appears within the periods when Corinthian material appears at Cretan sites. Cretan material is represented at several of the major panhellenic religious sites: Delphi, Delos, Dodona, the Samian Heraion. Late in the period, interaction between south-central Crete and the Greek North African colonies, possibly through Kommos, appears strong compared with other Cretan outflows. No Dark Age Cretan products have been reported at any site in Anatolia, the Levant, Mesopotamia, or Egypt, early or late. Products moving out of Crete are mostly pottery, although the finds at the panhellenic sanctuaries include bronzes as well. Some gold jewelry

appears, as does some terracotta, some ivory, and some remarkably surviving pieces of Daedalic woodwork at Samos.

The imbalance between the number of foreign products found in Crete and the Cretan products found at overseas sites is striking. If we look for some rough balance in terms of apparent value, the Cretan products overseas clearly are not so valuable as to redress an apparent imbalance in volume: Crete was not sending out a small volume of gold for a large volume of clay. Also striking is the apparent mismatch between origins of foreign products found in Crete and the locations of Cretan products found overseas, although some simple mapping suggests less geographical mismatch with sites outside the Near East and Cyprus. The Cretan products found overseas are not such as would be highly likely to be mobile after their first overseas move: they do not appear to be products that might have been taken first, say, to Attica, then to Italy, although that direction of subsequent movement is itself not preposterous. The imbalance between finds in Crete and in the Levant and Egypt is particularly striking, and a secondary move hypothesis applied to that area finds even fewer nearby sites with Cretan objects; a secondary move from, say, Egypt to Italy is far-fetched. However, some triangular trade, with Phoenicians playing a prominent role, will be explored further when I return to the Cretan material.

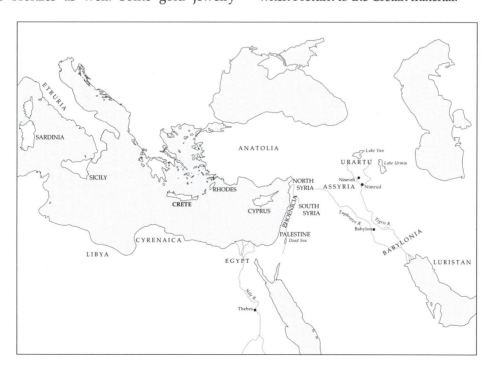

Map 1. Crete and Other Lands in the Ancient Mediterranean

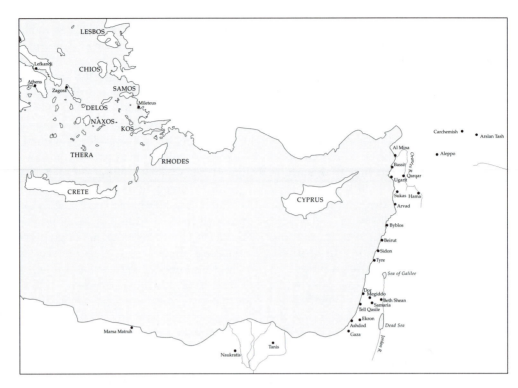

Map 2. Sites in the Eastern Mediterranean

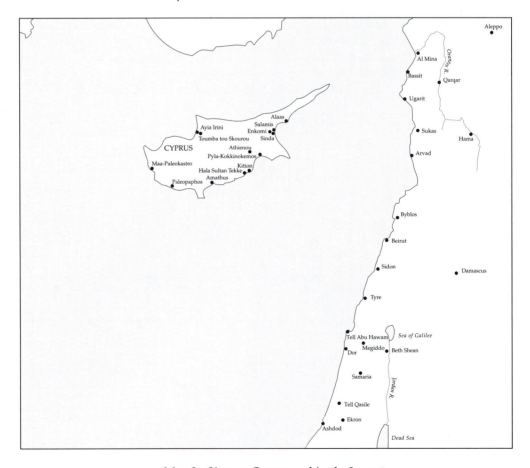

Map 3. Sites on Cyprus and in the Levant

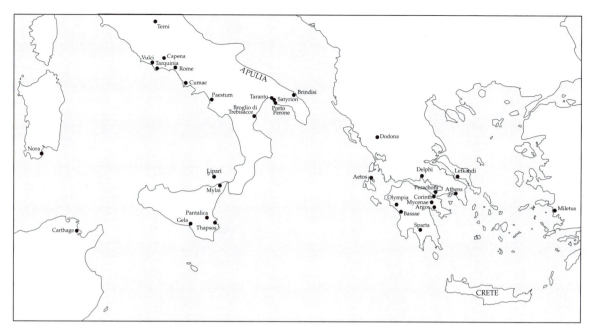

Map 4. Sites in the Aegean and Central Mediterranean

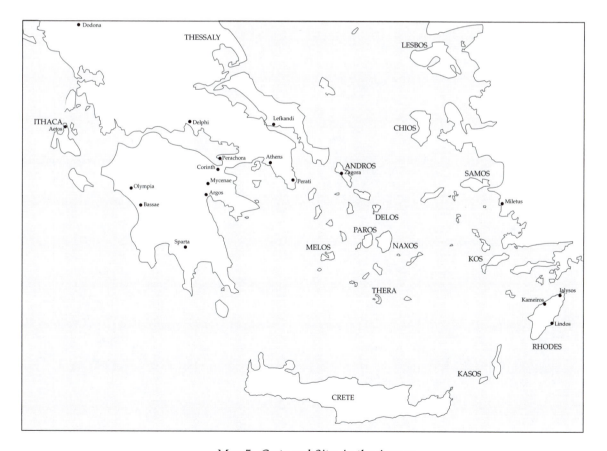

Map 5. Crete and Sites in the Aegean

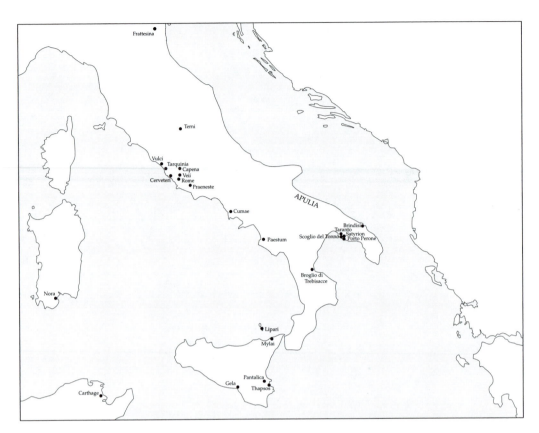

Map 6. Sites in Italy and the Central Mediterranean

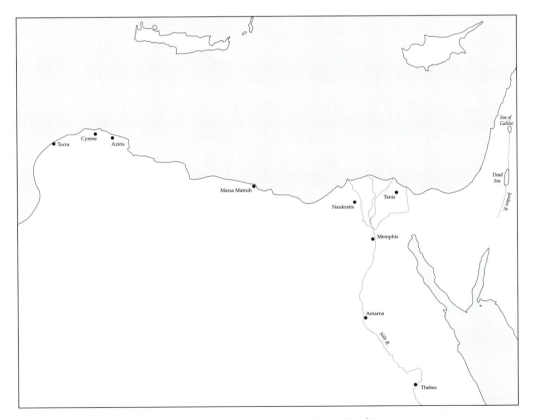

Map 7. Sites in Egypt and North Africa

III

TRANSMITTING EXTERNAL INFLUENCES IN DARK AGE GREECE

One of the principal questions about the foreign artifacts found in Crete and the Cretan artifacts found overseas is whether they represent some kind of regular commercial intercourse that reasonably could be called trade. One part of my approach is to see if evidence exists that sheds light on this issue. First, I address the evidence on ships: Did ships exist that might have been designed and used for overseas trade? Next, did harbors exist, or were they necessary under the circumstances? Third, was piracy so rife as to preclude seaborne trade during the period? Finally, I address the subject of trade directly, equipped with information on these related subjects. Some readers may be easily satisfied on these subjects—for example, large merchant ships unequivocally existed in the Late Bronze Age; could any reasonable person doubt that they continued to exist in Greek waters in the Dark Age? In fact, reasonable people have held, and still hold, different opinions on this

issue. So, too, on piracy: though it may be considered unreasonable to claim that piracy *eliminated* trade, it is not uncommon to find references to piracy as the transportation mechanism for metal artifacts in Dark Age Greek graves, with no clear way of evaluating the suggestion.[1] The disagreements concerning harbors appear to be fewer and less far-reaching, but the association with shipping warrants at least a few words on their land contacts. In the discussion of each topic, I attempt to integrate social reasoning with the archaeological and historical material from the literature.

SHIPS

The survival of good-sized merchant ships across the discontinuity of the disasters associated with the Sea Peoples a little after 1200 B.C. would hardly seem to be an issue worth consid-

---

[1] For recent examples, cf. Sandars 1987: 186, on Perati cemetery artifacts; and Watrous 1982: 19, on Karphi. Basch (1986: 429–30, 435–36) perceives a community at Kolonna, on Aegina, that lived off what could be called industrial piracy from the Saronic Gulf to Crete, from the beginning of the Middle Helladic to the end of the Late Helladic. The elements of his reasoning include a warship depicted on a Middle Helladic pithos from the excavation at Kolonna, the strength of that site's fortification walls, Thucydides' references to Aegean piracy, and Renfrew's estimate of Aegean regional populations in the major periods of the Bronze Age (1972: 251). Basch constructs a story for these pirates raiding the Chrysolakkos cemetery at Mallia, on Crete, of the Aegina Treasure around 1700, and an Aeginitan pirate family keeping them as heirlooms for three or four centuries before depositing them, between 1350 and 1150, in the tomb where they were found in the nineteenth century A.C. More recent interpretations of the articles in the Aegina Treasure loosen their linkage to Crete and Chrysolakkos. Gates (1989: 215 n. 4, 224) attributes them to Aegean craftsmen who amalgamated Near Eastern, Egyptian, and Cretan artistic and iconographic influences into a new, Mycenaean art. Niemeier (1995: 77), relying on the example of the rich shaft grave found just outside the east suburb wall of City IX at Kolonna, considers it likely that the articles were indeed robbed from a tomb, but that the tomb was Mycenaean and on Aegina.

ering except for the fact that Dark Age Greek historiography has been guided for over half a century by the belief that they disappeared from Greek waters for over half a millennium, between c. 1200 and c. 600–550. The clear evidence of Levantine maritime activity early in the eleventh century, as illustrated in the tale of Wen-Amun, indicates that the real issue is not whether the concept and application of the merchant ship survived the disruptions at the end of the Bronze Age, but whether those ships plied Greek waters before the great Greek revival of the Late Geometric and Archaic periods. Admittedly, evidence on this revised question has been primarily, but not exclusively, literary until excavations at Athens, Lefkandi, and Knossos have demonstrated undeniably an eastern presence, as likely Phoenician as any (although North Syrians have their champions currently), in the eleventh and tenth centuries.[2] The eastern artifacts in eleventh- and tenth-century Greece are reflected, if not exactly paralleled, by the presence of Greek pottery at eastern sites by the tenth century: mid-tenth century at Bassit,[3] the second half of the tenth century at Amathus on Cyprus,[4] late tenth century at Tyre,[5] followed by late-ninth-century finds at Al Mina,[6]

Hama,[7] Sukas,[8] and Tambourit, near Sidon.[9] Relatively early Greek pottery has been found at several inland sites as well: a fragment of a low-footed, Thessalo-Cycladic skyphos with concentric circles in Stratum III at Tell Abu Hawam is contemporary with Attic Early Geometric (c. 900–860/850), and a Thessalo-Cycladic glazed, one-handled cup may date as early as the second half of the ninth century; two rim sherds from Attic broad, shallow skyphoi, dating to Early Geometric II to Middle Geometric I at Megiddo; and about a dozen Geometric sherds from Samaria, all Attic or Atticizing according to Coldstream and none dating later than Attic MG II—although one sherd with a single wavy band between horizontal bands has closer parallels with Protogeometric than Geometric examples, and decoration on several of the pieces is reminiscent of patterns at Lefkandi.[10]

With contacts early in the first millennium established beyond the point of plausible deniability, the question of whether there were merchants on ships in Greek waters reverts to whether the ships were merchant ships or warships (possibly a moot point), and whose ships they were. Were they warships because of pirates, or were they warships because there was

---

[2] Summarized by Köpcke 1990: 91–92.

[3] Courbin 1993: 98, 103.

[4] Desborough 1957: 215–16; Coldstream 1987b: 22 n. 10.

[5] Over 100 Early Iron Age Greek vases have been found at Tyre: Bikai 1979: pls. 22.1, 30.3; Coldstream and Bikai 1988: pt. 2, 35–44. One Mycenaean vessel they date to the period 1200–1070/50.

[6] Boardman 1980: 39–45; Coldstream 1968: 312–13.

[7] Riis 1970: 150–52.

[8] Ploug 1973: 12–13.

[9] Courbin 1977: 147, 157.

[10] Tell Abu Hawam: Hamilton 1934: 23–24, nos. 95–96, pls. 12–13; Heurtley 1934: 181, pl. 88; Desborough 1952: 140–41, 181–85; Coldstream 1968: 153, 302–3. Heurtley recommended both artifacts as Thessalian, with close parallels to vases from tombs at Marmariani, dating possibly as early as c. 925; Desborough called the skyphos fragment Thessalo-Cycladic but discussed the one-handled cup as Thessalian; Coldstream called the skyphos alternatively Thessalo-Cycladic and Cycladic and leaned toward a Cycladic origin for the cup. Verdelis (1958: 92) considers the skyphos sherd to be Thessalian of late-tenth- or early-ninth-century date, the cup somewhat later. Megiddo: Clairmont 1955: 99–100, pl. 20.1–5; Coldstream 1968: 303–4. Samaria: Reisner, Fisher, and Lyon 1924, 1: 281–83, figs. 157–58; 2: pl. 69; sherd with wavy band is 1: 283, no. 21a, fig. 158; 2: pl. 69g (no. 2909). The wave pattern on no. 21a is of a rather high amplitude but is not quite angular enough to be characterized as a zigzag pattern; in addition to a number of modest correspondences with sherds from the Protogeometric building at Lefkandi, a closer affinity to no. 21a (pl. 69g) is a sherd with a zigzag softened somewhat on the bottom (Catling and Lemos 1990: pl. 38, no. 758). The meander and dots around the rim on sherd no. 1 (pl. 69d) from Samaria are quite close to a Euboean PG/SPG sherd from Xeropolis: Popham and Sackett with Themelis 1980: pl. 26, no. 738. Samaria sherd no. 3 (pl. 69j) has a concentric circle flanked by vertical stripes, similar to Popham and Sackett with Themelis 1980: pl. 29B, left, from Area SL at Lefkandi (Euboean SPG II–III; latest date for deposit is early Attic MG I). Samaria no. 23a, pl. 69h (a snakelike figure–or high-amplitude wavy band–with cilia): Catling and Lemos 1990: pl. 19, no. 329. The Greek sherds from Samaria were all found in disturbed contexts that provided little chronological information.

so little trade that there was no justification for building separate merchant ships? Why would anyone want a warship? Would warships have been justifiable without merchant shipping to protect?[11] How would warships have been financed—from strictly nonmaritime activities? Commerce clearly thrived along the Levantine coast during the eleventh and tenth centuries, and would have been conducted in ships tailored to the appointed task as much as the current technology permitted. If the eastern activity in Greek waters was indeed the "sporadic presence of Phoenician merchants … rather than organized trade,"[12] would such activity have dictated an alternative type of ship? Clearly, the subjects of ships, piracy, and Aegean economic, social, and political organization have become thoroughly intertwined as evidence has gradually emerged and pushed against intellectual convictions. Consequently, some readers may find a review of evidence on ships of the early first millennium perfunctory, but others may find useful a comparison of this evidence with the questions and doubts held by a number of scholars.

There is not a great deal of direct evidence on merchant shipping during the period 1100 to 600, but there is evidence for the preceding and following periods, and there are a few models and vase paintings from the period itself. More evidence exists for warships of this period than for merchant ships, possibly, Johnston suggests, because of the greater familiarity of merchant ships and hence the greater attractiveness of warships as novel artistic subjects.[13] Still, Casson cites

paintings of merchant ships in two Egyptian tombs of c. 1400.[14] The first contains two ships, which he concludes represent an Egyptian's view of Syrian ships; from the absence of rope trusses for bracing, he infers that the Syrian ships had the structural strength to sail over open water. The ships in both paintings have sails and rounded hulls indicative of a cargo-carrying design, and the crews in both are Syrian. The ship of the second tomb painting has a downward-curving yard, which is unattested in Egyptian sails of the period. Casson also describes a ship on a Cypriot vase of c. 1200–1100 as a merchant ship: the ship is large and has a deck and a "roomy hold."[15] Kirk cites a painting of a ship with mast and oars on a Cypriot Mycenaean amphora from Enkomi as a merchant ship; it has a deck but no ram.[16]

Then there are the excavations of the Ulu Burun merchant ship, dated tentatively to the late fourteenth century,[17] likely a ship of one of the larger sizes, and the Gelidonya ship, a smaller merchant vessel dated to the late thirteenth or early twelfth century.[18] Wrecks of three ships, dated to c. 1400 (?), the fourteenth to thirteenth century, and the thirteenth to twelfth century, and all carrying metals in one form or another, have been found off the Israeli coast in recent years. The earliest of these, at Hishuley Carmel, one-and-a-half kilometers south of Haifa, left four 250-kilogram stone anchors thought to be of Cypriot or Ugaritic origin, altogether hinting at a substantial size of ship. The middle-dated ship, found at Kefar Shamir, three kilometers south of Haifa, yielded five stone anchors, one bearing

---

[11] Gray (1974: 116–29) considers several *uses* of ships—purposes of state, trade, transportation of emigrants, and war—but does not relate her use categories to one another.

[12] Aubet 1993: 45. I am reluctant to cite Aubet's excellent book for such a quotation, but the expression captures common sentiment about early-first-millennium Aegean exchange, which is secondary to her own contributions.

[13] Johnston 1985: 127. For the past four decades, the Revelle Corporation has sold plastic models of battleships, aircraft carriers, destroyers, and cruisers of at least four nations, which are largely indistinguishable to the untrained eye except for the numerals painted on their hulls and flight decks, but not a single model of a freighter, ore ship, oil tanker, or other type of cargo ship; a model from the late 1950s of the *RMS Queen Elizabeth* is a notable exception to the "no-civilian-ship-model" rule. Basch (1983a: 139) is skeptical of a conclusion that "hardly any merchant ships existed" in the Archaic period in Greece because of the predominant depiction of warships relative to merchant ships. Gray (1974: 56) raises the question, for the Late Bronze Age, of artists' preferences for warships over merchant ships as a possible explanation for apparent regional differences in ship representations in the Aegean.

[14] Casson 1986: 35–36, figs. 57–58.

[15] Ibid.: 36, fig. 59.

[16] Kirk 1949: 116, 119.

[17] Bass 1986: 275.

[18] Bass 1967.

the Egyptian sign *Hafr* ("life"), but all with shapes consistent with a Late Bronze Age Syrian or Cypriot origin. The latest of these three ships, found about 100 meters from shore near Kibbutz ha-Hoterim, was found with two "very large" stone anchors, again suggesting a sizeable ship carrying scrap bronze either during or not long before the period of the region's difficulties with the Sea Peoples. No trace of any of these three ships was found, but Parker interprets the stone anchors as excluding simple jettisons of cargoes.[19] Most recent is the discovery of a Late Helladic IIIB2/IIIC shipwreck about 100 meters off the west side of Point Iria, about five kilometers east of Asine, on the Argolic Gulf coast of the Peloponnese. Pithoi, amphorae, stirrup jars, stone anchors, and various sherds and bits of wood were found spread over some thirty meters of bottom at depths of seventeen to twenty-five meters. So far, the pottery finds include five Cypriot pithoi dated to LC IIC/IIIA, six to

eight Cretan stirrup jars dated to LM IIIB2, several Mycenaean deep kraters resembling some LH IIIB2 examples from Prosymna, and several fragments of Mycenaean cooking ware. Two of the Mycenaean kraters are of Furumark shapes that continue as late as LH IIIC1, but the excavators have dated the cargo to about 1200. Neither the size of the ship nor its architectural characteristics has been determined yet, but the extent of the sherd scatter is some indication of the former.[20] Gillis has suggested that the Iria ship may have been bound for Asine, which itself, she suggests, may have been a major, or the, port of entry for the Argolid at the time.[21]

Moving clearly into the Dark Age, two ships on a Cretan Protogeometric vase from Fortetsa also have rounded hulls, and Casson and Basch pronounce them merchant ships, as did Kirk.[22] Nevertheless, Morrison and Williams have considered this pair of ships to be warships, and the issue remains open.[23] The ships (one under each

---

[19] Parker 1992: 209. The Hishuley Carmel ship (ibid.: 211–12, no. 503, Map 14; Galili et al. 1986; Maddin et al. 1977: 44–45) contained five small (2–4 kg each) tin ingots with possible Cypro-Minoan signs and a copper oxhide ingot with a cast or impressed sign. The Kfar Shamir ship (Parker 1992: 225, no. 540, Map 14; Raban and Galili 1985: 326–28, figs. 4–5; Galili and Shmueli 1983: 178) left eight bar and two hemispherical ingots of tin; five small, lead ingots; an Egyptian plaque; and an Egyptian sickle-sword with its wooden handle remaining. The ha-Hoterim ship (Parker 1992: 209, no. 494, Map 14; Wachsman and Raveh 1981: 160; 1984: 169–76; Raban and Galili 1985: 329; Galili et al. 1986: 35–35) had carried what may have been scrap bronze—horse bits, a ploughshare reminiscent of some from the Cape Gelidonya wreck, and various tools—and some fragments of copper and lead ingots. Gillis (1995: 64 n. 20) reports recent, informal communication from Wachsmann that the ha-Hoterim and Kefar Shamir wrecks are indeed two separate ships.

[20] Pennas 1992: 39; Pennas and Vichos 1996a: 4; 1996b: 7, 14, 16; Vichos 1996: 17; Lolos 1995: fig. 1, 72–78; 1996a: 4; 1996b: 21, 27–28, 31.

[21] Gillis 1995: 73; see 74, fig. 2 for map showing location of Iria. Gillis (1996: 1203) notes the discrepancy between the richness of the burials at Asine, relative to those at nearby Berbati, Dendra, Mycenae, and Prosymna, and its excavated settlement. Based on the burials, she believes that Asine must have been a very important center in the Argolid at the time, even if the impressive parts of the settlement have not been found.

[22] Brock 1957: 12, Tomb VI, no. 45, pls. 4, 135; Casson 1986: 36, fig. 60; Basch 1987: 159; Kirk 1949: 118–19, fig. 6.

[23] Morrison and Williams 1968: 12. Whereas Kirk (1949) judged that the ships faced to the right, Morrison and Williams believe they faced to the left, leaving them with different interpretations of the small, downward-pointing protrusions at the left end of the hull of each ship. Kirk believed them to be steering oars, but Morrison and Williams believe the somewhat squarer left-hand end of the ship to be its bow, because later warships had high, squared-off bows supporting their rams. Van Doorninck (1982: 281), in an assessment of whether the introduction of the ram on the Greek warship could be dated as early as the Protogeometric period, supports the Morrison and Williams interpretation. Snodgrass (1971: 437 n. 8) tacitly endorses the Morrison and Williams interpretation, but notes Kirk's earlier opinion without comment; Casson (1986: 42 n. 4), addressing Kirk's discussion, thinks rams to be a later development, but he considers "a distinction between oared merchant vessels and warships ... not only unproven but most unlikely at this age." Gray (1974: 57) calls the Fortetsa ships caïques, as distinct from the galley, which she considers the Halicarnassus ships (note 24 below) to represent. A recently excavated pyxis from tomb 61 at the Toumba Cemetery of Lefkandi, and dated to c. 850–835, has an unquestionable steering oar at its stern and a square bow with an equally unquestionable ram jutting straight out from the hull: Popham 1978: 356. The steering oar looks considerably like the protrusion on the Fortetsa

handle) on the Protogeometric krater from Halicarnassus, tentatively dated by Bass to the second half of the tenth century (by comparanda from Marmariani), are galleys, although whether war or merchant seems to remain under discussion; van Doorninck sees a forefoot, comparable to what he believes is represented on the Fortetsa ships, on the bow, whereas Gray saw the ships' importance as indicating a larger, heavier galley than previously (to 1974) had been thought to have existed prior to the eighth century. Both Gray and van Doorninck consider the Fortetsa and Halicarnassus (or Bodrum or Dirmil) ships to indicate the continuation of Late Bronze Age ship types into the Protogeometric period.[24] A clay model of a merchant galley from Cyprus, dated to the ninth or eighth century, has a deep, rounded hull.[25] Casson offers a painting of a merchant ship on a seventh-century vase from Cyprus and a drawing of the rear of a merchant

ship from a seventh-century votive plaque from Corinth (one of the Penteskouphi plaques).[26] Johnston tentatively identifies a seventh-century ship model from the Samian Heraion as a merchant vessel by its rounded proportions and relatively great depth.[27] Avigad has published a ninth-century Near Eastern seal depicting what he describes as a Hebrew-Phoenician ship, perhaps of the "Tarshish" type.[28] The ship has a rounded hull, a square sail, an identifiable stern and prow, and a clearly identifiable rudder or steering oar that is longer than, but reminiscent of, the protrusion on the lower hull of the Fortetsa ships. All in all, the ship looks like a merchant vessel.

From the persistence of the drawings of the rounded hull, Casson concludes that the rounded-hull design on merchant ships persisted throughout this period, and Johnston contends that the evidence shows continuity in ship architecture from the Late Bronze Age through the

---

Note 23 continued

ships, but the ends of the Fortetsa ships with the protrusions are more squared at the bottoms than are the other ends. Westerberg (1983: 51) notes that rams appear on both long and round boats in Cypriot material. She suggests that the projecting elements that later developed into rams on warships were only extensions of the keel or the kelson and had no implication for the classification of the ship as warship or merchant ship. Steffy (1985: 88 n. 8) reports a sixth-century Cypriot model in the Metropolitan Museum of Art that is sometimes credited with a ram bow; Steffy thinks the modeler was trying to portray an outer stempost knee construction instead of a ram. Basch (1969a: 143) unambiguously identifies the Fortetsa ships as merchantmen, reflecting either Levantine influence on Greek construction or, in his opinion more likely, a common eastern Mediterranean merchant ship; he believes the latter interpretation would carry the further implication of continuity across the twelfth-century gap back to the Late Bronze Age. Cf. Basch 1969b: app. II, 245, for Basch's assessment of the Fortetsa ships' developmental relationship to Levantine and Mycenaean ships. Basch (1987: 159) considers the protrusions pointing down from the hull to be steering rudders. Wallinga (1993: 38) sees the ram as part of a merchant ship's defensive equipment, but I have difficulty envisioning a fleeing merchantman turning round and trying to ram a pursuing pirate vessel.

On the issue of which end of a ship was bow and which stern, Raban (1984: 13–17) discusses bidirectional ships in the Late Bronze Age "and even after 1200" as an architectural concession to the location of Levantine ports on narrow, coastal estuaries; steering oars could have been switched from one end of the ship to the other as required. Basch (1991: 47–52) has considered at length which ends of ships depicted in Late Bronze Age drawings and inscriptions were prows and which were sterns. Much of his attention is devoted to ships with asymmetrical hulls, but in addressing symmetric ships, such as the later drawing on the Fortetsa vase, suggests bidirectionality for some ships of the Bronze Age. This proposal would leave the steering oar or ram still a question, but a steering oar could be moved from one end of the ship to the other with little problem; elsewhere Basch (1983b: 395–96) has suggested that bow and stern appendages, which can be difficult to distinguish from rams, were cutwaters, intended to increase hull stability.

[24] Bass (1963: 358–59, pl. 15, fig. 15) considered the ship figures to be "crude 'horns.'" Gray 1974: 21, no. D.3, 57. Van Doorninck 1982: 283, figs. 1–4.

[25] Casson 1986: 65–66, figs. 86-87. DeGraeve (1981: 130) cites the ship on the Cypriot vase as a merchant ship.

[26] Casson 1986: xxi, figs. 95–96 (Cyprus), 98 (Corinth).

[27] Johnston 1985: 46, 60, Arch. 14. Johnston notes that four models of merchant vessels of the Archaic period are known from Amathus on Cyprus (46 n. 2).

[28] Avigad 1982: 59–61.

Late Geometric period.[29] Morrison and Williams also claim that the representations of Mycenaean ships indicate that the main features of the ships of the Geometric period were already present in the Mycenaean period.[30] The hull construction of the Ulu Burun shipwreck is similar to that of the Kyrenia ship of a millennium later, lending strength to a suspicion of continuity over a considerable period.[31] Wallinga prefers to see the technical developments that led to the variety of ship designs present at the end of the eighth century as an eighth-century phenomenon, but he also believes there is a reasonable probability that those developments may be survivals from as early as Mycenaean times.[32] His preference, on balance, for the eighth-century revival of Greek nautical technology appears to be grounded in, or at least strengthened by, the "very sharp decline of Greek trade after the Mycenaean collapse," and somewhat more indirectly based on his acceptance of Finley's conception of "the ancient economy."[33]

Merchant ships appear to have been large enough to have required a regular commercial traffic for justification. A document from Ras-Shamra from c. 1200 refers to a ship of some 450 tons' burden as if it were not unusual.[34] A stone anchor found in the temple area at Kition, dated to c. 1100 and estimated to weigh 1471 kilograms, is thought to imply a ship with displacement of at least 100 to 120 tons and length exceeding 20 meters.[35] The clay merchant-ship model from ninth to eighth-century Cyprus has fourteen oar ports,[36] and the "broad merchantman" to which Odysseus refers in Book 9 of the *Odyssey* had twenty rowers.[37] Casson suggests that Homer may have had in mind a merchant galley with twenty rowers. According to Morrison and Williams, a standard-sized ship of the period may have used forty oarsmen, and perhaps there was a smaller size that used about thirty.[38] Referring to

[29] Casson 1986: 36; Johnston 1985: 35. Meijer (1986: 23–26), on the other hand, contends that warships and merchant ships of this period differed little in design, and that the rounded hull on the merchant ship of the second millennium reappeared only in the seventh century, under Phoenician influence. He contends that, with the upsurge of commerce in the seventh century, heavier and more spacious ships were developed, with concessions to speed and maneuverability. Casson's evidence seems to dominate Meijer's assertion, but Meijer may have in mind Greek adoption of Phoenician hull styles. Casson's evidence for the rounded hull does not distinguish between nationalities of ships, and it is entirely possible that Greeks made models and vase paintings of Phoenician merchant ships. It is certainly plausible that the vase painting, from the late sixth century, of the pirate ship (presumably) attacking the merchant ship may represent a Greek pirate ship attacking a Phoenician merchant ship, with implicit approval of the attack. If Phoenician ships did most of the carrying in Greek trade of the Dark Ages, Greeks may have had to adopt the most competitive merchant ship style when they were able to enter the carriage themselves on a large scale.

[30] Morrison and Williams 1968: 44. The statement is for warships, but the same conclusion appears to hold for merchant ships. They cite several possible Mycenaean Age merchant ships in Vermuele 1972: 259, fig. 43, and pl. 32. Heichelheim (1957: 507–8 n. 47) also believed "that there was more of Mycenaean shipbuilding preserved after the Dorian Migration than is usually realized." Heichelheim based his belief on his observation that most of the technical innovations that appear to arise in the eighth century are already present in drawings of Egyptian ships of the Pharaonic Bronze Age. He believed that the Minoan and Mycenaean ships were at least as well built as the Egyptian. His reasoning implicitly excludes Early Iron Age relearning of Bronze Age nautical technology.

[31] Bass 1986: 275; cf. Steffy 1985: 72–95, on the Kyrenia ship's hull construction.

[32] Wallinga 1993: 64–65.

[33] Ibid.: 8 n. 7, 29 (describes Finley's view as "the new orthodoxy"), 64–65 (quotation).

[34] Casson 1986: 36; Sasson 1966: 132.

[35] Frost 1982: 270, assuming the anchor was indeed used on a ship and was not strictly votive. However, anchors over one-half ton in the Middle and Late Bronze Ages are common. This particular anchor from Kition was designed to be used as one of a pair—it could not be used singly. Cf. Frost 1969: 238–39, where she estimates that a "half-ton anchor presupposes a wooden ship of at least 200 tons and a length of 20 m."

[36] Casson 1986: fig. 86.

[37] Ibid.: 169 n. 5; *Od.* 9.322–23. The "twentier" was a common term to refer to a seagoing ship and need not have indicated that it had twenty oarsmen. Morrison and Williams (1968: 46) suggest that twenty oars may represent either a small ship or a larger one in which there is plenty of room for cargo in addition to the oarsmen.

[38] Morrison and Williams 1968: 40.

the Classical period and later, Wallinga warns against a search for an average ship size, which he considers a meaningless concept: there was a wide array of ship types and sizes, each designed for a particular shipping niche, with size related to type.[39] For the end of the eighth century, he perceives only four basic ship types in Greece.[40] Nevertheless, he sees considerable scope for size variations within those four types and believes that "privately owned galleys certainly were very heterogeneous."[41] The recent discovery of a late-fifth- or early-fourth-century shipwreck at Alonisos, in the east-central Aegean, reinforces this concept of distinct ship types for a period that has been thought to have had only smaller ships, in the size range of the Kyrenia ship, about 40 feet long. The Alonisos ship appears to be about 85 feet long and possibly of 150-ton burden, likely intended for uses different from those of ships such as the Kyrenia ship.[42] Similar forces may have produced a variety of ship designs and sizes earlier in the first millennium B.C., although the variety may have been more in size than in hull or interior compartment construction.[43] Burn's description of a Dark Age merchant ship as "little more than a half-decked whaleboat" appears misleading for the period.[44]

The clearest evidence is for the period just before the Greek Dark Age (i.e., before c. 1200)

and the period just toward its end (beginning c. 800/750). At the beginning of the time between these two periods, throughout the eastern Mediterranean and the Aegean, states and economies collapsed, trade contracted, and the demand for ocean shipping would have declined accordingly. To accommodate smaller loads, the size of merchant ships would have been decreased, although there would have been limits, perhaps quite tight ones, on how much smaller they could be made without unacceptably compromising seaworthiness. It is likely that the decrease in trade would have affected the number of merchant ships more sharply than it did the size of the remaining ships. Likewise, the proportion of merchant ships to warships might have fallen, although, following the suggestion of Johnston above, merchant ships still may have remained more common than warships.

Would the art of marine architecture have regressed during this period (c. 1200 to c. 800/750) as well? Despite the apparent regression of many arts in Greece during the early part of this period, Levantine technology appears to have remained at a high level, primed by military requirements as well as commercial opportunities early in the first millennium.[45] Ships being mobile, local shipmakers would have had no advantage over more advanced shipping tech-

---

[39] Wallinga 1964: 25. Thureau-Dangin's (1931: 228–30, tablet no. 5) identification of at least twenty-four different kinds of ship on a Sumero-Akkadian tablet at Ras Shamra reinforces the concept of Late Bronze Age ships designed for specific niches. These are primarily riverine ships. The Ugaritic dialect knew a much smaller number of ship types, one of which, the *any kn*, appears to have been the prime, seagoing transport ship: Sasson 1966: 131 n. 23. Referring to Egyptian cargo ships in the Eighteenth Dynasty, T. Säve-Söderbergh (1946: 16) noted that designs were tailored to specific uses. Cargo ships used in the eastern Mediterranean, where distances between ports were not great, were designed for maximum loading capacity, whereas ships intended for the Red Sea were designed for speed because of the substantial distances and the scarcity of fresh water on shore between ports.

[40] Wallinga 1993: 63–64.

[41] Ibid.: 38, 47 (quotation).

[42] Wilford 1993. I am indebted to Dr. E. L. Will for directing me to this reference. For a preliminary excavation report, see Hadjidaki 1996: 37–45.

[43] Steffy (1994: 43, 77), discussing the fourth-century Kyrenia ship, indicates that hull design flexibility was limited at the time but implies relative ease in adjusting size within the eastern Mediterranean-Aegean design parameters.

[44] Burn 1937: 245.

[45] Sherratt and Sherratt (1991: 373–74) suggest that ship sizes were reduced after the collapse of the eastern Mediterranean-Aegean palace system, c. 1200. Smaller and more maneuverable ships, with a comparative advantage in carrying smaller volumes longer distances and in eluding pursuit, economically undercut the larger vessels designed for the preceding trade regime. They suggest the Sea People's ships depicted in the Medinet Habu reliefs of the early twelfth century are representative of the type of ship that became the trading standard of the early first millennium. Though the pictorial evidence of the larger ships of the Late Bronze Age exists, the Ulu Burun and Cape Gelidonya ships, from the late fourteenth and late thirteenth centuries, reveal a range of Late Bronze Age ship sizes, the latter being small relative to the larger, pictured examples, the former large enough to carry hundreds of metal ingots as well as numerous transport amphorae.

nologies from elsewhere; in this direct competition, the more sophisticated technologies would have tended to drive out less sophisticated technologies in other parts of the eastern Mediterranean and Aegean, simply because of mobility. Without this direct competition, the less mobile land-based technologies could have progressed at much different paces. In all, it seems reasonable to suppose that there was considerable continuity in the character of merchant shipping in the eastern Mediterranean and, by consideration of the interaction patterns, in the Aegean between c. 1200 and the Classical period.[46] Although marine technology developed rapidly between the eighth and fifth centuries, there is no evidence it had declined during the earlier period. Ships may have appeared less frequently in Greek waters during the lengthy depression from c. 1200 to c. 1050, but it would be inaccurate to conclude that shipping was unavailable.

There are contrasting, or at least varying, opinions in the literature, that only toward the end of the Dark Age, in the eighth and seventh centuries, did merchant ships and warships become distinguishable.[47] According to Heichelheim, whose summary is technically dated, although its outlines still reflect a major branch of current opinion, Greek and other Mediterranean ships became considerably more seaworthy during the eighth century, merchant vessels increased in size, and a separation developed between war and merchant ships. These developments coincided with the growth of Greek trade between 700 and 560, according to his dating, and probably would have been drawn forth by increased demands for merchant shipping. Wallinga's recent assessment of Greek shipping, although more detailed technically, reaches essentially this same conclusion.[48] This interpretation is not at clear variance with the evidence presented above, but it confers less of a sense of continuity with merchant shipping of the earlier Dark Age and thus lends a different impression. Certainly, the improvements in the rowing system, and the consequent importance of the ram, for warships in the eighth century encouraged rapid developments in warships that may have hastened their divergence from merchant ships. Likewise, the growth of trade would have stimulated technological developments in merchant shipping.

Humphreys's influential discussion of merchant shipping emphasizes a discontinuity around the end of the sixth century. She finds that

> representations of ships on West Greek vases of the eighth and seventh centuries confirm that the ships which visited or sailed from the Greek colonies in southern Italy and Sicily were of the same type as those portrayed on the vases displaying the warrior exploits of the Athenian elite in the Dipylon cemetery. . . . The first Greek representations of large "round-ships" which clearly relied entirely on sail and could carry bulk cargoes with only a small crew belong to the end of the sixth century.[49]

Humphreys buttresses this artistic-archaeological evidence with historical evidence from Herodotus that the Phokaians used pentekonters for long-distance trade in the western Mediterranean in the fifth century.[50] It certainly may be the case that several types of ship, such as the pentekonter and its later, enlarged version, the *samaina*, routinely served multiple purposes. MacDonald interprets the Phokaian merchant traffic in pentekonters and the introduction of the "big-bellied *samaina* as attracting the attention of Herodotus through their exceptional quality."[51] He endorses the view that "the round ship, driven by sail or oar," was the primary cargo ship of the eastern Mediterranean "dating back to the Bronze Age," and presumably throughout the earlier Dark Age. MacDonald attributes Humphreys's belief in the late emergence of the round ship to

---

[46] Basch (1969a: 142) reaches exactly this conclusion.
[47] See, e.g., Heichelheim 1957: 244.
[48] Wallinga 1993: 33–65.
[49] Humphreys 1978: 166, 168.
[50] Hdt. *Histories* 1.163; Humphreys 1978: 168 n. 13.
[51] MacDonald 1986: 192 n. 7. I am grateful to A. M. Snodgrass for bringing this reference to my attention. MacDonald endorses the opinion of C. M. Reed (1984: 39), who believes that Herodotus's passage on the Phokaians should be interpreted as emphasizing their exceptional practice.

her focus on Greek trade and Greek ships, isolating events in the Aegean from their wider Mediterranean context.[52] Wallinga's observation of a wide array of ship types, each serving a particular niche, probably is valid throughout the Dark Ages, even if reduced demand for shipping thinned out the array somewhat.[53] Humphreys does not cite the ninth to eighth-century clay merchant-ship model from Cyprus, the Cretan Protogeometric vase from Fortetsa, or the seventh-century examples cited by Casson.[54] As with Heichelheim, her observations are accurate but are sufficiently circumscribed that their implications are rather narrower than they occasionally have been treated. Salmon accepts Humphreys's observation, but softens its implications by suggesting that the merchant ships depicted on vases may have substantially predated their artistic appearance.[55]

Humphreys, however, raises an insightful question: Who among the Greeks would have had the capital to construct and furnish a solidly built merchant ship in the Archaic period, much less earlier?[56] Her answer is that Greek aristocrats were the only group with the required wealth, which, combined with that group's attitudes toward commerce, reinforces her suspicion that commercial trade among communities in the

Archaic period was accordingly circumscribed and often indistinguishable from the piracy more favorably viewed by the aristocracy. By extension, commercial trade would become nearly meaningless in the Geometric and Protogeometric periods. This answer overlooks the possibility that a good deal of the freight of these periods may have been carried on Phoenician ships, funded by more developed capital markets, earlier recovering states, or both, in the Levant.[57] Wallinga, however, believes that the technological developments in Phoenician ships did not differ from those in Greek shipping through the end of the eighth century.[58]

Snodgrass relies on Humphreys's analysis of the array of ship types available in the Archaic period to circumscribe the scope for commercial trade in that period. He contends that the Penteskouphi plaque from seventh-century Corinth, which Casson identifies as a merchant ship from its rounded hull, is indistinguishable from the war-galleys on other plaques.[59] To Salmon, on the other hand, the Penteskouphi plaque "appears to have proportions very like those of the rounded merchantman, and its sail is prominent; no oar-ports are shown," and indeed its hull shape is fundamentally different from the hull shapes of warships painted on

---

[52] MacDonald 1986: 192 n. 10.

[53] Wallinga 1964: 25.

[54] Humphreys 1978: 166.

[55] Salmon 1984: 152: "The character of vessels used for trade before the mid-sixth century is difficult to determine ... the first clear signs of purpose-built merchant ships are not before the late sixth century, but they had probably then existed for a good deal longer."

[56] Humphreys 1978: 166: "Any man might own a small boat capable of crossing the Gulf of Corinth, but to build, equip, and man a `broad, cargo-carrying ship of twenty oars, fit for open-sea crossings' (Odyssey 9.322–23) required both material and social capital." Steffy (1994: 27, 43) notes the large quantities of wood, including much with naturally grown curvatures, for both Bronze Age and Classical period vessels. The labor time and skills—both design and carpentry—required for construction also were considerable, and maintenance on some ships may have required quite a bit of labor time (28). He notes, "Our knowledge of ancient Greek ship [construction] contracts and shipbuilding economics is practically nonexistent" (43), but comparison of the production requirements identified qualitatively above with the magnitude and intricacy of other machinery of the time points to the order-of-magnitude conclusion that ships were relatively expensive pieces of equipment.

[57] The ownership, or funding, of warships seems to have been addressed very little. A warship would seem to have been a community's property—why would a private individual other than a pirate want to tie up his resources in one? From this question I would not deduce that all apparent warships were pirate ships. It would seem that a community structure capable of requisitioning resources is a prerequisite for warships; do the social requirements for financing merchant ships demand more or less community structure? Wallinga (1993: 26–30) raises the issue of financing warships in Archaic Greece and does not believe that state fiscal capacity to maintain sizeable navies went far back into the Archaic period, if at all, for many states.

[58] Wallinga 1993: 30, 60–63. His reasoning seems to be based on evidence late in this period and does not deal either with the overall technological levels of the two regions throughout the period or with apparent demands for ships in the two regions.

[59] Snodgrass 1983b: 16, 17; Casson 1986: fig. 98.

vases.[60] Meijer suggests that the prevalence of pirates in the Dark Age encouraged the use of warship forms as merchantmen, presumably for superior speed, and that the reemergence of trade encouraged the further development of merchant ships.[61]

It is easier to believe that merchant ships need not have existed as a distinct class of vessel if one also believes in the irregularity, infrequency, and general weakness of overseas commercial contacts during the period, as several of these authors do. This association is reasonable, since conclusions regarding merchant ships and trade should not be independent. However, the archaeological evidence seems clear on the existence and possibly on the commonplace character of merchant ships in the Early Iron Age. The existence of a separate class of merchant ships suggests the persistence of ocean commerce during this period. Finally, considering ships as an element in a social system that includes their financing rather than as an independent technological system, the existence of warships may imply the existence of commercial shipping as their raison d'être.

HARBORS

What sorts of harbor facilities were required for the shipping of the period, and what evidence is there for the existence of harbor works? Once again, the subject of harbors presents the situation in which relatively clear evidence exists for preceding and succeeding periods, making due allowances for coastal geomorphological, eustatic, and isostatic changes.[62] Greek harbor works appear late in this period (700–600 B.C.), and major Cretan ones possibly only earlier and later, but there are hints of earlier harbor works on the eastern Mediterranean coast. Although merchant ships were big enough to require quays in the middle of the second millennium, no harbor works that early have been identified; Blackman, however, claims that "there is little reason to doubt that they existed," and the technical knowledge required to create artificial harbor works on the sea coast was present in the Late Bronze Age.[63] Maritime structures at Dor have been dated to the thirteenth to twelfth centuries: a cargo of conical jars of c. 1200 help date some of the works, the construction of a new landing stage in the harbor has been dated stratigraphically to the thirteenth century, and the Sikels cut a flushing channel through the rock shelf at the northwest corner of the lagoon in the twelfth century.[64] A breakwater at Tabbat al-Hamman, on the mainland opposite Machroud, south of Tartous and near the mouth of the Orontes, has been dated to the ninth or eighth century,[65] and underwater remains at Sidon have been dated to the Bronze or Iron Age by evidence of sea-level changes.[66] Tyre and Aradus have similar cut and

---

[60] Salmon 1984: 113, fig. 15, and 152. Snodgrass (personal communication) remains unconvinced of the seventh-century date of this plaque and notes that most of these plaques are of "decidedly later date." Reed (1984: 40) disagrees with Snodgrass's assessment of indistinguishability of the ship on the plaque in question from war galleys, contending the former is "clearly a sail-driven merchantman."

[61] Meijer (1986: 23–24) relies indirectly on Humphreys 1978, via Snodgrass 1983b. If weight were a feature demanded of warships of the early first millennium, as it was of the ram warships of the late first millennium, the speed advantage of warships over merchant ships in eluding pirates could be easy to overstate: cf. Steffy 1991: 33. But cf. Casson's suspicion (note 23 above) that there may have been little difference between warships and merchant ships in the early first millennium.

[62] Raban 1991: 130–33.

[63] Blackman 1982: 90, 92.

[64] Raban 1988: 273–76. On the rock-cut channel, Raban 1990: 106; also described are other harbor and estuarine engineering projects, dating from Middle Bronze II to Early Iron Age, designed to alleviate siltation problems (104–8); Raban 1987: 125–26.

[65] Braidwood 1940: 208, pl. 20.1, 2, for the sea leg of the breakwater, and pl. 25, for the land leg.

[66] Frost 1973: 89. Some of the remains she dates to the Persian period probably, from the presence of quartzite revetment, with bolstering from historical evidence of Sidonian prosperity during that period. The winds and current patterns in the area make some artificial barrier necessary for protection of shipping anchored near shore (88), which Sidon clearly served in the Early Iron Age. Poidebard and Lauffray suggested that the South Harbor, the *crique ronde*, may have been the Bronze Age "Egyptian Harbor," but they found no evidence of maritime construction there (1951: 53–54, 83, fig. 1 bis, pls. 1, 6–8). In the Northern Harbor, Roman remains rested on earlier constructions of dates they were unable to determine, but which they suspected of being at least as early as those at Tyre (89). Cf. Muckelroy 1978: 75–78, on the early Lebanese harbors.

built-up reef-breakwaters, and although it is not yet clear that these are ancient harbor works, Blackman recommends Frost's case for Sidon.[67] Altogether, the harbor evidence from the Near East suggests the continuation of commercial maritime activity in the early first millennium. What does Greek evidence of the same time period show, and what does it suggest?

What were once identified as Bronze Age harbor works at Amnisos have been identified as the underwater remains of houses, although Schäfer believes that the physical characteristics of the bay and shoreline at Amnisos would have favored it as a ship-landing in the Geometric period. Cuttings in bedrock have been identified as ship slips at Mallia, Nirou Chani (Ayia Theodori) east of Herakleion, Rethymnon, and east of Sitea, although the ship slips at the last

site have so far eluded dating. A cut channel and a silted-over Bronze Age harbor have been identified at Mallia. Making the Late Bronze Age harbor at Mallia more intriguing is a vase fragment with the grafitto of a merchant ship of Mycenaean type with sail, found by a tourist at Mallia in the spring of 1993. The sherd has been dated to the Late Minoan period, probably LM II-III, and the author publishing it considers it an indication of maritime commerce at Mallia in the post-palatial period. Evans reported remains of Minoan harbor works under the Venetian port at Candia (Herakleion), as well as possible remains of a Minoan port at Hagia Pelagia, some twelve miles west of Herakleion.[68] Davaras suggests Minoan and Hellenistic use for the slip near Sitea, but without any clear chronological evidence. Harbor remains of the Roman period

---

[67] Blackman 1982: 92; Frost 1973: 92. On the underwater remains at Tyre, Poidebard (1939: 23–37) reports moles, breakwaters, and quays; the blocks of which the submarine walls are composed differ from the material of which the underlying reefs are made (74). Frost's reexamination (1971: 105–7) of two of Poidebard's submerged structures, identified by buoys OP and AQT, on the southern reef at Tyre found no evidence of masonry. She suspects that Alexander's causeway provoked heavy depositing of silt, which may still hide earlier constructions. Katzenstein (1973: 13) favors an early-ninth-century construction date for the port of Tyre, in the reign of Ethbaal I; by mid-ninth century, he believes, Tyre had both north and south harbor facilities. Aubet (1993: 27–29, 36) describes Tyre's early-first-millennium harbor facilities and their upgrading by Hiram I in the third quarter of the tenth century. Aradus (modern Arwad) is at the northernmost end of a reef some 8 kilometers long, at the south end of which is the island of Machroud; Frost (1964; 1966: 25–27) determined the submerged architectural features on both Machroud and Arwad to predate the Iron Age and to have gone out of use by sometime before the fifth century B.C. The pre-Iron Age initial date is judged from the independently estimated timing of sea-level changes (1966: 25–26), and the date of disuse from the location of amphoras from fifth-century wrecks in areas with earlier, terrestrial architectural remains (ibid.: 27). At least part of the submergence appears to have been caused by earthquakes. Drillings at Arwad have yielded Iron Age sherds: Frost 1995: 7–12.

The age of the submerged harborworks at Pharos, the western harbor of Alexandria, remains unknown, although they may date to Ramesside times or earlier. It is quite likely that some considerable facility was on the site at least as early as Greek Late Geometric times, as Menelaus mentioned the location in *Odyssey* 4.354–59: "There is an island there in the heavy wash of the open sea, in front of Egypt, and they call it Pharos . . . there is a harbor there with good anchorage, whence they put forth their balanced ships to sea." Jondet's survey early in this century (1912: 254; 1916) did not yield satisfactory material for dating, although he suggested the possibility of Ramesses (III) building it with prisoner-of-war labor after turning back the Sea Peoples' and Libyan's attacks (1916: 73). Alexandria was built on or near the site of an existing Egyptian settlement called Raqote. Baines and Málek (1980: 169) characterize the remains as "pre-Ptolemaic sea walls north and west of the island of Pharos," and in the (unnumbered) map at the top right of that page, "pre-Hellenistic harbor works." Subsequent investigations in the area have focused on the Ptolemaic remains of the Pharos light tower, several hundred meters to the east, and other submerged remains in the eastern harbor (Frost 1975: 126–28; 1995: 5–6, 7). The only pre-Ptolemaic remains emerging so far in these investigations have been a fragment of an obelisk with the titular inscription of Seti I and an architrave from the Twenty-Sixth Dynasty, both of which the excavator believes to have been only some pharaonic memorabilia used in Ptolemaic sanctuaries or gardens (Empereur 1995: 759; La Riche 1996: 74, photographs on pp. 62–63, 75). Other remains of ancient jetties at Dékhéla, some 10 kilometers to the west of the western port at Alexandria, are equally of unknown date, although Malaval (1909: 372) suggested a Ptolemaic date. The founding date of an ancient settlement at Rhakotis, less than a mile from Pharos Island, remains subject to debate, ranging from the second half of the New Kingdom to the Thirtieth Dynasty; located beneath present Alexandria, excavation has not settled the question (Mokhtar 1993: 28–30). Altogether, the dating of the submerged harbor remains has little supporting information.

[68] Evans 1921: 298.

have been found at Chersonisos, east of Ayia Theodori, and carefully squared blocks without cement may be remains of earlier harbor works. A shipshed and quay from the Greco-Roman period have been found at Matala, two miles south of Kommos; few Minoan sherds have been found at Matala, and no Minoan structures are known.[69] Publications from the recent excavations at Kommos have not dealt in detail with the harbor. While possible submerged remains in the water were noted early, the excavation has looked in vain for years for any underwater constructions at Kommos, and Shaw doubts any will be found. Nonetheless, clearance of Gallery 3 of Building P, from the Late Minoan III period, has yielded evidence that supports the argument that the galleries of this building may have sheltered ships during the nonsailing season.[70] Excavations at Phalasarna in West Crete give a fourth-century date for the harbor construction there.[71] Any harbor remains at Itanos have been submerged with the subsidence of the eastern end of Crete in the first millennium A.C. and have been little explored. For the Bronze Age, Shaw recommends attention to shoreside buildings in addition to offshore remains, as the latter may be difficult or impossible to date and are especially subject to destruction.[72] At Kommos, Building Q has been associated with commercial, or at least nondomestic, activity, but it is not a direct maritime structure, as Building P appears to have been in the Late Minoan period. No other Cretan sites have revealed Early Iron

Age counterparts to Building P at Kommos. But what does the absence of Early Iron Age harbor facilities on Crete imply?

The great age of Greek harbor construction began toward the end of the Dark Age, with the works at Delos in the eighth century; Lechaeum, the Corinthian Gulf port of Corinth, possibly in the late seventh century; and Samos in the late sixth century.[73] Blackman contends that Greek cities of the Iron Age probably had little need to build much in the way of protecting moles: "Perhaps they built a shoreline quay or projecting jetty for larger merchant ships to berth against, but quite possibly nothing at all."[74] Casson concurs: craft that sailed between coastal towns and between small islands often loaded and unloaded off beaches without harbor installations of any kind "throughout Greco-Roman antiquity," and he suggests that Bronze Age ships did the same.[75] Odysseus's description of the fine harbor of the Phaeacians reveals a simple but effective row of berthing sites, probably in the sand, with shacks for the ships' gear.[76] Wiseman's assessment of the use of the western Corinthian port at Lechaeum is that the use of the beach for ships "must extend well back into the prehistoric period."[77] Basch describes beaching a boat on Samos: hooking a rope from shore through an iron hook screwed to the hull, then pulling the boat in. He believes the technique could have been used from c. 1500 B.C. on.[78]

This is a convenient place to draw together some behavioral relationships between ships,

---

[69] J. W. Shaw, personal communication, October 28, 1992.

[70] Amnisos: Marinatos 1929: 94–104; Shaw 1990: 425; Schäfer 1991: 114. Mallia: Blackman 1982: 93; Guest-Papamanoli and Treuil 1979: 668–69; Hue and Pelon 1991: 117–27; Van de Moortel 1994: 389–90, 396–97; Van de Moortel 1994: 389–90, 396–97. Nirou Chani: Marinatos 1925–26: 141–47; Frost 1963: 107–9; Blackman 1973: 132; Shaw 1990: 425–26. Sitea: Davaras 1967: 84–90. Rethymnon: Blackman 1982: 206. Chersonisos: Leatham and Hood 1958–59: 266. Matala: Leatham and Hood 1958–59: 266; Shaw, personal communication. Kommos: Whittlesey, Myers, and Allen 1977: 187–88; Shaw, personal communication. On Building P at Kommos, Shaw 1990: 426 and fig. 9, 425; 1992: 2.

[71] Hadjidaki 1988: 463ff.; Frost and Hadjidaki 1990: 513–27.

[72] Shaw 1990: 433.

[73] Pâris 1916: 5–73, on Delos and Mykonos; Salmon 1984: 148, on the construction of Lechaeum under Periander. Lehmann-Hartleben (1923: 148) also dates Lechaeum to the Archaic period, but Shaw (1969: 371) reports that archaeological finds do not support such an early date.

[74] Blackman 1982: 93.

[75] Casson 1986: 361–63; fig. 191, xxvii, from the third century A.C., is a mosaic from a tomb chamber near Sousse (Tunisia) showing a coastal craft unloading bars of lead onto a beach. The projection of this evidence backward nearly a millennium may not be unreasonable in this instance.

[76] Ibid.: 362; Od. 6.263–69.

[77] Wiseman 1978: 87.

[78] Basch 1983b: 401.

harbors, and trade. It can be shown that the cost-minimizing size of a ship tends to increase as the square root of the length of voyage and to decrease as the square root of variable costs of unloading in port.[79] If a larger ship cannot be unloaded more quickly, per ton of cargo, than can a smaller ship, the relationship is exact. For ships touching many ports, unloading part of their cargoes and taking on some more at each place, the measurement of this length-of-voyage effect would be more intricate, but the concept of the distance and length of time a cargo is carried survives this complication. If congestion is an issue in a port—that is, if ships have to wait to unload—larger ships are more cost-effective since they are cheaper per ton to operate. Two corollaries follow from this effect of idle time. Shipping costs in a congested port that is unsuitable for large ships will be higher than those for an equally congested port accessible to large ships. Correspondingly, harbor developments that reduce congestion reduce costs of using small ships more than the costs of using large ships.

How would these relationships be reflected in the events at the turn of the Late Bronze Age and the beginning of the Early Iron Age? A reduction in the demand for shipping—because, say, of a reduction in quantities of goods traded—would tend to reduce congestion at any available or surviving ports, which in turn would make smaller ships more cost-effective. If the typical length of voyage also fell, there would be a second force tending to reduce ship size. Steffy implicitly has suggested that ship size was more amenable to variation than was basic hull design at this time,[80] and if that was in fact the case, ship size should have shrunk at the very end of the second millennium and the beginning of the first. Addition of both berths and warehouse facilities would reduce port congestion. Now, if manmade port facilities did not exist, but instead ships loaded and unloaded via lighters to the shore, would small ships be encouraged relative to large ships? To the extent that the large ships' operating costs per ton are lower than those of smaller ships, the larger ships would have an economic advantage in such situations. Thus, the absence of fixed harbor facil-

ities is not an economic obstacle to the use—and consequently the existence—of larger ships. However, if such sites were physically unapproachable by larger ships, trade absorbs the cost of ships more expensive to operate as well as the cost of lightering. Whether the dangers of piracy (discussed below) and nature would tend to increase or decrease the minimum-cost ship size depends on ownership as well as a number of characteristics of equally or more speculative nature, such as the relationship between ship size and defensibility and trade-offs between defensibility and speed. We need not know the answers to these implicit questions to acknowledge their importance to the progress of ship size.

I have discussed the relationships between port facilities and ship characteristics as if ships responded to port characteristics and not vice versa. In a longer time horizon, port facilities may be developed to accommodate desired shipping characteristics, but manmade harbor facilities are very large and costly fixed capital items that could respond less rapidly to current conditions than could additions to the stock of ships. Nonetheless, less costly shore-side facilities such as warehouses could respond more quickly to shipping demands, so Shaw's recommendation to pay more attention to such structures has theoretical as well as practical force.

PIRACY

Piracy has been cited as a factor inhibiting, and occasionally terminating, overseas trade as well as causing considerable disruption on land during the Greek Dark Age. It is not uncommon to find an exotic artifact, particularly a metallic one, at a Dark Age Greek site attributed to piracy rather than to trade. With little unequivocal evidence one way or the other, should such an interpretation be given equal, or even greater, weight than suggestions of commercial origin? This is the problem facing interpretations of a good bit of artifactual evidence.

Though evidence for Dark Age piracy is indirect at best, nonetheless both archaeological and historical traces exist. Apparently, piracy of the period was directed against targets on both sea and land. The withdrawal of coastal settlements during the earlier part of the period is attested in the archaeological evidence and is reported in the literary evidence by Thucydides,[81] but the reactions of shipping have left less tangible traces.[82] A. R. Burn believed that pirates cut off Phoenician access to areas of the Aegean north of Rhodes for at least some period in the ninth century.[83] The *Odyssey* makes references to piracy in the form of raids on settlements as well as legitimate traders kidnapping and murdering. The raids are accepted as honorable, aristocratic methods of accumulating wealth, and Homer is equally accepting of kidnapping as a legitimate source of slaves.[84] Piracy clearly was not so prevalent in the Aegean and the eastern Mediterranean as to have virtually eliminated seaborne trade during some part of the Dark Age,[85] but it undoubtedly affected trade as well as settlement locations.

Piracy and its landward cousin, highway robbery or brigandage, were not new. Hammurabi's law code of the first half of the eighteenth century excused traders from repaying loans if they lost their goods through enemy attack and required local authorities to compensate victims of highway robbery in their territory.[86] Brigandage, as well as piracy, continued to characterize Mediterranean land travel for the next three thousand years.[87] The problem at hand is not to establish whether piracy existed or was new in Dark Age Greece, but to obtain some hints, perhaps insights, into how it might have interacted with commerce and related production and consumption activity during the period.

The Mediterranean and Aegean coasts offer numerous natural hiding places from which pirates could attack ships that hugged the coast, which much of the shipping of the period did. Across the open seas, shipping followed fixed routes with prevailing winds at particular times

---

[81] Thuc. 1.7. This withdrawal may have been overstated and its causes possibly misattributed. For instance, the recent Vrokastro archaeological survey, around the eastern end of the Gulf of Mirabello, on the eastern end of Crete, has found sufficient remains of pithos sherds dating from Late Minoan III through the Geometric period at coastal promontory sites at Nisi Pandoleimon and Priniatikos Pyrgos to "indicate continued, though perhaps limited, use of the exposed coastal region (possibly for fishing, agriculture, or trade) even at the close of the Bronze Age": Hayden, Moody, and Rackham 1992: 329 n. 102; fig. 20, 330; 343, 344. On alternative views of possible refugee settlements, "dual" settlements, and piracy and alternative sources of settlement disturbance, see Nowicki 1990: 178–80; 1994: 235–68; Haggis and Nowicki 1993: 334–36.

[82] Sandars (1987: 186) notes that "archaeologically the evidence for piracy is difficult to catch, but the Cypriot, Egyptian and other trinkets that turn up in Dark Age sites and in graves may be just such evidence."

[83] Burn 1960: 43 n. 4. Reaching forward in time for better-documented cases of endemic piracy that are suspected to have largely choked off trade, Dell (1967: 349–50) examined the opinion that endemic piracy accounted for the lack of Greek settlement and trading activity in the northern Adriatic before the fourth century, finding both temporal limitations until the third century on references to Illyrian piracy in the ancient texts and the silent, archaeological testimony of Greek sites on the Adriatic coast as early as the sixth century.

[84] Aubet (1993: 103–4) notes the ideological component to the Greek characterization of Phoenicians as piratical and generally untrustworthy. Cf. discussions of the social acceptability and respectability of piracy in the Greek Dark Age (or at least in the ninth to eighth centuries) in Nowag 1983: ch. 4; Jackson 1985: 656–57; van Wees 1992: 213–14.

[85] Ziebarth (1929: 1) observed that the flourishing of piracy is at least indirect evidence for the flourishing of trade, off which it lives. Garlan (1989: 174) seems inclined to dismiss Ziebarth's study as mixing a modernist study of commerce with a mechanical treatment of piracy, but these criticisms do not affect the logic of Ziebarth's observation.

[86] Casson 1974: 30, 38–39.

[87] Braudel 1972, 2: 743–54. It is a good antidote to consider Braudel's conclusion on Mediterranean highway robbery and piracy before further considering the rise of piracy in the Greek Dark Ages: "Like piracy and just as much as piracy, it [highway robbery] was a long established pattern of behaviour in the Mediterranean. Its origins are lost in the mists of time. From the time when the sea first harboured coherent societies, banditry appeared, never to be eliminated. . . . Let us not be tempted then as historians sometimes are who rarely look outside 'their' specialist century, to say that banditry made its first appearance in Corsica say in the fifteenth century or in Naples in the fourteenth."

of the year, so that pirates would know where to find prey.[88] Without armed escort, individual ships must have been at considerable risk, and it is unlikely that the volume of trade was sufficient to have justified convoys for protection.

The simple term "piracy" blurs a considerable range of activities during this period, and indeed, a number of modern writers conclude that the Dark Age Greeks blurred the distinction between piracy and trade.[89] It was difficult to distinguish between piracy and privateering during the Archaic and Classical periods, and law gave legal rights of reprisal on the open seas to private individuals seeking compensation from citizens of other cities (σύλη).[90] Within the category of simple piracy there are issues of motivation, sponsorship, and professionalism, and the business of piracy itself involves physical flows of goods that may require some intricate accounting on the part of the scholar, particularly if the volume of goods moving through pirate channels is large relative to the volume of goods moving through regular shipping channels.

During some portion of the Dark Age, it certainly is possible that aristocratic adventurers led plundering raids against settlements, probably of nonkinsmen, and possibly against shipping. Adventure, honor, and booty, perhaps even a regular income, gave motivation dampened only by the prey's ability to protect itself. Certainly attitudes in the *Odyssey* reflect a general lawlessness in the casual approach to kidnapping and murder as well as to adventurous plundering,[91] but of greater seriousness for shipping is the possibility that professional pirates were encouraged by the absence of international law or diplomatic protocol and weak or nonexistent military protection of shipping. Because of the difficulty of eking out a living from agriculture, as well as the weakness of intercommunity protocols, predation on shipping could have presented an attractive supplement or alternative.[92]

[88] Ormerod 1924: 15–16. Bass (1986: 270) observes that three shipwrecks from the sixteenth or fifteenth to the late twelfth century B.C. have been found in a pattern he interprets as hugging the coast around the Bay of Antalya off southwestern Anatolia. Semple (1916: 135) notes the benefits to pirates of the intricate coastlines in the eastern Mediterranean and Aegean; her attribution of the region's piracy to geographical conditions is more starkly environmentally deterministic than contemporary scholars would feel comfortable endorsing without qualification (cf. 138–39 on causes of the region's piracy).

[89] E.g., Roebuck 1951: 214: "Seventh century Greek trade was so nearly akin to piracy that the regulations [at Naukratis] were designed to prevent pillaging in the Delta rather than to enable the collection of import duties." Cf. Burn 1960: 47: "In the eighth [century], Greek traders, no doubt also pirates when opportunity offered, were already conducting their own commerce with Levantine ports." Badian 1970: 834: "Piracy, in early antiquity, was not clearly distinguished from trade on the one hand and war on the other." Zimmern 1931: 315: "This early period [seventh and sixth centuries] when pirate, trader, and naval officer were merged into one." Cf. ibid.: pt. 3, ch. 4, for discussion of the ethics, economics, sociology, and practicalities of late Dark Age piracy. For likely official attitudes, Burn 1984: 145: "In the early seventh century, contacts were growing closer; the worst human hazard to shipping was probably casual piracy, on which the state authorities, with an eye to legitimate trade, probably frowned, like the men of Ithaca on Eupeithes when he raided friendly people." Mele (1979: 61, 72) considers trading and piracy to have been interchangeable during the eighth century. "Handel, Seeräuberei, und Krieg erschmalzen unmerklich": Gray 1974: 117.

Van Wees (1992: 245) has explored the internal logic of the standard Homeric question to a stranger, "`Are you traveling at random, like freebooters, or on some business?' ... The standard question ... would have little meaning if those who are `on business,' no less than freebooters, start plundering at the first opportunity." He believes in a small overlap of the two categories, trader and pirate, by at least the ninth to eighth centuries.

[90] Ormerod 1924: 61–64; Cary 1970: 1026; Bravo 1980: 675–987. Pritchett (1991: 68–152) offers severe objections to Bravo's organization, methodology, and findings.

[91] E.g., *Od.* 15.415–81.

[92] Thucydides (1.5) assigns among the motives of Dark Age piracy profit for the aristocracy and support for needy families at home. Nowag (1983: 176–78), who does not believe in a high prestige of piracy in the ninth and eighth centuries, finds *Versorgungsschwierigkeiten* to be the primary motivation of plundering raids against land targets. Largely accepting Finley's interpretation of virtually no trade in this period, he sees piratical attacks on shipping prior to the seventh or sixth century as apparently modest forays against Phoenician shipping (117). Mele (1979: 59) believed piracy to have been honorable among Greeks of the Dark Age. Bravo appears to have modified his position on the question. In 1980: 976–77, after considerable debate with himself regarding the Homeric *temoinage* (or *Zeugnis* seems to capture the use of the epic record more satisfactorily than

Ormerod suggested that the typical pirates were highly competent, professional seamen and notes that amateurs, especially "inexperienced landsmen," were generally quickly eliminated, by the weather if not by local policing crews.[93] This kind of seamanship probably would not be acquired on a part-time basis by individuals seeking to supplement agricultural incomes. The ill discipline of Odysseus's apocryphal crew with which he raided Egypt attests to the problems facing amateurs.[94] While fishermen would acquire the seamanship skills and the intimate geographical knowledge of at least limited areas, the typical fishing craft would make an unlikely pursuit vessel. An alternative to individual entrepreneurship in part-time piracy would have been a community division of labor, with village or city sponsorship of piracy.[95] In the Hellenistic and early Roman periods, a number of cities in Crete were noted for piracy that appears to have been of this latter sort, although Davies interprets a diplomatic strategy in such sponsorship.[96] As an example of the casual appeals to piracy in the current literature, Fagerström endorses the notion that piracy was a sort of

---

Note 92 continued

does the English "evidence"), he proposed that Dark Age Greeks held both condemnatory and honorable opinions of piracy, largely depending on the region in consideration; he believed that piracy was considered both legitimate and honorable in Aetolia and Crete in the eighth to seventh century, largely on interpretation of the epic *temoinage*. Later, however (idem 1984: 103), he shifts to the opinion that Dark Age piracy was a marginal activity of no particular honor, if in fact led by a noble, although both he and Mele share an outlook on Dark Age economic activity along the lines of Hasebroek and Finley (136), so major differences in doctrinal perspectives are not responsible for their differing interpretations. Mele (1986: 67–69) does not accept Bravo's later interpretation of the epic *temoinage*, but both authors may place greater weight on literal interpretation of that *temoinage* than the literary devices will support.

Van Wees (1992: 209 n. 87) notes that Homeric raiders ("Homeric" in the sense of being described in the epics; he would ascribe them to roughly the ninth to eighth centuries), whom he calls freebooters rather than pirates, attacked only land targets, not shipping. This observation reduces somewhat the pertinence of the epic raiding evidence to the transportation of goods by sea. Rather than suggest consequently that piracy at sea was of little issue because the epic examples focus on land targets, it is safer to accept the existence of attacks on shipping while reserving somewhat the direct applicability of the Homeric evidence for shipping problems. Consequently, Van Wees's account of the motivation of settlement-oriented raiding in the ninth to eighth centuries as a mechanism for simultaneously increasing wealth and prestige at a time when peaceful means of rapidly increasing the former were severely restricted technologically (246–49) is of limited relevance to the present focus on the piracy-trade relationship, unless one is willing to extend that motivational hypothesis to sea piracy, which Van Wees, with his textual focus, has not appeared inclined to do.

Reviewing the evidence on the activities of the Illyrian pirates, Dell (1967: 357) concluded that hunger at home was responsible for the few episodes of Illyrian sea raiding prior to the mid-third century.

[93] Ormerod 1924: 30–31.

[94] *Od.* 14.243 et seq. Ormerod (1924: 30–31) pointed to events in the Jewish Wars of the Roman period in which refugees seized Joppa, built ships, and "endeavored to plunder the trade route from Syria and Phoenicia to Egypt." Vespasian attacked them; they fled, were caught in a squall, and were driven ashore and destroyed. McKechnie (1989: 106 n. 41) expresses reservation on the issue of pirates' sailing skills, at least for the much later fourth to second centuries, on the grounds that pirates operated even more on land than on the sea. See Garlan 1978: 1–16, on the integration of land and sea operations of Classical and later pirates. Nonetheless, competition with professional sailors would have pitted skills against each other; luck would have been an erratic compensation for professionalism.

[95] O. Murray (1980: 53) appears to view the raids of Odysseus's Cretan character as such publicly sponsored activity, of benefit to the home community. McKechnie (1989: 111–12) mentions pirate establishments (fourth century), whether camps or permanent communities, but does not address such issues as long-term provisioning, recruitment (by enlistment or birth), and retaliation, all affecting the stability of the pirates' own organizations.

[96] In an unruly international environment, the communities (cities, states, etc.) sponsoring or allowing piracy could have been using the extracted wealth as a bargaining chip for improved terms of diplomatic recognition; if the ploy failed, they at least retained the goods: Davies 1984: 288–90.

evolutionary predecessor of trade but does not specify the evolutionary laws.[97]

The material flow of goods must be considered in a social analysis of piracy. Different cargoes (or different compositions of booty from settlements raided) would have had different immediate consumption values. Precious metals could have had honor and prestige value in honor/adventure-motivated aristocratic raids, but, for pirates motivated by hunger, imports of gold booty would have required further transactions before they could accomplish their ultimate purpose. If, say, pirate gold were brought back to the pirates' home community with an eye to increasing consumption rather than enhancing prestige, exchanging the gold for locally produced items simply would have altered the community's price level in terms of gold (i.e., the implicit or explicit valuation of different goods in terms of gold), possibly leaving some community members worse off than they were before the booty arrived.[98] Only if some unused resources, most likely labor, existed in the community would the entry of pirate gold have increased consumption for the entire community. In general, unless pirates captured major food shipments

such as grain, they themselves would have had to trade their booty to feed themselves.[99] Even with community sponsorship of piracy, cargoes other than food would be unlikely to expand immediately the livelihood of the community. Unless metals were captured that could be converted to agricultural implements, the routes from pirate booty to increased community well-being are indirect. Materials that could be put to military uses could reduce the resources the community would have to devote to producing such equipment themselves and allow them to devote more resources (probably primarily labor) to agriculture or other production. Possibly slaves captured from crews could have been put to work in agriculture, but their probability of escape may have been high in dispersed rural settings.[100] The intimate connection between piracy and slavery during the period is acknowledged, but it would have made better business sense (although the term itself may be an anachronism) to sell captives to third parties or ransom them back to their families rather than employ them directly. If the community of the capturing pirates were to keep the captives as workers, it would run the risk of incurring raids launched to free them.[101] In gener-

---

[97] Fagerström 1988: 146. Fagerström suggests that the Dark Age Greek pirate would have derived "a not negligible proportion of his livelihood by means of force or violence" (147), which obviously suggests professionalism, somewhat less obviously specialization, and still less directly, a sizeable volume of traffic to be intercepted (or coast-dwelling victims) that could have sustained the pirates' income. The shipping volume must have been large enough that a good living for pirates (roughly, what they could have made doing something else) must have been a small enough proportion not to have deterred merchants (but successful piracy must not have attracted more pirates than the commerce could bear). Also, coastal dwellers of the period frequently are identified jointly as likely pirates and potential victims; would not land-raiding pirates have sought out less redoubtable victims? Genuine pirate communities probably were less common than sometimes supposed today.

[98] Redistribution of possessions, and consequently consumption, could result if the people bringing the gold into the community and selling the first units of it for other commodities would sell their gold at pre-gold-import prices. Subsequent sales of gold for goods would be made at lower prices of gold, with those prices eventually reaching the final relative price of gold in terms of goods. People making exchanges at the earlier, higher prices of gold would have obtained more goods for their gold than could be obtained on average at the final price of gold.

[99] In his analysis of Mediterranean piracy in the sixteenth and seventeenth centuries A.C., Braudel (1972, 2: 870) observes, "Privateering required above all a market for its spoils."

[100] Finley (1959: 159–60) believed that in the Classical period, fugitive slaves were a "chronic and sufficiently [sic] numerous phenomenon in the Greek cities," but that the countryside was a dangerous place for escaped slaves, particularly non-Greeks such as the Thracians and Carians.

[101] Bielman (1994: 234) notes that forcible rescues of prisoners tended to occur when capturing and origin communities were nearby, characterizing capture in warfare between neighboring cities. Pirates in her sample of inscriptions tended to take their prisoners off some distance quickly their poorer, landward cousins—the brigands—were less likely to; cf. Brulé (1978: 161) on the relative wealth of pirates and brigands. As a related case in point, she (180–84, decree no. 51) reports an Ephesian decree, from the last decade of the second century or the first decade or so of the first, honoring the Astypalaeans for rescuing some captured citizens. Some pirates, probably Cilicians, had abducted a large group of citizens and slaves from the sanctuary of Artemis Mounychia at the small, fortified town of Phygela, south of Ephesus. An Astypalaean squadron intercepted the pirate flotilla before it could get away with the prisoners; they executed the pirates, in a clear demonstration of the virtue of anonymity to captors.

al, however, piracy would need to be followed by external exchange.[102]

Sensible piracy should not have been so rapacious as to choke off shipping altogether, but sensible piracy could have been difficult to achieve. "Optimal" piracy would be much like optimal harvesting of any renewable resource, in which the absence of proprietorship of the prey would have led to "overfishing." If enough independent communities were engaged in attacking shipping, each could have attempted to appropriate as many ships as possible in the belief that if they did not, a neighbor would.[103] Again, agreements among communities sponsoring pirates could have mitigated that competition, but such agreements could have been difficult to maintain. Piracy, as well as land brigandage, was common throughout the second millennium A.C., and trade flourished. Braudel notes that during the years A.D. 1560–65, the Barbary pirates were so rapacious in the western Mediterranean as to virtually close the region to shipping and, as a consequence of eliminating their ordinary prey beyond a level that could sustain themselves, began attacking the coasts of Languedoc and Provence.[104] Archaeological evidence of the removal of settlement sites away from coasts in the Dark Ages could reflect a comparable situation of pirates' having overfished their waters, although archaeological survey is beginning to modify beliefs about desertion of sea coasts in the Submycenaean/Subminoan period.[105]

Just how bad could "bad" piracy have been? What proportion of ships could have been expected to be snared during a period of piracy characterized as "extensive"? We need not expect quantitative evidence from the Early Iron Age in the eastern Mediterranean, but some is available for the early eighteenth century A.C. that may give some suggestions. Insurance rates on shipping runs from England to the American colonies give some indication of the premium attributable to piracy. By the 1720s, the common peacetime trans-Atlantic rate was 2 percent of the manifest value (one-way); Jamaican rates were higher because of the piracy rife in the Caribbean in the early years of the century. Outward rates from London were 2.5 to 3 percent, and the return rate was 4 percent. The round-trip rate between Jamaica and New York, passing by the dangerous Carolinas, was 5 percent in 1720. Insurance at this period covered cargo and ship, to within 1 to 2 percent of the loss.[106] The differential between the insurance rates on the routes at no (or low) risk to piracy and those on routes at substantial risk (whatever that term may have meant) bears a close relationship to the additional losses to piracy on those routes. It is probable that shippers incurred additional costs of precautions against piracy—ship tonnages and armaments were adjusted to the risks on the different routes—beyond the insurance differentials.[107] When piracy is more prevalent and more effective, these costs of precaution and of insurance (in case precaution was insufficient) rise; as they do, the volume of shipping will be reduced, the balance between piratical predators and their prey will change, possibly reducing the number of predators, and eventually, the entire system of investment, shipping, and piracy will come into (or at

---

[102] Pritchett (1991, 5: 312–63) compiles literary evidence of Aegean piracy in the Classical and later periods, emphasizing geographical conditions and warfare. He takes for granted the importance of external disposal of booty (322, 401–8). Ormerod (in Ormerod and Cary 1932: 351) notes that the Cilician pirates' role in slave wholesaling in the early first century probably was responsible for Roman tacit toleration of their nuisance for a number of years.

[103] Cf. Pendlebury's (1930b: 91) concept of Mycenaean participation in the Libyan attack on Egypt in the late thirteenth century. De Souza (1995: 188) uses the predator-prey analogy to characterize the relationship of piracy to trade.

[104] Braudel 1972, 2: 872.

[105] See note 81 above.

[106] Shepherd and Walton 1972: 77, 83; on insurance coverage, Davis 1962: 87. Cf. note 310 below, on evidence from the late sixteenth and early seventeenth centuries A.C. in the Adriatic, suggesting similar proportions.

[107] Attempts to shift the financial burden of shipping protection among various parties with multiple relationships can produce counterintuitive results. In the early sixteenth century, Spanish royal regulations required armaments on private Spanish merchant ships operating in the Atlantic Triangle (Spain-Caribbean-northwest Africa), but the crown and Spanish merchants disagreed on the methods of financing protection against pirates. Owners of merchant ships frequently circumvented the armaments regulations, being reluctant to devote valuable cargo space and weight to cannon and ammunition: Hoffman 1980: 28–29, 62.

least tend toward) an equilibrium, in which the differential insurance rates will reflect the differential risk of capture. The first observation on the numbers cited above is that covered losses must have been small, even in a period during which localized piracy was considered to be a serious problem. Second, the losses to piracy on routes where that was a problem were nearly equal to the losses from natural hazards on other routes. This rough estimation abstracts from any differences in natural hazards and exposure times (roughly speaking, distances) on the different routes. Extrapolation of this information to a period twenty-five to twenty-seven centuries earlier naturally requires care. Losses to natural hazards undoubtedly were higher, but how high, and how total losses between nature and man were allocated, remain open questions, which may, in fact, be unanswerable.[108]

Would a general improvement of well-being throughout the region have led to an increase or a decrease in piracy?[109] To the extent that piracy was dangerous for the pirate as well as for honest shipping, it should have led to a decrease. Easier ways to make a living would have made the risks of piracy less appealing. To the extent that wealthier communities could better protect their shipping, it should have led to a decrease.[110] To the extent that greater wealth meant fatter prey, piracy would have increased. To the extent that it was simply fun, increasing wealth could have led to an increase in piracy, although ethics and the sources of honor could have changed along with

wealth.[111] For the mid-second millennium A.C., in a conclusion that, as far as it goes, appears largely transferable to the first millennium B.C., Braudel finds a "positive correlation between piracy and the economic health of the Mediterranean: and I would stress that it is positive: they rise and fall together. When piracy has little impact on peaceful trading, it is probably because prizes are hard to come by and possibly corresponding to a general falling-off in trade."[112] This is a splendid statement, but it is capable of inflicting considerable deception inasmuch as it mixes together many effects. As Braudel himself ponders the relation, this "positive correlation" does not distinguish whether the "increase in piracy" is an increase in the absolute value of plunder or in a percentage of shipping plundered, or even whether it represents a more articulate complaint about the piracy.[113] And because piracy is a genuine occupation, a way of making a living, alternative opportunities must have an effect on the number of men who offer their services to piracy, especially as the risk of piracy is likely to increase as wealthier prey can better protect themselves. If an increase in well-being were unevenly spread across communities, and individuals had difficulty in transferring themselves to the communities that were improving more rapidly (as probably was the case in Dark Age Greece), an increase in the region-wide, average well-being might have attracted even more piracy from lagging communities. In sum, it is no easy task to decide whether an increase in wealth

---

[108] In the United Kingdom, registry data prior to the second quarter of the nineteenth century A.C. were inadequate to form incidence statistics on wrecks. By mid-century, estimates were in the range of 4–5% per year. Lindsay 1876: 465–69. Davis (1962: 87, 156) notes Lindsay's estimate and can say only that he believes it to be a lower bound for loss incidences a century earlier. For yet earlier centuries, Davis mixes the effects of Moorish corsairs with those of natural hazards to obtain only the qualitative judgment that losses must have been yet higher, which remains uninformative on the effects of either hazard separately.

[109] J. Bouzek (1985: 243) suggests that in the period after c. 1100, during the Greek Dark Age, some piracy in the Aegean-eastern Mediterranean was conducted in response to the increased Phoenician trade.

[110] Convoying and increased naval patrolling by wealthier communities certainly would have been effective protective actions, but more subtle measures could have been taken as well by those who could afford them: e.g., slight modifications of ship designs to improve speed, maneuverability, or defensibility; addition of a marine or two to tip the balance in case of boarding. Neither of these types of change need have been noticeable enough to cause remark in later literary sources or to be apparent in drawings or models.

[111] According to Van Wees's model (1992: 257), the growing importance of sources of prestige alternative to demonstrations of physical prowess in piracy largely eliminated prestige as a motivation for at least the land-oriented raiding, although its material profitability may have continued.

[112] Braudel 1972, 2: 887.

[113] Ibid., 2: 866, on the politics of distinguishing between piracy and privateering; 883, on the difference between rhetoric and reality of pirate depredations; and 886–87 n. 268, on difficulty in distinguishing absolute and relative amounts of shipping plundered by pirates.

as the Dark Ages gave way to the late Archaic and Classical periods would have ameliorated or exacerbated the piracy problem, or left it about the same. It is possible, however, that piracy retarded trade in general, occasionally cut it off on certain routes, and at times directed its attacks against land targets when seaborne prey became less attractive either through scarcity or through increased protection.

To draw together this assessment of the effects of piracy in the Greek Dark Age, I offer a brief, comparative view of subsequent piracy that may elucidate more general principles that can be used to help understand the Greek Dark Age and other ancient cases.[114] A number of differences distinguish the circumstances of the ancient cases of piracy from the better-recorded episodes of the second millennium A.C., many of which can be captured in the categories of more extensive development of the state and maritime technology. Nonetheless, many of the social and economic interactions that I have suggested underlay Dark Age piracy are encountered repetitively in subsequent piracy. I enumerate and discuss eight principles, none of which runs counter to the ancient evidence, and most of which suggest the generality of the principles operating in the Greek Dark Age case.

First, piracy, privateering, and brigandage are physically equivalent, any differences between them flowing from differences in legal sanction. Second, most accounts of piracy have been written by the victims' societies, although the accounts of the seventeenth-century English pirates, and one Dutchman, are exceptions to this rule of thumb. The accounts of Aegean and Mediterranean piracy by several of the ancient historians tend to be relatively uninquisitive political and military narratives from the point of view of Rome, emphasizing effects on and inconveniences to Roman affairs.[115] Others, more interested in causes and correlates of piracy, were at a disadvantage for detailed information on the societies supplying piracy. One account (App. *Mith.* 93) reveals incidentally that the pirates' warfare style tended to baffle the regular military establishments of the day by failing to conform to expectations.

Third, the terms "pirate" and "piracy" commonly are political denotations imposed on an opponent.[116] The second and third principles should caution scholars in their interpretations of all reports of activities characterized as piracy in contemporary accounts.

Fourth, piracy is a labor specialization. Pirates are full-time professionals, not part-time amateurs. Nautical and military skills and discipline are required. Psychological preparation is necessary for the constant life-threatening and life-gambling nature of the labor. This attitude is acquired,

---

[114] The episodes upon which I draw for this assessment include: the Cilician piracy during the second and first centuries B.C.; piracy in the early modern Aegean; Illyrian piracy in the northern Adriatic, of the late fourth to third centuries B.C. and of the sixteenth and early seventeenth centuries A.C.; the Caribbean piracy of the sixteenth and seventeenth centuries; the Barbary and Maltese piratical legacy of the seventeenth and eighteenth centuries; northwestern European piracy of the seventeenth century—English, French, and Dutch primarily; North American and Indian Ocean experiences with piracy in the late seventeenth and early eighteenth centuries; Caribbean and Gulf of Mexico piracy of the nineteenth century; South China piracy of the late eighteenth and early nineteenth centuries; and piracy in the southwest Pacific and South China Sea in the mid-nineteenth century.

[115] Plut. *Vit. Pomp.* 24, 29; Strab. 10.4.9–10; Livy *Epit.* 37.27, 60; Diod. Sic. 27.3, 31.45; Cic. *De Imp. Cn. Pomp.* 31–33.

[116] Searching a university library catalogue via computer brought this point home to me forcefully: a subject search for "piracy" elicited only titles on late-twentieth-century international copyright violation, a much more peaceful crime (again, in the eye of the beholder) than attacking cargo ships by hand. On Polybius's dislike of Cretans in general, see 4.8.11–12, 4.53.5–6, 7.16.4; Walbank 1967: 421, on this prejudice of Polybius; de Souza (1995: 185) expresses skepticism regarding both Polybius's and Livy's vilification of the Spartan king Nabis's "commercial policies" at the turn of the third century. On the effects of the victims writing the records, some aspects of Cilician piracy–the expansion of the sea warfare to Italy in the early first century, and the willingness of seemingly unrelated pirate leaders to coordinate and cooperate with one another in emergencies–appear to have been generalized resistance against Roman expansion eastward: Flor. *Epit.* 1.41; Ormerod and Cary 1932: 372; Cic. *De Imp. Cn. Pomp.* 64–65 on the hatred of Romans in first-century Anatolia. Rhodes's wars with Cretan cities in the middle and end of the second century over frustration with Cretan piracy may have been in fact trade wars, written from the perspective of the Rhodians' Roman friends; cf. Willetts 1965: 145, 154–55; Errington 1989: 248; Habicht 1989: 381.

and the acquired attitude toward risk is not consistent with success in either farming or fishing.[117]

Fifth, labor supply is critical to piracy, from the perspectives of both the pirates and the scholars studying them.[118] Pirates' life expectancies generally have been short—three to five years. Poverty, even desperation, of the host population has been necessary to ensure the continual supply of pirate recruits.[119] When communities have supported piracy, either willingly or grudgingly, there is little evidence that pirates form the social

and familial relations to furnish an adequate supply of recruits organically, that is, from their own families, although the occasional pirate chieftain surely managed to die of old age in his own bed, attended by his granddaughters. Although pirate bases may last well over a century, the political structure tends to be unstable, and the continuity of the settlement (archaeologically speaking) masks the fluidity of the occupying population's kinship structure.[120] Training of pirate recruits commonly has come from extended periods of

---

[117] Garlan (1978: 5; 1989: 189) notes the tendency for the personality of a pirate to eschew commerce—except to sell his booty—but he does not seem to consider the pirate's personality characteristics ("adventurous" is an encompassing euphemism) as an acquisition from occupational hazards.

[118] Sir Henry Mainwaring, the reformed English pirate of the early seventeenth century, recommended to James I that "devis[ing] some more universal employment than now we have" would be a more effective means of suppressing English piracy than increased naval patrolling. Mainwaring and Perrin 1922: 41. The principle surely is more general than early-seventeenth-century England; cf. Thucydides' commentary on motivation, note 92 above. Several early historians noted Pompey's understanding of the relationship between economic desperation and pirate recruitment revealed by his policy of resettling former Cilician pirates after their suppression: App. *Mith.* 96; Plut. *Vit. Pomp.* 28; Luc. *Phars.* 2.635–36.

[119] Garlan (1978: 4–5, 11–12) emphasizes the role of slavery in fostering and perpetuating piracy, but sufficiently desperate economic conditions can blur many distinctions between slavery and various conditions that pass for free, or nonslave. The opportunity to sell slaves increases the demand for piracy, while the ability to escape either from slavery or from nonslave, desperate poverty increases its supply. Jackson (1973: 244–45, 248) has given detailed consideration to the social sources of supply of pirates in the Classical to Hellenistic periods—exiles, friendly or neutral states' subjects, and fugitives (slaves, debtors, etc.)—although he is willing also to consider pirates as solid family men occasionally (248). Willetts (1965: 147) sees piracy and mercenary service as activities that "could drain off their [Cretan city-states'] surplus manpower." Hind (1994: 163) notes the destruction of cities, financial ruin of survivors, liberation of slaves, and reenslavement attending the Mithridatic Wars of the second century as prime sources of Cilician pirates. Cf. Dio Cass. 36.20 on the relation between economic desperation and piracy at this time. Jonkers (1959: 20–21) relates the Cilician piracy to even more widespread distresses during the period as well as to opportunism. In a search for the origins, but not necessarily the causes, of the Cilician piracy, Marasco (1987: 126, 128–29) attributes its emergence to the extended period of dynastic wars between c. 145 and 95. As has characterized the background of subsequent, more amply documented episodes of piracy, this lengthy period of turmoil fostered the development not only of two generations of soldiers, apparently with few nonmilitary skills, who off and on found themselves without an employer, but also of business opportunities at which some of their skills serendipitously were useful–supplying slaves.

Dell (1967: 357–58) associated the flowering of the Illyrian piracy to the weakening and collapse of the Molossian monarchy in Epirus in the third quarter of the third century, when the Illyrians discovered a serious local power vacuum. He concluded from close examination of the ancient texts that the Illyrian piracy in earlier centuries had not, in fact, been endemic but instead had consisted for the most part in occasional raids for food.

[120] It may be objected that the continuity of Cretan cities that sponsored piracy from the third to the first centuries contradicts this claim about the fundamental instability of pirate bases as communities. Certainly much of the internal instability experienced by Cretan city-states in this period derived from adjustments forced on their rigid, archaic social systems by both external and internal developments. Intercity interactions certainly were a continual source of external political instability. But most of the cities survived, and by and large with the descendants of their earlier populations, with a few glaring exceptions. Why did piracy not contribute to a more fundamental instability? First, some of what is reported as piracy from the third century on may be interpreted as the slave trade–a different industry from piracy, although since overlapping skills are useful in both piracy and slaving, some of the same individuals could have participated in both industries, and probably did. Although pirates have not shied away from dealing in the slave commodity under the proper circumstances, slavers have not always been pirates, and pirates have not always engaged in slaving, even while the two activities have been conducted simultaneously in the same regions. It could prove personally satisfying as well as politically useful to call slavers who kidnapped one's friends and relatives "pirates," but surely the legal cir-

warfare in which relatively poor states' naval forces were expanded with legally sanctioned privateer fleets.[121] Wars not uncommonly have lasted a decade or longer. Two generations of sailors have passed through the privateer life without ever knowing any peaceful sea life. By the ends of such wars, these men were unfit for the routine and discipline of peacetime maritime service. An excess supply of seamen commonly has attended the end of such wars. Peacetime trade does not seem to have absorbed the full postwar slack of unemployed seamen, and the states initially sponsoring the piracy lose control of them because the incentives they once had to offer disappear with the arrival of peace, and the sanctions they can offer are weak deterrents—execution commonly has been seen as the next best alternative to piracy because of desperate economic conditions. Even during times of official hostilities, some people came to piracy from nonnautical occupations such as farming and nonship-related crafts, but the proportions have been small enough to be absorbed for rapid training without compromising the efficiency of the crews.

Sixth, naval and military (land) skills are complementary in piracy, but do not necessarily reside equally in all individual pirates. There is specialization among pirates. Pirate operations frequently have had what we today would call an amphibious character, but such operations have been contingent on the political setting of the piracy. Such operations tend to be larger than strictly sea attacks. Land targets are riskier than sea targets and require correspondingly lucrative prospects.[122] Raiding poor and relatively defense-

less settlements for slaves requires a market for those slaves that is wealthy enough to make the capture worthwhile: even "defenseless" farmers can be dangerous to capture.

Seventh, and related to the characteristics of pirate operations, pirates generally have been willing to fight harder to capture a ship than the victim ship's sailors and marines have been willing to fight to protect someone else's property. The prospect of being enslaved would factor into this equation, but included as well are the type of slavery and the conditions of the current occupation. Regular soldiers on land and regular naval personnel at sea also have less incentive to fight pirates than vice versa. Social considerations underlying the supply of military and naval recruits is important on that account, as a community might have felt, "If they will just take what they want and go away, we will be satisfied."

Eighth, piracy requires disposal of the booty. Booty does not provide a sufficiently reliable supply of the balance of necessities to sustain life. The booty must be exported, either directly or indirectly, from the community sustaining the pirates. Otherwise, the booty would serve only to destabilize a closed community. Relative prices of booty would fall (leading to a type of inflation—possibly continual—in terms of the local store of value, if that is what the booty is). If the booty were food, nonexported booty eventually would wreck the local agriculture or depress the value of booty below what would sustain piracy.

Several of these principles already have appeared directly in the focus on the Greek Dark Age. Others give reason for pausing before mak-

---

Note 120 continued

cumstances, as well as many of the economic ones, differed. Second, other actions reported as piracy were the leasing of naval mercenaries–reported by "the other side." Third, in the absence of settled, international commercial diplomacy, community-sponsored or -tolerated attacks on nonlocal shipping must remain subject to interpretation as efforts to (1) establish or negotiate maritime territorial claims, (2) carve out a niche in the carrying trade, by force if not by superior productivity, and (3) strike out at foreigners who may have enjoyed demonstrably greater power and economic success within one's own community as well as elsewhere. (Brulé [1978: 157–58] considers commercial antagonisms between wealthier Rhodes and less-successful Crete, jealous of its richer neighbor, in the late third century to have nourished the Cretan piracy, particularly as it targeted Rhodian interests.) Fourth, perhaps there was a bit of genuine, freelance piracy for the raiders' own accounts only, and perhaps it did indeed contribute a measure of the political instability experienced by individual Cretan cities, instability that has not been accounted for correctly. Altogether, relying on my first three principles of piracy, I am reluctant to accept the ancient accounts and interpretations strictly at face value.

[121] The term "privateer" may appear to be an anachronism, but the concept, in which a state uses unofficial naval forces to attack its enemies, through whatever legal mechanisms appear warranted in the age, surely is time-honored. In the Third Macedonian War (171–168 B.C.), Cretan cities supplied naval forces to both Perseus and Rome. These forces were called "pirates," probably by opposite sides: Willetts 1965: 145, 155.

[122] Dio Cassius (21) noted the better defensibility against land attacks from pirates than against attacks on the seas.

ing simple statements about the operation and effects of Dark Age piracy. The recent discussions of Dark Age Greek piracy have tended to focus on motivations, usually either hunger or prestige, sometimes both. These two motivations do not distinguish piracy from many other activities, and either of these two explanatory approaches runs the risk of largely conceding its conclusion in its premise. The discussion here has begun with the resource requirements of engaging in piracy, the overall production requirements of a self-perpetuating (sustainable) community, and the return resource flow from piracy. This approach may prove a useful supplement to the motivational approaches to the extent that it facilitates deductions about some limits on the practice of piracy and on its economic and social roles.

So what is the implication of piracy for seaborne trade in the Early Iron Age? First, if there is no trade to offer targets at sea, should pirates not live as well off targets on land? I believe not. The land targets available tended to be poor themselves—the wealthier ones could have defended themselves better—and in a repeated game, pirates could have skimmed off only the "surplus" from each town attacked. Where such surpluses were slender, pirates either would have required many communities in their "herds," from which to skim a satisfactory living for themselves, or would have been willing to kill off prey communities. Harvesting, not mining, is the proper analogy for piracy. One could build a case in which, say, each pirate community "harvests" from some twenty prey communities—but to avoid predictability, the twenty communities must be varied (say, exchanged with other piratical communities for a while?); in which each pirate community manages to keep its identity and location secret from its prey; etc. Before long, a model like this collapses under its own weight. After considering the possibilities, I accept that piracy probably was evidence of trade, although occasional attacks on land targets by both professional pirates and prestige or famine raiders may complicate inferences from the archaeological record.

Second, does the absence of attacks on seaborne targets in the *Odyssey* imply the absence of such attacks in fact? The tales of raiding in the epics have lent themselves to alternative interpretations, of which competent scholars have been equally confident. Inferring the absence of sea piracy from the *Odyssey*'s omission of it is an argument from silence, but it also is not obvious

to me that the social problem that Odysseus's character, the Cretan Kastor's son, is solving by raiding is the same as the social problem to which piracy that preys on ships at sea is an adaptation, if not necessarily a solution. The similarities between the career of Kastor's son and that of the seventeenth-century A.C. Caribbean's Henry Morgan are superficial, and the differences I believe are more important.

Third, was piracy always a problem during this period? Possibly, but not necessarily in the same places throughout the period. A half millennium and the Aegean and the eastern half of the Mediterranean offer considerable scope for variation in historical experience, despite the connections among the regions.

Fourth, would piracy have eliminated trade? Trade is part of a set of activities encompassing production and consumption at opposite ends of the trade network. Cessation of trade, even relatively small volumes, could require serious rearrangements of social and economic relations in the trading communities. Piracy so rapacious as to threaten the continued existence of trade would be resisted before the trade was given up. Some reduction in volume would occur as an adjustment to higher expected costs, and a few routes might be avoided for a while, but the cessation of trade is in the interest of neither the pirate nor the trader. My interpretation, considering these complications, is that piracy is evidence of the regular movement of targets by sea, whether one prefers to call those movements "trade," "commerce," or something else, in sufficient quantity to make the organization of piracy worthwhile. General social and economic upheaval might have eliminated trade, but piracy should not have done so, any more than fleas eliminate dogs.

Fifth, can we identify pirate's booty empirically in the archaeological remains? I doubt it. Pirates will take anything, and we have no models that can assign greater or lesser probability to a particular artifact, metal or otherwise, having arrived at its find site via piracy rather than via a less exciting mechanism.

Sixth, I suspect that much of the well-documented detail of Aegean and eastern and central Mediterranean piracy in the fourth (even the fifth) to first centuries may not transfer too well to the early centuries of the first millennium. It is widely recognized that the piracy (and actions called piracy) in the Hellenistic and Roman periods were elicited in large measure by the extensive disturbance to local political structures following the removal of Persian administration in Asia Minor and exacerbated by the continuing instability of their Macedonian successors, and following that period, by Roman policy. Roman economic policies of mining the provincial populations (figuratively, not literally) opened the door to poverty-driven piracy as well as to guerrilla-type wars of resistance that looked like piracy to the Romans, who meantime offered plenty of shipping targets.[123] The circumstances of the early first millennium appear to have differed. Although political and social disruptions were widespread, they were not accompanied by the establishment of a small cadre of new overlords ruling extensive territories to the advantage of their foreign homelands. Additionally, shipping targets undoubtedly were neither as common nor as fat as they were later in the millennium. The emergence of the extensive slave trade, probably by the fifth century, would have offered an attractive new commodity for the industry to acquire and distribute.[124] (At that point, industry lines blur between slaving and what I consider more narrowly defined piracy.) I do not see evidence that such "labor market conditions" characterized the early part of the first millennium, even if (though) slavery was not unknown to the Greeks of those centuries.[125]

TRADE: EVIDENCE IN THE BRONZE AGE AND STORIES FOR THE GREEK DARK AGE

At this point in the discussion, the questions turn naturally to trade. Was there trade during the period? If so, was it more than casual? Was it simply gift exchange à la Mauss? Could it be called commercial? Were exchanges orientated toward, or motivated by, profit or gain? To move beyond personal predilections about how Dark Age Greeks should have been, we must find what answers we can from the evidence of the period, but with the assistance of modern intellectual devices, of which the concept of gift exchange is but one.

EVIDENCE FOR THE END OF THE LATE BRONZE AGE AND THE BEGINNINGS OF THE IRON AGE

My strategy in addressing the information gap the Greek Dark Age interposes between the better-known periods preceding and following it is to summarize what is known about the earlier edge of the gap and to see to what extent the gap can be narrowed, or its darkness lightened somewhat, by identifying continuities.[126] There appears to have been extensive commercial trade in the third and second millennia in the eastern Mediterranean. Evidence is reasonably clear for Old Babylonia, Old Assyria, Hatti, as well as Egypt, which may have been somewhat less outward-looking at times. From the late third millennium through the first millennium, the equivalent of international commerce, or international trade, was conducted, often by private merchants, but with the state and religious institutions playing varying roles at different periods, although the participation of the state appears to have increased in the Late

---

[123] On Rome's economic policies of mining the provincial populations, see Pohl 1993: 55-56, 99.

[124] Certainly Homer refers to slaves in the late eighth to early seventh centuries, and Finley (1959: 145) was impressed with how Hesiod's advice to farmers in the early seventh century seems to have taken slaves for granted. However, the organization and operation of a large slave industry is less apparent at that time. The issue here is not whether slavery existed then in Greece, but whether the demand for slaves was extensive enough to have provided the raison d'être for the industrialization of slaving, as occurred later. I suspect that that demand was not nearly as great in the eleventh to ninth centuries.

[125] Brulé (1978: 184) offers a clear summary of his views regarding the very special conditions that produced the Cretan piracy of the fourth to second centuries. Cretan political elites endeavored to solve island-wide, domestic social problems externally via the legal, international commercial market in slaves and captured goods, enriching themselves and redistributing the labor force in a way that raised the standard of living of the ordinary Cretans.

[126] Winter 1988: 210, in discussing Near Eastern-eastern Mediterranean trade in the early first millennium, recommends a similar strategy of bracketing a lesser-known period with information from better-known periods and searching for discontinuities that would preclude assumptions of continuity of activity.

Bronze Age.[127] Egypt and Crete enjoyed relations of some kind in the mid-second millennium, according to Egyptian tomb paintings and Egyptian artifacts in Minoan Crete, although there is not the literary documentation for the Egypt-Crete exchanges that exists for the Mesopotamian commerce.[128] The relative importance of private traders and the state (the "palace sector," as well as trade organized by relatively independent temples) in Egyptian overseas trade throughout the Bronze Age appears to have weighted the latter heavily, and

---

[127] For historical evidence, see Oppenheim 1977: 64, 91–92; Leemans 1950: 113, 119–25; Veenhof 1972: 348–57; Larsen 1967: 2–4, 178; Gledhill and Larsen 1982: 200–213; Gurney 1990: 15–16, 70–71. For the late third millennium, scholarship has begun to modify the temple-economy model, emphasizing decentralized economic decisions in addition to institutional participation: Foster 1977: 31–43; 1981: 225–41; Powell 1977: 23–29; Postgate 1992: 211–16, 235–37. Heltzer's studies of the economy and society of Late Bronze Age Ugarit (destroyed c. 1200) conclude that "the principal socio-economic unit in Ugarit was the [private] rural community, and the wealth of the kingdom was based on its productivity": 1976: 102. Heltzer's characterization of the royal sector both portrays extensive centralization of diverse economic activities, ranging from urban crafts to rural agricultural production, and observes individually initiated activity within that system of royal ownership and accountability to the palace. Heltzer's view proposes a large, possibly dominant, but not exclusive, role for the palace in foreign trade: 1982; 1978; and 1984: 183–86, 192–93. Knapp (1983: 42–43) observes royal-private interactions in international trading activity at Ugarit, with an Alashiyan merchant requesting approval from the king of Ugarit for the purchase of some ships from private merchants of Ugarit, c. 1400–1200. Larsen reiterates his interpretation of changing balances of power between the state and private traders in Middle Bronze Age Mesopotamia: 1987: 49–50. Foster (1987: 11–16) offers a short overview, oriented to the Aegean archaeologist, of long movements in state-private proportions in the economies of the ancient Near Eastern kingdoms from the Early through the Late Bronze Age, demonstrating considerable variation by time and region. The most recent, new archaeological evidence for the Late Bronze Age is the Kaş shipwreck: Bass 1986; Pulak 1988: 1–38.

[128] Vercoutter's works (1954, 1956) are early but basic treatments of the artifactual record to that date as well as examinations of the identity of the Keftiu. Leclant (1996) largely reinforces Vercoutter's conclusions regarding Egyptian-Aegean interactions in the Bronze Age and the identification of the Keftiu with the Minoans, from a perspective of thirty-five years of subsequent research. Smith (1965: 130–37) endorses Cretan presence in Egypt during the Middle Kingdom. Warren (1969: 105–15) cites Egyptian stone vases in Crete, and (1991: 296) records more recent finds of Egyptian stone vases. Helck (1971: 107, 167, 283, 402–3, 501, 503) notes implicit and explicit indications of Cretan interactions with Egypt, from the Old Kingdom to the middle of the Eighteenth Dynasty, although by the reign of Tutmosis III, he considers Crete to have dropped outside the circle of Asiatic great powers. Phillips (1991) reports 461 Egyptian and Minoan egyptianizing artifacts; most appear around Knossos and Phaistos, with a tendency for a larger proportion of Minoan copies at Phaistos (947–76). A scattering of both genuine Egyptian artifacts and Minoan copies appear at a handful of eastern sites as well, and at Chania, but the less-central sites tended to attract the copies more frequently. Sapouna-Sakellarakis and Sakellarakis (1984: 200) consider, "It is evident from the pictorial and inscribed sources . . . , and not from the limited literary sources, that these relations were commercial." The Sakellarakises consider the Keftiu to have provided the Egyptians with the products of a number of different lands, but they dismiss the Egyptian characterization of these commodities as gifts. Bleiberg (1984; 1996: 115–23) interprets the word *inw* as a gift to the pharaoh, or as an official gift between persons of unequal stature, inferring a robustness that weathered unspecified changes in meaning between the First and Twentieth Dynasties. Gordon (1983: 386–90) found substantial variation in the meaning of *inw* from the Protodynastic period through the end of the New Kingdom and inferred that the Egyptian characterization of goods as *inw* tended to glorify as tribute goods that entered Egypt in a variety of mechanisms, not the least of which was ordinary trade. He concluded that the characterization as *inw*, especially on pharaonic monuments, was royal propaganda that bore no necessary relationship to *how* the originator of the goods viewed the transaction. Warburton (1997: 221–36, esp. 232, 236) considers Bleiberg's inferences unduly influenced by modern doctrinal categorizations of exchanges and concludes with Gordon that *inw* encompassed a variety of transactions, including trade. The dating of Cretan-Egyptian relations is complicated by the vast chronological discrepancies between the recognized dates of a number of early Egyptian artifacts appearing in Late Minoan contexts across Crete. Pomerance (1973: 21–30) makes a plausible case for Late Minoan importation of Egyptian antiques, such that the find *contexts* faithfully indicate the entry date of earlier overseas material. The most recent evidence of Minoan-Egyptian relations is M. Bietak's discovery of apparent Minoan bull-leaping frescoes in a Sixteenth Dynasty building at Tell el-Daba'a, in the northeastern Delta; Bietak 1994: 45–58, pls. 14–22; see Shaw 1994: 331; Dickinson 1994: 164, 244, 247, pl. 7.1; Bietak 1995: 73–79, pls. III–VIII; Bietak and Marinatos 1995: 49–62.

there is little evidence that those relative weights fluctuated as much as they did in Mesopotamia.[129] However, the state or private participation has no implication for the commercial character of the trade.[130] Although the palace sector's transactions would have includ-ed exchanges or purchases of diplomatic good-will between royal houses, values certainly attached to such intangibles, and equally certainly, agents outside the palace sector consumed at least some of the traded commodities at both ends of the transactions.[131]

---

[129] Davies and Faulkner (1947: 45) describe the painting in the tomb of Kenamūn, the mayor of Thebes and superintendent of the Granaries of Amūn, probably in the reign of Amenophis III. The painting includes three wharfside stalls of apparently small, independent shopkeepers buying articles from the same ships that are discharging other cargo, apparently under the direction of Kenamūn. Davies and Faulkner say, "Although the main cargo of incoming ships was apparently sold through the agency of men in high authority like Kenamūn, there seems to have been no regulation against small-scale private trading." It seems possible to take the pharaonic inscriptions at too close to face value and reach conclusions of extensive centralization of the entire Egyptian economy through the Middle Kingdom. Helck (1987: 17) makes such an acceptance of an inscription of no less bold a pharaoh than Ramesses II, and reaches conclusions of remarkable economic centralization. The information requirements for the coordination involved in implementing the claims of the inscription would have been enormous, such as helped bring down the centrally planned economies of Eastern Europe in the twentieth century A.C. Helck's conclusions about the social, economic, and moral consequences of such centralized palace control in Egypt (18) further require considerable faith in the Egyptian common people's docile compliance with each restrictive edict, although such compliance allegedly kept them on the margin of existence. Kemp (1972: 667–76; 1992: 126–27, 184, 195, ch. 6) has developed the case for an extensive, private, profit-oriented economy underpinning the well-recorded pharaonic public economy throughout the New Kingdom. Janssen (1992: 316–17) objects to Kemp's equation of *gain* and *profit*.

   In the case of Cypro-Egyptian exchanges during the Eighteenth Dynasty, Merrillees (1968) considers that the "quantity, comparative value, geographical distribution and social setting [of the Cypriote Base-ring I and II ware found in Egypt] together weigh against every argument that they may have been acquired in any other way than by ordinary commercial transaction" (168); "the comparatively large quantities of Cypriote pottery in the city [el-Amarna] suggest that Akhenaten was responsible for creating a favourable climate in which overseas merchants could operate with ease" (186). From the long continuation of this pottery in Egypt, with little change in its physical appearance, Merrillees infers that this trade was "no chance exchange between Cyprus and Egypt but the exploitation of a sales potential in Egypt based on known preferences, for which the Cypriotes specifically sought to cater" (157). In "Opium Trade in the Bronze Age Levant" (1962: 288), Merrillees develops the idea that the stability of the container shape and appearance must have been a principal advertising device for foreign merchants among a population who, if they were literate, must have read only their own language. Holmes (1973: 93) reports varying quantities of Late Bronze Age Cypriot pottery found at some fifty sites scattered all over Egypt.

[130] Davis and Lewis (1985: 89) point to the invariance of external competition to local administration of production and trade in the Late Corinthian I and II periods: "Whether it is the individual potter or his lord who trades his pottery abroad, both must compete for consumers in other polities."

[131] Wiener (1991: 327) notes that such ceremonial gifts do not "constitute `archaic' non-profit-maximizing behaviour." For the later, Neo-Assyrian period, Winter (1988: 209–10) characterizes such "royal gifts . . . as cementing palatial and even possibly commercial alliances. . . . Gifting is not . . . separate from, or outside of the commodity-system, . . . even if . . . exchange is delayed." There is the additional, natural role of a state in supplying "public goods" (and services) such as provision of safety for overseas trading activities, whether private or royal, and underwriting of some of the risks of distant ventures. Köpke (1987: 256–57) suggests these roles for the Cretan palaces, although there is less reason to see the palace sector as the major source of capital advance as well. In fact, wealthy private families may have been a major financial resource for the palaces. The term "public good" is a disciplinary economic term referring to goods or services that have the characteristic that, once provided, it is difficult to exclude anyone's use of them; public safety is an apt example. Consequently, if such a good or service is provided by a private individual who has no ability to command payments reflecting the good's value to others as well as to himself or herself, that individual will provide less of it than society actually wants. The state has the coercive capacity to command payment sufficient to cover the cost of providing such goods.

The Aegean was integrated with this world in the second millennium.[132] However, there is a shift at this point from the relatively secure evidence of commercial activity in Mesopotamia and the Levant in the second millennium to an interpretation of archaeological evidence showing interaction between the Aegean and the Near East over the same period. Still, I see no reason to conclude that the nature of the Aegean transactions, as contrasted with their possible volume and commodity composition, differed from those of the groups identified in the cuneiform texts.[133]

---

[132] Kantor 1947: 79–83. Furumark (1950: 213–15) believed that Kantor had overstated the case for the intensity of interactions between the Aegean and the east in general; furthermore, he specifically considered the available evidence insufficient to support hypotheses that one group or another carried the goods that were found in excavations: "No further conclusions [than that the vases were made in one place and brought to where they were found] can be drawn from this material without the aid of other evidence." I return to this theme below, in note 143. More recently, see Crowley 1989: 245–68. Stubbings (1951) reports ceramic evidence of Mycenaean presence in Syria, Palestine, and Egypt, as well as Rhodes and Cyprus from Late Helladic (Mycenaean) II through IIIB. Hankey 1967: 107–47; 1970: 11–30; and 1972: 143–45 add to Stubbings's finds. Hankey (1973: 131 n. 15) reports additional ceramic finds in the Levant through Mycenaean IIIB; she maps the finds in the Levant and in Egypt (135–36, figs. 2 and 3). The Greek ceramic finds at Amarna, from a variety of contexts, suggest decentralized, commercial trade, possibly via private, Syrian traders, and extend through Mycenaean IIIB:1: Hankey 1973: 128–30; Merrillees 1973b: 176, 178, 182–83. Hankey (1980) appears of two minds on the method of arrival of the Mycenaean pottery at El Amarna: the shapes do not suggest a "royal deal or gift" (43), although she believes that the sherds filtered down from the palace and aristocratic houses (44); on the other hand, from the relative infrequency of Mycenaean pottery elsewhere in Egypt and the Egyptian plaques at Mycenae, she infers the likelihood of a single royal visit that was responsible for the plaques at Mycenae and the Mycenaean pottery at El Amarna (45–46). Physical analysis indicates that at least some of the Mycenaean pottery at El Amarna was produced in the northern Argolid, probably in the Mycenae-Berbati area: Catling, Richards, and Blin-Stoyle 1963: 109; and Mommsen, Beier, Diehl, and Podzuweit 1992: 293–302. Bell believes that the Late Helladic IIIA:2 and IIIB stirrup jars—both small (fineware) and large (coarseware)—found at the workmen's village at Deir el-Medina belie the characterization of the imported Aegean contents as luxuries at any of the Egyptian sites at which these vessels are found: 1982: 151–53; and 1983: 18.

Lambrou-Phillipson (1990) assesses the published Near Eastern and Egyptian artifacts in the Aegean to the end of the Late Bronze Age. She characterizes the relations between Greece and Egypt, and between Crete (Kommos) and Egypt, during the Eighteenth Dynasty as organized commercial activity, possibly conducted by both Mycenaeans and Egyptians in the former case and without intermediaries in the latter (153). Cline (1990: 210) suggests that Laureion characteristics of lead glaze on apparently Egyptian faience plaques found at Mycenae could indicate Egyptian imports from Greece. This suggestion is strengthened by the apparently Laureion provenance of lead objects found in Eighteenth Dynasty Egypt—El Amarna and Abydos: Gale 1980: 178. The common suggestion that the higher-quality Mycenaean material was sold off mostly in Cyprus, and only the leftovers were carried on to Egypt, is worth remarking for its counterintuitive economic quality: e.g., Hankey 1980: 45. Ordinarily, more-expensive goods (before adding shipping costs) are able to bear greater shipping costs and hence travel farther than less-expensive goods, other things equal (such as shipping costs per item on cheap and expensive goods). Because of the existence of resource constraints, it is difficult to accept the interpretation of an inverse relationship between distance shipped and quality (cost) of an item as evidence that the people of the later second millennium were "unlike us." It seems more natural to think of contents of those less-interesting vessels as contributing the value that was able to bear the larger shipping cost. Cf. Silberberg 1987: 345–49, on the effect of transportation costs on the relative delivered costs of low-quality (cheap) and high-quality (expensive) goods. Wachsmann 1987: 106–13, 124–25) doubts that Mycenaeans themselves ever reached farther east than Cyprus: that Cypriots carried any Mycenaean goods to the Levantine coast and to Egypt. He interprets the tomb paintings of Minoans as indicating two diplomatic missions of Cretans to Egypt (122–24), but does not speculate on the purpose of diplomatic missions if other, more commonplace contacts did not exist to make the diplomatic effort worth the trouble. The most recent possible evidence of Mycenaean interaction with Egypt is the painted papyrus fragment from Amarna showing possible Mycenaean equipment on some soldiers, found in a room with an intact Mycenaean vase. The painting was executed by an Egyptian artist and shows possible interpretations of boar's-tusk helmets and metal-edged tunics, both of which have parallels in the Aegean but have not been found in preserved Egyptian battle scenes: Schofield and Parkinson 1994: 169, frontispiece. On the distribution of the boar's-tusk helmet and possible parallels that could have contributed to the helmets represented on the Amarna papyrus, cf. Hencken 1971: 18–21; Borchardt 1972: 16–18 on the Aegean zone helmet, 18–37 on its boar's-tusk variety, fig. 3 on the distribution of the

Cline's review of Mycenaean objects in Egypt in Late Helladic IIIA and IIIB finds that "simple, ordinary" Egyptians—from grave contexts at Deir el-Medina (across the Nile from Thebes; see Map 7)—could afford to own Mycenaean pottery and that Egyptian-Mycenaean relations continued beyond the end of the Amarna period into the Ramesside period.[134] From his recent analysis of the imported pottery at Late Minoan Kommos, on the south coast of Crete, Watrous reaches two

important conclusions relevant to Late Bronze Age Aegean-Near Eastern interaction. First, from the appearance beginning in Late Minoan I of Egyptian pottery—frequently large container jars—and their relative scarcity along the Levantine-southern Anatolian coastal shipping route, and from the eight-to-one ratio of southern Canaanite jars to northern ones at Kommos, he believes that direct commerce from Egypt to Crete during this period is a justifiable hypothe-

---

Note 132 continued

boar's-tusk helmet, 91, 92, no. 28.II.3, pl. 24.2,4 on a fifteenth-century Egyptian representation of a Syrian helmet with modest similarity of its vertical armor plates to those on the Amarna papyrus, and Beil. F for a convenient, graphical presentation of the geographical and chronological distribution of helmet types in the Late Bronze Age Aegean and eastern Mediterranean regions; Borchardt 1977: 61–64.

Cline (1994) reviews the opinions on the character of international exchanges during the Late Bronze Age—state gift exchange or private commerce (85–88)—and thoroughly documents the array of both eastern (Egyptian, Near Eastern, Anatolian) and western (Italian, other European) artifacts recovered from sites around the Aegean (his Catalogue II, 132–233). He finds adequate room for a variety of transport mechanisms for these objects. He also (1995b: 147–49) discusses relationships between royal gift-giving and ordinary commercial trade, and suggests that the Near Eastern and Egyptian artifacts found in the Aegean are simply too numerous to have been all the results of diplomatic missions. Cline (1995a: 265–83) reviews artifactual evidence for the presence of Aegean individuals in Egypt and various regions of the Near East during the Middle and Late Bronze Ages; the following record of discussion (284–87) reveals considerable diversity of opinion on the methodology of making these inferences as well as on the specific artifactual interpretations.

[133] The evidence of the Aegean-Near Eastern exchanges is primarily from the second half of the second millennium, during which time the role of the state in regulating, and possibly conducting, foreign trade was greater than it was in the late third and early second millennium. Private traders, however, appear to have conducted much of the royal trade, were able to grow wealthy from it, and still were able to undertake some private trade, although it was relatively heavily regulated: Leemans 1950: 119–22, 125; Oppenheim 1977: 92. Köpke (1987: 259) suggests that "the importance of the private trader in the Near East is likely to have been part of the Cretan [LM II–IIIA] tradition as well." Palaima (1991: 309) reports that the Linear B tablets from Pylos and Knossos, despite an "extensive poverty of references to trade or shipping activities . . . record foreign trade products and foreign individuals and ethnic groups, proving that overseas contacts were strong." The tablets indicated that relations with Cyprus were strong. Palaima believes that Mycenaean ships probably carried the intra-Aegean trade, but that Near Eastern ships may have brought the Near Eastern imports. Uphill (1984: 213) discusses the Twelfth Dynasty diorite statuette of User found probably at the palace at Knossos in an unclear context ranging from possibly somewhat earlier than Middle Minoan IIB to Late Minoan. From a comparison of contexts of other such statues around the eastern Mediterranean outside Egypt, and their funereal contexts within Egypt, he concludes that it probably is a votive left by a private Egyptian merchant to lower his probability of dying in a foreign land. Cf. Wotzka 1990: 449–53. Melas (1988: 62–63) characterizes the relations of Late Minoan I Crete with Cyprus, the Levant, and possibly Egypt as "commercial intercourse." He considers the Cretan pottery as probably trade goods because the "Minoan pottery was the finest pottery of its day," although he acknowledges that agricultural products such as textiles also must have been included in Crete's export merchandise (63). Melas also cites evidence that "Minoan [sic] trade of course continued into the Postpalatial times both within the Aegean and beyond" (63). Liverani (1986: 411) concludes that the Mycenaean trade with the Near East in general and with Ugarit in particular was primarily private and commercial. He is also critical of the biases in assessing trade introduced by uncritical tracing of pottery (410). Hooker (1976: 29, 54, 115, 174) interprets the archaeological evidence from the Shaft Grave period through Late Helladic IIIC as reflecting Mycenaean "commercial contacts of . . . long standing" (174), rather than as results of warfare, territorial expansion, and other coercive programs.

[134] Cline 1987: 13–17. Stos-Gale and Gale (1982: 476) suggest that part of the Mycenaean-Egyptian trade might have been Egyptian gold, which, earlier, made the Mycenae Shaft Graves so spectacular, for Greek lead and silver. Cf. the heirloom discussion in Cline 1991: 41–42, regarding two faience monkey figurines, possibly related, with the Tiryns example found in a Late Helladic IIIA context; Cline does not find sufficient grounds to lean toward either a royal gift or a bric-a-brac (ordinary trade?) hypothesis.

sis, in addition to the more commonly cited, counterclockwise circulation along the Anatolian peninsula, between the southeastern Mediterranean and Crete.[135] Second, and more central to my own suggestion that Egyptian-Aegean economic relations differed little in character from other Egyptian overseas economic interactions, he suggests that the representations of Minoans in late-sixteenth- and early-fifteenth-century Egyptian tomb paintings may reflect "Aegean-Egyptian commerce" rather than "rare embassies."[136] Though Watrous does not commit himself to the further step that this suspected commerce was indeed mercantile trade rather than a regular exchange of presents between royal houses, he implies such. With no palace found at Kommos, why would a stream of royal gifts not arrive at Knossos directly instead of at a port at the head of a splendid oil-producing region such as the Mesara?[137] It seems reasonable to suspect that royal gifts would have landed at a port close to the principal palace and, concomitantly, that evidence of foreign activity in a port town located next to an agricultural region that probably had little trouble producing far more oil than it could use itself suggests trade in commercial quantities of that product, regardless of who conducted the trade or owned the products—the palace or private individuals.[138] Haskell has suggested that a vision of highly centralized economic direction on Late Minoan III Crete imposes an unreasonably high degree of centralization, which would imply more independence from Knossos for the activity seen indirectly at Kommos.[139] And certainly Egypt was not the only Near Eastern region to interact with Late Bronze Age Crete: in a thirteenth-century text from Ugarit, Ammistamru II, king of Ugarit, gives a trader a franchise to import grain, wine (beer?), and oil from Crete (Caphtor).[140] Would these products have left Crete through Kommos? Additional evidence of contact between Crete

---

[135] Watrous 1992: 176. While the wind patterns in the eastern Mediterranean have been cited commonly in justification of the more traditionally accepted counterclockwise shipping pattern, Watrous cites the alternation of northerly and southerly winds in the Aegean between March and September and points to the south wind from Libya, which frequently warms an already hot Crete during the summer (177). He also is willing to consider supplementation of sails by oars, even in the open sea (178). Clearly, the only resolution that is required to make the two shipping routes compatible is to accept that both are likely to have existed simultaneously and to adjust our beliefs about the proportions of freight moving along each route, possibly varying by subseason. Gilmour (1992: 119) suggests a direct shipping route between Kommos and Marsa Matruh on the western Egyptian coast, thence eastward to the Nile Delta. The large proportion of Cypriot vessels, many of them coarseware, excavated at Marsa Matruh, with a small number of Minoan, Mycenaean, and Egyptian sherds from the thirteenth century, and possibly the fourteenth, suggest a Cypriot trading station and hint at the possibility of trade with Crete, despite the wind pattern, since Marsa Matruh (Bates's Island) is west of the Nile Delta and both Cypriot and Egyptian material is found at Kommos: Hulin 1989: 120–21, 125–26. Helck (1983: 81–82, maps on 93–94) derives from the Homeric and classical references a series of settlements along the North African coast west of the Nile Delta, which he associates with a direct trade route between Egypt and Crete in the second and early first millennia. Georgiou (1991: 62) produces a more striking departure from the current wisdom regarding ancient shipping routes by studying the flexibility of rigging systems to establish Bronze Age ships' ability to sail to windward. In fact, he considers sailing fully with the wind in a Bronze Age ship to be hazardous. Cf. Chapter 4, note 396.

[136] Watrous 1992: 172.

[137] For the later fourteenth and the thirteenth centuries, Watrous (ibid.: 178) does commit himself to the concept of "regular international trade" with the Levant, including Egypt. On the basis of the continuous presence of Syro-Palestinian and Egyptian pottery and a large number of coarse stirrup jars, sixty-five of seventy-five examples apparently of local Mesara fabric, he concludes that Late Minoan IIIA2–IIIB Kommos was an important center of oil exportation. Five pieces of a balance-weight set consistent with the Egyptian metrological system have been found in a Late Minoan IIIA grave at Katsambas, an early port of Knossos, suggesting Knossian trade with Egypt: Petruso 1984: 303.

[138] Of course, it is possible to envision "royal" influence—"control," ownership, taxation, extortion, or whatever—from Phaistos, depending on one's beliefs about relationships among the Cretan palaces.

[139] Haskell 1989: 102, 109. Palmer's interpretation of what she calls a "direct exchange system" at Pylos supports a more decentralized vision of the Mycenaean economies than is sometimes proposed: Palmer 1989: 272.

[140] Nougayrol 1955: 101, 107–8; Heltzer (1988a: 10–11) identifies Sinaranu as one of the wealthiest men in midto late-thirteenth-century Ugarit and infers the high importance the king of Ugarit placed on his trade relations with Crete (13).

and the Levant about the same time (LM IIIB in Minoan chronology) comes from Nami, a coastal site fifteen kilometers south of Haifa. The excavations at Nami found, in a hilltop sanctuary, some improvised conical cups with pumice placed in them. The practice is foreign to the Levantine coast but has been found on Crete at Zakros, Nirou Chani, and Chania. The port town at Nami was an international maritime center, and the remains in the sanctuary could represent dedications from Cretan sailors or from Syrian sailors who had visited Crete. Thirteenth-century Mycenaean and Cypriot pottery has been found in the cemetery of Nami East.[141]

In general, focus on hypothesized motives in foreign trade and identities of personnel involved in the production, ownership, transportation, and consumption of externally traded items, to the exclusion of the patterns of resource allocation and transfer involved, evolves into an intractable array of models of trade that are poorly testable.[142] Additionally, the resource allocation and transfers involved, and important social relationships, are simply invariant to many of the intricate model variations. The proportions of domestic and overseas economic activity operated by private agents or the palaces (the "royal sector," the state, or the "government," to use a

---

[141] Artzy 1991: 203–5; 1994: 125–26; 1990: 76.

[142] Adams (1974: 239–49) reached a similar conclusion in considering the evidence of ancient Mesopotamian trade. Renfrew (1972: 465–71, amplified in 1975: 41–51) has provided a now-well-known set of trade models with a strong emphasis on spatial characteristics of exchanges, which is intended to address distributional characteristics of archaeological evidence for trade. Runnels (1985: 30–43) has used the spatial and temporal incidence of millstones as evidence of trade, with no inferences regarding the social organization of the exchanges. Renfrew has distanced himself somewhat from his earlier efforts at inferring social underpinnings of trade from artifactual evidence on the basis of what he calls "equifinality" of the models he used—different models leading to the same result: 1977: 82–83, 88. Hodder (1982: 202) has equated that equifinality problem with mathematical analysis, which he says may not be able to distinguish between alternative social processes generating the same visible pattern. This inability to distinguish is clearly a problem, and it is a problem of method, but it cannot be attributed simply to "mathematical" analysis. The approach in Renfrew's work, and indeed underlying Hodder's earlier work (e.g., Hodder 1974: 172–89), is to produce a mathematical formula, *deus ex machina*, that is thought to characterize empirical regularities in data without *deriving* those formulae from prior specifications (also mathematical) of the behavior thought to produce the regularities. Sometimes a single representation is inadequate, and the disentangling of variations in data to determine the correspondence to hypothesized behavior requires intricate specification of several behavioral relationships, not just one. This complication of empirical testing is known in economics and econometrics as the identification problem, and its analysis has been brought recently to palaeopathology by Wood, Milner, Harpending, and Weiss (1992: 343–58).

The social interpretation of the different spatial patterns of evidence has led to an emphasis on the persons, or personae, involved and their functions in the transactions, which, while interesting, has tended to obscure more fundamental issues of resource allocation and the possible effects of trade on the well-being of the participants. However, much of the interest in ancient trade has resided in its potential as a mechanism for transferring ideas and for facilitating cultural diffusion in general. Does a direct focus on these questions yield robust answers? Would participants have felt themselves better or worse off for having been exposed to elements of outside cultures? What opinions would nonparticipants—those indirectly affected—have held? Focus on the resource movements can approach the culture questions from this direction. Wiener (1987: 264–65) finds that "the categories suggested for trade [gift exchange, trade, administered trade, trade for profit, barter, trade at a market price, down-the-line exchange, prestige gift exchange, freelance commercial trade, directional commercial trade] often tend to dissolve in the disorder of reality." In an attempt to apply Renfrew's trade-classification scheme to imported pottery from Late Cycladic I Phylakopi, Cherry and Davis (1982: 338) conclude, "It seems clear, then, that none of these models of exchange is wholly satisfactory." Their alternative proposal implies the continuous turnover of merchandise inventories at sequentially visited ports of call; the proposal gives the logical and empirical freedom to envision a flexible mix of private and state-sponsored traders (339–40). Schofield (1982: 19, 21–22) also suggests the concept of a mix of state and private trade circulating among ports of call in the western Cyclades in Late Cycladic I/Late Minoan I, on a route between Crete and the mainland. She declines to use Polayni's port-of-trade concept to characterize the ports of call. In this "tramping" concept of Late Bronze Age Aegean trade, the sequential character of the ships' calls is not random or in any way unplanned. Smith (1987: 156) notes several difficulties faced in applying these descriptive models of trade to archaeological data. She substitutes some concepts regarding the identification of colonists and finds considerable interpretive latitude applying that model also to the Italian information from the Late Helladic III period (159–61).

term with a more contemporary ring) are an interesting issue, but one that is separable from the issue of commerce versus gift exchange. It seems unreasonable to assume that palaces could more afford, or would have been more willing, to lose resources through failure to calculate the value of outputs derived from the cost of inputs than could private families. If palace sectors happened to participate in a larger proportion of trade with Crete and the Aegean in the Late Bronze Age, those proportions could reflect, at least in part, greater commercial risks associated with longer-distance transportation than was the case in Levantine interstate trade. The reduction in the capabilities, or the willingness, of states to fulfill their roles of public-good provision in overseas economic activity could have been a major factor in the interruption of foreign trade at the end of the Late Bronze Age.

R. S. Merrillees has devoted considerable attention to the practical implementation of models of Late Bronze Age trade in the eastern Mediterranean, focusing on individual traders, whether they represented only themselves or royal principals. His characterization of trade emphasizes the identification of merchants with specific cities, rather than with entire regions (or, anachronistically, countries), a characteristic that will apply to a large portion of Early Iron Age trade, with exceptions for imperial Assyrian and Egyptian trade.[143] He emphasizes trade between, say, Enkomi and Ugarit rather than between Cyprus and north Canaan. Within this set of interacting cities, Merrillees envisions a trading system with merchants of various city affiliations moving goods between various cities, stockpiling goods from diverse regions at commercial centers, with reexport of some of these goods by different merchants. In such fashion, goods could be moved throughout the Levant by a series of traders, often indirectly, rather than by the same individuals carrying them from origin to final destination. This is a sensible, conservative reconstruction that does not appear to appeal to anachronistic business practices, or to anachronistic information or shipping technologies. The same structure of interactions is quite plausible for Early Iron Age trade as well.[144]

Continuing with trade in the east, the external contacts of Cyprus throughout the Bronze and Iron Ages are relatively well-known, and I cite evidence for some of those relations around the end of the Late Bronze Age and the beginning of the Early Iron Age only to round out the picture being developed in this section of traffic during the last years before the Greek Dark Age. Cyprus is a large island with numerous excavated and well-published sites, and I strive to be representative rather than complete in this brief review. Although overshadowed quantitatively by Mycenaean pottery, Cretan LM IIIB pottery has been found at a number of Cypriot sites.[145] Enkomi, just inland from the east coast, and Kition (present-day Larnaca) on the southeast coast, have yielded Late Minoan IIIB pottery from Chania—eight fine vessels from tomb 9 at

---

[143] Although a number of Merrillees's publications contain elements of his practical approach to theorizing about Late Bronze Age trade, possibly the most compact expression of his thinking on this topic is the Discussion in *The Mycenaeans in the Eastern Mediterranean* (1973a: 325–26).

[144] Merrillees (1973a: 326) expresses the opinion that the twentieth-century A.C. focus on the balance of payments as a key variable in international trade has distracted scholars from the city-specific orientation of ancient trade. This is reasonable and possibly correct. However, his subsequent rejection (327) of accounting constraints on the small-scale, reexport trading system he envisions for the period is incorrect (unless he has in mind a parallel, capital account), although the error (in the absence of a capital account) does not affect the structure or operation of his model of trade. Merrillees shares this belief about the inappropriateness of applying the balance-of-payments concept to Late Bronze Age overseas commerce with Hooker (1976: 133), who believes that the use of the concept requires a centralized agency such as a state to keep track of the accounts, but such an agency is unnecessary for an accounting balance to impose itself on individuals in unorganized, or decentralized, transactions. Hooker's example of Mycenaean settlers abroad as a possible source of demand for Mycenaean pottery exports does not avoid the constraint those settlers would have faced in persuading fellow Mycenaeans at home to send pots. While the moral suasion of blood kin might have had some persuasive effect, simple payment should have been sufficiently persuasive. In both cases—Merrillees's and Hooker's—the values of material flows will be the same in both directions. Any device introduced to avoid this constraint merely adds another account that is subject to the same conservation law.

[145] Åström 1972: 403–8 reviews Minoan ware found in Cyprus through the 1960s: thirty-one vases from LM IIIA2–IIIB, one from LM IIIA1.

Kition—and Cypriot White Slip II material has been found at Chania. (See Map 3 for locations of sites on Cyprus, and Map 8 in Chap. 4 for sites on Crete.) Two Late Minoan IIIB octopus kraters have been found in a house at Toumba tou Skourou, and two Late Minoan IIIA:1 vases were discovered in a well at the same site.[146] A relatively high proportion of Late Minoan IIIB pottery—late thirteenth century—has been found at Pyla-Kokkinokremos, another site near the coast, between Enkomi and Kition. At Athienou, inland about midway between Nicosia and Larnaca, several Cretan stirrup jars from the second half of the thirteenth century have been found, along with, in an early-twelfth-century stratum, a bell-shaped bowl that may be Cretan. A few oatmeal stirrup jars, identified as Cretan, have been excavated in Late Cypriot IIC contexts—thirteenth century—at Kourion, toward the western end of the south coast.[147] Kanta notes a Late Minoan IIIC amphoroid krater at Sinda, inland from Enkomi.[148] Levantine material from Late Cypriot IIIB (1150–1050) has been found at Alaas, north of Salamis, with one or more Levantine flasks in nearly every tomb, and at least twenty Syro-Palestinian torpedo-shaped jars have been found in the Ingot God Sanctuary at Enkomi, particularly in eleventh-century levels, and elsewhere at Enkomi, as well as at Salamis, Enkomi's coastal successor. Late-eleventh-century Palestinian pottery has been found in the cemetery of Palaepaphos-Skales, in the southwest of the island. A bowl with an Ugaritic inscription has been found in a first-quarter twelfth-century context at Hala Sultan Tekke. From the mid-twelfth century to the mid-eleventh, there is no evidence of direct trade between Cyprus and Palestine, but by the mid-eleventh century, a good bit of Levantine pottery

was reaching Cyprus, and some Cypriot White Painted I ware was reaching sites in Israel.[149] Egyptian material reached Cyprus during the Late Cypriot IIC–IIIB period (1300–1050), and Palaepaphos-Skales demonstrates renewed contact with Egypt during Cypro-Geometric I (1050–950).[150] I have noted the Sardinian connection above: inter alia, a bronze coal shovel (from a private collection) nearly identical to examples from Sinda and from the foundry hoard at Enkomi, dated by the latter to the twelfth century or the beginning of the eleventh; a rhyton from Nuraghi Antigori with an exact parallel from a Late Helladic IIIB:1 context at Enkomi; a number of bronze mirrors, possibly as early as the thirteenth century, probably from the twelfth and eleventh; and some Late Cypriot IIIC rod tripod stands, which probably arrived on Sardinia shortly after LC IIIC.[151] Late Bronze Age Cypriot pottery has been found at the emporium of Thasos on Sicily, and Cypriot bronze mirrors have been found in Late Helladic IIIC:1 contexts (shortly before 1200) at Pantalica North.[152] (See Map 4 for locations of the Sicilian sites.) The twelfth century and the first half of the eleventh in Cyprus appear to have been a period of major social and territorial reorganization, after arrival of people probably from the Aegean—both Minoans and Mycenaeans—and the Levant. Contact with the Mycenean Aegean, frequent over the previous two centuries, virtually ceased at the beginning of the Late Cypriot III period (c. 1190), and Mycenaean-style pottery on the island began to be made locally.[153] External contacts from the later twelfth century were more heavily weighted to the east than previously.[154] Subsequent imports from Greece, other than possibly Crete, appear not to have reached Cyprus before the late tenth century—the

---

[146] Vermeule and Wolsky 1990: 384. The authors suggest that later Minoan vases may have come off ships from Bates Island, off the western coast of Egypt, which has yielded Late Minoan IIIA and Late Helladic IIIA sherds mixed with White Slip II.

[147] Enkomi: Popham 1979a: 184. Kition: ibid.: 185; Karageorghis 1976: 29. Pyla-Kokkinokremos: Vermeule 1985: 359–60. Athienou: Dothan 1979: 175; Dothan and Ben-Tor 1983: 49–53. Kourion: Dothan and Ben-Tor 1983: 53; Catling and Millet 1965: 32–37.

[148] Kanta 1980: 313; from Åström 1972: 404.

[149] Alaas: Karageorghis 1975; 1990: 30. Cook 1988: 17–20. Palestinian relations: Mazar 1989: 102–3; Stern 1993: 331–32. Hala Sultan Tekke: Stieglitz 1984: 193.

[150] Peltenburg 1986: 163, 166. Palaepaphos-Skales: Karageorghis 1990: 31.

[151] LoSchiavo et al. 1985: 7, 25, 27, 29, 35–42, fig. 14; Ridgway 1990: 66.

[152] Holloway 1991: 35, 39.

[153] Jones 1986b: 593–608.

[154] Cook 1988: 16.

Euboean vases found at Amathus.[155] There appears to have been a hiatus in traffic with Crete during Late Minoan IIIC, although there may be some artifacts from each island on the other during the Subminoan period (roughly, the eleventh century). Summarizing this distillation of evidence from Cyprus, various parts of the island appear to have remained in one external-connection network or another throughout the closing years of the Bronze Age and the opening of the Iron Age, apparently connecting, at least indirectly, points east and west.

Moving farther east, to mainland Asia, at Tel Abu Hawam, on the central Palestinian coast below Acre, among a group of Late Helladic IIIB sherds that demonstrated typical Argolid compositions under neutron-activation analysis, are three sherds of a Late Minoan IIIB stirrup jar that match a Khania composition.[156] A scattering of other Cretan ceramics from Late Minoan IIIA and B have been found throughout the Levant, including some coarseware stirrup jars at Minet el Beida (the harbor town of Ugarit) and Tel Abu Hawam, a fragment of a Late Minoan III stirrup jar in a Late Helladic IIIA:2–IIIB:1 stratum at Sarepta,[157] and Late Minoan IIIB pottery at Lakish in southern Palestine.[158] Mycenaean IIIC pottery has been identified at Tell Sukas, fifty-five kilometers south of Ras Shamra, at Beth Shean, at Sarepta, and perhaps at Ashdod, with some genuine imports dating to 1200 or slightly after.[159] Though the Late Helladic IIIA and IIIB stirrup jars found at sites in Palestine, as well as Rhodes, Cyprus, and Egypt, appear to be gen-

uine imports, mainly from the Mycenae/Berbati region, some of the IIIC stirrup jars in those regions, from the results of neutron-activation analysis, appear to have been made locally, suggesting a twelfth-century reduction in the volume of trade between Greece and the eastern Mediterranean.[160] Leonard's recent catalogue of Late Bronze Age Aegean pottery in Syria and Palestine includes nearly 2,300 entries (including some figurines, minus a dozen or so unused catalogue numbers), of which sixty-one may be Late Helladic IIIB or IIIC; another twenty-one are reasonably secure IIIC, including one IIIC–Late (Submycenaean) deep bowl (FS 285) from Tyre Stratum XIV; another twenty-one vases are of IIIC type, but possibly or probably were made locally in the Levant; and fourteen are IIIB–Late.[161] The latest Minoan vase Leonard reports in the Levant is an amphoroid krater from Ras Shamra, which he alternatively identifies as "LH IIIB–C?"; otherwise, Late Minoan IIIB is his latest Minoan material.[162]

The most explicit evidence for international commercial intercourse in the eleventh century is from the Levant, the literary evidence provided by the tale of Wen-Amun at the end of the first quarter of that century.[163] Although Wen-Amun's own journey was not a commercially motivated venture, the citation is offered of seventy Levantine ships in the harbor at Tanis, in the eastern Nile Delta, at any one time. This count includes only those from Byblos and Sidon, and those cities are said not to have had a monopoly on the Egyptian trade at the time. Mention is

---

[155] Desborough 1957: 215–16; Coldstream 1986: 321.

[156] Asaro and Perlman 1973: 222–23. Jones (1986b: 564) concurs with this opinion. Hankey 1979: 149, no. 8, pl. 18.4; Humbert 1982: 63; Balensi and Herrera 1985: 108, fig. 13.1. Glass seals from the same mold have been found in Argos and at Tell Abu Hawam, although their dates are uncertain: Pini 1990: 116.

[157] Koehl 1985: 105 no. 104, 143–44, figs. 4, 16.

[158] Hankey 1979: 144–57. She reports a large, Late Minoan IIIB coarseware closed vessel, not a stirrup jar, from the Airport Temple at Amman (151, no. 14); she also reports that no Late Minoan IIIC vessels have been found in the Levant, and that Mycenaean IIIC vessels are rare (155). On Lakish, Hankey 1972: 144.

[159] Hankey (1966: 171) suggests a date of c. 1190 for some of these vessels. See also Hankey 1967: 113, 127–28, 143, 146; she suggests that the sherds found at Beth Shean might indicate the "last Mycenaeans in Palestine," who might have been refugees or mercenaries (128). Mazar (1993: 216) reports further Late Helladic IIIC vases, distinct from the Philistine ware produced at Ashdod, Ekron, and Ashkelon. Sarepta: Koehl (1985: 146–47) reports some Late Helladic IIIC Cypro-Mycenaean sherds dating to c. 1200.

[160] Leonard, Hughes, Middleton, and Schofield 1993: 121.

[161] These pieces come from seventeen sites: Byblos, Sarepta, Tell Abu Hawam, Ras Shamra, Ras Ibn Hani, Kamid el-Loz, Ashdod, Beth Shean, Megiddo, Ain Shems, Tell Miqne, Bassit, Tell Keisan, Sukas, Sidon (Qraye'), Gezer, and Akko; none from the Amman Airport. Leonard 1994: ch. 3.

[162] Leonard 1994: ch. 5, esp. 196, no. LM#18 (= "Mycenaean" #292).

[163] I deal with Wen-Amun's story in detail in the section below on travel. For references, see note 338 below.

made of a person named Werekter, presumably a Phoenician merchant resident at Tanis, with whom the fifty Sidonian ships did business.[164] The port of Dor is described as a thriving port city. These incidental facts portray a healthy commercial trading system in the Levant in the early eleventh century, and surely a generation or more of activity must have been required for the intercourse to have reached such a volume.[165] This literary evidence bolsters the archaeological evidence for Levantine trade in the early eleventh century, and possibly a half-century earlier.

Turning to the west, while the Mycenaeans had been in contact with Italy in the sixteenth and fifteenth centuries, the fourteenth and thirteenth had seen extensive Mycenaean interest in that region. (See Map 4 for locations of sites in Italy.) Some of this activity survived the IIIC period's disruptions, even extending into IIIC:2/Submycenaean. Taylour's pioneering

study reported a small number of nonlocal Mycenaean IIIC vases at Scoglio del Tonno (just southeast of Taranto), and Smith's recent summary reports IIIC pottery from some thirty-five sites in Italy, Sicily, and Sardinia. Cyprus and Rhodes had been the principal overseas correspondents with Italy in IIIA and B, and they appear to have retained some connections with Scoglio del Tonno in IIIC: a fringed octopus stirrup jar and two kraters from Rhodes, and a stirrup jar from Cyprus; and another krater sherd with IIIC date that may have a Cycladic origin.[166] A number of IIIC vases at Apulian sites show Kephallenian affinities, although Taylour identified no certain imports; but LoPorto subsequently reported IIIC material at several Apulian sites.[167] Taylour concluded that "maritime trade, of a restricted scale, was maintained [through the late phase of IIIC] in the Western Mediterranean, in spite of being cut off from the Aegean."[168] Since

---

[164] Maisler (1946: 10) considers Werekter to have been the head of a great trading company. Albright (1942: 36–37) believed the Wen-Amun tale reflected the continuing prevalence of piracy on the Levantine coast, but also accepted the role of Werekter's mercantile organization (the *khubûr*) as finding the capital to build and outfit trading fleets as well as protecting them once they were built.

[165] Themistocles' rapid expansion of the Athenian trireme fleet six centuries later was financed by the silver bonanza at Laureion, but there are no hints of such external financing of a Levantine merchant fleet at the end of the second millennium. A slower growth rate to a combined fleet size of seventy ships at Byblos and Sidon, financed predominantly from retained earnings from shipping, is a reasonable belief. About eighty years probably would have been the maximum life of a ship at the time, so the fleet in Wen-Amun's time was not simply the remnants of the Sea People's fleet celebrated in the Medinet Habu reliefs, however that representation is to be interpreted. (Cf. Steffy 1985: 95–99, on the age of the Kyrenia ship, admittedly some eight centuries later; the economic lifetime of a ship could have changed for both technological and economic reasons, but an eighty-year *physical* lifetime of a wooden ship in continuous use in the Mediterranean may not be unreasonable. Might the Kyrenia ship have sunk *because* it was eighty years old?) At a net investment rate (gross investment minus maintenance and replacement) of 5% per year, an initial fleet size of ten ships would have required thirty-nine years to grow to seventy. A beginning fleet size of twenty ships would have required twenty-five years at a 5% net rate to reach seventy. If the fleet size of seventy ships had been reached only in the year of Wen-Amun's trip, a fleet of at least ten to twenty ships must have been in operation twenty-five to forty years prior as well. If the fleet had reached a steady-state size of seventy bottoms twenty years before, profitable Levantine shipping would reach back to somewhere between 1140 and 1120.

[166] Some of the material identified as Rhodian may be from the Ionian islands instead: Fisher 1985: 330. Holloway (1992: 41 n. 9) accepts Fisher's characterization.

[167] Taylour 1958: 108, nos. 113, 114, fig. 11, pl. 14:12; 109 nos. 117 (pl. 13:14), 118; 110, no. 120; 165. Vagnetti (1970: 368–69) reaffirms some of Taylour's suggestions. LoPorto (1986: 14–15) adds other Apulian locations with IIIC pieces. Many of Taylour's visual assessments have been sustained with contemporary chemical and petrographic methods. Jones (1986a: 208) indicates that allegedly imported sherds from Scoglio del Tonno do not correspond to local products. Jones and Vagnetti (1991: 132) confirm a number of the Late Bronze III Rhodian, Cretan, and Peloponnesian compositions previously identified visually by Taylour.

[168] Taylour 1958: 184–85. It is not clear, from the evidence Taylour presents, that the western Mediterranean was cut off from the Aegean in IIIC. French (1986: 281) interprets the evidence from the eastern and central Mediterranean: "The threat [to external trade, from the end of IIIB through early IIIC], if such it is, does not last long. . . . By this time [LH IIIC] the bureaucratic systems in the mainland have broken down but free enterprise (or piracy if you prefer) is rampant. The position of the islands and of the trading sites like Miletus and Rhodes in the East . . . and Taranto and Nuraghe Antigori in the West is very relevant. We still see a wide range of contact but it has become much more irregular. This is the world of the much maligned Peoples of the Sea."

Taylour's publication, a more extensive distribution of Late Helladic IIIC material in Italy has been published, and although in general the quantities still are not described as large, the geographical distribution is wider than previously, including inland sites for the first time.[169] Sites in southern Italy up to Etruria, Sardinia, Sicily, and the Aeolian islands report Late Helladic IIIC pottery, and IIIC:2 material has been reported from three sites around Taranto and at Paestum. At Satyrion, the acropolis of Porto Perone near Taranto, 179 IIIC:1 and 88 IIIC:2 sherds have been reported, compared with 17 IIIB sherds. Local pottery at Broglio di Trebisacce in Calabria has close stylistic connections with Cretan Late Minoan pottery.[170] Only a single Late Helladic IIIC:1 sherd has been published from Sicily, however: a jug sherd from Pantalica North Cemetery, dating to shortly before 1200. Lipari, in the Aeolian islands, has yielded a good bit more Late Helladic IIIC pottery. Several IIIC and earlier sherds have been found in Etruria and Latium Vetus.[171] Late Helladic IIIC pottery has been found with imported ivory and an ostrich-egg shell fragment at Frattesina at the head of the Adriatic, a 0.9-hectare site containing indications of a wide array of industrial activity—bronze-smelting, lead-working, and glass production.[172] In addition to the Late Helladic IIIC pottery, several bronzes of "Ionian Island and Cretan type" were found at Frattesina.[173] At Torre Mordillo, near Broglio di Trebisacce, a comb of elephant ivory decorated with concentric circles, similar to

the ivory at Frattesina, has been found in a Final Bronze Age context.[174]

Alongside the genuine Aegean imports in Italy is a complex array of locally produced pottery in Mycenaean style at sites throughout Italy.[175] Whether this material represents visiting craftsmen, immigrants, colonists, refugees, or other types of interaction remains speculation, but it does not lessen the indication of contact between the Aegean and Italy at this time.[176] The appearance of Aegean bronze typological series (e.g., fibulae, swords, and hammers) in Italy and vice versa from the thirteenth century through the eleventh has led Bietti Sestieri to infer that Aegean-Italian contacts continued throughout that period. Bronzes from Sicily, the Tyrrhenian coast, and southern Italy provide evidence of continued linkage with the Aegean, prominently Attica and Crete, in the eleventh century.[177] Marazzi and Tusa note the reports of some Submycenaean sherds at two sites in northern Latium, and Taylour reported a continued trickle of Greek Protogeometric and Geometric pottery at Scoglio del Tonno, Porto Perone, and Torre Castelluccia; these finds indicate some continuing interaction between Greece and the west in the early years of the Dark Age, possibly down till the colonization period.[178] Of potentially greater significance, however, is the emerging evidence of a long-standing and largely uninterrupted traffic between the Levant and Cyprus on the one hand and Sardinia on the other, from at least the fourteenth century, and continuing

---

[169] Smith 1987: 123, 125.

[170] Vagnetti 1982: 99–113; Smith 1987: 123.

[171] Vagnetti 1980: 151–52, 163–64. Casale Nuovo in Latium Vetus: Angle et al. 1993: 199, 211, fig. 4.6; Jones and Vagnetti 1992: 234–35.

[172] Bietti Sestieri 1984: esp. 62–63, 74, 80, 89, 118; Holloway 1981: 71–74, 80–82, 91, 109–10;1991: 29–41; Lukash 1984: 22, 30. Smith 1987: 112, 138.

[173] Bietti Sestieri 1982: 203; Smith 1987: 138.

[174] Ridgway 1995: 94. Another parallel is in a twelfth- to eleventh-century tomb at Enkomi.

[175] Benzi and Graziado (1996: 1524–28) report pottery in the style of Late Helladic IIIC Middle to Late, with close parallels from the Argolid and Corinthia, on the southern Adriatic coast of Italy at Punta Meliso. The clay appears quite close to local clay, visually, and they believe that, if chemical examination substantiates its local origin, the extensive Mycenaean pottery from this site may indicate the arrival of Mycenaeans from the Peloponnese.

[176] A useful progress summary is Vagnetti and Jones 1988: 335–47; see also Jones and Vagnetti 1991: 132–36. Though the Mycenaean presence appears to have been restricted to coastal sites in the Italian peninsula, and its material cultural influence relatively restricted, there is evidence of more extensive Mycenaean presence inland in Sicily, suggesting relatively simple trading with the Italian sites but possibly settlement on Sicily: Bietti Sestieri 1988: 34, 40–41.

[177] Bietti Sestieri 1973: 395, 407–12.

[178] Marazzi and Tusa 1979: 349; Taylour 1958: 136–37, 140–42, 148–52.

through the Phoenician period of the eighth to seventh centuries.[179]

I turn to activity in Greek lands themselves. Kilian, speaking of the continuity of civil life after the destruction of the palace around 1200, cites new building activity in the lower citadel at Tiryns. He reasons that some kind of political organization, possibly including some synoecism, was required to sustain the twenty-five-hectare settlement around the fortress, with an estimated population of 10,000, after the destruction of the citadel. He further suggests the continuation to some extent of the Mycenaean bureaucracy, even if official recording seems to have stopped. A single grain of rice was found in a Late Helladic IIIC—eleventh-century—context at Tiryns; Sallares considers this definitely an eastern import at this time.[180] Kilian appeals to similar events and processes at Asine, Argos, and Mycenae.[181] Archaeological evidence exists for continued relationships, including commercial trade, during the Late Helladic/Late Minoan IIIC period, although the interactions are clearly on a smaller scale than in LH IIIA and B. Shelmerdine concludes from her examination of the perfume industry at Pylos, which she considers to be a favored export industry using imported inputs (ingredients), that the Pylians went to considerable trouble to obtain henna, which does not grow in Greece, from times late in the Late Helladic IIIB period, when traffic in the Aegean and the eastern Mediterranean

increasingly was being interrupted, down to the final year of the palace.[182] Haskell believes that the Pylian international trade in oil, probably with Cyprus and the Levant, continued into the second half of the thirteenth century.[183] Elsewhere in the Peloponnese, Kanta reports two Late Minoan IIIC octopus stirrup jars at Monemvasia and a female head from the shrine at Asine, indicating clear Cretan influence in the IIIC period.[184]

Moving north on the mainland, one piece of Late Helladic IIIC:1 ware found at Kouklia on Cyprus has been determined by neutron-activation analysis as well as by stylistic considerations to be "almost surely" from Perati.[185] Lead and silver finds with atomic indications of Laureion provenance at Perati, Athens, and elsewhere in Attica indicate that the Laureion mines were operating as late as Late Helladic IIIC:1 (possibly as late as c. 1075), certainly a source of potential prosperity.[186] At neighboring Porto Rafti, Kanta notes another Late Minoan IIIC octopus stirrup jar.[187] Nearby Lefkandi has produced Italian material from a IIIC context and a Syro-Palestinian juglet from an Early Protogeometric grave, some two hundred years before the founding of Al Mina.[188] Harding, whose rigorous assessment of Mycenaean relations with Europe, reports a widening of the distribution of European amber within Greece and points east in the Late Helladic IIIC and Submycenaean periods, relative to its appearance in IIIA and B.[189]

---

[179] LoSchiavo, Macnamara, and Vagnetti 1985: esp. 25, 28–30, 35, 45, 58. Knapp (1990: 124–27, 138–41) reviews recent artifactual evidence of exchange between Cyprus and the Aegean on the one hand and the central Mediterranean on the other, including Sardinia, from the Late Helladic I period. Knapp proposes a decentralized challenge-and-response phenomenon in the twelfth century whereby Cypriot copper producers reoriented their export sales from the depressed eastern Mediterranean to the central Mediterranean and, as well, away from local markets eroded by the introduction of iron (152).

[180] Sallares 1991: 23.

[181] Kilian 1988: 135. Iakovidis (1996: 1044–49) develops a similar, or even more continuous, story for the developments at Mycenae during Late Helladic IIIC.

[182] Shelmerdine 1985: 30, 153.

[183] Haskell 1984: 106–7.

[184] Kanta 1980: 256, 300.

[185] Perlman 1973: 334.

[186] Stos-Gale and Gale 1982: 470–71, 476–80, Table 5.

[187] Kanta 1980: 300.

[188] Popham and Sackett 1968: 18, fig. 34; Desborough 1980: 347–48.

[189] Harding 1984: 82, 83 figs. 20–21. Harding casts the distributional evidence into Renfrew's proposed trade typology (see note 142), suggesting that the earlier (IIIA–B) amber trade appears as "directional commercial trade," while the IIIC-Submycenaean pattern appears more to fit the "prestige chain exchange" category, with the earlier material probably coming from Britain and the later from central Europe via the Adriatic (85–86). I prefer what I believe is a simpler accounting: that Mycenaean income distribution became less concentrated in IIIC, yielding both the reduction in volume and the greater dispersion in spatial distribution. At any rate, the continuity through the changes of the times warrants emphasis.

To the east, on Rhodes, imported Mycenaean pottery declines from Late Helladic IIIA, and is rare by Late Helladic IIIC. However, Mee considers the range of imports at Ialysos in Late Helladic IIIC to be remarkable; some thirty Late Minoan IIIC octopus stirrup jars have been found at Ialysos, most of which look Cretan, and several of which have had their clay compositions traced to Cretan correspondences. Additionally, an apparently Cretan Late Minoan IIIC:1 bull's head rhyton was found at Lardos near Lindos. Mee contends that "the evidence is not overwhelming but the re-establishment of trade routes does suggest that the Eastern Mediterranean cannot have been in complete turmoil at this time."[190] Elsewhere around the Dodecanese, Cretan and mainland pottery has been found in IIIC contexts at Eleona/Langadha on Kos, and a Late Minoan IIIC stirrup jar has been found at Iapili, a few kilometers east of Seraglio, also on Kos. Three LM IIIC stirrup jars have been excavated on Kalymnos.[191]

Desborough similarly concluded earlier, from the nonceramic objects from Late Helladic IIIC tombs on Rhodes, Kos, Naxos, and at Perati in Attica—"a fair amount of gold, and semi-precious stones ... objects of Egyptian origin ... little figurines, scarabs, faience—and also cylinder seals, which probably derive from Syria or its neighborhood"—that the central and southern Aegean remained in contact with the east.[192] On the nearby Asian mainland, there appears to be evidence of continued Mycenaean contact with Anatolian sites at least through Late Helladic IIIC:1, including Sardis in western Anatolia, Müsgebi in southwestern Anatolia, and Tarsus in Cilicia.[193] Kanta believes that three sherds from Tarsus may be Late Minoan IIIC.[194] Late Helladic IIIB/C amphoroid kraters, possibly from Miletus, or alternatively Kos, have been found at Ugarit (Ras Shamra) in deposits dating from just after 1250 to just after 1200.[195] Several Late Helladic IIIC imported vases and local imitations have been reported from Gindaris, about fifty kilometers

---

[190] Mee 1982: 32–33, 73, 91–92; Jones and Mee 1978: 469–70; Benzi 1992: 10. On the bull's head rhyton, which is in the Karo collection, see Karo 1911: 260, fig. 11. C. F. Macdonald (1986: 149–50) interprets the pattern of Rhodian imports and exports in IIIC as suggesting that Rhodes was involved passively in trade as a port of call rather than in any more active manner. Activity on the island during IIIC appears to have relocated and concentrated in the northwest, around Ialysos: Benzi 1988b: 261–62, and 1988a: 69–70, Table 1. Papadopoulos (1988: 74) believes that the Achaean evidence justifies a conclusion that "Achaea and the rest of the West Peloponnese had long-standing commercial and possibly cultural contacts with the Aegean, and especially the Dodecanese, ranging ... from LH IIIA2 to and including the LH IIIC period." He cites IIIC western Peloponnesian objects from Ialysos and Passia on Rhodes and from Eleona and Langadha on Kos (73). Jones and Mee (1986: 510–13) find no support for a Rhodian origin among a sample of twenty Late Helladic IIIC sherds from Aigira in Achaea; cf. Papadopoulos and Jones 1980: 232–35, for the original chemical analysis. Papadopoulos (1988: 74) considers Jones's chemical results to be based on a sample that is too small and restricted in area to justify revising his conclusions regarding the Rhodian-Achaean connection.

[191] C. F. Macdonald 1986: 142–47.

[192] Desborough 1964: 228; cf. 1973: 83. Iakovides (1980: 84, 86, 111) reports imports from Egypt, Syria, Crete, the Aegean islands, central Europe, and the Baltic in the twelfth century, gradually constricting in range of origins, and dwindling in quantity by the second quarter of the eleventh century. Sandars (1987: 186) suggests that the Perati artifacts and similar ones in other Greek tombs of the time may be pirates' loot rather than trade goods. Mee (1982: 92) considers the possibility that "these Mycenaeans were not honest merchants but mercenary warriors," but concludes that the grave goods in Rhodes "do not give the impression of a martial temperament." Cadogan (1973: 170) characterizes the overall evidence as showing that Mycenaean pottery in the Levant dropped sharply in the Late Helladic IIIC period, while Syro-Palestinian objects continued to reach Greece much as they did in LH IIIA:2 and IIIB.

[193] Mee 1978: 156. Re (1986: 351–53) reports Late Helladic IIIC and Submycenaean pottery, apparently imported from the Aegean region, at various sites in Anatolia, in substantial quantities in Cilicia, other than Tarsus, where much of the IIIC pottery appears to be locally made. Much of the LH IIIA–C pottery at Miletus previously was thought to have been imported from Mycenaean Greece, but recently physical analysis has shown it to have been made from local clays: Gödecken 1988: 310–11.

[194] Kanta 1980: 308; from Goldman 1956: nos. 1327, 1341, 1338, fig. 333.

[195] Courtois 1973: 149–64; fig. 12, 164. Mee (1982: 91) considers Kos the more likely provenance; C. F. Macdonald (1986: 144) disagrees. Åström (1973: 359) contends that the Ras Shamra kraters are not later than Mycenaean IIIB; he reports that Furumark also held this opinion.

northwest of Aleppo.[196] Crete appears to have maintained relations with the west as well as the east during the Late Minoan IIIC period: Pålsson Hallager reports Italian finds at Chania in a IIIB house, IIIB/C rubbish pits, and a IIIC floor deposit; a handmade bowl at Kommos; some Italian ware in an early IIIC context at Knossos; and a stop ridge knife of a northern Italian or Alpine style in another IIIC context at Knossos. The Italian plain and coarseware at Chania range in date from the second half of the thirteenth century into the beginning of the twelfth. Altogether, Pålsson Hallager suggests that the contacts with such areas as Scoglio del Tonno and Sardinia and other sites such as San Cosimo d'Oria, Broglio di Trebisacce, and Milena were most intensive in the thirteenth and twelfth centuries.[197] She believes the Chania artifacts represent the presence of Italian merchants, with their families. She also notes Egyptian finds at Chania in Late Minoan IIIB.[198] Also at Chania, the skull of a young woman from a tomb dated to Late Minoan IIIB:1 by associated pottery demonstrates craniometric characteristics dissimilar to those of Aegean populations and more consistent with those of Predynastic Egypt, Bronze Age Troy, and Neolithic Macedonia; with it were found two silver signet rings with possible parallels in Cyprus. The skull might reflect Levantine immigrants resident in the port town of Chania at this time.[199] On the south coast, Kommos has produced a corpus of Italian finds ranging in date from Late Minoan IIIA1 until the site's abandonment toward the end of the thirteenth century, but peaking in LM IIIB. Watrous reports fifty-four impasto vessels of probable Italian origin, similar to finds at Chania and with fourteenth- to thirteenth-century paral-

lels on Sardinia, as well as gray ware similar to that at coastal sites along the Gulf of Taranto. Most of the Italian vases were large enough to have been storage jars, using bowls for lids. Considering the evidence for bronze-smelting at Kommos, Watrous suggests that some of the larger storage jars may have carried scrap bronze from Italy. However, he finds no grounds for thinking that any of these vessels were made locally by resident Italians.[200] Kommos also has produced small numbers of pottery imports in contexts as late as Late Minoan IIIB from Egypt, the Cyclades (probably Naxos), the southern Peloponnese (probably Lakonia and Messenia), and some in Late Minoan IIIA/B contexts from Cyprus and Syro-Palestine (southern and northern Canaan).[201] A number of Italian bronze artifacts appear in Crete in Late Minoan III (late B or C) contexts: five Peschiera-type daggers and two Matrei-type knives at the Diktaean Cave, a Peschiera dagger in a tomb at Zapher Papoura, Matrei knives in tombs at Knossos and Phaistos, and some razors at Tylissos.[202] Violin-bow fibulae dated to Late Minoan IIIB and C have been found in a number of sites in Crete in votive and funerary contexts; at least some of them may be of Italian or other northwestern origin rather than of local manufacture.[203] A Late Helladic IIIC stirrup jar from the northwest Peloponnese has been found recently at Tourloti-Plakalona in the Sitea district of eastern Crete.[204]

The incursions of the Sea Peoples are credited with interrupting this trade network from the Near Eastern end, and the collapse of the Mycenaean palaces remains largely a mystery. The artifactual evidence has suggested a hiatus in foreign exchanges involving Greek communi-

---

[196] Weiss 1997: 119.

[197] Pålsson Hallager 1985: 295, 303 n. 110, 305; 1983: 113, on the find at Kommos. She believes some of the wares were imported from the regions of Apulia and the Gulf of Taranto (116): they "are identified as non-Minoan on the grounds of fabric, shape, decoration, and surface treatment" (111). She suggests that some of the pieces may have been made, apparently locally, by the wives of the merchants.

[198] Pålsson Hallager 1983: 116. Vagnetti has suggested that Pålsson Hallager's plain wheelmade gray ware at Chania, rather than the work of Italian immigrants, may have been a local ware found at a number of sites in Crete. She believes that some of the handmade pottery associated with Italian presence at Chania may instead be "Barbarian ware" found throughout the Aegean and that some of the ware reported as Italian at Kommos may be the same. Vagnetti 1985: 31 n. 11, 32.

[199] Hallager and McGeorge 1992: 16–17, 42–43, 44, 45; from Tomb 8, a pit tomb.

[200] Watrous 1989: 70–71, 75–76; 1992: 163–68, 182.

[201] Watrous 1992: 153–63.

[202] Smith 1987: 36, Table 5.

[203] Sundwall 1943: 3; Desborough 1964: 54–58; Sapouna-Sakellarakis 1978: 34–35.

[204] Tsipopoulou and Vagnetti 1995: 186.

ties from around the late thirteenth century to the eighth to seventh centuries, when Greek trade began to reemerge. There is some evidence regarding trade in the Levant during part of this time, but little for Greece. The evidence for Greece includes Homer, Hesiod, and archaeological finds, and the interpretations of these scraps of evidence have found them consistent with different stories. How much detail can be interpolated for this dark period? It probably is unsafe to reason that because commercial trade existed before and after the Dark Age, it must have existed during the Dark Age. Social institutions *could* have broken down, and economies *could* have retrenched and receded sufficiently to virtually eliminate earlier activities.[205] The character and extent of exchange between members of different communities in Dark Age

Greece is an empirical matter rather than one of logic alone. However, theories are intended to describe what is not apparent to the naked eye as well as what is, and their employment in interpreting the evidence will find its way into any stories that are constructed. Some arguments from better-known periods, either later or earlier, can be useful, but care must be taken to ensure that conditions are similar enough to satisfy the conditions of the analogy.[206] Nonetheless, research of the 1980s has separated the end of Mycenaean civilization and the collapse of the palaces, finding the impression of considerable continuity and vitality of organized social activity in the twelfth century. The eleventh century still witnesses the end of the Mycenaeans as a recognizable group, though, and the gradual deterioration of apparent prosperity.[207]

---

[205] Recently, Morris has expressed belief that a good deal of the social hierarchy of the Minoan-Mycenaean civilization survived the fall of those civilizations and that Greek society was "always much more sophisticated than contemporary urnfield Europe." Morris 1987: 2, 161–62. Cf. Dickinson 1986: 25: "The Dark Age did not involve a total social breakdown requiring an entirely new start." Burkert (1985: 48–59) notes the linguistic evidence for the continuity in religion from the Late Bronze Age into the Dark Age, even if archaeological evidence of continuity at cult sites is slender at best. Deger-Jalkotzy (1991a: 62–64; 1991b: 146; 1991c: 27–28, on Achaea in particular; 1995: 375–77) has devoted considerable attention to the series of sociopolitical bumps on the downward slide from the last Mycenaean palaces to the contracted (re-)occupations of some of the former palace sites in the progressive phases of Late Helladic IIIC; while not directly addressing the issues of continuity or discontinuity between the Mycenaean period and the early Greek Dark Age, her assessment shows that the downward leap required at the very end of the Mycenaean period to get early Greek society to the level of political organization and economic prosperity (or lack thereof) that appears in the epic descriptions of the early Dark Age was not all that great. The opening up in the past two or three decades of the archaeological understanding of the Late Helladic IIIC period has revealed a kind of social and political tenacity that would have given time for many components of Mycenaean social structure (legal, political, etc.) to have adapted to the more constrained circumstances of the Postpalatial period rather than simply being swept away. Writing at the same time, Vanschoonwinkel (1991: 513–14, 518) has reached similar conclusions: that despite the apparent break with the destruction of the palaces in Late Helladic IIIB, the continued operation of Mycenaean culture through the IIIC period at many sites across Greece gave time for transformation into Early Iron Age Greek culture rather than yielding a complete break with the institutions of the past. Foxhall (1995: 244–46) explicitly develops the case for political and economic continuity into the Protogeometric period.

Wood (1989: 90), reasoning from the stability and clarity of property rights in Greek society as it emerged from the Dark Age, believes that the Mycenaean kingdoms were an integral part of a long and complex prehistory of Homeric society: "No available anthropological evidence from other societies has provided analogous cases which might help to account for such a development out of a pristine, 'primitive' social order. Anthropology offers no comparable example of a 'fully stabilized' regime of property, with this degree of individuation in combination with a political organization so rudimentary as to invite comparison with tribal chieftanship."

[206] Starr (1977: 14–17, 58–59) perceives the use of parallels from other times in the analysis of ancient Greece as offering possibilities of useful analogy but sees the application of modern social theory as more likely to produce serious distortion. He appears to find intellectual constructs from modern anthropology less distortionary than those from economics, or at least as a useful counterdistortion to other modern social theories.

[207] Rutter 1992: 70. Muhly (1992: 19) goes so far as to suggest that the fall of the palaces benefited commerce by removing the burden of that system's excises from entrepreneurial citizens. The concept is interesting and may point to some genuine correspondences in the social logic, but the physical evidence of foreign artifacts in Late Helladic IIIC Greece and IIIC Mycenaean artifacts overseas does not seem to burgeon in the twelfth century, even in contacts with the west, which did not experience the same level of devastation the coastal Near East

STORIES ABOUT TRADE IN THE GREEK DARK AGE

Confronted with the question, "Was there trade in the Greek Dark Age?" few scholars would feel comfortable giving an unqualified "yes" or "no" answer. Conditions after the fall of the Mycenaean palaces clearly were not business as usual, yet evidence of external contacts of some sort has been emerging from Greek sites from the Submycenaean (Subminoan) and Protogeometric periods. Wide differences of opinion exist on the meanings of these artifacts. Despite common demands for hard evidence, hardness is an elusive quality in many of the artifactual remains. Ceramic vessels probably are the most solid type of artifact in terms of interpretability, but contexts frequently are disturbed and absolute chronologies are not without their uncertainties. Local copies of external shapes and decorations are frequent, although sometimes fabric helps in identification of provenance. Metal objects—jewelry and weapons primarily—ivories, and faience frequently are more difficult to assess, and questions sometimes linger about place of manufacture, if not about source of material. And then there is the heirloom, a concept that, because of its ability to strip so many artifacts of their information content, warrants more study than it has received. Thus, even the presence of the artifacts yields ambiguities about whether external contact is indicated and, if so, when and with whom, all basic facts in assessing the prehistory of trade.

These are knotty problems, but they are compounded by the subsequent (some might say *prior*) issue of the social mechanisms underlying the movement of artifacts. Differences of opinion that appear to be most difficult to bridge with dialogue arise about this subject. Did markets exist? For what activities were markets necessary? What concepts regarding resource allocation existed in various societies at particular times? What natural forces existed to channel scarcity? Considerable interest has arisen regarding the social and political structures of ancient communities, with the attendant possibility that such structures imply particular types of resource allocation, at both organizational (community) and behavioral (individual) scales. As a consequence, different scholars are inclined to see quite different social structures and behavioral mechanisms underlying the artifactual remains. It is hardly surprising that sharply divergent interpretations of artifacts emerge.

Given these major sources of artifact ambiguity on the one hand and differential inferrability, as I shall call it, on the other, there are a number of what I would call (with some apprehension) historical questions about external contacts, concrete issues where these ambiguities and differences find expression in practice. When did contacts occur? Between which points or areas? In what frequencies and volumes? What administrative structures and rules may have been present to assist and regulate contacts? The role of the Phoenicians in the early first millennium has become a well-focused research issue in recent years, raising questions of timing, activities, and routes at the very least. A discussion of longer standing, although occurring later in the Dark Age, concerns the relationship between Greek western colonization and prior trade—the trade before the flag question. In recent years, this discussion has been merging with the Phoenician issue. Related to the colonization and trade issue is the matter of Greek presence in the east—Al Mina has been a scholarly focal point—issues of timing, type, and level of activity. The presence of foreigners—craftsmen as well as traders and refugees—in Greek communities has been considered an alternative in some instances to importing, particularly in reference to jewelry, but in the cases of ivories and even some pottery as well.

These issues and the literature addressing them form the background to any inferences that may emerge from my own research program on

---

Note 207 continued

did in the late thirteenth and twelfth centuries. Both of these papers emphasize continuities between the Mycenaean palace culture and subsequent culture, but to my mind they misleadingly deemphasize the magnitude of the disasters that resulted in and certainly attended the substantial decline in population in Greek lands that seems to have begun in the late twelfth century. Various social and cultural structures appear to have continued in modified form through clearly difficult times, and even some external communications were maintained. Nevertheless, "entrepreneurial initiative" (Muhly 1992: 19) was unable to support a regeneration of population for several hundred years.

Cretan external relations. Accordingly, it is useful to review an array of opinions on trade in the Greek Dark Age—some old, some recent, some influential, others demonstrating more the influence of other compelling opinions. As such, this review will not be a complete historiography of Dark Age trade, but will focus on issues of timing, routes, frequency and volume, and what might be called sophistication, the character of the contacts—commercial intercourse or something else—and emphasizes the variety of views held. Most of the opinions still find adherents. Although I venture into some stories about Archaic trade, I am less concerned with the later eighth and seventh centuries in this review, not because there is more consensus on events of that later time,[208] but because of the vast scope of the literature on later activity and its relatively heavier emphasis on literary than archaeological evidence. I do not find a topical organization particularly helpful in this endeavor. Nearly every possible opinion has been expressed about almost every topic, and little coherence emerges from such an organization. Consequently, I have chosen a scholar-by-scholar approach, occasionally combining two or more scholars when dialogue has been engaged. The arrangement is generally in chronological order of appearance in the literature.

Few scholars have been willing to venture any stories for the earlier part of this period, but several have ventured stories from roughly the ninth or eighth century forward, and a few have considered earlier centuries.[209] Blakeway took to task Gwynn's assessment of early Greek commercial retardation in a debate about "trade before the flag," asking whence came the geographical knowledge of suitable settlement sites in the West.[210] Blakeway cited the finds of Greek Geometric pottery, and local imitations of it, earlier than the earliest colonial burials at Syracuse at twenty-eight sites in Italy, Sicily, and France; he believed that no mechanism other than commercial interaction could have been responsible for so wide a distribution of Greek pottery.[211] He concluded that the first commercial contact of the Greeks with Etruria was "certainly earlier" than the foundation of Cumae,[212] and that Greek commerce and influence on Etruscan art began not later than the early ninth century.[213] Since the time of Blakeway's articles, more Greek artifacts have been found in Italy, of even earlier date. La Genière includes in her review some tenth-century Greek vases, probably Cycladic, found at Porto Ceseareo in southern Italy as well as Submycenaean vases of western Greek origin found at Satyrion and at Porto Ceseareo.[214] On the basis of such finds, she suggests that the interruption of maritime traffic between the Aegean and southern Italy after the fall of Mycenaean civilization was not complete. More recent

---

[208] In fact there is less consensus. If anything, the differences of opinion on later economic activity, including trade, are sharper and wider and are considered more consequential for associated beliefs about Greek civilization.

[209] I choose the term *story* rather than *theory, hypothesis, model*, or one or more of a host of other words that find frequent use, without any pejorative sense, but rather in the rhetorical sense of a method of telling why or how. Metaphor or analogy is the alternative choice of explanation, although ideally the two methods reinforce each other. For insightful applications of literary methods to the analysis of exposition and persuasion in the writings of economics in particular, see McCloskey 1983: 481–517; 1985; and 1990.

[210] Blakeway 1932–33: 170 n. 3. Gwynn 1918: 91–92.

[211] Blakeway 1932–33: 171. Gwynn did not take full advantage of the archaeological evidence available at the time he wrote, but neither did he entirely ignore it. While he did not refer to the Italian finds published by 1910 (as Blakeway acknowledged, some of the individual Italian artifacts still were not published at the time of his own writing: ibid.: 173), Gwynn used the site of the settlement at Cyrene on cliffs rising steeply from a low-lying shore as evidence that the settlement was agricultural rather than commercial: traders would have chosen a port as the site of their new home; Gwynn 1918: 97. Arguments could be made for and against his reasoning, but scholars have moved away from the implied either-or characterization of ancient motivation and behavior. Blakeway (1932–33: 172 n. 1) rejected the traveling-potter hypothesis as a mechanism for precolonization contact of Greeks with the west and was scornful of it as a postcolonization mechanism: "As a general explanation of the distribution of Greek pottery in Greek settlements in the post-colonization period, the `Travelling Potter' hypothesis does not deserve serious refutation. . . . One is almost tempted to ask whether the engraved ostrich eggs of the various Etruscan cemeteries were laid by a traveling ostrich with a traveling egg engraver in attendance."

[212] Blakeway 1935: 129.

[213] Ibid.: 147.

[214] La Genière 1979: 77: "Submycenaean (IIIC2: ninth century B.C.)."

assessments of precolonization Phoenician presence in the area—including Sardinia and the Italian mainland—synthesized by David Ridgway have both modified and supported Blakeway's conviction in an early Greek presence in the west.[215]

Glotz's views on Greek trade in what he called the Homeric period, which he delimited as extending from the twelfth century to the end of the eighth, introduced what were considered, since at least the 1930s, structural and behavioral anachronisms. However, he raised issues that still cannot be avoided, and offered answers, with greater confidence than generally is considered safe today, some of which may be vindicated yet.[216] He saw most of the shipping conducted by the Phoenicians, with the two exceptions of the Pelasgian Lemnians and the Eteocretans.[217] He interpreted Odysseus's explanations of himself as a Cretan to suggest that it was common to find Cretans doing business outside their island, but he was less explanatory about the Lemnians. As for the prevalence of traded goods, he pointed out that even Laertes, in his rustic cabin, had a bathtub and scented oils.[218] He perceived a clear division of ships: the warship or pirate ship was long and narrow, and the cargo ship was the "hollow ship."[219] Where Austin and Vidal-Naquet find the use of the term *emporos* to mean only a passenger on a ship rather than its later meaning of a maritime trader to imply the rudimentary character of foreign commerce, Glotz interpreted its meaning of "passenger who pays a fee" to imply a regularity of passenger traffic.[220] Where Austin and Vidal-Naquet see the

Phaeacians as an inward-looking people who rejected maritime commerce and lived instead from the land, Glotz got from Homer's characterization of Scheria a glimpse of a commercial town of the "Homeric Age" (Glotz's chronological definition).[221] In arrangements between Odysseus's Cretan impersonation and the Phoenician, which eventually landed the former in trouble in Phoenicia, he saw the possibility of "a Cretan and a Phoenician found[ing] a house for export to Libya."[222] He thought that Hesiod's "countryman who goes by sea to sell a part of his produce . . . both husbandman and trading boatman . . . must have been frequent in the VIIIth century [and] did not disappear very quickly" in the Archaic period.[223] Finally, rather than seeing the quasi-legal status of piratical agreements noted by both Solon and Aristotle as representing Greek difficulty in distinguishing piracy from trade, at least in practice if not in their minds as well, he saw the emergence of commercial law from pirate custom. Clearly, this story does not have enough change in it for a 500-year period, but its alternative interpretations of some well-known facts are provocative. Glotz may have intended the joint founding of an "export house" to appeal to a facetious sense of the anachronistic, but the concept of a Cretan and a Phoenician cooperating to conduct business between Crete (possibly Kommos?) and Libya before the Theran foundation of Cyrene (how did Korobios come to know the North African coast well enough to guide the Theran colonists there?) must not have been implausible to a Homeric audience. While Homer's

---

[215] Ridgway 1990: 69; 1992a: 85–92; 1992b: 7, 13–29.

[216] The period that the Homeric epics describe has long been the subject of debate, with answers ranging from the late Mycenaean period itself to the eighth century. Snodgrass (1974a) concluded that the epics were a hopeless tangle of social and technological practices from all the times between the Mycenaean period and the eighth century. Morris (1986b: 115) emphasizes the probable flexibility and contemporaneous diversity of social structures and practices in Dark Age Greece and disagrees with Snodgrass's interpretation of temporal inconsistencies, particularly in marriage customs, concluding that Homer describes eighth-century society. Whitley (1991a: 343) notes Morris's eighth-century date but accepts a tenth- to ninth-century date for the more archaic social structures, and suggests c. 800 as a date for "Homeric society" (365).

[217] Glotz 1926: 49–51.

[218] Ibid.: 48.

[219] Ibid.: 51–52.

[220] Austin and Vidal-Naquet 1977: 43; Glotz 1926: 57.

[221] Austin and Vidal-Naquet 1977: 44; Glotz 1926: 58.

[222] Glotz 1926: 58. On the basis of the archaeological evidence on the coincidence of Greek and Phoenician presence in eighth-century Italy, Ridgway (1992b: 140) accepts the story as reflecting the normal range of possibilities in commercial activities of the period.

[223] Glotz 1926: 117.

Phaeacians may well have been inward-looking in the story, despite some practical difficulties, Homer may have gotten his image of Scheria from observations of thriving, outward-looking maritime towns of his own time. The proposed derivation of commercial law from pirate customs is, at the least, a brilliant stroke of cynicism. Glotz's concession that "household economy still predominates," throughout his Homeric period, is, in fact, compatible with his commercial interpretations of the epic scenes.[224]

Heichelheim's reasonable story about eastern Mediterranean and Greek foreign trade in the first millennium is that archaeological evidence clearly confirms its interruption and decrease, and that the Iron Age brought "a more marked commercial autarky to most lands." Foreign trade reawakened only gradually, and the growth of Greek trade began between 700 and 560. Greek vases dated before c. 640, which may appear to have been imported, he thinks were local imitations, although he does not consider how the ideas were transmitted for local imitation.[225] I mention the Heichelheim reference, which of course is seriously dated in its details now, because the basic outline of his story maintains the same structure in a number of more recent accounts that differ in more current archaeological detail.

Humphreys, as noted above, develops a story about Dark Age trade simultaneously with her observations about Archaic merchant shipping. Her story combines Greek aristocratic piracy and disdain for commerce demonstrated in the Homeric epics, the latter continuing through the Classical period, with a Maussian interpretation of hospitality and gift exchange in the epics: "The `commander of sailors out for gain, always thinking about his cargo' (*Odyssey* 8.159 ff.) . . . did not necessarily restrict his activities to peaceful trade. . . . A rigid distinction between `trade' and the transfer of goods through war, raiding, hospitality, and gift-exchange cannot be imposed." Her two routes to ownership of a sea-going ship are aristocratic wealth sufficient to build, equip, and operate such a ship, and what amounts to an occupational ladder climb by either an *emporos* who traveled with his merchandise on others' ships or a career pilot or steersman emerging to the situation of *naukleros*, whose exact financial circumstances continue to be a question, even in the Classical period. However, she very nearly merges the distinction between these two types of participant in overseas exchange. To her, the aristocrat seeking goods overseas for his own consumption or for use in gift exchange differs from the "commander of sailors out for gain" by "little but an ideological hairline."[226] The latter may resort to piracy, and implicitly the former's motivation differs little if at all from the commercial trader's. A young nobleman might "give" passage on his ship to traveling craftsmen, or even to traders. The primary difference between the aristocratic shipper and the commercial merchant in her story is that the former "buys his own," whereas the latter performs the task for others who are less particular about how they obtain their foreign products. In fact, the merchant in this story appears in a position to achieve some economies of specialization that would lower transaction costs of trade. The distinction between the participants hinges on the identification of the Homeric hospitality with the twentieth-century A.C. intellectual construct of gift exchange. The volume of trade increased around the end of the sixth century B.C., but the "professionalism" of trading may not have changed.

Reasoning from archaeological evidence, Coldstream ventures the earliest specific hypotheses about Early Iron Age Greek trade. With the Mycenaean collapse between c. 1200 and c. 1150, commerce in the Aegean declined sharply, and travel was equally sharply restricted in the Early Dark Age. However, by the second half of the tenth century, Attic Protogeometric pottery styles began to inspire styles in other Greek communities, and the late tenth century in particular was one of peaceful progress: the spread of Attic Protogeometric style across the Aegean "implies improvement in sea communication, and the existence of trade on a small scale."[227] External contacts among Greek communities declined during

---

[224] Ibid.: 58, 60.

[225] Heichelheim 1957: 200, 239 n. 26, 244. He also suggests the introduction of iron as a disruptive force on foreign trade on a scale comparable with the incursions of the Sea Peoples, although his price data do not unambiguously support that interesting hypothesis (197–99, 204).

[226] Humphreys 1978: 167, 169.

[227] Coldstream 1968: 340.

the first half of the ninth century, possibly—but speculatively—as a consequence of piracy: "Merchants seldom traveled now beyond the land of their immediate neighbors."[228] Trade with the eastern Mediterranean was "extremely rare." Greater homogeneity of the pottery marks an improvement in Aegean communications in the second half of the ninth century, including a sudden increase in trade with the Levant. Levantine traffic continued to increase in the first half of the eighth century. The Assyrian conquest of the Levantine coast in the second half of the eighth century was not fatal to Greek trade with that area.[229] Coldstream reasons by a process of elimination, with some admitted intuition, that "commerce supplied by far the strongest motive for the export of Geometric pottery," and that the existence of commerce may be assumed whenever there is no contrary evidence that might imply the movement of people.[230] The principal alternatives are traders' wares, chattels of colonists or resident aliens, or votives left by foreign visitors, but Coldstream observes that peripatetic potters cannot account for the circulation of a single style of pottery around the Aegean: "The Athenian Potters' Quarter would have been seriously depopulated in LPG and MG times!"[231]

Boardman's characterization of Early Iron Age Greek trade is much less explicit than Coldstream's, particularly before the eighth century, and he concentrates on trade with non-Greeks. However, he notes the archaeological evidence of the Greeks' awareness of the countries of the Levant between the fall of the Mycenaeans and the widely acknowledged resumption of trade in the eighth century. These remains "suggest a pattern of casual trade with one part of the Greek world in particular,

Crete."[232] Cyprus appears to him the intermediary between Crete and the western Asian mainland. In other parts of Greece, the evidence is very slight for eastern, including Cypriot, trade before the eighth century, although Euboea (Lefkandi) yields eastern pottery and jewelry from the ninth century, and Athens yields several metal objects from around the mid-ninth century.[233] Boardman finds it difficult to fit the Phoenicians into his picture of international relations in the Early Iron Age Aegean, but although there is no clear evidence of Phoenician trading colonies in the Greek Aegean (excluding Cyprus) before the Greek appearance at Al Mina, he suggests that the Phoenicians still may have been the carriers of what little commerce did reach into the Greek world before the eighth century.[234] With another decade for more evidence from Lefkandi to emerge and be evaluated, Boardman recently has modified his earlier proposals somewhat, to allow for greater Euboean participation in shipping between the Levant, including Cyprus, and the Aegean, as well as the coast of Italy, in the late ninth and early eighth centuries, before the establishment of Al Mina.[235]

From the chronological and regional pattern of the appearance of iron in Greece in the late second millennium and early first millennium, Snodgrass inferred a disruption in the supply of tin used in bronze production. According to his complex hypothesis, Greek trade, through Cyprus, with the Near East was broken in the aftermath of the destructions in the Levant associated with the Sea Peoples. He dates the break in trade to between c. 1025 and 950, although his story would have Crete still in trade contact with Cyprus during this period.[236] Waldbaum, while seeing more scope for independent Greek activi-

[228] Ibid.: 343.
[229] Ibid.: 383.
[230] Ibid.: 334.
[231] Ibid.
[232] Boardman 1980: 36.
[233] Ibid.: 37.
[234] Ibid.: 37–38.
[235] Boardman 1990a: 179–80, fig. 2. Negbi (1992: 615 n. 95) disagrees with Boardman's assessment of the role of Euboean traders in the carrying trade between Al Mina and the Aegean. She disputes Boardman's assessment that the inhabitants of Al Mina were Aramaeans rather than Phoenicians and that, consequently, the culture of Al Mina was North Syrian rather than Phoenician. She believes that Al Mina was Phoenician, established about the same time as the Temple of Astarte at Kition. Graham (1986: 51–65) traces the evolution of opinions regarding the origins of Al Mina and the erosion of opinions that it was founded by Greeks or was populated largely by Greeks in its early history.
[236] Snodgrass 1971: 237–53; 1980: 348; 1982: 293.

ty in the development of iron technology, tacitly accepts the cut-off of trade and the Greek tin supply at the heart of Snodgrass's thesis.[237] Morris has offered an alternative interpretation of the relative disappearance of bronze and its apparent replacement with iron that relies on changes in deposition in graves rather than on a change in the availability of bronze in circulation.[238]

Snodgrass is willing to venture more specifics in the story of Archaic Greek trade that he develops from the archaeological and literary evidence. He develops his story by asking how the nonlocal artifacts found by excavations could have come to reside where they were found.[239] Some, of course, were found at panhellenic sanctuaries and are reasonably interpreted as votive offerings, with no clear implication for "international" economic relations, and certainly not for commercial activity, in his opinion.[240] Snodgrass also stresses the gift exchange, guest friendship, and hospitality that appear throughout the Homeric epics. Reasoning again from the archaeological evidence, he notes the rarity of commercial quarters in excavated settlements of Archaic Greece and assigns a small weight to a commercial element motivating the movement of the artifacts. Greek appearance at Al Mina on the Syrian coast shortly before 800 and the establishment of the trading enclave at Naukratis in the Egyptian Delta around 630 are important times in his story of Archaic Greek trade. In the second half of the Archaic period, roughly corresponding to Heichelheim's date, the commercial character of Greek trade grew with its volume. Snodgrass also accepts the appearance of the "purpose-built merchantman" around the end of the sixth century.[241] Impersonality in transactions is an important defining characteristic of trade to Snodgrass's story: "If `trade' is defined ... [as] the purchase and movement of goods without the knowledge or identification of a further purchaser, then it seems that a substantial component of archaic Greek maritime shipments could not be classified as trade."[242] However, the resource-allocation consequences of trade are unaffected by anonymity or identifiability of participants, and in fact, in a period of poorly developed international law and weak enforcement of any protocols, personal identifiability may have been a key element in conducting any transactions at all.

Starr also is willing to venture a story about Archaic Greek trade, albeit more from a historical than an archaeological perspective.[243] His story develops the motivation of trade and the question of its commercial character as well as physical characteristics such as trade volumes and composition and the timing of its growth or resurgence. He concludes that bulk commodities were traded from at least the eighth century, and that trade grew markedly thereafter in volume and variety. The motivation component of his story reveals mixed feelings about the role of gain-seeking. He endorses Marcel Mauss and Marshall Sahlins on gift exchange and stresses the aristocratic Greek aversion to the appearance of peacefully seeking material gain, but seems to find the Homeric references to motivations of gain ultimately persuasive. On the gift exchange, he notes the regretted exchange in the *Iliad* between Glaukos and Diomedes of gold armor for bronze.[244] From the Phaeacian youth's taunt of Odysseus about being a trader, he reasons that, "All in all, it would be unreasonable to assume that most traffickers [seaborne traders] endured the dangers of the sea without serious economic

---

[237] Waldbaum 1982: 338.

[238] Morris 1989: 502–6.

[239] Snodgrass 1980: 132–43.

[240] Kilian-Dirlmeier (1985: 215) lists a range of possible means of deposition of foreign objects in Greek sanctuaries, mostly involving *travel* but none necessarily external commercial activity. Strøm (1992: 57) suggests organized import on the parts of sanctuaries as a possible mechanism to account for the appearance of a particular class of Near Eastern bronze vessels in sanctuaries but not in graves.

[241] Snodgrass 1980: 151.

[242] Snodgrass 1983b: 26.

[243] Starr 1977: 15–20, 55–75.

[244] *Il.* 6.234–36. Knorringa (1926: 4–5) makes the same observation about the exchange between Glaukos and Diomedes; he finds Homeric gift-giving a closely calculated exchange and sees no reason to suspend or dilute economic motivations from the Homeric retinue. Knorringa published shortly after Mauss's essay (1923–24), and although it cannot be certain that he was unfamiliar with the essay or with Mauss's earlier "Une forme ancienne de contrat chez les Thraces" (1921: 388–97), he cites neither work in his *Emporos*.

intent. Overseas exchanges would not have grown so rapidly, and the evidence of the archaic poets attests that gain was an objective, even if a Greek trader could not calculate his profit from a voyage by modern bookkeeping techniques."[245]

Salmon's story of Archaic, and possibly earlier, trade is based on his analysis of the growth of Corinthian foreign trade, but is more general. Addressing the issue of distinguishing pirates' plunder from trade, he observes, "It is fashionable to draw attention to the difficulty of distinguishing, especially in the early period, between trade and piracy; but while theft can generate imports it can hardly generate exports."[246] Clearly, if some communities' exports are known beyond doubt, at least some of the foreign artifacts found at excavation sites must be genuine commercial imports and not pirate plunder. Salmon finds little doubt that specialist traders worked in the trade between Corinth and the west from the late eighth century, although questions remain about their status. However, he finds "powerful arguments" for placing the development of an independent status for traders, at least at Corinth, relatively early, and he believes that similar arguments might be applicable to Aegina and parts of the eastern Aegean. This argument is that Greek aristocrats simply were not flexible enough to have been responsible for the development of trade such as had occurred at Corinth by c. 750. Salmon offers a specific example of the resource-allocation effects of Corinth's trade: encouraged by the regularity of grain imports from the west, the Corinthians replanted some of their grain land in vines in order to pay for further imports.[247] This change of crop mix would alter the productivity of both land and agricultural labor, and the latter would have an effect on labor used in both

household and specialized manufacturing activities. Morgan has strengthened much of Salmon's story recently, citing the establishment of apparent trade relations between Corinth and Medeon (on the north coast of the Gulf of Corinth, southeast of Delphi) early in Corinthian Late Protogeometric period (first quarter of the ninth century), and Corinthian pottery on Ithaka dating to c. 800, and in Epirus at Arta (possibly as early as the ninth century) and Vitsa (early eighth century?), where a faience necklace also was found in a grave.[248]

Osborne recently has challenged Finley's conception of relatively random, sporadic, and not-for-gain trade directly, with a tripartite investigation of trans-Mediterranean movements of goods and people in the eighth to sixth centuries. First, he tabulates the find locations, from the eastern Mediterranean to central Italy, of Attic Black-Figured pottery, by pot shape and by painter, from the "early sixth century" and the second quarter of that century. This display of data indicates that different shapes went disproportionately to different locations, which, together with other evidence on Attic vases at Italian locations, suggests to him that Attic workshops specifically prepared some vase types for particular markets; that is, the overseas sales were planned in advance and were not simply overstocks from the local market. He calls this "directional" trade, in the contrasting sense to random, tramping trade.[249] Second, he reflects on the rapid rise of the Greek population at Pithekoussai in the second half of the eighth century, going from nearly nothing to some 5,000 souls in roughly twenty-five years. Reasoning that the new Greek residents had not immigrated to farms, and that their arrival in a single, large flotilla seems unlikely, he infers a regular

[245] Od. 8.161–64; Starr 1977: 60.

[246] Salmon 1984: 148.

[247] Ibid.: 152–53, 156.

[248] Morgan 1988: 315–19, 331; 1990: 112–25. Cf. Coldstream 1977: 177, 182–84, 186.

[249] Osborne 1996: 34–38, Tables 1–8. I suspect that many if not most of the frequency differences that Osborne reports from his tables would not be statistically significant. There are too many categories of vases, and too many possible locations; the proportion of the vases remaining in Athens and other Attic sites is too large, and there are too few pots altogether to generate sufficient variance for statistical identification. Nonetheless, the logical direction of his inquiry seems sound to me. Another logical extension of this part of his inquiry, which he acknowledges only implicitly, is that the knowledge of these overseas markets possessed by either Attic pottery workshops or their buyers, or both, represents an investment in knowledge, on which a return would be expected and required. Corresponding knowledge about the locations of demands for and supplies of other products could help repay the investment in knowledge about prospects for pottery sales; thus regular trade in other products would support an inference of regular, planned trade in painted pottery, and vice versa.

traffic of ships carrying immigrants—and products—over this period. From what is known of ship sizes, he estimates something in the neighborhood of fifty ship arrivals per year at Pithekoussai, carrying "perhaps 3500–4000 tons of goods." Despite the peculiar locational advantages of Pithekoussai, Osborne believes that it "demonstrate[s] the possibility of regular, frequent and ... directional, long-distance trade as early as the third quarter of the eighth century."[250] Third, his interpretation of the advice of the *Works and Days* and the fictional situations of the *Iliad* and the *Odyssey* is that people routinely produced for nonlocal buyers and that merchants or traders commonly found themselves in unfamiliar places.

The Sherratts recently have offered a relatively explicit view of Mediterranean trade between c. 1200 and c. 1000, which includes early post-Mycenaean Greece in its story.[251] According to this view, the collapse of the palaces in the eastern Mediterranean and Mycenaean Greece around 1200, rather than eliminating trade, changed some of its characteristics. The Sherratts appear to suggest a revised interpretation of the destruction of the Near Eastern kingdoms: they appear (the text is not entirely clear) to propose that the destruction was not the result of population movements traditionally identified with the Peoples of the Sea, but rather an endogenous interaction between the competitive hiring of mercenaries by the competing Near Eastern kingdoms and the ability of the people hired as mercenaries to squeeze into niches in the trading system, thereby precipitating extensive disruption of the political and economic hegemony of the principal kingdoms and eventually bringing them down. The extent to which the Sherratts' view of foreign trade between 1200 and 1000 depends on the acceptance of their reinterpretation of the collapse of the palaces traditionally credited to the Sea Peoples is not clear. However,

in this setting, they propose the emergence in the twelfth century of a diversified, small-scale, international trading system, possibly with Cyprus as a hub, connecting the eastern Mediterranean with Greece—Attica, Euboea and coastal Boeotia, and Chalcidice[252]—and areas as far west as Sardinia, the Po Valley and central Europe. A brief recession follows in the eleventh century with the dislocation of Cypriot settlements. The tenth century witnessed a revival with the opening of the Red Sea and overland trade with western Arabia, which fostered the growth of the south Levantine coastal cities, from which the Phoenicians emerged as major international traders. Crete and the Dodecanese are identified as way stations on the far-flung western routes in both parts of this period. The suggestion is daring and finds some, but not overwhelming, support in archaeological evidence.[253]

As a result of the past several decades' excavations and analysis, it has become more difficult to separate the subject of Dark Age Greek trade from Phoenician activity, and recent syntheses offer different interpretations of the evidence. Current opinions on Phoenician-Greek interactions are still in flux. In her recent monograph, Morris has presented a vision of relatively continuous trade between the Levant, the central and western Mediterranean, and the Aegean, motivated by eastern demand for western metals, from the Late Bronze Age until the conquest of the Assyrian empire by the Babylonians at the very end of the seventh century.[254] The twelfth century saw the dispersal of Phoenician entrepreneurs to Greek sites like Ialysos, Lefkandi, and Perati, as well as Cyprus and Italy, and the eleventh century was a busy and profitable period for independent entrepreneurs. Morris would assign the prosperity of early-first-millennium Knossos to a Phoenician presence, including Coldstream's proposed unguent factory, and sees Crete's relatively abrupt decline around 600 reflecting the termina-

---

[250] Ibid.: 41.

[251] Sherratt and Sherratt 1991: 373–75. The Sherratts' story is quite close to that of Vincent (1924a: 427–28, as well as 1924b: 181–85), discussed by Dothan and Dothan (1992: 62–63).

[252] Sherratt and Sherratt 1991: 378 nn. 22, 23.

[253] See ibid.: 378–79 nn. 21–28, on archaeological evidence and approaches to it.

[254] Morris 1992a: 118–22, 131–41, 169–71. Niemeyer (1984: 21, 62, 89) conceptualizes two major phases of Phoenician activity, the first of which, from the end of the Bronze Age until c. 800, was prior to any colonization; the first phase yields indications of more sophisticated demands in Greek areas than in Italy and Spain and an overall lower density of Phoenician material in the Mediterranean. Bisi (1987: 229) interprets continuous Levantine interaction with the Aegean and the western Mediterranean from before the fall of the Mycenaean palaces, through the times of the Sea People's movements, with Cyprus as an important staging center.

tion of Assyrian demand for Cretan iron. This vision rests on a triad of archaeological artifacts, subsequent literary testimony, and coincidences of artistic motifs and mythico-religious parallels. Regardless of one's reaction to Morris's placement of the Phoenicians, her impressions reinforce David Ridgway's more restricted conclusions regarding the activity of the Phoenicians around Italy prior to the Euboean colonization at Pithekoussai, noted above. Günter Köpcke, in his thorough review of the artifactual evidence for Greek external relations, accepts a period of easy communications in the southern Aegean in early Late Helladic IIIC, but deduces a lengthy period of serious depression in Greece in the twelfth century, until c. 1050.[255] Nonetheless, interaction between Cyprus on the one hand and Sardinia, Sicily, and Italy on the other continued throughout the eleventh and tenth centuries. Throughout this depressed period, however, Köpcke believes that the Greeks never lost their experience with the sea, which they had developed in the Mycenaean period. In the late eleventh and the tenth centuries, he believes Knossos, Athens, and Lefkandi to have been prominent commercial centers in the eastern trade, with Knossos and Lefkandi in particular in a network that linked them to Phoenicia and Egypt in the tenth century. His interpretation of Greek involvement at Al Mina, and earlier evidence for interaction at Tyre (late tenth century), is of regular market trade, with Greeks, of whatever class, motivated by the opportunity for profits: for "gain ... self-interest ... [and] enterprise."[256]

The course of trade and commerce in Late Bronze Age and Early Iron Age central Europe surely is relevant to the progress of trade in Dark Age Greece. The views of Peter Wells, as well as his reviews of a large volume of literature on European archaeology of the period, are a useful complement to the study of the same subject for Greece. In his first monograph, Wells applied the analogy of clans and the relevant anthropological theory to the behavior of central Europeans in the first half of the first millennium B.C.: "Late Hallstatt central Europeans probably did not operate according to the economic principles with which modern Westerners are directly familiar."[257] Wells reports that by the period 1000–800, bronze, graphite (for pottery decoration), and glass were being imported at the site of Hascherkeller—not in large quantities, but enough that the community was in active contact with the outside world.[258] Throughout central Europe, some trade was apparent in all periods, but after c. 1000, trade was "much more regular and of larger scale than previously." By 1000, circulation of various materials was very active in central Europe, and the typical small community was receiving a variety of goods from the outside.[259] With the construct of the clan society whose activities would have been directed by a chief, Wells proposes, "In order to supply Greek traders with products they sought, central European chiefs had to organize the production of surpluses for export. Chiefs in traditional societies can increase the productive activities of their groups by providing incentives for members' greater application to production."[260] To secure a larger surplus for trade, the chief gets at least some of his people to specialize more in their productive activities.[261] In subsequent work, Wells suggests that the social exchange depicted in the Homeric epics and emphasized by Karl Polanyi, Johannes Hasebroek, and Moses Finley as characterizing ancient Greek society may have characterized at least some of the economic behavior of the elites in central European society, but that peasants probably secured their traded goods through ordinary exchange. In the European Late Bronze Age (c. 1200–800), "the metal [bronze] was being traded according to principles of value determined by distance from sources. Too many people were involved, over too great distances for coherent social relationships to have existed. From the Late Bronze Age on, the sheer mass of goods being traded argues against circulation being primarily socially

---

[255] Köpcke 1990: 78–128.

[256] Köpcke 1992: 104, 112.

[257] Wells 1980: 76.

[258] Wells 1983: 139–40. After c. 1000, roughly one-third of the ceramic vessels in central Europe were decorated with graphite, which gives some idea of the scale of trade in this product alone. Its source is yet to be determined: Wells 1984: 74.

[259] Wells 1983: 140, 153.

[260] Wells 1980: 97. This is an application of Sahlins's big man-chief model.

[261] Ibid.: 98–99.

based."[262] Trade between Greece and central Europe, possibly up the Rhône Valley, is well accepted for at least the sixth century and later. It is not absolutely necessary to establish whether the European trade of the earlier centuries in the first millennium involved the Greeks to make the reasonable case that if the less-sophisticated Europeans were involved in commercial trade around 1000 B.C., it is quite likely that the more-sophisticated Greeks had at least resumed their apprenticeship in trading, if they had not yet remastered the art.[263]

RECENT DEVELOPMENTS: LEFKANDI AND THE APPLICATION OF THE GIFT-EXCHANGE MODEL

Twin developments have characterized thinking in the past decade about Dark Age Greek trade. First, the archaeological evidence of overseas artifacts found at Greek sites and elsewhere in Europe has increased. Second, in what appears to be the continuation of the modernist-primitivist discussion in ancient history, archaeologists have become interested in applying contemporary anthropological theories to individual behavior and social interaction in prehistoric Greece and elsewhere.[264] Marcel Mauss's gift-exchange model[265] and Marshall Sahlins's ideas about economic behavior of tribal societies[266] have proven popular. It is not clear that these two developments have fit together particularly comfortably, however. The excavations at Lefkandi have revealed a considerable number of foreign artifacts, which the excavators have interpreted as demonstrating that trading links between Lefkandi and the Near East, as well as with areas to the north of Euboea, "were already established by LPG."[267] The earliest import found so far at Lefkandi is a Near Eastern bronze bowl, dated to near 900. The grave, a single burial of a woman, contained other Near Eastern imports as well: faience rings and three other bronze bowls. An Attic pyxis from the grave provides a firm dating to the Early Protogeometric period. This bowl is earlier than the Middle Geometric I Kerameikos bowl and raises the date of earliest Eastern contact at Lefkandi from LPG/EG1 Transitional or EG1.[268] Those authors have not discussed options for the transportation of these objects, but rather appear to have thought naturally of the general category of "trade." Morris, who otherwise has found gift exchange an attractive model of product circulation, considers the Lefkandi finds as evidence of the possibility of direct contact between Greece and Egypt in the tenth century

---

[262] Wells 1984: 28–29. Harding (1984: 24–39) reviews the gift-exchange and substantivist models of ancient economic behavior in some detail and reports his disbelief in the existence of markets in the great Near Eastern civilizations (28, 39), but suggests that the archaeological remains of metalsmiths' hoards in Bronze Age Europe imply the involvement of individual initiative, in addition to corporate effort, at least in distribution if not in mining and smelting (37). Nonetheless, Champion (1986: 554) takes Wells to task for devoting insufficient attention to literature on relationships between power, status, and exchange in the Iron Age. See Champion, Gamble, Shennan, and Whittle 1984: 292–94, for a presentation of that contrasting approach to economic organization. In subsequent work, Wells (1992) characterizes the widespread distribution of bronze tools and ornaments in twelfth-century central and eastern Europe as "tempt[ing] one to envision a prehistoric `free market' in which bronze was produced on a large scale and traded to any communities that could offer acceptable exchange goods. . . . There is no question that lively contact existed between the regions [Mediterranean world and central-eastern Europe] and it probably took the form of trade, among other mechanisms" (37, 38).

[263] Dietler (1989: 134–36) suggests, for the sixth and fifth centuries, some trading arrangements among the indigenous people of the upper Rhône-Saone Valley that would have permitted Greek products to have arrived in Hallstatt Europe without either direct participation by or the conscious interest of the Greeks themselves.

[264] Sherratt and Sherratt (1991: 352–54) offer an intellectual genealogy of this difference of opinion, from Max Weber through Johannes Hasebroek, Karl Polanyi, and Moses Finley, to Keith Hopkins. They note that trade is a more commonly accepted concept among Bronze Age archaeologists "at a time when Iron Age archaeologists (taking their lead from ancient historians) are most hostile to it" (351). The questioning of trade in such a disrupted and little-known period as the Early Iron Age seems quite natural, particularly when so much about the period is unknown, but the emergence of more information about the Dark Age has revealed greater continuity with the Late Bronze Age than earlier scholars had considered safe to assume.

[265] Mauss 1954. Subsequent page references are to this translation.

[266] Sahlins 1972.

[267] Popham, Touloupa, and Sackett 1982: 247.

[268] Popham 1995: 103.

and feels that the volume of traffic between Greece and the Near East has been underestimated previously.[269] Whitley, who also has found gift exchange a useful model to apply to this period in Greece, and generally finds Dark Age Greece as fitting more a tribal than a peasant paradigm, assumes that trade was taking place at both Athens and Knossos and that Knossos was in contact with the Levant "from a very early date." He views the diversity of Near Eastern and Near Eastern-inspired material in the Knossian graves as evidence of a steady flow of Near Eastern material into Knossos in a volume too great to be controlled by an elite.[270]

What sort of role should be given to gift exchange as a mechanism for moving around the Aegean and Mediterranean the artifacts unearthed by archaeologists? While Coldstream has given commercial trade the principal role in distributing Greek Geometric pottery to foreign sites,[271] he also has suggested gift exchange as the means of distributing a small number of large, mainly open vessels, with high prestige value yet still utilitarian, found in tombs and at some palace sites in the Near East.[272] Elaborating with an example from tomb 1 in the royal cemetery at Salamis on Cyprus, Coldstream suggests that the presence of an Athenian Middle Geometric II pedestalled krater and twenty other Attic skyphoi of the same date indicates the exchange of gifts between aristocratic families in Attica and Cyprus.[273] In the discussion of Coldstream's paper, Murray objects that Coldstream has oversimplified his use of the theory of gift exchange by overemphasizing the strength of the reciprocal relationship, and suggests that the Glaukos-Diomedes armor swap in *Iliad* 6.234–36 is the only example in Homer of a true gift exchange,[274] in contradistinction to Finley, who sees it everywhere.[275] Murray emphasizes the implication of Coldstream's suggestion, that "either some Knossians were visiting Athens or Athenians visited Knossos; there was a cultural

---

[269] Morris 1986b: 98. Morris (1986a: 1) considers that the limitation of gift exchange to clan societies is empirically too restrictive.

[270] Whitley 1991a: 360–61 and 1991b: 188. Morris (1989: 507) relies on control of metal artisans by an elite as a critical element in his thesis regarding the replacement of bronze by iron; such a social structure is closer to a peasant-and-elite society than to a tribal one.

[271] Coldstream 1968: 334.

[272] Coldstream 1983: 201. He has suggested (1994a: 159) the mechanism for the appearance of an Attic Late Geometric Ia kantharos recently excavated from Tomb I at Kition because of the fineness of its figural decoration and its uniqueness overseas at this time.

[273] Coldstream 1983: 201–3. Coldstream endorses an earlier suggestion of Desborough(1979: 122), of "an exchange of gifts ... between one family in Cyprus and two others, of diverse origin, in the Aegean?" In the same place, Desborough suggested the alternative interpretation that the important family represented by tomb 1 bought vases from both Euboean and Attic traders and used them as cremation gifts. Desborough's suggestion should be viewed with Gjerstad's reasoning (1979: 93) from the evidence of that tomb—that it represented a royal, or at least aristocratic, marriage between a Cypriot man and a Greek, probably Attic, woman; the Attic pottery was from her dowry. This account leaves the Euboean material unexplained, but that material poses no awkwardness for Gjerstad's proposal.

[274] Murray 1983: 207. This difference of opinion points to an important disagreement in the contemporary literature on gift exchange. Mauss himself emphasized the reciprocal element of gift exchange, but Weiner (1992: 2, 28–33) develops at length the thesis that Mauss's reliance on reciprocity in gift exchange represented the imposition of western rationality on nonwestern societies and that reciprocity is in fact a much weaker element than is the motivation to retain possessions. Beidelman (1989: 227–59) uses the gift-exchange concept to analyze social relations expressed in the *Iliad* and the *Odyssey*, but does not extend his purview to the analysis of Dark Age or later Greek social and economic relations. In contrast to Mauss's stress on the ability of gift exchange to temper—socialize—aggressive behavior and eventually convert it to legally circumscribed trade, Beidelman emphasizes the continuing use of competitive social exchange to rearrange political hierarchies in a contestant's favor. Hirschman (1977) develops a tempering argument for capitalism similar to Mauss's use of ritualized reciprocity. Hirschman does not cite Mauss or rely on the gift-exchange construct, and he cites concepts of Simmel much different from those Beidelman uses (55–56 n. 73). Altogether, Hirschman's results are more similar to Mauss's emphasis of the social-channeling consequences of competition with economic means than to Simmel's and Beidelman's emphasis on the construction of a relatively nondestructive social-competition mechanism.

[275] Finley 1979: 61–66, 95–98, 120–23, 145. Donlan (1989: 1–15) offers a sophisticated and illuminating assessment of the Glaucus and Diomedes incident, from which the entire exchange appears fully rational within the two warriors' society.

relationship that made these gifts useful or symbolically important."[276] Finley recognizes the reciprocation of "proper recompense" in gift exchange as it occurs in the Homeric epics and considers it to have been a distribution mechanism for metals across *oikos* lines in Homeric society (whenever that might have been).[277] He emphasizes the use of gift exchange for the transfer of services—"to compensate for a service, seal an alliance, or support a friendship"[278]—while ordinary trade involved the exchange of goods that were needed for themselves.[279] He sees gift-giving as the means by which status relations were created and political obligations secured and discharged:[280] that is, "the gifts of guest-friendship were the archaic forerunners of articles of agreement."[281] More recently, Morris has endorsed the concept of gift exchange as a social device in Geometric (and earlier) Greece. He sees metal grave goods and votive offerings as evidence of competitive destruction of wealth, used to rank households,[282] likening those depositions to the potlatch of the northwestern American Indians, which was one of Mauss's most prominent expository examples of gift-exchange mechanisms.[283] Whitley uses the term "gift exchange" to refer to guest friendship, but does not suggest that gift exchange need preempt other means of more mundane exchange such as commercial trade.[284] Herman follows the spirit of Finley, suggesting, "In Homeric society, gift-exchange was the chief method of organizing the supply of goods and structuring social relations," but she offers remarkably little and weak support of this contention.[285] Snodgrass has developed possibly the closest reliance of any of these authors on gift exchange as a theoretical device, having recommended its substitution, as a matter of factual correctness, for what others have called commercial trade.[286] While Coldstream and other scholars

---

[276] Murray 1983: 207. Coldstream has proposed an Attic belly-handled amphora from tomb 219 of the Knossos North Cemetery as another example of possible gift exchange: Coldstream 1983: 204–5, fig. 5.

[277] Finley 1979: 63–64.

[278] Ibid.: 67.

[279] Ibid.: 66–67. The literature on gift exchange does not yield such a clear dichotomy between ritual goods and services and the exclusion of utilitarian objects. Even proportional arguments (e.g., a lower proportion of utilitarian objects) would be difficult to support empirically. Weiner (1992: 191 n. 2) discusses theoretical arguments against this distinction and focuses her own emphasis on the inalienable-possession concept: that this concept is central to gift exchange and that individualistic shifting of any object between the categories of alienable and inalienable possession is the critical element in gift exchange.

[280] Finley 1979: 98. Renfrew (1986: 161) suggests that a shift of emphasis from the transitory gesture of gift-giving to ownership may have conferred greater permanence of prestige through the resource-commanding power of physical wealth.

[281] Finley 1979: 123.

[282] Morris 1986a: 11–12. Morris cites the nearly exclusive retrieval of metal objects from contexts of deliberate disposal—graves and, after c. 750, sanctuaries—and the few metal finds from settlements as suggesting that little metal was used in everyday activity. The apparent limitation of metals to the deliberate disposal contexts then yields the interpretation of "gift exchange as an integrative and competitive mechanism" (12). This interpretation does not account for the liability of metals not deposited in graves to recycling, as noted vividly by Wiener 1991: 326.

[283] Morris 1986a: 12–13; Mauss 1954: 32–37. While the northwestern American Indian potlatch may be the most familiar to nonspecialists, Mauss stresses the potlatch as the major institution of gift exchange in societies throughout the world at the developmental stage of total prestation, Polynesian and, particularly, Melanesian examples being prominent but far from exclusive: 3–4, 18. "Total" refers to the simultaneous expression of multiple institutions—religious, legal, moral, and economic—in a single social phenomenon (1). The destructiveness of the potlatch, and the extent of goods entering it, can be overstated: Weiner (1992: 41) notes that "Kwakiutl chiefs schemed to keep their most renowned cloaks and coppers out of exchange. . . . When an extremely valuable copper was given to a rival chief at a potlatch, only a piece of the metal was broken off. . . . At a later potlatch he would be able to reclaim the metal and rivet it back onto the original." Weiner's figure 3 is a late-nineteenth-century photograph of a high-ranking Kwakiutl woman displaying such a repaired copper ax blade.

[284] Whitley 1991a: 363–64, 360–61.

[285] Herman 1987: 78. Moving forward to the period of the *polis*, Herman concedes that "goods can also be exchanged outside the context of friendship—in trading relationships, for example. . . . The simple trading of benefits was certainly practiced in the ancient world, and may have been important. But we hear remarkably

often refer to gift exchange rather casually as the simple exchange of gifts rather than as involving a complex web of obligatory social relationships, Snodgrass proposes the more extensive use of the

concept as applying to Dark Age Greek society. On a more questioning note, both Bisi and Morris have noted the potential gap between the external acquisition of foreign artifacts—specifically

---

Note 285 continued

little of it" (80). The period to which "the ancient world" refers is not defined. In a work that otherwise is closely documented, Herman makes the remarkable leap with gift exchange that "the majority of loan transactions in fourth-century Athens—and hence, presumably in the whole of the ancient world—involved interest-free loans" (94). Again, the generalization to "the whole of the ancient world" neglects any reference to evidence and unwarrantedly assumes a homogeneous world, while the belief in the predominance of the Athenian interest-free loan is based on the excessively sweeping conclusion of Millett (1983: 47–48), which itself relies partially on a spurious distinction between production and consumption loans (43 n. 16). P. Millett has elaborated his notions of the foundation in gift exchange, from the Late Geometric to early Archaic period, of Classical period loans in *Lending and Borrowing in Ancient Athens* (1991: esp. 27–52); his assessment can be compared with that of Cohen 1992, which is especially well-grounded in the theory and practice of banking. Herman's chapter 4 offers a number of citations of gifts in the late Classical and Hellenistic periods with insufficient analysis of the implicit *quid pro quo* character of the transactions, which range from procurement of favors for the state, to transferring property from less-stable *poleis* to more-stable ones, to foreign economic and military assistance to actual or potential allies. Even the procurement of a large amount of grain from a friendly king during a famine is an incomplete transaction until it reaches the final consumers, and the mechanism for that final distribution may well have been sale at prices that the state attempted, with only partial success, to control. Herman's chapter 4 details transactions of grain, timber, money, and military manpower that were large enough to have wrenching effects on resource allocations in both the sending and the receiving regions, and, if this was the case, the impression that the transactions were arbitrary, even whimsical, surely overlooks the likelihood that the parties involved were capable of anticipating those impacts and took account of them in their decisions—or at least suffered the consequences if they did not. The chapter leaves the impression of having compressed many different types of transaction, with different motives and calculations, into a relatively undifferentiated model of ritual friendship and gift exchange. The result blurs distinctions between public and private actions, between self-interest and altruism, and between calculation and whim. While the collection of textual material is a substantial scholarly achievement, the theoretical evaluation is too naive to be credible.

[286] Snodgrass 1980: 57–58, 132–33; and 1991: *passim*. The notion that Snodgrass claims (1991: 18), that "gift exchange almost by definition excludes profit," is incorrect and probably derives from insufficient attention to definitions. In common parlance, profit is the difference between revenues and expenses and is an indicator of an individual's craft and thrift, while in disciplinary economic terminology, it simply represents the net product of effort and reflects impersonal forces of interactions, often indirect, among producers. If people do not get as much out of their efforts as they put into them (think of food production for concreteness, but the concept is more general), eventually they will starve. Certainly the literature on contemporary and recent gift exchange in the southwest Pacific reveals considerable thought given to maximizing expected gains from ritual exchanges. Late Bronze Age royal or palace sectors did not amass the wealth indicated by their archaeological remains by being nonprofit organizations, and considering the natural tendency of "things" to "run down" (the entropy law), it seems likely that the personnel responsible for administering those palaces gave considerable thought to how to produce more than they expended. Admittedly, this is a thought experiment rather than artifactual evidence, but the implications of the null hypothesis seem inconsistent with the artifactual evidence. The occasional pursuit of economic policies (often incidental policies) that weakened the productive capacity of the overall economy, particularly the private elements upon which the palace sector ultimately rested, is not counterevidence to calculation on the part of the palace personnel. We are quite capable of pursuing destructive economic policies, in the name of greater good, in the late twentieth century A.C.

The reciprocity-redistribution concept (Snodgrass 1991: 16) does not provide the scholar with the accounting discipline necessary to analyze the profitability conditions that must be satisfied for reciprocal and redistributive transactions to be sustained. Similarly, the absence of "mutually agreed prices" (17) in gift exchange follows possibly from considering price as a determinant of a transaction rather than as a consequence. In fact, in real terms, a price is nothing but the physical ratio of two goods exchanged, whether that concept is recognized by the transacting parties or not. Use of the gift-exchange concept cannot offer an escape from prices. It is difficult to understand the referent of the term "minimalist." Rather than impose minimal a priori restrictions on interpretations of archaeological evidence, minimalism appears instead to sanction one set of interpretations to the exclusion of others.

Phoenician in their cases—and their possible uses as gifts among Greek aristocrats: how were the gifts acquired before they entered a Greek gift exchange system?[287] Van Wees's empirical and logical assessment of gift exchange in Dark Age Greece leads him to reject the concept of nonconvertibility among exchange spheres (treasure and nontreasure), accept maximization of production as a household or estate goal, and separate gift-giving into two types that are not part of an agonistic, prestige-building system. He retains a third category of gift exchange (parting gifts) that he believes may have been used as a wealth-building mechanism, but he rejects the actuarial basis underlying generalized reciprocity for the system, suggesting instead what he calls hierarchical reciprocity, whereby lower-rank hosts give proportionately greater gifts to higher-rank guests than vice versa.[288]

Is it possible to identify empirically archaeological remains that moved via gift exchange? Intellectual constructs (models) can tell us what kinds of goods should have been suitable in such exchanges, agonistic or otherwise, but I can think of no characteristics of the goods themselves or their contexts that could be used to reject a null hypothesis of gift exchange or not-gift exchange. The motivations behind the artifacts are unobservable, and the possible transmission mechanisms are insufficiently distinguishable from one another. This seems to put considerable weight on the quality of the logic in the intellectual construct inasmuch as it guides interpretations of finds. The interpretations of gift exchange seem to rest as often as not on assumptions (sometimes considered to be inferences from subsequent literary sources) such as the eschewing of profit (in the midst of an agonistic exchange), which, *ex hypothesi*, rules out most nonritual types of exchange. At the risk of directing discussion away from its empirical base, it seems that the most informative analysis of gift exchange in Dark Age Greece lies in the intellectual construct itself.

Turning to Mauss's model of gift exchange itself, it is not a comforting alternative to the impersonality of the market. As he says himself, "Although the prestations and counter-prestations take place under a voluntary guise they are in essence strictly obligatory, and their sanction is private or open warfare. . . . The agonistic character of the prestation is pronounced . . . essentially usurious."[289] Mauss emphasizes, nonetheless, that markets coexist beside gift exchange in societies practicing the latter.[290] The model is a highly elastic concept, which can be stretched to fit nearly any observation, ancient or modern.[291] Sahlins takes a step beyond Mauss-style gift exchange with his big man/chief model of exchange and, to

---

[287] Bisi 1987: 233–34; Morris 1992b: xvi.

[288] Van Wees 1992: 222–37. The actuarial basis of the generalized reciprocity model of using parting gifts to build wealth is that recipients depend on enough of their hosts dying before they can return the visit and deplete their own gift-acquired treasure—essentially a Ponzi scheme, of which the chain letter is a familiar contemporary example.

[289] Mauss 1954: 3, 4.

[290] Ibid.: 2.

[291] Firth (1965: 331) shows some ambivalence about this characteristic of the model: "M. Marcel Mauss in his admirable *Essai sur le Don*, a stimulating theoretical treatment of the subject [primitive exchange] . . . stresses the binding nature of the obligations underlying much primitive exchange. . . . Each of these propositions could aptly cover some aspects of the Tikopia situation. But they must not be stressed too strongly. . . . These [exchanges] involve a strong response to complex social obligations. But these may be considered as part of a rational economic choice, if a preference for other types of advantage or satisfaction than mere increase of wealth be regarded as legitimate. . . . Moreover, one must not ignore the more purely material aspects of the transactions. Again, while from a general standpoint . . . exchanges . . . may be viewed as group-exchanges, . . . group-exchange conceived as a set of individual transactions is a more adequate formulation."

Working backward to earlier sources in the literature is easier than working forward from an early, known piece of scholarship to contemporary work, but working intellectually with Mauss's 1925 contribution (Mauss 1923–24) is equivalent to relying on Adam Smith ([1776] 1936) and Alfred Marshall (1920) for economic concepts. Although I do not attempt to review its development comprehensively, the thinking based on gift exchange appears to have taken several divergent paths. Sahlins (1972: ch. 4) and Weiner (1992: 23–32, 44–46) discuss the development, as well as antecedents, of the gift-exchange concept, Sahlins emphasizing relationships to the development of exchange and international diplomacy, Weiner stressing the ritual aspects of gift exchange and its roles in maintaining social continuity, in the nineteenth- and twentieth-century A.C. Western world as well as in noncomplex societies. The importance of ritual to gift exchange has emerged as one promi-

some extent, production, in which he relies upon Karl Polanyi's concepts of various degrees of reciprocity in exchange.[292] Sahlins brings the gift-exchange model to a point of development at which it is offered as an intellectual competitor for contemporary economic models of economic organization and behavior in tribal societies in particular and, for many students, in peasant societies as well.[293] At this point in the intellectual development, the issue is no longer whether gift exchange replaces markets in archaic societies, but whether the model of a generalized, gift-oriented system of production and exchange organized by big men or chiefs should replace the

intellectual structures offered by contemporary economic theory for the analysis of ancient economic activity regardless of the institutional mechanisms through which exchange operated. While the existence or nonexistence of markets is of some interest in the study of intercommunity trade, the only relevant issue in the application of conventional economic analysis to early economic activity is whether physical production and personal satisfaction can be conceptualized so that in a mathematical representation, their first partial derivative has a positive sign, and particularly so that their second partial derivative has a negative sign.[294] This is a very weak condition and

---

Note 291 continued

nent theme in the literature subsequent to Mauss, and this development appears to have downgraded the quantitative role of gift exchange in the economies of noncomplex societies (Finley 1979 follows this approach). Weiner's thesis in fact focuses on a quite restricted range of objects involved in gift exchange and appears to find ordinary (nonritual) consumption and production outside the purview of the concept. Similarly, Reheja (1988), while finding such ritual exchanges widespread throughout a Hindu village, restricts the scope of gift exchange to apotropaic behavior and payment for ritual services, leaving the other consumption, production, and resource allocation exogenous. Sahlins (1960a, 1960b, 1963, 1968, 1972), *inter alia*, has developed the reciprocity concept in gift exchange into models with wider reach into the economies of noncomplex societies, but ritual gift exchange recedes in prominence in his more generalized models of socioeconomic reciprocity. Following the historical-linguistic aspect of *Essai sur le don*, with a focus on Mauss's earlier interest in classical Greece and Rome, Benveniste (1948–49: 7–20; reprinted in 1971: ch. 26) worked from words for *gift* to various meanings of *exchange* toward interpretations of ancient Greek and Roman economic relations. In this literature is Derrida's recent deconstructionist analysis of Mauss's concept of gift exchange: 1992: chs. 1–2. Derrida questions the name "gift" and emphasizes the exchange relationship in Mauss's examples and the potential for disguised aggression in such transactions. His interest is the concept of the gift rather than the position of gifts in wider economic relations.

[292] The works by Sahlins that appear to be the most insightful are 1960b: 495–500 (which is a précis of his dissertation), and 1963: 285–303. Sahlins 1960a: 390–415 is a contentious essay that is compromised by unfamiliarity with contemporary economic analysis and attendant conceptual confusions. Later, consolidated statements of Sahlins's integration and generalization of gift exchange, reciprocity, and the big man/chief model of exchange and production are 1968: ch. 5, and 1972: 132–48, 246–63.

[293] Cf. Douglas (1990: xiv) on the use of the gift-economy concept as a means to improve the discourse on elusive social subjects—as a device for systematically squeezing "subjective hunches and concealed political pressure" from scientific discourse.

[294] In production, the positive first partial derivative describes the phenomenon that more of some input gives more of an output; the negative second partial derivative means that the positive increments of output attributable to increases in one input get smaller as more of that input is used, holding constant the quantities of any other inputs that may be used. In preferences or consumption, a positive first partial derivative says that having more of what one likes gives more satisfaction, while the negative second derivative says only that the person eventually (slowly, or bit by bit) will get sick of it. Cf. North 1985: 561, on the irrelevance of markets to the analysis of choice, and Posner 1980: 10–18, for an interpretation of gift-exchange interactions as partial insurance contracts. Akerlof (1982) has modeled a problem of employer-employee relations of pay and effort as a gift exchange, in which each party gives more than the minimum necessary. This conceptualization differs superficially from the more commonly used neoclassical model of the labor market, in which all parties, in equilibrium, do only what they must. In fact, several transactions are occurring simultaneously in Akerlof's model—prestige, pay, job security, work hours, and effort. A contract with a single term—such as the simplest version of the neoclassical labor-market model—could not equilibrate all these transactions, and in Akerlof's model, the gift exchange operates within a market, as a device to expand the number of terms in the contract so as to give all parties more satisfactory exchange outcomes. Nonetheless, all the parties to the labor-market contract in Akerlof's model maximize, which yields important mathematical similarities between the gift-exchange and neoclassical models.

has nothing to do with the separation of economic organization from kinship structures.[295] In summary, the gift-exchange model, if we accept its restriction to ritual, and generally agonistic, events, shows limited potential as a mechanism for distributing the Dark Age artifacts addressed in this study, and the generalizations of that model to encompass the totality of resource allocation in preindustrial societies, technically speaking, demonstrate neither necessary nor sufficient conditions for rejecting the application of contemporary economic analysis to economic activity in those societies.[296]

Empirically, the evidence of commercial interactions in the eastern Mediterranean and Aegean in the Late Bronze Age and their reappearance, if not their continuation, in the Early Iron Age in the eastern Mediterranean inclines me to accept a strong relative importance to ordinary, nonritual commerce in the external movement of surviving artifacts, and what I think must have been a larger corpus of nonsurviving commodities, in the Early Iron Age Aegean. Could the nonagonistic giving of gifts have facilitated such nonritual exchange? Why not? (It works today, only we have attempted to drive it underground and call it bribery unless conducted officially by organs of the state, and states are striving to restrict even those gifts.) Conceptually, while the gift-exchange concept aims at helping the scholar understand the integration of economic, political, and religious activities in a society (noncomplex or complex, archaic or modern), the development of the concept has not produced intellectual mechanisms that permit the scholar to analyze detailed effects of events in one arena on behavior in another: for example, if events in the external political arena bring forth an increase in, say, cloth moving out of the community, how will the choice and quantities of crops planted and harvested be affected? Under prevailing rights to distribution of the harvest, will the subsequent harvest foster discontent on grounds of perceived fairness? These are the sorts of question that interest me, and I do not find the gift-exchange model particularly helpful in addressing them, regardless of whether items move in commercial markets or as ritualized gifts. Other scholars with different interests may continue to find archaeological applications of the gift-exchange model intellectually satisfying, but I will not rely on it to a major extent in the remainder of this study.

---

[295] The explicit joining of economic activity (literally, hammering and sawing as well as more intricate activities such as merchandizing) with activities otherwise characterized as social or "noneconomic" can be accomplished by taking advantage of each individual's (and hence each community's) time constraint: Becker 1965: 493–517. On rationality, Becker also has observed that rational behavior requires definition, which opens the possibility—even the necessity—of specifically defining and modeling irrational behavior (there may be numerous varieties of irrationality): Becker 1962: 1–13. With these concepts, a wide variety of social organization becomes amenable to explicit modeling. Hunt (1987: 168 n. 17) points out that Sahlins's construct in *Stone Age Economics* (1972) implies that the only constraint on (cost of) increased production is leisure, whereas "it is very attractive for us to think that levels of production are constrained. It is entirely possible that Sahlins's position is correct in some circumstances. I know of no demonstration of such a condition for agriculture in civilizations." Rationality and efficiency sometimes are distinguished insufficiently from each other, the former being a weaker condition—i.e., more easily satisfied—than the latter; see, e.g., Liverani 1979: 22. Rationality is little more than making one's means consistent with one's goals, with no judgment of the goals, while efficiency is getting the most of what one wants with what one has, and may be subject to numerous constraints that impede obtaining maximum satisfaction of one's goals.

It is not difficult to find discussions that mix together the topics of cultural beliefs and rationality or irrationality, which, of course, have little, if anything, to do with each other. Greif (1994: 921, 943) uses game-theoretic concepts to characterize relationships between cultural beliefs and equilibrium behavior. Defining cultural beliefs as expectations about others' actions in various contingencies, expectations may differ rather than equilibrium actions involving strategic behavior. This characteristic does not imply that all people behave similarly, but that common strategic interactions may be recognized as defining the best opportunities for interacting individuals under a wide range of beliefs about how others will behave in out-of-equilibrium situations. Game theory, as the systematic study of contingent, interactive behavior, offers innumerable opportunities for specifying situations involving alternative cultural beliefs. This richness comes at a high price in mathematical sophistication, however.

[296] Elsewhere (Jones forthcoming a and b) I have studied the behavior of an *oikos* leader engaging in gift exchange as a constrained maximization problem with material and time constraints. Such a nonmarket situation is readily amenable to choice-theoretic analysis.

In the cases of both ancient Greece and pre-historic Europe, the modern constructs of tribal economics, including gift exchange and the leading role of the chief in directing resource allocation, operate in the direction of predicting less-pervasive interregional interactions, greater restrictions on trade, and later appearance of trade. The scholars referring to these theories also identify or concede the existence of trade early in the first millennium, even in volumes not amenable to control by the very elites to which the tribal economic theories appeal. The actions that Wells proposes for the central European chiefs in redirecting the efforts of their people to produce surpluses that could enter trade are the same actions that contemporary economic explanations would predict, even in the absence of markets. For analytical purposes, the chief is a redundant agent in obtaining the increase in output required for, or induced by, trade, although there is no denial that chiefs existed in the central European societies.[297]

FURTHER EVIDENCE ON CHARACTERISTICS OF DARK AGE TRADE

In this section I assemble further evidence and offer some brief reasoning on several topics dealing with trade during the Early Iron Age. The first topic treats the regularity of trade, although not particularly conclusively; the second addresses products traded; the third involves ship size; the fourth explores motivations for trade; and the fifth involves risk in shipping and its implications. These topics are not entirely independent in every case. As much as possible, I rely on evidence belonging to the Dark Age, usually literary and indirect, but I use several analogies from other periods.

REGULARITY OF TRADE

Did Dark Age traders, Greeks, Phoenicians, or others, move crisply among planned destinations, or did they wander with loose schedules and irregular destinations? For a 500-year period in the eastern half of the Mediterranean and the Aegean, we can expect variation in this characteristic. In Eumaeus's tale in the *Odyssey*, the Phoenician traders who ultimately kidnapped him with the conspiracy of his nurse spent an entire year on the island by the time they had collected a full cargo.[298] Greek trading ships to the west were said to sometimes put into an unoccupied site for a growing season, sow a grain crop, and remain long enough to harvest it to provision themselves. Neither of these examples demonstrates what would be called rapid turnaround, nor does either necessarily represent unplanned wandering. Herodotus's account of the legend of Io's abduction from Argos provides an interesting contrast.[299] The time to which Herodotus refers would be, in contemporary terminology, Late Mycenaean times, so it falls outside the Dark Age, but the details of his version of the story may reflect later, including Dark Age, practice. A Phoenician (Canaanite? Syrian?) ship carrying Assyrian and Egyptian goods stopped in Argos. The crew displayed their wares on the beach, presumably where ships loaded and unloaded at the time, and within five or six days they were nearly sold out. Some women came down to the beach to see what was left, and while they were standing around looking for something to buy, the Phoenician sailors made a rush at them, caught a few, including Io, and sailed away. Notable in the story are the civil reception given the Phoenicians, suggesting diplomatic acceptance as well as familiarity; the offloading at the beach without built port facilities; the rapid sale of the

---

[297] From the perspective of analyzing resource-allocation behavior of some society, a chief is equivalent to the "auctioneer" or "central planner" in Walrasian models of general economic equilibrium: while that "individual's" actions implement the particular resource-allocation mechanism that directs activities ("sets the rules"), that individual himself is not modeled, only the action of the rules he (or she) implements. For an introduction to contemporary perspectives on the implementation of resource-allocation rules, of which those composing a private-property market economy are only one case, see Campbell 1987. See also Yoffee 1993: esp. 64–65, on what he sees as preoccupation with chiefs and chiefdoms in archaeological research, while the anthropological research tradition from which it developed has gone on to produce alternative approaches to the issue of social development.

[298] *Od.* 15.455. An entire year clearly is a stock phrase, but it indicates a period of time longer than a simple port stop for quick watering and loading.

[299] Hdt. *Histories* 1.1 (trans. de Sélincourt 1972: 41–43).

wares with the anticipation that the sailors would soon embark again; and the abduction, which, although it created a fuss among the Greeks, suggests that kidnapping for the slave trade was not unusual. This is the Greek story, according to Herodotus. The Phoenician account of the affair, also according to Herodotus, is that Io got pregnant by the ship's captain and, when she discovered the fact, sailed with the ship to avoid embarrassment with her family. To make the Phoenician version plausible, it should have been not uncommon for a trader's ship to put into a harbor for well over a month, but two-and-a-half to three months would probably not have been an unusual length of stay.

PRODUCTS TRADED

Odysseus's account to Eumaeus of the last time he saw Odysseus fabricates his impersonation's embarkation from Thresprotia on a Thresprotian ship bound for "Doulichion, rich in wheatfields."[300] Thresprotia was in southwest Epirus, and the best current guess about Doulichion is that it was a city on the coast of Acarnania, opposite the Echinades, perhaps at Traganesti or more probably at the harbor named Pandeleimona or Platyá.[301] Knorringa accepts this account as a fabricated voyage to obtain wheat.[302] However, Knorringa wrote before Milman Parry's analysis of the structure of oral epic, and the epithet of Doulichion, "rich in wheatfields" (πολύπυρος), describes Doulichion rather than the reason for the journey there. The same epithet appears with Doulichion in *Odyssey* 16.396, the only other time Doulichion appears in either the *Odyssey* or the *Iliad*. However, πολύπυρος is used to describe the isle of Syria at *Odyssey* 15.406 and is used of Argos at *Iliad* 15.372. This epithet of Doulichion cannot be used safely as evidence that trade in a bulk commodity such as wheat would not

appear jarring to a mid-eighth-century audience.[303] Nevertheless, Homer offers no other motivation for the Thresprotian voyage to Doulichion, and motivation may be implicit in the choice of destination, although this remains weak evidence for wheat trade.

The following account of traded items comes from Knorringa's examination of the Attic comic fragments of the fourth and third centuries for items that were imported into Athens.[304] Undoubtedly, the variety of traded goods increased between the eleventh century and the third, and I make no suggestion that the variety of the later period is representative of the variety available seven or eight centuries earlier. What is striking, however, and may apply to the earlier centuries, is the variety that exists within commodity groups often thought of as relatively undifferentiated. Standing thirty centuries away, we may be hard pressed to conceive of what various Dark Age Greek communities may have found to sell to one another that they could not find at home and that they were willing, possibly eager, to have, or that someone else could produce cheaply enough to sell to them and still cover shipping costs. Consider this apparent demand for variety. Among the fish mentioned in these fragments are: from the Hellespont, tunny (σκόμβρος) and various kinds of salt fish; from Skyros, crayfish (κάραβοι); from Pontus, mussels (μύες); from Megaris, another variety of tunny (θύννοι); from Boeotia, eels (ἐγχέλεις); from Carystus, *Maena vulgaris*, a small sprat-like fish similar to herring or anchovy, which was salted (μαινίδες); from Eretria, *Pagrus vulgaris* or bream (φάγροι); from Gades, dried or smoked fish (τάριχη); and from Sikyon, conger eel (γόγγροι).[305] Among the references to fruits, nuts, and vegetables in the fragments: from Euboea, pears and apples; from Paphlogonia, acorns and almonds; from Phoenicia, dates; from Samothrace, onions. Other agricultural products

---

[300] *Od.* 14.334–35.

[301] *OCD* 2, 1062; Smith 1873: 803–4; Lenk 1937: 63–69.

[302] Knorringa 1926: 9. Bravo (1983: 17–18, 25; 1984: 120–21) believes that various regions of Greece were trading in grains as early as the eighth century, some regions exporting to the Phoenician Near East and others importing from Sicily. He does not consider this to have been "mass commerce," although he does not attempt to define that term.

[303] I am indebted to David Tandy for assistance with this assessment.

[304] Knorringa 1926: 74–76.

[305] Some writers have interpreted some lines from the *Odyssey* as indicating that fish was a despised food, eaten only by the poor, during the Dark Ages. In the Classical period, fish was an article of passion with the Greeks. Both Glotz (1926: 37) and Mitchell (1940: 286–87) dispute the notion that Homeric Greeks despised fish

include silphium and cowhides from Cyrene, pork and cheeses from Syracuse, fine wheat flour from Phoenicia (which is usually noted for manufactures), and mustard from Cyprus. Manufactured goods include couches, pillows, and earthenware from Sicily; papyrus, perfumes, and other unguents from Egypt; incense from Syria; carpets and pillows from Carthage; and kettles from Argos. Among natural-resource products, talc comes from Sicily, cypress from Crete, and ivory from Libya. Slaves come from Pagasae and Phrygia, and wines come from too many locations to enumerate. Mustard grows well in central Greece. An entire ship's cargo of mustard is unimaginable; what else would have occupied a ship sailing from Cyprus to Crete, and need the ship have originated in Cyprus? The point to emphasize here is variety. A theme through the literature on trade in prehistoric and early historic Greece is the satisfaction of mutual needs through trade, but through the sparse evidence that remains shines the shreds of variety that spiced these peoples' lives, as well as bulk commodity items.

From the archaeological evidence of an earlier period, it is worth reviewing the items found on the Ulu Burun shipwreck of the late fourteenth century.[306] The ship appears to have been heading west along the southern coast of Anatolia. First, Mycenaean, Cypriot, and Syrian pottery have been found on board. The Mycenaean ware may

have been personal items of some of the ship's crew. Pithos KW251, the largest of six storage jars visible in the vessel, contained eighteen pieces of Cypriot pottery, still neatly stacked. The pottery does not represent a cargo of significant commercial value, and Pulak suggests it may represent trade goods the crew would have used to acquire necessary supplies on their trip. Second, downslope of pithos KW250 was a large deposit of several hundred fish bones, including complete skeletons of small fish. As of 1985, it had not been determined whether these are the remains of spilled contents of a container or accumulated excrement of a large predator once living in the pithos, although the complete skeletons do not sound consistent with excrement. This may be evidence of a load of dried, salted, or smoked fish. Third, a similar deposit of hundreds of the opercula of murex shells (their "doors") was trapped between several copper oxhide ingots and was preserved by being impregnated with copper. Their stacking suggests that the deposit is the remains of a shipment carried in a bag and probably represents a by-product of the purple-dye industry. Pliny noted medical uses of murex opercula, but Pulak suggests that these opercula may have been a shipment of incense. Fourth, by 1985, sixty-seven Canaanite amphorae, roughly half of those on the wreck, had been raised. Several yielded fig seeds, which Pulak suggests may be intrusive but may nonetheless represent former con-

---

Note 305 continued

as food. Noting the *Odyssey*'s epithet for the sea as "abounding in fish," Glotz believes that the Aegean waters must have exercised a strong attraction on the Greek coastal populations. Gallant's detailed study of fishing in the ancient Aegean concludes that fish could not have been a major component of the ancient Greek diet, because of both the relative scarcity of fish in the waters of the region and the labor-intensive technology of fishing. Nonetheless, he assesses an important role for trade in fish as a means of offsetting fluctuations of crop yields. Fresh fish he envisages as having been a quantitatively minor delicacy in antiquity (principally in the Classical period): Gallant 1985: 40–44. For archaeological evidence from the fifth century of trade in preserved fish at Corinth, see Williams 1979: 111–18: whole and cut fish, some identifiable as sea bream and tunny, in Punic as well as Aegean-region transport amphorae. Rather than being the simple result of millennia of overfishing, the relative infertility of the eastern Mediterranean and parts of the Aegean, presently and in antiquity, is attributable to interactions of water temperature, salinity, and limited entry of river water combining to retard the regeneration of nutrients. The northeastern Aegean, the southern Levantine basin, and the Adriatic are the most fertile parts of the eastern Mediterranean: van Andel 1987: 50. Such local marine fertility differences would have produced trade opportunities based on differences in resource availability. Sakellarakis (1974: 389–90) believes the scarcity of representations (on vase paintings, reliefs, and seals) of fishermen reflects the humble and peaceful character of that activity within an artistic tradition that, since the Mycenaean period, had favored the heroic in its art. He contrasts the Mycenaean and even the Minoan disinterest in fishing with that of Egypt, where fishing was a favorite royal pastime. (This disinterest in fishing is not to be equated to a disinterest in marine life, amply expressed in Minoan and Mycenaean vase painting; cf. N. Marinatos 1993: 195–96; on a ritual interpretation of the boys with fish on the fresco from Thera, ibid.: 216–17.)

[306] The following account is taken from Bass 1986; Pulak 1988: 5, 10–12, 14, 37; Bass and Pulak 1989: 1–12; Haldane 1990: 57–59; 1993: 352–54.

tents. In smaller vessels such as flasks, fig seeds may represent the remains of a dried fig used as a stopper, but over 1,000 fig seeds have been recovered. Some 120 Canaanite jars contained organic deposits of Chios turpentine, or terebinth (as much as one metric ton), from the tree *Pistacia atlantica*,[307] and another contained pomegranate seeds, flower parts, and fragments of skin, and appears originally to have contained whole pomegranates; others contained digital bones of sheep or goats as well as shells of land snails. Frankincense and myrrh were present in some amphorae. Coriander seeds appear to have been carried in baskets or woven bags. Additionally, safflower seeds, an amphora full of olive pits, several almond shells, sumac fruits, black cumin, and several varieties of grape seeds have been recovered. The coriander, pomegranate, and safflower are consistent with a trade in inputs for perfume-making. Fifth, consider some manufactured items. By 1985, twenty-one glass ingots in the shapes of truncated cones had been raised. Among the tools recovered are sickles, axes, adzes, chisels, drill bits or awls or both, and a pair of tongs. Some of these may be ship's equipment, and some could have belonged to an itinerant craftsman, but some may have been cargo. The jewelry contained some excellent items that suggest a royal consignment, but other pieces have the appearance of having been scrap that could have been for sale. Bronze weapons could have included personal items as well as cargo. A final manufactured item of particular interest is a wooden diptych, or writing tablet, of two rectangular wooden leaves joined by a three-piece ivory cylindrical hinge, an interesting representative of crafted or manufactured items that we of thirty or thirty-five centuries later are unlikely to think of. Sixth are a number of raw materials. Most striking are several hundred copper ingots, the number of which contrasts with the eighty-odd found on the Gelidonya wreck, as well as several dozen tin ingots.[308] There are also pieces

of elephant and hippopotamus ivory and logs of "African ebony." Seventh, among the miscellaneous finds were twenty-two balance weights, which may indicate that the ship carried items that would be sold by small, individually weighed lots rather than in bulk. Spices and incense come to mind as possibilities.

These recovered artifacts indicate a combination of bulk cargo and smaller items, but altogether a wide and varied array. The provenances of the artifacts indicate a cosmopolitanism that is unlikely to have lasted into the Greek Dark Age, but the multistop character of the voyage implied may have carried over. The presence of the Cypriot pottery in a ship that does not otherwise appear particularly Cypriot suggests a mechanism for the transmission of a class of ceramic goods and even metal art items between communities. These items themselves may not have borne transportation costs well, but subsidized by a larger cargo of bulk items and high-value, highly transportable items like spices and incense, they may have been able to support a crew and pay for ship repairs.

The interpretation of the cargo of the Ulu Burun shipwreck is still under discussion in the literature, but that of the late-thirteenth- to early-twelfth-century Cape Gelidonya shipwreck probably has reached a narrower range of consensus by now.[309] The Gelidonya ship appears to have been a Syrian, or possibly Cypriot, merchantman, headed west with an assorted cargo of raw materials and finished products from various origins in the Levant. A load of broken bronze items suggests an active market in scrap metals,[310] while the oxhide and other ingots clearly indicate a market in raw materials, although interpretation of state or private sponsorship of the latter appears to be a matter of scholarly preference. At any rate, the ship is clear evidence of foreign trade very close to the time of the Sea Peoples' attacks on Egypt.[311]

---

[307] Mills and White 1989: 37–44.

[308] Bass 1986: 274, 294; Pulak 1988: 6, 8–10; Bass 1967: 52–83. By the 1993 season, the count of copper ingots had reached 354: Gates 1995: 223.

[309] Bass 1967: 164–67. Bass responds to varying interpretations of the finds in 1973: 29–38.

[310] Knapp, Muhly, and Muhly (1988: 257–58) interpret the appearance of scrap as evidence of a thriving and mature industry rather than of one simply stressed for raw material. This interpretation parallels the changing locational characteristics of the United States' iron and steel industry as the availability of scrap became a weightier factor: Perloff, Dunn, Lampard, and Muth 1960: 451.

[311] Muhly, Stech Wheeler, and Maddin (1977: 361) suggest that the attempts to determine the origin and destination of this ship have obscured what they consider the most important information the wreck contains: that at least part of the Late Bronze Age metals trade appears to have been in private, entrepreneurial hands.

Mallowan's account of trade in sheep dung in A.D. 1938 is worth citing for the sheer humbleness of the products involved. Bartered for baked clay amphorae carried empty in ships from Sidon (modern Saida), the dung was shipped 150 miles and occasionally further as fertilizer for orchards and gardens. Mallowan cites Odysseus's use of mule and cow dung as fertilizer in *Odyssey* 17.296–300.[312]

SHIP SIZES

Hesiod recommends, "Compliment a small ship, but put your cargo in a big one; bigger will be the cargo, bigger the extra gain, provided that the winds withhold their ill blasts."[313] The admonition suggests greater safety in a larger ship, but the last clause indicates the susceptibility of even larger ships to natural dangers. It does not, however, include human dangers, which Braudel noted to be nearly as great as natural dangers at the turn of the sixteenth century A.C.[314] In addition, it suggests that a potential shipper would have had a choice of ships on which to consign or otherwise ship his goods. Would social norms have permitted an eighth-century Greek aristocratic shipowner of Humphreys's description to accept a shipment from a farmer, and if so, under what conditions?

MOTIVATIONS FOR TRADE

Hesiod again: "When you want to escape debt and joyless hunger by turning your blight-witted heart to trade, I will show you the measure of the resounding sea."[315] This merges gain with survival, which is instructive for the Dark Ages. There need have been little difference between concepts of improvement of well-being and material survival. With the emphasis on luxury products dominating earlier periods, it is singularly interesting that Hesiod, writing in the early to mid-seventh century, recommends trade as an element in a much more basic strategy. Redfield suggests that local droughts could have been an impetus to trade among agricultural communities.[316] He recognizes that this trade would have required some payment mechanism, since the normal income stream would have been interrupted, and suggests hoarded valuables, usually metals, as a means of payment.[317] I doubt whether the typical Dark Age Greek farming community would have had sufficient valuables to trade for enough food to make up a serious shortfall, but trade could have offered a buffer against risk via a mechanism other than giving a trader the piggy bank in a bad year. That mechanism proceeds along the lines developed by Salmon in his story of how Corinthian trade affected that community's land use. The opportunity to trade on a regular basis would allow farmers to put some of their resources, probably labor mostly, into activities other than the main food crop. Such activities would be chosen so that their returns, or prosperity, would be relatively uncorrelated, or possibly even negatively correlated, with the main

---

[312] Mallowan 1939: 86–87.

[313] *Works and Days* 643–44 (trans. West 1988: 56). The usability of *Works and Days* in interpretations of Hesiodic society has been subjected to searching examinations, as has the usability of the Homeric epics. Hesiod himself has been described alternatively as a peasant and an aristocrat on hard times, and his admonitions and recommendations have been considered both as cogent advice and as possibly metaphorical representations. Altogether, it is difficult to believe that the poem would have been an effective vehicle for any message had its referents not corresponded fairly well to the audiences' intuitive understanding of them. For a representative array of recent literature on the subject, see Quiller (1981: 109–55), who refers to Hesiod as a peasant (124); Millett (1984: 84–115) takes up the what's-in-a-name issue regarding peasantry in Hesiod; on the metaphorical structure of sailing in *Works and Days*, Rosen 1990: 99–113; and Nagy 1990: 77–80.

[314] Braudel 1972: 886–87, citing Tenenti 1959: 67–561. Between 1592 and 1609, of 1,021 voyages underwritten by two major Venetian houses, pirates claimed between 250 and 300 ships (Tenenti's plate II) departing the port of Venice, whereas there were 300 shipwrecks, including ships run aground (Tenenti's plate V); it is unclear how many of the groundings were actual losses. This ratio is not certainly transferable to the Greek Dark Age, but the implied relative hazard is noteworthy.

[315] *Works and Days* 646–48 (trans. West 1988: 56).

[316] Redfield 1986: 41.

[317] Morgan (1990: 199–200) suggests that the demand for metals as just such insurance may have been an important motivation for the resurgence of Corinthian non-elite trade with western Greece and the Adriatic region c. 800.

food crop, so that income would be available to cover a food shortfall from local production in a bad year.[318] Such diversification would tend to be across food crops if trade were not a regular option, but would tend to extend to nonfood crops or even nonagricultural activities if the opportunity for external trade existed.[319] Evidence for external trade could exist in geomorphological and possibly pollen remains. In Appendix A, I discuss the measurement and

[318] Several authors have studied ancient Greek agricultural organization, including methods of dealing with risk. Gallant (1991: 36–38, 41–43, 94–98, respectively) and Garnsey (1988: 49–53, 48–49, 53–55, respectively) discuss crop diversification, spatial dispersal of land holdings, and storage. Both also recognize exchange, or trade (reciprocity in Gallant's work), as a mechanism contributing to the stabilization of agricultural incomes, but neither places particular importance on it (Gallant 1991: chap. 6; Garnsey 1988: 56–58). Gallant notes losses as high as 50% to 80% in the storage, but nevertheless believes that ancient Greeks may have attempted to hold ten to sixteen months' supply of food in storage (97), and Garnsey notes the existence of losses in storage but does not venture a percentage (55). Gallant bases his estimate of storage losses on contemporary Third World reports and beliefs about medieval Europe (94), but his estimates seem excessive. McCloskey and Nash (1984: 178) estimate average medieval English stocks at around 5% of annual consumption, on the basis of the behavior of grain prices and imputations of the interest rate. They also note that average barn size, either in records or in excavated remains, is a misleading guide to actual stocks held. Barns or other storage buildings would have been built for the maximum maximorum, immediately postharvest, rather than for any average holdings (176). Opportunities for trade can alter the autarkic trade-off between risk and return that can be derived from crop diversification and plot fragmentation, but trade as a mechanism for reducing or dispersing agricultural risk requires a means of payment in the event of crop failure. Bravo (1983: 23; 1984: 120–21) considers that distress (famine) was a principal motivation for the Dark Age grain trade. Sen (1981a: 433–64; 1981b: chap. 5) has conceptualized this sudden failure of an agricultural community to come up with means of securing food when its own crops fail, in his "entitlement" approach to the analysis of famines. While credit would be a theoretically acceptable payment device in such an event, it is unlikely to have been a prevalent payment means in Dark Age Greece. Regular reciprocity relations may be a candidate in the absence of an adequately developed capital account, but could require a relatively sophisticated level of diplomacy, and certainly would require effective and timely communication and transportation. Sen's principal message is that the absences of a capital account and alternative diplomatic means of securing loans have set the preconditions for the twentieth century A.C.'s greatest famines. The principal risk-management alternative I see is the diversification into activities that are little, or not, subject to agricultural risks, and that produce items that could be sold in the event of crop failure. Gallant (1991: 181–82) reports diplomatic arrangements between Greek states (fifth to third centuries) guaranteeing rights to import food in times of crop failure ("social storage"), but he notes the need to have something with which to buy it. Garnsey and Morris (1989: 99–101) rely on Hesiod for evidence of mechanisms that individuals could have used in the later Dark Age to deal with agricultural risk, citing that writer's focus on storage and trade; but most of their attention focuses on later periods and the involvement of the *polis* in meeting food emergencies, rather than on risk-reduction or consumption-stabilization strategies. They see trade as one way of dealing with agricultural risk—"mobilizing a surplus"—in the Dark Age (100), but do not include the nonagricultural tradable goods as part of the mechanism. Halstead and Jones (1989), from a study of contemporary (A.D. 1980–81) farming on Karpathos and Amorgos, emphasize field dispersal (50) and crop diversification (51) as methods of reducing risks from pests and weather. They characterize "overproduction" as a risk-reduction mechanism, without explicitly identifying it as self-provided insurance, although they acknowledge the mechanism's own risks from fire, theft, and pests (51–52). They view both recent and ancient grain trade in the Greek islands as responses to "short-term conditions of surfeit and shortage" (54), although the symmetry of trade in the two conditions requires some other category of item available for trade, either commodity or medium of exchange. For recent analyses of interactions among agricultural risk-reduction and dispersion mechanisms in medieval England and contemporary western India, see Townsend 1993; 1994: 539–91. Townsend's results reinforce findings of low carryover (storage) as well as the inadequacy of storage by itself as an insurance mechanism; the results from India suggest the importance of intra-family transfers as insurance devices; both studies point to the importance of external trade opportunities in conditioning risk-avoidance strategies at the village level. Walker and Ryan (1990: 262–64) point to both the importance of and the limitations on intervillage or interregional connections in determining the effectiveness of agricultural risk-reduction efforts.

[319] Such a spatial-temporal pattern following the ebb and flow of trading opportunities has been suggested for the southern Argolid on the basis of geomorphological evidence for land-use change: van Andel, Runnels, and Pope 1986: 103–28; Runnels and van Andel 1987: 303–34; van Andel and Runnels 1987: chap. 8. Most recently, Wells, Runnels, and Zangger (1993: 57–58) report evidence from an archaeological survey of the Argive plain

conceptualization of agricultural risk as it may have been faced by Dark Age Greek communities. Altogether, I find agricultural risk probably to have been of limited scope as a motivating force behind Dark Age trade in the aggregate.

Much archaeological and ancient historical literature on ancient trade focuses on exchange of resources that simply did not exist, or of products that are not known to have been produced, at the destinations. As a result of this focus, the importation of products that *could* have been produced locally is not considered. For the Mycenaean period, Palaima has recognized this issue and dealt with it in a very sophisticated manner.[320] Linear B tablets from Knossos indicate that olive oil was being sent to Cyprus in the Late Minoan III period, but objection to this interpretation has been raised on the grounds that no reference is made to perfuming of the oil, and since Cyprus could have produced plenty of olive oil, why

would it have imported any? Palaima is reluctant to presume that the oil *was* perfumed, in the absence of any such reference in the tablets, but he suggests two reasons why Cyprus could have been willing to import olive oil. First, and relatively obvious but nonetheless cogent, the Cypriots may have had a demand for variety in olive oil, which could have been supplied by Cretan imports.[321] Second, but more subtle and far-reaching, Palaima suggests that the Cypriots, although they could have produced all the olive oil they wanted, had alternative uses for their resources, such as ore extraction and processing, which could have taken labor away from olive-oil production, leaving the island with an excess demand for olive oil that would have to be supplied with imports. The products that absorbed labor that otherwise could have been employed in oil production would have been replaced less easily through trade. The general lesson of

---

Note 319 continued

around Mycenae that suggests more intricate interactions, however. Agricultural production, with export products including grain, olive oil, and woolen textiles, was intensified in the fourteenth and thirteenth centuries with little evidence for increased erosion, apparently because of extensive and competent infrastructural engineering such as terrace walls and dams. Nonetheless, there is evidence of massive erosion around Tiryns and the southern edge of the Argive plain around 1100, without any evidence of increased pressure of use on the land. Although some engineering works date from this period, they did not halt the erosion. Wells et al. imply that the Mycenaeans may have been unable to maintain the infrastructure, possibly because labor was stretched too thinly on other projects involving defense. The causation in this interesting proposal runs from unobservable, but reasonably suspected, changes in income, to archaeological evidence of land-use change rather than the reverse. Cf. Wells, Runnels, and Zangger 1990: 223–28, for details on finds from the Mycenaean period. The prior assessments of both Hooker and Kilian reinforce this interpretation. Hooker (1976: 177), while less precise on the forces operating from the Mycenaean public economy (especially construction) to the civilization's environmental stability, finds the archaeological and linguistic evidence leaving a major role for natural reverses, such as drought and famine, in accounting for the quickly successive palace destructions. Kilian (1988: 134), using Tiryns as an example, explicitly relates the Mycenaean collapse to the connections between what could be called public spending in contemporary terminology and overall economic stability. He attributes "agricultural over-expansion" to the "excessive building activities" of roughly the previous three generations before the collapse c. 1200: the new (LH IIIB) citadel at Tiryns "almost certainly ruined the ruler economically." On the basis of geomorphological analysis and review of the archaeological stratigraphy around Tiryns, Zangger (1994: 212) concludes that "the political collapse of the Mycenaean palatial culture was most likely accompanied by natural catastrophe in the Argolid." Cf. Chapter 4, notes 323 and 325, on the integration of environmental causation into human history, traditionally a ticklish matter methodologically.

[320] Palaima 1991: 284.

[321] The demand for variety has attracted considerable attention in the literature of international economics lately as an alternative or supplement to theories of the determinants of foreign trade that focus on relative supplies of inputs possessed by trading partners: Helpman and Krugman 1985: chaps. 6–8. Related to the role of differentiated products (i.e., products from the same industry but distinguished from one another by various characteristics) in determining trade patterns (the ratios of exports and imports of different countries or regions) and the locational patterns of industrial production is the potential importance of being the first producer in a new line of products: 1991b: 80–83; Krugman 1991c: 651–67; 1991d: 483–99; or, more accessibly, 1991a. Although the importance of being the first to produce an item may be clearer when labor is mobile between production locations, the possibility of long-standing economic advantages accruing from early innovation underscores the importance of the timing of Cypriot innovations in iron production and use, a very active subject of examination and speculation for several decades.

Palaima's example is that countries or regions do import products they can produce for themselves, paying for them with exports that the trading partner also can produce itself. The motivation for the trade is different relative production costs at different locations, and the volume of trade is regulated by the equalization of those relative production costs, within the margin of transportation costs; producing greater volumes of a product, with given resource supplies, gradually decreases production-cost advantages. The relevant empirical implication is that we need not restrict ourselves to products with unique production locations in reconstructions of ancient trading patterns. Even the (frequently implicit) characterization of metal ores as items of trade that went from where they were found to where they were not found has been modified recently by physical analyses, particularly lead isotope analyses of bronzes, which have revealed a wider array of known and unknown sources than was previously suspected. Cyprus may at times have exported copper to other regions, for example, Crete, which also supplied some of its own consumption of the metal and could have supplied more than it did, had not local production beyond a certain volume (rate) been costly enough to permit Cypriot exports, plus transport costs, to be competitive. Many regions may have been—in fact, probably were—both local producers and net importers of metals, simply because their local deposits were not rich enough or accessible enough, or their ores were not sufficiently easily worked.

RISKS OF TRADE

The riskiness of Dark Age seaborne trade is difficult to overlook, and it is interesting to obtain glimpses of how participants adjusted to it. Again, Hesiod recommends, "And do not put all your substance in ships' holds, but leave the greater part and ship the lesser."[322] Not putting all one's eggs in a single basket is a simplistic maxim of modern portfolio theory, and it is reassuring to see its early application. The implications are more widespread, however, and the maxim extends directly to shipowners as well as to agents consigning shipments. If a man is suffi-

ciently wealthy for a single merchant ship to represent a small part of his wealth, he would be little harmed by the total loss of one, to either nature or man. It appears that ship construction may have changed little between Mycenaean times and the later Dark Ages, or even the early Classical period, but whether ship costs changed over that period also depends upon whether the costs of the inputs into a ship changed (timber, metals, labor costs); furthermore, the cost of a finished ship may have changed relative to the wealth possessed by the "average" wealthy man or family.

Thus, the relative costliness of a merchant ship may have changed for any of several reasons over this period. Even with a relatively concentrated distribution of wealth, if assets such as land had limited fungibility, "wealthy" aristocrats may have found the cost of a seagoing merchant ship a relatively large proportion of their readily disposable wealth. The potential loss of one could have posed an unacceptable risk, although limited fungibility also could have sealed off the effects of such losses. This issue bears directly on the apparently much later issue of whether *naukleroi* were independent ship owners or were routine debtors, as were the *emporoi*. The question actually should be, and probably was in the Dark Age as well as the Classical period, if you *can* own a ship, *should* you? What proportion of a person's wealth would be sunk into an asset that could be totally lost? The most sophisticated treatment of this question, but dealing with the Classical period, is in an oddly popularizing little book by Calhoun.[323] In discussing the court case dealing with Hegistratus's attempt to sink his own ship to perpetrate a fraud, Calhoun observed that either the cargo was worth more than the ship or there was a heavy lien on the ship that would have been absolved in the event of its natural loss. On the grounds that the typical ship captain was not wealthy and should have preferred to take out a loan on his ship rather than put such a large share of his wealth into a single, highly risky asset, he preferred the latter explanation. A lender of large means could afford to put his resources into this business, as the occasional loss of a ship would not wipe out his resources, and the interest rate was high enough to ensure a profit.[324] For the Dark

---

[322] West 1988: 57.

[323] Calhoun 1926.

[324] Ibid.: 62, 65–66.

Ages, when such lenders were probably few and far between, if they existed at all, this risk-avoidance criterion could have put the Greeks by and large out of the merchant ship-owning business. Less poorly developed Levantine capital markets, more powerful Levantine states, or both, could have put Phoenicians in the shipping business during the Early Iron Age throughout the eastern Mediterranean and the Aegean by virtue of a superior ability to disperse the financial risks of shipping: earlier, longer, and possibly stronger capital-market traditions in the Near East may have survived the period of disorder at the end of the second millennium better than did any such institutions in the Aegean.[325] The consequences for the resource-allocation effects of foreign trade would have been largely unaffected by the "nationality" of the owner of the shipping, a subject that has claimed a share of attention in the literature out of proportion to its importance.

Also related to the risks of intercommunity shipping, Calhoun noted the characteristics of the type of loan contract used for Classical period Athenian shipping, the respondentia loan. Its major defect from the point of view of risk allocation is that from the time the lender has parted with his resources until the loan is repaid, or a return cargo representing its value is turned over to the lender or his agent, the lender has practically no security beyond the integrity of the absent borrower. The fact that Athens depended so heavily upon this trade "under a type of contract that depended almost entirely on the good faith of the contracting parties would seem to indicate that a majority of the men engaged were honest and upright, and the standards in the business were fairly high."[326] This contradicts the claim of Herodotus regarding the dishonesty of the typical merchant, but Herodotus may represent the aristocratic attitude toward commerce.[327]

This implication regarding ethical standards of the contracting parties harkens back to the evidence of nearly a millennium and a half earlier regarding the pride of the Old Assyrian merchants in their high ethical standards as well as their social status.[328] It is easy to fit a straight line between two data points, but it is worth considering the possibility that the standards of behavior in intercommunity commerce may not have been strictly Hobbesian during the Greek Dark Ages. The alternative hypothesis is that the Greek mentality changed from predominately piratical to remarkably reliable between the time of the Homeric epics and the Classical period, and such a large, rapid change seems improbable.

TRAVEL

Personal travel, other than for trade, could have had a number of motivations: adventure, tourism, a visit to a religious shrine, travel by itinerant craftsmen. What characteristics would such travel have had in the Greek Dark Age, and how could such individual movement have contributed to the pattern of artifactual remains?

INCONVENIENCES AND DANGERS

As dangerous as Dark Age sea travel was, considering the elements, the possibilities of attack, and the equally real chance that a ship's captain and crew might sell a traveler into slavery, Dark Age land travel may have been even more problematic.[329] The road systems of Minoan Crete and Mycenaean Greece were impressive, usually one lane, but with occasional widths of eleven-and-a-half feet, sufficient for two-way traffic.[330] By the Dark Age, however, lack of maintenance and repairs would have reduced the utility of these

---

[325] Aubet (1993: 95–96) believes that the palace dominated Tyre's overseas trade in the tenth century, contributing to an overall scale of operation, going both east to Babylonia and west to the Mediterranean and the Aegean, which would have been able to disperse the risks of ship-owning. In the ninth to seventh centuries, wealthy private Phoenician merchants attained operational scales sufficient to bear risks of ship-owning. Aubet sees both palace and private participants as having been in the business for profit.

[326] Calhoun 1926: 49.

[327] Cf. Knorringa 1926: 23–24; Hdt. *Histories* 1.93; 2.141, 164; 3.89.

[328] Oppenheim 1977: 92.

[329] André and Baslez (1993: 483–503) summarize the contemporary accounts of the miseries of the ancient voyage, from Classical to Roman times: from prolonged exposure to the elements to language barriers, nausea, exposure to epidemics, untrustworthy guides, bad and unaccustomed food, general discomfort aboard ship, and poor lodging.

[330] Casson 1974: 27.

roads for vehicles.[331] Foot traffic and pack animals probably dominated land transportation in Early Iron Age Greece, and Crouwell believes that it is easy to underestimate the role of land transportation in this period and that the scarcity of figural evidence represents the lack of interest in the subject to the patrons of art.[332] Most of the physical evidence for Early Iron Age roads comes from the seventh century and later.[333] Writing primarily of the Classical period and later, Pritchett emphasizes the overall primitive character of Greek roads as a decline from Mycenaean construction. On roads through mountains, he notes the difficulties of dating and distinguishing intentionally engineered grooves from worn ruts, although he believes, again from the Classical period, that most mountain travel used animals, leaving wagons to dirt roads on the plains.[334]

Highway brigandage was quite common during the Bronze Age in Mesopotamia and Egypt, and one of the features of the Minoan highway system on Crete may have been a series of fortified posts for highway police.[335] Though inns had been a common feature of the Bronze Age Near East, traffic in the Greek Dark Age apparently was of insufficient volume to justify them, although they were common by the fifth century along major roads, in most towns, and in ports. Dark Age travelers were left with no central authorities for personal protection and relied on the hospitality of strangers for shelter during the period.[336] Although religion clearly enjoined hospitality to, and protection for, strangers, our own lack of knowledge of diplomatic protocols of the period and the ancients' fear that strangers might be raiders leave some ambiguity about how travelers from either land or sea might have fared among strangers. Casson concludes that in Dark Age Greece, sea travel was the most expeditious means of moving between communities.[337]

The story of Wen-Amun's trading voyage from Egypt to Lebanon for cedar around 1076 is instructive on several of these points.[338] A brief review of the story, and of the report itself, is a useful point of entry. The story itself comes from a papyrus, P. Moscow 120, which was found at el-Hibeh in Middle Egypt, a fact considered important in the evaluation of the manuscript. The political importance of the town at el-Hibeh begins with the Twenty-First Dynasty, and it is seen as a stronghold of the Theban partial secession from Pharaonic sovereignty. The manuscript long was considered a literary version of an administrative report, but Černý's conclusion that "it is almost certainly the original report," on the basis of its style, language, and particularly its vertical composition on the papyrus fibers, has gained wide acceptance by Egyptological scholars.[339] Wen-

---

[331] Ibid.: 46.

[332] Crouwell 1992: 101, 104.

[333] Ibid.: 23.

[334] Pritchett 1980: 143–96.

[335] Evans 1927: 66, 78; Casson 1974: 38–39. Crouwell (1981: 31) does not find support for the extensive Minoan road system claimed by Evans but accepts that the existence of roads for wheeled traffic on Crete and the mainland can be inferred from the evidence of chariots in figures and Linear B tablets. Recent Greek surveys in eastern Crete seem to corroborate Evans's interpretation of a well-developed and controlled road network in Middle Minoan II–Late Minoan I. Some of the defensive buildings associated with the roads were reused in Late Minoan III and Protogeometric times. The surveyors' preliminary assessment is that the roads were satisfactory for pedestrians and pack animals but not for wheeled vehicles: Tzedakis, Chryssoulaki, Voutsaki, and Venieri 1989: 59, 72; 1990: 62.

[336] Casson 1974: 46–49, 87.

[337] Ibid.: 45.

[338] There are numerous translations of the report, with later works frequently contributing subtle but significant reinterpretations. Among the more prominent and more commonly available in English are Gardiner 1961: 306–13; Wilson 1958: 16–24; Wente 1973: 142–55; Lichtheim 1976: 224–30. Goedicke 1975 offers a thorough, critical analysis of the entire text. I have relied substantially on Goedicke's interpretations. There are occasional retellings of the story in the literature on Classical Greek and Roman subjects, using a previous translation and frequently offering its own interpretation, e.g., Casson 1974: 39–43; 1991: 47–53. Casson emphasizes the dangers of sea travel exemplified by the tale rather than the elements of order.

[339] Goedicke 1975: 4–5; Černý 1952: 21–22. Goelet (1996: 126) believes that Wen-Amun's report is indeed a "21st Dynasty copy of an official document recording events in the later part of the 'Repeating-of-Births' era of Ramesses XI's reign; the grammar and vocabulary are in keeping with the language of non-literary Late Egyptian in the latter part of the 20th Dynasty, and the manuscript avoids certain constructions commonly found in literary works of the period." Lesko (1992: 151) appears to retain reservations.

Amon was a priest of the great Egyptian god Amūn, and lived at Thebes. Around 1075, according to the Egyptian low chronology, he was charged, probably by the high priest at Thebes, with procuring lumber from Lebanon to repair the river bark of the god Amūn.[340] These repairs appear to have recurred roughly every eighty years. Through coordination between the effective ruler of northern Egypt, Smendes, and the high priest of Amūn, who effectively ruled southern Egypt, Wen-Amun departed from Tanis (see Map 7), Smendes' capital in the eastern Nile Delta, on a Syrian ship chartered by Smendes. Goedicke believes that the procurement was not a straight commercial purchase, but rather involved some traditional religious and political obligations between the Egyptian pharaoh and the prince of Byblos, although ample recompense had been made on the side in the past.[341] Wen-Amun's ship put into port at Dor, where, out in the harbor, one of the crew stole the silver that was intended for use in procuring the cedar. Beder, the ruler at Dor, declined to make good the loss, apparently on the grounds that the thief was not a person under his jurisdiction and that the theft had happened on the sea rather than on land. Beder nonetheless recommended that Wen-Amun wait around for a while to see what Beder could turn up in the way of either a thief or Wen-Amun's silver. After waiting to no avail for a while, Wen-Amun proceeded north to Byblos, holding up a Tjekker ship on the way to recompense himself for what he had lost. When he arrived at the harbor of Byblos, one interpretation is that the Tjekker had arrived before him and complained to Zeker-Baal, the prince of Byblos, about the theft. Rather than receive Wen-Amun in a friendly fashion, Zeker-Baal forbade his disembarkation, leaving him cooling his heels on his ship in Byblos harbor for twenty-nine days before admitting him. Apparently in the politically confused condition of Egypt, Wen-Amun naively had left his letters of introduction from the high priest at Thebes with Smendes, a serious diplomatic faux pas. Zeker-Baal recognized the traditional relationship in which the prince of Byblos supplied cedar for the bark of Amūn, but also demonstrated official records showing much more generous compensations from the Egyptians than that with which Wen-Amun had either begun or shown up on Zeker-Baal's harbor step. As part of the verbal exchange establishing their relative positions, Zeker-Baal told Wen-Amun that Byblos had twenty ships regularly in port at Tanis and that Sidon had seventy; he also implied that these cities had no monopoly on the commerce with Tanis. Zeker-Baal forced Wen-Amun to send back to Tanis for another cargo of goods to make an acceptable gift (effectively a price). Eight months later, the goods arrived, the cedar was cut and loaded, and Wen-Amun was ready for the voyage back to Egypt when eleven Tjekker warships sailed into Byblos harbor demanding justice for the stolen silver. Zeker-Baal told the Tjekker that he had no right to detain an emissary of Amūn, but that they were free to pursue Wen-Amun's ship once it left his harbor.[342] Once out of the Byblos harbor, a southeasterly squall came up and saved Wen-Amun from the Tjekker, but it shipwrecked him and drove him ashore on Alasiya, most likely Cyprus. There he appears to have been given the dubious welcome of a suspected pirate by the natives. He claims to have been nearly

---

[340] The trip was undertaken in a fifth year, possibly of the high priest at Karnak, Hrihōr, at the end of the Twentieth Dynasty or the beginning of the Twenty-First. Gardiner 1961: 306. Kitchen 1973: 251. Goedicke (1975: 9) anchors the date of Wen-Amun's departure at 1075 (low chronology) or 1095 (high chronology).

[341] Goedicke 1975: 73–75 nn. bd–be. Liverani (1990: 247–54) interprets the exchange in Wen-Amun's report as a relatively straightforward commercial transaction, with Egyptian pretensions on one side offset by Byblian clear-sighted pragmatism on the other. He infers from a number of Amarna Letters a pattern of court-to-court trade negotiations common to earlier relations with Alasia, Mitanni, and Hatti as well.

[342] The interpretations of Zeker-Baal's solution to the Tjekker's demand differ. Casson's cynical description of the events (1974: 39–43) is that Zeker-Baal, to wash his hands of a ticklish matter, persuaded the Tjekker to give Wen-Amun, with a boatload of cedar logs, a running start ahead of eleven fast warships, hardly a sporting chance for the Egyptian. Goedicke (1975: 123–25 nn. dz–ea), on the other hand, grants Zeker-Baal a genuine acceptance of his religious role in the worship of Amūn as well as of the Semitic god Seth, which requires him to treat Wen-Amun well—once the preliminary relationships and mutual obligations are recognized—and interprets the prince as telling the Tjekker that in fact he has no legal cause to detain Wen-Amun, since he committed no crimes within his jurisdiction, but that they are free to pursue him on their own. Goedicke believes that a strong residual remained at this time of the former structure of relationships between Egypt and the Levantine cities, and that legal jurisdictions were well defined, if not necessarily complete.

killed before he found someone who spoke Egyptian. He managed to find the palace of the queen, where he found the Egyptian speaker and was given hospitality by the queen. At that point the papyrus ends and the story is broken, although it is apparent that Wen-Amun eventually reached home.

The story is instructive, and surprising, on a number of relevant points. First, the extent of commercial trade demonstrated by the seventy Levantine ships regularly calling at Tanis is striking. Second, the exposure of travelers to theft and brigandage is quite apparent. Third, and more surprising, is the extent of the codification of legal jurisdictions. However, external, or foreign, protocols appear to have had some glaring hiatuses that individual princes were reluctant to fill with unilateral decisions. Although the extent of commerce implies considerable protection for individuals in foreign lands, there were international loopholes that would have encouraged predation by virtue of the difficulty of prosecuting offenses. Fourth, the danger from nature exacerbated that from man. Fifth, Wen-Amun's reception on the shore of Alasiya suggests the prevalence of dangers from the sea. Sixth, the language barrier between Wen-Amun and the Alasiyans who found him reveals some of the difficulties a traveling stranger might encounter. However, the fact that someone at the Alasiyan court understood Egyptian indicates that international contacts were still extant in the early eleventh century despite the relatively recent (a century prior) incursions from the Sea Peoples. The fact that the knowledge of Egyptian was located at the court may suggest that trade was centralized through the local ruler or that any trade that transpired was centered on a port town where the court happened to be located, or it simply may be evidence of diplomatic contact between economically autarkic communities. At Byblos, the negotiations between Wen-Amun and Zeker-Baal apparently were conducted in Egyptian. Finally, on what was expected to be a routine mission, it took Wen-Amun probably two years, and possibly more, to return home; some of his predecessors at Byblos had remained there seventeen years, and had died and been buried there. A multiplicity of dangers awaited the traveler, for any purpose, despite a substantial volume of regular international commerce and despite a considerable degree of regularization of diplomatic relations. Travel in the times was dangerous, but primarily because of nature and technical difficulties both in international coordination of social institutions and in enforcing the protocols that existed. It would be oversimplifying to characterize the times as "wild and woolly."

THE ITINERANT CRAFTSMAN

Wen-Amun's story may provide an excessively dreary light in which to consider travel of itinerant craftsmen, but it does suggest that some sort of diplomatic arrangement between the craftsman's community and that of his destination would have been instrumental in offering protection to visitors from outside the community, particularly in the sensitive cases in which such outsiders might compete with community members in local craft production. Proxenoi (citizens of City A who agree to represent commercial and legal interests of citizens of a "foreign" city, City B, in City A) began to appear in Greek cities only by the mid-sixth century, later than the time period under consideration here.[343] Consider three issues involved in expatriate activity by craftsmen who intended to return home. First, how did they pay for their voyage? It is possible they traveled for free, as guests, on merchant ships or warships. I do not find this possibility compelling, but it is not out of the question. For the moment, however, consider means of payment by paying travelers. Coins were first minted in Ionia in the late seventh century, so that easily transportable medium was unavailable for all practical purposes throughout the Dark Age. In the later part of the period, however, definitely

---

[343] Starr 1977: 71, 218 n. 55; Wallace 1970: 191–94. Wallace argues the case for a date no earlier than the early sixth century, and more probably the mid-fifth century, for the cenotaph of Menekrates of Oianthea found in Western Lokris, on the grounds that proxenoi were a constitutional institution, with rights, honors, and duties conferred by the citizens. A date in the late seventh century, as proposed, as much on ceramic as on epigraphic grounds, by Jeffrey (1961: 232), would violate this logical criterion, as well as place Menekrates' cenotaph much earlier than any other known proxenoi. Wallace notes that the tyrants of the eighth and seventh centuries tended to conduct the business later conferred upon the proxenoi through ties of blood, marriage, and friendship. It is questionable whether this aristocratic protection would extend far enough down the social ladder to include itinerant craftsmen except of the very highest order of skill and the most far-reaching fame.

by the mid-seventh century and possibly in the eighth century, weighed, unstamped "dumps" of silver and gold were available and acceptable and served several functions of coins. Such dumps appear in archaeological remains, and their origins may be narrowed down, but their itineraries are indecipherable. An itinerant craftsman might offer to pay for his voyage in kind of his own making, which, depending on the durability of the material in which he worked, might appear at a foreign location, possibly the home of the ship's captain or at some port where it was traded. If a craftsman had been invited to work in a foreign town by a resident or deputation of that town, the hosts probably would have paid for his voyage, in which case some artifact would represent the destination of an itinerant craftsman rather than his origin.

The second issue is how the foreign craftsman would have lived in the foreign town. The answer is obvious: he would have made his crafts and sold them locally, in which case the archaeological evidence may be difficult, but not impossible, to distinguish from traded articles, partly on the basis of fabric in the case of pottery and partly on the basis of stylistic concessions in the cases of both pottery and metal objects.[344] A foreign craftsman making and selling his wares locally brings us back to the issue of competition raised in the previous paragraph. Competition seldom has been looked upon favorably except by economists, certainly not by the noninitiating participants in that game. Local demand for craftsmen's wares must have been small, and probably inelastically responsive to the appearance of new designs and competitively depressed prices, although the demands for individual varieties within categories of crafts may have been volatile (i.e., a new variety—say, a new vase form or decorative style—might have temporarily eliminated the demand for a more con-

ventional, local variety). Without some form of effective personal protection, such outsiders, without a strong family system to avenge their murder, must have been at considerable personal risk. Generally, an itinerant craftsman should have been sufficiently local for his own community to be able to guarantee his safety on his circuit of other communities.

As another category of outside craftsmen, refugees fleeing devastation and death at home might have made reasonable sympathy cases for a while, providing they could communicate sufficiently well with the local population to relate their plights. But even relatives deserving sympathy wear out their welcomes, particularly if they become successful at the visible expense of their hosts. The economic politics of outside craftsmen in small markets, then, does not lend support to a widespread existence of such craftsmen. Dark Age Knossos and Athens, and possibly some of the contemporary Cypriot towns, might have been large enough to accept *resident* outsiders as well as itinerant foreigners in addition to simply local, mobile craftsmen.[345]

The final question is how any saved earnings might have been repatriated without the assistance of money. Pre-coin precious-metal dumps are a possibility, but the archaeological evidence they would leave, if any, would be ambiguous. Purchase of goods to exchange upon returning home is another option; this is nothing more or less than trade, however, the sole distinction being in the movement of the resource of one community (the skilled labor) to another to produce the products to be sold in the latter. It is possible, if not especially persuasive, that itinerant craftsmen would not have earned enough to have anything left to take home with them, in which case the sole archaeological evidence for their presence could be artistic influences of one community found in another with no further evi-

---

[344] Boardman (1967: 63; 1980: 56–60, 270 n. 73) and Lembesi (1975b: 173) have given considerable thought to how to distinguish native copying of foreign models from the work of immigrant craftsmen, in terms of combinations of styles, shapes, and fabrics. Burial customs, for example, may provide additional information, but would be less useful in cases in which foreign craftsmen were only temporary residents. Hoffman (1990: chaps. 4 and 5) addresses this issue at length, but with ambiguous conclusions.

[345] Jones (1986b: 601–2) raises the question of the social acceptance of hypothesized Mycenaean potters on Cyprus in his analysis of the origin of Mycenaean Pictorial Style pottery on Cyprus. However, the diplomacy and international law regarding trans-state fugitives seems to have been well developed by the second half of the second millennium in the Levant: Buccellati 1967: 58–61. The progress of Greek political sophistication in the first two centuries of the first millennium is important to interpretations of artifactual remains that suggest the presence of foreign groups in Greek communities, such as the possible goldsmith at Knossos or the inverted funerary pots at Arkades in the first half of the seventh century: Boardman 1980: 60–61.

dence of exchange of goods through which to transmit the influence. This story certainly fits the pattern of much Cretan evidence, but the social difficulty of a craftsman having no durable form of accumulated wealth to take home with him is a weak link in the story.[346] The distinction between products made locally by a foreign craftsman and retained in the local community and imports from the craftsman's community is an interesting twist on the usual trade in products with productive resources remaining immobile. However, as long as the craftsman returns to his home community and takes his accumulated earnings with him, the implicit trade in resources is very similar to an explicit trade in products.[347]

The hypothesized activity of itinerant craftsmen would muddy the analysis of Dark Age trade, but not terminally. The ideas for distinguishing the local work of native craftsmen imitating foreign models and foreign guests working for local customers suggest that we may be able to develop guidelines for distinguishing what is evidence of itinerant (as contrasted with permanently resident) foreign craftsmen and what is evidence of trade in the archaeological record. First, the medium may narrow the range of ambiguity. Clay fabrics will usually give good clues to whether a ceramic piece is local or nonlocal, regardless of the ethnicity of the potter.[348] Whether a foreign pot in a grave or a well was brought to its resting site through commercial trade or as repatriation of earnings by an itinerant craftsman (he could be a carpenter or a bronzesmith as easily as a potter) who has returned home is probably impossible to distinguish, but it is also not of first-order importance, since the effective mechanism of its transfer is still trade or commerce; this holds true for other media as well. What is at issue is the scale of the trade, which may be interesting in its own right, but will have only a secondary impact on the effects of the exchange. Other media will leave less telltale signs of where they were made. Lead isotope analyses may be able to narrow down the ore sources of a number of metals, but they cannot help identify whether a piece was made near where it was found by a foreign craftsman or imported. Lembesi hypothesized that visiting foreign craftsmen would have made objects with local shapes but foreign decoration, and vice versa for local craftsmen imitating foreign models, but this rule of thumb seems risky.[349] Would exoticism or familiarity have been more valued by local customers of a foreign craftsman? Would a visiting craftsman have attempted to capitalize on his difference from local craftsmen or to try his hand at some new things he could learn from his native colleagues or competitors? Answers to these questions could differ from customer to customer and across craftsmen with different temperaments.

For nonceramic products, most of the information needed to distinguish commercially or personally imported items from items made locally by a foreign craftsman will be too detailed ever to be recovered from remaining evidence. Fortunately, a large majority of foreign artifacts are ceramic, and the difficulty of Dark Age travel would seem likely to restrict the scope for such peripatetic craftsmanship. When we also consider the likely reactions of local competitors in a time when people were at some risk in foreign communities, we may further restrict the scope for such occupational travel. We may be likely to find itinerant craftsmen at the very top and very bottom of the social and

---

[346] The ability to repatriate profits is a choke point in theories of foreign branch plants, such as the Phoenician unguent factories proposed by Coldstream for Rhodes and Knossos. I have analyzed that problem at some length elsewhere: Jones 1993: 293–303. Rowlands (1971: 214–15) reports little ethnographic evidence of itinerant metalsmiths, who, he finds, generally are integral members of their own communities.

[347] But not exactly. The earnings the foreign craftsman spends on consumption during his residency goes to residents of the host community rather than to the home community of the craftsman. Much of the production cost of, say, a vase made in Knossos by an expatriate Attic potter would have been directed to Cretan food rather than Attic food—assuming, of course, that both locations produce their own food, which would not have been the case in fifth-century Athens. It probably would take a rather large expatriate work force for this mechanism to have a noticeable effect—a larger work force than was the case in Dark Age Greece.

[348] This assumes no, or little, trade in potter's clay. Boardman (1956: 56) suggests that a limited trade in the finest pottery clay and slip between locations as far apart as Chios and Naukratis in the early sixth century could have been "a sound venture for an enterprising potter." Lemos (1991: 117–18) considers that the balance of current evidence suggests Chian production, although decisive physical evidence is still absent. See Chapter 4, note 201.

[349] Lembesi 1975: 173.

professional scales: the renowned worker in a relatively rare or specialized material like marble and the slave craftsman who is sent where his owner wants him, or the local specialty potter from the next village. Neither case is likely to affect materially the interpretation of the majority of excavated foreign artifacts.

I return to the subject of resident foreign craftsmen and other immigrants, in Crete specifically, in the following chapter.

Religious Travel

The abundance of foreign artifacts left as votives or other dedications at the major panhellenic shrines reveals the willingness of Dark Age Greeks, as well as others, to travel for religious purposes, even considering the likelihood that some of the votives were deposited by through travelers such as merchants and seamen. Again, this travel was costly: fares on ships most likely had to be paid, and the traveler had to eat. It is possible that Homeric hospitality could have kept some of these travelers alive during these pilgrimages, but it is difficult to see how the return payments required in gift exchange would have been made by the vast majority of such travelers. Traffic of the volume the major shrines experienced could have worn hospitality thin, particularly closer to the shrine—a sort of congestion effect. Leaving aside the matter of whether some pilgrims traveled on hospitality,

consider how the others might have paid for transportation and food. Since portable forms of money were not readily available during much of the period, people of sufficient income to make such journeys may have been accompanied by one or more slaves or other servants bringing food. In fact, the pilgrims may have traveled in groups for protection against robbers, spreading the cost of an attendant or two to carry food and any high-value items that might have been useful for exchange. I see no major confusions that could arise involving evidence for trade and artifacts associated with religious travel.[350]

Mercenaries

Egypt is known to have employed Asiatic mercenaries in its navy in the Twelfth and Thirteenth Dynasties, and records of the employment of Asiatic and Nubian soldiers go back to the First Intermediate period.[351] There is evidence in Egyptian records of the employment of mercenaries from the end of the Second Intermediate (employment of Nubians to help expel the Hyksos) and in the Late Bronze Age (the Medinet Habu reliefs, Papyrus Harris).

The seventh-century use of Ionian mercenaries by Psammetichus is well known. Other Near Eastern principalities may occasionally have supplemented their frequent regional alliances with the rental of mercenary services in the first millennium during the wars with the expanding

---

[350] Strøm (1992: 57) raises the possibility that some of the foreign votives at some Greek shrines might have been imported by the shrine priests specifically as votives. Rather than complicate the interpretation of foreign artifacts at religious sites, this would put those artifacts on the same footing as imported olive oil—straightforward commercial trade. On a more fundamental level, objection may be made to a scholar's mixing business (resource allocation, economics) and religion on the grounds that either (1) they are separate spheres, not to be mixed by Dark Age Greeks or other eastern Mediterranean peoples of antiquity, or (2) they are inseparably intertwined, possibly with religion the dominant strand, so that resource-allocating behavior in religious activities is an oxymoron. In this context, N. Marinatos's suggestion (1993: 104) regarding some social dynamics of Minoan religion is interesting: "Performance and display must have been integral elements of Cretan rituals, suggesting that the Minoan elite used religion as a means of self-presentation and aggrandizement." The concept of religion as a means of social control by ancient elites, i.e., religion as a device (albeit a complicated one) subject to deliberate manipulation, has been studied extensively, but religious practice, and eventually religious belief, as one among a number of resource-absorbing activities subject to choices and possible substitutions with other activities has been a less prominent topic of study. On resource-allocation decisions involved in religious practice, see Anderson 1988: 1066–88. On the relationship between an increasing variety of consumption opportunities associated with economic growth and the allocation of resources to religious ritual and dedication, see Smith 1937: 755–56. Along the lines of Smith's reasoning, changes in grave dedications would be linked to material prosperity but not necessarily in the direction commonly assumed: richer grave offerings might imply nothing better to do with one's resources than to bury them in the ground, while sparser—or less costly—offerings may suggest a greater array of consumption opportunities above ground, which would have the effect of reducing the share of any particular item (including funeral outlays) in total consumption.

[351] Posener 1957: 145–63; Bietak 1996: 14.

Assyrians and with one another, but I am not aware of evidence of specific instances. The service of Cretans on behalf of the Spartans in the First and Second Messenian Wars, reported by Pausanias, is well known, but there is little other tangible evidence of Cretan mercenary activity before the Classical period. Of course, in Hellenistic and Roman times, the island became known for this service export. Thus, the existence of a demand for foreign military assistance in the Aegean-eastern Mediterranean region in the Early Iron Age is only modestly attested, with little detail about numbers and timing; it remains largely an empirical challenge.[352]

Assuming for the sake of discussion that there *was* a reasonably steady demand for mercenary service during these earlier centuries of the Early Iron Age, what could have been the economic implications of supplying mercenaries? Would the mercenary service providers have returned with riches? Could the rewards of mercenary service have accounted for the military equipment found in tenth- and ninth-century graves around Knossos? Would the withdrawal of military-age men have affected the food supply or general level of well-being on Crete during their temporary absence—or permanent loss, in the event of extreme lack of success?

The archaeological evidence on Crete could be interpreted to represent the success of mercenary captains, but any number of other, less dramatic stories could account for the military equipment found in Early Iron Age burials on the island. Seeing mercenaries returning with either plundered or earned wealth reflected in these artifacts casts greater informational content on the remains than they possess. Assuming for the moment that Crete *did* export mercenary services early in the Early Iron Age, and, further, that those mercenaries *did* return with more wealth than they left with, what could that wealth have done for the island? The *form* of the wealth would have been critical to any answer to the question. Precious metals might have conferred prestige, although it is an open question whether some minimal level of prior prestige would have been required for additional pre-

cious metals to confer a permanent increase in prestige. If mercenaries working overseas operated as companies with their own ranking systems, it seems unlikely that the officers would have come home with less than the men. Possibly younger sons among the officers would have increased their prestige relative to older sons who stayed home, and possibly returning common soldiers would have had enough to purchase some additional assets, such as land or agricultural equipment. However, once we move to this point in the disposition of any precious metals repatriated from mercenary work, we have very much the same situation discussed previously of pirates spending precious metals imported from abroad. Unless additional indigenous resources could be brought into productive use on the island, or unless Crete as an economic accounting unit could import goods with the precious metals, the principal economic impact of the imported riches would have been to depress the local value of the precious metals. Some rearrangement of the local prestige ranking might occur in the process, but it is not clear that that could be distinguished archaeologically from other events. Productive assets, including unshaped base metals providing they were formed into productive equipment, could have expanded productivity and material well-being on the island. One critical issue in evaluating the effect of the material returns to mercenary-service exports is whether the mercenaries brought home enough material of value to make up for the assets they had to take with them to ply their trade—that is, did they get a positive *net* return on their investment, and was it as good as they could have gotten if they had used the resources at home instead of abroad?

The withdrawal of labor supplies from an economy with the structural features I have used in Appendix B to characterize an Early Iron Age Greek region such as Crete could have had sizeable effects on economic well-being: the removal of 1 percent of the labor force into mercenary activity could have raised the level of well-being of the remaining population by about one-third of a percent. This analytical (not empirical) result is

---

[352] Parke (1970: 672–73) notes that from the end of the Late Bronze Age until the Peloponnesian War, mercenaries played a small role in Greek warfare. Snodgrass (1964: 143, 147, 199–200) casts doubt on the wide employment of Cretan mercenaries during the Early Iron Age, although he acknowledges that the presence of Cretan mercenaries on the mainland "is suggested by the archaeological record, and supported by slight literary reference" in the eighth and seventh centuries, in the First and Second Messenian Wars.

consistent with the much later reports, from the second and first centuries B.C., that Crete supplied mercenary troops because of a surplus of manpower.[353] The economic result would have been to relieve some of the depressing effect of population pressure on the productivity of remaining labor. If the mercenaries came back with anything to show for their efforts, so much the better.

---

[353] Brulé (1978: 162–63) considers the Cretan mercenaries of the Hellenistic period to have been, effectively, temporary emigrants.

IV

CRETE'S EXTERNAL RELATIONS IN THE EARLY IRON AGE

I begin this chapter with descriptive discussions of the foreign material found at Cretan sites and of Cretan—and suspected Cretan—material found overseas. I follow this description with five sections devoted to analysis of various aspects of the artifactual record. The first four of those sections discuss the relations with regions of particular importance to Crete—Attica and Corinth, Cyprus, the Near East, and the West—that may be implied by the artifactual record. Some of the possible relationships require topical discussions—on trade and agricultural risk, heirlooms, etc.—to help identify restrictions on interpretations; discussion of one of these topics is expanded in Appendix A. In addition to archaeological material, the Near East (unlike the Aegean and west-central Mediterranean regions during this period) offers historical records, and I identify what seem to be the principal political and economic trends from that region that may be important determinants or conditioners of the foreign artifactual record in Dark Age Crete. The last section returns its focus to Crete itself and addresses how the issue of importance can be inferred from this artifactual record. This assessment requires the employment of some social models, which I develop and discuss at some length in Appendix B, but I report the results in the text.

THE SITE REPORTS

I devote separate sections to Knossos and Kommos, the former because of its large number of foreign artifacts and its long-standing social and political prominence, the latter because of its

striking implications as a long-forgotten port town with far-flung overseas connections during the Early Iron Age, as well as in the Late Bronze Age. The other sites I treat in three regional groups, one covering the eastern and northern part of the island to just west of Knossos; the second covering the south-central part of the island; and the third, the western sites. The eastern group contains the most sites and the western group the fewest. Clearly, some alternative regionalization could be justified at the edges of these regions, but the the regionalization is motivated more by descriptive convenience than by analytical purposes, and I do not attempt to derive conclusions based on the regional assignments, which are particularly sensitive to the regional boundaries. Clearly, alternative groupings could have been used, some geographical, others not—for example, sanctuaries versus towns versus cemeteries. There were many other entirely different ways to organize the data rather than by site: by material, by type of artifact, by origin, by date, etc. Each of these alternatives could have produced interesting information. The organization by site highlights the site as the focus of a community, and I am particularly interested in the behavior of individuals within the communities they compose. Map 8 identifies the locations of the Cretan sites from which I report foreign artifacts.

KNOSSOS

Across the four groups of sites, the foreign pottery comprises a wide variety of types, although on the whole it is conditioned by the

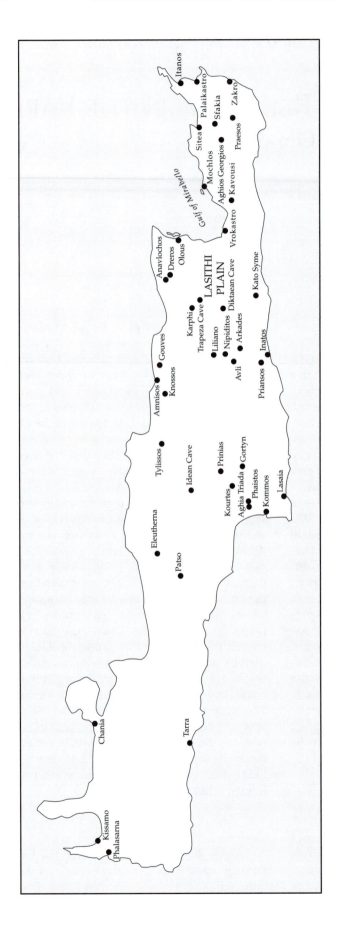

Map 8. Sites in Crete with Overseas Artifacts

fact that most of the pottery was found in graves. Some pots are clearly containers of relatively valuable material such as perfumes or unguents. Some fine vessels are utilitarian rather than container vessels: the kalathoi, the skyphoi and kotylai, various kraters, the oinochoai, and some of the larger amphorae and pithoi may have been part of an early funerary monument industry. As noted earlier, most of the items are Attic, Cycladic, Corinthian, and Cypriot. Ceramic outliers in terms of provenance are two Euboean amphoriskoi, two Late Protogeometric pieces from KMF Tomb 285 and KAM Tomb 12 (KNC.20–21),[1] a Euboean (or Cycladic) Protogeometric skyphos and krater from Zapher Papoura (KN.22–23), an amphora from Thessaly (KNC.23), and an askos from Khaniale Tekke Tomb II, which has been identified recently with Sardinia (previously with Cyprus) and dated from Protogeometric to Early Orientalizing (KN.40).[2] Perhaps the Euboean amphoriskoi were items traded off a ship from Euboea to the West, to help provision the crew or simply to turn over some inventory on a port call. A similar origin could account for the Sardinian askos.[3] The Euboean Protogeometric items lend themselves less easily to a known transmission story. Among the artifacts published to date, there is little Euboean material at Knossos, or anywhere on Crete. In addition to the four items cited above, there is a Euboean Protogeometric amphora shoulder from the town (Ktwn.2) and two gold nuggets from Tholos Tomb II at Khaniale Tekke (KN.47), which agree with the weights of the Euboean stater and the gold Babylonian shekel. The Late Geometric amphoriskoi were identified by chemical analysis as being compatible in composition with clay from the Lelantine Plain in Euboea, but could not be distinguished between origins at Lefkandi, Chalcis, and Eretria. Six pendant semicircle skyphoi from Tekke Tomb G, suspected to be Euboean by their design, were subjected to the same chemical

analysis as the two amphoriskoi from the North Cemetery, but could not be attributed to the same clay, although their state of severe weathering could have altered their chemical composition. Popham is unwilling to call them Euboean, but Kearsley was willing to so designate them, and I have included them in the catalogue with Euboean attributions (KNC.25–27).[4] Full publication of the pottery from the North Cemetery may yield a different picture of Euboean material at Knossos, but the presently available material has only a minor Euboean presence.[5] However, the present evidence does not rule out a Euboean carrying trade between the Near East and Italy, with Crete as a way station, prior to the establishment of the trading station at Al Mina, probably between about 825 and 775, although the Late Geometric amphoriskoi are of the Al Mina period.[6] Euboea operated a carrying trade with the goods of other lands rather than a direct trade with Crete, and was not noted for the small votives and trinkets for which the Near East was known; thus there is little reason why Euboean pottery would find its way to Crete in any major quantity. This is, of course, an argument from silence, but it simply reminds us that the negative evidence of Euboean interchanges need not rule out Euboean trading activity touching Crete. The appearance at Lefkandi of cast-bronze tripod legs with lines of linked spirals, dated to c. 900, has been connected to the same design on the tripod from Fortetsa Tomb XI, raising the suspicion of direct connections between Knossos and Euboea, and involving Cyprus as well.[7]

Conspicuously absent, even from the Knossos town excavations and the other nonfunerary contexts, are coarseware transport amphorae, save three recently excavated fragments of a Euboean SOS transport amphora (KN.122), found in an Early to Late Orientalizing context in a reoccupied Late Minoan II house west of the Southwest House, southwest, naturally, of the palace. They are not to be expected, of course, in

---

[1] Popham, Pollard, and Hatcher 1983: Table 1, 283; Coldstream 1991: 291, fig. 3.

[2] Vagnetti 1989: 354–60.

[3] Cook (1959: 123; 1979: 153) develops this explanation for appearances of pottery of minor schools, i.e., other than Attica and Corinth, particularly for the Laconian fine pottery of the sixth century.

[4] Popham et al. 1983: 289; Kearsley 1989: 40–41.

[5] The final publication of the North Cemetery, which appeared late in 1996, did not fundamentally alter the prepublication impression regarding the frequency of Euboean pottery. Coldstream (1996: 403–4) reports only six Euboean imports.

[6] The suspicion of Boardman (1990a).

[7] Popham, Sackett, Jeffrey, Catling, and Catling 1980: 97.

graves, and such large, heavy vessels may have remained around a port area, which would have been a natural break-of-bulk point in the absence of circumstances conducive to a large, inland collection center such as the Minoan palace at Knossos in earlier times. The excavations at Amnisos did not yield any Dark Age commercial facilities, as have the excavations at Kommos; excavations at Katsambas have yielded Neolithic and some Minoan remains, but nothing from the Early Iron Age; and the harbor founded in the ninth century under present-day Herakleion has not been excavated.[8]

The metal objects come primarily from Cyprus and the Near East, with the exception of the three dress pins suggested to be of Argive origin (KN.1) and the spectacle fibula from Mastabas (KN.124).[9] The bronze rod tripod from Cyprus (KN.30) may be an arrival from Mycenaean times, although it was found in a Cretan Late Protogeometric context, so it might not represent any

exchange from the Early Iron Age. The carriers of the Hittite-style lead lion (KF.1) and the bronze pendant of the naked female figure of a type from Luristan (KF.28) pose an interesting question. (See the southeastern corner of Map 1 for the location of Luristan.) The former is from an Early Protogeometric context, the latter from mid-ninth to mid-eighth century, representing contact with the hinterland of the Levant over as much as 200 years.[10] Both of these pieces would have needed middlemen. The Luristan piece (assuming Luristan is its provenance) likely accompanied cavalry horses bought by Assyria, whence it worked its way to North Syria or Phoenicia. Its presence on Crete demonstrates immediate contact with North Syria or Phoenicia, not with Luristan. A similar, indirect set of movements would have brought the lead lion to Crete.

Fortetsa also has yielded a Phoenician bronze bowl dated by Brock to the mid-seventh century from the tomb context, but more recent-

---

[8] Marinatos 1932: 76–94; 1933: 93–100; Coldstream 1984b: 319.

[9] For a number of years, Cyprus has been accepted as the precursor to Greece in iron production in the Early Iron Age, and there has been a tendency to accept uncritically a Cypriot provenance for bimetallic (iron and bronze) products, particularly but not exclusively iron knives with bronze rivets, found at Greek sites. Waldbaum (1982: 327–37) has confronted this attribution of Cypriot origin with the cumulative archaeological evidence and has found more variation in the shapes, chronologies, and find sites of bimetallic, utilitarian artifacts in the eastern Mediterranean than clearly sustains the attribution (even if the evidence does not clearly point to another story about attribution). She consequently is reluctant to endorse Cypriot origins for such artifacts found in the Aegean. Snodgrass (1982: 286–87) disputes some of the inferences Waldbaum makes from her data. He finds clear evidence of Cypriot temporal leadership in iron technology in the twelfth and eleventh centuries, but he does not address the issue of Cypriot attribution of bimetallic objects found in the Aegean in twelfth- to tenth-century contexts. While evidence of ancient iron-working exists on Crete, near Karphi among other sites, the dates of the slag heaps are indeterminate: Faure 1966: 61–66; Waldbaum 1978: 63.

[10] The possible Luristan figure is one of the few bronze artifacts from Luristan, which itself remains relatively poorly known, to derive from a known archaeological context: Muscarella 1977: 33 n. 4, fig. 1; idem 1988: 33–34; Herrmann 1968: 26. Dating has proven difficult, with "Luristan bronzes" in general, as various types of so-called Luristan artifact have ranged from the late third and early second millennia to the seventh century. Pieces similar to the Fortetsa piece have been dated to the Luristan Bronze Age, which ranges from c. 1200/1150 to 700/650. None of the canonical bronzes identified with burials of this period are exact comparanda to the Fortetsa figurine, although some relatively close parallels appear in Godard 1931: 67–68, nos. 111–18, 153, esp. no. 116, pls. 31, 32, 36; and Moorey 1971: 129, no. 136, pl. 25. Moorey, in contrast to all other opinions on the Fortetsa piece, doubts the Luristan origin for this pendant. His discussion of it (ibid.: 26 nn. 4–6) is uncharacteristically confused. He interprets P. Jacobsthal's statement of doubt about Luristan origins as applying to the Fortetsa piece as well as to the belt clasp from Perachora (Payne et al. 1940: 34, 139, fig. 20, pl. 44.5), but Jacobsthal's text clearly seems to refer to the latter only (Jacobsthal 1956: 77 n. 1). Moorey recommends an origin in the Caucasus rather than in Luristan, so in fact the resulting difference is not great. One difficulty in relating the Fortetsa piece to the Luristan harness trappings is that the figure in the circular pendant crosses in the center of the circle, leaving no clear slide for a harness trace. Böhm (1990: 68–69) believes the motif of the naked woman and the lions on the outside of the ring on the Fortetsa piece is not Luristanian, but possibly of Mesopotamian production.

The mechanisms for the transportation of this figure to Crete are unknown, although some middleman in the Assyrian or Babylonian region would appear to be a reasonable speculation for some link in the chain: Calmeyer 1969: 179–80; Moorey 1974: 26. Muscarella (1977: 46) prefers a route through Assyria and North Syria to the overland route through Anatolia. The latter route would have passed through Urartu, and Muscarella disputes the prevalence of Urartian products in the west. However, on the overland route, see notes 370 and 373 below.

ly suggested to date to c. 800 on grounds of motif (KF.47).[11] Probably the most remarked metal piece from the Knossos area is the inscribed Phoenician bronze bowl from Tekke Tomb J, near the North Cemetery (KNC.7). (I include Tekke Tomb J with the North Cemetery section of the Knossos catalogue because it appears to be an extension of the same group of tombs.) Though it was dated by Sznycer to the end of the tenth century, Cross has strongly recommended a dating no later than the end of the eleventh century on the basis of the typological features of the script, and Puech has recommended a date a quarter-century earlier. Cross also claims that bowl KNC.7 "provides direct evidence for Phoenician presence in the West before 1000 B.C."[12] Its dating about a generation earlier than the other material from the tomb suggests that it was an heirloom. While a host of detailed mechanisms for its transportation to Crete could be imagined, it is more useful to group them into two categories: mechanisms operating through what may be called "commodity accounts," and those operating via a "population account," for want of a more commonly used term. The commodity-account mechanisms share the feature that a return flow of resources to the land of origin, albeit possibly indirectly, is required. Transportation by the population account involves the unrequited, permanent movement of people accompanied by their personal possessions. No reverse flow need occur. The population account would seem to be a more likely channel through which an heirloom would have moved between the eleventh and ninth centuries. The bowl, and even its find context, is earlier than Coldstream's suggested dating of Phoenician unguent-makers around Knossos.[13] If it is in fact Cypriot or Cypro-Phoenician, it still would antedate the period of Boardman's proposed North Syrian goldsmith of the Tekke tomb.[14] The inscription on the bowl leaves it looking more like a personal possession than a trade good. It certainly was a personal possession by the time it was deposited in its

tomb, but it is not impossible that it was inscribed on Crete after its arrival through a commodity account. Either transportation method has the bowl arrive prior to other evidence of regular Phoenician, or North Syrian, activity around Knossos. The indisputable fact surrounding the bowl is that it was transported from some land to the east and is evidence of one of these means of transportation. If we are reluctant to accept immigration as a transportation method at this time, we are left with one of the commodity accounts—trade.

Among the metal objects from Knossos that have been little remarked upon are the silver and gold dumps, all from vase 104 of Khaniale Tekke Tomb II (KN.45–47). Hutchinson identifies KN.45, a silver dump of 7.25 grams, as consistent in weight with half of a Phoenician shekel. Three gold dumps of 18.10, 18.95, and 19.00 grams respectively (KN.46) agree well with the weight of the Egyptian double kedet, and two rectangular gold nuggets of 16.65 and 16.90 grams are closely consistent with both the Euboean stater and the gold Babylonian shekel standard.[15] It is a commonplace that if communities of this period did trade, it was without money, and consequently trade would remain balanced. The exception to this rule of Attica, with its Laurion silver mines, is also a commonplace. The existence and role of a separate precious-metals account, even in the absence of any monetary system or other commonly accepted standards of fineness, have been ignored in implicit assumptions of barter, and consequently of balanced, trade. Whether or not these three sets of precoinage dumps were brought to Crete by a ninth-century B.C. Silas Marner and never left a mattress until they accompanied him to his grave, they point to the presence in Dark Age Greek territory of such international, quasi-standardized precious metals that could be used for settlement of accounts. A community could run a merchandise trade ("current account") surplus for some time, taking in these metals, and in

---

[11] Falsone 1987: 181–94; 1988: 236.

[12] Cross 1980: 15–17; 1986: 118, 124, 125–26 n. 12; Sznycer 1979: 89–94; Puech 1983: 374–89. Falsone (1988: 238) claims c. 950 as a terminus post quem on "archaeological grounds," otherwise unexplained, but this does not seem necessary.

[13] Coldstream 1979: 261–62; 1986: 324; 1984a: 137.

[14] Boardman 1967: 63.

[15] Hutchinson and Boardman 1954: 219; Skinner 1967: 38; cf. Powell 1989: 510–16, on the influence of the Babylonian system on, and the complexities of, the first-millennium Assyrian system of measures.

other periods run a sustained current account deficit, sending the metals out again. In fact, attempts to spend an accumulation of these precious-metal dumps locally rather than externally would simply reduce the value of the metals. Could Dark Age Crete have had sufficient quantities of these internationally acceptable metals to run the kind of trade balance deficit that would be consistent with the imbalance of artifacts at home and abroad? Crete has some minor deposits of argentiferous lead and even more minor deposits of gold, but none of significance, and there is no evidence that these were worked or even known in Minoan times or in the Early Iron Age, so Cretans must have imported—or stolen—any gold and silver of consequence that they possessed.[16] There is a fair bit of scattered evidence of ancient iron-mining and slag heaps from ancient iron-smelting, and Faure notes the proximity of stronger Cretan cities of the Geometric and Archaic periods to beds of iron, but there is no literary evidence of Cretan iron exports, although I discuss archaeological evidence below.[17] A final possibility is that Minoan and Mycenaean gold and silver remained in the island and slowly surfaced and leaked out through merchandise imports. This last possibility seems far-fetched; any such remains of precious metals probably would have been looted and exported—converted into consumption or prestige—very quickly in desperate times such as the twelfth and eleventh centuries. These considerations bring us back to the greater likelihood that the import and export of quasi-monetized precious metals in Crete were coordinated with reciprocal exports and imports of other products. The questions remain what those other products were and how large their aggregate value was. We may get some hints of the former, but probably not of the latter.

The four Knossos site groups report nineteen East Greek artifacts—fourteen securely attributed and five estimated as possible to probable. The provenances include Rhodes, Miletus, Miletus or Kos, and East Greece. Three pieces come from Fortetsa, five from the North Cemetery, one from the town, and ten from the other Knossos sites. The earliest, an outlier chronologically in this group, is a Protogeometric or Early Geometric amphora shoulder fragment (KN.16), identified only as East Greek, from near the edge of the Little Palace. Otherwise, the East Greek artifacts—all pottery—begin to arrive in the later eighth century and continue at about the same frequency through the mid-seventh century. A few pieces continue to appear through the seventh century. Atomic Absorption Spectroscopy of some 300 sherds from the North Cemetery has found a wide range of chemical compositions, indicating a wide range of sites in East Greece as origins, to suspected East Greek sherds across five clusters.[18]

Among the abundant imported pottery at the Knossos sites is a Transitional to Early Corinthian alabastron from Phoinicia, to the southwest of Knossos, which is the name-vase of the Painter of Candia 7789 (KN.153).[19] Considering the volume of Corinthian imports to this part of Crete in this period, the piece stands out for surviving sufficiently intact to permit art-historical analysis as well as for being of sufficiently high artistic quality to be identifiable. Other pieces of this painter's work have been identified at sites on Sicily, in southern and central Italy, on Delos, at Corinth, and possibly on Samos.[20] It would appear that central Crete was able to participate as a consumer in the mainstream of this Corinthian craft, whether the craft was high or low.

The complete absence of Near Eastern artifacts among the finds in the Knossos town area is a striking contrast to their appearance at all three of the cemetery sites. Many of the ceramic items in the graves would have found everyday, or at least special-day, uses during the lifetimes of the people with whom they were interred,

---

[16] Faure 1966: 68-71.

[17] S. Morris (1992a: 131–36, 169) stresses a key role for Cretan iron exports in Phoenician activity on the island during the Dark Age and for the chronological pattern of Cretan interactions with the Levant. The story is exciting, but I do not find the evidence for it compelling enough to support such a detailed reconstruction. Cf. note 9 above, and notes 265-69 below.

[18] Liddy 1988: 29; 1989: 568.

[19] I am indebted to George Rethemiotakis of the Herakleion Museum for information on this piece's provenance on Crete and its acquisition: personal communication, January 24, 1995.

[20] Amyx 1988, 1: 82; Neeft 1986: 14, 18.

but on the whole, the Near Eastern items appear to have been nonutilitarian, not items that would be dropped in a well by accident or discarded in a rubbish heap after being broken. I am reluctant to describe the contrast between the Near Eastern items and the Greek items as luxury versus nonluxury, because many of the Greek vases appear to fit the luxury label as well, while some of the Egyptian faience items may have been relatively inexpensive trinkets.[21] Possibly the transport distance from the Near Eastern ports to Crete influenced the types of product that reached the latter point, with the more compact items that characterize the Near Eastern artifacts capable of being squeezed between other cargo items without fear of breakage. The ostrich-egg rhyton fragment from the Khaniale Tekke tomb (KN.118) does not fit this characteristic and may, in fact, be Carthaginian rather than Levantine, although it would still be culturally Phoenician.[22]

This discussion of cargoes raises the question of what the other cargo items on the westbound Levantine ships were; and the historical, as well as the archaeological, evidence indicates that by the tenth and ninth centuries, at least Tyre, and probably the other Phoenician coastal cities, were developing industries and accepting a greater reliance on imports for foodstuffs. In the eighth and seventh centuries, these cities also were acting as middlemen securing raw materials for Assyrian and Babylonian industry as well as their own.[23] The Near Eastern products at Knossos, as well as at other sites, are consistent with a Phoenician carrying trade as well as with Phoenician industrial exports.

The finds from the North Cemetery, excavated in the late 1970s but not fully published yet, may alter some of the conclusions about geographical orientations of Knossos and possibly about the chronology of contacts, but the presently published array of foreign artifacts does much more than hint at widely cast geographical connections from an early date. The partial publication of the North Cemetery's foreign artifacts is heavily skewed toward Cyprus, by virtue of Coldstream's publication of at least part of the Cypriot and some Phoenician material, although he notes that finds from at least ten overseas areas were recovered.[24] Coldstream's publication of the Cypriot material reinforces the impression of Knossian connections with Cyprus yielded by the Fortetsa finds. However, Coldstream estimates the Attic pottery, the largest group of imports, to account for about 3 percent of the total corpus from the North Cemetery. It appears chiefly in the Attic Late Protogeometric and Middle Geometric periods. Considering the limited time period during which Attic material is prominent in the North Cemetery, it would have accounted for a much greater share of the material at any one time, possibly as much as 5 to 7 percent in the early periods. The eastern Mediterranean objects account for about 1 percent of the North Cemetery corpus, beginning in the ninth century.[25] Possibly the most far-reaching new evidence that could emerge from the final publication of the North Cemetery tombs would be the addition of a wide array of Euboean material, probably from the ninth or even the tenth century. Additional material from the west—Italy, Sardinia, Phoenician North Africa—would reinforce impressions given by currently published material. To date there is very little published material from the west at Knossos—the Sardinian askos (KN.40), some

---

[21] Earlier faience items are likely to be Near Eastern, either Egyptian or Phoenician imitations. Greek faience appears around mid-seventh century and appears to have lasted somewhat over a century, made principally on Rhodes and at Naukratis: Webb 1978: 5–10. However, aryballoi nos. 1557–8 from Tomb P at Fortetsa appear to be Cretan: Brock 1957: 133, 208; Webb (1978: 263) agrees. There are difficulties in distinguishing Rhodian faience flasks from Phoenician and even Carthaginian versions in seventh- and sixth-century deposits. Rathje (1976: 99) discusses this problem for finds from Etruscan tombs, in which the weight of other Phoenician articles—scarabs, amulets, faience figurines, silver, glass, ivories, *tridacna squamosa* shells, and undecorated ostrich-egg shells—gives a higher probability for Phoenician or Carthaginian origins. At the Cretan sites, other Near Eastern objects often outnumber the clearly Rhodian items.

[22] Moscati (1988: 456) notes the role of North Africans as middlemen in supplying the eggs, but not always the art.

[23] Frankenstein 1979: 267–68, 270, 273.

[24] Coldstream 1984a: 122.

[25] Coldstream 1994b: 116, 118.

amber beads from Fortetsa (KF.46) and the North Cemetery (KNC.85), and the amber inlay in the Tekke penannular gold pendant (KN.44).[26]

A bronze cow figurine, dated to the second quarter of the eighth century and found near the palace, has similarities to an Argive piece from Olympia, but its abdomen shows similarities to another figurine from Aghia Triada.[27] I have not included it in the catalogue. It is one of a number of bronze animal figurines found on Crete but having similarities to Argive and Laconian votives at Olympia, dated to the eighth century.[28] The recording of this bronze piece is a convenient place to introduce a number of bronze figurines found (some *probably* found) on Crete that have external parallels, although identification of them as imports may be hasty. Pilali-Papasteriou cites bronze figurines from Aghia Triada and Patsos as having parallel elements in examples from Ayia Irini and Myrtos Pigadhes on Cyprus; the artifacts on Crete range in date from the twelfth/tenth to the ninth century, with a chronological outlier dated to the early seventh century.[29] She cites another eleven figurines with known Cretan provenances—Aghia Triada, Phaistos, Psychro, and Lasithi—as having parallels with Argive and Laconian bronze figurines found at Olympia. The Cretan figurines are dated to the eighth century, one in the first quarter, two in the second, three in the third, and five in the fourth.[30]

Another thirty figurines of unknown provenance, but possibly Cretan, are from the Giamalakis Collection, located in Herakleion: twenty-five have parallels at Olympia, twelve of those of Argive origin and another seven of Laconian origin. Three more have Argive parallels, one a Laconian parallel, and another an Argive/Spartan parallel.[31] The Cypriot parallel elements are curious, and any connections seem indirect at best. The pieces involved also show Cretan elements as well as Cypriot. The pieces with the parallels at Olympia are more intriguing: are they imports to Crete, made by artisans in the Peloponnese, or did Cretan artisans at Olympia pick up Argive and Laconian elements that they applied at home in Crete? Zimmerman has raised a similar question regarding the bronze horse figurines from the Giamalakis pieces presently located in various museums: were they made in the Peloponnese for buyers at Olympia and on Crete, or in Crete?[32] With the current evidence, there do not seem to be adequate grounds to discriminate between these possibilities. I discuss these pieces further at points in the sections on regional site reports, and I discuss the Giamalakis pieces further in the section on Cretan artifacts found overseas.

Over a dozen sites in Crete have yielded fine, handmade clay beads and some vessels of a type that has become known as "Attic" Dark Age Incised ware, raising a question of origin. Although known previously from excavations at Eleusis, this material first attracted wider attention in excavations in Attica, from a Geometric house on the north slope of the Areopagos, in the Kerameikos excavations, and at Nea Ionia; hence the use of the term "Attic" in quotation marks.[33] The ware stood out in Late Protogeometric Attic graves. The ware comprised dolls or idols, some pyxides and other small vases, small tripods, hollow balls, spindle whorls, and, especially, beads, mostly in female and child graves. While the issue of the origin of this material in Attica arose early, its appearance in Crete, first pointed out explicitly by Boardman, raised the question of whether the Cretan artifacts were imports from Attica or were local productions manifesting another type of external influence.[34] Some 250 of these beads were excavated at Protogeometric tomb V at Aghios Ioannis, a number far greater than the total num-

---

[26] Strong (1966: 19) believes the amber spacer bead from Tekke Tomb 2, vase 57, to be a Bronze Age survivor; Hutchinson and Boardman 1954: 217, pl. 28.5; Boardman 1954: 226, no. 5; Harding and Hughes-Brock 1974: 167.

[27] Pilali-Papasteriou 1985: 48–49, 179, no. 110, pl. 10. Cf. note 100 below.

[28] Cf. notes 88, 98, and 99 below.

[29] Pilali-Papasteriou 1985: nos. 17, 4, 219, 10.

[30] Ibid.: nos. 49, 80, 81, 72, 228, 92, 94, 193, 147, 206; the Lasithi pieces are from the Giamalakis Collection in the Herakleion Museum.

[31] Ibid.: nos. 142–44, 148–55, 158–59, 194–99, 203–4, 206–12, 214.

[32] Zimmerman 1989: 299–300.

[33] Eleusis: Skia 1898: 105, pl. 2.14–15; 1912: 35, fig. 15.2, grave 44. Attica: Burr 1933: 554, 557, 565, nos. 7 and 35–36 from the child's grave, nos. 83–93 from the floor of the house, fig. 24; Kübler 1943: pls. 29–32; Smithson 1961: 170–73, pl. 30; for later material, into Attic MG I, Smithson 1968: 103–9, nos. 35–63, pls. 29–30.

[34] Boardman 1960: 146–48, pl. 39; 1961: 132.

ber excavated in Attica. Boardman was able to cite similar beads at twelve other Cretan sites and a suspended vase from one other site: six Dark Age sites and six Early Geometric.[35] Subsequently a single bead of this kind has been published from the Subminoan-Protogeometric house in front of the temple at Gortyn, and a handmade incised cup is reported (but without illustration) from the Geometric Grave V at Gavalomouri in western Crete.[36] Boardman brought attention to one bead of this type reported from Delos and a handful of beads and vessels from Lindos on Rhodes. Since then, a doll and some beads, clearly of this ware, have been found in Subminoan-Protogeometric graves in the Palaia Perivolia cemetery at Lefkandi in Euboea.[37] The Lefkandi excavators considered the doll from tomb 22 to be an import, probably from Attica, but otherwise were reluctant to commit to a particular origin for the beads, local or otherwise.[38] Smithson pointed to handmade ware at Mycenae and Corinth of similar date, but in neither case does the material appear to be of this fine, incised ware.[39] At present, Crete remains the region with the largest number of sites reporting this handmade incised ware, and Attica still yields the greatest variety of ware. The Cretan beads have a greater variety of shapes than the Attic beads; the artistic level of the Cretan beads ranges below that of the Attic, and the Attic beads are frequently larger than the Cretan. Additionally, the Cretan beads may be somewhat earlier than their Attic counterparts. Boardman left open the question of import into Crete; Desborough raised the possibility of Cretan export to Attica or vice versa,

considered the latter more likely, but in the end thought the origin of the ware remained an open question.[40] Bouzek has reviewed the evidence on this ware at all the sites at which it has appeared and favors local production in Attica, Crete, and Rhodes, although the origin of the bead from Delos remains an open question, and he wrote before the definitive publication of the Lefkandi material.[41] The external influence on Greece itself represented by this incised ware has been debated since Milojčić's initial suggestion of a North Balkan-Middle European origin for the Attic incised ware.[42] Both Smithson and Boardman considered that the evidence supporting Milojčić's European attribution of the ware was weak, but Bouzek has supplied additional evidence, particularly in the form of dolls or idols, for the north Balkan-Danubian (Çirna-Žuto Brdo group) origin of this material.[43] Snodgrass, having pointed to the lack of artifactual evidence for interaction between Greece and the Balkans between the Late Mycenaean III period and the eighth century, favors a local origin for the Attic incised ware, probably based on a revival of traditions going back to the Middle Helladic period. He sees some precedents for the Late Protogeometric incised ware in some earlier pyxides and in the coarse handmade ware.[44] Reber settles on an Attic origin for this ware on the grounds that there are no other sufficiently close parallels elsewhere, but he does not treat the items of this ware found on Crete.[45] In the most recent contribution to this discussion of origins for this ware, Bouzek refers again to the frontier area between Rumania, Serbia, and Bulgaria as the

---

[35] Dark Age: beads at Aghios Ioannis, Fortetsa, Knossos, Mavro Spelio (probably derived from Iron Age burials above LM graves), and Phaistos (probably PG despite apparent association with the First Palace) and a suspended vessel at Petrokephali, near Phaistos; Geometric and later: Anavlochos, Dreros, Vrokastro, Arkades, and Amnisos.

[36] Rizza and Santa Maria Scrinari 1968: 5, fig. 4; M. Andreadaki-Vlasaki 1985: 29.

[37] Popham and Sackett with Themelis 1980: 143, no. 30, 150–51, no. 30, 344, pls. 125, 214, 269.

[38] Kourou (1988: 314) considers the beads found at Lefkandi an "exportable ware," but in the final analysis does not attempt to judge the origin of the beads at Lefkandi.

[39] Smithson 1961: 170; for Corinth: Weinberg 1943: 78; Argolid: Desborough 1955: 240–42.

[40] Boardman 1960: 146–48; Desborough 1972b: 142–44, 229, 232.

[41] Bouzek 1974: 34, 48; 1985: 200–201.

[42] Milojčić 1948–49: 29–33.

[43] Smithson 1961: 171; Boardman 1960: 147; Bouzek 1974: 36–42, fig. 15.

[44] Snodgrass 1971: 97, 329; on the apparent chronological gap in contacts between Greece and the Balkans between the end of the Mycenaean period and the eighth century, idem 1965: 229–40, esp. 235–36. Desborough (1972b: 144) considers the revival of Early Helladic crafts improbable.

[45] Reber concedes northern or northwestern Greek influence of an undefined sort but ultimately places responsibility for the Attic ware in Attica. He also notes the evidence of local production in most regions during most (but not all) periods (1991: 15–16).

TABLE 1. Origins and Dates of Overseas Artifacts Found at Knossos, All Sites

Period	Period frequency	Attica[a]	Corinth	Cyprus	Egypt	Phoenicia	Cyclades	Near East	East Greece and Rhodes	Argos	Euboea	Italy and Sardinia
1100-1050	11	0	0	4	1	1	0	3	0	1	0	1
1050-1000	2	1	0	0	—	0	0	0	0	0	1	0
1000-950	45	15	0	3	5	0.5	7	10.5	1	0	3	0
950-900	28	24	1	1	0	0	0	0	1	0	3[b]	0
900-850	17	4	0	1	0	0	3	2	0	2	4	0
850-800	51	18.5	1	8	2	3	14.5	2	1	0	0	1
800-750	76	16	8	31	1	5	5.5	4.5	0	0	3.5	2
750-700	46	1	7	11	1	1	11	2	4	2	5	1
700-650	63	0.5	16	9	6	2.5	1.5	8.5	16.5	0	1	0.5
650-600	26	0	23	0	1	0	0	1	2	0	0	0
Origin frequency	370	80	56	68	17	13	42	33.5	25.5	5	20.5	5.5

[a]Includes several Boeotian, or possible Boeotian, pieces.

[b]One from Thessaly.

location of the best parallels. This culture apparently moved south around 1000, and one fragmentary idol of the class in question has been associated with the South Bulgarian Cepina group. Bouzek believes that the dolls probably were transmitted through wooden versions that became preserved in clay imitations in the Attic and Euboean graves.[46] In any event, while the extra-Greek origin of this pottery may continue to be in question, the production of the Cretan material in either Attica or Crete seems to remain in presumption of the latter.

It may be useful to aggregate the finds from the four sites (groups of sites) in which I have presented the Knossos material so far, on the grounds that Early Iron Age Knossos was a single, coherent community, integrated economically and otherwise.[47] Table 1 summarizes the four Knossos tables from the Catalogue. It presents only artifact counts in the cells of the table; catalogue numbers of the specific artifacts and their likely dates can

be found in those catalogue tables. A column near the left margin of Table 1 reports the period frequency of artifacts (the number of artifacts dated to the corresponding fifty-year period), and the bottom row reports the origin frequency (the number of artifacts from particular origins). Cyprus (with 68 reported artifacts), Attica (80), and Corinth (56) are the three principal origins of published foreign material, although aggregation of Egypt, Phoenicia, and Near East into a single Eastern group (excluding Cyprus; this aggregation is not shown in the table) reveals Knossos's strong Eastern orientation as well (53.5 artifacts— the half of an artifact indicates an uncertain provenance, which I have divided between proposed origins). Several patterns emerge easily. First, Attic material appears early but pretty much ceases by the middle of the eighth century— except for two Attico-Boeotian fibulae. Second, Corinthian material does not appear until the eighth century (a single artifact, dated from c.

---

[46] Bouzek 1994: 230–31.
[47] Coldstream 1984b: 312–13; Hood and Smyth 1981: 16–18.

835–750, appears possibly earlier) and is the only source to continue clearly through the end of the seventh century (a single Chiot vase, dated to c. 630, is the exception to this observation). The greatest frequency of Corinthian material is in the seventh century. Third, the Cypriot material is scattered across the entire time period. The 650–600 cell for Cyprus is empty, but that only indicates that no Cypriot artifact is clearly no earlier than 650; several Cypriot pieces may in fact date to sometime within that last half-century. Fourth, the aggregate Eastern material, excepting that from Cyprus, is nearly as large as either the Attic or the Corinthian corpus. Adding the Cypriot material to the other Eastern material gives 121.5 artifacts, compared to 136 from Attica and Corinth, or 229 from all Greek origins. I reiterate the danger of drawing sweeping or precise conclusions from counts of this sort—recall the effect Coldstream's publication of Cypriot material from the North Cemetery has on the apparent Cypriot tilt of that site—but I believe some reasonably cautious inferences—preliminary, if one wishes—may be drawn. The overall Eastern presence at Knossos is large relative to the corpus of other Greek material; whether the true number

from one region is larger than that from the other may be immaterial to the conclusion that the relative proportion of Eastern material at Knossos is substantial. This Eastern material is present from the very first of the Early Iron Age, although its pace seems to quicken in the second half of the ninth century. Fifth, the Cycladic material appears relatively early—in the first half of the tenth century; it has a relatively strong presence in the ninth century, and continues through the first half of the seventh. Sixth, the East Greek material is strongest in the first half of the seventh century; the Argive and the Euboean material both appear scattered throughout the majority of the period under study.

Maps 9 through 12 summarize the regions in contact with Knossos. Each of these maps indicates the foreign contacts, direct or indirect, implied by the provenances of reported artifacts with a line from Knossos to the foreign site or region. I have not attempted to vary the thickness of the contact lines to represent the absolute or relative frequency of artifacts. Map 9 reports the eleventh- and tenth-century pattern of contacts as indicated by the artifact provenances; it also includes the one reported overseas contact of

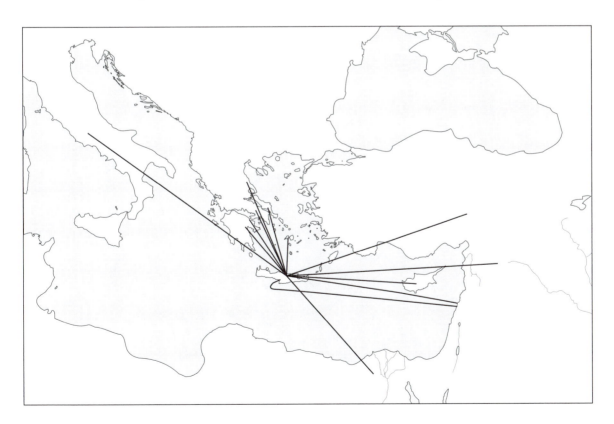

Map 9. Origins of Overseas Artifacts at Knossos and Kommos, Eleventh and Tenth Centuries

Kommos during this period. In the first two centuries of this period, Knossos reached nearly the full geographical array of external contacts it would maintain through the first half of the first millennium: East Greek sites, Argos, and Sardinia do not appear in this contact list. Maps 10 through 12 show very much the same diversity of external contacts in the ninth through the seventh centuries. None of these lines should be interpreted as trade *routes*: I have not attempted to trace prob-

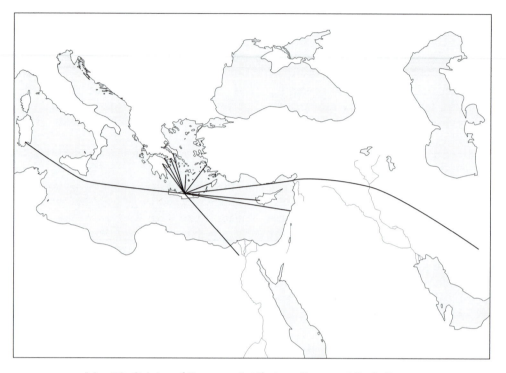

Map 10. *Origins of Overseas Artifacts at Knossos, Ninth Century*

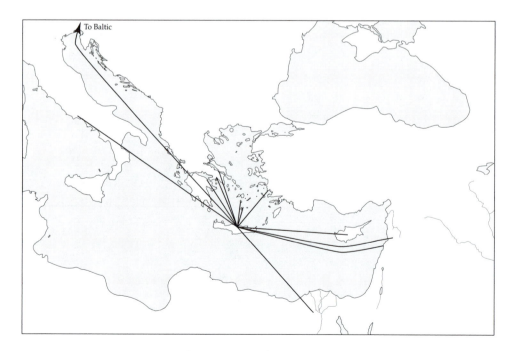

Map 11. *Origins of Overseas Artifacts at Knossos, Eighth Century*

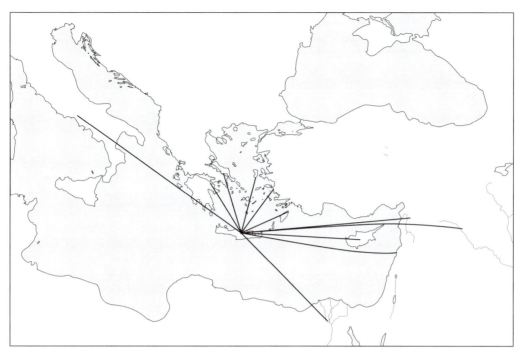

Map 12. Origins of Overseas Artifacts at Knossos, Seventh Century

able shipping routes since there is no assurance that a number of the foreign sites may not have been linked together on shipping circuits.

KOMMOS

The site of Kommos lies on a modest hill, and the ancient port appears to have had an offshore anchorage behind a sheltering reef.[48] It was an ancient port for Phaistos, and could have served the Mesara Plain from its western end.[49] Dating to the Middle Minoan period, with a wide range of contacts both east and west, Kommos was abandoned in the second half of the thirteenth century, and very few LM IIIC (1200–1100) sites have been found in its Mesara hinterland. Survey indicates that resettlement of the western Mesara behind Kommos began in the Geometric period,

---

[48] Shaw 1981: 251.

[49] Shaw 1982: 193. Shoreside Building J, from Minoan times, appears to have been a commercial building, perhaps a public warehouse. Its LM III floor contained a number of abandoned storage vessels: Shaw 1980: 240. Evans thought he had traced the Minoan transit road from near the beach at Kommos all the way to Knossos and considered it capable of having permitted four-wheeled wagons, at least in sections, as well as pack animals: Evans 1927: 88–89, 155; map following 70. J. W. Shaw reports, however (personal communication) that there are no traces of wagon ruts on the road pavement north of Building J; neither has he seen wagon ruts on other Minoan roads or pavements on Crete. Watrous, who made the hike with Shaw between Knossos and Kommos, concludes that although they could find no physical evidence for Evans's hypothesized royal road, ". . . tracks between the Mesara and the north coast undoubtedly existed in Minoan times": 1992: 171. K. F. Vickery (1936: 86) concluded that Minoan Crete traded olives and olive oil to Egypt and that the port of Kommos was the terminal for the Egyptian trade, part of which traveled overland to Knossos on the road described by Evans. Both Evans and Vickery may have reached these conclusions with inadequate evidence, although the finds at Kommos tend to support them. Physical remains of both Bronze Age and Early Iron Age roads for wheeled vehicles are found mostly in mountainous and relatively remote areas. In low, flat country, construction did not need to be particularly durable, and what there was would have been subject to destruction by subsequent construction. More extensive rock-cutting would have been required in mountainous areas less subject to other human disturbance. Crouwell 1981: 30; 1992: 12, 104. Cf. Evans's observation that, "The plain of Mesarà once reached[,] all traces [of the road] cease" (1927: 80).

although by the seventh century, settlements were more common.[50] Early Iron Age excavations published so far have been of various phases of the buildings of a sanctuary and its outlying buildings rather than graves, yielding an impression substantially different from that given by Knossos and other sites where graves have predominated. Foreign artifacts are found beginning probably at least as early as the early ninth century and possibly as early as the early tenth century. Activity began in the Greek sanctuary, Temple A, as early as the Subminoan period (1020–970 according to Brock's chronology).[51] With the exception of one Cycladic skyphos (KM.4), the foreign artifacts are all from the East, including some Cypriot amphora fragments dating between 900 and 700 (KM.3), until the last quarter of the eighth century when Corinthian pottery begins to appear. Over half of the foreign artifacts are attributed to Egypt and the Levant, with Phoenicia the prime suspected provenance in the Levant. Unlike the Near Eastern artifacts from elsewhere in Crete, the Phoenician (or Levantine) artifacts are coarseware amphora fragments. The Egyptian artifacts still are all faience objects that may be votives and have been found within and near the temple area.

Under a floor of Greek Temple B was found a tripillar altar that appears to be of Phoenician design. Correspondences exist between depictions on later Phoenician funerary stelai and the Kommos shrine. Its three low pillars are set into a base in mortice-and-tenon style, and several bronze and faience votive objects were found between the pillars. The tripillar altar appears to have been a center of worship in the late ninth and eighth centuries, and sometime after 750, a shield was placed behind it.[52] The concept of Near Eastern votives being left at Greek shrines near coasts by sailors and traders carrying Near Eastern goods agrees with the artifactual evidence.[53] Over 200 sherds of Phoenician transport amphorae, as well as a few Levantine flasks, have been found in contexts around Temples A (c. 925–800) and B (c. 800–600). Some of the later amphorae tentatively identified as Phoenician may be North African Phoenician.[54] From the pottery, it appears that Phoenician activity at Kommos peaked during Temple Phase A2, around 875–800, prior to the Phoenician colonization era, and judging from the scarcity of Phoenician pottery in Temple B, the Phoenician use of the temple may have been short-lived. Shaw suggests that Kommos may have served as a watering and trading point for ship crews and passengers; he also notes that travelers by sea could get to the shrine at Mt. Ida from Kommos,[55] although the deposits in the Idaean Cave do not, in general, look like travelers' votives. In his discussion of Kommos as a likely port for Minoan trade with Egypt, Evans noted that it was only 180 miles distant across the Libyan Sea to the North African coast, and thence east along the coast to the mouth of the Nile.[56] This route certainly could have been used by tenth- and ninth-century Phoenicians.

Building P, which appears to have been a ship shed built in LM IIIA2, was abandoned

---

[50] Watrous 1985: 7–18; 1989: 69–79; Watrous et al. 1993: 229–30.

[51] Shaw and Shaw 1993: 175.

[52] Hoffman (1990: 119–23) disputes the Phoenician attribution of the tripillar altar on two principal grounds. First, the shrine postdates the period of the greatest intensity of Phoenician artifacts, which prompts her to question the contemporaneity of commercial contact and worship. Second, she questions the willingness of Greeks to accept Phoenician religious apparatus in one of their temples. Shaw appears to have considered the first issue in translating the effect of Phoenician worship practices in the period of Temple A into influence possibly on Greek practices in Temple B: Shaw 1984: 284. On Hoffman's second point of dissent, I see little reason to doubt Greek openness to foreign religious forms, either integrally into their pantheon and beliefs or experimentally into their practice. Negbi (1992: 608–9) reviews Shaw's reasoning and accepts the Phoenician attribution of the tripillar shrine. Elsewhere, she has suggested the interpretation of small- to medium-size, asymmetrical buildings at Phylakopi and Mycenae as road temples built to serve Canaanite traders and seafarers engaged in eastern Mediterranean trade in the fourteenth and thirteenth centuries: Negbi 1988: 356–57.

[53] Winter 1988: 210, and Winter's personal communication with G. Köpcke cited there.

[54] A. Johnston (1993: 371) refers to "other sites under Phoenician influence (e.g., Carthage)" and uses the term *Punic*. On the use of *Punic* to refer to Western Phoenicians, and particularly sites under Carthaginian influence, beginning in the sixth century, see Aubet 1993: 11–12.

[55] J. W. Shaw 1989: 165–83.

[56] Evans 1927: 89.

around 1250, but stood for centuries thereafter. A Canaanite jar was found on the original floor of gallery P1, mixed with LM IIIA2/B cups and domestic ware. The wooden roof beams of the building finally collapsed in the eighth century. The western (shoreward) end of the building was used for several centuries, possibly by visitors to Temples A and B. The building lends a further air of seaward orientation to the town, both in its days of prime use and in its time as a useful derelict.[57]

Building Q, probably built in the seventh century, appears to have been a commercial warehouse of sorts, and has yielded transport amphora fragments from Chios (KM.26), Lesbos (KM.27), Samos (KM.53), other East Greek points (KM.28, 52, 61), Attica (KM.29), possibly Laconia (KM.52), and Phoenicia (KM.58). Phoenician transport amphora fragments (KM.18) have been found beneath its floor.[58] Only one Corinthian transport amphora has been reported, from south of Building Q. Room 38 of Building Q contained a mass of some 2,000 crushed *Murex trunculus* shells, which leave a strong impression of association with a purple-dye industry.[59]

The Early Iron Age artifacts give a distinct feeling of a commercial town going back into the tenth and ninth centuries. The early orientation is toward the Near East, where urbanization of Tyre, Byblos, Arados, Sidon, and other cities depended on food and other raw-material imports. The Mesara could have been one of those suppliers, but the survey evidence does not indicate a flourishing agricultural population in the western Mesara in the tenth and ninth centuries. The transport amphorae found in Building Q suggest storage of liquids, possibly grain, but they date to late in the seventh century. The foreign character of the amphorae in Building Q suggests that they may have held imports, but they equally well could have held local products for export. A reasonable, mixed possibility is that they carried in imports, but,

once emptied in Kommos, may have been used to hold exports from the Mesara.

The scatter of amphorae from the eastern Aegean and Attica dating to the last quarter of the seventh century suggests that Kommos may have been invigorated as a stopover point on newly emerging runs between East Greece and Cyrene and between Attica and Cyrene, and it may not have been out of the way on the East Greece-Naukratis run, which would have arisen about the same time. Some triangular trade between these first two sets of points may have emerged, with something like Cretan oil, Cyrenaean grain, and East Greek wine in one triangle and Attic oil, Cretan fruits, and Cyrenaean grain (and hides and silphium?) in the other. The Attic trade does not seem to have included much pottery, but at the end of the seventh century, Corinth's products had captured most of the international fine pottery market in the Greek world, and Corinthian pottery does appear at Kommos. Cretan pottery has been found in the Greek pottery at Tocra, to the west of Cyrene, in the last quarter of the seventh century, and at Aziris to the east, presumably for the years 637–631, when the Therans lived there.[60] In an East Greece-Crete-Egypt triangle, a plausible set of commodities is East Greek (especially island) wine, Cretan oil, and from Egypt, grain and an array of specialty items ranging from medicines to spices. An obstacle to the proposed Greek contents of this triangle is the paucity of Greek pottery fragments found in Egypt that could have held either wine or oil.[61] Cretan woolen textiles, which would not have required ceramic containers, may have been of limited use in Egypt, whose inhabitants would have appreciated linen more.[62] An alternative hypothesis that could place East Greek and possibly Attic transport amphorae at Kommos, in a triangular trade with Egypt, is more complicated. Possibly East Greek wine went to Kommos, where Cretans ran a surplus in grain or oil with Attica, with net payment

---

[57] M. C. Shaw 1985: 22–23; Shaw and Shaw 1993: 167, 175, 187, fig. 9.

[58] Johnston 1993: 339–82.

[59] J. W. Shaw 1986: 229–30. Nonetheless, 2,000 shells would not yield a large amount of dye.

[60] Boardman 1966: 149–50; Boardman and Hayes 1966: 78–80.

[61] Cook 1937: 227–37; Milne 1939. Milne (1945: 233) suggests that Egypt sent grain to Minoan Crete, which (following Evans) had a larger population than it could feed domestically, but concludes that the primary Greek export to Naukratis was silver traded for grain.

[62] Woven cotton fabric does not appear in Egypt before Coptic times: James 1979: 235. Lucas (1962: 147–48) cites Herodotus's knowledge of "tree-wool" used in India (3.106, 7.65) and Assyrian knowledge of "trees that bear wool" in the seventh century. The earliest mention of cotton in papryi is the second century A.C.

in silver (recall the silver and gold dumps in the Khaniale Tekke tomb); the silver, now the property of East Greeks, went to Egypt to pay for grain that went back to Asia Minor and the eastern Aegean islands. The greater simplicity of the first two proposed triangles may commend them relative to the third. Yet another alternative is that the transport amphorae were reused, and their place of manufacture therefore is not a reliable guide to the sources of the goods they carried or of the destinations of exported goods.[63] The fact that three of the manufacture sites of the amphorae are close together suggests that reuse, if these amphorae were indeed reused, may not be geographically misleading in this case.

Fitting somewhere in these possible regional interaction patterns are ten locally made cup sherds inscribed with graffiti in various regional Greek alphabets, indicating the presence, possibly residential, of outsiders at Kommos.[64] Comfortably accommodated with the East Greek interactions through Kommos is sherd I45, inscribed after firing, in what is possibly an East Greek alphabet, dating by context to the second half of the seventh century. Less clearly accounted for, in terms of other imported pottery sherds, are two sherds inscribed, *before* firing, in Central Greek alphabets, probably Boeotian, and one inscribed after firing, in another Boeotian script. One of these, from within the Temple B dump, dates stratigraphically to the seventh century. A fourth cup sherd (I26) uses yet a different Greek alphabet. In these cases of inscriptions before firing, literate users of a non-Cretan Greek alphabet had a sufficiently sustained presence at Kommos to interact with potters (presumably local and probably nonliterate). Such literate foreigners would more likely have been merchants than sailors.

With the absence of Early Iron Age grave items from Kommos and of clearly commercial items of that period from the Knossos region, it is difficult to compare the artifacts from the two areas. Yet some similarities appear even across the contextual differences: the scarcity of Attic pottery after the mid-eighth century (Attic fine pottery has not appeared in the published reports from Kommos), the appearance of Corinthian fine pottery in the eighth century, and the persistence of nonutilitarian Near Eastern items throughout the entire period of activity. The appearance of a few pieces of Attic fine pottery before the middle of the eighth century in the nonfunerary Knossos town deposits contrasts with the complete absence of Attic fineware in the town at Kommos. No other foreign fine pottery, with the exception of a ninth-century Cycladic skyphos, appears at Kommos either, but reports of grave excavations could change this.

Map 9 above records the earliest Early Iron Age external contact reported at Kommos, with Phoenicia. Maps 13 through 15 show the site's external contact patterns in the ninth through the seventh centuries. The ninth-century pattern is relatively restricted (Map 13), with an eastern pattern to Cyprus and Phoenicia and a northern one into the Cyclades. The array of external contacts shows a little wider dispersion in the eighth century (Map 14), but again only three in number. The seventh-century pattern (Map 15) is widely dispersed, diversified, and quite interesting. Kommos has two major northern contact routes, one north and east to East Greece, Rhodes, and the islands of the northern Sporades and Lesbos, the other virtually straight north from the western end of Crete—to Attica, Corinthia, and Laconia. It is tempting to connect a line from Kommos to Cyrenaica, since Cretan pottery has been found at Aziris and Tocra, although those finds appear closest to pottery from central Crete. A contact line may be in order between Kommos and Phoenician North Africa, but I have not included one. A due eastern route leads to Cyprus and Phoenicia, and a southeast one to Egypt. The northern routes certainly leave Kommos looking like a way station on routes between Greece and Africa. The separate line between Rhodes and Kommos should not be interpreted as an actual trade route, or even as indicating the existence of a separate Rhodes-Kommos shipping run; it is not unlikely that Rhodes and Cyprus, and possibly even Phoenicia, would have been on a single circuit. The appearance of a relatively late date for foreign material certainly is encouraged by the predominance of Building Q in the published material to date. More complete publication of the Early Iron Age material from Kommos could alter this impression.

[63] Grace 1979: 4–5.
[64] Csapo 1991: 211–16; 1993: 235–36.

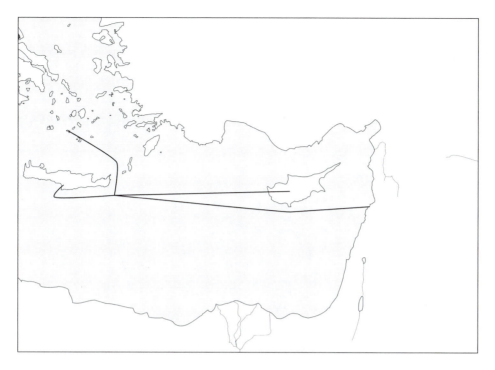

Map 13. Origins of Overseas Artifacts at Kommos, Ninth Century

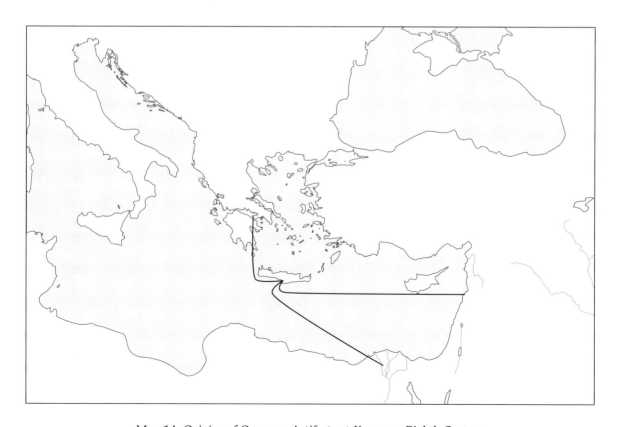

Map 14. Origins of Overseas Artifacts at Kommos, Eighth Century

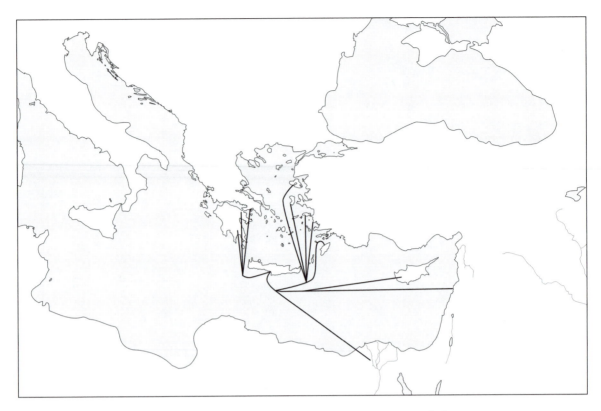

Map 15. Origins of Overseas Artifacts at Kommos, Seventh Century

Sites in Northern and Eastern Crete

The majority of the foreign artifacts from these sites are from grave contexts, but some are from temple areas or shrines, in addition to those from the Diktaean Cave, and several from Vrokastro and Arkades are from houses. The north-central part of this section of the island shows signs of possible exchanges with Attica, Cyprus, and Egypt early in this period. The bronze rod tripod from Vrokastro (VR.3) was found in a grave and may be a Mycenaean-period heirloom or a Subminoan period import, but it was found in a context that could make its placement in the grave as late as Early Geometric.[65] The six faience seals and blue faience beads found in the same tomb with the tripod may be quite early in the period, or even prior to 1100, or from the mid-tenth century to the late eighth. Their appearance in the same tomb may suggest a rather more regular interaction with points east. The early Cypriot, or suspected Cypriot, products are metals, but the two later ones, from the

Geometric period (VR.14–15), are ceramic. The Attic and Cycladic fine pottery (VR.6, 8, 9, 16) is all from nongrave contexts, indicating utilitarian use of those areas' products, although funerary uses simply may be lost.

Kavousi, a few kilometers east of Vrokastro, is farther from the coast than Vrokastro by several kilometers. The Vronda site is in the foothills of the Sitea Mountains, while the less accessible Kastro site is on a peak a kilometer or so farther south. The foreign artifacts from Kavousi, predominantly from Vronda and scattered foothill sites, show an orientation toward Cyprus similar to that at nearby Vrokastro, both in early appearances (cf. KV.2—firedogs—with VR.2–3—a knife and a rod tripod) and in later (KV.4, 9—a bronze bowl and a ceramic aryballos—and VR.14–15— vases). For non-Cretan Greek orientations, the Kavousi area has produced a Euboean hydria (KV.3), while Vrokastro has produced a larger array of material, both pottery and fibulae, from the mainland (VR.4–6, 8, 10–13) and the Cyclades (VR.9, 16). Both have produced faience associat-

---

[65] Hall 1914: 132–35.

ed with Egypt (KV.5, VR.7), and generally from the East Kavousi has yielded both blue glass beads and some thin, blue glass pieces, possibly inlays (KV.6–7). The four iron ship firedog fragments bought by Evans (KV.3) appear to have been from Kavousi.[66] I have not included the thin bronze plaque from Kavousi, found by Boyd, among the imports.[67] Reed has suggested that its Syrian elements are strong enough to justify calling it imported or, if a Cretan product, made by an expatriate Syrian.[68] Boardman had considered it a product of a Knossos workshop, in the second half of the eighth century, and beginning to show a mechanical repetition; Coldstream offered a similar opinion, and both he and Boardman noted its similarities to other local finds.[69]

From the "Sitea area" is an oral report of an Egyptian shawabti in the possession of an antique dealer, relayed by Pendlebury.[70] The circumstances are unsatisfactory, but the provenance is not out of keeping with the foreign finds in the area. In the same area, Mochlos has produced an attractive and interesting find. Mochlos is an island a few hundred meters off the north coast, although it probably was connected to the mainland in the Bronze Age by a narrow isthmus. It lies toward the east end of the Gulf of Mirabello, roughly half as far from Kavousi as from Sitea. Mochlos has been long known for the spectacular Minoan artifacts found by Seager in his 1908 excavation, but was re-excavated in the 1970s and again from 1989, continuing to the present. The 1994 excavation unearthed the bottom part of a Middle Protocorinthian oinochoe from a trench beneath the Hellenistic fort at the island's peak. The piece appears to a product of Amyx's "Early Monumentalists."[71] This is one of the few products of an identified Corinthian (or Protocorinthian) painter or workshop on Crete (cf. KN.153, the name piece of the later Painter of Candia 7789, found near Knossos). This part of Crete does not give the impression of having

been particularly cosmopolitan in the mid-seventh century,[72] so it is natural to wonder how this piece arrived at its resting place. Assuming it is in a contemporaneous deposit, perhaps it represents a finer piece of a more well-to-do estate owner (basileus?) of this region. From the other side of the Isthmus of Ierapetra is a fragment of an Egyptian statuette of black-green stone, broken and in battered condition. It was found in the late nineteenth century near Ierapetra and presently is in the Ierapetra Museum. Missing the royal uraeus, it is undatable and may be an import of either the Late Bronze Age or the Early Iron Age.[73]

A Cypriot bronze pendant dated in a range from Subminoan to Cretan Protogeometric (KRΦ.1) and a possible Italian/Sicilian fibula (KRΦ.2) from the Subminoan period are reported from Karphi. Snodgrass has identified a bronze arrowhead at Karphi as of Anatolian form (KRΦ.3); I have included it as a possible import, although I certainly do not envision transmission as straightforward and routine as a barrel of Anatolian arrowheads imported to Crete. More likely are the possibilities of a Karphiote spending some time as a mercenary in Anatolia, or someone selling or trading a few arrowheads acquired in Anatolia. A fragment of faience (KRΦ.4) and a biconical faience bead (KRΦ.5) could be Late Bronze Age survivals. In grave 8 of the Ta Mnemata cemetery at Karphi, Pendlebury found a group of "the remains of a collar of bronze discs sewn on to some material."[74] Lorimer speculated that this might just possibly be the remnant of a scale corslet from the Near East, via Cyprus, because she believed that the Cyprus-Crete connection remained open throughout the Dark Age; but Snodgrass found the evidence "of the most questionable kind" and declined to accept Lorimer's suggestion.[75] While Young's preliminary notice described a *collar*, the final excavation report described evidence of triple or quadruple bands

---

[66] Gesell, Day, and Coulson 1983: 389, 412–13.

[67] Boyd 1901: 147, figs. 10–11.

[68] Reed 1976: 366, 371–72, 375, no. 1.

[69] Boardman 1961: 134–35; Coldstream 1974: 163–64; 1977: 284–86.

[70] Pendlebury, Eccles, and Money-Coutts 1932–33: 97.

[71] J. Soles, personal communication, January 12, 1995; Soles and Davaras 1995: 312–13.

[72] Dreros, just to the east of the Gulf of Mirabello, is an exception to this characterization, with its sanctuary area and bronze-covered statuary.

[73] Phillips 1991: 802–3, no. 407.

[74] Young 1938: 233–34; Snodgrass 1964: 147.

[75] Lorimer 1950: 202; Snodgrass 1964: 85.

around the *border* of some garment.[76] The exact number of the discs was not reported, but was described as "many"; they are small—0.8 centimeter in diameter—and *hollow*, "with clips at the back for attachment to leather or material."[77] Although these discs remain unillustrated, from comparison with the photograph of disc no. 419, also described as hollow, that term indicates that the disc is bulged out in the center rather than flat;[78] hollow does not appear to imply that the discs had hollow centers, like washers, through which a strip of leather or thick cloth could be inserted like a string of beads. The thickness of these discs is not reported, so their potential strength cannot be assessed. It is not difficult to imagine explanations for the fact that no remains of other armor scales were reported from the tomb, but one should have believed already that these discs imply a scale corslet to make such an explanation necessary, a prior belief that Snodgrass was unwilling to concede. Nearby Karphi, Watrous collected a sherd from a Protocorinthian juglet or aryballos at Augousti in his survey of the Lasithi Plain.[79]

Graves at Anavlochos have yielded Middle to Late Geometric Cycladic pottery and Protocorinthian pottery, as well as an undated terracotta statuette that Demargne attributed to Egypt.[80] The objects from Dreros and Olous are all grave goods and range from quite early in the period under study until the last quarter of the eighth century: OL.1 is a pair of possible Attic Submycenaean stirrup jars, and DR.6 is a bronze fibula of Attic or Boeotian appearance.[81] Dreros shows some signs of connections with the mainland, with an Attic Geometric fibula, a Dipylon-style krater sherd that does not appear to be a local copy as others are, a Corinthian oinochoe, and the Attic or Boeotian fibula mentioned above. Once again, Egyptian blue beads appear in a Geometric grave. Desborough reports a single Attic Protogeometric skyphos from a grave at Rhiza and a similar one at nearby Kanli Kastelli.[82]

Much of the ancient town of Itanos is underwater and has not been excavated, but Deshayes reports four foreign sherds from the Geometric period to the late seventh century.[83] The earliest is the rim of a bowl that he calls Parian Geometric, followed by a sherd from a Boeotian Late Geometric oinochoe and two Corinthian sherds from the late eighth to seventh century. The alleged Phoenician associations with Itanos are not borne out, but neither is any interaction with Thera, whose colonists found Korobios to guide them to North Africa in the early 630s. Itanos's location at the northeast corner of Crete could have made it a natural stopping point on Phoenician shipping runs from Rhodes and from Cyprus, and despite Demangel's disagreement with Février's interpretation of the Punic inscription from Sousse, the books should not be closed firmly on Phoenician activity there without further excavation.[84] Korobios was a murex fisherman, the Phoenicians were famous for their dye industry, and there is evidence around Palaikastro, not far to the south, of murex fishing in the Minoan period for both a dye industry and food.[85] The Phoenicians could have had an established distribution system for dyed textiles, and they may not have been averse to distributing Cretan dyed materials as well as their own, particularly if their products were distinguish-

---

[76] Pendlebury, Pendlebury, and Money-Coutts 1937–38: 113, no. M8.169.

[77] Ibid.: 104.

[78] Ibid: 113, 119, pl. 29.1.

[79] Watrous 1982: 55, Map 12; pl. 20:d, C.

[80] Demargne 1931: 401.

[81] Van Effenterre 1948: 29, 42.

[82] Desborough 1952: 83, 259.

[83] Deshayes 1951: 208.

[84] Demangel 1949: 395; Boardman 1961: 151. On Korobios and the Theraeans, Hdt. 4.152.

[85] Reese 1987: 203, 206. In the dye industry, various colors could be made with different combinations of species used (there were three major ones, all present at Palaikastro), the amount of sunlight and air allowed, and the weave and type of textile used. The color could vary from pale pink to dark violet or black-purple. There is also widespread evidence of these shellfish having been eaten at many Cretan sites during the Minoan period, which may suggest another Cretan product available for trade overseas in the Early Iron Age. Reese (1982: 249–50) reports seashells from what appears to be MM IIIA domestic rubbish: inter alia, several recent *Murex trunculus* shells and a large Tun shell. There is no evidence that the murex was associated with dyeing activity rather than food, and the Tun shell may have been a votive object.

able. At any rate, it would not have hurt to keep an eye on the competition; even if Dark Age Greek ideas of commercial competition may have been blurred with more aggressive activities, the Phoenicians surely were more cosmopolitan. The only foreign artifact from the Early Iron Age reported from Palaikastro is a fragmentary set of bronze tripod legs of Attic style found near the temple precinct (PLK.1) and dated by Benton to between the Protogeometric period and the end of the eighth century. I know of no corroboration of this suggestion from the eastern coastal sites, but it may indicate something for which to look. Hogarth reported some Egyptian blue paste beads in a Late Geometric grave at Hellenika near Zakros.[86]

Praesos shows an array of foreign artifacts similar to those found at the other northern and eastern sites: a scattering of mainland pottery from Attica, a relatively large amount of Corinthian material, and some Eastern connections with Egypt, Cyprus, and possibly Syria or Phoenicia. Additionally, there is a bucchero oinochoe, dated from the Cretan Late Geometric to Early Orientalizing period (PR.10), which may be from Italy. The Diktaean Cave, being a shrine, differs in character from the other sites in the region, and the foreign artifacts found there are of the sort suitable as votives. Several Egyptian objects associated with the Early Iron Age are not dated (DC.2–4), but the two other Egyptian objects are relatively late (DC.27) or possibly earlier than 1100 (DC.1).[87] Two bronze cow figurines are similar to votives found at Olympia. One, parallel to a Laconian cow, is dated to the third quarter of the eighth century; the other, with an Argive parallel, is dated to the fourth quarter of that century.[88] Considering some differences from the Olympia pieces, it is difficult to estab-

lish clearly overseas origins for these two pieces, and I have not included them in the catalogue. If they *are* imports, they might have been brought back to Crete by Cretan visitors to Olympia rather than representing direct connections with Laconia and Argos.

An "Argive Monochrome" aryballos has been found in a tomb near Agios Georgios, a few kilometers northwest of Praesos.[89] Argive Monochrome ware is found at widely dispersed sites throughout the mainland, the islands, and the western colonies, and there appear to be several workshops in different regions, although the greatest quantity may derive from Corinthian and possibly Argive ateliers.[90] The ware, with a floruit of the second half of the eighth century into the seventh, roughly contemporaneous with Protocorinthian, is handmade, commonly of fine clay, and is either undecorated or decorated with incised designs. Kourou believes the aryballoi and poppy-shaped vases of the ware were used to transport opium.[91] The Agios Georgios aryballos has been identified chemically as probably Corinthian, but definitely Peloponnesian, and Tsipopoulou places it in the third quarter of the eighth century.[92]

With or without including the votives from the Diktaean Cave, the heavy proportional representation of artifacts from the Near East characterizes these sites as a group (the Near Eastern proportion of artifacts is higher when the Diktaean Cave is not included than when it is included). This proportion distinguishes them from those finds in the central, southern, and western parts of the island, and their Near Eastern proportion is even heavier than it is at Knossos, although a bit lighter than at Kommos.[93] However, including the Idaean Cave, the Near Eastern proportions are roughly the same as in

---

[86] Hogarth 1900–1901: 145.

[87] Again, an amber bead from the Diktaean Cave is believed to be from the Late Bronze Age, by virtue of its similarity to the amber in the wire wheel from the Tiryns Treasure: Boardman 1961: 72–73, no. 352, fig. 32.352; Strong 1966: 21, 23; Harding and Hughes-Brock 1974; cf. Karo 1930: 127–28, Beil. 31–32.

[88] Pilali-Papasteriou 1985: 43–44, 179, 180, nos. 92 (Argive) and 94 (Laconian), pl. 8.

[89] Tsipopoulou 1987: 266–67; 1990: 139.

[90] Dunbabin 1962: 314–15; Kourou 1987: 31–53; 1988: 315, 318, fig. 1, for distribution map. Bouzek (1994: 230) considers the Argive Monochrome ware as a continuation of the Dark-Age Incised ware, considered above.

[91] Kourou 1988: 321–22.

[92] Tsipopoulou 1987: 266–67.

[93] If one were inclined to apply statistics to these samples, which I am not, in view of their susceptibility to rapid change with new finds, the proportion of Near Eastern artifacts at Kommos and at the northern and eastern sites probably would not be significantly different. The Near Eastern presence in those two samples, however, probably would be distinguishable from that proportion in the Knossian, south-central, and western sites.

the northern and central sites including the Diktaean Cave. There does appear to be a hiatus in Near Eastern items between the early tenth century and the early ninth century, when the Near Eastern finds assume some regularity. Attic, and possibly Cypriot, artifacts continue during this period, however. The apparent (or possible) Boeotian items in the second half of the eighth century (IT.2 and DR.7) may be the odd items picked by a ship leaving Corinth from the west and making several loading stops before heading south or by Euboean ships from the other coast of Boeotia. The chronology of these items antedates the seventh-century Egyptian trade as well as the Cyrenaean colonial trade.

Despite being occupied continuously from the Neolithic through Archaic times, Amnisos has yielded only a few, mostly late, foreign objects, all but one from the East, although publication is a problem for evaluation of that site. A Syrian bronze reported by Dunbabin, and dated by him from 900 to 700, is one of the earliest pieces.[94] A Protocorinthian skyphos from the Cave of Eileithyia and a PC kotyle from the Sanctuary of Zeus are the only imports from mainland Greek areas. A bronze handle with lotus blossoms on the ends (AMN.4), dated to c. 745–710, is all that has been found of an Egyptian bronze lotus bowl like those found at Fortetsa and the Idaean Cave. A number of loosely dated Egyptian faience items and a bronze bowl may be from the late seventh century but are said to be possibly earlier or later.[95] There is nothing in the Early Iron Age finds at Amnisos to connect it, as a port of entry, with foreign artifacts found at Knossos. The eastern orientation of the site is notable, however, particularly at the recently republished Sanctuary of Zeus Thenatos, with its high proportion of late (early Archaic) Egyptian faience votives (AMN.9–11, 13, 17–20, 23; 8, 15–16, 22, and 25–26 may be Egyptian or East Greek, and AMN.14 may be Egyptian or Rhodian). These Egyptian votives, as well as some that are possibly Phoenician (AMN.24), Cypriot (AMN.14, 21), and Rhodian or other East Greek, seem sufficient to keep open the notion that Amnisos served a port town, probably nearby Thenai, at least late in this period; the scarcity of earlier foreign material may

reflect destruction of shoreside remains or selectivity of excavation, as well as the possibility of genuine inactivity in shipping. Gouves, a few kilometers east of Amnisos, has produced a grave with a Protocorinthian kotyle (GV.1), dated c. 680–630. The economic role of Amnisos may have its appearance distorted by the fact that the Early Iron Age excavations have been centered on sanctuary sites. No Early Iron Age buildings apparently connected with shipping, such as Building Q at Kommos, have been found. Such edifices may have been of impermanent construction, may have been destroyed by the sea, or both.

The foreign artifacts at Arkades show a strong eastern orientation, including Rhodian. They include one Attic MG I amphora neck fragment (ARK.3), a small bit of Cycladic Middle to Late Geometric pottery (ARK.5), and a relatively large amount of Corinthian pottery (ARK.9–15, 40–44) beginning around mid-seventh century. Some of the pieces identified in the catalogue as possibly Corinthian have been noted elsewhere in the literature but not identified as secure Corinthian vases, although they have comparables outside Crete; I have included Levi's description of fabric and finish in the catalogue entries for these vases. The Rhodian material does not begin until around the mid-seventh century. The faience crouching lion (ARK.35), dated to mid-seventh century, probably is a local copy of an Egyptian original—an import "shadow."

At Mingilísi, near Avlí Pedhiádos, northwest of Arkades, a large scarab with a hieroglyphic design (AVL.1) was found in 1957. The decoration has been assigned to the seventh century.[96]

The geographical pattern of Corinthian products relative to Attic is striking. At the Knossos sites, Corinthian and Attic materials are in about equal proportion, but in the other sites in northern and eastern Crete, Corinthian artifacts outnumber Attic three to one. The Attic material appears to dwindle to virtually nothing about the time of the Protocorinthian expansion on Crete—the latter probably representing growth in both Crete and Corinth. Otherwise, the distribution of Corinthian material across Cretan sites in the later part of the period is only slightly wider than that of the Attic material in the earli-

[94] Dunbabin 1957: 36.
[95] Marinatos 1929: 98; 1933: 98–99; 1934: 128–33.
[96] Hood 1958: 20.

er part, a difference that could be attributable to growth in the number of available sites.

Rather than attempt to map the external contacts of each of the sites, or of all of them together, I rely on a more selective set of maps to represent the sites in northern and eastern Crete. Map 16 reports the external linkages of a wide array of sites, including several from the other two regions, during the eleventh and tenth centuries. While none of the sites individually has the diversity of overseas contacts that Knossos did, when combined they virtually repeat the Knoss-

ian pattern, suggesting Knossos as the principal port of entry during these two centuries. This interpretation would, of course, imply intra-island contacts. Maps 17 and 18 trace the external contacts implied by artifacts at Amnisos during the ninth through the seventh centuries. The dashed line from Amnisos to Cyprus, with the question mark at its Cyprus end, in Map 17 represents the uncertainty of the Cypriot provenances of the ninth- to eighth-century Amnisos material, as do the dashed lines to Rhodes, Cyprus, and Phoenicia in Map 18. Those geo-

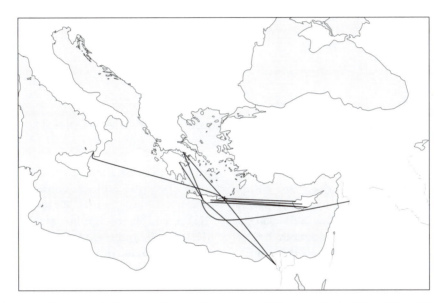

Map 16. Origins of Overseas Artifacts at Sites in Northern and Eastern Crete, Eleventh and Tenth Centuries

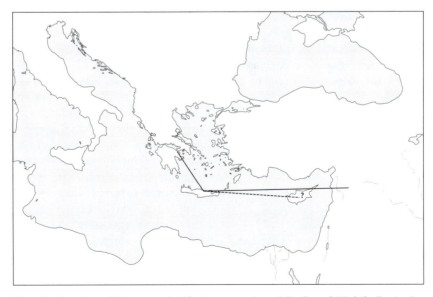

Map 17. Origins of Overseas Artifacts at Amnisos, Ninth and Eighth Centuries

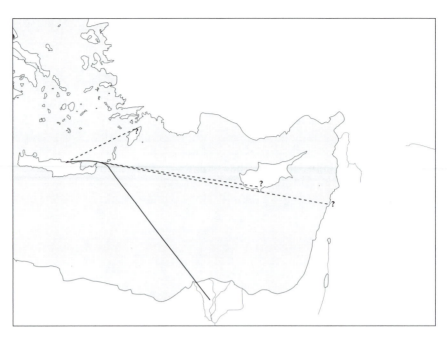

Map 18. Origins of Overseas Artifacts at Amnisos, Seventh Century

graphical patterns are neither highly diversified nor numerous. The ninth- and eighth-century pattern indicates an eastern link to Syria, possibly via Cyprus, and one to Corinthia, whereas the seventh-century pattern shows a definite link to Egypt, and possible connections to three areas that could have been on a single shipping circuit—Phoenicia, Cyprus, and Rhodes. None can be assured, however. Identifying Amnisos as a port town for Knossos would be difficult but for the relatively special character of these finds: virtually all are from sanctuaries of one kind or another—the Cave of Eileithyia or the Sanctuary of Zeus Thenatos—and no town or grave finds are reported. Of course, Katsambas, still beneath contemporary Herakleion, may have been an, or the, important port for Knossos, dating to the ninth century,[97] but the circumstances of the finds from Amnisos do not give an unbiased image of its own functions. Maps 19–22 show origins of finds from the Geometric to the Orientalizing periods reported at Arkades, the Diktaean Cave, Praesos, and Vrokastro.

SITES IN CENTRAL AND SOUTHERN CRETE

The Attic presence in the sites of central and southern Crete excluding Kommos is somewhat greater than at Kommos itself. At these other sites, the Attic artifacts consist of (possibly as many as) three vases at Phaistos (FS.2, 10, and 11), a couple of fibulae at the Idaean Cave (IC.99–100), and eight vases reported to be from Lasaia. Graves from Kommos might show a higher proportion of Attic pottery. The East Greek presence is proportionally stronger than elsewhere except in the North Cemetery at Knossos. At least two, and possibly three, of these East Greek artifacts are Rhodian, although the earliest (FS.4) may be a local imitation. The two Rhodian bird vases from Gortyn (GRT.2) are from the first half of the seventh century. Also from Gortyn are two or three fragmentary faience votives (GRT.5–7; 6 and 7 may be from a single piece) that may be East Greek, Levantine, or Egyptian. While the secure and possible Rhodian material may reflect the collaboration involved in the cofounding of Gela with Rhodians around 688/89, they do not indicate any long-standing connections between Cretans and Rhodians preceding that colonization. Map 23 shows the external linkages of Phaistos in the eighth and seventh centuries. The pattern is predominantly (possibly all) Greek. Though the pattern of external contacts resembles that of Kommos in the seventh century, the dates of the

[97] Coldstream 1984b: 319 n. 21.

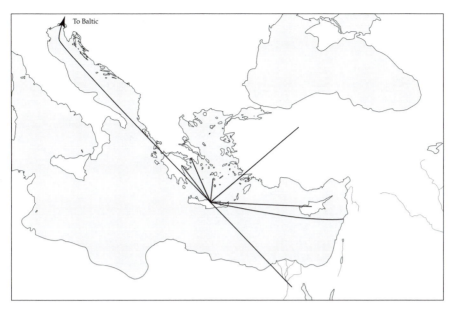

Map 19. Origins of Overseas Artifacts at Arkades, Ninth to Seventh Centuries

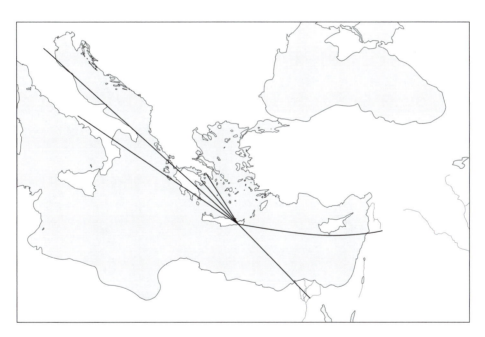

Map 20. Origins of Overseas Artifacts at the Diktaean Cave, Geometric and Orientalizing Periods

material at Phaistos are earlier and more spread out than the dates of the Kommos material, so there is little solid evidence here to suggest that the material found at Phaistos arrived through Kommos rather than through Knossos—or elsewhere. Three bronze cows and one possible cow from Phaistos have some similarities to Argive votive statuettes at Olympia, but they also demonstrate Cretan, and even occasionally Minoan, influences. All four date, by the Olympia examples, to the last quarter of the eighth century. One from Aghia Triada has an unprovenanced partial parallel at Olympia, which dates to the first quarter of the eighth cen-

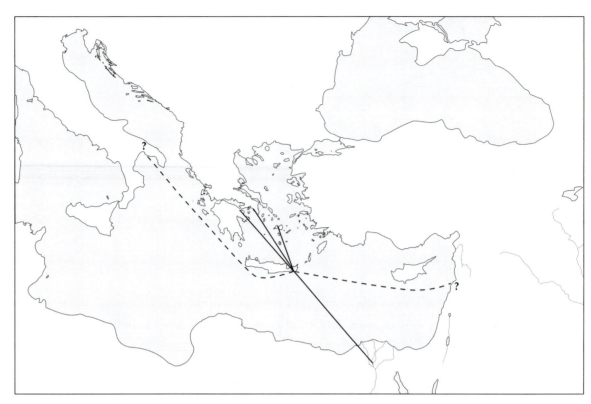

Map 21. Origins of Overseas Artifacts at Praesos, Geometric and Orientalizing Periods

Map 22. Origins of Overseas Artifacts at Vrokastro, Geometric Period

Map 23. Origins of Overseas Artifacts at Phaistos, Eighth and Seventh Centuries

tury.[98] As in the previous cases of bronze animal figurines with features parallel to examples from Olympia, the evidence for inferring importation is not compelling, but the parallels may indicate a prior Cretan artisan presence at Olympia.

Tylissos, the northernmost of the sites in this regional division, has yielded an interesting bronze piece (TYL.1) with a striding male figure following a bull, both on the same flat base, thought to be Cypriot or Syrian, probably dating to about 1000. The man's Near Eastern headpiece has no parallels on either Crete or the Greek mainland.[99] In contrast to the other bronze figurines published by Pilali-Papasteriou, this piece

seems to warrant identification as an import. Also from Tylissos, although of uncertain find circumstances, is a small ivory figurine of a seated female, possibly a goddess (TYL.2). It possesses a striking similarity to a figurine from the Sanctuary of Artemis Orthia, and it is believed to be a genuine Spartan product of c. 650–620.[100]

The Idaean Cave sanctuary has yielded a great number of foreign dedications, preponderantly from the East: North Syria, Phoenicia, possibly South Syria, regions in the Assyrian empire, and Egypt. I have listed 109 objects in the catalogue, including ivories, bronzes, jewelry, faience, and pottery, but many more have been excavated and identified. As many of the ivories

---

[98] Pilali-Papasteriou 1985: 28–29, 181, no. 49, fig. 16, pl. 4 (Aghia Triada); 36–37, 39–40, 92, 179, nos. 72, 80–81, 228 pls. 6, 7, 22 (Phaistos; nos. 72, 80–81 only possibly from Phaistos). Aghia Triada has three other bronze cow figurines, dating from the twelfth to tenth century, the ninth century, and the early seventh century, with partial parallels from Cyprus, sometimes in clay rather than bronze. Nonetheless, each also has Cretan affinities as well, and none of the cited Cypriot parallels is especially compelling: 14–15, 177, no. 4, pl. 1 (ninth century); 16–17, 178, no. 10, figs. 32–33, pl. 1 (early seventh century); 19, 20–21, 178, fig. 34, pl. 2, no. 17 (twelfth–tenth century). No. 4 also has two bronze comparables from Olympia.

[99] Pilali-Papasteriou 1985: 98–99.

[100] Levi 1927–29: 701, 704 n. 2, fig. 663; Lane 1933–34: 178 n. 12; Kunze 1935–36: 218 n. 1; Boardman 1961: 154 n. 1; Marangou 1969: 194. The comparable figurine at the Sanctuary of Artemis Orthia: Dawkins 1929: 220–21, pls. 122.5–7, 123.1.

appear to have been furniture inlays or other furniture decorations, the number of ivories listed in the catalogue may overstate the number of separate imported items represented. There are several ivory items from western Phoenician (North African?) locations, as well as some amber pieces that ultimately are attributable to the Baltic region. Many of the ivories must derive from the same Syrian and Phoenician workshops that produced the Layard and Loftus ivory groups from Nimrud, but several pieces must have been made locally by Cretan craftsmen. Though local production is accepted for the Idaean Cave shields, either by or under the tutelage of Eastern bronze artists, the idea of local production of most of the ivories by expatriate craftsmen seems too strained to be credible. The Nimrud ivories were produced over a period of at least a century, possibly more, and in different locations. The Assyrian palace at Calah simply assembled them at one place, and the destruction of the palace sealed their simultaneous stockpiling (possibly an indelicate term for a royal art collection). Local production in Crete of the entire array of styles sealed by the destruction at Nimrud is unlikely. A group of ivory seals (IC.86–90) dated to c. 725 is, in contrast, of local make, even though the raw material must have been imported. A number of ivory pieces that cannot be attributed with any security to particular regions I have identified as coming from the "Near East," in which I include Egypt.[101] A daedalic ivory figurine of a woman (IC.104) clearly is a Cretan product carved with imported raw material. To date, there is no tangible evidence of ivory carving, such as half-carved pieces or ivory chips, near the cave, but the vast majority of the ivory artifacts found in the cave

are so closely related to the Nimrud ivories that imported final products are virtually certain. (See Map 1 for the location of Nimrud, and Map 2 for Arslan Tash, a possible origin for some of the Nimrud ivories.) A number of the imported ivories are pyxides (e.g., IC.9, 10, 16, 17, 21–24, 27, et al.), several are figurines not associated with the pyxides (e.g., IC.29–30), and many are flat, incised reliefs that probably were furniture decorations. Were entire pieces of furniture (assembled or disassembled) imported to Crete, or were detached ivory attachments only imported? Sakellarakis notes Pythagoras's report of seeing an intact throne in the Idaean Cave, which indicates that at least some, if not all, of the ivory reliefs came with furniture.[102] Inlaid furniture and ivory pyxides and fly whisks do not seem to be the kinds of objects with which a hastily departing refugee would want to be burdened, and it is correspondingly difficult to see these objects as the dedications of Near Eastern refugees of ninth- or eighth-century Assyrian conquests. Once again, less-exciting mechanisms for delivery of these objects to Crete seem more plausible to me.

The foreign metal—bronze—finds from the Idaean Cave parallel the ivories.[103] They are Egyptian, North Syrian—some comparable to finds from Nimrud—Phoenician, and Cypriot, with other oriental shapes that cannot be attributed to particular origins; most seem to be earlier than the seventh century. About a dozen small Egyptian bowls (IC.3) with lotus-ornament handles in low relief probably date to the ninth to eighth century. There is also an Egyptian situla (IC.56). A Phoenician piriform jug (IC.61), of the type common later in the western Mediterranean, probably dates to the eighth century. A well-pre-

---

[101] Sources of elephant ivories were probably several: East Africa, via Sudan and Egypt; savannah Africa, farther to the west; Syria and Iraq through the ninth or eighth century possibly; and India. Hippopotamus ivory seems to have been rare in the first millennium, but more common in the second: Caubet and Poplin 1992: 94–95, 100. Barnett (1982: 7) discusses discernible distinctions between Indian and African elephant ivory and between African woodland (east) and savannah ivory, although such close identification of ivories has been published infrequently. Collon (1977: 219–22) presents evidence for importation to Assyria of live elephants from India during the first millennium. Gill (1992: 233–34) points to literary evidence from the Classical period of ivory from Phoenician northwest Africa arriving in the central Mediterranean and Aegean, but the ultimate origin of that ivory must have been the sub-Saharan savannah belt. Some of the otherwise unidentified ivories to which I have assigned a Near Eastern origin may have arrived via the west, but probably only some late in the period under study. It is possible also that African savannah ivory could have reached Crete both via Sudan and Egypt and via a trans-Sahara route in the west.

[102] Sakellarakis 1993: 361.

[103] Dr. Hartmut Mätthaus graciously supplied the information in this paragraph in personal communication; it is based on a presentation he delivered at the Taverna at Knossos early in 1994. I am grateful for his permission to cite this material.

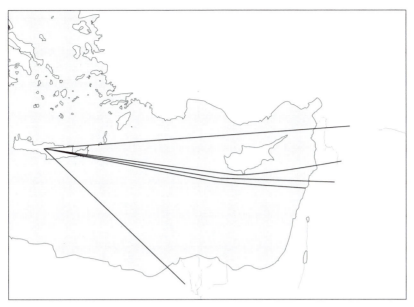

Map 24. Origins of Overseas Artifacts at the Idaean Cave, Ninth and Eighth Centuries

served North Syrian bowl, decorated with pairs of bulls and comparable in shape to a bowl from the Athenian Kerameikos (IC.2), dates to the ninth century. Several other fragments of North Syrian bowls with figured decoration date to the ninth century (IC.4), and there is a North Syrian bowl with animal friezes (IC.83), dating to the eighth century, comparable to the shields from the cave. Two Phoenician bowls are decorated with egyptianizing sphinxes (IC.79), and one of them is closely comparable to finds from Nimrud. There are several other fragments of decorated Phoenician bowls: part of a bull bowl (IC.80), a fragment with scarabs and falcons (IC.81), and a fragment with pseudo-hieroglyphs (IC.81). From Cyprus there are several bowls with lotus handles and other types (IC.57–58). A number of items are certainly Oriental but cannot be attributed closely to particular regions: some bowls with movable swing-handles (IC.54), bowls with ribbed decoration (*Zungenphialen* in German; IC.55), and one bowl with a spike omphalos (IC.53). Another small bronze jug has close parallels at Megiddo (IC.59). Conspicuously absent from the Idaean

Cave bronzes are omphalos bowls, and cauldrons with lion or griffin protomes, so common at Olympia, Delphi, and Samos.

For small objects consistent with travelers' dedications, there are a scarab (IC.64) and a cylinder seal (IC.65), a faience statuette of Bes (IC.105) and a faience figurine of a flute player, and two fibulae (IC.99–100).[104] Even allowing that this is an incomplete listing of such finds from the cave, these dedications have a different character from those at the Samian Heraion and Perachora, where a large number of votives has been found. Despite the relative proximity to the port town at Kommos, the foreign finds at the Idaean Cave do not give the appearance of the cave's having attracted travelers wishing for luck.[105] That kind of dedication appears to have lodged with the successive temples at Kommos. The small finds that could be interpreted as the votives of travelers are Cretan. Maps 24 through 26 plot the foreign sources of artifacts, dating from the ninth through the seventh century, found in the Idaean Cave. Map 24 records the provenances of the early items, dated to the ninth or early eighth century. They are

---

[104] Catalogue item IC.66 is a large array of faiences, some broken pieces from vessels, but otherwise undescribed. These and other faiences from the Idaean Cave are under study by Dr. E. J. Peltenburg: personal communication from Dr. I. A. Sakellarakis.

[105] Compare the foreign dedications at the sanctuary of Artemis at Pherai, the Perachora sanctuaries, the Samian Heraion, and Olympia, catalogued by Kilian-Dirlmeier (1985: 244–53), and even those in the Sanctuary of Zeus Thenatos at Amnisos, catalogued by Schäfer (1992: Area D).

exclusively from the Near East, including Egypt but excluding Cyprus. Map 25 indicates the origins of items dated clearly to the eighth century; the eastern orientation is still the strongest, including possible Cypriot material, but there are possible western connections now. The seventh-century connections are shown in Map 26. The eastern connections have become less diverse, while there are links to central Greece—Attica/Boeotia and Corinthia—and to Phoenician North Africa. Table 2 summarizes the origins and chronologies of the artifacts from the Idaean Cave.

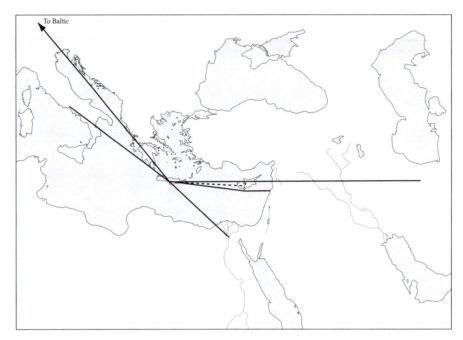

Map 25. Origins of Overseas Artifacts at the Idaean Cave, Eighth Century

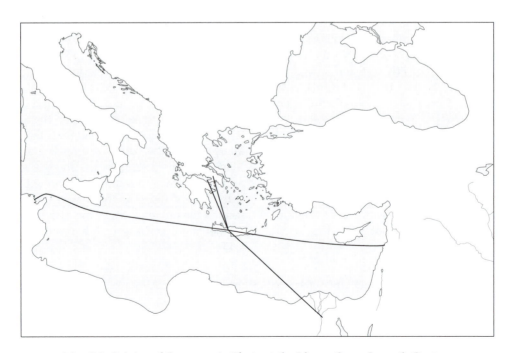

Map 26. Origins of Overseas Artifacts at the Idaean Cave, Seventh Century

TABLE 2. Origins and Dates of Overseas Artifacts Found at the Idaean Cave

Period	Period frequency	Egypt	North Syria	Syria	Phoenicia	Near East	Cyprus	Other
1100–1050	0	0	0	0	0	0	0	0
1050–1000	1	1	0	0	0	0	0	0
1000–950	0	0	0	0	0	0	0	0
950–900	0	0	0	0	0	0	0	0
900––850	1	0	1	0	0	0	0	0
850–800	61	5	25.5	13	0.5	15	2	0
800–750	24	1	1	1	16.5	2	0.5	2[a,b]
750–700	11	0	5	0	2	0	0	4[c]
700–650	7	1.5	0	0	1.5	0	0	4[d]
650–600	4	2	0	0	1	1	0	0
Origin frequency	109	10.5	32.5	14	21.5	18	2.5	10

[a] Italy.
[b] Balkans.
[c] Italy, Baltic, Mainland Greece.
[d] Corinth, Attica/Boeotia, Western Phoenician sites.

The period from the second half of the ninth century to the first half of the eighth is clearly the period of its most intense overseas connections, with some likelihood of a heavier weighting in the earlier half-century. The first half of the ninth century features some foreign artifacts, in roughly the same proportion as they appear in the second half of the eighth century. The items listed in the North Syria column have a strong presumption of being from that region, but some of those listed under the Syria column also may be North Syrian. The artifacts listed in the Near East column, with a few exceptions, simply could not be assigned to closer origins. The clearly identified Phoenician artifacts appear in the following half-century, with overlapping of the North Syrian/Syrian/"Near Eastern" artifacts. This suggests that many of the artifacts identifiable no more closely than "Near Eastern" may in fact be Syrian. Coldstream has identified the second half of the ninth century as a period of eased Assyrian pressure on North Syria, which permitted the kingdoms of that region a short period of prosperity, during which Al Mina was established within the territory of Hama.[106] The beginning of that period probably could be lowered to about 835, and the period lasted until probably the third quarter of the eighth century in North Syria, and until around mid-eighth century in Phoenicia.

What exactly is to be made of this chronological correlation between Assyrian activity in the Levantine coast and its hinterland and Syrian and Phoenician artifacts at the Idaean Cave is not obvious. The first half of the ninth century could have been a period of strong Syrian demand for foreign goods, accompanying the region's relative prosperity, resulting in Syrian exports overseas. The identity of the people who carried the Syrian material to Crete—and to Greece in general during this period—has been much debated, but the importance of answering that question is disproportionate to the energy spent discussing it. Syrians clearly were compensated for the Syrian material found in Crete, whether in Cretan goods, in the goods of a third-party carrier who received Cretan goods, or in

---

[106] Coldstream 1977: 93.

the goods of some fourth, fifth, or whatever, party. And equally clearly, Cretans paid for this material, either to Syrians or to someone else. The only story that avoids this set of payments is a dedication by a traveling Syrian—in fact, quite a number of Syrians over a generation or a little more—that seems on the border of incredibility; even then, the Syrians' food and lodging while in Crete are likely to have required some form of payment. An accounting of the chronology of these contacts should not overlook the continued appearance of Phoenician and other Near Eastern artifacts outside this century at other sites on Crete (see Table 3, p. 1XX). Sakellarakis himself implicitly characterized the Syrian dedications at Ida as the consequence of "the commerce of the period."[107]

The early, possible Argive fibulae from Phaistos (FS.1) are outliers in terms of provenance. Considering the strength of the eastern material at this group of sites, even excepting the Idaean Cave, the Argive provenance might be reconsidered as Cypriot; but there are no other reported Cypriot finds either. A fibula could have traveled overland between sites in Crete, say from Knossos, probably more easily than pottery could have, so we need not think only in terms of direct contact. However, Argive material is not common at the Knossos sites either.

Kaloi Limenes, on the coast just west of Lasaia, is reported to be the find site of nine imported vases (eight Attic, one Corinthian) from the Mitsotakis Collection, dating between about 750 and 675. Unfortunately, no information about the find context is available for these pieces. As noted below, Lasaia is a site with ancient slag from high-phosphorus iron, although it has not been identified as an occupied Early Iron Age site. The relatively large number of Attic vases contrasts with the relative scarcity of Attic material published from nearby Kommos. Around 100 faience votives have been found in the cave sanctuary of Eileithyia at Inatos, on the south coast about fifty kilometers east of Lasaia, and a bronze wall-bracket for a torch, with a remarkably close Cypriot parallel, has been found in a grave near Priansos, slightly to the northwest of Inatos, with Cretan pottery dating from the Protogeometric to the Orientalizing periods. Fragments of four-sided stands of Cypriot style have been found at the open-air sanctuary of Hermes and Aphrodite at Kato Syme Viannou. Catling has suggested them as Cypriot imports, but Matthäus and others have declined to so identify them, and evidence of bronze casting has been found on the site.[108] I have not included the Kato Syme bronzes in the list of imports. However, a fragment of a bronze sistrum (KTS.1), probably Syrian or Phoenician, just possibly Cypriot, is a late eighth- to seventh-century find from Kato Syme, and one faience scarab (KTS.2), probably East Greek or Egyptian, is reported from a seventh-century deposit there.

The eastern material from the Cave of Eileithyia recently has been analyzed and reported in detail. At least eighty-eight pieces of Iron Age Aegyptiaca are reported to have come from the cave, some thirty of which are in the Metaxas Collection.[109] Several pieces are securely Egyptian (INT.13–14, 54), and for thirty-seven pieces, analysis of design only cannot distinguish between an Egyptian or a Rhodian provenance. The dedicators appear to have understood the Egyptian significance of the foreign votives. The Egyptian votives appear to have been selected for their reference to health in childbearing, which is appropriate in dedications to Eileithyia, and even the numerous scarabs may have represented an appeal to the Egyptian reputation for medical knowledge, spells, and charms.[110] Several of the scarabs have close, datable parallels among the Perachora-Rhodes scarabs from Perachora, which may place some of the Inatos dedications as early as the late eighth century rather than bunching the vast majority of them in the last third of the seventh century. The proximity to Kommos cannot be ignored as a possible point of entry for these votives, and there appear to be

[107] Sakellarakis 1988: 210.

[108] Catling 1984: 89; Matthäus 1988: 290; Blome (1982: 25) considers the Kato Syme material to be of conventional, Cretan Geometric type. The excavator considered it Cretan: Lembesi 1975a: 329. On the bronze casting, French 1992: 59.

[109] Skon-Jedele 1994: 1768–1804. Phillips (1991: 786–89) reports four earlier Egyptian pieces, one of which (no. 391) she believes might be of Iron Age date, a white faience scarab in the Metaxas Collection. Alternatively, it could be as early as the Twelfth Dynasty, or possibly a Minoan copy.

[110] Skon-Jedele 1994: 1779–80.

Levantine or perhaps Phoenician artifacts at Kommos at a consistent time (KM.10–11, 14–15, 18, 29), as well as some Egyptian dedications in the Greek Temple B (KM.8–9, 12–13). The Rhodian and other East Greek presence at Kommos otherwise appears late in the seventh century.

In a recent reexamination of Temple A at Prinias, Watrous has inferred a number of Egyptian influences in the architecture of that building, from the clenched fists in the monumental goddesses' laps, characteristic of Egyptian but not Near Eastern sculpture, to the position of the goddesses on the lintel above the recessed and sculpted door jambs. To date, the Prinias temple is the earliest known example of architectural sculpture in Greece, and it appears in a fully developed, sophisticated combination of frieze, orthostate, and lintel sculpture, lending the impression that its development is to be sought elsewhere. Comparing a number of the characteristics of the facade of the temple at Prinias with the Sixth Dynasty mastaba of Tjetu at Giza, Watrous suggests that the Egyptian influence probably is attributable to observations by Cretans visiting Lower Egypt.[111] The Egyptian architectural elements are combined with substantial Cretan and Near Eastern imagery into a thoroughly Greek temple that Watrous believes to have been devoted to Artemis and the Kouretes. Some thirty-five years earlier, Boardman had suggested that the relieving triangle over the door of Temple A at Prinias may have been a feature borrowed from Egypt, and he believed that these influences, in combination with this Cretan experiment in monumental stone sculpture at Prinias and the limestone palm capitals from Arkades, pointed to direct Cretan contact with Egypt, unmodified by a circuit through the Near East.[112] Additionally, Boardman found the hairstyle on the bronze figure of a youth from Phaistos, dated to the late (or even the mid-) seventh century, strikingly un-Cretan and persuasively similar to original Egyptian types, closer than to Near Eastern imitations of the Egyptian type. The body of the figurine is very much like those of Greek kouroi, altogether suggesting local production under a strong and, Boardman believed,

direct Egyptian influence, although he did not elaborate on the sort of influence that might have produced such an Egypto-Cretan amalgamation.[113] A few miles to the southeast of Prinias and Phaistos, Lembesi reports very close copying of Egyptian motifs of animal- and offering-bearers in bronze cut-out plaques found at the sanctuary of Kato Syme Viannou. Plaque A7, dated to c. 670–650, is very close to the Egyptian motif of the animal-bearer, whereas plaques dated from c. 650/40 to 600 show greater modification with Cretan elements. These plaques appear to be products of a single workshop, which Lembesi calls the Syme Workshop, although its location at or near the sanctuary remains undemonstrated.[114] These Egyptian influences in the small arts as well as the monumental may reflect different elements of closer interactions between Crete and Egypt in the seventh century.

Foreigners resident in Crete are a well-discussed topic, as I note below, but suggestions that Cretan archaeological evidence points to Cretans having traveled abroad have not commanded similar attention as a component of Crete's external relations. Certainly, Cretan copies of Cypriot and Protocorinthian pottery shapes and decoration are common throughout the island, possibly even more common than the genuine imported articles themselves, and though there have been suggestions of Cretan visits to Cyprus in the twelfth and eleventh centuries, these pottery imitations have not compelled suggestions of Cretan visits overseas to get the ideas to be copied at home. The architectural similarities, with their differences in transportability of the objects involved, reasonably demand a different explanation, while the statuette from Phaistos falls into an intermediate category. If the Egyptian elements in the temple at Prinias are attributable to observations of Cretans abroad, not just any Cretan traveler is a reasonable candidate. The traveling Cretan must have been socially and intellectually capable of both making the observations and influencing costly architectural work at home. A common sailor would not do, nor would an ordinary mercenary, although the latter must have had his

---

[111] Watrous 1995: 5, 9–10.

[112] Boardman 1961: 152, 170. On the palm capitals from Arkades, Levi 1927–29: 187, 451, 700, figs. 206 and 586.

[113] Boardman 1961: 119–20.

[114] Lembesi 1985: 229–33, 238. No contextual evidence survives for the plaques at Syme, so the chronological assignments are made on the basis of parallels with Protocorinthian, Corinthian, and Protoattic pottery (82, 224).

leaders. Neither would the architectural observer be likely to have made the bronze figurine from Phaistos with the suggestively Egyptian head: a bronzesmith and a monumental stone architect seem far from one another to my way of thinking. The latter's work commits a society to far greater outlays than does the former's, and I believe their social orbits would have differed correspondingly. Both these architectural features and the bronze figurine seem plausible candidates to represent the results of Cretan experience abroad. Not all of the foreign artistic influences on the island seem compatible with such an accounting—for example, the bronze shields from the Idaean Cave and the Tekke jewelery, which I discuss below.

Sites in Western Crete

Western Crete has been far less explored than the central and eastern parts of the island, and what appears to be lack of ancient activity may instead be, at least partly, lack of excavation. The recent excavations at Chania have begun to alter ideas about the Late Minoan period, but little Dark Age material has emerged from Chania, and only two Dark Age foreign artifacts have been reported from the recent Greek-Swedish excavations at that site.[115] The first foreign artifact at Chania is a Late Geometric krater, possibly Euboean or Parian (CHN.2), from beneath the Kastelli, which Tzedakis permitted Coldstream to publish.[116] The second is a neck sherd of a Euboean SOS amphora (CHN.3), probably Chalkidian, which Johnston and Jones date to the last quarter of the eighth century.[117] It was probably an oil container.[118] Together these two artifacts may be quite significant as an indication of commercial activity between Euboea and western Crete despite the paucity of the finds. Two mold-made terracotta Astarte figurines (CHN.5) from Chania are attributed to Phoenicia or North Syria, and several writers have suggested that

immigrant craftsmen from the Assyrian empire may have been involved in the carving of the limestone building slab (CHN.4) first reported in the publication of the German excavations of 1942. The three archers on the slab, one above another, are a characteristically Assyrian motif. Excavation of a pit at Chania has yielded some imported Archaic pottery, none of which is necessarily later than the sixth century, although more precise dating does not appear to be possible.[119] The pit was thoroughly mixed, with LM IIIB material appearing in the same strata as Geometric and Archaic. The earliest sherds are from MM IIIB, continuing through all the phases of LM IIIC, and into Protogeometric. The Geometric group was the most numerous, followed by the Archaic. Most of the imported pieces are too small to date very precisely; one small body sherd (no. 82) shows a ray pattern, but it neither helps distinguish the origin (Athens or Corinth) nor narrows down the date. The excavators suggested "perhaps Athens" for some of the sherds with a very fine black glaze. It is not certain whether any of these pieces are as early as the late seventh century. From a pithos grave in a river bank just outside Chania comes an imported lidded pyxis said only to be from "the Aegean" (CHN.1) and dated to the Protogeometric period.[120]

Foreign artifacts have been found in both older and recent excavations at Eleutherna and, from nearly a century ago, in the Cave of Hermes Kronaios, near modern Patso and the site of ancient Sybrita. Eleutherna is roughly one-third of the way between Herakleion and the west end of the island, about ten kilometers from the north coast. At least one of the foreign artifacts at Eleutherna, an Egyptian faience seal said to be of the Twentieth to Twenty-Second Dynasty, suggests contact sometime between the Subminoan and the Cretan Protogeometric periods. Pieces of a large bronze bowl and its tripod base have been found in the recent excavation in a deposit

---

[115] Hallager and Tzedakis (1984: 19–20; 1985: 26, 28; 1986: 26; and 1988: 48) note the abandonment of Chania during LM IIIC and its reoccupation during the Geometric and Archaic periods, but report no foreign material between the LM IIIB and Hellenistic periods. Though Chania has yielded a considerable number of foreign artifacts from the Late Minoan period, nothing has been noted for the Early Iron Age in the site's progress reports; but the excavations there have been quite restricted in area.

[116] Coldstream 1971: 8, pl. 3e.

[117] Johnston and Jones 1978: 114.

[118] Ibid.: 140; Klein 1971: 206.

[119] Tzedakis and Kanta 1978: 30–34, 40, pl. 16.82.

[120] Andreadhaki Vlasaki 1991: 414.

that may range from Geometric to Archaic, but Stampoulidis suggests it may have been an heirloom, produced in the eleventh or tenth century, probably in Cyprus.[121] Among the earlier ceramics are larger pottery pieces of Attic and Corinthian Middle to Late Geometric (EL.3–4) and some Cycladic Late Geometric sherds, one possibly Theran (EL.7), others possibly Naxian (EL.8). Later pottery is all Corinthian. A Near Eastern representation appears in the form of fragments of a molded glass phiale (EL.6) and hundreds of multicolored faience beads (EL.5), assigned to Phoenicia or Egypt. Four ivory heads (EL.15), possibly from a piece of furniture, were recovered from the remains of a funerary pyre; they seem to have been carved locally, or at least in Crete. Considerable chronological disagreement surrounded the early Laconian III krater (EL.16) shortly after its publication.[122] Boardman's reassessment of Spartan chronology could put it well into the second quarter of the sixth century or later, but recent developments in excavations at Sparta tend to raise the segment of Laconian chronology affected by the sand layer—between the late seventh century and the early sixth—above Boardman's downdating.[123] It seems reasonable to place this krater from Eleutherna around the very end of the seventh century or the beginning of the sixth.[124]

Map 27 displays the external linkages of Eleutherna over a fairly lengthy period, but altogether, Eleutherna does not appear to have been as cosmopolitan as the diversity of its external contacts would suggest. The links to Greece are more clearly identified; the eastern linkages are no less real, but their exact provenances are less certain. Nonetheless, the diversity of Eleutherna's overseas linkages is striking; but it may represent a relatively well-to-do area whose occupants were prosperous enough to acquire

occasional foreign items arriving at a site like Knossos rather than an independent, western importer. That is, from the perspective of Eleutherna, these contacts may be the result of interregional rather than international exchange.

The Cave of Hermes Kronaios is near the road running from Phaistos and Kommos in the south to the north coast, passing through Eleutherna. The cave is to the west of Mt. Ida and is roughly two-thirds of the way to Eleutherna from Phaistos.[125] That cave has produced a much-remarked-upon Near Eastern-style bronze figurine of a god, presumed to be Reshef. Evans considered it to be a Mycenaean-period import, although it previously had been judged to be an early first-millennium Syrian or Phoenician piece.[126] Helck has considered it Syrian but has been reluctant to commit to a chronology.[127] Hoffman has studied the artistic characteristics of the piece and the historiography of its provenance assignments. She concludes that it definitely is not Cretan and favors a Near Eastern origin and an eleventh-century date for it, although there are insufficient known parallels from the Levant to attribute it to any specific workshop group or region at present.[128] The cave at Patso also has yielded a bronze figurine that Pilali-Papasteriou calls a goat and for which she notes a Cypriot ceramic parallel from Myrtou-Pighades, as well as a ninth-century Argive bronze statuette to which it has similarities.[129] The figurine from Patso has the horns of an agrimi, quite similar to those on vase 45 from Fortetsa Tomb VI—the famous ship-and-goat vase.[130] I have not included the figurine in the catalogue. Recent reinvestigation of Patso Cave has identified a fragment of a clay stand made of Attic fabric, with Attic Late Protogeometric decoration (PTS.2). Two similar stands have been found in Grave 48 of the Kerameikos Cemetery in

---

[121] Stampoulidis 1990a: 388, 393 nn. 38–40.

[122] Hartley 1930–31: 111, fig. 34.6–7; 1931–32: 251–53; Droop 1931–32: 247–48.

[123] Boardman 1963a: 4.

[124] Raising the date of the sand layer at the Sanctuary of Artemis Orthia are Catling (1977a: 36) and Cavanagh and Laxton (1984: 34–35). Carter (1987: 358) tentatively accepts the updating implications of the recent analyses.

[125] Pendlebury 1939: 8, 13, map 2. Dunbabin 1947: fig. 2, 187.

[126] Evans 1901: 125 n. 2, fig. 15.

[127] Helck 1979: 179–80 n. 44.

[128] Hoffman 1990: 26–27, 91–95.

[129] Pilali-Papasteriou 1985: 88–89, 178, no. 219, pl. 21.

[130] Brock 1957: 12, no. 45, pl. 135. Brock also called the animals goats. For comparison of Cretan and Cypriot goats, see the array of goats on Cypriot Proto-White Painted ware in Iacovou 1988: figs. 2, 26, 36, 62, 71–73 (all her cat. no. 30), 74, 83.

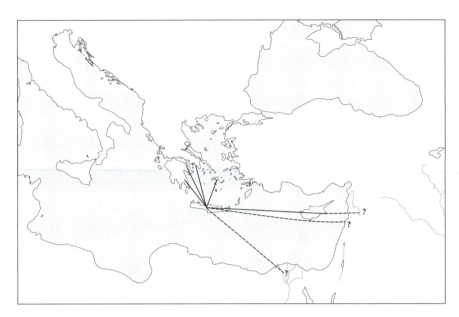

Map 27. Origins of Overseas Artifacts at Eleutherna, Geometric to Late Orientalizing/Early Archaic Periods

Athens.[131] Levi cited an unspecified number of fragments of miniature faience vases in Late Geometric to Orientalizing material from the Patso Cave (PTS.3).[132] They sound Rhodian, but I have listed them in the catalogue only as from the "East."

From Kissamo is the bronze pomegranate (KSM.1), presumably from a stand and attributed tentatively to Cyprus. In a vase purchased by Evans, together with a wide chronological mixture of Cretan items, it was said to have come from a chamber tomb at Kissamo, but its context is irretrievably lost. It remains an intriguing item, and speculation about it, which could be unbounded, is best cut short. A possible Attico-Boeotian fibula in the Chania Museum (KSM.2) is probably from somewhere in western Crete, and I have included it with the finds from sites around Kissamo simply for convenience. A glazed-composition (faience) bead (KSM.3) and an unidentifiable fragment of "blue frit" (KSM.4) probably are either East Greek or Egyptian. Late seventh- to early sixth-century Corinthian vases are reported from Polyrhenia (KSM.6), about five kilometers south of Kissamo, and at Phalasarna

(KSM.5), on the west coast, nearly due west of Kissamo.

Although excavated foreign artifacts from western Crete are sparse, several vases have been found in that part of the island that have led the excavators and other scholars to point to overseas contact, probably trade in some cases. Coulson has noted close parallels between several tenth- to ninth-century vases at Modi and Vryses in western Crete and Dark Age II (975–850) vases in Messenia, particularly at Rizes, and at Sparta.[133] He concluded that either the pottery of the two regions—the western Peloponnese and western Crete—developed from the same Mycenaean stock, or, "despite the assumption of a general low ebb in the seagoing trade in the Dark Age, contacts existed between Messenia and West Crete." Graves at Gavalomouri have produced three locally made flasks closely related to the Cypriot flask, two dated to the early eighth century, one to the late eighth century. In this connection, Coulson notes that two of the bell-shaped skyphoi shapes at Modi and in Messenia also have parallels at Alaas on Cyprus.[134]

---

[131] Kübler 1943: pl. 25, inv. nos. 2028, 2029.

[132] Levi 1927–29: 460; cited in Skon-Jedele 1994: 1904, 1908.

[133] Messenia: Coulson 1986: 10, 28 n. 5; 1983b: 76, 80, 320; McDonald and Coulson 1983: 320. Sparta: Coulson 1985: 57; cup type P1, of the mid-tenth century, is found at Sparta, Nichoria, and Vryses.

[134] Tzedakis 1979: 192–98; Coulson 1983b: 76.

Grave I at Gavalomouri has yielded three Attic Middle Geometric II vases and one Cycladic skyphos of the same time period. Reported in the same grave is a late eighth-century skyphos similar to a Rhodian Late Geometric example from Kameiros, but it is unclear whether the Gavalomouri specimen is a Cretan copy or an import, and I have not included it in the catalogue.[135]

Among the few Early Iron Age pieces from the 1942 German excavations in western Crete are two sherds from Aptera that warrant attention, although I have not included either piece in the catalogue, to risk erring on the conservative side about adding sites with foreign artifacts.[136] Drerup reported three Geometric sherds from the sanctuary at Aptera, one with circles joined by running tangents (from lower left to upper right), another with wavy lines, the third a shoulder fragment with a band of hourglasses in frieze.[137] The circle-and-running-tangent motif was quite popular on Thera, although it is not unknown on Naxian pottery—and even Attic—and a motif of that general type has appeared on a local pithos lid from Fortetsa.[138] The Theran circles connected by running tangents generally have a dot at the center, as does the Aptera sherd—as well as Hartley's sherd from west of the acropolis at Eleutherna, which she suggested as possibly Theran.[139] The motif on the Fortetsa lid does not have the central dot and has a heavier outer concentric circle than do the Theran examples or either the Aptera or the Eleutherna sherds. Drerup did not suggest that any of the three Geometric sherds from Aptera were non-Cretan, but he did accept that possibility for the Eleutherna sherd.[140] The vertical wavy-line motif on Aptera sherd 72.1 also differs from the

appearance of the vertical wavy-line motif found on various Fortetsa pieces, and I can find no other Cretan example comparable to the Aptera motif.[141] The lines of the Aptera motif are thinner and less regular in the wave pattern than the Fortetsa vertical wavy lines, and they taper toward the bottom; the irregularity of the Aptera motif corresponds more closely to Theran examples (but not all Theran vertical wavy lines) than to the Fortetsa motif and other Cretan examples. A sanctuary location for imported pottery in western Crete would not be extraordinary, although the other major Cretan sanctuaries have not yielded large concentrations of imported Greek pottery. The Diktaean Cave offers four Corinthian vases from the seventh century (DC.23–26); Kommos shows a few Corinthian pieces from the Temple area (KM.16–17, 19, 22); two Corinthian kotylai are reported from an Early Orientalizing context at the Idaean Cave (IC.102); Amnisos has a Corinthian piece each from the Sanctuary of Zeus and the Cave of Eileithyia (AMN.6–7); and only a single import, probably East Greek or Egyptian, is reported from the Sanctuary of Hermes and Aphrodite at Kato Syme, whereas the Cave of Eileithyia at Inatos has yielded imports only of East Greek and other Near Eastern votives.

Only one foreign artifact from before the sixth century—the aryballos from Phalasarna (KSM.5)—has been reported along the far western coast. The pattern of provenances from the sites yielding foreign artifacts before the sixth century is scattered, but is representative of the sources of foreign artifacts in the rest of Crete. Subsequent excavations may reveal a more distinct regional pattern of external interactions. In the sixth century, Corinthian vases are very

---

[135] Andreadaki-Vlasaki 1985: 27.

[136] On the German excavations during World War II, Matz (1951) reports Minoan and later graves in western Crete but declares no foreign artifacts; Jantzen (1964: 60–62) reports no foreign artifacts.

[137] Drerup 1951: 105, pl. 72.3 for the running-tangents sherd and pl. 72.1 for the wavy-lines piece. Coldstream (1968: 234 n. 3) casually refers to the Aptera sherds 72.2 and 72.3 as west Cretan, but does not mention the wavy-lines piece.

[138] Fortetsa: Brock 1957: 69, 176, no. 767, pl. 49, motif 9ah. Thera: Dragendorff 1903: figs. 141, 143, 148a–b, 170, 312–14, 320–21, 324, 330–32, 334, 343, 344a, 346a–b, 350, 361–62; none of these, of course, has a recommended Cretan provenance. Naxos: Coldstream 1968: pl. 35. Athens: Brann 1962: 68, nos. 325–31, pl. 19 top; note some of the tangents running from upper left to lower right; 71, no. 357, pl. 21.

[139] Hartley 1930–31: 109–10, fig. 34.5. Hood and Boardman (1961: 77 n. 8) suggest Hartley's Eleutherna sherds of fig. 34.3–4 and fig. 35 as possibly Naxian on the basis of Hartley's brief description of the fabrics, but do not mention the sherd with the running tangents.

[140] Drerup 1951: 105 n. 2.

[141] Fortetsa: Brock 1957: 175, motif 8c. Thera: Dragendorff 1903: figs. 23a, 49a, 134a–b, 195.

prominent at Phalasarna, to be superseded by Attic vases in the fifth. Gondicas notes that the passage of Attic merchants through Crete in later times, beyond the period of this study, is well known, and that the island was a station on the grain route between Attica and Africa.[142] No such evidence for external contact has been found for the Geometric period on the west coast of Crete, but the island's role as a way station between various end points on trade routes may apply to sites in other parts of Crete in earlier times. Ships may have stopped specifically for Cretan products or for revictualing, repairs, or crew replacements.

FOREIGN WORKERS AND OTHER IMMIGRANTS IN CRETE

Cases have been made in greater and lesser detail for the presence of foreign workers or other immigrants in Crete. North Syrians have been detected in the goldsmith's tomb at Fortetsa, in the limestone warrior's head at Amnisos, in the urn burials and local ceramic versions of North Syrian artifacts at Arkades, and in immigrant (or at least foreign) construction workers (architects?) in the foundation deposit of the temple on the acropolis at Gortyn.[143] The discourse over the presence of North Syrian bronze workers behind the shields from the Idaean Cave, at one or more removes, is well known, while Barnett's tentative suggestion of expatriate ivory carvers has sustained less attention.[144] Resident Assyrians have been inferred from the bronze belt at Fortetsa and from the limestone stele at Chania.[145] Coldstream's Phoenician unguent factory at Knossos, along the lines of his similar suggestion for Rhodes, is familiar by now.[146] I have relied on several of these suggestions in the catalogue to indicate the possible presence of foreign labor on Crete—AMN.3 and CHN.2. Several different bases of reasoning have been used in these identifications: artistic motifs in the

cases of the Fortetsa bronze belt and the Chania relief; artistic motifs and artisan techniques in the cases of the Idaean Cave shields and the Khaniale Tekke goldsmiths; burial practices in a supporting role in the case of the Tekke goldsmiths and, together with foreign-inspired, locally produced ceramic artifacts, in a leading role in the interpretation of foreign residents—but not craftsmen—at Arkades. The choice of subject was the basis of suspicion that a North Syrian craftsman carved the warrior's head found at Amnisos. The apparent vegetable contents of the foundation deposit beneath the temple at Gortyn suggested the presence of North Syrian workmen to Burkert.

In each case, further attention to detail of motif, technique, or burial practice can weaken the case for immigrant presence as easily as strengthen it. Hoffman's detailed examinations of the proposed immigrants at Arkades and Khaniale Tekke in particular reveal the sensitivity of conclusions to the level of detail that one believes to be relevant.[147] Her project was an initial effort to find whether a set of principles could be derived to infer foreign craftsmen from artifacts themselves and components of their excavation circumstances, short of unambiguous inscriptions—which, of course, would take most of the intellectual burden from the logical exercises.[148] She concluded that a substantial amount of detailed work focused on artifacts, by numerous scholars using a common analytical framework, might eventually be able to distinguish products of foreign craftsmen to a reasonable degree of satisfaction.

Carter finds striking iconographical similarities between the sculpture of Temple A at Prinias and the Prinias steles on the one hand and the reliefs on ninth-century orthostat blocks from the Processional Entry at Carchemish on the other—with sufficiently detailed correspondence to suggest a connection between them, although the

---

[142] Gondicas 1988: 302–6.

[143] The goldsmiths: Boardman 1967: 57–66; Lembesi 1975b: 173. Amnisos warrior's head: Adams 1978: 5–8. Arkades urn burials: Boardman 1970a: 20–23; 1980: 60–61. Construction workers at Gortyn: Burkert 1985: 52; 1992: 55.

[144] The literature on the Syrian bronzesmiths at some distance behind the Idaean Cave shields is extensive, and I refer to Hoffman's thorough review of it (1990: 144–48). The North Syrian ivory carvers: Barnett 1948: 6.

[145] Boardman 1978: 11; 1980: 74; Adams 1978: 11–13.

[146] Coldstream 1984a: 137; for Rhodes, Coldstream 1969: 1–8.

[147] Hoffman 1990: 134–43, 162–80.

[148] It is not obvious that we would be able to identify a Cretan presence at Gela if it were not for the historical record that a consortium of Rhodians and Cretans colonized the site. The identifications of certain artifacts at Gela as locally made by Cretan immigrants would be insupportable without the assistance from Thucydides.

work demonstrates the integration of Levantine elements into Cretan forms.[149] But did Cretans visit Carchemish and bring the idea back to Prinias, or did inhabitants of Carchemish resident around Prinias suggest the sculptural program? Carter favors the latter mechanism on the basis of chronology. The Prinias architecture dates to the later seventh century, but the Carchemish relief procession was visible till Nebuchadnezzar's destruction of the city in 606/5; Til Barsib eclipsed Carchemish as a river port during the seventh century, making the latter city a less likely site to be visited—and copied—by foreigners, including Cretans, as the seventh century progressed. Carter's alternative is expatriate Carchemish residents, departing after that city's capture by Sargon in 717, resident in the vicinity of Prinias, persuading local Cretans to copy some magnificent architecture of their home city. I have no quarrel with this chronological justification for Syrian emigrants rather than Cretan travelers, but it does not seem compelling to me. I have no difficulty envisioning Cretans visiting a secondary city on a trip in Assyrian territory—Cretans who were capable of absorbing the Syrian symbolism—and I see no forceful reason to prefer one mechanism over the other. The mechanism of Carchemenes in Crete gains force from the other instances of hypothesized Syrians in Crete, but few of those cases seem compelling on their own, and the compounding of individually uncompelling cases need not lead to a compelling aggregate case, particularly since they are independent rather than correlated cases.

Elsewhere, relying primarily on economic models of relevant behavior and organization, and secondarily on characteristics of artifacts, I have found Coldstream's hypothesis of Phoenician unguent factories to be difficult to sustain if one insists on seeing those factories as part of a centralized Phoenician network benefiting owners in the homeland.[150] The associations of the archaeological material in Coldstream's hypothesis are insightful and interesting, but I believe the behavior required to sustain such "factories" as overseas branches rather than as independent operations to have been unlikely. The branch unguent-factory hypothesis lends itself particularly well to behavioral scrutiny because it involves a particular set of activities.

In general, the other hypothesized cases of foreign craftsmen or other immigrants do not offer enough of a story behind the immigrants to explore the logical structure of any behavior. Expulsions or evacuations from Near Eastern wars are the most detailed speculations anyone has ventured, and it is possible that those events alone would not distinguish their behavior from that of native residents. Lembesi has offered a behavioral correspondence between several characteristics of artifacts and the identity of the craftsmen: the subject and decoration of a product made by an Eastern craftsman working in Greece would be Greek since the object would have been ordered by a Greek patron, but the style would be Eastern because of the craftsman's inability to adjust immediately to local styles. Greek character with a shape and decoration from the East would indicate a Greek craftsman. These rules of thumb are not entirely unlike those used by Boardman in thinking about the ceramic objects he considered to have been ordered by Eastern immigrants around Arkades. One problem with implementing Lembesi's rule of thumb lies in defining and gaining agreement in practice on Greek and Eastern techniques or "character." And ultimately, the behavior Lembesi attributes to the artisans is automatic, leaving no flexibility for individuals to take advantage of opportunities or otherwise to adapt to circumstances—but also not distinguishing between alternative motives for the presence of foreign craftsmen. Were they invited guests, there of their own accord to seek their own advantages, there to save their skins from the flames back home? These motivations for emigration from the East could give different objectives to foreign craftsmen in how they served local demands. An Easterner in Crete of his own accord might find it to his advantage to maximize the distinctiveness of his products, while a refugee might simply try to fit in. These particular objectives are speculations, of course, but they exemplify the types of relationship that could have existed between motivation for emigration and practice in Crete.

Burkert's suggestion that the characteristics of the foundation deposit under the temple at Gortyn indicate the presence of North Syrian workers leaves open what I believe are some

---

[149] Carter 1995: 14–15.
[150] Jones 1993: 293–303.

important specifics, the devil being in the details. Would the North Syrians have been master craftsmen or architects—possibly *the* architect (surely these skills were distinguishable at this time, at least in the Near East, even if they were combined sometimes in Greek lands)? What sort of occupation involved in raising a temple would be permitted to define or otherwise contribute to the contents of a foundation deposit for a religious building? The Greeks were fairly catholic in their religious practices, so letting a foreigner conduct one of his dedicatory practices would not have been out of the question, but would a master stone craftsman, say, have had sufficient prestige to be allowed such a liberty, or would one have to have been more critically involved in the design of the building?

To conclude a lengthening discussion, I have found no independent grounds on which to evaluate the hypotheses regarding immigrants in Crete and have tacitly endorsed several cases only on the basis of the plausibility of the accounts of artistic influence or source.

CRETAN PRODUCTS FOUND AT SITES OVERSEAS

Though I have found over 800 reports of apparently foreign artifacts at Cretan sites, I have found only 153 reports of apparent or suspected Cretan artifacts at overseas sites, at least six of which were made overseas under, or reflecting, Cretan influence. The only area with Cretan artifacts from the eleventh century is Cyprus. Some, but not all, of these artifacts may indicate population movements rather than exchange of items between groups at fixed locations. Some of the artifacts reminiscent of Crete that have been found in Cyprus may in fact be either from Crete or made by Cretans in Cyprus. From Salamis are a three-legged coarseware cooking pot (8),[151] which may have accompanied a Cretan immigrant, and an incised pitcher (9), both with similarities to examples from Karphi.[152] Also reminis-

cent of Karphi is the incised pitcher from Enkomi (10), dated to the Subminoan period. The terracotta goddesses with upraised arms (11), found at Kition, seem distinctly Minoan and have been considered evidence of Minoan immigrants on Cyprus. Desborough mentioned a krater sherd at Kition of about mid-eleventh century (2) as possibly Cretan. No Cretan, or suspected Cretan, artifacts are found in Cyprus after the eleventh century.

Two artifacts at Mycenae indicate the possibility of continued contact with the mainland during the first half of the eleventh century. Wace excavated a pithos burial containing two stirrup jars and a small jug on the terrace of the Cyclopean Terrace House and dated the burial to after the final destruction at Mycenae. Desborough suggested that the pithos itself, 1.7 meters high, with three rows of running tangent circles separated by wide bands with three wavy lines, would be "more at home in Crete than elsewhere," and Furumark considered stirrup jar no. 1 to be Cretan, dating both to his period LH IIIC1a. Mountjoy, without discussing provenance, dated stirrup jar no. 1 to the later part of her LH IIIC Late.[153] I include the stirrup jar (3) and the pithos (4) in the catalogue. From a Protogeometric cist burial in the west room of the House of Shields at Mycenae, Desborough cited a three-legged askos as having the origin of its shape sought in Crete, Kos, and Cyprus rather than in the Argolid. He recommended only that "there may at this time [tenth century] have been some connection between the Argolid and one or more of these areas."[154] The shape of the body is round, unlike the oblong shape of the duck askos, and the decoration—hatched triangles and wide, dark bands—is more compatible with Cypriot patterns of the time than with Cretan.[155]

Also as early as the eleventh century, but reflecting possible Cretan influence rather than transported products, are house models and house urns found in Latium (in the vicinity of Rome and in the Alban Hills) dating from the

---

[151] Arabic numbers in parentheses in this section refer to the artifact numbers in the catalogue of Cretan artifacts found overseas.

[152] On the three-legged pot, Yon 1971: 28–29; and Seiradaki 1960: 7. On the incised pitcher, Yon 1979: 242; Dikaios 1969a: 316–17; 1971: 492–93; 1969b: pl. 95 no. 26, cf. pl. 106 no. 5.

[153] Wace 1921–22: 406–7, pls. 62.1b (Cretan stirrup jar), 62.2 (relief pithos); Furumark 1944: 197, 200; Desborough 1964: 36; Mountjoy 1986: 186 nn. 11–12, 188.

[154] Desborough 1954: 259–60, pl. 43.

[155] Cf. Pieridou 1973: pls. 16.11, 17.9 (stirrup jars), 23.8 (krater); Karageorghis 1975: pls. 9.13 (amphora), 15.13, 22.B6 (stirrup jars), 40.A7 (hydria).

Late Mycenaean to Subminoan periods (1). Identifying these artifacts as possible representatives of unspecified Cretan influence may be considered controversial, but there seems to be sufficient evidence of movement between the Aegean and Tyrrhenian regions to justify leaving open the possibility that more substantial transmission mechanisms will emerge.[156] If these represent Cretan influence, the people involved may have been the successors of the commercial connections between the Aegean, especially Crete, and southern Italy and Sicily, and predecessors of the founders of the later Greek colonies. Somewhat more substantially, in terms of currently available evidence, Cypriots or Phoenicians traveling between the eastern Mediterranean and Sardinia, or points even farther west, could have been responsible for transportation of these models as early as the eleventh or even the twelfth century. Later house urns found in graves around Tarquinia (11) show less resemblance to Cretan models than do the earlier Latian ones, although they may reflect Cretan and possibly Near Eastern influence via Latium.[157] They are not products of Crete carried overseas, although they may reflect other direct transportation such as population movements at the end of the Late Bronze Age. A number of leech-shaped fibulae with thickened bow (12) appear in Villanovan IA graves just to the east of ancient Tarquinia, and probably reflect some kind of Cretan influence, although they themselves likely are of local manufacture. They have parallels in Subminoan to Protogeometric finds from Vrokastro.[158] The same is the case with the "candelabra" from around ancient Tarquinia, which have similarities to the stand with birds from Fortetsa and are approximately contemporary; according to Hencken, "Some connection may be suspected."[159]

---

[156] Hencken 1968, 2: 467. Recently Mercereau (1993: 2–4) has ruled out links between the commonly termed hut urn (hut models, naiskoi, cylindrical models) found on Crete and those found elsewhere in the Mediterranean, including those in Italy. She rejects Italian influence on the Cretan examples because of the timing involved (fourteenth to eleventh centuries for Crete, tenth to ninth for Italy), as well as Cretan influence on Italian examples, with more involved reasoning: LM III commercial interaction of Crete with Italy, which she accepts, if it survived the twelfth-century disruptions, was not the "substantive and sustained" sort of contact required to affect Italian burial customs. Additionally, find contexts and uses differ between the Cretan and Italian examples. Mercereau accepts the reasoning of Gjerstad (1961: 381–82) and Mavriyannaki (1972: 167–68), *contra* Müller-Karpe. She does not discuss the views of Hencken, who finds Müller-Karpe's chronology preferable to Gjerstad's competing Italian chronology (1968, 2: 657–60) and is unwilling to rule out the possibility of Cretan influence on the hut urns despite the differences in uses and contexts between the Cretan and Italian examples (ibid.: 464–67). Boardman (1961: 170) considered that "there may well have been some connexions [between Crete and central Italy in the early stages of Roman-Alban culture in the tenth century], although not as close as [Müller-Karpe] suggests." Boardman notes the votive character of the objects in Crete and their funereal use in Italy, and believes that Müller-Karpe understated or ignored the Near Eastern origins of, *inter alia*, the house models with figurines within. The currently accepted chronology for early Latium is closer to Müller-Karpe's than to Gjerstad's: cf. Bergonzi and Bietti Sestieri 1980: 62; Bietti Sestieri 1980: 66–67; 1992: 86. Hägg (1990: 100), in searching for origins for the Cretan models, also rejects Italian influence on the Cretan models on the grounds of chronology but notes striking similarities in the arrangements for opening and closing doors in the two regions' models. He does not discuss Cretan influence on the Italian examples in that article, but Mercereau (1993: 3 n. 13) expresses surprise that he could fail to reject the Cretan influence on the Italian examples in Hägg and Marinatos 1991: 304. While Mercereau criticizes both Hägg and Alexiou (1950b: 441–62) for not specifying a transmission mechanism (for transmission of Syrian examples to Crete), her own reliance on what she characterizes as an insufficient trade volume for a Crete-to-Italy transmission is not sufficient to reject a connection. The equation of currently inadequate knowledge of a mechanism with the nonexistence of a mechanism is not warranted. Considering the LBA connections, the points of correspondence between the hut models from the two regions, the chronological possibility, the other possible Cretan influences on local Italian artistic productions, and the apparent continuity of commerce between the Levant and the central Mediterranean via Crete, it seems more prudent to retain, for the time being, the hut models as possible indicators of Cretan influence in Italy. Regarding the intensity of interaction required to transfer burial customs, a barrier on which Mercereau partially relies, since the urns were not funerary equipment in Crete, their funerary use in Italy would have been not a transfer of burial customs but simply the introduction of an object that struck a funerary fancy, so to speak, in the destination region.

[157] Hencken 1968, 2: 463–64, 532.

[158] Ibid.: 534–35.

[159] Ibid.: 538–39.

The historiography of Cretan pottery in Italy and Sicily leaves several opportunities for confusion, depending on where one enters the literature. The early identifications of Cretan pottery in Italy and Sicily by Pellegrini, Orsi, Gabrici, Johansen, Payne, and Blakeway have undergone extensive revision, with some pieces being reidentified as Rhodian, others as Euboean, and yet others as Italian Geometric.[160] Johansen suggested that the aryballoi from Cumae with concentric circles around the shoulder and groups of undulating vertical lines (spaghetti lines) were Greek island products, probably Cretan.[161] Payne also considered a number of vases from Cumae and other sites on the Italian peninsula to be Cretan imports.[162] Shortly after Payne's suggestions in *Necrocorinthia*, Blakeway relied on the authority of Payne to a considerable extent in his citation of vases from a number of Italian sites as Cretan, although he made a number of independent identifications.[163] About a decade later, Åkerström corrected several of Blakeway's Cretan attributions to vases at Terni, making a wide range of alternative attributions himself. In his publication of the Rhodian material from Exochi, having had the opportunity to study the material published in the *Clara Rhodos* volumes and the earlier publication of the Vroulia excavation, Johansen amended his own previous Cretan attributions of the aryballoi with concentric circles and spaghetti lines in a systematic way to Rhodes, designating the design *Kreis- und Wellenband*.[164] After a decade of excavation at Pithekoussai, Buchner offered a systematic replacement of Cretan attributions at Cumae with Euboean, considering the similarity in the pottery at the two sites.[165] In publishing further excavations at Gela, Adamesteanu and Orlandini used the term *rodio-*

cretese to describe vessels at Gela of types other than Johansen's *Kreis- und Wellenbandstil*, pieces that appeared to incorporate both Rhodian and Cretan backgrounds in shape and decoration but that they consider to have been made locally in Sicily.[166] LoPorto offered a thorough review of the Cretan vase attributions in Italy and Sicily, largely endorsing the revisions offered by Åkerström, Johansen, and Buchner. She accepted only one of nearly a dozen previous Cretan attributions at Cumae, accepted most of the previous Cretan attributions at Gela and several at scattered sites in southern Italy, and considered several of the Etrurian and Latian finds as local copies of Cretan imports.[167] Both LoPorto and deMiro used the Rhodio-Cretan concept to discuss the characteristics of vases at Gela.[168] In no case does a Rhodio-Cretan designation of a vessel indicate that it might have been produced in Crete; such pieces are strictly local products, generally of Gela, but possibly of some other Sicilian sites as well.

Another potential source of confusion is Blakeway's early use of the term "Creto-Cypriot" to describe several vases in Sicily and Italy.[169] Blakeway's concept of Creto-Cypriot bears no relation to the concept of the same name used by Brock to classify a group of lekythoi, oinochoai, and alabastron-aryballoi at Fortetsa that appeared to be derived from Cypriot imports to Crete.[170] The Creto-Cypriot vases from the Fortetsa-Knossos area generally are not direct copies of Cypriot prototypes, but rather are distinctive adaptations. Blakeway's use of the term is best illustrated by his designation of the four vases from Cerveteri as Creto-Cypriot. Two of the vases are pedestaled bird askoi, corresponding roughly to Desborough's Type I, inasmuch as the small head is at the front and a pouring spout is at the opposite

[160] The original excavation reports are Pellegrini 1903: 201–94; Orsi 1906: 5–763; Gabrici 1913: 5–872.

[161] Johansen 1923: 42.

[162] Payne 1931b: 4 n. 2, 5 n. 1.

[163] Blakeway 1932–33: 181–83, 194–98; 1935: 130.

[164] Johansen 1958: 158. Buchner and Ridgway (1993: 733) identify the vast majority of *Kreis- und Wellenband* aryballoi at Pithekoussai as Rhodian imports, and only two as local copies of the *KW* style.

[165] Buchner 1964: 268–70.

[166] Orlandini and Adamesteanu 1956: 278–79, 307–8. Levi (1927–29: 698) used the term *rodio-cretese* to describe apparent mingling of Cretan and Rhodian motives in some vases from Sicily.

[167] LoPorto 1974: 182, 187, pl. 19.2–3, 5.

[168] Ibid.; Fiorentini and deMiro 1983: 61, 79, figs. 13, 39.

[169] Blakeway 1932–33: 188, no. 45, at the Sicel settlement at Tremenzano on Sicily; 195, nos. 63–66, pl. 29, from Capodimonte (region of Bisenzio); 198, no. 4, from Cerveteri. Cited again in idem 1935: 130.

[170] Brock 1957: 155–56, oinochoe class III; 157, aryballoi class I.F; 158–59, aryballoi class II.E(iii), the Creto-Cypriot lekythoi. Cf. Coldstream 1984a: 135.

end.[171] These two items are clearly reminiscent of the Subminoan/Submycenaean bird askoi from the Aegean, and Blakeway calls them local Geometric products imitating Greek models, although Geometric would seem late for the appearance in Italy of Greek or Cypriot productions of these askoi. Åkerström discussed the Cypriot and Cretan antecedents of these two askoi but made no comment on Blakeway's commentary, implicitly leaving them with an Italo-Geometric origin, which is probably correct.[172] Of Blakeway's other two Creto-Cypriot vases from Cerveteri, one is an oinochoe with a long, barrel-shaped belly, a long neck, and a high pedestal foot; the other is a pedestaled krater. The decorations on both could be Cycladic or even Euboean in inspiration, but neither appears particularly close to either Cretan or Cypriot pieces. The aryballos from Cerveteri, now in the Louvre, Blakeway calls a genuine Greek Geometric import, and it is the sole piece he cites from Cerveteri on which Åkerström does not offer an opinion.[173] The final piece Blakeway describes as Creto-Cypriot is the vase from Tremenzano on Sicily, which he calls a local Geometric piece made by Sicels but copied directly from a Greek Geometric original. He does not illustrate the piece. Thus, it is clear that the early use of the term "Creto-Cypriot" does not indicate vases of the type later so designated at Fortetsa and the Knossos North Cemetery, and that vases in Sicily labeled with this term generally do not appear to be either Cretan exports or copies of Cretan exports.

The pyxis from the sanctuary of Bitalemi (78), in the territory of Gela, has a Protogeometric motif that persisted in Crete through the seventh century and has Late Geometric parallels at Kavousi and Arkades.[174] In Latium and Etruria, several apparent local copies of imported Cretan vases dating to the mid-eighth century have been found in tombs at Terni and Vulci (24–25), Cerveteri (26), and Vetralla (27). A bronze lion head at Veii reminiscent of the Cretan shields is dated to the eighth century, and some bronze cauldron stands from graves at Praeneste and a bronze bowl from Capena probably are from the same workshop that made the tympanon from the Idaean Cave.[175] All are sites in northern Italy: Terni, well inland, some eighty kilometers northeast of ancient Tarquinia, in the Apennines; Cerveteri, near the coast, some thirty-five kilometers west of Rome; Vetralla, fifteen kilometers northeast of ancient Tarquinia; Veii, twenty kilometers north of Rome; Praeneste, forty kilometers east of Rome; and Capena, thirty-five kilometers north of Rome.[176]

Five Cretan vases have been found around Gela and dated to the eighth century, prior to the colonization period (29, 76–79); two others have been dated from precolonization to about 640; and three others are dated to the early seventh century or the first years of colonization (89–91). One vase and a patera at Gela (95–96) date to the first half of the seventh century and are believed to be Cretan, and three other apparently Cretan vases from the seventh century have been found at Gela (106–8); a fourth (102) is a local product that closely resembles a vase at Arkades. Within a half-century of the founding of Gela, the Cretan pottery dwindled out, while the Rhodian pottery became more prevalent. The Cretan finds overlap the far more common Corinthian pottery at Gela.[177] The Cretan-style vases at Gela have no parallels with pottery found in the Knossos area; their closest relationship is to material found in or near the Mesara, which has prompted Coldstream to suggest that the Cretan co-founders came from the southern part of the island.[178]

Mylai, on the northeast coast of Sicily, was established around 716 as a colony of Gela. Several cemeteries there were excavated in the early 1950s, several graves from which yielded five unpainted aryballoi that Bernabò Brea and Cavalier identified as Cretan. These aryballoi are roughly of the shape of the vases Johansen identified as *Kreis- und Wellenbandstil*—flat lip, squared to slightly raised handle flush with the top of the lip—but undecorated. Two were

---

[171] Desborough 1972a: 246–47.

[172] Åkerström 1943: 62, 64–65, pl. 13.1–2.

[173] Ibid.: 54.

[174] LoPorto 1974: 179; Coldstream 1968: 375.

[175] Assuming that the tympanon was made in a Cretan workshop, just possibly by Urartian refugee bronze-smiths, more likely by other resident foreigners.

[176] See maps in Hencken 1968, 1: 2; 2: 472–74; and in Talbert 1985: 82, 86.

[177] Dunbabin 1948: 226–30.

[178] Coldstream 1968: 257, 375.

miniature examples, only about five centimeters high. Orlandini published some similar aryballoi from the later excavations at Gela but did not discuss or mention them in his text.[179] LoPorto suggested that the Mylai aryballoi were Rhodian or Cypriot rather than Cretan, while Coldstream identified two of them, as well as Orlandini's from Gela, as *Kreis- und Wellenbandstil*, but ignored the rest.[180] Dehl cites all five as "Kretische?" without discussing alternative origins.[181] I have excluded the aryballoi cited by Coldstream, but the variation in shape represented in the remaining three spans comparable elements of shape in a number of aryballoi from Fortetsa.[182] I have included these three aryballoi from Mylai in the catalogue (74), but with a question mark.

Several other possible Cretan artifacts have been found at scattered points in southern Italy: possibly one vase at Cumae dated to the end of the eighth century or the early seventh (75); three vase fragments from Taranto (93, 120, 141), a terracotta from the third quarter of the seventh century (49); a vase fragment from Satyrion (92); two terracotta relief fragments from unknown sites in southern Italy (135–36); and a pyxis at Brindisi (121), dated to about 660. From further north again, in the vicinity of Rome, the ivory lions (94) found in tombs at Praeneste (approximately forty kilometers east of Rome) and Cerveteri in the first half of the seventh century are in the same tradition with the lion's head protome on the Idaean Cave shield (Kunze, KB no. 10) and could be of Cretan origin.[183] Boardman describes the Cretan artifacts in the southern parts of Italy in the late eighth and seventh centuries as trade objects carrying perfumed oil.[184]

Schweitzer suggested a Cretan origin for the square-bodied ring vase found in Tomb 67 at Cumae on the basis of the published description of the decoration on a ring vase from Praisos.[185] The Cumae ring vase has a well-executed meander pattern on its outer section, rhomboids on its face, and circumferential lines on the inner face and the foot. It has a high, moderately flaring, slightly concave foot, but the neck and handle are broken and missing. Payne tacitly endorsed Schweitzer's assessment of several aryballoi from Cumae, particularly that of plate 36.2, as Cretan, but made no reference to his suggestion regarding the ring vase.[186] In fact, the decoration on the ring vase from Praisos is difficult to assess from the published photograph, but the photograph does reveal it to be round in section and without a foot, although it does have a neck and the handle is broken and missing. Inspection of the Praisos ring vase in the Herakleion Museum by Geraldine Gesell on my behalf reveals a decoration distinctly different from that of the Cumae example. Gabrici himself suggested that the ring vase was imported,[187] or at least made from a proximate foreign model, but the meanders reminded him of Dipylon vases, and he noted ring vases from Argos, Thera, and Attica.[188] The ring vase from Argos appears to have a squared inner section, although whether the outer section is squared or rounded cannot be ascertained from the photograph; the decoration used guilloches and lozenges rather than meanders, and the foot was straight rather than flared. Some half-dozen of these vases were found at the Heraeum. The Theran ring vase is odd, with squared edges, but with a strap handle and a curved

[179] Orlandini and Adamesteanu 1956: 292, fig. 6, from grave 7.

[180] LoPorto 1974: 176 n. 24, 177 n. 61; Coldstream 1969: 4 n. 33.

[181] Dehl 1984: 98 n. 406, 223.

[182] Brock 1957: nos. 466, 683, 734, 772, 787, 815, 869, 871, 917, 1063.

[183] Brown 1960: 2–3. They are also in the tradition of the Nimrud and North Syrian ivories and could have come directly from the Near East.

[184] Boardman 1961: 156–57.

[185] Schweitzer 1918: 44; ring vase is from Gabrici 1913: 270–72, pl. 39.2. The Praisos ring vase is published in Droop 1905–6: 26, no. 3850, fig. 1, middle row, fourth from left. The description of the decoration is not totally inconsistent with that of the Cumae ring vase: "The ornament was mostly in parallel lines, but on the outside was a field of oblongs, decorated with perpendiculars alternating with diagonal lines." It does not seem unreasonable to interpret this as a description of meanders filled with diagonal lines, and concentric circles on the inner and outer sections, as in the Cumae vase. I am indebted to Geraldine Gesell for taking time from her own research to study the decoration on this vase for me.

[186] Payne 1931b: 5 n. 1. LoPorto (1974: 175) identifies the aryballos from Cumae, pl. 36.2, as Euboean.

[187] Gabrici 1913: 316.

[188] Waldstein 1905: 143, fig. 83; Dragendorff 1903: 313, no. 45, fig. 501; Böhlau 1887: 56, no. 14, figs. 21–22.

spout; it is decorated with concentric circles. Another Theran ring vase, described as a pilgrim flask, has a more rounded body and a wavy decoration.[189] Dragendorff points to Eastern Geometric styles for the origin of these vases—Cyprogeometric and Melian Geometric.[190] The body of the vase from the Athenian acropolis is round-bodied, has a very low foot and a broken neck and handle, and is decorated with large lion heads reminiscent of a Protocorinthian alabastron; Böhlau called it a ring-formed Corinthian alabastron. The poor correspondence of these ring vases with the Cumaean example, at least with the hindsight of subsequently published ring vases, may have left the Cretan suggestion quite reasonable. The square section of the Cumae ring vase clearly is a distinguishing feature, and Ure has noted the Boeotian ring vases as "generally rectangular in section (not round as in normal Corinthian examples)."[191] Indeed, the meander pattern on the Cumae vase does correspond reasonably to Boeotian Geometric, and the style of its foot seems to appear more commonly among Boeotian Geometric vessels than in other regional styles.[192] A similar style of foot appears not uncommonly among the Late Geometric pottery from Lefkandi, but no ring vases appear among those finds.[193] Johansen includes the Cumae ring vase in his corpus of Corinthian (Sicyonian) vases, although its meander pattern and its rhomboids are purely Geometric, as he notes, while the tomb context appears to be consistent roughly with a Protocorinthian dating.[194] Johansen shows a Corinthian ring vase with square section, with flat-lipped mouth and thin handle but no foot; the decoration on the face of this vessel is a series of wavy lines (zigzags) perpendicular to the circumference of the section,

and the inner face is decorated with circumferential lines comparable to those on the Cumae vase.[195] He refers to Italian imitations within the Protocorinthian-Corinthian style.[196] Altogether, the provenance of the Cumae ring vase remains unclear, and there is no better reason to think that it came from Crete than that it may have come from Corinth or may have been made locally under a mixture of foreign influences.

Recent excavations at Akragas have yielded an imported clay head from the oldest stratum of the western sector of the Temple Hill, which deMiro has suggested may be either Cretan or Rhodian.[197] The similarities to a number of Cretan clay figurines are striking. The long, straight, narrow nose extending to raised eyebrow ridges, the protuberant eyes, and the pinched mouth closely recall a Protogeometric clay head from Kalokhorio, in northern east-central Crete, as well as the Late Minoan III to Subminoan clay goddess figurines with upraised arms from Gazi, Karphi, and Kavousi.[198] A painted clay head from the Diktaean Cave and another from Aghia Triada are softer in facial features, yet retain similarities to the Akragas head in their sharp noses, eyebrows, and relatively narrow mouths. The closest Rhodian correspondence to the Akragas head I have found is a small, human-shaped vase from Tomb 145 at Ialysos, an infant burial.[199] The vase has Geometric or Protogeometric painted decoration, otherwise reminiscent of the Cretan goddesses with upraised arms, but has the arms stretched out to the side as in an embrace. In the same tomb were found a bird askos, two flasks, and two amphoriskoi, all with Protogeometric or Early Geometric designs. All these Cretan pieces, as well as the Rhodian piece, are much earlier than the founding of Akragas in 580, so the relation-

[189] Dragendorff 1903: no. 53, fig. 505.

[190] Ibid.: 314–15.

[191] Ure 1946: 45; Böhlau 1887: 56.

[192] Cf., e.g., Ruckert 1976: pl. 8.3, for an example quite close to that of the Cumae ring vase, although the Boeotian example is an amphora.

[193] Popham et al. 1979.

[194] Johansen 1923: 26–28, pl. 7.4.

[195] Ibid.: pl. 8.4.

[196] Cf. Sieveking and Hackl 1912: 74, no. 623, pl. 26, for a square-section example with trefoil mouth, high handle, and wide, flat foot, decorated with transverse stripes on the outer circumference and a single wide band on the flat surface.

[197] Fiorentini and deMiro 1983: 100–101, fig. 112.

[198] Karphi goddesses: Pendlebury et al. 1937–38: pl. 41. Kalokhorio head: Pendlebury 1939: pl. 41.3. Gazi goddesses: Davaras n.d.: 27, pl. 89. Kavousi goddesses: Gesell et al. 1995: 79, pl. 22.d.

[199] Jacopi 1929: 149, fig. 142.

ship between the Akragas head and either Crete or Rhodes is unclear. The Akragas head certainly could be a local, possibly Gelan, product influenced by a Cretan import to Gela, although the timing of such an import even to Gela seems problematic.

The excavations at Aetos on Ithaka have yielded a gold finial (88), dated to the early seventh century or possibly as early as the last quarter of the eighth century, which is quite similar to the one from the goldsmith's tomb at Khaniale Tekke. A late eighth- to early seventh-century date on the gold finial from Aetos would be too early for an Ithaka stop on the run to southern Italy, but not too early for the traffic to Etruria. It is also tempting to try to exploit the relative proximity of Ithaka and Dodona; that it might be simply pirate's loot would be difficult to disprove, but the extra baggage that interpretation carries with it should be kept in mind. It is safer to develop explanations for the appearance of ceramics and even bronzes than for the appearance of precious metals. Some late seventh-century pottery matching local items at Arkades has been found as well on Ithaka (133).[200]

A small number of apparently Cretan ceramic pieces appear in the Aegean islands, but with no tighter dating than the Geometric period. At least one pot has been found at Zagora on Andros (16), a skyphos fragment on Samos (17), and some aryballoi on Aegina (18).[201] On the nearby mainland from around the same time period,

apparently Cretan aryballoi have been found at Corinth (19) and in the Argolid (20). Also from around 800 is a Cretan pithos from grave 39 at Kameiros on Rhodes, identified by Brock, who said it was not Knossian.[202] From the late eighth century (after about 725) are several Cretan vases at Delos (54), probably carried on religious visits, and three vases on Melos (55). Two Cretan Orientalizing vases have been found on Delos as well (103). Two (38–39), and possibly as many as four (also 23 and 82), Cretan vase fragments from the Cretan Middle to Late Geometric period (early eighth to mid-seventh century) have been reported from the nearby island of Kasos, about fifty kilometers east of the northeast tip of Crete.

On the mainland, several fragments of a large Cretan Geometric vase has been found at Athens (56). Sakellarakis recently has pointed to the striking similarity in the design of some locally carved ivory seals found at the Idaean Cave (IC.86–90) that date to after c. 725, and some of the stamped gold bands from graves at various sites in Attica (51). A similar gold relief band from Corinth (53), allegedly from a grave, also is likely to be Cretan. The similarities are very close and suggest a Cretan origin for the gold artifacts in Athens, either as exports from Crete or as products of Cretan artisans in Athens. On the Peloponnese, considering Sparta's autarkic reputation, the pyxis from the acropolis of Sparta (144), thought by Payne and Hartley to be Cretan, as well as the Cretan terracotta head (145) from the Spartan acropolis, prob-

---

[200] While our attention is directed still to the north and west, it may be useful to note Hencken's thesis on the Hersprung shields, with a modest parallel he cites between a Cretan example and one found in Denmark. The Cretan example, with V-notch, is from the Idaean Cave, is dated to c. 800, and is only a *representation* of this shield type on Kunze's shield no. 67. The Hersprung shield may be a Cypriot development, and Hencken correlates its finds and chronology with the amber trade from the Baltic, through central Europe, and into Italy and Greece in the eighth and seventh centuries: Hencken 1950b: 259; 1950a: 297, 305–7, figs. 8 (Idaean Cave) and 25 (Denmark); Kunze 1931: 30, no. 67, pls. 43, 46; Snodgrass 1964: 55, 210–11. These shields are less direct evidence of external relations than I generally rely upon here, but the parallels are worth maintaining in the background because of the other appearances of interaction between Crete and central and north-central Europe at this time.

[201] Payne (1931b: 138) suggested that the Ram Jug from Aegina might be Cretan, but since Cook (1934–35: 189) pronounced it Protoattic, that provenance has remained firm, although S. P. Morris (1984: 21) has suggested recently that it is Aeginetan. Morris also discusses the possibility of trade in pottery clay between Attica and Aegina. Arafat and Morgan (1989: 314–15) demur in the case of Attica and Aegina, but Boardman (1956: 56; 1980: 123) has suggested that clay may have been shipped as ballast from Chios to Naukratis. Jones (1985: 26) notes the difficulty of empirically distinguishing Boardman's hypothesis from a simple case of trade in pottery. He notes, however, that most contemporary Greek potters get their clay within 1 or 2 kilometers of their work site. He has been unable to corroborate or document Casson's claim that earlier twentieth-century A.C. Siphniot itinerant potters carried their clay with them on their caïques: Casson 1938: 464–73.

[202] Brock 1957: 217 n. 2. A lidded pyxis from grave 85 at Kameiros was recommended by Jacopi as Cretan, but Johansen studied it at length and judged it to be Rhodian: Jacopi 1932–33: 203, fig. 243; Johansen 1958: 148–54, fig. 219. Coldstream (1968: 274–75, pl. 62a) calls it Rhodian LG.

ably represent some noncommercial interaction.[203] The recent survey of the southern Argolid has yielded a single Subgeometric/Orientalizing sherd that could be Cretan at Dhroukoulina, on Dhouroufi Ridge, about two kilometers south of Koiladha, itself about two kilometers southwest of Franchthi: the body fragment of a large vessel, either a krater or an amphora. Its gritty, greenish fabric is not local. The publishing author considered it probably an import from a Cycladic, Rhodian, "or even a Cretan site." Near a possible handle attachment is an outline, matte-painted serpentine creature, with a circular eye, line teeth and tongue, and a loop ear, and with an asterisk-like star behind the neck. No parallels to this creature's details seem compellingly close, and the star is common in many areas, including the Argolid. It is not included in the catalogue.[204]

Cretan origins have been suggested for two additional vases found on Rhodes, but in both cases those suggestions are either incorrect or doubtful. Pfuhl called attention to a Geometric trefoil oinochoe in Berlin as of Cretan origin, and Payne, possibly independently, considered that vase a later version of a Cretan Protogeometric oinochoe from Knossos; but Johansen assigned that vase to his group of Elfenbeinimitierende Vasen, Rhodian vases that he believed attempted to reconstruct in clay several decorative characteristics of North Syrian ivories: cables, circles with centers, and impressed dogteeth.[205] The Berlin oinochoe has tangent concentric circles on its shoulder, a series of narrow concentric bands separating the shoulder from the belly, and a series of nontangent concentric circles that overlap the lower two separating bands. Inside each concentric circle on the belly are circles with central dots that Johansen characterizes as imitations of ivory work. The vase has a high foot, and its handle arcs slightly above the trefoil lip. The lower part of the belly and the moderately high foot are painted dark. Johansen cites an oinochoe from Exochi as similar: it has nontangent concentric circles, each with a central x, around the shoulder, with vertical series of tangent circles with single, small circles in their centers running between them. The belly zone has rows of pendent circles (semicircles) with the single, small central circles inside them. The vertical rows of tangent small circles are repeated on the lower part of the belly, which surmounts an unpainted, low foot. The series of concentric circles, tangent and nontangent, are of course common on Cretan vases, especially pithoi and aryballoi, but not particularly so on the oinochoai. The shape of the Berlin oinochoe is not closely paralleled by Cretan oinochoai that I can find: bodies tend to be more globular, necks tend to be thicker, thin necks are longer (cf. the trefoil oinochoe with moderately high foot, the foot and lip painted dark, from Milatos:[206] decorations of chevron rows, opposing offset dogteeth, concentric bands, and short, vertical stripes—totally unlike the decoration of the Berlin oinochoe). Altogether, the variable correspondence of the elements of the Berlin oinochoe's shape with the shapes of other Rhodian oinochoai, and the limited correspondence of its decoration to that of other Rhodian vases, even in Johansen's Elfenbeinimitierende Gruppe, seem to leave it less certainly of Rhodian origin than Johansen believed, although its correspondence in decoration *and* shape in the same vase in Cretan oinochoai does not leave it a clearly Cretan import. Jacopi suggested that a pyxis from Kameiros Tomb 85 was a Cretan import on the basis of its shape, but Johansen included it also in his Elfenbeinimitierende Gruppe.[207] The cable pattern is recognized now as characteristically Rhodian, and Johansen surely is correct in this assessment. Coldstream identifies this pyxis as Rhodian Late Geometric.[208]

---

[203] Payne 1931b: 5 n. 1, 342 no. XII; Hartley 1930–31: 61 nn. 5–6; Droop (1926–27: 58, pl. 6) previously had identified it as local on the basis of design, paint, and fabric.

[204] Langdon 1992: 71, nos. 1210, 221, 236, figs. 64, 136. On the location and characteristics of site B2, see Jameson, Runnels, and van Andel 1994: 437–38, figs 0.1 and 4.31, for maps. The site extends over roughly 0.6 hectares, where remains were found of at least two structures with worked limestone foundations. Among small finds were 255 sherds, eighteen roof-like tile fragments, three ceramic spoons, a loom weight, and a lead clamp.

[205] Pfuhl 1923: 89; the Berlin oinochoe was published originally by Furtwängler (1886: 137), from a grave on the southwest side of Kamerios. Payne 1927–28: 251, no. 85, pls. 6.13 and 10.5; and 297, fig. 42, another PG oinochoe. Johansen 1958: 148–54 on the Elfenbeinimitierende Vasen, 152, 154, fig. 220, on the Berlin oinochoe. Cf. Coldstream 1968: 275, on Johansen's grouping of Rhodian imitations of Levantine products.

[206] Levi 1927–29: fig. 623; Johansen 1958: 35, fig. 62.

[207] Jacopi 1932–33: 203, fig. 243; Johansen 1958: 150–52, 154, fig. 219.

[208] Coldstream 1968: 274–75, pl. 62a.

On the sea lane to Rhodes, two Cretan Late Geometric vases have been reported from the island of Kasos, between Crete and Karpathos (KAS.38–39). A possible earlier appearance of Cretan material on Kasos is a rim of a large Middle/Late Geometric krater, which might be either east Cretan or local Kasian (KAS.23). Similarly uncertain in origin is the later, possible Cretan krater fragment, dated to the first half of the seventh century; its fabric is "rather Cretan," whereas its decoration recalls Cycladic animals.[209] Turning from the northeast of Crete to the northwest, and moving slightly later, three Cretan vases are reported from Kythera, but with little contextual information available. An alabastron and an aryballos from the first half of the seventh century emerged from the excavations of the 1960s (KYΘ.126–27). An askos in the form of a siren (KYΘ.153) found in the nineteenth century also appears to be Cretan. The aryballos has parallels at Fortetsa and Arkades, and the askos has design parallels at Arkades.

No certain Cretan artifacts have been reported in either Euboea or Sardinia.[210] Nonetheless, Coldstream has identified a lentoid flask (pilgrim flask) from Skoubris Tomb 33 (S33,3) at Lefkandi as an import with similarities to vases found on Crete, although he is reluctant to call it Cretan because of the dearth of Cretan exports in the early ninth century.[211] The pale, powdery clay of this flask is reminiscent of some eastern Cretan Geometric pottery, and Coldstream cites a pilgrim flask from Adhromyloi in eastern Crete as a possible parallel.[212] I have not included the Skoubris flask in the catalogue, but the possibility of a Cretan origin for it should remain open. Certainly, Euboean material had reached Knossos by the early ninth century, and there is no reason, a priori, that some Cretan material should not be found at Lefkandi.[213]

The bronze bull figurine found in a rural sanctuary near Doukos, outside of Chalkis, might be a Cretan product; its forehead contains a triangular depression to take some possible filling of another substance to represent some jewelry worn by the beast, a characteristic of one bull figurine found at the Sanctuary of Hermes and Aphrodite at Symi Viannou, as well as several others from Aghia Triada and a possible Cretan example found at Delphi.[214] If it is indeed Cretan, the method by which it arrived at its excavation site remains a matter for speculation: Did a Euboean sailor who had been to Crete come home to retire, bringing a good-luck piece with him? Did a sailor, of whatever "nationality," trade it for something else to a farmer he met in port? Did he get drunk and lose it? (Would he even have carried it with him during such activities, or would he have kept it safely with his belongings aboard ship?) How did he get it on Crete (assuming that's where he got it, even if it is of Cretan origin)? Such speculation appears to put some cloth on what otherwise would be dry bones, but it is unclear that it advances our understanding of the means of transport of this item. The Euboean material on Crete, especially at Knossos, suggests that it is not unreasonable to think in terms of a Euboean acquiring this item on Crete, but how it was acquired remains beyond our knowledge. Direct mercantile actions could have been at the base of this item's transportation overseas, just as well as our hypothetical sailor's personal acquisition.

Cretan artifacts from the late eighth century have been found on Thera (83–86). It is claimed by some that Crete's most regular exchange remaining in the artifactual record appears to have been with Thera. Boardman describes these artifacts as reflecting "considerable traffic," while Cook calls the implied Crete-Thera intercourse as

---

[209] Melas 1995: 161, no. 4.

[210] Themelis (1983: 153) suggested possible Cretan—or Cypriot—origin for the late Submycenaean bird vase (duck askos) from grave S16, but other assessments have not suggested either origin. Spectrographic analysis indicates that it is not Cypriot, and its form differs from other Cretan examples. Cf. Popham, Sackett, and Themelis 1980: 114; Desborough 1980: 334; 1972a: 256, no. 54.

[211] Coldstream 1977: 42 n. 33, fig. 9h; 1980b: 353, pl. 101; Popham, Sackett, and Themelis 1980: 121.

[212] The Adhromyloi example is published in Droop 1905–6: 54–55, fig. 22, row 3, nos. 2, 4.

[213] Rocchetti (1988–89: 248) cites two lentoid flasks from the Palaia Perivolia cemetery at Lefkandi as Cretan imports: Popham, Sackett, and Themelis 1980: 142, Tomb P3, no. 8, pl. 261f; and 150, Tomb P22, no. 19, pl. 270a. The excavators identified P22.19 as a "Cypriot Bichrome II(?)" lentoid flask, and P3.8 as a trefoil lentoid flask, presumably of local origin. For the latter piece, Desborough suggested for its origin either (1) survival of a Mycenaean shape or (2) innovation with (a) Crete or (b) Cyprus, more likely the latter, as the source region; he noted that no flasks with trefoil lip had been found to that date in Cyprus (1980: 330, 332).

[214] Schürmann 1996: 185.

Crete's "least infrequent."[215] The interactions between Thera and Crete are accompanied by two legends. I have already noted the well-known story of Korobios of Itanos leading the Theran colonists to the coast of North Africa in the early 630s. The other refers to the generation before the founding of Cyrene. Etearchos of Axos wrongly suspected his daughter, Phronime, of promiscuity and ordered her thrown into the sea. He entrusted a Theran trader to carry out the sentence; however, the trader took her back to Thera instead, where a high-ranking Theran citizen took her as a concubine, and her descendants were distinguished Therans.[216] Whether or not the legend has a basis in fact, it not only reinforces the idea that the two islands were engaged in trade, but also suggests that foreign traders were making their way inland. Could foreign traders have gone inland on Crete on buying missions for relatively transportable items like wool and textiles?

Cretan dedications have been found at a number of the panhellenic shrines. Olympia has produced Cretan bronze material from the second half of the eighth century through the end of the seventh, primarily armor (99, 124, 146–49), but also figurines (43–45), jewelry—pins (48, 150)—and a relief (98). Dedications at Delphi begin slightly later—the last quarter of the eighth century—and appear through the last quarter of the seventh century. As at Olympia, only bronzes are attributable to Crete, and they are mostly armor (62–65, 143–44), but they also include an openwork stand (57) and a statuette (66).[217] The "Crowe" corslet and its fragmentary companion piece once were considered Cretan, but an origin somewhere in the Peloponnese is generally accepted now.[218] I have not included in the catalogue a bronze pin from an unknown find site at Olympia, which has markings similar to a seventh-century Cretan pin from the Sanctuary of Demeter at Knossos.[219] While there may be some evidence for Cretans casting bronze figurines (the horses) on site at Olympia, the finds at Delphi do not imply such residence. The reported Cretan dedications at the Samian Heraion include no metals, but rather three wooden korai (128, 131–32) and an ivory musical instrument (130), from the late eighth to the mid-seventh century. The well-preserved wooden Daedalic kore (128), dated to the first half of the seventh century, is said to be a good candidate for having been carved on Samos by a Cretan artist[220]—the accounting may be good for the other two as well—although an alternative explanation would be a votive either carried by a Cretan or picked up by a non-Cretan stopping in Crete. This kore is similar to others found at Gortyn and Arkades. Two Cretan terracotta relief plaques were found at Perachora, one from the end of the eighth century (71), the other from the mid-seventh (97). Both were made with a Cretan matrix from local clay. Also from the mid-seventh century is a terracotta relief plaque from the Argive Heraeum (128), apparently made from local Argive clay, but with the same Cretan matrix used to form the later terracotta from Perachora (97). Waldstein also cited a Cretan parallel for a vase fragment at the Argive Heraeum.[221] He believed the Argive Heraeum fragment to have been a pithos lid with a modest knob, but did not discuss the dissimilarity of the decoration, and it is not clear whether he meant to suggest that the piece may have been Cretan. Courbin has published this fragment as a ceramic pomegranate, of Argive origin, and his discussion is convincing.[222]

The bronze votive animal figurines—horses and cows—of the Giamalakis Collection pose

---

[215] Boardman 1961: 156; Cook 1972: 145.

[216] Jeffrey 1976: 191.

[217] Shield 6948 (catalogue no. 57.DL here) has been considered Cretan by a number of analysts, and analysis of the metals has indicated that several others, as well as some openwork stands, are probably Cretan: Filippakis, Photou, and Rolley 1983: 119. However, the origins of several others remain undecided. In particular, two votive shields with lion (or other animal) protomes, similar to the shields found in the Idaean Cave, have been considered possibly Syrian and Luristanian, as well as Cretan (inv. nos. 7177 and 7227): Lerat 1980: 103–14; Magou, Philippakis, and Rolley 1986: 132.

[218] Hoffmann 1972: 50–53.

[219] Kilian-Dirlmeier 1984: 210–11, 219, no. 3423, pl. 85; Philipp 1981: 57, no. 104, pl. 30. Cf. Coldstream 1973b: 145–46, no. 116, fig. 35.

[220] Kyrieleis 1980: 100–101.

[221] Waldstein 1905: 115, no. 3, pl. 58.3. The Cretan parallel is in Wide 1899: 36–37, fig. 15.

[222] Courbin 1966: 234, no. GR2, pl. 90.

problems that do not yield any solutions yet. A number of these pieces appear to have come from Olympia, while others have alleged, but unprovable, provenances on Crete—the Lasithi and Mesara regions. The pieces contain both Cretan and Peloponnesian characteristics, and it is undecided yet whether they come from a Cretan workshop influenced by Peloponnesian styles and traveled to Olympia with Cretan visitors, or were made on the Peloponnese, with some of them finding their way to Crete in antiquity, or were perhaps made at Olympia by Cretans.[223] Physical analysis of the metals may prove helpful on the issue of provenance of these pieces. In the catalogue I have presumed that an unspecified number of the horses were made either on Crete or by Cretans at Olympia.[224] The Giamalakis cow figurines pose a slightly different problem from that presented by the horses. Pilali-Papasteriou describes twenty-one Giamalakis bronze cow figurines (her nos. 139–59); for fifteen of these, she cites similarities to Argive or Laconian (or unprovenanced) examples from Olympia.[225] With insecure find sites on Crete—if indeed they are from Crete—there is no assurance of importation to Crete. In general, the Giamalakis cows—and bulls—differ in appearance from most of the other bovine figurines Pilali-Papasteriou presents, so there is less of a case for their Cretan production, either on Crete or at Olympia, than there is for some of the horses.

Provenances frequently are difficult to identify for pins, as for bronze figurines, and Cretan parallels have been noted for several pins that I have not included in the catalogue but that may warrant notice nonetheless as possible Cretan articles. First is a bronze pin from a Submycenaean grave in the Forum at Corinth: it has a flattened (or squared) section of shank near the head, which is paralleled by a gold pin from Grave J at Knossos-Ambelokipi, the same tomb with the bronze bowl with Phoenician inscription (KNC.7), as well as pin B.4 from Subminoan burial II at Ayios Ioannis, also near Knossos.[226] The eleventh century is earlier than any Corinthian material found on Crete, but Attic material of such a date does appear at Knossos—the town and the North Cemetery—as well as at Vrokastro, and subsequent movement of Cretan material between Attica and Corinth seems plausible, although the grave in question contains no Attic material. Also from the Submycenaean/Subminoan period is a bronze pin from Karpophora in Messenia, about two or three kilometers in from the coast along the northwest curve of the Gulf of Messenia, which has correspondences at Argos and in Tomb VI of the Upper Gypsades cemetery.[227] Finally, an iron pin probably from the Sanctuary of Athena and Poseidon at Asea in southern Arcadia, between Megalopolis and Tripolis, also has similarities to the pin noted above from the Sanctuary of Demeter at Knossos.[228]

Earlier Cretan finds at Samos are ceramic: a Geometric skyphos or pyxis fragment (17). Dodona and Miletus both have produced a single votive bronze shield thought to be Cretan (69, 70), dated to the last quarter of the eighth century. Delos has produced mostly reported ceramic finds from Crete, ranging from Geometric (21, 54) to Orientalizing (103), but also a lone bronze horse figurine from the late eighth century (47). The Sanctuary of Artemis Orthia at Sparta has produced an ivory seal (52) related to some found in the Idaean Cave and dated to the last quarter of the eighth century. At Bassae are later deposits of miniature armor, dated to the mid-seventh century (122). Snodgrass develops the case that these last are offerings crafted locally to the specifications of Cretan mercenaries from Lyttos and Aptera who were fighting for Sparta in the Second Messenian War. He sug-

---

[223] Pilali-Papasteriou 1985: 60–67, 79–87; Zimmerman 1989: 298–306.

[224] E.g., Zimmerman 1989: nos. GIA.23, 43b, 43c, 47, 49, 50, 55, 65, pls. 70–71.

[225] Cf. Pilali-Papasteriou's discussion of individual pieces with her identification of "Entsprechungen außerhalb Kretas" in her concordance of type-groups (1985: 177–82). Not all the pieces for which similarities to examples from Olympia are noted in the discussion (60–67) are identified as having correspondences outside Crete in the concordance.

[226] Kilian-Dirlmeier 1984: 67, 69, 81, no. 191, pl. 6; Catling 1977b: 12, fig. 25; Williams 1970: 15, no. 14, pl. 6–two child burials, the pin with earlier burial, a Submycenaean lekythos with the second; Hood and Coldstream 1968: 212, fig. 4, pl. 54g.

[227] Kilian-Dirlmeier 1984: 67; Choremis 1973: 70–72, no. 732, pl. 38; Hood, Huxley, and Sandars 1958–59: 236, pl. 60a.

[228] Kilian-Dirlmeier 1984: 210, 219, no. 3422, pl. 85; Coldstream 1973b: 145–46, no. 116.

gests they were thank-offerings made after the capture of Phigaleia, around 668.[229] Small though it is, the resource transfer reflected by this votive armor is nonrepatriated labor earnings, analogous to overseas expenditures by itinerant craftsmen. While no Cretan artifacts have been identified beyond reasonable doubt (or within reasonable interest) at Perachora, Dunbabin highlighted one aryballoid jug "of uncanonical shape" as possibly Cretan by virtue of its shape, which was not paralleled at Corinth, although both clay and paint were "like those of LG Corinthian vases." The date proffered for it was "perhaps soon after the middle of the seventh century."[230] Considering the characterization of the clay, I have not included it in the catalogue of Cretan artifacts found at sites outside Crete.

A dozen Cretan vases dating from the last third of the seventh century (108–19) have been found in the excavations at Tocra, on the coast of North Africa, west of the Theran colony at Cyrene.[231] One Late Orientalizing hydria is similar to a hydria from Gortyn, and the decoration on some jug fragments is similar to decoration from Fortetsa. The Tocra excavations antedate the Kommos excavations by some fifteen years, and to date, a comparison of the Cretan ceramics found there with the local ware at Kommos has not been published; such comparisons might prove fruitful now, although the chronological overlap may be frustratingly short. Stepping slightly beyond the nearer time boundary of this study, Stucchi reports a very small percentage of early sixth-century Cretan pottery from the agora of Cyrene: 2.27 percent of all vase sherds, 3.33 percent of all imported, non-Corinthian and non-Attic vase sherds. He offers similar estimates for percentages of Cretan vases at Tocra (0.99 percent of all vases, 2.39 percent of imported, non-

Corinthian and non-Attic vases) and the Sanctuary of Demeter at Cyrene (3.03 percent of imported, non-Corinthian and non-Attic vases).[232]

A final possible Cretan artifact found at an overseas site is very close to the Near East, outside the areas where any securely identified Cretan artifacts have been reported to date. Barnett suggested that the mouth fragment of an aryballos of Creto-Cypriot type, found at Mersin, just west of Tarsus on the southeastern coast of Anatolia, might be Cretan.[233] The piece is dated generally to the Orientalizing-Archaic period, and was accompanied by a number of Protocorinthian, Corinthian, and East Greek imported vases (and fragments). The piece in question has a collared neck and a flaring lip, with a design of triangles around the lip and a zigzag line on the collar. The clay is a fine buff, and the paint is matte black. From the photograph, no handle is apparent, either at the lip or joining the neck at the collar. I have been unable to find close parallels to the fragment's shape and design among Cypriot, Rhodian, or other East Greek artifacts. From the photograph, the lip appears closer to the Creto-Cypriot lekythoi from the North Cemetery at Knossos than to aryballoi, but the zigzag decoration around the collar is not paralleled.[234] Both Mersin and neighboring Tarsus appear to have been native Cilician towns refounded after some Mycenaean occupation in the twelfth century, although the later settlements may have had some small Greek quarters. Coldstream suggests that the Greek material at both sites may have come from the Rhodian colony of Soloi, on the coast slightly further southwest, although no deep soundings have been made there.[235] The location of Mersin for a Cretan artifact is not implausible; while Cretan artifacts have not been reported east of Rhodes

---

[229] Snodgrass 1974b: 196–201.

[230] Dunbabin 1962: 27, no. 121, pl. 2; cited in Index IV, 563, at "?Cretan vases."

[231] Boardman and Hayes 1966: 78–80; Boardman 1966. Boardman and Schweizer (1973: 275 Diagram XX, 280) identify three pieces from Tocra as definitely Cretan; they refer to pieces 921 and 924 from Boardman and Hayes 1966 as early sixth century, whereas Boardman and Hayes had called them "LO to early sixth century." I have noted these two pieces as Late Orientalizing to early sixth century in the catalogue. Boardman (1968: 134) interprets the Korobios story as indicating that Cretans "clearly . . . had long [by 637] been visiting this coast."

[232] Stucchi 1984a: 141; 1984b: 164–68.

[233] Barnett 1939: 114, pl. 78.16; Garstang (1953: 253, 255) accepts Barnett's Cretan interpretation. Cf. Coldstream (1968: 321, 386), who notes generally only East Greek pottery at Mersin.

[234] Coldstream 1984a: pl. 26.

[235] Garstang 1953: 254; Coldstream 1977: 95–96. For Tarsus, see Hanfmann 1963: 115 n. 93, 129, 132–39; regarding the problematically early dating surrounding Tarsus, see Boardman 1965: 5–12; Coldstream 1968: 321; Snodgrass 1971: 115.

subsequent to the possible eleventh-century vases on Cyprus, the inflow of eastern material to Crete, some of it possibly along the southern Anatolian coast, was significant in the late eighth and the seventh centuries. It is certainly possible for a Cretan vase on Cyprus to have found its way to the nearby Cilician town through subsequent exchanges or personnel movements. I have not included this piece in the catalogue.

Although Cretan artifacts found outside Crete are small in number, the geographical pattern of their occurrence is quite diverse. Maps 28 through 31 record the locations of these overseas finds of Cretan material for the eleventh and ninth through the seventh centuries. The eleventh-century finds (Map 28) are all on eastern and southern Cyprus, and there are no finds in clear tenth-century contexts. Map 29 presents the

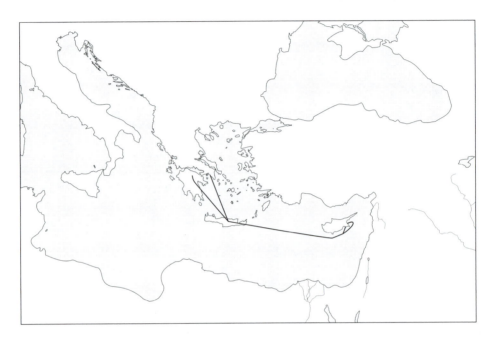

Map 28. Locations of Cretan Artifacts Overseas, Eleventh Century

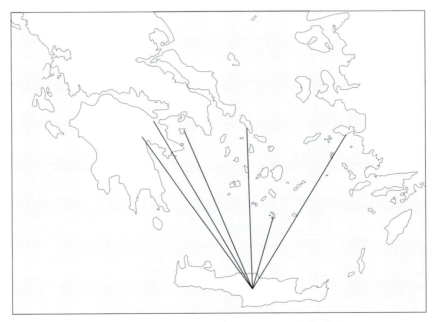

Map 29. Locations of Cretan Artifacts Overseas, Ninth Century

ninth-century finds, which span an arc across the central Aegean, from Samos on the east, to Andros, Aegina, Corinthia and Argos, and Thera to the south. Of these locations, the Samian and Sparta finds are at sanctuary sites. The eighth-century finds (Map 30) are even more widespread, but again span an arc across the Aegean, this time from Ialysos on Rhodes at the eastern end, to Miletus, Thera, Delos, and mainland sites—

Athens, Delphi, Dodona, Sparta, and Olympia. Cretan artifacts appear at western sites during this period—at Taranto, at a cluster of sites in Etruria and Latium, and at Gela on Sicily. During this century, Cretan finds increase at sanctuaries—Miletus, Delos, Delphi, Dodona, Sparta, and Olympia. The seventh century pattern (Map 31) is similar to that of the eighth century, with the Aegean arc spanning from Kameiros to Samos,

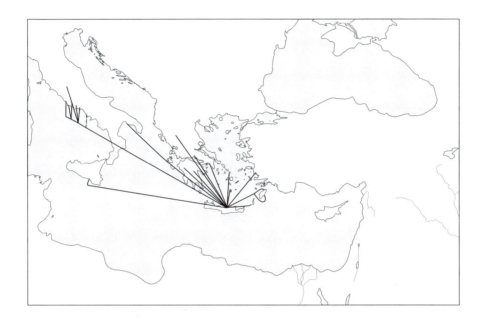

Map 30. Locations of Cretan Artifacts Overseas, Eighth Century

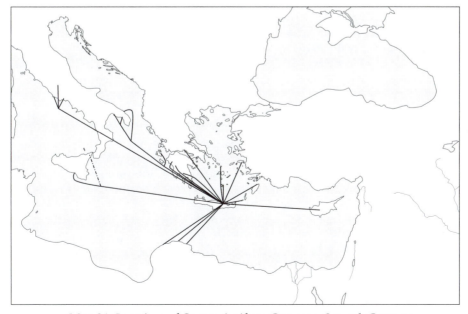

Map 31. Locations of Cretan Artifacts Overseas, Seventh Century

Thera, and Delos, and continuing across mainland Greece, exclusively at sanctuary sites—Delphi, Bassae, Olympia, and Sparta. Going westward, Cretan material appears at Aetos on Ithaka, in the heel of Italy at Brindisi and Taranto, at a smaller number of Etruscan and Latian sites, and again in Gela. Toward the end of this century, and possibly going into the early sixth century, are links to the three North African sites—Aziris, Cyrene, and Tocra. A striking feature of this collection of maps—both of overseas artifacts on Crete and of Cretan artifacts overseas—is that, for all the discussion of the lack of evidence of reciprocal contacts between Crete and many of the regions that contributed the foreign material found on Crete, the lines from Crete in Maps 28 through 31 fairly well parallel many of the lines in Maps 9 through 27. There are not exact correspondences, and we cannot identify Cretan locations for most of the Cretan artifacts found overseas, but there is sufficient aggregate parallel, especially with the Greek connections and to some extent with the Italian connections, that it is difficult not to envision shipping routes with an array of material moving in both directions. Granted, many of the Cretan artifacts overseas, particularly in the seventh century, come from sanctuaries, which presumably did not send out material exports (but rather spiritual ones) for their votive deposits received from overseas, but simply the rough directions of flows to and from Crete yield the appearance that Cretan material found at sanctuaries could have been deposited on more worldly trading trips. That certainly would have cut the transportation costs of devotion—and Cretans need not have carried the Cretan votive material, although they may have. There is no need to see Crete as the final destination for many, or even any, of these runs, but Crete certainly emerges looking like a member of bilateral interactions—but only to Greece and the west, not to the Near East and Cyprus. The maps do little to illuminate the reciprocal basis of Crete's strong eastern connections.

CRETE AND MAINLAND GREECE: ATTICA AND CORINTH

Attica and Corinth are major contributors to the foreign Early Iron Age artifacts found in Crete. Although Cretan exports are not common, even by the standards for Cretan artifacts, both Attic and Corinthian finds of Cretan objects appear to be underrepresented, considering their imposing presence at Cretan sites. There are enough traces of relations between Crete on the one hand and both Phoenicia and Cyprus on the other that those relationships have attracted speculation. Crete once was considered to have exerted a major artistic influence on Corinth,[236] but that is now generally discounted, and no other stories have replaced it, nor has a story been added for Attica. The artifactual evidence does not leave much to go on, and reasoning from historical patterns of the three regions' resource endowments has not inspired much speculation in the literature beyond gift exchange between Knossos and Athens.

The record of Corinthian external relations in the eighth and seventh centuries is much the inverse of Crete's throughout the Early Iron Age: despite the extensive ceramic record of Corinthian activity overseas, Corinthia itself shows remarkably little evidence of imports in its own ceramic record. There was no mining activity in Corinthia, so metal objects themselves—gold, silver, bronze, even iron—are evidence of importing, as are the ivories; but an extensive array of foreign pottery is absent in Corinth.[237] Athens, on

---

[236] Johansen 1923: 54–59, 64–66; Payne 1931b: 4–5, 53.

[237] Weinberg 1943: 32, 73. Blegen, Palmer, and Young 1964: in an otherwise unspectacular cemetery, no material from the forty-nine Geometric graves could be established as foreign–in fact, most were empty of offerings (13–14), and from the sixty-five graves of the Protocorinthian period, foreign material amounted to a green faience scarab, possibly Twenty-Sixth Dynasty, possibly earlier, and an ivory brooch (61, 66). Next to no foreign material was found in the Potters' Quarter: Stillwell and Benson 1984: 258–59: three pieces out of nearly 1,500 were "virtually the only possible traces of physical contact with outside ceramic influences during the 8th and 7th centuries on the part of ceramists of the Potters' Quarter." Pemberton (1989: 1, 138), working with PC and later material, finds only two foreign pieces, both Attic, dating before 550. Amyx and Lawrence (1975) report no imported material at all; the well may have been dug as early as the first decades of the seventh century (63), and the other material begins a little before mid-seventh century (13). Stillwell (1948) reports no imported material prior to some fourth-century glass objects (130–31), although the earliest pottery is LG (6) and the terracotta molds are as early as the early seventh century (88). Salmon (1984: 128) summarizes the evidence for Corinthian imports prior to the Classical period as negligible by comparison to later materials. Cf. Amyx 1988, 2: 678.

the other hand, received a flood of Corinthian pottery beginning in the second quarter of the eighth century, and by the last quarter of that century, roughly 10 percent of every well group is Protocorinthian or Early Corinthian.[238] The common appeal to nonsurviving—probably agricultural—exports from Crete is paralleled by the likelihood of a great extent of nonsurviving agricultural imports to Corinthia during its great expansionary period.[239]

The Attic or Corinthian artifacts found in Crete are predominantly ceramic, in contrast to, say, those of the early Cypriot connection and most of the Near Eastern products. The individual pieces do not look like plausible candidates for Homeric gift exchange, despite Coldstream's suggestion,[240] and there is no evidence for migrations from either Attica or Corinth to Crete, as may have been the case with Italy and Cyprus. Neither do the Attic or Corinthian ceramic products in Crete look, in general, like the consequences of expatriate craftsmen resident in Crete. First, the presence of both Attic and Corinthian products lasts several hundred years, longer than would be expected as a consequence of resident aliens without absorption by the local population and culture. Second, the timing of the virtual disappearance of Attic pottery and the surge in Corinthian pottery coincides with the replacement of Attic pottery exports by Corinthian pottery throughout the Hellenic world.[241] Finally, the fabrics on the Attic and Corinthian vases are

Attic and Corinthian, and it seems implausible that clay, rather than the vases themselves, would have been imported to Crete to be made into fine vases by expatriate potters, on a scale sufficient to account for the Attic and Corinthian pottery found in Crete. Trade appears to be the only mechanism by which the great majority of the Attic and Corinthian products could have gotten to Crete.

What could Cretans have offered to Attica and Corinth? First consider wood. After 600, Crete sent cypress to Athens for the main, weight-bearing timbers for the Parthenon, and an Attic comedy produced during the early years of the Peloponnesian War included cypress from Crete in a list of Athenian imports.[242] Discussing the Minoan period, Branigan suggests that oar-propelled ships would have been unlikely to take on heavy cargoes like timber,[243] but the evidence of sails even on merchant ships equipped with oars reveals no major obstacle to a Dark Age timber trade. But how much timber could Attica and Corinth have used, and would it have come from the regions of Crete showing evidence of Attic and Corinthian imports?

Both Attica and Corinth were natural grain-deficit regions,[244] and Crete was not a natural granary, as were Egypt, Sicily, and Cyrenaica. Crete is, and undoubtedly was in the Early Iron Age, a "natural" olive-oil producer, but Attica was a "natural" oil producer as well, and was much closer to Corinth as a trading partner if Corinth

---

[238] Brann 1962: 28. Brann, nonetheless, dissociates the smaller quantities of East Greek pottery from trade, but questions why there was "no Cycladic or Cretan pottery to speak of" if there had been a direct trade route to the east. She apparently sees Aegina and Corinth as having been intermediaries in Athens's trade with the East, despite the equally small quantities of Cretan material, in particular, at either site. She prefers traveling potters and other travelers carrying personal goods to account for the foreign material other than Corinthian and Aeginetan at Geometric Athens. This interpretation leaves open the question of why shippers would prefer to transship at these alternative sites, at some expense, rather than take advantage of direct (but not necessarily nonstop) shipment to Athens's accessible port facilities at Phaleron.

[239] Salmon 1984: 129–31.

[240] Coldstream 1983: 204–5.

[241] The only Attic materials reported on Crete in the seventh century are a few transport amphora sherds from Kommos. In a study of Attic Black-figured (ABF) pottery found in the Mediterranean, Rosati (1989: 19, Tables 1–2) reported no ABF material from Crete in the period 630–600, and only one ABF piece from the period 600–575, a dinos from Gortyn by a painter in the circle of Sophilos (ibid.: 35–37, 355, no. 1110, Tables 10–11), which Bakir (1981: 59, 72, no. B.2) dates to probably 570–560. For the period 575–560/50, Rosati again reports no ABF pottery from Crete (1989: 146–49, Tables 143–44).

[242] Meiggs 1982: 99, 200; Knorringa 1926: 75.

[243] Branigan 1970: 189–90.

[244] Garnsey (1985: 74–75) recalculates Attic grain-supply capacity and suggests that Attica was much less dependent on external grain than has been believed, until "well into the post–Persian war period," although he does not dispute the existence of earlier grain imports.

had been a net importer of olive oil.[245] Again for the Minoan period Branigan suggests, intuitively, that olives, olive oil, and dried grapes were the only foods that Crete may have been able to offer abroad.[246] This would appear to rule out several major candidates for Cretan exports, but in fact it does not. Comparative, not absolute, advantage is sufficient motivation for exchange, and at relatively low levels of exports of both grains and olive oil, Crete may have been able to supply both Attica and Corinth competitively, that is, at prices that would have permitted the sale of their products in Attica and Corinth. For example, suppose that Crete could produce wheat and olive oil at relative costs such that a family of six could produce three medemni of wheat and two choes of olive oil, but in Attica production conditions were less favorable to wheat and the same family could produce two medemni of wheat and two choes of olive oil. The Cretan wheat:olive oil ratio of 3:2 exceeds the Attic ratio of 1:1. It would pay the producers of both Crete and Attica for Cretans to produce more wheat than they could consume, the Atticans to produce more olive oil than they could consume, and the two groups to exchange the difference. This clearly happened between Attica and the Black Sea region in subsequent centuries, but

whether such divergent production conditions existed between Crete and its mainland pottery suppliers is an open question. Transport costs also were high, and may have been high relative to the cost of grain and other agricultural commodities. Could comparative production advantages have outweighed transport costs?

How much difference in relative production costs could have existed? Using anachronistic data on some agricultural yields for the Cyclades in 1916, Crete in 1947, and all of Greece in 1934–38, offers at least some notion not only of comparative advantages that may have existed, but, more importantly, of how comparative advantage would have worked.[247] I begin with the grains. The ratio of wheat yield per hectare to barley yield per hectare is 0.643 for the Cyclades, 0.805 for Crete, and 0.761 for all of Greece. Statistically, the Cretan and all-Greek ratios probably are indistinguishable, but the difference between the ratios of Crete and the Cyclades probably is meaningful. Shifting a hectare of barley into wheat would cost 25 percent more in the Cyclades (on average; the islands could differ substantially among themselves) than on Crete, according to these figures. Crete could trade wheat to some of the Cycladic islands for barley, and producers and consumers at each place

---

[245] Boardman (1977: 190, 193) observes that there is less evidence for the olive in Dark Age Greece than in Mycenaean times: oil lamps are absent from the archaeological remains, and the stirrup jar largely disappears, although other slow-pouring, small flasks with narrow round mouths appear, which would have been logical oil containers. The olive is of minor account in the Homeric epics, and Hesiod does not mention olive cultivation. Nevertheless, Boardman believes that "it is impossible that the cultivation of the olive was one of the things which the Greek Geometric Renaissance had to relearn." Wright (1972: 195–96) reports a substantial rise in the olive pollen curve in cores from Osmanaga Lagoon, at the head of Navarino Bay, between c. 1100 and 700, following the Mycenaean collapse. Another core from Lake Voulkaris, north of the Gulf of Patras, yields a radio-carbon date for a rise in the olive pollen curve of c. 1190±120, also following the Mycenaean period (198–99). (The bidecadal radiocarbon curve is well behaved [single-valued] in this range: Pearson and Stuiver 1986: 844, fig. 1B, unsmoothed curve; cf. 848, fig. 2B, smoothed curve.) Wright dismisses the hypothesis that these increases represent the replacement of the domesticated olive with the wild olive, because the olive trees would not seed in that way. He does suggest that the olive might have made a good subsistence crop during dangerous times because it needs far less attention than do grain crops. However, the length of time required for an olive tree to begin producing is great, as much as two human generations, and such a delay in the output would reduce its value during troubled times, when high rates of time preference (i.e., heavy discounting of the future) would prevail. Greig and Turner (1974: 193) support Wright's interpretation of continuous olive cultivation in Messenia. Their radiocarbon datings from Philippi in Macedonia show a gap in olive pollen between c. 1350 and 1000, with a weak peak representing local cultivation resuming between c. 1000 and 500 (182, Fig. 3; 183, Table 3). At Nichoria, also in Messenia, Coulson (1983a) reports the use of olive wood as a major building construction material (probably roofing) in Dark Age II and II/III Transition periods (38) and its use as firewood in the same periods (27). From the same site, Shay and Shay (1978: 56, Tables 5-9 and 5-10) report 16% of Dark Age I–II wood charcoal samples and 25% of DA III samples to be olive.

[246] Branigan 1970.

[247] Data for Crete are from Allbaugh 1953: Tables 47, 48; data from the Cyclades are from Sanders 1984: Table 3; all-Greece olive-oil yield is from Hutchinson 1962: 41.

would be better off. The relative yields of olive oil to wheat are (were) 0.595 for Crete and 0.278 on average for the rest of Greece (the olive-oil yield is not available for the Cyclades). The use of other, twentieth-century A.C. data on grains and legumes in Crete, Attica, Corinth, and Lesbos suggests that Cretan comparative advantages in field agriculture are greater vis-à-vis the northern islands than with Attica and Corinth, but there is no information on agriculture-manufacturing comparative advantages, and certainly nothing that would be valid for the Dark Ages.[248] I do not have comparable data on Attic and Corinthian wine and olive-oil yields, but Cretan comparative advantages in oil with both those regions could have permitted Cretan communities to send olive oil and possibly even some wheat to Attica and Corinth for manufactured goods, not restricted to pottery, which I presume was a small share of manufactured production, but may in fact represent the net direction of movement of manufactured goods. The Cretan wheat exports need not have been enough to attract notice, but they could have helped offset the cost of manufactured imports. The comparative production advantage that would have been necessary to outweigh transport costs is an open question.

Wool is another product that Crete may have been able to sell abroad in some regions, possibly in both Attica and Corinth. From the age-at-death distribution in remains of animal bones at Early Iron Age sites, it may be possible to find evidence of sheep and goat husbandry

for wool. Keeping animals for milk results in a large proportion of young animals being killed, with only, say, 40 to 50 percent surviving past the first year, and a slow drop-off thereafter. Wool husbandry is associated with some 80 percent of the animals surviving through the first year, and some 50 to 60 percent surviving through six years. Keeping animals for meat leaves a distribution between these two patterns.[249] These distributions of animal-survival ages will be affected by the interest rate, whether that rate is a pure rate of time preference in consumption in an autarkic community or whether it reflects the importation of the interest rate determined in a more sophisticated community's capital market.[250] It is possible that tenth- or ninth-century trade (or eleventh-century trade, for that matter) with the Near East, where tamkāru were making and taking loans at interest, would have brought Cretan interest rates closer to the rates determined by the more populous and more prosperous Mesopotamian and Levantine regions. Although Near Eastern interest rates were high (ranging from 20 to 50 percent, depending on the location, date, and type of loan[251]), the personal danger in Crete that sent communities to remote, crag-top settlement sites like Karphi and the Kastro at Kavousi early in the Dark Age would have sent local Cretan interest rates (essentially rates of time preference in consumption) even higher.[252] Opening trade of any sort should have brought down these Cretan interest rates. Lower interest rates

---

[248] These other comparative-advantage figures are presented and discussed in Appendix A.

[249] Payne (1973: 282–84, figs. 1–3) presents three diagrammatic models of flock-management strategies. He corroborates killing strategies underlying these models through discussions with contemporary residents of the area and discusses some possible interruptions to the simple interpretations of the archaeological remains with his age-survival curves from a known population (299–301, fig. 17). If a community either exported some of its animals or purchased its animals or meat from another community, the interpretation of age-survival curves from archaeological remains would be compromised seriously. Halstead (1987: 82), in assessing the application of Payne's age-survivor model, suggests another potential interpretive problem: if there were economies of scale in flocks such that the retention rate of female lambs could be reduced, proportionally more males might be kept alive in larger flocks. Halstead appears to have in mind that the female lambs kept in reserve for breeding might be a fixed number rather than a fixed proportion of flock size, at least within a certain range of flock sizes. The case is hypothetical, and no evidence is presented suggesting that such scale economies exist.

[250] Trade, or exchange by any other name, involves an exchange of production costs as well as products, and the interest rate is simply one component of production costs.

[251] Goldsmith 1987: 14–15.

[252] The interest rate as a rate of time preference is simply the premium a person would require to defer consumption in the present period to the next period. The period used is frequently the year, but monthly interest rates are not uncommon, and conversion from a monthly to a yearly base is straightforward. Financial markets are unnecessary for interest rates to exist, although they facilitate the exchange of present and future consumption among people with different arrays of assets.

would have made it more agreeable to keep sheep and goats longer, for their wool. In a consideration of Dark Age Greek wool production, Snodgrass's hypothesis of a post-Mycenaean return to a pastoral economy characterized by a meat-based diet cannot be ignored.[253] Isager and Skydsgaard are reluctant to accept this thesis,[254] and I do not find the logic or the evidence offered in support of it compelling. In risky times, reliance on herds that could be killed in a stroke and take years, even a human generation or more, to replace would expose a community to an avoidable chance of starvation.[255] Any kill-off (or survival-age) pattern emerging from archaeological data should be considered in the light of whether community herd size was at a desired steady state or was subjected to a radical change in either direction over the period from which bones are available.[256] Hesse raises the possibility that a change in the product mix desired from a herd might change the desired herd size, independent of external stability considerations, by virtue of those products' having different human labor efforts associated with them;[257] this, of course, adds a complication to the straightforward interpretation of apparent herd sizes. With these cautions in mind, evidence from Kavousi, cast into Payne's frame-

work, yields an age-at-death distribution of caprines close to a meat-production curve, although the authors take care to point out that any pure strategy was unlikely.[258] It cannot be inferred from these findings that wool was not produced, even in exportable quantities, in the Kavousi area, and it is difficult to compare these findings with the documentary evidence of the importance of wool in Minoan times.[259] Many scholars have suggested textiles as a medium for transferring designs that appear on locally made pottery when genuinely imported pottery is absent,[260] but Schweitzer and Barber have taken a further step in specifying the mechanisms involved.[261] Schweitzer identified the checkerboard, saw-tooth, and lozenge patterns on Geometric pottery as direct developments from weaving technique, while Barber, as a textile scholar, identifies specific weaving techniques as the basis of different Geometric vase designs and has reproduced a number of those designs in weaving. The color scheme of the Fortetsa Late Geometric-Early Orientalizing funerary pithoi particularly strike her as reproductions of cloth colors. Artifactual proof of these suggestions will be difficult to deliver, but they lend strength to other bases of suspicion that decorated textiles were produced in quanti-

---

[253] Snodgrass 1987: 197–200, based on a review of animal bones (at Nichoria), dedications of animal figurines (Pherai, Olympia), seeds (Iolkos), and settlements (Epirus and Euboea).

[254] Isager and Skydsgaard 1992: 19 n. 11.

[255] The twenty-year age profiles for sheep presented in Cribb 1987: 392–99, figs. 2–7, demonstrate the potential for difficulty and slowness in herd recovery from decimation. Cattle, with twice the gestation period of sheep, would take a considerable time to replace.

[256] Rosen (1987: 547–57) examines a number of counterintuitive responses of herd size to various cost and demand factors. Long-term and short-term changes (i.e., changes that are expected to be either permanent or long-lasting, as contrasted to changes that are expected to be impermanent) can have different effects in both desired herd size and the process by which that size is reached. On cattle as capital and consumption goods with cyclic responses to demand and cost changes, see also Jarvis 1974: 489–520; Rosen, Murphy, and Scheinkman 1994: 468–92.

[257] Hesse 1988: 590.

[258] Klippel and Snyder 1991: 185, fig. 1.

[259] Cf. Killen 1964: 1–15. Young (1965: 111–22) questions Killen's assessment of the importance of wool to the Late Minoan economy.

[260] *Inter alios*, Frankfort (1936–37: 116–17) deduced Cretan imports of western Asian decorated textiles in the Minoan period. Demargne (1947: 120–21) emphasized Phoenician textiles in transmitting Near Eastern artistic ideas to Crete. He suggested that the Phoenicians carried Egyptian, Arabian, and Mesopotamian fabrics as well. Referring to the Egyptian, Phoenician, and Assyrian artistic influences and artifacts at the panhellenic shrines as well as on Crete, Kunze (1931: 263) referred to "die restlos untergegangene Textilekunst." Schachermeyr (1979: 184) infers Cretan production in the Dark Age. On the transfer via textile trade of Assyrian motifs in particular to several Greek regions in the late eighth and early seventh centuries, see Payne 1931b: 19 n. 2.

[261] Schweitzer 1971: 30; Barber 1991: chap. 16, esp. 365–66, 370 n. 10. On the basis of changes in the woven textiles depicted in Egyptian paintings, Barber believes that Aegean textile exports of the Mycenaean era continued until early in the twelfth century (351).

ties large enough and qualities high enough to be exported, as early as the tenth century in at least some parts of Greece.[262]

It is also possible that local dye industries using murex shellfish continued at various coastal sites. Evidence of probably seventh-century dyeing activity was found in Building Q at Kommos, and although I have seen no other Early Iron Age reports of such activity on Crete, this would be one category of artifact for which to look elsewhere. Evidence of a dye industry in the same community with evidence of animal husbandry suggesting extensive wool production could be indicative of external economic relations.

During the Bronze Age, Crete had been known for perfumes,[263] and Melena has made a case for identifying Late Bronze Age Cretan exports of coriander for use in aromatics.[264] In a different product group, Varoufakis has identified some ninth-century iron tripods from Olympia with an unusually high phosphorus content that appear to be consistent with iron from Chania prefecture in western Crete. He has suggested that the iron was, in fact, exported from Crete during the Geometric period.[265] The phosphorus hardens steel made from ores with low to moderate carbon content, and this could have been recognized by metalsmiths of the time, Varoufakis believes. The Early Iron Age site nearest to these phosphorus-bearing iron ores, for which there is evidence of external economic relations, is Eleutherna, which is too far east to have been within economic exploitation of these deposits. Nevertheless, several of Varoufakis's sites of high-phosphorus iron ore are close to sites that Faure has identified as having traces of ancient occupation, if not necessarily

ancient slag heaps or mines. Varoufakis identifies Skines as a high-phosphorus iron site, and it is very close to Meskla, which is one of Faure's iron sites (also copper).[266] Faure identifies Gribiana as an iron site with LM III and Geometric sherds; it is one kilometer from Colimbari, which is one of Varoufakis's sites.[267] Ravdoukha is identified by both Varoufakis and Faure, and the latter notes Late Minoan(?), Archaic, and Classical building remains in the area.[268] Both also identify Sklavopoula, in the southwest corner of the island, near ancient Pelkis, with an Archaic floruit.[269] Varoufakis reports two other known sites with high phosphorus-content iron in the Aegean: a large metallurgical slag of probably the third to second century on Rhodes, and a slag found at Lasaia Chora on Crete, just to the south and east of Kommos. Varoufakis cites Lasaia as a Roman site, as Pendlebury lists it,[270] but Faure's description of the site as a copper-bearing location notes sherds ranging from Early Minoan to Late Minoan III in the area,[271] and I have included in the catalogue nine of the eighth- to seventh-century imported vases reported to be from Kaloi Limenes, just to the west of modern Lasaia. Sarah Morris has relied on Varoufakis's conclusions to make her case for the critical role of iron production in the Cretan economy during the first half of the first millennium, but the locations of Geometric iron-working and of prosperity on Crete in the Geometric period do not correspond particularly closely. The locations of the stronger Cretan cities cited by Faure experienced their periods of power and prosperity in the sixth and fifth centuries, after Morris's proposed collapse of Crete's Assyrian-driven iron-export industry. I can see a place for

---

[262] Seiradaki (1960: 37) suggested that the weavers at LM IIIC/Subminoan Karphi were using their grandmothers' textile designs as inspirations.

[263] Faure 1987: 101–24.

[264] Melena 1974a: 133–63; 1974b: 307–36.

[265] Varoufakis 1982: 318; map 1, 320.

[266] Faure 1966: 65; 47, map–fig. 1; on copper at Meskla, 56–57.

[267] Ibid.: 65.

[268] Ibid.: 66; Varoufakis 1982: 320, map 1.

[269] Faure 1966: 66.

[270] Pendlebury 1939: 366, map 23, and 374; Varoufakis 1982: 318.

[271] Faure 1966: 52; 53, figs. 4–5. Faure does not include Lasaia among his iron-bearing sites. Sanders (1982: 160) reports Lasaia (site 10/25) only as a site 8 kilometers west of Lebena, with some amphorae found off the coast nearby. Blackman and Branigan (1975: 28–32) report a 90-meter-long breakwater extending from the shore at Lasaia, out toward Trophos Island. The breakwater turns westward and extends another 25 meters, leaving a channel 10–15 meters wide between its tip and Trophos Island (29, fig. 7). Blackman and Branigan say the city was never important, and identify it as a Hellenistic site from sherds on the acropolis and at a nearby cemetery.

iron or iron products—intermediate or final—in an array of Cretan exports, but not as an economic linchpin, like gambling in Monaco or banking in Luxembourg.[272]

The logical next question is: What other goods besides ceramics could Attica and Corinth have traded to Crete? In the later parts of this period, both Attica and Corinth were noted for manufactured products, but Attica also exported silver and lead, and Attic transport amphora fragments from the late seventh century have been found at Kommos. With the expansion of Corinthian vine-planting as Corinth's grain trade with the west opened, it is surprising that no Corinthian transport amphorae have been found on Crete. Though it is common to think of ancient trade as involving exchanges of relatively undifferentiated items that were made nearly exclusively by each trading partner, the literary evidence from the Attic comedy fragments highlights variety (although fourth-century evidence may overstate tenth- to seventh-century variety). Hesiod's recommendation of relaxing with "Bibline" wine may refer to wine from Byblos, but regardless of the reference of the term "Bibline," the phrase suggests an interest in variety at an earlier period.[273]

CRETE AND CYPRUS

Trade clearly took place between Crete and Cyprus in the Minoan period, although the Cypriot export of copper to Crete probably has been overstated.[274] Relations between Crete and Cyprus were strong during some parts of the period 1100–600, but remain somewhat mysterious, and in the second half of the period are intertwined with relations of Phoenicia with both islands. A good deal of the mutual influence between the two islands takes the form of artistic influences of the other in locally produced vases and metalwork.[275] The mechanisms of these transmissions are unclear, although there are some candidates. What sort of island was it that seems to have been so elusively important to Crete? I have introduced evidence of Cypriot external relations over the

---

[272] Morris 1992: 132.

[273] *Works and Days* 589 (trans. Evelyn-White 1914). Burn 1960: 47: Considering "the penetration of European liquor to the remotest outposts reached by early modern trade, even among peoples who had their own native alcohol, it seems not impossible that the mysterious `bibline' wine, mentioned by Hesiod as a luxury drink, may actually have been wine of Phoenician Byblos." West (1988: 306) points to a number of complications. First, βίβλινος in the phrase βίβλινος οἶνος may refer to papyrus reeds rather than to the Phoenician city, although papyrus would appear to be an especially unusual stock with which to make wine, or even beer, since οἶνος need not specifically imply wine. Grapes would appear to have been the stock of choice for wine in Greece; growing conditions were excellent, and papyrus, being imported, could well have been too expensive to use as a substitute for grapes, particularly considering the quality of beverage each is likely to provide. Second, there is a secure fifth-century reference to a wine from Thrace known as Bibline. Third, there is little evidence otherwise of wine from Byblos. However, the term "Bibline" may generically refer to Levantine wine, as "twentier" was a common term for seagoing ships rather than specifically one with twenty oarsmen. See Chapter 3, note 37. Finally, the texts are corrupt around these lines. It would be unwise to rest a hypothesis of trade with Phoenicians on this reference, but it could offer further support in the presence of other evidence, which there is. I am indebted to David Tandy for bringing West's commentary to my attention, although he is not to be held responsible for my use of it.

[274] Gale and Stos-Gale (1989: 185–89) subjected nine of nineteen oxhide ingots from Aghia Triada (MM I or early LM IA) to lead isotope analysis and found that none were consistent with Cypriot copper fields or with Laurion in Attica. Of twenty-three bronze artifacts from the LM II destruction level of the Unexplored Mansion at Knossos, most were made from Laurion copper, and only three from Cypriot. From the LM I site of Nerou Kourou in western Crete, all fourteen objects examined were consistent with Laurion copper, as was the case with LM III objects from Samonas and Armenoi.

[275] Demetriou (1989: 75–77) details forty-two instances of Cypriot influences on Cretan pottery and metalwork and twenty of Cretan influence on Cypriot products, the latter mostly early in the first millennium, but only the Cretan vase similar to the incised one from Karphi (ENK.10 in my Catalogue of Overseas Artifacts) is believed to be an actually transported product; Popham (1979b: 318) suggests the Karphi vase might equally well have been an import. The remaining cases are locally produced items influenced by the other island via unknown mechanisms. Iacovou (1988: 83–84) would loosen some of the presumed Cretan influence to include influence from the Greek mainland as well, and even northern Syria; cf. note 284 below.

juncture between the Late Bronze Age and the Early Iron Age above, and in the subsequent section on activity in the Levant, I explore in further detail Late Bronze Age and Early Iron Age Cypriot relations with the Near East, including Egypt. I begin here with a brief discussion of Cyprus's internal Late Bronze Age background and some events that seem to have been important in determining the subsequent character of the island. I follow that sketch with a somewhat more detailed discussion of several topics in Creto-Cypriot relations between 1100 and 600.

Bronze Age Cyprus was a rich island, famous for copper, and an exporter of timber and possibly ships as well, among other items.[276] Egypt's pharaoh addressed the king of Alasia—with all its elusiveness, possibly but not certainly Cyprus[277]—as "brother," if a junior brother, as were most of Pharaoh's brothers. In the thirteenth century, the Hittites may have commanded some influence over at least part of Cyprus and seem to have fought a memorable sea battle against the Cypriots.[278] After some 350 years of commerce with the Aegean, Cyprus seems to have absorbed a migration of Mycenaeans (possibly two such migrations), probably peacefully, around 1200, after the period of great destructions of the Mycenaean palaces. The timing was, of course, close to the Levantine destructions blamed on the Sea Peoples, and several scholars have seen Cyprus alternatively as a staging area for and a victim of the Sea Peoples. Also shortly after 1200, Cyprus appears to have received immigrants from northern Canaan, possibly from destroyed Ugarit, who brought with them particular ashlar masonry practices and cultic architecture elements.[279] The ensuing century-and-a-half saw the abandonment of a number of major Late Bronze Age sites and the disappearance of Cypriot Bronze Age pottery types, but the island never went through a Dark Age

equivalent to that in Greece. There is debate over the extent and type of Mycenaean influence during this period (Were they rulers or neighbors? Were the Cypriot kingdoms listed on Sargon's stele in 709/7 the descendants of Mycenaean kingdoms or post-Phoenician developments?), and over when Cyprus "became Greek" (a Late Bronze Age Cypro-Minoan script, still undeciphered, was superseded by the Greek alphabet in the first millennium). The earliest Greek—not Mycenaean—pottery on Cyprus is the tenth-century Euboean material from Amathus, first published by Desborough, and contemporaneous Cypriot influences are present at Athens and Lefkandi. Levantine pottery of the mid-eleventh century has been found at Palaepaphos-Skales and Salamis and is not at all uncommon in the tenth century at a number of sites. Phoenicians from Tyre set up an operation of some sort in an abandoned part of Kition early in the ninth century, possibly as a way station for western trading ventures, and by late in the century, Kition appears to have been a Tyrian colony administered by a Tyrian governor. The entire island was claimed by Sargon II of Assyria in 709/7, beginning a forty-year period of relatively little-known Assyrian domination. The Cypriot kingdoms seem to have been independent for the remainder of the seventh century and experienced a brief and also little-known period of Egyptian domination in the sixth century prior to the Persian period.

CYPRUS AND CRETE IN THE ELEVENTH CENTURY: TRADE AND MIGRATION

In the eleventh century, various Subminoan elements appear in Proto-White Painted ware, quantities of which have been found on floor II at Kition.[280] At Alaas, the amphoroid krater and the amphoriskoi with two vertical handles from the rim to the shoulder may have been inspired

---

[276] Holmes 1975: 91–92.

[277] Hellbing 1979 offers a wide-ranging but inconclusive review of evidence. Cf. Merrillees 1987 for a sharp assessment of how the question of Alasia's identity has been studied. He concludes that there are inadequate grounds for firm beliefs about any particular identification to date, that philological, archaeological, and historical research have not been sufficiently coordinated to yield consistent results that meet standards of scholarship demanded on other topics. Masson (1990–91: 231–35) remains satisfied with the aggregate weight of the evidence supporting the equation of Alasia with Cyprus.

[278] Güterbock 1967: 80.

[279] Cook 1988: 21–22; Hult (1983: 89–90) interprets a modest immigration from the remnants of Ugarit, possibly extending not much beyond some craftsmen and merchants.

[280] Karageorghis 1968: 182–83; 1976: 90.

by a Subminoan prototype.[281] The pyxis was particularly popular in Subminoan Crete, and the Proto-White Painted pyxides of Cyprus, although relatively few in number, may have been inspired by Cretan examples.[282] Yon sees considerable Cretan influence on Cypriot ceramic-fabrication techniques in the eleventh century,[283] and Desborough identified a number of similarities in ceramic shapes and decorations on the two islands in the first half of the eleventh century.[284] A small number of Cretan, or suspected Cretan, ceramic pieces from the Subminoan period have been found at Salamis and Enkomi: a three-legged coarseware cooking pot (SLM.6) and an incised pitcher at Salamis (SLM.5), and a vase at Enkomi (ENK.7).[285] Desborough found confirmation of the links between Cyprus and Crete in the first half of the eleventh century in the similarities and the short-lived contemporaneity of the bird vases found at numerous sites from Cyprus to Achaea. He recommended transmission of the Type II bird vase (with a spout where the head would be) from Crete to Cyprus around 1100, although he would not rule out the reverse transmission.[286] The Cypriot (and possible Cypriot) artifacts found in Crete during the eleventh century are all metals: iron spits and a bronze tripod stand at Fortetsa (KF.2, 19), an iron knife with bronze rivets and a bronze rod tripod

at Vrokastro (VR.2,3), a bronze bowl and tripod base from Eleutherna (EL.2), a bronze pendant at Karphi (KP.1), and two arched fibulae at Phaistos (FS.1).[287] The clay stands found at Karphi are obvious imitations of similar ones in bronze found in Cyprus, and flasks at Vrokastro were inspired by Cypriot examples.[288]

Several writers have seen, around 1100, a migration to Cyprus of Cretan—Minoan— refugees from the Late Minoan IIIC disturbances. Desborough found evidence for this in the coincidence of the vase types and decorations, particularly the Type II bird vase. Further evidence for such a movement has been interpreted in the terracotta figurines of the goddess with upraised arms and high polos found in a ninth-century deposit of votive offerings in the temple area at Kition as well as terracotta centaur figurines of the early eleventh century at Enkomi and Aghia Triada, which Karageorghis believes represent a movement from Crete to Cyprus. Also found there were three fragmentary clay models of sanctuaries of a type that originated in Subminoan Crete.[289] Yon describes these finds as representing a movement of religious expression from Crete to Cyprus in the eleventh century.[290] Desborough saw the Cretan refugees in Cyprus as a natural source of continuing contact between the two islands during

---

[281] Karageorghis 1975: 48.

[282] Ibid. None of the pyxides from Alaas appear Cretan.

[283] Yon 1979: 245.

[284] Desborough 1972b: 57. Vase types: the feeding bottle (a spouted jug), the bird vase, the bottle, the kantharos, the amphoriskos with false spout by one handle, and the high-handled pyxis; decoration: the triangle enclosing a semicircle, the agrimi, and possibly the birds. The high-handled pyxis very well may have been transmitted from Crete to Cyprus. While Iacovou (1988: 35–36) accepts the likelihood of Cretan influence on Cyprus in the pyxis, she concludes that the goat/agrimi motif does not represent certain Cretan influence and, if there is a relationship at all, may indicate Cypriot influence on Crete (26, 80, 82–83). Yon (1970: 315–16) believes the Cypriot goats are derived from Syrian examples. The other motifs could have gone in either direction, and Iacovou (1988: 83) suggests LC IIIB influence on some LM IIIC vase shapes and motifs. Kling (1989: 174) detects Minoan influence in the Cypriot LC IIIB alabastron with vertical handles attached to the body.

[285] Salamis: Yon 1971: 28–29, no. 55; and 1979: 242. Enkomi: Dikaios 1969a: 316–17; 1969b: pl. 95, no. 26; Betancourt 1985: 186.

[286] Desborough 1972a: 275.

[287] Yon (1979: 242) and Desborough (1972b: 119) would add the iron knife with bronze rivets found in the Gypsadhes cemetery at Knossos, but this may be earlier. See the Catalogue of Artifacts Found Overseas for descriptions and sources.

[288] Desborough 1972b: 118–19.

[289] Desborough 1972a: 269, 275; Karageorghis 1976: 9; 1968: 184–85; 1965: 53. Karageorghis believes the later Ayia Irini centaur is derived essentially from the earlier Cretan transfers to Enkomi. Desborough, Nicholls, and Popham (1970: 28–29) would call the Cretan and Cypriot pieces sphinxes rather than centaurs and hesitate to accept these pieces as evidence of outright migration, although they do see them as evidence of close contacts between relatively new Mycenaean populations in both Crete and Cyprus.

[290] Yon 1979: 245.

a period in which commercial relations otherwise may have dwindled considerably: some of those who had left Crete for Cyprus would have returned either permanently or temporarily, "assuming that this move did take place, . . . or there may have been trade connexions."[291] Tzedakis, endorsing the hypothesis of the earlier population movement from Crete to Cyprus, sees Cypriot influence on pre-Geometric Crete, possibly via Rhodes, reflected in the Cypriot-inspired, locally produced, lentoid flask in both eastern (Vrokastro) and western (Gavalomouri) Crete.[292] Nikolaou dissents on the population movement on the grounds that there is not enough daily ware in Cyprus besides the terracotta goddesses to indicate such a large, resident Cretan population. He suggests that the Cretan artifacts found in Cyprus indicate Cretan traders engaged in a triangular, direct contact between Attica, Crete, and Cyprus in the early eleventh century.[293] Yon refers to the presence of Cypriot-style iron knives and bronze tripods in Crete as the result of isolated travelers or of merchants.[294] Demetriou endorses the Cretan migration around 1100, but ventures some further detail to the story on the basis of the chronology of the appearances of one island's artistic concepts on the other island. He believes that two-way contact between Cyprus and Crete remained intense for the first half-century after the presumed Cretan migration. The Cretan influence on Cyprus ended abruptly around 1050. The continued contact of the Cretan emigrants on Cyprus with their former Minoan homeland diminished around 1000 as they encountered post-Minoans on Crete, with whom their relations were not entirely cordial. The contacts were suspended for about a half-century between 1000 and 950, after which the people on the Cypriot end of the connection discovered that the new, possibly mixed population on Crete indeed formed a good market for Cypriot products. Demetriou attributes the apparent one-way traffic between Cyprus and Crete after the tenth century to the alleged introverted character of the post-Minoan Cretan population.[295] There is no need to question the characterizations of post-Minoan Cretan initiative, but the characterization of trade between the two islands as unidirectional clearly requires supplementation.

THE EASTERN CONNECTION

Large Canaanite storage jars and other Near Eastern material at Enkomi, on the eastern coast of Cyprus, suggest continuing contact between the Levant and Cyprus over the transition from the Late Bronze Age to the Early Iron Age.[296] In Enkomi's coastal successor city, Salamis, eleventh-century infant burials in undecorated Syro-Palestinian jars, a Phoenician custom, are scattered across the town, and Phoenician inscriptions begin in the ninth century. North of Salamis, nearly each tomb in the earlier cemetery at Alaas (LC IIIB, about 1150–1050) contains at least one imported Levantine flask.[297]

In western Cyprus, seventeen Phoenician vessels have been found in thirteen tombs at Palaepaphos, dating from LC III to Cypriot Geometric IA (about 1150–1000).[298] On the northwest coast, in the Paleokastro cemetery near Ayia Irini, a Phoenician tomb with a funerary inscription in Phoenician script has been dated to the second half of the seventh century; a single Geometric skyphos was the only Greek item in the cemetery.[299] On the south coast, just west of center, Amathus appears to have been a port of call on the trade route between Tyre in the east and Lefkandi, Crete, and even Sardinia in the west and northwest before the Phoenician foundation at Kition, although there is no evidence of resident foreigners there. The Greek material at Amathus is the earliest on the island, beginning well before 900, and there is a high percentage of Levantine flasks in tenth-century tombs. In nearby Limassol, six kilometers to the west, Phoenician pottery appears in eighth- and seventh-cen-

---

[291] Desborough 1972a: 269.
[292] Tzedakis 1979: 197.
[293] Nikolaou 1979: 255.
[294] Yon 1979: 245.
[295] Demetriou 1989: 84–85.
[296] Bikai 1987: 125.
[297] Salamis—Yon-Calvet 1973: 299; Yon 1987: 371–72; 1985: 205. Karageorghis 1990: 30–31.
[298] Bikai 1987.
[299] Quilici 1985: 186; Pecorella and Rocchetti 1985: 193–94.

tury tombs, and a Phoenician dedication to Baal has been dated to the eighth century.[300]

Kition, on the east-central part of the southern coast, may be most celebrated for its Phoenician influence. The city, parts of which were derelict by the late eleventh to early tenth century, came under Tyrian influence around the beginning of the tenth century and was a Tyrian colony by the end of the eighth century.[301] Coldstream identifies Kition as the most likely origin for the Phoenician unguent merchants who subsequently established branch factories on Rhodes, Kos, and Crete in the early eighth century. According to his hypothesis, Phoenician unguent merchants established at Kition first exported their wares to Crete, principally Knossos, then established a branch factory there, also presumably in the region of Knossos, where they commissioned local potters to make suitable containers that properly signaled the original contents.[302]

Accepting a ninth-century dating of the Nora Stone, Bikai concludes that the Tyrian shipping run, via Cyprus and Crete to Sicily and Sardinia, must have been established before mid-ninth century,[303] but it is reasonably clear that such a Phoenician route touching Cyprus must have existed a century to a century-and-a-half earlier.

Continuing Interactions between Cyprus and Crete, Tenth through Seventh Centuries

For the period 950–800, Coldstream cites evidence of "direct links" between the two islands: the Cretan attempt to copy pseudo-bucchero pouring vessels of Cypriot Black Slip I and II,

shaped like an opium poppy; a comb motif, which Coldstream thinks was transmitted from Cyprus to Crete before the end of the tenth century; and the appearance in Crete of the Cypriot motif of an eye painted on the trefoil lip of miniature oinochoai.[304] In the following period, the Cretan bird style of pottery decoration, with long necks, fan tails, and two leaf-shaped wings on cremation pithoi from about 750, appears nowhere else in the Aegean but is extremely common on Cypriot pottery toward the end of Cypriot Geometric III (850–750). Coldstream suggests that the coincidence of bird paintings implies either imports of Cypriot painted vases into Crete or a Cretan revival of Late Minoan IIIC birds.[305]

Coldstream describes the physical interaction after 800 as a steady trickle of Cypriot pottery imported into Crete, mainly in the Knossos area, although the catalogue of items reported in this study suggests the period around 850–700 as the major period of Early Iron Age Cypriot material on Crete, with very little Cypriot material found on Crete after about 650. Most of the imports are slow-pouring vessels, suitable for the export of unguents, and most are Black-on-Red ware, the fabric associated with the Phoenician penetration (colonization) of Cyprus and Coldstream's hypothesized branch unguent factories. Trade between Cyprus and Crete slowed considerably in the first half of the seventh century, not immediately following, but within a generation after, the Assyrian takeover of Cyprus. In the late seventh century, imports from Cyprus become scarce, possibly as a lagged response to the Assyrian seizure of the Tyrian colonies on Cyprus, dating to about 708, late in the reign of Sargon II,[306]

---

[300] Hermary 1987: 379–80; Coldstream 1986: 325; Coldstream and Bikai 1988: pt. 2, 43; Karageorghis and Iacovou 1990: 75–100.

[301] Karageorghis 1976: 95–96; Nicolaou 1976: 306–17; Michaelidou-Nicolaou 1987: 331–32.

[302] Coldstream 1969: 3–4; 1982: 268, 271.

[303] Bikai 1987: 125. Cross (1986: 120–22) dates the Nora Stone to c. 825 and the Nora Fragment to no later than the end of the eleventh century, contemporary with the bowl from the North Cemetery at Knossos (KNC.7). Aubet (1993: 181) points out that the eastern epigraphic parallels to the Nora Stone's inscription extend to the end of the eighth century, and she remains reluctant to endorse such an early chronology for Phoenician colonization in the west.

[304] Coldstream 1979: 257–59.

[305] Benson (1961: 74–75), in discussing the possible Bronze Age Philistine inspiration for the birds of the Knossos Reverse Head (RH) Painter, originally suggested by Payne (1927–28: 288), rejects the Philistine hypothesis and Cyprus as an intermediary. He finds insufficient similarity between the Philistine and Cretan birds, in the absence of a transmission mechanism, and much greater similarity between the Cretan birds and Mycenaean examples. The Cypriot birds generally do not have fishtails or reversed heads, as do the RH Painter's birds, and appear closer to 700.

[306] Boardman 1979: 268.

although possibly the Assyrian card should not be played automatically, considering the outward orientation the Assyrians appear to have encouraged on balance in their Phoenician clients.[307] The relative scarcity of Cypriot artifacts on Crete in the seventh century could be a consequence of Tyre's unsuccessful revolt against Assyrian rule in the reign of Essarhaddon (681–668). Following the revolt, Assyria restricted Tyre's freedom of trade, and these restrictions may have extended to Tyre's Cypriot interests if Assyrian authority was able to reach that far.[308] No Cretan pottery has been found in Cyprus in the Geometric or Archaic periods.[309] This pattern of artifactual remains leaves the impression of a one-sided relationship with, as Coldstream has expressed, "Cyprus always the giver, Crete always the receiver."[310] Demetriou deduces likely Cretan origins for two pottery shapes found on Cyprus—a pierced lug-handle on some plates, trays, and shallow bowls and a type of side-spouted jug—the former circa 800 or slightly later, the latter circa 725.[311] A clay goddess with upraised arms, which Karageorghis believes to be a local Cypriot product of the mid-seventh century, was found at Toumba tou Skourou. Karageorghis considers it a copy of an earlier Cretan goddess figurine that found its way to Cyprus probably in the twelfth or eleventh century.[312] Alongside the more extensive indicators of Cypriot influence on locally produced Cretan pottery, this west-to-east influence is modest indeed.

With the sparsity of information available, writers understandably have been reluctant to propose more specific mechanisms of contact. Desborough's suggestion of possible home visits by Cretan refugees in Cyprus, as well as of possible trade contacts initiated by those people, are the most specific in the literature for the years before the Phoenician colonization of Cyprus. Yon also suggests travelers or traders as agents

behind the movement of artifacts. Coldstream's proposed Cypro-Phoenician unguent activity culminating in the branch factory in Crete is quite specific as a vehicle for taking Cypriot materials and ideas to Crete, but is open-ended regarding how any reverse flows might have transpired before the establishment of Cretan production.[313] Canciani, however, ventures the reasonable hypothesis for the later centuries of this period that easily perishable products of nature, such as fabrics, were of considerable commercial importance in Creto-Cypriot relations, although he does not suggest who might have sent fabrics to whom in exchange for what.[314] Along the lines of Canciani, Boardman says that "material exports from Crete to the east [including, but not exclusively, Cyprus], if there were any, were not of a nature to have survived."[315] The difficulty and personal danger of travel during the entire period makes trade a more reasonable contact mechanism than personal travel, with the exception of travel for religious purposes, although international or panhellenic shrines existed in neither Cyprus nor Crete.[316] Particularly for refugees who had once fled a location, return visits, either temporary or permanent, do not seem particularly plausible. However, if the population movement from Crete to Cyprus at the beginning of the eleventh century, assuming it did occur, had more the character of later Greek colonizations, such return visits would be more plausible, if no less costly and only slightly less dangerous. Even with this modest revision of the population movement, some two-way contact mechanism is needed to account for the cultural contacts apparent in the art of the two islands, and trade may be the least implausible candidate.

It is time to see what summarizing will yield. There is a strong Cypriot artifactual presence on

---

[307] Köpcke (1992: 106) notes that the archaeological evidence does not indicate a downturn in Phoenician prosperity under the Assyrian domination—if anything, it shows the opposite.

[308] Bondi 1988: 42.

[309] Gjerstad 1977.

[310] Coldstream 1979: 263.

[311] Demetriou 1989: 31, 44, 77.

[312] Karageorghis 1959: 339–40, fig. 4.

[313] On branch factories in general in this period, cf. Jones 1993.

[314] Canciani 1970: 197–98.

[315] Boardman 1979: 264.

[316] Casson 1974: chaps. 2–4. The Cretan cave sanctuaries, despite the international array of artifacts found in them, appear to have been more local than panhellenic shrines. The Idaean Cave may have attracted a few foreign merchants and seamen, but it probably attracted few Dark Age pilgrims from overseas on its sole account.

Crete, beginning around 850, peaking, if that is not too sharp a term, in the eighth century, and dwindling to next to nothing by the second half of the seventh century. Most of this physical presence is on the northern side of the island, and Knossos dominates the finds; more thorough excavation there should account for only a part of this differential incidence. Cretan material on Cyprus after the Subminoan period is virtually unreported—a possible single bronze head-vase (CYP.136) suggested by Boardman. Neither are Cretan artistic influences prominent on Cyprus during this period—Demetriou suggests a total of two relatively specialized pottery shapes on Cyprus that he attributes to probable Cretan influence, even if the actual Cretan models have not turned up. The absence of Cretan material in Cyprus should not trouble us excessively, considering the general scarcity of Cretan material outside the island, but Cypriot artistic influence in Crete probably exceeds that of most other regions whose material is found in Crete. The constraint that the value of goods flowing into Crete from Cyprus must have been equated to the value of goods flowing out of Crete to pay for them cannot be ignored. It is easy to appeal to nonsurviving Cretan exports, possibly too easy for any real informational rewards. Keeping this balance-of-payments constraint in mind, what sorts of interaction could account for such a pattern of material artifacts and artistic influence? Two nonexclusive possibilities come to mind: the carrying trade and triangular trade, possibly combined. On the carrying trade, traffic from Cypriot ports, whether originating there or farther east, could have used Knossos as a victualing stop, offloading some Cypriot textiles (flax?), occasional pots, now and then metal items, to pay for supplies and water. Taking on bulkier Cretan products for sale farther west or north would have depended on space on the ship and what was unloaded in Crete; presumably captains tried to avoid having empty hold space both entering and leaving Crete. A triangular trade (or one with more corners), in which ships from Cyprus carried goods to Crete and took on Cretan goods that were sold before touching Cyprus again is another possibility, but one for which positive demonstration is hindered by the apparent ephemerality of Cretan exports. Such a triangular trade would have been principally out of the Knossos area, judging from the scarce incidence of Cypriot Early Iron Age material around Kom-

mos. A triangle between Cyprus, Athens/ Lefkandi, and Knossos is not unreasonable, and the shipping need not have been in the exclusive hands of any one group—Phoenicians, Cypriots, Eubeoans, Athenians.

CRETE AND THE PHOENICIANS: THE NEAR EASTERN AND EGYPTIAN BACKGROUND

In assessing Crete's opportunities for external relations, particularly economic relations, during the Dark Age, the progress of events in the Near East, including Egypt, is relevant and important. Cretan relations with the Phoenicians offer a clear entry into this subject, and from those relations I work backward to activities on the mainland of western Asia that form the context and background of Phoenician activity. Although Dark Age Cretan material has not been reported at any Near Eastern sites, Near Eastern material and artistic concepts have been prominent in finds at Cretan sites, demonstrating the potential importance of Near Eastern events to Cretan activities. This study spans five hundred years, far too long a period about which to generalize regarding economic activity. The importance of Greek relations with the Near East in the Greek Dark Age has long been recognized, but as scholars of the Greek regions have recognized as well, the Near East was far from a homogenous region. There was not a single trajectory of "events in the Near East" to which trading activity in Greek lands can be correlated. Different kingdoms were paramount politically at various times; others differed in their degrees of political and economic independence. The orientations of interkingdom trade changed over the period, sometimes sharply. The prosperity of the entire region varied over this half-millennium, with some apparent correlation across the various kingdoms. The period of this study begins shortly after the arrival of the Sea Peoples, which was the last straw for Late Bronze Age political arrangements, and questions may be raised regarding the degree of continuity, in a number of dimensions, between the relatively well-known Late Bronze Age and the Near Eastern Early Iron Age. Since differences of opinion exist on just what the economic organization of that context was, I devote some attention to reviewing evidence bearing on the continuity between the

Late Bronze Age and the Early Iron Age, the public and private participation in the economy and in external trade in particular, the progress of events in different parts of the region, and the relations among various kingdoms and empires. More than simply setting a backdrop against which invisible relations with Crete occurred, this review portrays the levels of economic sophistication to which Dark Age Greeks, Cretans, and others would have been exposed in transactions with these eastern regions.

Artifactual evidence of Phoenician contact with Crete extends throughout this period. The earliest pieces are the bronze bowl incised with early Phoenician script (KNC.7) found in the North Cemetery at Knossos and the fragments of transport amphorae (KM.1) found at Kommos. The bronze bowl may have been the personal possession of a Phoenician resident at the time of its interment, but its entry into Crete nevertheless represents a resource flow of at least one kind.[317] It may be earlier than the amphora fragments at Kommos or roughly contemporary. Coarseware amphora fragments continue at Kommos through the ninth and eighth centuries. The North Cemetery at Knossos also has yielded two Phoenician vases (KNC.34–35) dated to the mid-ninth century that are more suggestive of commercial contact than is the earlier bronze bowl. The late ninth century saw the establishment of the shrine with the tripillar altar in Temple B at Kommos, an apparent indication of Phoenician commercial presence that lasted possibly a century. Coldstream's hypothesized establishment of a Phoenician unguent factory at Knossos around 800 is the next major date in Phoenician-Cretan relations. There are Phoenician or possibly Egyptian artifacts, dated loosely from the Geometric to Archaic periods, in a grave at Eleutherna (EL.5–6), as well as bronze bowls at Fortetsa (KF.47) and the Idaean Cave (IC.80–82, 97) dated eighth to seventh century. The goldsmith's tomb at Khaniale Tekke con-

tained one item of Phoenician provenance (KN.63) from the late eighth to the seventh century, and two other artifacts (KN.92–93) may be of Phoenician origin or association, or of Egyptian or other Near Eastern origin. Not a single Cretan artifact has been reported in the Phoenician Levant or the surrounding regions, or at any Phoenician colonies to the west.

Relations between Cretans and Phoenicians represented by these artifacts may be illuminated better by considering Phoenicia's external politico-economic environment during this period rather than by continuing an exclusive, direct focus on Crete. The economic history of this period is rather thin, but the political history, or chronology as it were, of the time may serve to orient this examination to order or disorder that could have been reflected in economic prosperity or hardship and to changing patterns of international relations.

THE BRONZE AGE BACKGROUND THROUGH THE TURN OF THE FIRST MILLENNIUM

From the beginning of the Late Bronze Age, the Levant had been in the spheres of influence of Egypt, Assyria, and the Hittites (Maps 2 and 3 above identify locations of sites in the Near East and Egypt). The Egyptians established their Asiatic empire in the sixteenth century in a contest with the kingdom of Mitanni, with considerable devastation to the Canaanite city-states, which may not have fully recovered before the arrival of the Sea Peoples some two or three centuries later.[318] Toward the end of the Amarna period (1350–1334), Egypt lost its access to Ugarit, but the Cypriot trade with Egypt appears to have continued throughout the Late Cypriot IIC–IIIB periods, although some change in the transfer mechanisms seems to have occurred.[319] About a generation after Mereneptah (reign c. 1212–1202) turned back an incursion of Sea Peoples attacking the delta from the west, Ramesses III turned back

---

[317] Coldstream 1982: 271.

[318] Gonen 1984: 61, 70.

[319] Weinstein 1981: 16. Gittlin (1981: 55–56) notes the arrival in Palestine of new Cypriot products in Late Bronze IB and deduces from the differences in the array of Cypriot pots available in Cyprus and in Palestine that the trade was well organized, planned, and selective, indicating a thorough knowledge of the market to which the products were traded. The LB Cypriot trade with Palestine appears to have gone as far south as northern Sinai, where a number of Late Cypriot vessels of modest value have been found and interpreted as representing a private trade parallel to official supply caravans. The distribution of the pots indicates that they arrived from southern Canaan rather than from Egypt: Bergoffen 1991: 71, 72–73. See Peltenburg 1986: 150, 166–67, 170, on the continuity of Egyptian and Egyptianizing material at Cypriot sites in the twelfth century.

three attacks of Libyans and Sea Peoples in the fifth, eighth, and eleventh years of his reign, between about 1177 and 1171, after which he renounced relationships with the Aegean world.[320] Subsequently, the Philistines, Tjekker, and Sherden settled, or remained if they had settled previously, on the Canaanite coast with Egyptian sanction. The Egyptian garrison at Beth Shean did not outlast Ramesses III, and between the death of Ramesses III in c. 1166 and the third quarter of the twelfth century, perhaps even by the reign of Ramesses VI (1141–1134), Egyptian presence in Palestine had completely disappeared.[321] By the end of the Twentieth Dynasty, around 1085, Egypt had lost the remnants of its Asiatic empire, but the extent to which it suffered economically as a con-

sequence—or a concomitant—is an open question; much remains unclear about this period.[322]

Ugarit, the great trading city, was destroyed a little after 1200,[323] but about the same time, Hittite Carchemish appears to have suffered not destruction but rather a political and economic decline reflecting the withdrawal of protection by the Hittites.[324] The Hittite empire itself also collapsed around this time, probably resulting from a combination of prolonged fighting in western and southeastern Anatolia and in the east against the Assyrians, persistent drought and famine in Anatolia, and attendant migratory pressures that eventually peaked with the appearance of the Sea Peoples, who may have contributed little more than the coup de grâce.[325]

---

[320] Kitchen 1973: 244–45. Wente and Van Siclen 1976: 218. The year identified as 1177 could be as early as 1193 if the chronology of R. O. Faulkner (1975: 217–51) is used. Lesko (1992: 153–55) suggests that the Medinet Habu inscriptions of Ramesses III may describe Mereneptah's campaigns against the Sea Peoples, and similarly for Ramesses's first Libyan War; Weinstein (1992: 148) expresses reservations about Lesko's hypothesis.

[321] Weinstein 1992: 146–47; Bietak 1993: 298–302.

[322] Whether this period was one of civil war in Egypt or only of rapid but regular succession among the sons and grandsons of Ramesses III has been interpreted differently from the inscriptional and textual evidence: Černý (1975: 611–13) interprets civil war from usurpation of Ramesses V's inscriptions at Medinet Habu by Ramesses VI and a papyrus recording some sort of killing and destruction; Kitchen (1972: 188 n. 5, 192–93) infers routine successions from the patterns of usurped and intact royal inscriptions. Cf. O'Connor 1983: 188.

[323] Schaeffer (1973: 327–29) believed that Ugarit's last disaster was natural, not manmade: there is "not a button found from a fallen warrior at Ugarit . . . at the end of the thirteenth century" (328). He suggests drought as the likely cause. Karageorghis (in ibid.: 340) concurred. Neumann and Parpola (1987: 163–64) concur with this interpretation of the archaeological evidence from Ugarit, but their primary evidence is directed at the later period of Assyrian relative decline, although their environmental evidence is not particularly strong. Nevertheless, Yon (1992: 117–19) presents more recent and convincing evidence that the city was indeed sacked, probably between c. 1195 and 1185 (120). There is a wide dispersion of arrowheads (but not stockpiles) throughout the ruins, suggesting intense street fighting.

[324] Sader 1992: 159; McClellan 1992: 167. Cf. note 373 below.

[325] Singer 1983: 217; 1988: 240, 243; Heltzer 1988b: 14–15; Hawkins 1988: 99–108; Yakar 1993: 3–28. Hallo (1992: 2–3, 6) rejects what he calls "field theories" of the collapse of the Hittite and other empires around this time, which attribute many of these major events to natural disasters. Hallo believes that these events were recurring and frequently recovered from, and that we have only accidental knowledge of a few instances, which accordingly appear more abnormal than they were. He prefers to keep humans as the active agents in history and assigns the causal role in the destructions of the late thirteenth and early twelfth centuries to massive population movements. I am sympathetic to these concerns for maintaining a focus on human choice and behavior, but great migrations themselves require explanation. Some scholars, including Hallo, accept population explosions as a sufficient cause for such population movements. Sallares (1991: 129–60) accepts a high variance in human fertility rates (roughly, birth rates) and consequently sharp bursts in preindustrial population growth rates. I do not believe that evidence and the present knowledge of human fertility behavior support such a conclusion: cf. Jones forthcoming b. The focus on natural disasters can foster what Dickinson (1994: 6) has characterized as an event-dominated approach to prehistory, which he contrasts with what he considers to be a more satisfactory, process-oriented approach, which has in fact been growing more common in archaeological accounts of Aegean and Near Eastern ancient and prehistory. Of course, the environment, and particularly human interactions with it, can be viewed as sets of processes, so any methodological dichotomy between human and natural influences in prehistory and ancient history is unnecessary. Cf. Zangger's geoarchaeological investigation of Tiryns's environmental experience, Chapter 3, note 319.

The Hittite cultural, and possibly some of the administrative, heritage appears to have passed to the surviving—or emerging—kingdom of Carchemish. Population redistributions in northern Syria, primarily among the Aramaeans, during the greater part of the twelfth century disrupted trade along the Euphrates, although the interior of Syria appears not to have suffered the destructions the coastal areas did.[326] Tiglath-Pilesar I of Assyria (c. 1115–1077) took advantage of the power vacuum left by the downfall of the Hittites and fought his way to the Mediterranean coast,[327] temporarily reopening trade with the ports of North Syria, which soon would be characterized by the culture now known as Phoenician.[328] After his reign, with the disturbances in North Syria, Assyria's economic vitality was interrupted by disruptions from the Aramaeans, and its military power declined rapidly, not to recover until the last quarter of the tenth century.[329]

The disturbances along the Levant appear not to have had much impact on southern and eastern Mesopotamia—Babylon.[330] The Babylonian Kassite dynasty was engaged in warfare with both the Assyrians to the northwest and its eastern neighbors, the Elamites, throughout much of the twelfth century. Despite the possibility of some significant environmental changes, the continuation of apparent long-term population decline, and dynastic instability, there is little indication that the events to the

west were related, even though there is artifactual evidence of trade relations with the eastern Mediterranean area and the Aegean from the fourteenth century through the early twelfth.[331] However, Babylonian departure from a gold standard, possibly as early as the last two decades of the thirteenth century and continuing through at least the first two-thirds of the twelfth, could reflect interruption of trade with Egypt or Anatolia, although sources of Babylonian gold are not well known.

The Levantine coastal region had been under Egyptian control of some sort, south of a line running roughly from Qadesh, on the Orontes River, through the Bekaa Valley, from the time of the Eighteenth Dynasty, in the sixteenth century. Various nations of the Sea Peoples began to appear in Canaan, beginning at least in the thirteenth century: the Sherden and several other Sea Peoples were mercenaries in the army of Ramesses II at the Battle of Qadesh against the Hittites in 1301 (1276 according to the low chronology), and are attested as early as the mid-fourteenth century in the Amarna letters.[332] From their earlier roles as mercenaries and pirates, the various Sea Peoples moved into confrontation with the Egyptians, both in the west, in Mereneptah's reign, and in the east, in the reign of Ramesses III as celebrated in the Medinet Habu reliefs. Farther south, along the southern Canaanite coast, the cities of the Late Bronze Age, under Egyptian supervision at the

---

[326] Sader 1992: 159–61; McClellan 1992: 166–69. Winter (1976: 47) discusses the preservation of second-millennium Hittite cultural and artistic features in first-millennium North Syrian artwork.

[327] Frankenstein (1979: 267) believes that Tiglath-Pilesar's movement to the Mediterranean coast was essentially peaceful. Cf. Wiseman 1975: 457–64, esp. 461. Neumann and Parpola (1987: 176, Table 2, App. A) note correspondences between possible indicators of climatic change and population movements in north Syria in the twelfth to eleventh centuries.

[328] The question exists whether the occupants of the Phoenician coast in the Iron Age were the same ethnic groups who lived there during the Bronze Age. Muhly (1970), Röllig (1983), Markoe (1990: 13–26), and Garbini (1993: 331) all raise questions regarding continuity between Late Bronze Age Canaanites and the Early Iron Age Phoenicians. Aubet (1993: 16–21) sees a relatively smooth continuity along the northern Levantine coast. Answers to this question would not affect the issues addressed here.

[329] Saggs 1984: 65–66, 70.

[330] Zettler 1992: 175–80; Oates 1986: 104.

[331] Among the Near Eastern cylinder seals from LH IIIB:1 Thebes were twelve Kassite seals: Porada 1965: 173; 1966: 194; Symenoglou 1985: 47, 226–27. An ox-hide ingot at Dur-Kurigalzu, on the outskirts of modern Baghdad: Oates 1986: 89, 91.

[332] For the Qadesh battle inscriptions, see Lichtheim 1976: 63, 64–65. Cifola (1988: 301–4) interprets the Egyptian narrative of the encounters with the Sea Peoples in Palestine as a literary condensation of a continuous and lengthy interaction. The Wilbour Papyrus, from the Twentieth Dynasty (c. 1142), includes sixty-eight Sherden, presumably retired soldiers, renting temple lands in Middle Egypt as farmers, hinting at some element of social continuity through these interactions: Kemp 1992: 218, 311, fig. 103.

least, demonstrated extensive trade relations with Cyprus, the Aegean, Syria, and Egypt.[333] Though the chronology and sequence of events is uncertain yet, various Sea Peoples appear to have taken over the existing urban system of Canaan, with at least some of its international trading network, around the end of the thirteenth century through the mid-twelfth century, apparently peacefully in the thirteenth century.[334]

The northern Levantine coast (Phoenicia in the Early Iron Age) and Palestine enjoyed about three centuries of independence, from c. 1200 to c. 900, but that period is less well-known than either the preceding or the following period, when the region is reported upon in the documents of the great powers into which it was incorporated.[335] Tyre, Sidon, and Byblos all were flourishing maritime cities just after the reign of Tiglath-Pilesar I. Although there is some evidence of a relative decline of Byblos in the eleventh century, Tyre, Sidon, and probably Arvad appear to have attained considerable political and naval power during that time.[336]

In southern Canaan, Ashdod (Stratum XIV), among other cities, was destroyed in the late thirteenth century, and Philistine pottery appears subsequently in Strata XIIIa and XIII.[337] By the end of the eleventh century, Ashdod had recovered under Philistine occupation and expanded to a size of about 100 acres in the Stratum X city.[338] Recently, a Canaanite jar from tomb 11 at Enkomi has been assigned an origin in Iron Age I Ashdod (1200–1000) by neutron-activation analysis.[339] In addition to this single jar from Ashdod, Mazar cites a group of some twenty others found in a secure twelfth-century context in the Ingot God Temple at Enkomi, all similar to Iron Age I jars from Strata XII–X at Tel Qasile, about forty kilometers north of Ashdod; however, similar jars are nearly unknown in northern Palestine.[340] Ashdod continued to enjoy prosperity and extensive commercial links with other regions—Egypt, Mesopotamia, and Phoenicia—despite several destructions (by King David of Israel in the early tenth century and possibly by Sheshonq I of Egypt c. 923[341])—into the late eighth century, when it was massacred and destroyed by Sargon II and repopulated with outsiders.[342] The Philistines apparently founded the town at Tel Qasile, north of the Yarkon River about two kilometers from the sea, around 1150, suggesting the continuing importance of the coastal trade to the Philistine economy.[343] The city of Ekron (Tel Miqne), also occupied by the Philistines, reached almost fifty acres in the first half of the twelfth century and flourished from the mid-twelfth century through the early tenth century,

---

[333] Gonen 1992: 236. By LB II–III (1400–1150), scarcely a tomb or excavated room in Canaan has not yielded at least one imported ceramic vessel (216, 248). However, the archaeological record has preserved far more evidence of foreign goods in Canaan than of Canaanite products abroad, suggesting Canaanite export specialization in products that have not survived. Gonen suggests that the textile industry may have been well developed in Canaan by the Late Bronze Age: heaps of split murex shells have been found in a LBA stratum at Accho, near the central Canaanite coast. Gonen also suggests that agricultural surpluses probably constituted the bulk of Canaanite LBA exports, based on the wide distribution of the Canaanite jar, which was designed specifically for the transport of liquids, probably wines and oils (247–48).

[334] Tubb (1988: 256–60, 264–65 n. 16) interprets the grotesque-style anthropoid clay coffins found at Beth Shean, dated to the thirteenth century, as burials of Sherden mercenaries serving in the Egyptian army prior to the arrival of the Philistines and the clashes of other Sea Peoples with Ramesses III in the early twelfth century.

[335] Weill 1980: 175. Stieglitz (1990: 11) describes the Phoenician coast of the Levant as a "political vacuum" during the twelfth century.

[336] Stieglitz 1990: 10–11.

[337] Dothan and Dothan 1992: 165.

[338] Mazar 1990: 308; 1992: 271. Ashdod was a large city by southern Canaanite standards, but for comparison with a major metropolis of the period, Nineveh covered nearly 1,800 acres: Barkay 1992: 372.

[339] Gunneweg, Perlman, and Asaro 1987: 168–72.

[340] Mazar 1988: 225–26. The jars from the Ingot God Temple are published in Courtois 1971: 249–51, fig. 91 and 256, fig. 96.

[341] Dothan and Dothan (1992: 184) suggest that Sheshonq was the destroyer of the Stratum IX city, but Ashdod was not on the list of Canaanite cities Sheshonq himself claimed to have destroyed: Barkay 1992: 307.

[342] Dothan and Dothan 1992: 184–87.

[343] Mazar 1990: Table 6, 300; 1992: 272.

with elaborate finds of that period indicating relations with Cyprus and the Aegean.[344] Nonetheless, the extensive international trade of southern Canaan/Philistia in the Late Bronze Age declined in Early Iron Age I, and imported Cypriot vases are rare in Palestine from the beginning of the twelfth century through the middle of the eleventh.[345] This trade was conducted on a reduced scale in the eleventh century, mostly with Phoenicia and to some extent with Cyprus.[346] In the second half of the eleventh century, Cypriot imports reappear in small numbers at Megiddo and Tel Qasile, although the continued presence of metal objects suggests that relations with Cyprus may have been maintained throughout Iron Age I without being reflected in pottery imports.[347] The earliest Cypro-Geometric pottery found at Dor, on the coast nearly due west of Megiddo, comprises at least eight different vessels found in a building, possibly of public function, on the street nearest the inside of the city wall. The pots are dated, from the local pottery, to the period between the second half of the eleventh century and the first decades of the tenth.[348] Dor was a thriving, independent port city, apparently of the Tjekker, in Wen-Amun's time (c. 1075; the Stratum XII city), but it was destroyed around the mid-eleventh century, probably by the Phoenicians. The Phoenicians appear to have destroyed Acco and several other coastal cities occupied by the Sherden about the same time. Stern suggests that the Cypriot White Painted ware found at Dor indicates trade between Palestine and Cyprus, or even an "internal transfer" of goods between Phoenicians at Dor and other Phoenicians on Cyprus.[349] Cypro-Geometric finds similar to those at Dor are

reported at fourteen other Canaanite sites, with dates from c. 1050 through the early tenth century.[350] The small quantities of this pottery suggest to Gilboa that they were secondary items of exchange in renewed trade.[351] Imported pottery, largely Cypro-Phoenician ware, begins to reappear in the southern Canaan area in large quantities during the tenth century, continuing through the remainder of the Iron Age.[352]

POLITICS AND ECONOMICS IN THE NEAR EAST, c. 1000–600

In the last years of the Twenty-First Dynasty, the first half of the tenth century, Egypt effectively split into Upper and Lower Kingdoms, with the High Priests of Amun ruling at Thebes and the kings of the Twenty-First and Twenty-Second Dynasties ruling in the north. The decline in the quality of Egyptian ivories after c. 1050, until the Saite period, may reflect an economic inability to sustain the skills in that craft, a decline not restricted to the arts.[353] Thebes became a political backwater, but northern Egypt under Sheshonq I and his successor Osorkon I, from the mid-tenth century to the early ninth century, renewed the secular friendship of Egypt with the princes of Byblos.[354] This relationship with Egypt did not restore Byblos to the preeminence it had held in the second millennium, but the Egyptian intervention may have helped Byblos remain outside the sphere of direct Tyrian domination in the tenth through the eighth centuries.[355]

Intriguing evidence of material interaction between Egypt and the Aegean region during this period comes from a mummy coffin in the Egyptian Museum in Stockholm. Found tucked

---

[344] Mazar 1990: 308–9.

[345] Gilboa 1989: 204.

[346] From tombs in Cyprus, Karageorghis (1982: 302) reports Canaanite jars, faience objects including stamps, and local imitations of Canaanite jars, altogether suggesting "quite a brisk trade with the Near East."

[347] Mazar 1992: 300–301.

[348] Gilboa 1989: 205. Three of the pieces have been subjected to instrumental neutron-activation analysis, on the basis of which two, a bowl and an amphoriskos, have been identified as Cypriot and very similar to a group from Kition. The third, another bowl, came from the region of Tel Dor, in contrast to Gilboa's provenance assignment on the basis of design: Yellin 1989: 226.

[349] Stern 1990: 27–34; 1993: 331–32.

[350] Gilboa 1989: 213–14.

[351] Ibid.: 217.

[352] Barkay 1992: 325.

[353] Barnett 1982: 22.

[354] Gardiner 1961: 330; Kitchen 1973: 292.

[355] Katzenstein 1973: 121.

inside the coffin as packing were some remains of a marine plant, *Zostera marina* L., which is common along European coasts and also reported from the northern and western coasts of Asia Minor, but is not found south of that region. G. Lugn (keeper of the Egyptian Museum) and T. Säve-Söderbergh (assistant keeper at the time) dated the coffin to the Twenty-First Dynasty or the end of the Twentieth, but reexamination by Professor Andrzej Niwiński of the University of Warsaw places it in probably the first part of the Twenty-Second Dynasty.[356] Although museum records contained no information on its provenance, the cartoon work on the mummy mask suggested a Theban origin for the mummy. Laurent-Täckholm suggested a Greek origin for the

Z. marina, inasmuch as Greek lichens have been found in Middle Kingdom tombs; she noted, as an alternative transportation mechanism to deliberate human carriage (trade), that the seaweed simply could have washed up on the Egyptian shore without human intervention, although she does not propose that explanation (it still would have had to reach Thebes as a commercial product). After some further investigation, I believe it probably was imported from the Aegean region, or from some location further north, as packing material for some other traded goods, most likely during the period c. 940–850, a period for which there is otherwise little direct evidence of interaction between Egypt and the Aegean.[357]

---

[356] Personal communication, March 15, 1998.

[357] Persson 1942: 177; Laurent-Täckholm 1940: 142–48, 159–60. Furumark (1950: 248 n. 6) questioned whether the eastern Mediterranean floral distributions of 3,000 years ago can be represented adequately by their present geographical distributions. As a general answer to a general question, "no" probably is correct, but Laurent-Täckholm considered such an extrapolation in the case of this particular seaweed, and Furumark's goal was to cast as much doubt on Helene Kantor's assessments of Aegean-Near Eastern interactions as possible. *Zostera marina*, commonly known as eelgrass, is the most common sea grass of the northern hemisphere. Its present geographical distribution includes the northern coast of the Mediterranean, the coast of Algeria in the Aegean, and the southwestern coast of Anatolia (but excludes Cyprus); however, the record of many of these finds are fifty to one hundred years old. It is not found on the Levantine, Egyptian, or North African coasts. Its growth is relatively insensitive to salinity but is sensitive to water temperatures above 25–30° C. The length of time the water temperature remains between 10° and 15° C is important to its vegetative development; above 22° C, the plants either produce flowers and seeds, becoming annual, or become moribund; and temperatures above 25–30° C inhibit photosynthesis and cause the death of the plant, including its rhizomes, although different subspecies ("races" in the literature) appear to have different temperature tolerances. *Zostera* prefers sheltered habitats–long, sloping, wave-damping shelf areas (estuaries, bays, etc.), and it attains its maximal growth rates at average current velocities slightly below one knot. The American and European coasts of the North Atlantic suffered an eelgrass devastation in the early 1930s, the most widely accepted explanation of which is a water-temperature rise. In parts of the North American coast, the situation quickly reached disaster levels, eliminating fisheries, silting up bays and estuaries, and causing major restructurings of marine flora and fauna. The consequences in Europe, particularly in the Baltic, were not as extreme, possibly because of different marine-community structures. When submarine erosion occurs following an eelgrass crash, reestablishment of *Zostera* is difficult. Den Hartog 1970: 31–32, 42–60; Rasmussen 1977: 4–5, 17–18, fig. 1; Burrell and Schubel 1977: 222–23; Biebl and McRoy 1971: 53–54; Zieman and Wetzel 1980: 97; Milne and Milne 1951: 53–55; McConnaughey and Zottoli 1983: 111; Phillips and Meñez 1988: 11–13, 28–30, 34, figs 10, 12, maps 3, 9.

Could the 1940 identification of the sea grass in the mummy case have been incorrect? The quantity of the material available (primarily leaves, but also one *Z. marina* seed) for examination was "as much as would fill a cigar box . . . almost exclusively *Zostera marina* L." (Laurent-Täckholm 1940: 145, 147). Another *Zostera* species, *Z. noltii*, grows throughout the Mediterranean, and has been reported in Egypt, particularly around Alexandria, although once again the reports are 95 to 170 years old (den Hartog 1970: 70). *Z. noltii* is smaller than *Z. marina*, although in some habitats in the Mediterranean, and commonly in northern European habitats, it occurs with smaller varieties of *Z. marina*. *Z. noltii* ranges from 2 to 25 centimeters in length, usually around 10 centimeters, and its leaf is around 2 millimeters broad, while *Z. marina* can exceed 2 meters in length (C. P. McRoy, personal communication, November 13, 1997). *Z. noltii* is in the subgenus *Zosterella*, while *Z. marina* is in subgenus *Zostera*. The specimen Laurent-Täckholm published in her figure 2a is 45 centimeters long and 6 millimeters broad. She noted the only other *Zostera* species in the region as *Z. nana* Roth, which den Hartog (1970: 64, 271) classifies as *Z. noltii*. Another sea grass species in the family *Potamogetonaceae*, subfamily *Posidonioideae*, that has leaf blades that might appear superficially similar to those of *Z. marina*, especially when dried, is *Posidonia oceanica* (Ronald C. Phillips, personal communication, December 1, 1997). However, Laurent-Täckholm (1940: 147)

In the time of Osorkon II, the second quarter of the ninth century, Egypt may have been in a paroxysm of intra- and interregional dissension and the efforts of the northern rulers to maintain

sovereignty, and this instability may have continued to the end of the dynasty, about 715. During this period, however, Egypt seems to have maintained ordinary commercial relations with

---

Note 357 continued

specifically noted that *Posidonia* grew in local habitats, washed up on the Egyptian seashore, and was used by residents for roofing material. One of the three classification systems of *Potamogetonaceae* current at the time Laurent-Täckholm studied this sea grass from the mummy case combined the subfamilies *Zosteroideae* (which contains *Z. marina*) and *Posidonioideae* (den Hartog 1970: 10–11), but without specifically referring to any of these three systems, Laurent-Täckholm apparently relied on one of the systems that separated the two. Professor den Hartog very kindly has examined the Laurent-Täckholm article in response to a query from me; he reports that the description of the seed found in the mummy case fits *Z. marina*, and certainly not *Posidonia* or another species rather similar to *Z. marina* and common along the Mediterranean coast of Egypt, *Cymodocea nodosa*. While he has seen three separate old collections from a location near Algiers, he has no data from Libya and confirms that there is no record from the eastern Mediterranean, including Egypt. His conclusion regarding the specimen in the mummy case is: "If the material came from Egypt, I would have expected that it was packed in *Cymodocea*. . . . The most likely solution is thus, that the material originates from the Aegean Sea" (C. den Hartog, personal communication, December 2, 1997). The evidence available presently suggests that the identification of the sea grass in the mummy case as *Z. marina* is correct. Dr. Ronald Phillips, another authority on sea grass ecology, concurs in the identification on the basis of the description of the seed (R. C. Phillips, personal communication, January 9, 1998). A recent catalogue of Egyptian flora does not list *Z. marina* among contemporary Egyptian flora in the *Potamogetonaceae* family (Täckholm 1956: 583).

Water temperatures in the eastern Mediterranean c. 1100 B.C. were roughly the same as now, although they warmed somewhat in the early first millennium B.C. They were not significantly cooler than their present temperature until before c. 7000 b.p. Paleoclimatic reconstructions do not imply a significantly different climate from today's for the southern Aegean during the Late Bronze Age, possibly 1° C warmer c. 3500 b.p.: Ryan 1972: 166, fig. 9; Cita and Ryan 1978: 56, fig. 5; McCoy 1978: 96. From these physical details, it seems reasonable to conclude that *Zostera marina* did indeed have effectively the same geographical distribution in 1500–1100 B.C. as presently. Its sensitivity to temperature variations and preference for wave-protected coastlines do not make it a reasonable candidate for an inhabitant of the Levantine coast, and its temperature sensitivity would seem to rule it out of Egyptian delta waters. Additionally, the potential for drastic habitat response to its withdrawal, for whatever reason, might not have let its departure go unnoticed during a geographical retrenchment. The acid test, of course, would be whether *Z. marina* remains can be found in situ along the (former) Mediterannean coast of Egypt. My nonexhaustive search for published reports on analysis of floral remains from archaeological excavations and geological corings in the Nile delta has turned up no sea grass remains, only domesticated plants and associated weeds and pollen from nondomesticated, terrestrial flora: see papers in the two conference volumes edited by van den Brink (1988; 1992).

Next, however, the Theban origin of the mummy and coffin remain uncontested ("die Herkunft nicht unwarscheinlich Theban ist": Diener 1968: 7–8), but the dating of the coffin offered by Säve-Söderbergh in 1940 must be revised. According to the research of Professor Andrzej Niwiński, "No cartonnages at all were used in Thebes during the XXIst Dynasty, while the material, cartonnage, the colors, the white and yellow-varnished figures, and the iconographic scene clearly suggest the XXIInd Dynasty. The brightly painted cartonnages of the period occur first of all in the first part of this Dynasty, under Sheshonq I and Osorkon I, with possibly a longer stay after this latter reign. Thus, the dates proposed for the NME 12 [the number assigned to this mummy in Diener 1968] is, to my feeling, about 940–850 B.C." (personal communication, March 15, 1998). (Note: the Laurent-Täckholm article referred to this mummy as that of a child; the x-rays reported by Diener [1968: 9] suggest the remains of an adult who had been eaten by a crocodile.) I am considerably indebted to Professor Niwiński for researching this particular mummy case for me, and to Dr. Beate George, chief of the Egyptian Department at the Medelhavsmuseet, Stockholm, for her assistance to Professor Niwinski in his efforts on my behalf.

As for the specimens in the mummy case being washed ashore by tides, the winds and currents move in the wrong direction from the nearest habitats–southwestern Anatolia–and an Algerian source seems unlikely because of the distance and the intervening stretches of coast where drift material could have washed ashore. This review of the sea grass *Zostera marina* suggests that the specimens Laurent-Täckholm published from the Theban mummy case were brought to Egypt as packing material for some traded goods. Professor Niwiński's research on the mummy cartonnage indicates that the sea grass specimens arrived probably between the mid-tenth and the mid-ninth century B.C.

the Levant, although no chronicles such as Wen-Amun's exist to record it. Egyptian influence in Phoenician artistic production rose during the ninth century, reaching a peak in the eighth century, and Egyptian goods of the Twenty-Second Dynasty appear widely throughout the Mediterranean.[358] Markoe interprets these patterns as evidence of renewed Egyptian political and commercial influence.[359] Against this interpretation of heightened Egyptian influence in the Levant in the ninth century should be placed the civil wars of the second half of the ninth century and the rise of the parallel Twenty-Third and Twenty-Fourth Dynasties in the north in the late ninth and eighth centuries.[360]

The situation further north in the Levant stabilized around the middle of the tenth century. As the urban development along the Levantine coast proceeded in the tenth and ninth centuries, Tyre in particular, and possibly the other Phoenician cities, developed fishing and textile (weaving and dyeing) industries as well as workshops for bronze and ivory and probably fine woodwork, breaking their dependence on the local hinterland for foodstuffs. Both before and after the division of the kingdom of Israel, the Phoenician cities certainly were involved in the distribution of Egyptian products and in the manufacture of other,

Egyptianizing articles; probably were engaged in the distribution of Assyrian products as well; and certainly exported their own manufactured products. Against these developments, Assyria began a major expansion to its northwest in the late tenth and early ninth centuries. Ashur-nasir-pal II (c. 883–859) was the first Assyrian emperor to reach the Mediterranean since Tiglath-Pilesar I, and he received tribute from cities as far south as Tyre, but Assyrian activity did not impinge seriously on the economic prosperity of the Phoenician cities in the ninth century.[361] Over the next century and a quarter, the Assyrian empire and the cities and tribes of Syria, Phoenicia, and Palestine jockeyed for suzerainty. Some northern Phoenician cities joined the alliance of the twelve kings of Hatti against Shalmaneser III sometime before the mid-ninth century and participated in the battle of Qarqar in 853, where the alliance fought the Assyrians to a draw. Tyre may have become the harbor for Damascus after Qarqar.[362] The Sidonian Kingdom (i.e., Tyre, not Sidon), though allied with the Kingdom of Israel, which was in the alliance of the twelve, did not intervene at Qarqar. The participation of 1,000 Egyptian troops at Qarqar on the side of the alliance hints at Egyptian commercial interests in the northern Phoenician littoral at the time.[363] The remainder of the ninth century witnessed a further

---

[358] Cyprus—Egyptian paste scarab at Salamis: Karageorghis 1969: fig. 15. Palaepaphos-Skales cemetery, on the southwest coast, shows evidence of somewhat earlier contact with Egypt, in CG I, c. 1050–950: Karageorghis 1990: 31. Italy—various sites from the second half of the eighth century: Hölbl 1979, 1: 144 and 2: passim; 1989b: 76–79. Greece—Samos: Jantzen 1972; Kilian-Dirlmeier (1985: 237, fig. 18) reports 12.6% of eighth-century dedications to be Egyptian. Egyptian artifacts at Perachora form a much smaller percentage of that material; Aegean in general—Hölbl 1981: 186–92; 1987: 128–33.

[359] Markoe 1990: 17–18, 22. Redford (1992: 334–37) reinforces this interpretation independently; he sees the rapid adoption of the Egyptian system of weights and measures by the Hebrew states in the Early Iron Age as an index of the importance of Egyptian trade with the Levant. Petruso (1992: 65) recommends a trade interpretation of foreign balance weights among recovered artifacts. Elat (1978: 21–23) reports what appear to have been Egyptian diplomatic gifts (sub-Saharan African animals) to Assyria from the eleventh century through the eighth, sometimes through Phoenician cities, and Egyptian manufactured goods and other products moving through Philistine cities from the eighth century: various linen fabrics, preserved fish, elephant hides (30–32). Katzenstein (1973: 262 n. 18) believes that much of the Egyptian and Arabian trade went through the Philistine mercantile centers, especially Gaza, in the early seventh century, despite the reasonably good (but not particularly cordial) relations between Tyre under Ba'al I and Egypt. Hölbl (1989a: 320) emphasizes the Phoenicians' clear understanding of the Egyptian iconography they used in their art, reflecting the thoroughness of the interactions between the two regions.

[360] Caminos 1958: 175–79.

[361] Katzenstein (1973: 170, 185) considers Tyre's payment as a tax to permit trade under a pax Assyriana rather than as tribute.

[362] Ibid.: 180. Katzenstein interprets the ivories at Arslan Tash as indicating that "mercantile relations" between Tyre and Aram (the Kingdom of Damascus) were prospering at this time (180–81).

[363] Acceptance of Egyptian participation hinges on the interpretation of the location of Musri. Katzenstein rejects the Egyptian equation, believing that Musri was a state in the border area between Syria and Asia Minor: 1973: 181–83. Most writers continue to accept the equation Musri = Egypt.

decade of Assyrian attacks in North Syria, followed by warfare between the kingdoms of Damascus and Israel, but there was little Assyrian pressure on the Phoenicians at that time. At the beginning of the eighth century, in the continuing struggles between the Assyrian empire and the independent North Syrian states, Adad-Nirari III reduced Damascus, but Assyrian attention soon was diverted to Urartu. The Urartian diversion left the Phoenician and North Syrian states relatively free to pursue their own interests with little threat from Assyria. Possibly as early as the late ninth century, possibly during the first half of the eighth century, disagreements within the royal family at Tyre sent Phoenician colonists to Carthage, although earlier commercial activity must have scouted the site.[364] It is difficult to associate that colony with Assyrian pressures.

Around 800, the kingdom of Urartu attracted the allegiance of the neo-Hittite principalities of North Syria, splitting Syria politically in two pieces during a lull in Assyrian attention to that region. Trade from the interior that had gone through the southern Phoenician cities of Byblos, Sidon, and Tyre was diverted to Al Mina at the mouth of the Orontes, once but no longer thought to be the site of legendary Poseideion.[365] The Assyrian resurgence in the mid-eighth century, combined with Cimmerian invasions, brought serious reverses to Urartu in the late eighth century, which Barnett, a number of years ago, conjectured may have sent Urartian metalsmiths to Crete, where they made the Zeus tympanon found in the Idaean Cave, a suggestion that further analysis of Urartian bronzes has not reinforced.[366]

Shortly after the mid-eighth century, Tiglath-Pilesar III returned his attention to the Mediterranean littoral and initiated efforts to bring the Phoenician coast under direct Assyrian dominion. He led two major campaigns against the Phoenician cities, the first from 743 to 738, against the northern cities, possibly including Byblos. Reorganizing the conquered coastal region as an Assyrian province called Simirra, whose southern border was north of tribute-paying Byblos, Tiglath-Pilesar provoked war with the Sidonian Kingdom, with

---

[364] Despite Carthage's legendary founding date of 814, archaeological evidence has pointed to about a century later. Recent excavations, however, have produced Euboean pottery and possible Cypriot and Phoenician sherds as early as the first half of the eighth century: Vegas 1989: 215–16, 222, 225; 1992: 181–89. Niemeyer (1993: 337) considers revision or confirmation of the traditional founding date premature with the available evidence.

[365] According to legend, Poseideion was founded by the Argive Amphilochus after the Trojan War. Woolley identified Al Mina as the legendary town, but subsequent excavations in the region by French archaeologists placed that site at Bassit, slightly to the south, because of a combination of archaeological correspondences with reports about the town during Roman times and the presence of Mycenaean pottery. Gurney 1990: 36–37; Boardman 1980: 42–54; Riis 1969: 438–39.

[366] Barnett 1950: 39. Despite the reported seriousness of the reverses to the Kingdom of Urartu in the second half of the eighth century, Urartian archaeological remains do not indicate that either the area or the wealth of the kingdom was greatly reduced: Zimansky 1985: 59–60, 99. Zimansky contends that the kingdom itself developed as an ecological-political response to perennial Assyrian invasions and that the mountainous terrain and small, separated, arable areas permitted flexible military responses to superior military forces that found it difficult to fix an opposing force, occupy enough territory to support itself, or seriously damage the indigenous enemy. The kingdom continued into the late sixth century, when it vanished quickly. It is not clear how such an interpretation of the Kingdom of Urartu affects hypotheses regarding far-fleeing refugee craftsmen, other than the putative makers of the Idaean Cave shields.
The interpretation of the pervasiveness of the artistic influence of Urartian craftsmen throughout the eastern and central Mediterranean in the Early Iron Age, which prevailed in the first half of this century, has been curtailed in studies since the 1960s, leaving a much more local scope for the influence of Urartian bronzes: Muscarella (1962: 320–25; 1978: 65–66) modifies his earlier position that no Urartian objects have been found in the west, to allow one bell at Samos, B474, probably early eighth century, and possibly statuette B1217 as well, as genuine Urartian products—but none on the Greek mainland; Muscarella 1992: 21–23; Herrmann (1966b: 114–25; 1966a, 1: 59–67) favors North Syrian over Urartian attributions of the bronzes found at Greek sanctuaries; van Loon (1966: 106–13) details the non-Urartian characteristics of bronzes at Greek and Etruscan sites, many of which pieces once were thought to be Urartian, and (1977: 229–31) identifies the Syro-Hittite border region as the production location of much bronzework found in Greece and occasionally considered Urartian. Similarly, Boardman 1980: 64–65; Seidl 1988: 169, 172. R. S. Young (1967: 150, 153) has warned against simple replacement of Urartian attribution with a blanket attribution to North Syria, which itself was an amalgam of Late Hittite, Assyrian, and Canaanite influences, *inter alia*.

its capital at Tyre, by 734, and conquered the entire coast down to the border of Egypt by 732. By 727, Assyria controlled the Levantine coast as far south as Gaza.[367] Although Tyre technically never fell to the Assyrian siege, the Assyrian empire assumed a protectorate of sorts over the kingdom, controlling its trading activities and its politics, including royal succession. Tyre revolted under a succeeding king, Luli, around 701.[368]

Assyrian policy exercised tighter control over North Syria than it attempted to impose on the Phoenician cities, probably because the former area was more accessible and consequently easier to control.[369] Additionally, North Syrian trade may

---

[367] Saggs 1984: 58–92; 1988: chaps. 2–3.

[368] Tadmor 1975: 36–48; Puech 1981: 544–62; Millard and Tadmor 1973: 57–64; Cogan 1973: 96–99; Oded 1974: 38–49.

[369] On economic activity and foreign trade in the Neo-Assyrian empire, Postgate 1979: Chart 1, 195, clearly reveals the skewing of evidence toward the palace "sector"; see 206–7, on the robustness of the private sector of the economy. Fales (1984: 207–20) interprets considerable decentralization of landholding in eighth- to seventh-century Assyria, as well as the possibility of reconcentration of holdings in private hands late in the empire's life, leading to a politically and possibly economically unstable situation. Saggs (1984: 175–79) considers the roles of military repatriation (war booty), tribute, and commercial trade in the Neo-Assyrian empire's foreign transactions. Saggs concludes that ordinary commercial trade, however regulated, coexisted alongside the other two international commodity movement mechanisms during the Neo-Assyrian period. In the eighth century, the Assyrians purchased timber from Tyre and alternately encouraged and prohibited that kingdom's timber sales to Egypt as well (ibid.: 177–78); idem 1955: 129, Letter 12. Postgate (1979: 206) cites several texts demonstrating official Assyrian encouragement of private foreign trade by the citizens of the Levantine city-states and Babylonia, although his text on Sidonian timber trade reveals official discouragement of timber sales to the Palestinians and the Egyptians. Frankenstein (1979: 269, 271) independently concludes that the Assyrian foreign policy in the eighth and seventh centuries allowed or encouraged foreign trading by its tributary states' merchants. Elayi (1988: 27–28, 37) cites an indeterminate mix of Assyrian tribute and commercial exploitation of Lebanese and Amanus timber. Linder (1986: 277) identifies the depiction of timber on ships as Phoenician riverine activity in commerce with the Assyrians but suggests that transportation difficulties prompted the Assyrians to prefer wood from the Amanus and the Zagros over the less-accessible Lebanese timber. Clearly, cost was an Assyrian concern.

The consequences of the tribute levied by the Assyrians on the Phoenician cities, as well as on other cities in Palestine during the eighth and seventh centuries, have structural similarities to the effects of export surpluses (albeit involuntary ones) on the parts of the tributary states. Additionally, the tribute has similarities to reparations payments such as those made by Germany to the Allies after World War I, as well as to the imposition of a tax without recirculation of the revenue. The exaction of tribute would have led to depreciation of precious metals in Phoenicia unless those were exported also. Further, the prices of goods subject to tribute would have risen relative to those of other goods. The depression of per capita income by the tribute would have decreased the demands for imports beyond the reduction induced by the fall in the relative price of nontribute goods. With full employment, which we can assume by virtue of the nonmonetization of the Phoenician economy at the time, as well as by its predominantly agricultural composition, the reduction in Phoenician demand for imports caused by its reduction in income would have occurred simultaneously with a reduction in its supply of nontributory exports, dampening the Phoenician role in international trade throughout the Mediterranean. Phoenician carrying trade need not have shrunk, but the Phoenician ships would have had to carry a larger proportion of other lands' goods. Katzenstein (1973: 170) explicitly introduces the issue of what benefits Phoenician cities—and, by extension, other tribute-payers—received for their contributions to the Assyrian coffers. His question brings greater sophistication to the study of Assyrian economic activity and influences, changing the structure of the economic problem from reparations to taxation and the provision of public goods. Such questions emerge as, "Did Assyria demand enough tribute (did they tax enough) or did they demand too much for its own economic well-being?" The answers to such questions must be based on empirical research. As an example of the sorts of benefit Phoenician cities might have derived from participation—required or voluntary—in such an Assyrian tribute league, consider the possible Assyrian clearing of pirates (perhaps Greek) from the northern Levantine-eastern Asia Minor coast c. 714 or 713: Saggs 1967: 76–79; Luckenbill 1927: §92; Katzenstein 1973: 237–40. The Assyrians clearly would have used Phoenician ships (probably Tyrian) in the strike, yet Sargon claimed the action as his own. Possibly only Assyria had interests across enough affected Phoenician cities to make taking action worthwhile, although the piracy would have affected each city individually: any one city's expenditure to scourge pirates would have benefited other, nonpaying cities as much as itself; rather than benefit their neighbor-competitors, they would take less-extensive actions individually. Assyrian financial sponsorship of Tyrian ships for the attack would have been a feasible combination of interests.

have depended partly on the traditional land routes across Asia Minor, which Assyria was able to influence heavily, if not outright control.[370] The North Syrians may have come to depend on Greek shipping for seaborne trade, while the Phoenicians undertook their own shipping. With the accession of Sargon II, Assyrian policy in North Syria became more destructive, resulting in serious damage to the economy of that region from the late eighth century through most of the seventh,[371] although Sargon tried to make the Samarians reopen trade with Egypt.[372] Sargon destroyed the great North Syrian trading (and probably manufacturing) city, Carchemish, in 717, after bringing most of that city-state's neighboring kingdoms within the orbit of Assyrian political and economic domination.[373] Oppenheim published two tablets from Uruk detailing the products carried by a Neo-Babylonian merchant between Mesopotamia and the Mediterranean coast and probably Anatolia in 551 and 550, an array of goods that Postgate considers to be representative of those traded internationally during the earlier period of the Neo-Assyrian empire. The goods included a substantial quantity of copper and iron from Yamana, iron from Lebanon, tin, various dyes, dyed wool, tumanu fibers, lapis lazuli, alum from Egypt, honey, wines, spices, and juniper resin.[374]

Assyrian impacts on the Phoenician economies grew in the eighth century. The Assyrian subjugation of Arvad around 740 finally may have interrupted Phoenician trade with North Syria and Rhodes, and also may have redoubled Phoenician attention westward with both trade and emigration. A reduction in Phoenician pottery in Level VII at Al Mina suggests conditions adverse to Phoenician commerce with North Syria in the late eighth century. While Assyrian influence in Phoenicia in the ninth century and the early eighth was looser than in North Syria, Assyrian influence in Phoenicia became outright political control toward the end of the eighth century, after the conquests of the late 730s, and grew more onerous over the following decades. Sargon II (722–705) held all Phoenicia in generally peace-

---

[370] Birmingham (1961: 185–95) organizes the artifactual evidence for the peak use of two overland routes—a northern one, Erzincan-Erzerum-Karaköse, and the Muş-Van road to the south—from c. 730 through the seventh century, although she thinks both roads were used continuously from c. 800 to c. 600, by which time the Cimmerian invasions halted traffic. Her case for Iranian traffic on the overland routes is based on acceptance of Urartian provenance of artifacts found at Altintepe and Gordion and of Phrygian contacts with regions farther west (192). However, her conclusions do not appear to require endorsement of Urartian influence on Greece, which lost most of its scholarly acceptance within a few years after her publication. Nonetheless, she refers to the cauldron attachments on Samos as Urartian (190). Sams (1974: 194) is reluctant to endorse transmission of specific North Syrian artistic ideas to Greece via Phrygia, although he finds the similarity between Phrygian and Parian crescent-shaped animal shoulders similar enough to warrant direct influence. Though his focus is on specific vase motifs, use of the overland caravan routes clearly is implied, as he finds the motifs on Phrygian pottery derivative from North Syrian art (181). The principal questions appear to ask who used these routes and what they carried. Perhaps Oppenheim's merchant's tablets from the mid-sixth century are reasonable guides to both who and what for the earlier periods: Oppenheim 1967: 236–54. Röllig (1992: 97–102) considers the harbor cities along the southern Anatolian coast as a trade route from the Levant to Greece.

[371] Winter 1976: 17–21.

[372] Postgate 1979: 206.

[373] Winter 1983: 190–94. Winter identifies Carchemish in the ninth and eighth centuries as a major producer of artistic bronzeworks and ivories, and luxury goods in general (186), as well as a major entrepôt in the metals trade between Anatolia on the one hand and Mesopotamia and the Levant on the other. She clearly sees the economic activity of the city, and the movement of goods in and out of it, as involving commercial trade as well as gift-giving, tribute assessment, and distribution of war booty (188–89). Winter reiterates some of these conclusions in 1988: 208–12. Sams (1974: 184 n. 41) notes that Carchemish apparently remained intact until its destruction by Nebuchadnezzar in 605/4, and its monumental sculpture remained a source of artistic influence on regions to the west. The names of two Assyrian overseers of the city are known, one dated to 691, the other to 649.

[374] Oppenheim 1967: 237; Yamana refers to the Greeks, according to Oppenheim (241). He develops the case that tumanu is not linen (247–51), but either cotton (251) or silk (252). He thinks the purple-dyed wool may indicate Phoenician participation. Postgate (1979: 207) is less certain that the tablets are representative of earlier trade in "coarser commodities." Moorey (1994: 246) considers Yamana to have referred "to Cyprus or some locality in southwestern Anatolia colonized by Greeks."

ful vassalage, and the kings of Cyprus submitted to him in 707,[375] but following the accession of Sennacherib (705–680), Elulaios (Luli), king of Tyre, led an insurrection, supported by Egypt, against Assyria. However, during this revolt, the other Phoenician cities supplied some sixty ships to Sennacherib rather than join with Tyre.[376] Luli was defeated and fled to Cyprus c. 701 or 700, where he died, or at least disappeared from Assyrian view.[377] Sennacherib imposed annual tribute on the Phoenician cities, in contrast to the sporadic exactions of his predecessors,[378] although it is not clear that this regularity was enforced uniformly.[379] The seventh century was coursed with unsuccessful revolts of Phoenician cities against Assyria, with ineffectual assistance from Egypt. The Assyrians destroyed Sidon in 676, and in 672 or 671, after the unsuccessful revolt of King Baal of Tyre, Assyria may have restricted Tyre's foreign trade somewhat,[380] although physically reducing the island city was impractical. Ashurbanipal (668–627) tightened the tribute required from the Phoenician cities, although it is difficult to correlate his increased exactions with Phoenician colonization efforts overseas.[381]

The Egyptians and Assyrians came into direct conflict in the reign of Sennacherib, when Hezekiah of Judah appealed to Egypt for assistance during a Philistine urban revolt. An Egyptian and Ethiopian army was dealt a major defeat at Eltekeh just before or just after 700, and the Assyrian usurper Essarhaddon (c. 680–669) drove the pharaoh Taharka as far south as Memphis. Taharka retook Memphis, Essarhaddon

died between campaigns, and Ashurbanipal in turn retook Memphis in 667, establishing in the person of Necho a local administration that became the Twenty-Sixth Dynasty. Egyptian tribute to Assyria lapsed under Necho's son, Psammetichus I, in the mid-seventh century. With the assistance of Greek mercenaries, Psammetichus reunited Upper and Lower Egypt. Assyrian strength was declining during the seventh century, and after mid-century, Babylon began to reassert its autonomy successfully. Ashurbanipal died in 627, and Babylonia under Nabopolassar dealt the Assyrian army a decisive defeat in the following year. By 616, Psammetichus had allied Egypt with waning Assyria against the rising Babylonian-Median alliance, but Nabopolassar sacked the Assyrian capital Nineveh in 612. The Assyrian king, Ashur-uballit II, continued to resist in the west until c. 609. Egypt under Necho II took the place of Assyria in opposing Babylonia. Nebuchadrezzar, the son of Nabopolassar, destroyed an Egyptian army at Carchemish in 605, but was himself driven back, with heavy losses, from a march on Egypt in 601. In the following century, Egypt fell to the Persians.

Such was the political setting of eastern Mediterranean economic relations in the first half of the first millennium B.C. Before seeing the extent to which these events correlate with the artifactual evidence of Crete's external relations with the region, I turn to the legacy of relations between Crete and Egypt as they evolved between Late Minoan times and the early centuries of the Greek Dark Age.

---

[375] Katzenstein (1973: 226, 240) and Reyes (1994: 56–60) both have a more benign view of the Cypro-Assyrian relationship commemorated by this stele. Contrary to the common interpretation of a predatory Assyrian empire, these scholars see the outlines of a regional trading union of sorts, with Assyria enforcing the peace and all participants benefiting from increased trade. Their view is compatible with Assyrian wars of expansion and enforcement. This view of Assyrian economic policy is shared generally with Oded (1979: chap. 3, esp. p. 67), who documents the imperial concern for and protection of deportees as part of imperial economic development policies designed to strengthen the agricultural base of the empire while relocating potentially troublesome populations. The deportees generally remained free, at least prior to Sennacherib's reign.

[376] Moscati 1968: 20.

[377] The alternative story about Luli is that Kition revolted against Tyre around the end of the eighth century, and Luli led an expedition to Cyprus to quell it and never came back. This rebellion also has been linked to the island's submission to Sargon II in 709: Gjerstad 1948: 437–38. Nicolaou (1976: 314) suspects a late-eighth-century rebellion at Kition may have been of Greeks rather than Phoenicians. Cf. Katzenstein 1973: 223.

[378] Culican 1970: 32.

[379] Elayi 1983: 50–53.

[380] Katzenstein (1973: 268) believes that the vassal treaty signed by Essarhaddon and Ba'al I actually was, commercially speaking, a good deal for Tyre.

[381] Elayi 1983: 57–58.

THE BACKGROUND FOR EGYPTIAN ARTIFACTS IN EARLY IRON AGE CRETE

The name Keftiu disappears from the Egyptian texts after a single surviving instance in the twelfth century,[382] but material exchanges between Crete and Egypt, as well as other Levantine sites, continued at least through Late Minoan IIIB.[383] Merrillees and Kemp have presented a conservative case for indirect trade between Egypt and Crete in the Minoan period (Eighteenth Dynasty and earlier), because of the absence of Egyptian artifacts in Crete that are not found also in Syria, as well as the relatively restricted classes of Egyptian artifacts found in Crete.[384] Warren, on the basis of finds subsequent to Kemp and Merrillees's publication, suggests a direct trading connection between Knossos and Egypt in Middle Minoan IIIB to Late Minoan II (Eighteenth Dynasty) contacts.[385] On the basis of the wide distribution of the stone vases throughout the city, from neopalatial times through Late Minoan IIIA, he proposes the existence of private merchants in these commodities, at least partly independent of the palace, with trade in other materials conducted by the palace sector.[386] From this level of Minoan activity with Egypt, direct or indirect, there is a decline to a relative scarcity of Egyptian articles found at Cretan sites from the period of the Twenty-First Dynasty, from roughly 1000 to 850. This dip may represent disruptions in Egypt, since Crete probably was beginning to regain order after the lengthy depression through the Late Minoan IIIC and Subminoan periods. Many of the Egyptian artifacts that may date as early as the second half of the ninth century alternatively may date as late as the late eighth century, and some as late as the mid-seventh, so disorder in Lower Egypt through the Twenty-Second Dynasty may have interrupted movement of Egyptian goods to Crete. It is possible that trade with Crete, direct or indirect, remained weak until the Assyrian-installed Saites began to restore order and foster a cultural resurgence in Egypt in the second quarter of the seventh century. Nonetheless, this contact appears to have resumed before the foundation of Naukratis (c. 615–610). Austin considers Odysseus's tale of a raid on Egypt (Od. 14.245–84) to be serious evidence of Greek knowledge of Egypt by at least the eighth century, derived from raiding activities down the Levantine coast to Egypt.[387] Austin and Brown agree that many of the small Egyptian finds at Greek Dark Age sites are not evidence of direct contact, since they appear to have traveled "from hand to hand," possibly as objects secured as votives by sailors and traveling mer-

---

[382] Vercoutter 1956: 115, Fig. 3.

[383] Kanta (1980: 308) reports LM IIIA and IIIB pottery at Tell Abu Hawam and IIIA sherds at Gezer, in the Levant. Though no LM IIIB material appears to be reported at Egyptian sites, Egyptian material appears in several Cretan sites in LM IIIA and IIIB contexts; but although she found none from IIIC (315–16), Italian or other western material has been found in IIIC contexts since Kanta's book was published: Pålsson Hallager 1985: 293, 303 n. 110. For concurring judgments on Minoan artifacts in Egypt, cf. Marazzi 1986: 326, Table 1; Vincentelli and Tiradritti 1986: 334. Phillips (1991: 170–80, 354–55) reports only a few, portable items like scarabs and beads from the Post-Palatial period, of which only a few items may be as late as the Nineteenth Dynasty, e.g., a green "stone" ape figurine from Palaikastro (711–12, no. 330).

[384] Kemp and Merrillees 1980: 283–84. They do not rule out direct trade other than exchange of prestige items between royal courts, but they consider the indirect route, along the Levantine coast, reaching Crete from the northwest, a more conservative interpretation of the artifactual data available in the late 1970s A.D.

[385] Warren 1991: 296–98.

[386] Ibid.: 299. Warren considers the proposal by Branigan (1989: 68–69) of private trading in the MM IB–II period, largely replaced by a palace trading monopoly in MM III–LM I, to be reasonable on the basis of 1969 data, but believes the more extensive finds do not warrant the belief in the palace monopoly. However, Wiener (1991: 330–31) believes that Branigan gives insufficient importance to the palace sector in trade in the earlier Palace period, for which Branigan uses the ratio of palatial to nonpalatial find contexts of several categories of Egyptian goods on Crete to suggest that trade was largely in decentralized, private hands (Branigan 1989: 65–66; Tables 1–2, 66, 67). The trade, however, is not disputed. Branigan also has suggested that, if Minoan colonies existed at Ayia Irini, Phylakopi, and Akrotiri, they were what he calls "community colonies," as likely as not privately initiated on the basis of opportunity and personal ambition, not of government or large-scale community sponsorship: Branigan 1981: 26, 31, 32.

[387] Austin 1970: 12.

chants.[388] Brown believes that the Egyptian trinkets could have been a major export item themselves, as they began to appeal again to Greek tastes in the Geometric period.[389] Pendlebury

---

[388] Ibid.: 13; Brown 1975: 122–23. Brown's catalogue excludes Crete, but Brown rejects a number of Pendlebury's chronological opinions in *Aegyptiaca* (1930a), preferring to date the grave items by context rather than by apparent date of manufacture, although later reproductions of earlier dynastic objects may make the latter problematic (Brown 1975: 111–13). For such a reproduction, note the scarab in Fortetsa Tomb II inscribed with the name of Amenhotep III, but dated to the Twenty-Fifth or probably the Twenty-Sixth Dynasty: Brock 1957: 208; Dunbabin 1948: 462–63. From his rejection of Pendlebury's early Dark Age dating of scarabs from the Isis Tomb at Eleusis, as well as Pendlebury's chronologies for finds at the Sanctuary of Artemis Orthia in Laconia, and at Athens, Brown derives the conclusion of a complete break in contact between Egypt and Greece between c. 1200 and c. 800. The finds from Lefkandi, excavated and published after Brown's work (Popham et al. 1983: 247), unambiguously revise that conclusion, and the finds at Cretan sites between c. 1100 and c. 800 certainly do not support such a conclusion for Crete. Snodgrass (1971: 116–17) discusses the heirloom problem in the case of the Isis Grave scarabs, which he dates to the eleventh century or earlier; he maintains that the scarabs could have been old when they were imported rather than being buried as heirlooms of local residents. The burial context can provide only a *terminus ante quem* for the scarabs, without further information. Elsewhere, Snodgrass cites a readiness to appeal to heirlooms as a problem for archaeologists, justifiable but vexing: 1983a: 151–52. Falsone (1988: 236) suggests that luxury articles such as the bronze bowl Fortetsa 1559 (KF.31) tended to be used for a long time before they were deposited in a tomb. Possibly such items derived the meaning that made them appropriate as grave goods by having been used in the deceased's family for a long time, although most ceramic deposits would not fit such a semiotic process. At the risk of introducing material that some may consider anachronistic, Gates (1990: 34–35) concludes that individuals at Mari did not automatically value old artifacts, and in fact reused many precious materials. She finds that antiquity enhanced an artifact's value only when combined with what the possessors considered to be historical merit.

Lambrou-Phillipson (1990: 55), following Pomerance 1973: 21–30, discusses the heirloom problem as it appears with Predynastic to Sixth Dynasty Egyptian vases found in Late Minoan deposits from north central Crete (Herakleion) and east Crete (Zakros and Palaikastro). Rather than accept a 1,000- to 1,800-year local holding of the vases, she endorses Eighteenth Dynasty tomb robbing and contemporaneous sale as antiques, to wealthy Cretans. Eighteenth Dynasty law gave strong incentive to rob royal tombs of previous periods by punishing those robberies with only a beating, but robberies of Eighteenth Dynasty royal tombs with death: Pomerance 1973: 25. In a case of such a great discrepancy between production period and deposition context, the tomb-robbery hypothesis seems reasonable, but its extension to other cases of chronological discrepancies in tomb deposits would seem contingent upon the type of artifact in question. The wealth of the Egyptian royal tombs found undisturbed or only partially looted clearly reveals the economic motivation for tomb robbery (strong enough to outweigh religious sanctions, when legal sanctions were only modest), but not all the material found in anomalous chronological contexts in Greek tombs are likely either to have been in target Egyptian tombs or to have had high priority for hasty removal in lieu of more lucrative items.

Like nearly all the topics archaeology treats, certain knowledge is out of the question, and the goal is to replace older, plausible stories with more plausible stories where possible, using new techniques, new concepts, or both. With this process in mind, I suggest that secondary markets—markets for used goods—are more sophisticated (in the sense that they may require more information) than are primary markets, in which newly produced goods are offered, in the ancient case probably offered as often as not by the producer. Although secondary markets are common in developing countries presently, the simple transfer to a Dark Age Greek setting may not be appropriate; the contemporary markets are long-established and sophisticated. An ancient antique market, particularly an international one, seems difficult to accept, particularly because of the confidence that would have to be posed in the marketing system to sustain prices people would have required to part with prized heirlooms; gold always could be melted down, but faience and pottery are a different matter. Although I would not assign a specific probability, the deposition of a local, family heirloom, possibly one imported years before, in a grave seems more likely than the conditional probability of the ancient purchase of a foreign antique and the subsequent deposition of a relatively recent acquisition with one's departed relative. The conditional probability is higher if the imported antique has been in the family for a generation or so, but it is still lower than the conditional probability of an imported new good held long enough to make it a family heirloom. This reasoning cannot remove the possibility of an ancient international antique market, but it persuades me to offer stronger weight to the probability of importation of goods, at least those other than precious metals—gold and silver—close to the time of their production. I belabor the point here because this reasoning guides some of my chronological recommendations.

[389] Brown 1975: 157–58.

romantically envisioned the Egyptian finds at Vrokastro, Kavousi, and Arkades as loot brought back by "the adventurers and the pirates."[390]

REFLECTIONS OF NEAR EASTERN EVENTS IN FOREIGN ARTIFACTS ON CRETE

Let us turn the focus to the role of the various Near Eastern regions in Crete's external relations in the Dark Age. The intermittent warfare in North Syria and along and inland from the Levantine coast between the ninth and seventh centuries would have been ample cause to disperse various groups of refugees, including the craftsmen who have been hypothesized for some Cretan artifacts, and could be consistent in timing.[391]

Against a background of three centuries of warfare and subjugation, the Phoenician cities were actively engaged overseas, carrying their own products as well as those of North Syria, Assyria, Babylonia and points east, probably Palestine, and Egypt. In addition to supplying their own industries, the Phoenician cities supplied raw materials to Assyria and Babylonia as tribute, trade, or both, and overseas commerce was a major means of securing these supplies.[392] The artifacts found in Crete and attributed to North Syria or Syria begin to appear in the first half of the ninth century. Those attributed specifically to Assyria, Babylonia, and Mesopotamia do not appear before roughly the middle of the eighth century. I cannot say whether this chronological pattern of provenances represents a shift in supply areas for the Phoenicians, a change in Cretan demands, a random variation in supply origins, or the introduction of Greek middlemen at Al Mina, or is simply an artifact of provenance assignments. No Cretan artifacts have been reported at Al Mina, but that may indicate a lack of participation of Cretan labor in merchandising and shipping rather than the absence of commercial interactions with the island, since Cretan artifacts are found nowhere else in the Near East either, yet Near Eastern artifacts are common in Crete.

It is almost inescapable that many of the Near Eastern artifacts other than Phoenician (e.g., KF.27, AMN.2, KF.75–76, and the Egyptian items) found at Cretan sites were brought to Crete by Phoenician traders on Phoenician ships. An alternative is that at least some of these, the North Syrian and Syrian, dated to just after 800 or a little earlier, were carried on Greek ships, say Euboean, plying a triangular trade from Al Mina.[393] There is little published artifactual evidence for Euboean activity on Crete, and what there is either is early (Ktwn.2) or is possibly Italian (FS.12) or Babylonian (KN.34). Nevertheless, it is an alternative that is not inherently implausible. Boardman has presented a strong case for Euboean management of the carrying trade between North Syria and the Aegean during the century before the establishment of Al Mina, mainly on the basis of the predominance of Near Eastern finds before the beginning of the eighth century in Euboea, primarily Lefkandi.[394] The number of Near Eastern artifacts datable to before c. 800 does not contradict Boardman's characterization of the Euboean dominance in overall eastern imports of the period, but there is remarkably little published evidence from Crete for a Euboean presence, certainly in artifacts but in motifs locally reproduced as well. The East Greek ceramic presence at the Knossos sites, Arkades, and elsewhere could represent Al Mina-Crete traffic carried by Ionian and Rhodian ships rather then Euboean, but this is in the Al Mina period rather than before it. Phoenician ships touching Crete surely did not have final destinations on the island, but were engaged in some triangular or multiple-stop trade. What may have begun as water and repair stops may have become regular, planned commercial visits

---

[390] Pendlebury 1930a: 4–5.

[391] Cf. Dunbabin 1957: 40–41, 61; Barnett 1950: 39; Maxwell-Hyslop 1956: 159; B. Goldman 1960: 321 n. 12; Peltenberg 1969: 87; Boardman 1980: 57–60.

[392] Frankenstein 1979: 273.

[393] Winter (1976: 18) suggests that Greek shipping carried North Syrian products west, while the Phoenicians carried their own goods, as well as those of other areas. Unless they have been dated too early, North Syrian artifacts appear in Greek and other western contexts before evidence of Greek presence at Al Mina, so this attractive hypothesis would have to be supplemented by earlier overland trade, other carriers for sea trade, or both. Muhly (1970: 19, 49) believes that the eastern metalwork reaching the Aegean in the ninth and eighth centuries was not Urartian work brought across the Anatolian overland route but rather North Syrian and Phoenician work carried by Phoenician merchants.

[394] Boardman 1990a: 177–78.

by the early ninth century on the north side of the island, and possibly by the late tenth century on the south. Crete may have been a market for artistic items from the Near East that were exchanged for ship's supplies and possibly for textiles for which Phoenician merchants would have known of third-party markets. The Phoenicians may have been mainlanders or Cypro-Phoenicians, or even Western Phoenicians. The paucity of North African material[395] in Crete suggests either that Crete was a stop on the west-bound voyages but not on the returns, or that only more ephemeral materials from the west were exchanged for supplies, that the manufactures of the west found no markets in Crete. The proposed Sardinian askos from Tekke (KN.27) could be such an item exchanged for ship's supplies on a return voyage from Sardinia and Italy. However, if Crete was a way station on Phoenician eastbound voyages, the scarcity of western Phoenician artistic work in Crete is remarkable. Although the tripillar altar at Kommos appears to have gone out of use in the later eighth century, suggesting that the Phoenicians stopped coming to Kommos, Phoenician amphora fragments, probably of the seventh century, were found under Building Q, and Phoenician and other Near Eastern artifacts continue to appear regularly through the end of the seventh century throughout the island. It is possible that some, but probably not all, of the East Greek items arrived in Crete on Phoenician vessels. Northern Crete may have been a stopover between the Levant and mainland Greece—Argos, Corinth, and Athens, possibly even Euboea.[396]

Elements of continuity existed between the Levant and Cyprus and between Egypt and the Levant throughout the period 1200–900, with a recession in evidence in Palestinian-Cypriot trade from c. 1200 to c. 1050. Trade throughout the Levant and areas to the south and east, and

involving Cyprus, continued throughout the entire period. When Cypriot material appears to grow scarce on Crete again, in the seventh century, other Near Eastern material also tapers off a bit, although the cluster of Egyptian votives in late-seventh-century contexts at Amnisos are an apparent exception to the more general trend across the island.

In the period from 1100 to 600, times of peace alternated with times of military campaigns, probably too closely interspersed to discern clearly in the artifactual record of imports in Crete, although suggestions have been made regarding occasional singular destructions such as those at Tell Halaf and Carchemish. It is tempting to correlate the chronological pattern of North Syrian and Phoenician artifacts at the Idaean Cave with the flux of Assyrian military activity in the region, but the Idaean Cave chronology of origins is not paralleled at other sites on Crete. Trade and economic relations in general were sophisticated, following sophisticated traditions that were neither altogether interrupted by the Sea Peoples' arrival and exploits of the thirteenth and twelfth centuries, nor completely forgotten over periods of localized recession. Crete was in contact with Cyprus during the earliest years of this period (1100–1000), and possibly throughout the period, if sometimes intermittently. Cyprus, in turn, appears to have been in contact, direct or indirect, with most of the rest of the Near East and southwest Asia during most of the 500-year period, and with at least parts of those regions for the previous 200 years of more precarious international relations. Crete surely had the opportunity for indirect trade relations with most of those areas, and the artifactual record on Crete supports such contacts. The pendant from Luristan (or northwest Iran) did not arrive as a result of a special trip to carry only itself, but instead

---

[395] The ostrich-egg fragments from the Khaniale Tekke tomb (KN.42) may be North African, and Sakellarakis (1993: 348) has noted a few western Phoenician ivories at the Idaean Cave (IC.103).

[396] Negbi (1992: 612, fig. 3) maps proposed Phoenician shipping routes from the Near East, through Crete and on to the west, during the early first millennium. Her routes proceed from Cyprus, westward along the Anatolian coast, past Rhodes, with a jog north to Kos, continuing to Crete, hitting the northeastern tip of the island around the site of Itanos, then bifurcating: along the north coast of the island as far as Knossos, and south and west along the south coast to Kommos, thence directly to North Africa and hence coastward to Sardinia, avoiding Sicily and Italy. No direct Egyptian routes are proposed. Lambrou-Phillipson (1991: 12–13) describes wind and current reasons to expect a direct route from Crete southeast to Egypt in the Bronze Age, but a shorter-time route from Egypt back to Crete counterclockwise along the Levantine and Anatolian coasts. Nonetheless, Watrous's reasoning (Chapter 3, note 135) requires consideration of the direct southern route from Egypt to Crete, as well as the indirect northern one.

probably arrived on one of not a few ships carrying goods supplied by ports and overland carriers from numerous points and areas in the Near East. These opportunities appear to have existed from the beginning of this period.

CRETE AND THE WEST

The central and western Mediterranean offer neither the literary nor the physical remains that the advanced civilizations of the eastern Mediterranean have left behind, and the stories that can be constructed for the corresponding Cretan component depends on a large number of excavations of relatively small and only loosely associated sites and a modest amount of possibly contaminated Greek legend.[397] Although the analogy of a relatively young and rather rough-edged culture seeking the benefits of more advanced civilizations in the east seems to characterize Aegean-Near Eastern relations in both the Late Bronze Age and the Early Iron Age, the analogy of advanced nations exploiting the natural resources of underdeveloped, even primitive, societies has been advanced to characterize the relations of the Aegean nations or polities with the west.[398] The scarcity of western pottery in the Aegean and farther east points to disposable western exports like metals as prominent, possibly dominant, among that region's exports. However, the western manufactured products, generally bronze implements, but an occasional ceramic piece such as the one at Lefkandi, and the winged ax mold from Mycenae, indicate that westerners were creating value-added themselves as well as exporting raw (smelted) natural resources. In the Greek colonization era, Sicily and Italy were veritable bread baskets for the Aegean, and the Western Phoenician colonists produced some manufactured exports as well as natural resources, but in both cases these were examples of implantations from societies more advanced than the indigenous westerners, whose

levels of political development, from current evidence, seem to have constrained them to activities that could be undertaken on a smaller scale than could be achieved farther east. Of course, Sardinia seems to have been an exception to this characterization of the residents of Italy, Sicily, North Africa, and places farther west, although its civilization currently remains more elusive than many of those in the east.

In this section, rather than attempt to reconstruct what is known of the situation in the central and western Mediterranean Basin, I organize the discussion around the evidence for Cretan interaction with various parts of the west. Previous sections of the study have touched on various elements of eastern and Aegean interactions with the west, and I will not repeat that information here.

BRONZE-AGE CRETAN PRESENCE IN THE WEST

The Bronze Age relations between the Aegean and the west central Mediterranean—Italy, Sicily, Sardinia, Malta, and the Aeolian Islands—began early and continued to evolve through the end of the Aegean Bronze Age and probably, in some form or other, through the (Greek) Early Iron Age. The evidence of Mycenaean activities in those regions and of possible Italian presence in Crete in the Late Helladic (Late Minoan) IIIC period was reviewed above to help establish the starting conditions for Cretan relationships with the west in the Greek Dark Age. Throughout the Mycenaean era, Mycenaean material greatly outnumbers Minoan material in the west, but some Minoan (Cretan) material is present.[399] Four Middle Minoan sherds have been found in Capo Graziano levels (c. 1600–1400) of the acropolis at Lipari.[400] In addition to the possible Cretan sherds to which Vagnetti pointed at Broglio di Trebisacce, physical analyses have identified possible or likely Cretan sources for several ceramic pieces around Italy, for which I have less precise information on chronol-

---

[397] Hdt. *Histories* 7.170; de Sélincourt translation, 1972: 500, on the unsuccessful Cretan (Minoan) siege of Camicus in Sicily before the Trojan War, the army's disastrous withdrawal, and the survivors' settlement on the Italian mainland. The town of Hyria, which legend says these Cretan survivors founded in Messapia, has never been found, and the factual basis of the story, if any, is unknown.

[398] Smith (1987: 145–51, 155) reflects this interest in the literature. Herodotus's story of the Carthaginians' silent trade with some people of the far western Mediterranean—or even the Atlantic—coast (Hdt. 4.407) is the touchstone in this interest.

[399] Smith 1987: 13.

[400] Ibid.: 115.

ogy. Some sherds at Termitito, in Basilicata, appear from petrographical analysis to be from western Crete, and others from Scoglio del Tonno, in Apulia, are from central Crete, according to atomic absorption spectrometry (AAS).[401] Petrographic analysis has pointed to a possible origin around Chania (although Calabria and Sardinia could not be excluded) for one undecorated handle at Vivara (a small islet off Naples, between Ischia and Procida), and AAS indicates sources in western and central Crete for eight sherds at Nuraghe Antigori on Sardinia.[402]

In addition to the slender physical evidence of Late Bronze Age Cretan presence in Italy and surrounding islands, Herodotus repeated a legend of how a Cretan community became established in southern Italy sometime before the fall of Knossos.[403] After giving up a siege on Sicily, a Cretan force was caught at sea in a storm and had its ships smashed on the shore of Iapygia. With no way to get back home, the Cretans stayed and built the town of Hyria. Eventually their identity as Cretans was submerged into the local population. The legend may be old or may have been invented to justify Greek colonization efforts of the late eighth century. Attempts to find archaeological justification for it are unlikely to survive disinterested scrutiny, but the legend remains a toehold that could be dismissed entirely only with some risk. This legendary Cretan presence is farther south than the catalogue items that I have included as indicating the possibility, if a slender one, of some form of Cretan influence in the earliest years of the Greek Dark Age (1.LAT, house urns [despite Mercereau's discussion]; 12.ETR, bronze cups with bulls' heads; 13.TRQ, house urns; and somewhat later for the same source or type of undefined Cretan influence, 14–15.TRQ, leech fibulae and ceramic pieces for which Hencken's term "candelabra" seems as appropriate as any). Retaining these pieces as subjects until future analysis has the opportunity to assign them more positively to some source rather than ruling them out of discussion out of concern for dangers of diffusionist intellectual tendencies seems to avoid committing a Type I error (rejecting a correct hypothesis) while not committing a Type II error (accepting a false one).

CRETAN RELATIONS WITH THE WEST FROM THE NINTH CENTURY

Possibly the earliest reasonably solid evidence for Cretan material in Italy or elsewhere in the west may date slightly earlier than the first Euboean colony at Pithekoussai, but certainly not by much. Several vases from the interior of central Italy have been regarded as local copies of Cretan originals—no. 23 from Terni and no. 26 from Vetralla. Both are similar to south Cretan vases, and LoPorto has endorsed both as local copies of original Cretan imports.[404] The Cretan models for these copies could have been carried by Euboeans stopping in Crete on voyages west, as is likely for other Cretan artifacts in central Italy—but not Cretan material in southern Italy, which is mostly later. No Cretan material has been reported from Pithekoussai, despite the regular appearance of Euboean material around Knossos, and only one Cretan vase fragment has been published from Cumae (70), a fragment with a tongue design that resembles those on some pithos lids from Knossos and Arkades.

The Cretan material at Gela reflects the joint colonization effort with the Rhodians, c. 688. That material includes genuine imports, locally produced, close copies of Cretan originals, likely by Cretan immigrants, and the artistic amalgamations called Rhodio-Cretan. To my knowledge, no inscriptions in Cretan script have been reported from Gela or elsewhere in Sicily. Several Cretan vases and terracottas have been found in southern Italy—Taranto, Brindisi, and Satyrion—that are roughly contemporary with the Cretan material at Gela. The artifacts from southern Italy may have accompanied Corinthian shipping that had stopped at Knossos before proceeding west. The Cretan material in southern peninsular Italy appears to postdate the tapering-off of the Euboean activity in the west, possibly the result of Euboean exhaustion in the Lelantine War.

A discussion of Crete and the west would be incomplete without mention of Sardinia. Direct Cretan interaction with Sardinia appears to have been slight, according to the artifactual remains, even in the Late Bronze Age, but relations between Cyprus and Sardinia seem to have been largely

---

[401] Ibid.: 19.
[402] Ibid.: 20–21, 23.
[403] Hdt. *Histories* 7.474.
[404] LoPorto 1974: 178, 187.

uninterrupted from around the middle of the second millennium well into the first millennium. By the ninth century, and possibly earlier, the Phoenicians, operating out of either Cyprus or the Levantine mainland, had taken up the route from previous occupants of Cyprus. Crete was a natural stopping-station on the route from the east to Sardinia. The Phoenician presence on Crete is quite early—Attic Late Protogeometric if the incised bronze bowl KNC.7 is dated by its deposit context, or even earlier if dated by the Phoenician inscription. Certainly by the mid-ninth century, Phoenician artifacts are in evidence around Knossos and at Kommos. The Sardinian askos in Khaniale Tekke Tomb II could date from mid-ninth century to mid-seventh century, but would appear to be evidence of the return trip from Sardinia to the east, probably by Phoenicians.

The evidence of interaction with Phoenician North Africa is slender and uncertain: a few ivory objects from the Idaean Cave (IC.105), dated to the seventh century or even later, and thirty-three storage amphora fragments from Building Q and nearby at Kommos (KM.60), dated to the seventh century. The ostrich-egg fragments from Khaniale Tekke Tomb II (KN.92) conceivably could be from North Africa; they have no decoration that would betray either origin or peregrination.

THE IMPORTANCE OF EARLY IRON AGE TRADE

A. R. Burn concluded that trade played a very minor role in the earliest Greek colonial movement, roughly the second half of the period under consideration here, but he emphasized that he was not implying that trade played "no part at all." He saw the primary historical importance of trade in this period as giving geographical experience to traders who subsequently guided colonists when the colonization movement began.[405] Extending this criterion to the earlier part of the Early Iron Age would render trade largely inconsequential, although clearly an exchange of ideas was sustained at some rate during the earlier period. Modern criteria for judging the importance of foreign trade concentrate on the impact of trade on the prices of productive inputs and hence on personal incomes.[406] Without disagreeing with Burn on the importance he assigns to prior experiences with trade in guiding the colonization movement, I explore the more conventional economic criteria of trade's impact on incomes.

With the scanty and fragmentary character of the artifactual evidence that bears on this issue, how can we judge it? This is largely a quantitative matter. First, how extensive in fact was trade during this period? Clearly the remains in Crete do not compare with the 15,000 Corinthian pots found at Megara Hybleia, representing well over half of the total finds, from the mid-seventh century forward.[407] For the entire period from 1100 to 600, some 3.5 percent of the catalogued artifacts from Fortetsa are likely (but not all certainly) foreign. Among the more recent excavations in the North Cemetery at Knossos, about 5 percent of the artifacts have been foreign, again over an extended period of time during which the importance of foreign products undoubtedly increased.[408] Throughout most of the twentieth century A.C., traded goods have accounted for 5 to 8 percent of

---

[405] Burn 1937: 232–33, 239. Subsequent research on early-first-millennium trade in the central and western Mediterranean, as summarized and interpreted by D. Ridgway (1992b), has raised the significance attached to Phoenician trading activity relative to the estimates during the period of Burn's writing, but gives essentially the same ultimate importance to the Greek activity.

[406] Another criterion that has become more prominent recently is the ability of trade to pass ideas across borders, under the rubrics of innovation diffusion and technology transfer. These concepts have been of major concern to scholars outside the field of international trade for some time and have never entirely left the field of trade itself, but have come back squarely to center stage largely as a consequence of the United States merchandise trade deficits of the 1970s and 1980s.

[407] Salmon 1984: 105. These are finds up to 1961, and Salmon thinks the estimate of 15,000 is far too conservative; he suggests 30,000 to 40,000 as closer to the true figure.

[408] Catling 1983b: 37. Coldstream (1984a: 122) reports approximately 1% of the North Cemetery pottery to be Cypriot or from other eastern sites. These percentages refer to physical quantities, in fact to proportions of *numbers of items*, without regard to size or, more significantly, to value. If the costs (prices) of these foreign items at the Knossian cemeteries were higher than the cost of the average local item (a terrible comparison) or of comparable local items (better but not necessarily available in the cases of unique items), the foreign share of the *value* of the deposited grave furnishings could be substantially higher than the foreign share of *number* of items.

national income in the United States, which, because of its size, has a relatively low share of traded goods compared with other industrialized countries.[409] The relative quantity of foreign products in the economies of the Early Iron Age Cretan communities, and of other Greek communities for that matter, is hardly a question: it is a matter of small proportions or very small proportions, possibly increasing from the latter to the former over this 500-year period. The bigger question is whether small amounts and shares of traded products could have had disproportionately large effects on Dark Age Crete's economic activity. Before delving into this second question, it is useful to review some outlines of what are probably the most important structural features of Greek economies during the first half of the first millennium—agriculture and individual food budgets.

There is general agreement that the Greeks gradually became better off over these five centuries. A number of Greek cities began to undertake major public construction projects, particularly temples but harborworks as well, by the late

seventh to early sixth century, indicating that they were producing greater aggregate surpluses.[410] Whatever the role of trade in the revival of Greek economic prosperity between 1100 and 600, improvements in purchasing power over foods—food security—must have been central to raising material well-being in the Greek world. Shares of consumption expenditures on food were large, so even small changes in agricultural productivity or food prices would have had a large effect on well-being. To what extent could trade have played a role in the improvement of well-being by working through the food component of budgets? To characterize the share of food in total expenditures (or the "food budget share"), I use data from the Classical period and discuss the appropriateness and limitations of the analogy.

The second half of the fifth century saw an inflationary doubling or more of prices, and it may be difficult to discern changes in relative prices. Consequently, care must be taken in comparing prices of slightly different times within this half-century.[411] During the latter part of the Pelopon-

---

[409] Moran, Larkins, and Webb (1994: Table 1.1) estimate United States exports in 1993 at 10.4% of gross domestic product (gdp) and imports at 11.4%. From 1834 through 1968, the United States's ratio of gross *national* product (close to gdp) ranged from 3.8% to 8.1%: Davis et al. 1972: 554, Table 14.1; Kuznets 1967: 113–14, Appendix Table I. Corresponding ratios of traded goods in European nations in the twentieth century A.C. prior to World War II ranged from 10% for Poland and 15%–16% for France, Germany, and Italy, to 26% for the United Kingdom, 35% for Sweden, and 50% for Norway: Svennilson 1954: 214, Table 64. Export/gdp ratios for some developing countries are an instructive parallel. For 1950–52 and 1978–80, percentages are: Afghanistan—4.1, 11.7; Brazil—9.0, 9.1; India—6.7, 4.9; Indonesia—18.9, 31.7; Iran—6.0, 26.8; Mexico—9.8, 6.1; Turkey—7.6, 3.9; Reynolds 1985: 410, Table 8. The share of trade in an economy is the outcome of many interactive factors, including location, development of markets, policy, size of country, and what a country has to sell. It might strike some as counterintuitive that in 1978, Afghanistan had a more internationally "open" economy than the United States had. Some of Afghanistan's measured 11.7% exports to gdp in 1978 may be attributable to measurement error in its gdp, such that a superior measure would lower the export share to something closer to the U.S. ratio around that time, but the two countries' roughly similar ratios do not reflect underlying structural similarities; Afghanistan's small share of traded goods probably was attributable to the state of market development in the country, whereas the United States's small share was due largely to the vast size of its domestic market and the diversity of its production base. There is not a simple continuum of the value of the trade/income ratio and any indicator of either "level of development" or size.

[410] Fagerström (1988: 167–68) notes the appearance of public architecture—temples—and more complex, private architecture in his Middle Iron Age, 900–760; on temple construction in the period 760–675, cf. 171. Several cities are known to have built city walls before the end of the seventh century. Smyrna had extensive walls built by the middle of the ninth century: Nicholls 1958–59: 122–27. Williams (1982: 15, 17) interprets the remains of the wall outside the Potters' Quarter, in the northwest of the city, as the foundations of a circuit wall dating to the mid-seventh century. Other cities with defensive walls before the end of the seventh century were Eleusis, with a Geometric enceinte, Halae in Boeotia, Eretria by the second quarter of the seventh century, Halieis in the southern Argolid, Vroulia on Rhodes, and Emborio on Chios: Nicholls 1958–59: 115; Williams 1982: 9 n. 1.

[411] In 451, daily pay of jurymen in Athens was 2 obols; in 425, it was raised to 3 obols. By 409/8, 1 drachma per day was the normal pay to construction workers, according to the Erechtheion accounts (Glotz 1926: 204). This may be partly attributable to the release of tribute money into the Athenian economy, combined in the later years of the war with a reduction in the supply of goods without a concomitant reduction in the money supply. French 1964: 129, 168.

nesian War, daily wages, as reflected by what the Athenians paid their rowers, were between 3 obols and 1 drachma.[412] This would have mirrored what a farmer working for himself would have been able to earn (although he would not have received wages), or possibly a little more in order to attract a rowing force.[413] Subtracting sixty days for Athenian holidays and accounting another 5 percent of the remaining work days as unemployed gives a yearly income of 290 drachmas.[414] Citations of wheat prices for this period range between 3 and 5 drachmas per medimnos, and barley around the same; olive oil around 1.5 drachmas per chous (or roughly 0.4 obol per liter); cheap wine between 4 obols and 1 drachma per chous (roughly 0.2 obol and 0.25 obol per liter).[415] Glotz calculated that a skilled worker with a wife and two children, earning 1 drachma per day, would spend 180 drachmas on food; the grain component is three adult daily rations of 1 choenix of wheat (nearly 2 pints), an amount considered large by Spartan soldiers, and the wine was watered as much as 3 to 1. The food budget works

out to 62 percent of income. Glotz added another 100 drachmas for clothing, housing, and incidentals, almost fully accounting for this income. To the extent that such work was not available year round, and the alternative was lower-paid agricultural labor, the income estimate above will be an upper bound, and the budget share of food will be a lower bound. There are differences of opinion regarding wage differences between skill levels of workers, and I accept the beliefs of those who think that unskilled workers earned less.[416]

Whatever generated the improvement in the standard of living in this half-millennium must have operated forcefully on the amount of food people could consume, or, equivalently, on the amount of food the typical farmer could produce. However, few avenues for major improvements in agricultural productivity existed. Earlier budget shares on food expenditures could not have been considerably higher, but the absolute quantities associated with those shares would have been lower in earlier years. First, increased political stability must have contributed to agricultural

---

[412] Thucydides (6.31.3) reports 1 drachma per day during the Sicilian expedition of 413. Xenophon (*Hellenica* 1.5.4) reports 3 obols a day for Athenian rowers in 406. Starr (1977: 72) reports up to 2 obols a day for workmen in Athens.

[413] Of course, farming was seasonal, so rowing wages need not exactly reflect foregone agricultural opportunities. See Osborne 1987: 13–16, fig. 3, for a comparison of agricultural and construction calendars in fifth-century Attica and Athens; the information is too patchy to be exceptionally informative about the resource costs of one type of activity in terms of the product of the other. At the most indirect, agricultural earning possibilities would have determined the value a (possibly idled) worker would have placed on his leisure; rowers' wages would have had to compensate such a person for his foregone leisure, to say nothing of adding a risk premium for the possibility of being killed.

[414] Mitchell 1940: 131.

[415] Glotz 1926: 286; French 1964: 129. On pottery prices as well as food prices and wages, with a discussion of implications of the former for trade, see Boardman 1988b: 29; Gill 1988b: 369–70; and Boardman 1988a: 371–73. Gill objects to the vision of a ship full of pottery, particularly empty pots, while Boardman's principal point is that pottery appears to have been able to compete with other cargoes, not that there might have been cargoes of nothing but pottery. The high stowage factor of empty, closed-shape vases would have precluded sending them in large consignments, but there would have been many alternatives to such a dangerous and foolish practice. Johnston (1974: 148–50; 1979: 32–35) discusses a number of difficulties in interpreting prices scratched on vases, either before or after firing. In the latter reference, he is struck by the results of his implicit assumption of linearity between apparent vase quality and vase price and does not rely on the concept of price-level change (or, alternatively, coinage debasement) when comparing vase prices separated by a century.

[416] Glotz (1926) comes down on both sides of this question, citing the uniformity of wages reported in the Erechtheion accounts of 409/8 (166, 204), but also commenting on his budget calculations that less-skilled workers could have managed only by dint of hard work and privations (286). Mitchell (1940: 131 n. 2), expresses skepticism at the notion of a uniform wage. Glotz is an older reference today, but his calculations tally well with more recent work, and his concept of the food portion of the typical budget is more useful than what I have found elsewhere. E.g., Larsen (1938: 412–14) segregates a consumer's expenditures into clothing, wheat or barley, and the opsonion, which "covered all expenses except cereals and clothing." Clearly, we cannot assess the total food portion of expenditures from this set of categories. Nonetheless, for the early third century to the early second century, Larsen calculates the cereal portion of expenditures as ranging between 39% and 48% for men. If cereals accounted for two-thirds of food expenditures, this would yield a figure very close to that which I have cal-

productivity. Second, some technological changes may have occurred in agriculture as iron became available for agricultural implements, or even as the use of iron in weaponry may have released bronze for cheaper use in agriculture over a transitional period of a century or so.[417] This would have been a one-time change rather than a source of continuing improvement, although the one-time change could have been spread out over a lengthy period. Agricultural techniques in the

---

Note 416 continued

culated from Glotz's figures. Pritchett's price data are not restricted to the Attic stelai recording the sale of property confiscated from the companions of Alcibiades in 415/4; they include agricultural prices from many places (Delos, Rhodes, Attica, Rome, et al.), scattered across a considerable span of time—some as late as the Edict of Diocletian in A.D. 301. It would be very difficult to use them to construct a coherent budget allocation that would refer to any particular point in time: see Pritchett 1956: 181–203, on agricultural prices. Foxhall and Forbes (1982: 58) note that the calorie content of these food budgets appears to be quite high, possibly in the range of 4,200 calories per day, adequate for a large (even by contemporary standards) man working strenuously. However, these are food acquisition, not intake, figures; Foxhall and Forbes point out the potentially large storage losses that ancient consumers could expect, which would lower substantially the consumption expected from such a daily ration (56–57).

[417] Catling (1964: 79–85) reports an array of humble, bronze agricultural implements from the Late Bronze Age, largely from Cyprus, and Crete certainly has produced LBA bronze agricultural tools: e.g., Bosanquet and Dawkins 1923: 119, pl. XXV.G–H. The Gelidonya ship also carried a number of bronze plowshares (or hoes) and a sickle, among other agricultural tools, possibly carried as scrap: see Bass 1967: 84–99, 117–18, fig. 130, on distribution of Bronze Age hoes. Iron agricultural tools have not survived in good condition in the soil (although weapons and jewelry have survived reasonably well in graves), so their relative scarcity among Early Iron Age artifacts need not imply their genuine absence or rarity: Schiering 1968: 147; Stech-Wheeler, Muhly, Maxwell-Hyslop, and Maddin (1981: 250, 253, ills. 2, 11) report iron plowshares and a fragment of a sickle or scythe blade from a late-tenth-century context at Taanach in northern Israel, with evidence of carburization in one of the plowshares and the sickle blade. So the metals revolution certainly touched agriculture even if we cannot assess readily what the productivity effect was—agricultural tools were *not* all stone, nor even necessarily predominantly stone, through the first half of the first millennium, as some have suggested; e.g., Morris 1986a: 514. Brinkman (1988: 140) notes that by the seventh century in Babylonia, most cutting implements that would have found agricultural uses—axes, knives, shears, sickles—as well as digging tools and branding irons were made of iron. Moorey (1988: 25) suggests that iron's early impact on agriculture in some regions—he highlights Palestine—may have exceeded its impact on military equipment. Thus it appears that the former category of effect—via iron's *substitution for* bronze in agriculture—is documented about as well as the evidence will permit. As for the possibility that substitution of iron in weaponry reduced the cost of bronze for some nonmilitary uses, it remains a possibility that could have helped extend the penetration of metals into agriculture, possibly restricted to particular use niches and locations, but it could be difficult or impossible to assess empirically, since there is little way of knowing how much bronze would have been used otherwise. Waldbaum 1978 contains some evidence on a possible partial substitution of bronze for iron in tools in general, not necessarily agricultural tools; but the results are inconclusive. Although the overall sample size, even for Crete alone, is not especially small, cell entries are too small to yield statistical significance (50, Table IV.9). Bearing in mind the risks of disregarding statistical significance, in Crete the ratio of tools to weapons was higher for bronze than for iron over the period of the twelfth century to the tenth, and in the eleventh century the percentage of iron weapons (the percentage of iron *and* bronze weapons) was greater than the percentage of iron tools. In the entire Near Eastern sample, the ratio of tools to weapons was greater for iron items than for bronze from the twelfth century to the tenth, but that ratio declined far more sharply over that period for the iron artifacts than for the bronze (56, Table IV.15). Cf. Morris 1986a: 512, Table 7, for counts from Nichoria. These calculations are rough: they have no statistical parameters, no accounting is made for the possibility of differential survival, either pre- or postdepositional, and of course, the tools are not restricted to agricultural implements. Nevertheless, these counts do not seem to leave the possibility of iron having freed bronze for some peaceful uses in agriculture any more farfetched than it may have seemed before the exercise. Moorey (1988: 25–26) points to the relative cost of bronze and iron: implements of the former metal were capable of being multiply cast, whereas those of the latter had to be forged individually at considerably greater cost in labor. Moorey thinks it likely that iron did not become cheaper than bronze, except where ore was locally available, before the middle of the first millennium. The superior technical suitability of iron for many agricultural applications could have been offset by bronze's relative cost advantage in many places.

Greek world by and large remained the same throughout the first millennium B.C.[418] Nonetheless, the introduction and gradually wider use of iron represented an expansion of resources available for production, even with a constant array of technology. Third, the population movements during the earlier part of this half-millennium would have brought many people to new environments that may have operated quite differently from those to which they were accustomed, especially in exceptional years, which may have governed how they farmed in ordinary years as well. It may have taken several generations to develop intimate knowledge of new farming environments, to construct new agricultural infrastructure such as terraces, dams and other water diversions, etc., and to prepare soils thoroughly for dry farming.[419] This learning and fixed capital stock would have raised agricultural productivity, but also probably as a one-time (or asymptotic) improvement rather than as a continuing source of productivity growth.

It is possible to stare at lists of foreign goods from archaeological contexts for years and still wonder whether they indicate anything important—in fact, that is largely what we have done. Much of the quandary can be attributed to insufficient attention devoted to defining criteria of importance. Without clear criteria for evaluating importance, it is difficult to assess how the values those criteria take on behave in the face of various changes. Provenances and dates are assigned to artifacts—primarily pottery and metals—using models of ceramics and metals, frequently in the form of typologies. We may be able to determine with a satisfactory degree of confidence that an item is from, say, Attica or Egypt, and even that it may date to, say, the ninth century, but whether any of those facts indicate importance requires further consideration. "Importance" is a social implication and requires a

model of some set of social activities for its assessment. I have attempted to take modest steps toward identifying some criteria of importance and assessing their behavior. Though there are scholars who might take issue with the particular criteria I use, some relatively well-defined proposals may have the merit of at least moving the discussion forward.

In Appendix B, I have developed a series of models of how and why particular economic changes might occur in an economy whose structure is probably quite similar in outline to the economy of many regions of Greece in the early first millennium: largely agricultural, trade limited to a small proportion of the total activity in the economy, not a major role for capital equipment. The models I have used there are simple, but the presentation is relatively formal, so that readers who wish to examine the assumptions and procedures in detail may assess them. I explore several issues related to trade, but I begin with situations that need not involve trade but rather are characteristic of responses to external events of an economy with these characteristics. First, in a largely agricultural economy, when some resources are diverted away from agriculture, what becomes of agricultural production? Does that sector somehow just "take up the slack" and continue to deliver the same volume of goods? The answer is a simple "no." The cost of agricultural goods rises sharply relative to the cost of nonagricultural products, with the cost change much more dramatic than the underlying quantity changes in agriculture. Next, I assess some particular reasons why agricultural production might change, instead of just supposing that it does, because the source of the disturbance might affect the society's response. If production changes derive from such external factors as weather fluctuations or climate changes or technological changes somewhere in the society, rela-

---

[418] Fussell 1967: 17. Isager and Skydsgaard (1992: 44) are reluctant to claim otherwise because of the difficulty of obtaining clear evidence, but they note that a number of tools that can be seen in a Greek market today do not differ noticeably from those of antiquity (66). Olive and wine presses may be exceptions to a rough technological standstill, although they are agricultural processing machines rather than cultivation equipment; the principal technical changes in this machinery may have occurred in the Classical and later periods, however (56–66); Hadjisavvas 1992: 7, 27, 116. Sallares (1991: 14, 345, 359, 361) suggests that selection of seeds during the early first millennium increased agricultural yields significantly. Nonetheless, the relatively low yields in agriculture, worldwide, through the later nineteenth century A.C. suggest that first millennium B.C. agricultural productivity growth probably was not great.

[419] Vermuele (1972: 4) emphasizes the region-specific experience required for farming and animal husbandry in the regions of Greece. Surely the same would have been true after population movements at the beginning of the Early Iron Age.

tive costs of agricultural and nonagricultural production would change, but some reallocations of productive inputs, such as labor and land, could be made between activities (agriculture and nonagricultural production such as the manufacture of simple, or complicated, products) to at least partially compensate for the external disturbances. The change in real well-being of the people consequently is overestimated generally by simple interpretation of relative production-cost changes.

The last model I develop in Appendix B describes a small economy with structural characteristics probably similar to corresponding characteristics of Dark Age Crete, and I examine its behavior in response to various changes in domestic and foreign-trade-related circumstances and the consequences of the changes and responses. To flesh out some main dimensions of this model, 95 percent of the labor force (or labor time) is devoted to agriculture, and 5 percent to what might be lumped together as "manufacturing"—making pottery, tools, textiles, etc. The economy exports agricultural products and imports other "manufactured" products; the total value of its exports amounts to 5 percent of the economy's agricultural production—4.75 percent of everything the economy produces.[420] Different percentages could be substituted for those I have used. Domestic changes—for example, changes in the local population, in the land available for agriculture, in the volume of resources used in local nonagricultural production, and in production technologies—have much stronger consequences for the model economy than do external changes of comparable magnitude—in shipping costs, income of foreign

trading partners, those partners' preferences for Cretan goods, and the foreign region's own relative production costs. This is not surprising, since the window through which foreign and trade-related events could be transmitted to the Cretan economy was so small—4.75 percent of the total activity of the island. This result is essentially unaffected by variations in the underlying production characteristics of agricultural and manufacturing activities. Even domestic changes that could have sharp effects on relative production costs and on the distribution of labor effort between agriculture and "manufacturing" generally have relatively dampened effects on real well-being, and the foreign events have virtually undetectable impacts.

Is the conclusion to be drawn from these results that external relations—foreign trade—were of virtually no consequence to Dark Age Greek economies? In characteristic economic fashion, the answer is "yes and no." On the "yes" side, unless some other compelling case can be made, we should accept as a fact that foreign trade could have had little effect on the overall structure of relative prices in Dark Age Crete and on the overall level of individual well-being. A lever from the outside world amounting to only 4.75 percent of the total volume of economic activity is simply too small to lift much, so to speak. For the "no" side, the structural features of the economy[421] by themselves contain a striking result: 95 percent of the "manufactured" goods consumed or otherwise used in the Dark Age Cretan economy would have been of foreign origin. If 2 percent of agricultural production had been exported, 38 percent of man-

---

[420] This composition of imports and exports is a simplification. Since virtually all artifacts that remain to tell of ancient product movements are from one variety or another of "manufactured" good, it is clear that just about all regions exported some manufactured products. In fact, most regions probably exported some agricultural products and some manufactured goods, although exported proportions of agricultural and manufactured products would have differed among regions. To show what might appear to be a modest expansion in detail would require a multisectoral model, which itself would require a geometric increase in information on parameter values (intersectoral flows as well as each new sector's own production and consumption parameters). This increase in parameter values to be specified expands the opportunities to misspecify—guess incorrectly about—absolute and relative magnitudes. Additionally, the results would be uninterpretable without numerical simulation, the usefulness of which would be limited—possibly quite severely—by the expanded scope for error in choices of parameter values. Consequently, I restrict the analysis to a model with two production sectors and three resources. Clearly the implicitly defined trading partners of the "country" illustrated in the model are net importers of agricultural goods and net exporters of manufactured products. For the Roman period, Sanders (1982: 32–35) characterizes agriculture as Crete's main source of wealth and as supplying the bulk of Crete's exports. This level of generalization, being approximately correct for the period two thousand years later is, I believe, also a safe generalization for a thousand years earlier.

[421] Admittedly assumed rather than derived from ancient evidence, but nonetheless conforming to contemporary characteristics of not particularly open, agriculturally based economies.

ufactured goods would have been imported, given the structure of this model. These figures are implied by the shares of agricultural production and external trade in the economy.[422] Manufactured goods, even simple ones, potentially contain vast amounts of information about production technologies. If such a large proportion of—an admittedly small class of—daily goods contained such information from the outside world, it would be very conservative to claim that external relations were unimportant to such Dark Age Greek economies. In fact, the models developed in Appendix B indicate that if imported manufactured goods contained information that could have been translated into technological changes in local, nonagricultural production on Crete, the impacts of foreign disturbances would have been eight to ten times larger than otherwise calculated without such a technology transferral effect; although impacts on Cretan well-being still would

have been small, they could have been noticeable.

This result returns us to Burn's claim noted at the beginning of this section, and to the attitudes and ideas implicit in the analyses of such scholars as Boardman and Coldstream, with their art-historical foci on intellectual transfers involved in the introduction of artistic motifs and craft techniques, not to speak of such far-reaching activities as the transmission of the Phoenician alphabet. There would seem to be considerable merit in Burn's assessment and in the art-historical focus on relatively intangible transfers. A concomitant implication seems to be that much of the economic revival involved in the eighth-century Greek Renaissance must have come from within the Greek regions themselves rather than being brought in from outside, although in such an interpretation, due regard must be given to the intellectual transfers that the existing small trade shares could have accomplished.[423] Indeed,

---

[422] If the model "Cretan" economy exported 2.5% of its agricultural output instead of the 5% used in the calculations, the imported share of manufactured goods consumed on Crete would drop to 47.5%. With only 1% of agricultural production exported, the imported manufactures' share would be only 19%.

[423] In recent literature addressing mechanisms in cultural diffusion, the issue has arisen regarding the necessity of an exchange of goods to effect a transfer of information. Watrous (1987: 65–66) reasonably has criticized the practice of simplemindedly inferring the importance of some set of interactions between different regions by counting the numbers of artifacts in particular classes. He does not pursue the reasons why this practice is simpleminded, but several are obvious: the archaeologically invisible goods problem, differential survival of artifacts, missing social context of the exchange, et al. Nonetheless, ignoring, or underestimating the importance of, the material exchange associated with a transfer of information leads to even more serious intellectual missteps. (Renfrew [1986: 8] and Cherry [1986: 40] appeal to the separation of information transfer from goods transfer, but without working through the implications.) There are good reasons to associate the transfer of information (cultural diffusion) with the exchange of material goods. Travel was expensive and dangerous. Simplistically stated, its costs had to be covered or the activity would cease to be supported. Would not the value of new information "cover the costs" of travel? Probably not, or at least not in a manner that the sponsor of the travel could capture. Information has unusual economic properties: once it is made available, it is difficult if not impossible to keep people who did not pay for its acquisition from using it. Stated alternatively, it is difficult for the person who furnished it ("imported" it, made it, or thought it up) to recover the full value of it. Knowing this in advance (implicitly, if not in the form of theorems or empirically tested hypotheses), potential suppliers of new information will be reluctant to invest much in that activity. This characteristic of information accounts for the large share of public support for information production in contemporary society, as well as for the patent system. This might be considered to constitute a sound reason for government (royal) participation in foreign trade in the Bronze Age and Early Iron Age and therefore a supporting rationale for believing in official "control" of foreign trade, but other factors, I believe, reduce that likelihood. Primarily, much of the information transferred between cultures via trade need not benefit the royal establishment. Some well-defined technological information might be sought specifically, but much of the information implicitly referred to in the cultural diffusion discussion is less specific, ranging from religious beliefs to fairly general, contemporary scientific concepts. Many trips could be made before some information was brought back that a royal sponsor considered worth the cost of the trips. These trips would have to cover their costs more quickly and more predictably to be continued. The same requirements would face private traders, who would not have much ability to capture the "external" benefits of information. Consequently, I have no qualms about tying information transfers to material exchange. Having said that, I hasten to point to information transfer that is not embodied in the goods themselves, although my own modeling here relies on that mechanism: traders' (and even their donkey drivers') observations of alternative ways of doing things (solving daily problems), ranging from agricultural practices to writing systems to noticing daylight differences.

formally modeling the transfer of foreign ideas to Crete raises the impacts of changes in foreign income and tastes by as much as an order of magnitude, although those impacts remain small relative to the most important domestic changes. The cumulative effect of some small changes also warrants attention. A 1 percent annual rate of productivity increase in shipping over a period of two centuries could have raised well-being by something like 80 percent. Whether the "true" increase was 80 percent, 40 percent, or even 20 percent, deriving from a more irregular productivity improvement in shipping, such a magnitude of effect warrants more detailed consideration of whether such causative changes are plausible.[424]

Another result of the model touches on the not-uncommon suggestion that a taste among late Dark Age aristocrats for eastern imports, for gift exchanges or deposition in graves, or for both, sparked an export drive to finance the acquisition of these goods, a drive that laid the foundation for the revival of trade and of the Greek economies in general by the eighth century. In fact, a shift in tastes toward an export good, which could be made in only modest quantities locally, would have no other noticeable effects than to depress aggregate income and individual well-being and to redistribute income to the owners of resources used in local production of the import-competing good. Only a change that

expanded the productivity of the local economy could have an expansionary effect.

The same model of trade indicates an impressive scope for redistribution of income in Dark Age Crete deriving from domestic changes—from expansion of land resources and from resources used in nonagricultural production, from population growth, from technological changes, even from changes in people's consumption preferences between agricultural and manufactured products. Such changes would have (could have?) sparked contests primarily between people deriving substantial amounts of their income from land and those getting their income from resources used in manufactured products. The part of the population deriving most of their income simply from their labor would have been relatively unaffected by many of these contests, although, in the case of expansion of land area, they would have found their interests aligned with the owners of resources for manufacturing, and in the case of population expansion, with the landowners. The only external change that could have had an effect on Greek income distributions comparable to those following domestic changes is a change in foreign preference for Cretan products (see Tables B.3 and B.4). The results of this study of income distribution may merit comparison with other evidence on these potential coalitions beyond what can be done here.[425] When idea transmission

[424] What is a reasonable range of rates of productivity growth in shipping over such a long period? It may not be inappropriate to consider some empirical information from a much later time. North (1968: 965–66, Table 3A) calculated an annual rate of productivity growth in English shipping (worldwide) of 0.45%, with no changes in load factor, sea time per voyage, prices of labor and capital, ship size, and ship-construction costs. Crew size, and thus victualing costs, fell by half, and port time fell equivalently. From 1814 to 1860, a period of more rapid technological change in shipping, productivity growth averaged 3.30% per year. Davis (1962: 194–98) similarly reports that improvements in on-shore commercial organization—assembling cargoes and negotiating prices and freight rates—reduced turnaround times in the seventeenth century by enough to reduce the cost of carrying a ton of sugar across the Atlantic by one-third between 1670 and 1770—an average rate of productivity increase of 0.40% per year. Davis stresses merchants' and ship's masters' connections in foreign ports as important elements in reducing port time (90, 197).

The fact that such changes in ocean shipping costs came, to a great extent, from institutional developments on land and from methods of operating technologically quite similar vessels rather than from critical changes in vessel design takes some of the burden away from hunting for radical (or at least observable) design changes in vase paintings and crude ship models. Less-extensive technical changes may have passed unnoticed by vase painters, if not by the mariners themselves. So, 1%-a-year improvement in shipping productivity is probably on the high side for the period between c. 1100 or 1000 and c. 800. More reasonable estimates may be 0.5 to 0.33 percent per year, but even a 0.25% average rate of productivity growth implies a 20% increase in well-being over a 200-year period with the models of Appendix B.

[425] Barnett (1957: 60) characterized the period from Ezekiel's time to the seventh century as a time of "enrichment of the land-owning aristocracy at the expense of the peasants" in Corinth, Lesbos, and other seventh-century Greek tyrannies as well as in Israel. Coldstream (1977: 70–71) raises the possibility of an association between the increased burial wealth at Athens in the mid-ninth century and the resumption (?) of silver pro-

accompanies external trade, changes in foreign income and tastes for the Cretan export can have limited effects on Cretan income distribution.

It is not impossible that a new concentration of wealth could have altered capital accumulation trends in ways that my modeling does not incorporate. These results suggest that, if trade with the Near East played a major part in the Greek Renaissance of the eighth century, the consequences of that trade must have operated through other than common price-and-income channels. One possibility is the transmission of skills, which could have revolutionized the ways Greeks went about their production activities (such a revolutionary event does not seem to have occurred, even with consideration of metallurgy); another is the communication of ideas about social organization that affected production (which does not seem any more plausible). This is the type of knowledge transfer to which a good bit of literature has appealed, but with little specificity about methods of transfer. Another alternative, which the present modeling does not incorporate but which could increase the contribution of trade to revived economic growth, involves interactions with risk. I turn to this possibility.

A major goal in recent and contemporary peasant agriculture has been to avoid risk, to keep risk within certain bounds.[426] In risky environments, higher average rates of return on productive farm assets (labor, equipment, land, animals, knowledge) are associated with greater riskiness. The positive aspect of this relationship is that farmers can reduce risk by selecting activities or procedures that will yield lower rates of return and hence lower average incomes. Autarkic communities must conduct these trade-offs within themselves, often over a relatively small area with limited environmental diversity, although mountainous areas do offer variety if not necessarily high average productivity. The cost of reducing risk can be a large sacrifice in expected rate of return. Opening trade with other communities not only opens their resource patterns to trading partners but also offers the opportunity to let them supply additional diversification of environmental risks. Trading farmers can afford to undertake local activities that offer higher incomes as long as they are able to secure essential foodstuffs, possibly at somewhat higher prices than in the best years locally, if the local crops are poor. Manufactured goods have a role to play in this strategy, since crops that do not come up cannot be used to purchase other communities' crops that do. It is not necessary, however, that each farmer or farm family engage in simple manufacturing activities as well as in agriculture, as long as some elements in the community are available to lend during food shortages, their lending being based on sales of nonagricultural (manufactured) products or loans secured outside the community on the security of those products. This could have been what happened to the Athenian rural income distribution in the decades before Solon's reforms. Experience with credit could have lagged the ability to dispense it with actuarial prudence, leaving the income gap between lenders and borrowers, lucky and unlucky, to widen intolerably.[427] Regardless of the individual and community mechanisms for reducing or spreading agricultural risks, the autarkic trade-off between risk and expected return can require a large increase in risk to achieve a relatively minor increase in expected return. Opening the local portfolio of activities to trade could alter the trade-offs in that relationship, or even shift the relationship to a higher plane of expected return for any given level of

---

Note 425 continued

duction at the Laurion mines (evidence of processing from Thorikos), also around the mid-ninth century. His example is one of increased resource exploitation (roughly equivalent to increased availability of resources) raising income and wealth rather than a change in the overall income distribution in favor of natural-resource owners, but the mechanism that he suggests would underlie income-distribution changes.

[426] Evidence for medieval Europe suggests that risk avoidance was a high priority in peasant agriculture then as well. McCloskey 1976: 124–70. Cf. Halstead 1990: 147–64, for description of precautionary behavior in contemporary Greek agriculture. Walker and Jodha (1986: 17–34) review agricultural risk management in contemporary developing countries; they find large changes in "socioreligious" expenditures in response to drought in India (23, Table 2.4). Isager and Skydsgaard (1992: 108–13) express concern for the introduction of anachronisms through application of contemporary ethnographic material to ancient Greek cases.

[427] This explanation roughly parallels the recent proposal of Gallant (1982: 123–24) for the origins of the Athenian land problem solved by Solon, but focuses on the underlying economic forces rather than upon reciprocity relations run amok.

risk. The volumes of trade required to accomplish this transformation remain to be demonstrated.

Some of the apparent prosperity of Crete in the later Dark Ages, through at least much of the seventh century, may have come from the ability to engage in a relatively small volume of agricultural trade. Crete was closer to the net food-demand areas of the Aegean and the eastern Mediterranean than was the Italian-Sicilian bread basket, which would have entered trade streams late in this period anyway. Additionally, Cretan suppliers may have been able to compete satisfactorily with the higher transportation costs of the more distant western colonies. The founding of Cyrene and the further opening of Egypt through Naukratis in the last third of the seventh century may have given Crete agricultural competitors who had natural advantages the Cretans could not meet well. The loss of markets would have had a magnified effect on Cretan producers, who not only would have lost income but also would have had to reorganize their activities to trade off even more income for less risk internally.

V

TAKING STOCK

The events of the close of the thirteenth and the opening of the twelfth centuries—the destruction of the Mycenaean palaces, the devastation of cities and reordering of kingdoms in North Syria, and the battles between the Egyptians and the various nations of the Sea Peoples—certainly disrupted the old international order in the region, but evidence indicates that economic life, including international transactions, continued. The scale was reduced, some trading partners reordered themselves, and by about 1100, entirely new political sovereignties had developed, although there were elements of continuity in the transition to the new political order. There is evidence of pottery from Kos, or possibly elsewhere in the Dodecanese, at Ugarit in the second half of the thirteenth century, and of LM IIIC Cretan artifacts on Rhodes. Kanta reports no mainland or Near Eastern artifacts in Cretan LM IIIC contexts,[1] but a small number of Near Eastern artifacts appear in Subminoan contexts, and Italian products appear in LM IIIC contexts at several sites. The Sea Peoples substituted themselves into the older Canaanite urban system, the northern Canaanites emerged as the Phoenicians, and the Egyptians, with economic and political problems at home, pulled themselves back somewhat from the Levant. The Assyrians benefited from the reduction of the Hittite empire to their northwest, and Aramaean kingdoms, which the Assyrians eventually subdued, arose in former southeastern Hittite terri-

tory. Trade appears to have continued among the different mainland kingdoms and principalities and between those states and Cyprus, although some sites show periods of interruption. The longstanding traditions of commercial sophistication, integrated with state involvement in the economy, appear to have continued to characterize the economies of mainland western Asia during the last century of the Late Bronze Age and the first centuries of the Early Iron Age, despite the turmoil of the times. Crete appears to have been indirectly, if at times tenuously, connected with this trading network, and probably in a role other than as a pirates' nest. Crete and Egypt probably engaged in a counterclockwise trade from the Middle Minoan period, because of the current and wind patterns in the eastern Mediterranean, giving the appearance and technicality of an indirect trade from Egypt to Crete, through the Levantine ports and Cyprus. Evidence exists for a southern route, clockwise and direct, from Egypt to Crete, use of which may have alternated seasonally with the northern route. These circulation patterns appear to have persisted into the Early Iron Age, the winds, currents, and shipping all having remained much the same, but Egyptian materials were finding their way to Crete probably in the eleventh century and certainly by the tenth. Nevertheless, the port of Kommos appears to have been infrequently used, if it was not out of operation altogether, in late LM IIIB and in LM

---

[1] Kanta 1980: 314–16. She notes that iron becomes somewhat more common in LM IIIC contexts than in previous ones, but iron per se is ambiguous evidence, at best, for external relations.

IIIC.[2] Economic interchanges between Cyprus and Crete appear to have persisted sporadically until the mid-ninth century, when they seem to have become more regular. Phoenician contact appears to have had a chronological pattern very similar to that of the Cypriot, although it seems to have been relatively more evenly distributed between the north and south coasts of Crete. North Syrian goods began to appear in Crete during the period when commerce with Cyprus and Phoenicia intensified. The western Asian wars of the 500 years studied here were dispersed over too many states and time periods for the Near Eastern artifactual material on Crete to yield clear effects on economic contacts of the ebb and flow of war and peace. Nevertheless, the trading activity of the Near Eastern states formed a continuous backdrop for Crete's external relations during the period.

Table 3 summarizes the chronological appearances of foreign artifacts on Crete, by probable origin. The century, roughly from about 850 to about 750, appears clearly as the boom period of overseas artifacts. The sharp increase in artifacts in the second half of the eighth century is boosted somewhat by the finds from Inatos. The regional patterns of artifactual origins in the second half of the eighth century and the first half of the seventh appear to differ from one another, although they might not be distinguishable statistically. The Egyptian and North Syrian shares drop, and the Phoenician and other Near Eastern shares rise; some, but not all, of this effect could be the result of greater difficulty in distinguishing between several of the more specific origins, which accounts for the rise in the count in the "Near Eastern" category. Attic origins continue their tapering trend in the first half of the seventh century, and the Cycladic share falls sharply. The decrease in the East Greek and Rhodian share may be more apparent than real. The constant overall number of foreign artifacts in the second half of the seventh century is, to some extent, an artifact of the large number of published votives from Amnisos. I say "to some extent" because the Corinthian material appears at a steady or increasing rate, and the

East Greek material from Kommos rises during this half-century. I should point out again that these half-century counts in Table 3 cannot be interpreted strictly as artifacts datable specifically to that half-century, but rather as artifacts that belong in that half-century or later.

The mechanisms for placing foreign artifacts at Early Iron Age Cretan sites include interactions associated with population movements, pirate loot, exchange of gifts, and various forms of trade. Artifacts that could be associated with previous population movements are restricted to Cypriot origin. Some smaller metal objects could be pirates' loot, but in general the artifacts are not what typically would be considered prime booty. Very few of the foreign items look appropriate for a gift-exchange network. A number of the sites in Crete have yielded only a small number of foreign artifacts, and I recall the admonitions voiced so well by both Cook and Clairmont regarding the interpretation of such finds. With a single site, it would be difficult to see much evidence of regular, external commercial contacts, but these artifacts are widespread throughout Crete, at both coastal and inland sites, early and late, too widespread to be consistent evidence of ancient nonbusiness travelers. As Clairmont expresses, "Everybody knows that in antiquity one did not sail the sea for mere pleasure."[3]

This leaves trade as the major mechanism for transporting most of these objects, although there may have been considerable variation in the characteristics of the interactions in this category.[4] Some of the interactions may have had Crete as an exclusive destination, but the appearance of much of the remains suggests that Crete was a way-station between various points on east-west and north-south voyages, from as early as the later eleventh century. Some of the exchanges in the trade category probably were purchases of ships' stores and living expenses during stopovers. It certainly is possible that this proliferation of sites was served with foreign artifacts through only two or three points of entry into Crete. Such a middleman trade involving some other community on the island would not detract from the fact that an end-

---

[2] Shaw 1984: 277–78.

[3] Clairmont 1955: 91; see Chapter 1, notes 5 and 9.

[4] Austin (1970: 35) uses a similar process of elimination to conclude that, despite the scarcity of hard, pre-fifth-century evidence, grain trade was the mid-seventh-century Ionian motivation for the contact with Egypt that led to the establishment of the Greek πόλις-ἐμπόριον at Naukratis.

TABLE 3. Origins and Dates of Overseas Artifacts Found on Crete, 1100–600 B.C.

Period	Period frequency	Egypt	North Syria	Syria	Phoenicia	Near East	Cyprus	Attica	Corinth	Central Greece[a]	East Greece & Rhodes	Cyclades	Italy & Europe
1100-1050	30	5	1	0.5	1	6	9	2.5	0	2	0	0	3
1050-1000	3	1	0	0	0	0	0	1	0	1	0	0	0
1000-950	40	4	1.5	0	1.5	10.5	3.5	10[b]	0	1	1	7	0
950-900	30	1	0	0	0	0	2	22	1	3	1	0	0
900-850	28	1.5	1.5	2.5	0.5	2	4	8.5	0.5	3	0	4	0
850-800	163	12.5	26.5	16	10.5	22.5[d]	15	24	5	7.5	4	19	1
800-750	117	4	1	0	25.5	8.5	31.5	14	7	8	0	7	10.5
750-700	169	29	5.5	1.8	3.3	8.5	12.3	9.5	34	5.5	38.5	14	6.5
700-650	127	14	1	1	8.5[c]	12.5	11	4	31	6	26	2	0.5
650-600	126	22.5	0.5	0.5	5	5	3	2	45	4	33	1	0
Undated	4	0.5	—	—	—	—	—	—	—	—	—	—	—
Origin frequency	837	97.5	38.5	22.3	55.8	75.5	91.3	97.5	138.5	40.5	104	54	21.5

[a] Boeotia, Argos, Laconia, Euboea, Thessaly.
[b] "Aegean region."
[c] 2 possibly from North Africa.
[d] 1 possibly Bronze Age.

point—say, Eleutherna—was in effective contact with a source overseas—say, Egypt. Indeed, the overall geographical pattern of overseas linkages of individual Cretan sites parallels the pattern of Knossos's linkages, suggesting Knossos as a major entry point from which foreign items might have scattered out to the rest of Crete relatively haphazardly through intra-island trade. Comparison of the set of maps showing overseas goods at Cretan sites with the maps of Cretan finds overseas shows a geographically reciprocal pattern of inflows and outflows—except with Cyprus and the Near East—that the literature has not reported before.

The small proportion of foreign artifacts found at Cretan sites and of Cretan objects found at overseas sites suggests at the very least that Cretan trade in the durable artifacts was not extensive. It is not transparent whether this also means that there was negligible trade in agricultural products and less-durable manufactured items between Crete and other regions that did not produce export-quality ceramics. The absence of transport amphorae in the artifactual remains may be an artifact itself of the high proportion of funerary to town sites excavated for the Early Iron Age, although organic containers may have been used for nonliquid products.[5]

The Phoenicians maintained a continual presence in the external relations of Early Iron Age Crete, although the volume of trade between Crete and Phoenician destinations is difficult to assess. The Phoenician presence, with the exception of Coldstream's proposed branch factory for unguents around Knossos,[6] if it in fact existed in that fashion, may have been primarily on stopovers on voyages to Italy, Sardinia, North Africa, and other sites in Greece, although the Phoenicians clearly brought culturally or artistically influential items, and they may have picked up Cretan products for export to some of their other customers. According to artifactual

remains, most of the Phoenicians' stops, for whatever purposes, appear to have been westbound. This interpretation leaves open the question of how they got back to the east if not via Crete. Hugging the North African coast appears to have been feasible and may have been the most common practice. Indeed, Aubet shows a generalized, counterclockwise pattern of shipping around the entire Mediterranean.[7]

The period of the most abundant Phoenician material is the century from about 850 to about 750, which corresponds with a resurgence of Cypriot material. The first half of this period (from c. 850 to c. 800) shows at least a local peak in material from all the Near Eastern origins. From about 750 through about 600, the Egyptian material continues in relative abundance. These are largely votives—amulets and scarabs mostly, although there are a few faience and bronze bowls. Of course, a large proportion of the other items from Near Eastern sites are votives as well. If the Phoenicians were purveyors of Egyptian material to Crete in the ninth century, it is curious that the Egyptian artifacts really increase in number after the peak in the material evidence of Phoenician visits.

Egyptian items, and items that look Egyptian, are prominent throughout the period and across the regions of Crete.[8] The genuine Egyptian items may be attributable to a triangular trade between Phoenicia, Egypt, and Crete, in which Phoenicians gave Phoenician or other items to Egyptians for Egyptian items, and then sold the Egyptian items elsewhere to pay for what they had given to Egypt. Multilateral exchanges of this sort are probably how the other Near Eastern items (North Syrian, Assyrian, Babylonian, Luristanian) got to Crete, although some of these items may have been carried by Greeks, possibly East Greeks or Euboeans, from Al Mina; recall the possible Cretan vase fragment from Mersin on the coast

---

[5] Boardman (1988b: 29) notes that whether grain was carried in sacks or skins, or was poured into a prepared hold, is unknown.

[6] Coldstream (1982: 268–69); cf. Coldstream's proposed Phoenician unguent factory at Ialysos around mid-eighth century: 1969: 4.

[7] Aubet 1993: 155–66, fig. 28.

[8] Demargne (1947: 112–13) emphasizes indirect Egyptian artistic influences on Crete, in addition to the direct contacts reflected in scattered Egyptian artifacts found at Cretan sites: "Ces exportations égyptiennes vers la Grèce demeurèrent en somme assez limitées et sans influence profonde. Et toutefois on réduiraie à l'excès les possibilités d'influence égyptienne sur la naissance de l'art grec si l'on ne se rappelait que de nombreux objets phéniciens ou chypriotes ou rhodiens sont parvenus en Grèce dans le même temps, lui transmetant des éléments égyptiens déformés." He points to the Phoenician role in carrying Egyptian products to Crete (111).

of Cilicia. There may have been an array of non-durable Egyptian items sold in Crete in such triangular trade with the Phoenicians. Although Minoan artifacts have been found in Egypt and Egyptian beans have been found in the storerooms of the Minoan palace at Knossos,[9] there is no clear evidence of a Greek presence in Iron Age Egypt before the founding of Naukratis; but Egyptian items clearly were getting to Crete in the Early Iron Age.[10]

There was commerce in painted pottery with Attica and the Cyclades from the tenth century through the first half of the eighth, when Corinthian pottery largely supplanted Attic throughout the Greek trading realm. The return flows were not in archaeologically durable products, but agricultural yields of the twentieth century A.C. illustrate how Crete may have possessed comparative advantages with different Greek regions in different crops in the early first millennium B.C. (but not necessarily for the same crops or vis-à-vis the same regions as in the twentieth century A.C.), and consequently may have been able to sell both wheat and olive oil on the mainland and in the Cyclades. The scarcity of Attic ceramics from c. 750 through the end of the seventh century may well imply a corresponding reduction of trade with Attica rather than only a change in the composition, because fine pottery is more a guide to end and intermediate points on shipping routes than an indicator of the composition. The presence of transport amphorae would indicate some type of commodity movement more certainly than would the appearance of fine cups and pyxides, but it still would leave wide latitude regarding commodity composition—in the absence of analytically legible residues. The transport amphora fragments from Attica, the northeastern Aegean islands, and East Greece found in the late-seventh-century commercial building at Kommos raise the possibility that Crete was a stop on Greek north-south trade routes as well as on Phoenician east-west trade routes.[11]

Cretan artifacts found overseas account for very small percentages of artifacts at those sites. The overseas regions where the most Cretan artifacts have been found are Italy and Sicily. Cretan contact in one form or another with Italy, from the vicinity of Rome to locations north, could have been relatively early, and may have been a continuation of Mycenaean or even Minoan relationships. Earlier population movements may have been involved. Actual Cretan artifacts in southern Italy are later, although a few still may be precolonization. The only Cretan artifacts at eastern sites are early finds on Cyprus, a vase at Kameiros dating from c. 800, some plates at Ialysos of about the same time, and a votive shield at Miletus in the last quarter of the eighth century. No Cretan artifacts have been reported at sites on the Near Eastern mainland. Cretan pottery appears on several Aegean islands, possibly as the result of commercial contact.

The substantial imbalance between foreign artifacts found at Cretan sites and Cretan artifacts found at overseas sites indicates that a good portion of Crete's overseas offerings was impermanent. The legendary evidence of the Theran trader at Axos in the late eighth or early seventh

---

[9] Evans 1927: 54 n. 2. Vickery (1936: 86) concluded that Minoan Crete traded olives and olive oil to Egypt, which "produces these things, but not in sufficient quantity to supply its needs; on the other hand there are many articles needed in Crete which can best be supplied by or through Egypt." The fact that Syrian supplies were closer to Egypt does not necessarily imply that Cretan products could not compete. There would have been times in the first half of the first millennium when Syrian supplies to Egypt would have been interrupted either by warfare in Syria or the Levant, or later by hostilities between Assyria and Egypt; and Cretan varieties of some articles may have been particularly valued.

[10] Cook 1937: 230, 237, lists Greek sherds in Egypt known in 1937, only three of which date as early as the last quarter of the seventh century: Early Corinthian aryballos fragments at Memphis and Luxor, and a Middle "Rhodian" stemmed dish at Edfu. Clairmont (1955: 100, pl. 20.6) notes a possible Ionian Geometric sherd of c. 800 found at Memphis. He attributes the Greek sherds at Luxor to modern trafficking by Egyptian art dealers rather than to an ancient Greek presence at that city.

[11] Long before the excavations at Kommos and the University Cemetery at Knossos, Demargne (1947: 326–27) suggested the key location of Crete on a number of Mediterranean trade routes: from East Greece to Naukratis, from Rhodes to the Argolid, from Rhodes to Cyrene, from Cyrene to the Epirote coast, and even from Cyrene to Sicily and Italy. Especially for the last route, alternatives are plausible, but the proposal itself is not implausible. Demargne suggests the importance of Kydonia on the Rhodes-Cyrene route; that region has not been intensively explored, and excavations in the area have concentrated on Minoan remains.

century (discussed in Chapter 4) offers a hint of foreign buyers searching inland sites for portable items they could sell at home. A reasonable possibility for a nondurable Cretan export is dyed woolens, for which there are several shreds of circumstantial evidence. First is the considerable evidence of a murex-based dye industry around Palaikastro in the Minoan period. Second is the remains of the crushed murex shells in the seventh-century commercial building at Kommos. Third is the identification of Korobios as a purple-fisher. Even if areas such as Palaikastro and Itanos engaged in such activity but have little to show in the way of foreign artifacts, they could have sold their products to Cretan intermediaries for other Cretan products. As producers and exporters of dyed textiles, the Phoenicians would have been able to offer a well-developed distribution network for Cretan products of this industry, and as international traders, they may have been commercially sophisticated enough to have availed themselves of this opportunity. A trade in designed textiles between Crete and Cyprus could account for the appearance of common vase motifs, and the trade could have been carried by Phoenicians.

The possibility of Dark Age Cretan export of high-phosphorus iron may warrant further investigation. Much remains to be excavated in western Crete, where some of these ores are found, but four of the sites identified as having this quality of iron ore show some remains from Late Minoan, Geometric, and Archaic, as well as later periods. Lasaia Chora, where one of the high-phosphorus iron slags has been found, is just around Cape Lithinos from Kommos, and nine mainland Greek vases recently published from a private collection are said to be from there. Iron ore would be a largely invisible export except for the ability of physical tests to detect characteristic trace elements.

The appearance of the gold and silver dumps in Tomb II at Khaniale Tekke suggests the existence of an international clearing account by the late ninth or early eighth century. This would have simplified multilateral trade and would have permitted regions to incur imbalances in their merchandise trade, at least for short periods. Regions such as Attica clearly had the ability to export precious metals from early times, but the existence of the precious-metal dumps would have extended this capability from merely a variant of commodity trade, largely restricted to proprietors or political suzerains of the

mines, to a more widely distributed capability of individuals whose activities were far removed from mining. Crete does not appear to have produced precious metals in the Dark Age in sufficient quantity to explain the apparently lopsided artifactual pattern by running a half-millennium-long deficit on a metals account. Whether the island produced a sufficient supply of base metals, particularly iron, which may have been used, like precious metals, for clearing external accounts, remains an open question.

It is well known that Greek trade revived in the seventh century and probably actually had begun its resurgence in the eighth. External relations of Greek communities in the eleventh through the ninth centuries have raised questions of the existence of trade as well as its volume or frequency. Crete clearly participated in the revival of trade in the late Dark Age, but its external contacts reached both north and east even in the eleventh century. Eleventh- to ninth-century artifacts are found at a half-dozen sites in Crete, although, considering the social realities of the early Dark Age, there may have been only two or three consolidated entry points on the island. If any of the foreign artifacts in Early Iron Age Crete suggest gift exchange or pirates' loot, they are some of the early metal objects. Nonetheless, ceramic items appear among the eleventh- and tenth-century artifacts, and they are much more likely to have been acquired by trade. Eleventh- and tenth-century items come from Attica, the Cyclades, Argos, Euboea, Cyprus, Egypt, and Phoenicia. The isolated or infrequent character of some of these provenances should not obscure their existence and the practical certainty that much has not survived. By the ninth century, the geographical dispersion of Crete's foreign contacts reached the level it maintained through the remainder of the period. Considering the smaller population of the earlier Dark Age and the greater likelihood that materials from that period would not survive, the level of external activity indicated by the earlier foreign artifacts is not insignificant relative to the later artifacts.

Did trade cause increased prosperity in Crete over this period, or did the reverse causation dominate? I have not attempted to develop archaeological indicators of income, which in itself would be a major task, particularly distinguishing broad changes in income from highly visible indicators of income distribution. However, analysis of the model economy in

Appendix B indicates three salient possibilities regarding the relationship between trade and income growth. First, with a small share of total production entering trade in a largely agricultural economy with limited opportunities for technological change in manufacturing, improved trading opportunities have very little scope for raising the level of income. Second, if the importation of implicit information accompanies the importation of manufactured goods, and if that information can be applied to local manufacturing, the scope for trade raising local income may be nearly an order of magnitude greater than in the first case—but still not strikingly large. Third, small improvements in shipping (ranging from changes in ship construction to the packaging and stowing of cargo to onshore storage and distribution systems) that lower ocean transport costs, occurring continuously for 200 years, could gradually raise the level of aggregate income in an economy of the first description by a substantial amount—20 to 25 percent would not be outside the range of possibility, with only a half-percent per year rate of improvement in shipping productivity. Such growth could produce a larger share of trade in the economy, which in turn could widen the opportunities for trade to affect the aggregate economy—for better or worse, depending on the external factors affecting trade.

The arrival of immigrant craftsmen skilled in the production of luxury manufactured products such as jewelry and related bronze products may have yielded highly visible artistic motifs—if one believes the signs—but the transformation of these skills into technological advances that would have improved productivity in a largely agricultural economy remains unaddressed. It is not clear that immigrant bronze-workers brought bronze-working skills that extended beyond applications to luxury products. The arrival of architectural skills would have had limited scope for raising the aggregate level of productivity in ninth- or eighth-century Crete.

Trade would have required considerable time to produce substantial income growth in Dark Age Crete—and the rest of Dark Age Greece, for that matter. The productive importance of immigrant craftsmen probably was smaller than that of trade. In this light, it is reasonable to look to local causes as well as external ones for the revival of prosperity by the eighth century. With an undoubtedly large proportion of the economy devoted to agriculture, the causes of increased prosperity in the later Dark Age must have affected productivity in agriculture, regardless of what their other manifestations may have been.

Appendix A

Agricultural Risk and Comparative Advantage

Agriculture was the dominant feature of Dark Age Greek economies, so agriculture will be a large factor in any discussion of trade or exchange at that time. Risk has always been an important issue in agriculture, and agricultural risk and trade have been linked in the literature on Dark Age Greece. Since I see comparative advantage as a more important basis for interregional trade during this period, it may be useful to discuss the alternative motivation, risk, in greater detail than is feasible in the main text. I follow this discussion of risk with a discussion of how the concept of comparative advantage operates.

Agricultural Risk: Measurement, Concepts, and Trade

How risky was Greek agriculture anyway? It might be possible to extract evidence on annual rainfall variance from tree rings or find some longer-period evidence from soils, but possibly the best insight currently available at reasonable cost is contemporary variability records, even if agricultural modernization may have found some ways to reduce variability a bit. Gallant presents coefficients of variation (the ratio of the standard deviation to the mean) of yields per hectare for six crops in twenty-six Greek regions; the range is from around 0.15 (the standard devi-

ation of the yield is 15 percent of the mean yield) to around 0.6 (the coefficient for broad beans in one region is 0.7).[1] Forbes reports similar statistics for a village in Methana, a district on the south coast of the Saronic Gulf, estimated from plot-specific wheat yields between 1962 and 1974, for odd- and even-year rotations.[2] The ranges of coefficients of variation are 0.13 to 0.50 for the odd-year crops and 0.13 to 0.41 for the even-year crops, with averages of 0.29 and 0.27. Garnsey and Morris present coefficients of variation of monthly rainfall as evidence of risk in agriculture; the spring and fall statistics range from 0.6 to 0.9, which they interpret as demonstrating the riskiness facing contemporary Greek agriculture, and hence ancient Greek agriculture. The substantial difference between rainfall variability and crop-yield variability indicates the inadequacy of the former to represent the latter; farmers know the weather variability (if not the precise timing of the variations) and structure their operations accordingly. Genuine surprises to farmers from the weather generally come from higher statistical moments than the variance (the variance is the second moment; the average, or mean, is the first moment)—that is, *deviations* from current expected values.[3]

How do these coefficients of variation of yields compare with those in contemporary agriculture elsewhere, and how well do these statis-

---

[1] Gallant 1991: 102, table 4.10. The time period over which the statistics were estimated is not clear; Gallant multiplies his coefficients of variation by 100.

[2] Forbes 1989: 92–93, tables 7.1 and 7.2.

[3] Garnsey and Morris 1989: 98; McGuire 1980: 347–49.

tics represent agricultural risk? Crop- and district-specific coefficients of variation of yields, averaged across districts, for eight crops across India, from 1954 through 1971, range from 0.19 to 0.39, with an unweighted average of 0.29; the variability across districts exceeds that within districts.[4] The coefficient of variation of total income from each of these crops (price times quantity) ranges from 0.55 to 0.76—a higher average variability than with the variability of yield alone, but about the same spread. The coefficient of variation of the total income from all crops together ranges from 0.50 to 0.59: the countermovement of yields and prices of crops within districts offsets the risk associated with any crop alone. An alternative measure of the risk of any single crop is called its covariance risk; this amounts to the additional contribution to the risk of all crop income contributed by any one crop. Some crops may be grown because of their general countercyclical behavior relative to other crops—that is, they help diversify income, moving down on average when other crops move up in success but improving when the others tend to deteriorate. The Indian evidence shows that crops with relatively high coefficients of variation of yields tend to reduce the overall variance of crop income, while the crops with lower coefficients of variation of yields actually add risk to the overall portfolio of crops.

Finally, the variability of income from agriculture represents only a portion of the variability in total income: some family members may produce income outside agriculture, and the returns to those activities may be uncorrelated or correlated negatively with the returns in agriculture. The proportion of such nonagricultural income in the family (or whatever the decision unit was in Dark Age Greece) production in Dark Age Greece is an important question for riskiness in general and for the ability of trade to mitigate risk. Such activities would have both stabilized income and contributed materials that could have been exchanged in times of poor agricultural production. It should be noted also that poor yields in any one crop need not imply poor yields in all crops, and Forbes's plot-specific yield variabilities indicate that even a single

household could experience quite different variability with a single crop, although Forbes's data do not indicate the correlation of yields across plots, which is an important consideration for the family's average crop income.

The variability of the yields of individual crops is only the first building block in the story of agricultural risk, and it cannot be relied upon to give either a reliable upper bound or a lower bound on agricultural risk in particular or the riskiness of total income. Risk facing individual households exceeds the risk facing all households in a region or village together, and the risk facing a village or region exceeds that facing groups of villages or regions that could, if conditions permitted, trade with one another. Local exchange around a village—interhousehold exchange—may be able to substitute reputation for capital to underpin borrowing,[5] but as more distant exchanges are contemplated, reputations are (or would have been in the first millennium B.C.; it is probably still the case) less clearly established, and sanctions for default (or nonreciprocity) are more difficult to enforce. Small-unit political leaders (household heads, village "bosses," "chiefs" or chief-equivalents, aristocrats of various sorts) may have been able to guarantee reputations over particular distances in the events of crop deficits, but I find that capital-market surrogate difficult to accept as the basis of trade across several hundred miles of sea, although I accept that other scholars may find its acceptance less difficult. It would be useful for scholars disagreeing on this topic to find a model *structure* on which they can agree; opinions that sometimes appear as vast philosophical differences, unbridgeable by evidence of any sort, might be converted to commonly accepted components about which differences of interpretation could be discussed with profit to all.

COMPARATIVE ADVANTAGES IN SELECTED AGRICULTURAL PRODUCTS

People in particular regions need not possess absolute advantages in some line of production to be able to engage profitably in trade with peo-

---

[4] Jones and Kaul 1983: 379–80, tables 1 and 2.

[5] See Townsend's finding from contemporary Indian villages (1994: 62, 570, 584) that individual household consumption varies much less over time than does individual household production, but that individual household consumption is highly correlated with aggregate *village* production.

ple in other regions. Each region can, rather, offer the product or products in which it has a comparative advantage relative to potential trading partners. The first table below presents yields per hectare in wheat, barley, broad beans, and lentils for Crete, Attica, Corinth, and Lesbos, over the period 1911–50. The average yields over the extended time period are likely to be more reliable guides than the yield of any single year, although I do not have the information required to calculate statistical confidence intervals on these averages. Average yields for all of Crete may not be representative of any particular region of the island, but the island-wide averages illustrate comparative advantages: the principle of comparative advantage does not imply that *all* locations in a region enjoy such conditions, but only that some place in the region does. In the first table, Crete shows the highest yields for every crop except broad beans, where Attica has a barely perceptible edge, which surely would not be statistically significant (Table A.1).

TABLE A.1. Yields (kg) per Hectare in Selected Greek Regions, 1911–50*

	Wheat	Barley	Broad Beans	Lentils
Crete	748.1	902.6	624.7	578.8
Attica	629.1	793.7	630.9	539.9
Corinth	611.0	708.8	537.2	484.6
Lesbos	662.6	689.2	539.6	465.1

*Source: Gallant 1991: 77, table 4.7.

Table A.2 uses the yield data in Table A.1 to reveal comparative advantages of Crete in wheat relative to the other three crops. The numbers of Table A.2 are created as follows. The wheat-barley yield ratio is created for Crete (it is 0.829, which is not shown in either table), Attica (0.793, also not shown), and similarly for Corinth and Lesbos. The comparative advantage of Crete relative to Attica in growing wheat and barley is 0.829/0.793 = 1.045, which is the number in the first row and first column of Table A.2. Crete can grow 4.5 percent more wheat for each unit of barley it grows than can Attica, despite the fact that the Cretan barley yield is 20 percent higher than the Cretan wheat yield (the Attic barley yield is 26 percent higher than the Attic wheat yield). Each unit of wheat that Cretans offer to Athenians for barley will get them 4.5 percent more units of barley than they could get by growing barley; and similarly for the Athenians: each unit of barley they trade to Cretans for wheat will get them 4.5 percent more units of wheat than they could grow themselves.

The comparative advantage figures of Table A.3, for barley versus other crops, and of Table A.4, for broad beans versus lentils, are constructed in the same manner. The barley:wheat comparative advantages in the first column of Table A.3 are simply the inverses of the wheat:barley comparative advantages in the first column of Table A.2.

According to the figures of Tables A.2 through A.4, Crete should trade barley for wheat, and lentils for broad beans, with Lesbos.

TABLE A.2. Comparative Advantages, Crete versus Other Regions, Wheat versus Other Crops, 1911–50

	Wheat:Barley	Wheat:Broad Beans	Wheat:Lentils
Crete:Attica	1.045	0.976	1.110
Crete:Corinth	0.962	1.054	1.025
Crete:Lesbos	0.863	1.202	0.907

TABLE A.3. Comparative Advantages, Crete versus Other Regions, Barley versus Other Crops, 1911–50

	Barley:Wheat	Barley:Broad Beans	Barley:Lentils
Crete:Attica	0.957	1.149	1.060
Crete:Corinth	1.040	1.095	1.067
Crete:Lesbos	1.159	1.131	1.053

Cretan comparative advantages vis-à-vis Attica are less pronounced than in the two Cretan-Lesbian cases, but Crete could trade wheat and barley to Attica for lentils and broad beans. The Cretan-Corinthian comparative advantages are much less pronounced for these crops, but any number of triangular trades could indirectly link Crete and Corinth in the products described here. The agricultural products presented here exclude wine, olive oil, and figs, as well as manufactured products, so the comparisons made here are far from exhaustive.

TABLE A.4. Comparative Advantages, Crete versus Other Regions,
Broad Beans versus Lentils, 1911–50

	Broad Beans:Lentils	Lentils:Broad Beans
Crete:Attica	0.923	1.083
Crete:Corinth	0.973	1.028
Crete:Lesbos	0.757	1.321

Appendix B

SENSITIVITY OF A DARK AGE GREEK ECONOMY TO RESOURCE REALLOCATIONS ASSOCIATED WITH TRADE

ISSUES AND APPROACH

Quantities of artifactual material suggest volumes of trade, subject to qualifications too numerous to mention here. Provenance and chronological identification tell where something came from and when it was made, if not necessarily when it was transported—again, both subject to well-known qualifications. The answers to none of these questions address the question, "But was it important?" Importance is a social phenomenon, defined by us moderns in an attempt to capture the circumstances of the ancients. Importance can have many dimensions: religious, intellectual, stomach-based satisfaction, etc. In any case, social models are required to evaluate the matter, and in this appendix I develop a series of models to help illuminate the importance of external trade in an economy with the major structural characteristics a Dark Age Greek region must have possessed.

Focus on the indicators of external trade cannot yield information on the consequences of trade that, themselves, have other indicators. This is intuitively obvious: if we suspect that one

effect of trade is to raise incomes, counting the number (or proportion or some other indicator) of foreign artifacts does not tell us anything about the progress of local prosperity. Only if we assume that more trade implies greater prosperity, and that more artifacts in our possession do in fact indicate larger trade volumes, can we make that latter inference. In this sense, the artifactual evidence of foreign contacts on the one hand, and the models of the importance of the trade that brought those objects and others that have not survived on the other, have a certain disjointedness. However, the models do yield hypotheses about the consequences and corresponding significance of such external contacts—and those hypotheses are interrelated and are derived from a model of behavior rather than pulled from a hat, with no clear idea what kind of behavior would have produced them. Calculating t- or χ^2-tests on counts of pot sherds or obsidian chips can yield information about differences in sample characteristics, but without behavioral models that produce hypotheses about those characteristics, behavioral inferences on the basis of the statistical tests are not supported by the tests.[1]

---

[1] For readers unfamiliar with statistical procedures, the t-test is a test of whether the means (averages) of two samples are different—e.g., whether one group of observations is, on average, heavier or larger, etc., than another group of observations. The χ^2-test is an index of dispersion and can be used to test whether the distribution of observations within a sample differs between samples; by "the distribution of observations within a sample" is meant, roughly, the relative number of observations taking each value in the array of, say, weights or sizes, from smallest to largest. The χ^2-test can be used to assess the probability that two samples come from the same population—e.g., do two samples of pot sherds come from the same, larger set of sherds or from different ones? In each case, the inference that can be made from the size of the test statistic (the particular value of the statistic t or χ^2) is restricted to the exact hypothesis being tested. The social interpretation of the rejection or accep-

Many of the hypotheses derived from the present series of models would be difficult, if not impossible, to test with contemporary, multivariate statistical methods (or even univariate ones).[2] Living in a world where such high-tech and demanding testing methods have become a standard against which to judge scholarly inference can foster a myopic vision of the alternatives, especially in fields where repeated-observation samples appear not to exist. With my own background, I approach models of the type I develop here with a particular confidence in the insights that analysis of them yields. This background includes both empirical referents that condition the models, with implicit or explicit analogues, and an awareness of corresponding analytical exercises that condition the degree of confidence I have in particular results. Other scholars, either without such a background or with backgrounds in alternative modeling traditions, may feel less confidence in the results of these models. Clearly, scholars of whatever modeling background have sufficient empirical referents to compare with model structures and results. The most fruitful path along which to proceed is not to demand levels of empirical testing of the other's models that, by precluding testing, would preclude consideration a priori, but rather to compare model components and to search for agreement on what kinds of information would indicate consistency or inconsistency with any of the implications of the alternative models. What are the archaeological indicators of changes in material prosperity, the distribution of income, production methods and production costs, shipping costs, foreign tastes and incomes, etc.? To what extent, and in what ways, in the case of Dark Age Greece, can the early literary evidence be used to inform about the preceding half-millennium (an issue about which much has been thought and written)?

Greek Dark Age communities were predominantly agricultural. Another way of stating this is that each farm family (or whatever the decision unit may have been) supported only a tiny fraction of nonfarm decision units. To put some hypothetical numbers in the discussion, suppose that 95 percent of the working population (which may have been just about the entire population above age four) worked full-time in agriculture. The other 5 percent may have been involved in crafts or in production of some luxury products that were traded, or may have provided some kind of service associated with towns. None of this 5 percent may have been engaged in nonagricultural pursuits full-time, but without assuming that this 5 percent was just more efficient at agriculture than the other 95 percent and therefore had extra time to perform other productive activities, we are left with the presumption that they produced less food than they consumed, leaving their food production spread among their fellows.

I want to know how much difference a bit

---

footnote 1 continued

tance of (failure to reject) a hypothesis is derived from a model that yields that hypothesis as one of its implications. A useful, introductory reference to hypothesis testing and the t- and χ^2-tests is Snedecor and Cochran 1967: esp. chs. 1, 4, and 9.

[2] *Univariate* and *multivariate* refer to statistical methods involving one variable and more than one variable. Statistical examinations of the relationship between two variables is, technically speaking, a multivariate analysis, but in many cases it is a particularly simple analysis: if one variable is thought to induce changes in another, some statistical methods are available to estimate such a relationship, but frequently such relationships between two variables are contingent on the behavior of some other variables; if a statistical analysis does not control for that behavior, the simple relationship estimated to occur between the pair of variables of principal interest will be contaminated by any movement in the omitted variables. While all statistical analysis of relationships between different variables is technically multivariate, an important difference exists between what are frequently called multiple and simple relationships in causal models; simple analyses estimate relationships between a pair of variables without controlling for the influences of other variables, while multiple analyses control for the influences of those other variables. Regression analysis is one such statistical technique; simple regression estimates the relationship between a dependent variable and a single independent, or causal, variable; multiple regression estimates the relationships between a dependent variable and two or more independent variables. Regression analysis has been the workhorse technique of statistical analysis in economics (commonly called econometrics) and other social and physical sciences, and it has been developed to test a wide variety of behavioral models. Not all multivariate statistical techniques fit the description of causal models, e.g., factor analysis, principal components analysis, and various clustering and scaling techniques.

more or less trade would have made in an economy like the one just outlined. Accordingly, the question I pursue here is, "What would happen to the cost of producing food in such a community if, for some reason, some people had their activities shifted from agriculture to nonagricultural production?" Why would such a shift happen? Possibly because some person with the authority or power to decide simply wanted something produced that could be traded for luxury imports. Possibly individuals themselves noticed small opportunities and decided to avail themselves of them in a decentralized manner. The question, "What would happen?" can be expressed more suggestively. Agricultural technology was not particularly dynamic at the time (stagnant may be a reasonable adjective), and it also may not have been particularly flexible, in the sense that a reduction in some resources may not have been able to be compensated easily by an increase in other resources. A reduction in the ratio of hands working at agriculture to mouths feeding may not have been accommodated easily. If the number of people to be fed by each agricultural family rose because of a shift out of agriculture that was not precipitated by an increase in the productivity of agriculture, all the people, on average, would have eaten less than they did before. Such a reduction in average food production per capita assumes that there were no slack, or unemployed, resources before the shift in resources. While that assumption may not characterize some of the islands of the Southwest Pacific in the late nineteenth and early twentieth centuries A.C., it appears to characterize a good cross-section of European traditional agriculture. Seasonal slack periods are compensated by seasonal peaks in activity, such as planting and harvest times, which create bottlenecks that constrain overall production. How would the reduced food per person have been allocated across producing and nonproducing individuals?

The answer I explore runs along the lines of a rise in the cost of producing food relative to the cost of producing whatever else the economy produces and is exchanged for food. Additionally, in an economy with the characteristics of those likely to have been found in Dark Age Greece—large share of agriculture and relatively stagnant and not particularly flexible agricultural technology—the change in relative costs would be large relative to the shift in productive resources that caused the cost change. Stated more concretely, a small shift of labor from agriculture to nonagricultural production would cause a rise in the cost of food relative to the cost of nonagricultural goods several times larger in proportion to the causal change. I will show four different ways of arriving at this conclusion.

I begin with a very simple analysis in which the supply of food is reduced a bit, for some unspecified reason. Although the absence of a clear reason for the decrease is not satisfying, this case illustrates how the interaction of technological and behavioral parameters affects agricultural production costs. As a next step, I construct a model economy that produces two types of good, agricultural and "manufactured" (using the term "manufactured" loosely; possibly only craft goods), using labor, land, and some natural resources; I specify the allocation of labor between the two activities rather than let labor be allocated endogenously. The exogeneity of labor allocations is unsatisfactory, since labor, given its own inclinations, might allocate itself differently, but this model allows us to approach more closely the question of production-cost responses to labor reallocations such as might be caused by a society reorienting some labor to traded products. In the next step, I allow the allocation of labor to be determined by the technological and behavioral parameters of the model, with changes in labor allocations and agricultural production costs deriving from population growth, increases in arable land, technological changes in agriculture and nonagriculture (manufacturing or crafts), and changes in personal preferences or tastes. This step allows clear, if simple, stories to be explored, with clear lines of influence from cause to effect. The final step takes the previous model of a closed economy or region (i.e., one that does not trade with societies outside) and converts it to a model of a country that does trade. With this model, I explore the impacts of domestic and external (foreign) events or disturbances on production costs, resource allocations, overall income, the distribution of income (consumption) among several groups of resource owners, and an index of individuals' perceived well-being—items that can be related to issues of "importance" of trade. I follow this trade model with an exploration of an alternative production technology in what is otherwise the same model. The final modeling exploration changes the model structure a bit to allow the importation of technological knowledge as well as products. For each model, I supply some parameter values that I believe are representative of an economy such as that of Dark Age Greece. I explain my choices here in the appendix text, although sometimes in footnotes, and the reader will have already encountered some in the section of the main text, "The Importance of Early Iron Age Trade," where I summarized some of the principal findings of this appendix, with the hope that both some repetition and spreading out of the lessons might help.[3]

Nevertheless, I do not expect that readers who are disinclined to approve of the use of my methods on a Dark Age Greek subject will be persuaded by my analysis, although other readers might find the methods more acceptable and some of the results of use. I *am* concerned to expose the method of my reasoning to scrutiny for any who may be interested in considering the implications of the results. The models I use are consistent with those used by Earle in his comparative analysis of food-procurement strategies in societies practicing hunting, gathering, and sedentary agriculture.[4] With the exception of a few differentiations, the mathematics I use below is all within the scope of a tenth-grade algebra course. I explain the intuition of both the economics and the mathematics, and the reader who prefers to do so can read around the equations, relying on the verbal explanations, and still pick up the most important elements of the analysis.

A SIMPLE SUPPLY MODEL

In the very simplest case, I consider only supply and demand curves for food, impose a change in the schedule of supply, and examine the ensuing change in the cost of food that people accept as a consequence.[5] I represent the supply of food by $Q^S = aP^\Phi$, where Q^S is the quantity of food supplied, a is a constant term, P is the cost of producing food relative to the cost of producing other items (or stated alternatively, the

---

[3] Small, analytical models that aggregate the production of complex economies into one or two, sometimes three, sectors have played an important role in contemporary economic analysis, both in purely theoretical investigations and in economic history. Two- and three-sector models have been used fruitfully in studying issues in the economic history of the United States and Japan: Williamson 1974; Kelley and Williamson 1974. Models with this degree of abstraction and generality are useful for studying certain classes of question. Other classes of question are subsumed in the aggregation, and other methods of analysis must be used to address them.

[4] Earle 1980: 1–29. Cf. Earle 1985: 107, for a synthetic view of formalist and substantivist approaches to economic problems as directed at individual optimization and systemic goals, respectively. This individual-group distinction is similar to the short-term (individual self-interest) versus long-term (social and cultural maintenance) transactional-sphere distinction developed by Bloch and Parry (1989: 25–27). In a number of social and natural sciences, when variables under analysis change at speeds three orders of magnitude apart, the more slowly moving variables may be considered exogenous for most purposes. To illuminate the relationship between these two major methodological groupings, Adams's citation of the old social-science joke is apt: "Economics is all about why people make choices, while sociology [anthropology] is all about why they don't have any choices to make." Adams 1990: 4. Expressed more prosaically, economic analysis addresses behavior within a given set of social constraints. In recent years, economics has begun to study the individual, behavioral foundations of societal institutions, but that work is still young. Anthropological analyses of economic behavior have relatively more intellectual tools for studying relations between a norm-setting social structure and individuals within it and relatively less fully developed constructs about purely individual behavior. I would not be surprised if my characterizations prompted some debate, but I think that, as a broad-brush depiction, they are satisfactorily robust.

[5] Some readers may wonder how I can justify using such models in a situation in which markets may have been weak or absent. Must I not model the actions of a chief who directs the economic operations of his local area? Markets are only one mechanism for allocating resources, and a market, while it can help, is not necessary to conduct the resources under one's control to their best uses. If a chief with such social responsibilities continually failed to allocate resources to their best uses, according to the paradigms of the society, he would be replaced with one who would. Each of the following models could be considered as having such a chief directing the allocations, with the objective of maximizing the chances of survival through consumption of two major types of good. The models are sufficiently general to correspond to a range of resource-allocation mechanisms, including, but not restricted to, markets.

relative price of food and nonfood or the price of food expressed in terms of nonfood—e.g., so many bags of wheat per hoe), and $\Phi > 0$ is the price elasticity of supply of food.[6] The demand for food is $Q^d = bP^\varepsilon Y^\eta$, where Q^d is the quantity of food the community consumes, b is a constant term, P is the relative price of food again, $\varepsilon < 0$ is the price elasticity of food, $Y = PQ + M$ (where M is nonagricultural production) is income, and $\eta > 0$ is the income elasticity of demand for food. For an equilibrium in production and consumption, $Q^s = Q^d$: the amount of food consumed (including any that people want to store) and the amount of food produced will be the same. We have two equations in two unknowns, food (Q) and the relative price of food (P). A change in a in the first equation represents a change in the

conditions of supply: an increase in **a** represents the ability of the community to produce more food at any given cost, because of either a change in technology or an increase in productive resources. A reduction in **a** would represent a reduction in resources available to agriculture, say, because labor is spirited away to some other production. In the following analysis, I ignore the additional production of **M** that would be contributed by resources diverted from agriculture, because it will be small. In subsequent analysis, I introduce that complication. Table B.1 collects and defines the symbols used in this model.

I represent percent changes in the variables with a caret: for example, $\hat{Q}$ is a percent change in Q, and $\hat{Q}/\hat{a}$ is the percent change in food pro-

---

[6] I assume a completely nonmonetized economy. Prices are simply relative prices—one good expressed in terms of another. Q is an abstract, aggregate measure of agricultural products—one might prefer to think of an index of weighted quantities; similarly with manufactures M, introduced just below.

Some readers may be concerned that prices abstract from the values people hold. This is incorrect, as I show. An individual's values can be specified in a preference, or utility, function, that relates his or her self-evaluated level of well-being to the levels of consumption of various items. It has the algebraic form $u = u(x_1, \ldots x_n)$, where the u on the left-hand side of the equal sign is the level of the well-being attained, the u on the right-hand side represents the specific form of the preference function (more specifics on that below), and the x_i are the quantities of items consumed. A specific form of such a function would be $u = \alpha x_1^{\delta_1} x_2^{\delta_2} \ldots x_n^{\delta_n}$, where α is a constant term, and the δ_i exponents are the weights that relate the consumption of item i to the value of well-being u. Those items naturally include goods such as food, clothing, shelter, trinkets, etc., but also can be specified to include "consumption" of less tangible items such as interactions with family, religious activities, etc. In fact, one's religious values could affect the values of the δ_i for particular items. (See page 199 for further discussion and use of a utility function.) Now, prices of these items are determined by equalization of aggregate demand and supply functions for each item. An individual's demand function looks like $Q_i^d = D(p_i, p_j, u)$, where Q_i^d is the quantity of item i consumed, D represents the specific form of the demand function, p_i is the price of a unit of item i, p_j is a vector of the prices of all other goods that may be substitutes for or complements to item i, and u is the level of utility that the individual can achieve with his or her income. (The relation between actual income and utility—well-being—is a relatively straightforward matter, in which utility is essentially "real income.") The demand function says that the quantity demanded of a particular item is related to its own price (negatively), the prices of other items (positively or negatively), and the available income the person has to devote to purchases, or, alternatively, the level of well-being the individual can attain with his or her resources. More specifically, at each level of price p_i, the individual will want to consume a specific quantity of that item, given his or her real income and the configuration of the prices of other items. The availability of the good can be defined by a supply function, $Q_i^s = S(p_i, p_k, X)$, where Q_i^s is the quantity of item i supplied at a particular price p_i, p_k is a vector of prices associated with other items used in production of the item in question ("inputs"), and X represents other relevant conditions affecting production. Convenient functional forms for these two relationships are $Q_i^d = ap_i^{\varepsilon_{ii}} p_j^{\varepsilon_{ij}} u^\eta$ for demand and $Q_i^s + bp_i^{\Phi_i} p_b^\theta X$ for supply. (The ε_{ii} and ε_{ij} are own- and cross-price elasticities of demand for item i, ε is the income—or "well-being"—elasticity of demand for that item, a and b are constant terms, Φ is the supply elasticity of item i, and θ characterizes the relationship between input prices and supply. The concept of an elasticity is explained in note 7 below. Aggregating the demand functions across all the individuals facing the given supply conditions (if they all have the same preference function, this is very easy; if their preference functions differ, the aggregation will be more complicated, but the manner in which the u term, representing a weighted set of individual preferences in that case, enters the solution for the price of item i will be unaffected), setting $Q_i^d = Q_i^s$ and solving for the price of a unit of item i, p_i, we get $p_x = (a^{-1}bp_b^\theta p_j^{-\varepsilon_{ij}} X u^{-\eta})^{1/(\varepsilon_{ii}-\Phi_i)}$. The term u, which contains the information on people's values, appears in the expression for the price of item i: people's most mundane and most cherished values affect the price they are willing to pay for any item i.

TABLE B.1. Symbols Used in the Supply Model

Symbol	Definition/Interpretation
Q^s, Q^d, Q	Quantity of food (agricultural good) supplied (s), demanded (d), and in equilibrium
M	Quantity of manufactured good (goods) produced
P	Production cost (price) of food in terms of the manufactured good (per unit of the manufactured good)
Y	Total regional income in terms of the manufactured good
Φ	Price elasticity of supply of food (% change in quantity supplied per 1% change in relative price of food)
ε	Price elasticity of demand for food (% change in quantity demanded per 1% change in relative price/cost of food)
η	Income elasticity of demand for food (% change in quantity demanded per 1% change in income)
θ_A	Share of agricultural production in total income
a	Constant term in food supply function (can represent technology or other external supply conditions)
b	Constant term in food demand function (represents tastes)

duced and consumed following a 1 percent change in the constant term of the supply function. Substituting the expression for **Y** into the food demand equation and equating **Q^s** and **Q^d**, I express the supply and demand equations in percent change form and solve for the percent change in the relative price of food that would follow a 1 percent reduction in the constant term of the supply equation, which could be caused by a shift of labor out of agriculture (or by poor weather for a season). The expression for that ratio of changes is $\hat{P}/\hat{a} = -(1 - \theta_A\eta)/[\Phi - \varepsilon - \theta_A\eta(1 + \Phi)] < 0$, where θ_A is the share of agricultural output in total income. The negative sign is intuitive: a reduction in the supply of food will raise the price of food relative to the price of nonfood. Assigning some plausible numbers to the parameters will yield an idea of the numerical magnitude of this relationship. A relatively inelastic supply of food characterizes traditional agriculture, and $\Phi = 0.2$ is a plausible value for the supply elasticity. The demand for food generally is both price- and income-inelastic; I use $\varepsilon = -0.2$ and $\eta = 0.1$ for price and income elasticities of demand.[7] To represent a community that is very predominantly agricultural, I let $\theta = 0.95$. Inserting these values into the expression the change in relative cost of food production, we get **$\hat{P}/\hat{a} = -3.16$**, which is a serious degree of sensitivity.[8]

---

[7] The price elasticity of demand is the percent change in the quantity of a good demanded (consumed) caused by a 1% increase in the price (cost) of that good; it is negative because, for most goods, when the cost rises, consumers take less. The income elasticity is the corresponding change in quantity demanded caused by a 1% increase in income; it is positive for so-called normal goods (as contrasted with "inferior" goods) because a larger quantity of income must be allocated across all expenditures (including savings), and for most goods ("normal" ones) some increase in purchases will occur. Agricultural goods are noted for low price and income elasticities of demand: since food items are commonly thought of as "necessities," we will not cut back a whole lot on them when their prices rise relative to those of other goods. Similarly, with the exceptions of a few luxury food items, we will not buy a whole lot more of them when our income rises, because we can only eat so much. For estimates of income and price elasticities of demand from contemporary developing countries, see Lluch, Powell, and Williams 1977: 243–47, 251–53.

[8] I amplify what I mean by "a serious degree of sensitivity." In an expression of the form $\hat{top}/\hat{bottom}$, the bottom variable is the causal variable, and the caret over it indicates "percent change in"; the top variable is the endogenous variable, which responds to exogenous changes in the bottom variable. The dimensions of this expression—the units in which it is measured—are the percent change in the top variable divided by a percent change in the bottom variable. This is a pure number, i.e., it is not measured in weight or length or value units, and consequently the measurement is unaffected by the units in which the top and bottom variables are measured. The interpretation of one of these expressions is the percent change in the endogenous (top) variable

A SIMPLE PRODUCTION MODEL WITH EXOGENOUS LABOR ALLOCATIONS

Next, I develop a slightly more detailed examination of this question. Rather than consider a change in the supply of food directly, I investigate a change in the allocation of labor between food production and other, nonfood production. As in the previous case, rather than attempting to build a story about why labor moves, I just assume it does and examine the consequences. An even more detailed model in which labor moved according to one story or another could provide some variation on the results I will present below, but the directions of effect should remain the same. Instead of working with a supply function, I employ production functions for agriculture and nonagriculture. The amount of agricultural output produced is represented by $Q^S = aN_A^\alpha L^\beta$, where N_A is labor and L is land; $\alpha > 0$ and $\beta > 0$ are output elasticities, and $\alpha + \beta = 1$, representing constant returns to scale in production; a is a constant term representing the level of production technology.[9] Consumption in the economy can be represented by the demand for agricultural output: $Q^d = bP^\varepsilon Y^\eta$, as in the previous analysis, in which $\varepsilon < 0$ is the price elasticity and $\eta > 0$ is the income elasticity of demand for the agricultural output; P is again the price of agricultural output in terms of nonagricultural output. Income is equivalent to

the value of agricultural output and nonagricultural output: $Y = PQ + M$. The economy produces the nonagricultural output according to $M^S = cN_M^\gamma S^\delta$, where N_M is labor used in nonagricultural production and S is "stuff," such as metal, clay, or other natural resources or processed material used in making nonagricultural (or manufactured) products. In equilibrium, $Q^S = Q^d = Q$, and $M^S = M^d = M$. The economy has a fixed amount of labor, $N = N_A + N_M$, which is fully employed across the two activities.[10] Table B.2 summarizes the symbols used in the present model.

Changes in N_M can be expressed in terms of changes in N and N_A. With substitutions, this model can be reduced to one equation in one unknown, P. In rate-of-change form, the change in the relative price of agricultural goods induced by a shift of 1 percent of the agricultural labor time to nonagricultural activity can be expressed as $\hat{P}/\hat{N}_A = [\alpha(1 - \eta\theta_A) + \eta\gamma n_A(1 - \theta_A) / (1 - n_A)] / (\varepsilon + \eta\theta_A)$. A new parameter in this system is n_A, which is the share of the economy's labor allocated to agricultural production. With the same set of parameter values used in the previous model, we get an intuitive, negative sign, comparable to $\hat{P}/\hat{a}$ in the previous model, but numbers give a better sense of the magnitude of the change. The output elasticities in the production functions correspond to income shares from the production process, which gives a more intu-

---

footnote 8 continued

induced by a 1% change in the exogenous (bottom) variable. Sometimes an expression of this sort will have a numerical value much smaller than one in absolute value (the changes can be positive or negative, depending on whether a change in the exogenous—bottom—variable causes the top—endogenous—variable to increase or decrease in value). In such a case, the endogenous variable simply does not respond very much to a change in the exogenous variable, and it is common to say that this endogenous variable is not very sensitive to changes in that particular exogenous variable. When the value of one of these expressions is greater than 1 in absolute value, the endogenous variable responds proportionally more than the initial disturbance that caused the change. Such a circumstance is characterized as relatively sensitive responsiveness of the endogenous variable to that exogenous variable. Values substantially greater than 1, say, 3 or 4 or even 8, I would characterize as serious degrees of sensitivity.

[9] Labor is measured in labor-hours, abstracting from interpersonal differences in skill, strength, desire, etc. Land would be measured in some constant-quality areal unit. The output elasticities, α and β, are the percent changes in output deriving from a 1% increase in the corresponding input quantity.

[10] Some readers may wish to think of leisure as an alternative activity, which is valued. I use the simplification of a fixed quantity of labor that is employed in constant effort and diligence. Extension to leisure would cause complications without compensating with additional insights into aggregate resource allocation and production. This is not to imply that the economic determinants and implications of leisure are without interest in some circumstances—only that they would not add materially to the present investigation.

Table B.2. Symbols Used in the Production Model with Exogenous Labor Allocation

Symbol	Definition/Interpretation
Q^s, Q^d, Q, M, Y, P, ε, η, θ_A, a, b	Same as in supply model (Table B.1)
M^s, M^d	Quantity of manufactured good supplied (d), demanded (d)
N_A, N_M, N	Labor used in agriculture (A), manufacturing (M), total labor
L	Land used in agriculture
S	Quantity of natural resource used in manufacturing
α	Output elasticity of labor in agricultural production (% change in output per 1% change in labor used)
β	Output elasticity of land used in agricultural production
γ	Output elasticity of labor used in manufacturing
δ	Output elasticity of natural resource used in manufacturing
c	Constant term in manufacturing production function (represents technology)

itive interpretation than the concept of output elasticity.[11] A wide range of empirical research suggests that labor shares around 0.8 and land shares around 0.2 would be representative of traditional agriculture (capital equipment is not particularly important quantitatively). Thus, $\alpha = 0.8$, and $\beta = 0.2$. In the nonagricultural activity, $\gamma = \delta = 0.5$ would represent production in which the raw material contributes a relatively large share of the output. To represent an economy with 95 percent of its labor allocated to agricultural production, $n_A = 0.95$. Using these parameter values, $\hat{P}/\hat{N}_A = -7.61$, which is quite large. Movement of 1 percent of agricultural labor to nonagricultural activities would precipitate a 7.6 percent increase in the relative price (cost) of agricultural output. An external change affecting the production function, such as a weather fluctuation or a permanent change in technology, could be represented by $\hat{P}/\hat{a} = -8.61$, which is even more sensitive than the consequence of a labor reallocation. Could the community compensate for the reduction in labor time devoted to agriculture by putting more land under culti-

vation? Could the increased supply of agricultural output derived from using more land dampen the relative price increase of agricultural goods? The answer to this question is contained in the expression $\hat{P}/\hat{L} = \beta(1 - n_A) / (\varepsilon + \eta\theta_A) = -1.72$. The increase in land under cultivation would have to be five times the reduction in labor used in agriculture. It is not impossible that a 1 percent reduction in labor could be accompanied by a 5 percent increase in land cultivated, but the possibility of meeting a 2 percent reduction in labor with a 10 percent increase in land area cultivated seems more remote.

A Model of Production with Endogenous Labor Allocation

Because our questions involve what happens to the relative cost of agricultural production as the agricultural labor force changes, the previous model is intuitively appealing inasmuch as it allows us to move labor in and out of

---

[11] These output elasticities strictly represent shares of output produced rather than shares of income received. If inputs are priced in a particular way (i.e., paid the values of their marginal products), income shares will equal output shares. The social rules of dividing the output among the individuals contributing labor and other inputs may diverge from marginal productivity input pricing, but the output elasticities still will represent the proportions of the output that can be imputed to the particular inputs. I do not specify any other income apportionment rules in the present analysis, so marginal productivity pricing is implicit but certainly not necessary; markets are unnecessary for allocation according to marginal productivity rules. Other income division rules would complicate the algebra.

agriculture directly. However, that model has several unsatisfactory features from a theoretical perspective. First, we have no explanation for the cause of the change in the allocation of labor between agriculture and nonagriculture. Might the cause of such a change also induce other changes in this economy for which we are not allowing? Second, such a reallocation of labor itself would cause the relative productivities of labor in agriculture and nonagriculture to change, and people might not be satisfied with the reallocation we have imposed; that is, they might do something different. I address these problems by making the allocation of labor between agriculture and nonagriculture endogenous and requiring that the productivity of labor be equalized between these alternative sets of activities.[12] This procedure uses the same equations as the previous model, but adds the relationship that the value of what labor can produce in agriculture and nonagriculture must be the same if people are to be satisfied with the allocation. Stated alternatively, and somewhat

more precisely, the reallocation of the last unit of labor to nonagriculture from agriculture must yield at least as much value of nonagricultural output as is lost in agricultural output, but it also must yield no more, or another unit of labor would be shifted as well. That is, the value of production from the last unit of labor moved between alternative uses must be the same in both uses. This condition is represented by $\alpha P a N_A^{\alpha-1} L^\beta = \gamma c N_M^{\gamma-1} S^\delta$. Each side of this equation is the derivative of the respective production function with respect to its labor input, and in intuitive terms is the addition to output conferred by that additional unit of labor. Multiplication of the value of agricultural output added by a unit of agricultural labor by P, the relative price of agricultural output in terms of nonagricultural output, puts the productivity contributions in comparable terms. With substitutions, we have two equations in two unknowns, P and N_A. I express the two equations in rate-of-change form and present them as simultaneous equations in matrix form:

$$
\begin{bmatrix} \varepsilon + \eta\,\theta_A & -\alpha(1-\eta\,\theta_A) - \dfrac{\eta\,\gamma\, n_A(1-\theta_A)}{1-n_A} \\[2em] 1 & -\beta - \dfrac{\delta\, n_A}{1-n_A} \end{bmatrix}
\begin{bmatrix} \hat{P} \\ \hat{N}_A \end{bmatrix} =
\begin{bmatrix} \beta(1-\eta\,\theta_A) \\ -\beta \end{bmatrix} \hat{L} +
\begin{bmatrix} \eta\,\delta(1-\theta_A) \\ \delta \end{bmatrix} \hat{S}
$$

$$
- \begin{bmatrix} \dfrac{\eta\,\gamma(1-\theta_A)}{1-n_A} \\[1.5em] \dfrac{\delta}{1-n_A} \end{bmatrix} \hat{N} +
\begin{bmatrix} 1-\eta\,\theta_A \\ -1 \end{bmatrix} \hat{a} +
\begin{bmatrix} -1 \\ 0 \end{bmatrix} \hat{b} +
\begin{bmatrix} -\eta(1-\theta_A) \\ 1 \end{bmatrix} \hat{c}
$$

Table B.3 recapitulates the symbols used in this model.

With this model, we need a story to explain why labor leaves agriculture, and one that appears satisfactory is that technology in nona-

gricultural production improves. In this case, $\hat{N}_A/\hat{c} = (\varepsilon + \eta)/\Delta = -0.05$, where $\Delta = \alpha(1 - \eta\theta_A) + \eta\gamma n_A(1 - \theta_A)/(1 - n_A) - (\varepsilon + \eta\theta_A)[\beta + \delta n_A/(1 - n_A)] > 0$.[13] Because the share of nonagricultural activity is very small, a change in technology in that

---

[12] This equalization of productivity in alternative activities does not require a labor market, although it certainly could be produced by one. All the labor reallocations could be conducted within individual households or other decision units. Small amounts of work undertaken for others outside the household, by some but not necessarily all households, could suffice to equalize labor productivity across households. See Nakajima 1986 on the analysis of such relatively self-contained agricultural households.

[13] Δ is the determinant of the 2x2 matrix presented above, and it can be calculated, among other ways, by

TABLE B.3. Symbols Used in the Production Model with Endogenous Labor Allocation

Symbol	Definition/Interpretation
Q^s, Q^d, Q, M, Y, P, ε, η, θ_A, a, b, c, α, β, γ, δ, N_A, N_M, L, S, n_A	Same as in supply model (Table B.1) and production model (Table B.2) with exogenous labor allocation
w	Earning per unit of labor (wage), in terms of the manufactured good
r	Earning per unit of land (rent), in terms of the manufactured good
p_S	Earning per unit of natural resource (price of the resource), in terms of the manufactured good
U	Index of individual well-being in terms of quantities of goods consumed (utility function)
u	Constant term in utility function
V	Index of individual well-being in terms of consumption costs (indirect utility function)
ψ, ξ	Weights in utility function (and indirect utility function) for food and manufactures

activity has a relatively small effect on labor in agriculture, but using the relationship between changes in labor allocation across the two sectors, $\hat{N}_M = n_A \hat{N}_A/(1 - n_A)$, we calculate that $\hat{N}_M/\hat{c} = 1.05$, which is both a noticeable and an intuitively reasonable magnitude of response. The relatively small reduction in the agricultural labor force is accompanied by (it does not cause) a change in the relative cost of the agricultural output: $\hat{P}/\hat{c} = \Delta^{-1}\{\eta(1-\theta_A)[\beta+\delta n_A/(1-n_A)] + \alpha(1-\eta\theta_A) + \eta\gamma n_A(1-\theta_A)/(1-n_A)\} = 0.46$. The ratio of the price change to the change in agricultural labor is even higher than the sensitivity of that price to the exogenous change in agricultural labor in the previous model: $(\hat{P}/\hat{c})/(\hat{N}_A/\hat{c}) = -8.33$. A very modest change in nonagricultural technology induces a relatively much greater change in the cost of agricultural production than in the agricultural labor force.

It is but a step from assessing the impacts of labor-force changes on agricultural production costs to considering the impacts of the same changes on incomes. As one measure of income, I use the productivity of a unit of labor as it was captured in the second equation of the last model. To use a shorthand term, this is the wage, although the connotation of that term may carry some unfortunate, if needless, baggage. It may be clear from the previous section that the wage, as the term is used now, is nothing more than the

value of what a unit of labor will produce. It is not required that an employer pay the wage; a self-employed worker generates his or her own wage, and whether he "pays himself" this wage, gives it away, or just eats it, is immaterial to the present analysis. It is the value of what a worker produces, and that amount is available for someone's consumption. From one side of the second equation in the third model, we obtain the relation that $\hat{w} = \hat{P} - \beta\hat{N}_A$, where w is the wage, or in the case of a change in nonagricultural technology which pulls labor out of agriculture, $\hat{w}/\hat{c} = \hat{P}/\hat{c} - \beta\hat{N}_A/\hat{c} = 0.47$. In the second model, in which the change in the labor used in agriculture is exogenous, $\hat{w}/\hat{N}_A = \hat{P}/\hat{N}_A - \beta = -7.8$. In both models, both w and P are measured in terms of nonagricultural goods, which clearly is not the only standard for measuring changes in income. The other obvious standard is the agricultural good. To derive the change in the wage in terms of the agricultural output, we simply can subtract the $\hat{P}$ term from both sides: $(\hat{w}-\hat{P})/\hat{c} = -\beta\hat{N}_A/\hat{c} = 0.011$ and $(\hat{w}-\hat{P})/\hat{N}_A = -\beta = -0.20$ for the two models. Both of these wage changes are "real" changes; that is, they are changes in terms of one of the goods rather than in money terms. The change in both cases is measured in terms of the nonagricultural output. In the case of the second model, the "real" wage change lies between 7.81 and 0.2, exactly where depending upon the proportion in

---

footnote 13 continued

Cramer's rule, which in this 2x2 case is simply the product of the upper-left and lower-right elements of that matrix, minus the product of the lower-left and upper-right elements.

which people feel themselves better off by virtue of the consumption of the two goods. In the third model, the real wage change, relative to the causal change, lies between 0.47 and 0.011. In current economic parlance, these proportions are characteristics of people's utility functions, which are simply an analyst's construct of how an individual thinks about how well off he or she is. For example, a simple utility function would be $U = uQ_A^\psi M^\xi$, in which a person evaluates well-being in terms of physical consumption; the exponents ψ and ξ are weights, which sum to 1, describing how changes in consumption affect the overall assessment of well-being. In this particular utility function, the exponential weights are budget shares, in which case $\psi = \theta_A$. Our evaluation of real income change is in terms of prices, however, rather than quantities. The utility function can be inverted and expressed as an indirect function of prices and income: $V = (w/u)[P_A^\psi P_M^\xi]^{-1}$, in which P_A and P_M are the separately expressed prices of agricultural and nonagricultural goods. Expressed as the relative price we have used so far, the indirect utility function would be $V = (w/u)P^{-\psi}$. Thus, to obtain a more balanced assessment of the real wage change in each of the cases we have considered, we can weight the relative price change in terms of people's evaluations of their relative importance. We can express the change in the real wage in terms of the indirect utility function, $\hat{V} = \hat{w} - \psi\hat{P}$, or with an adjustment to the expression for the wage: $\hat{w} - \psi\hat{P} = (1 - \psi)\hat{P} - \beta\hat{N}_A$. Using this formulation, the real wage change following the arbitrary shift of 1 percent of agricultural labor is $(\hat{w} - \psi\hat{P})/\hat{N}_A = \hat{V}/\hat{N}_A = 0.58$, while that following a technological change in nonagricultural production is $(\hat{w} - \psi\hat{P})/\hat{c} = \hat{V}/\hat{c} = 0.034$.

Labor, of course, is not the only source of income. Two other income sources are land and the raw materials used in nonagricultural production. Income to land—call it rent—is a residual after the payment or imputation of labor's income; derived from the agricultural production function, it may be expressed in rate-of-change form as $\hat{r} = \hat{P} + \hat{a} + \alpha\hat{N}_A - \alpha\hat{L}$, in terms of nonagricultural output. With the price index derived from the indirect utility function, the change in rent following removal of 1 percent of agricultural labor is $(\hat{r} - \psi\hat{P})/\hat{N}_A = (1 - \psi)\hat{P}/\hat{N}_A + \alpha = -3.00$. An improvement in nonagricultural technology yields a modest increase in rent in terms of nonagricultural output, $\hat{r}/\hat{c} = 0.40$, and

small decreases in terms of agricultural output and in terms of the weighted price index: $(\hat{r} - \hat{P})/\hat{c} = 0.044$ and $(\hat{r} - \psi\hat{P})/\hat{c} = -0.022$. With a fixed amount of land available, or with expansion only at considerable difficulty in terms of clearance costs or marginal transportation costs, this reduction in rent in real terms could account at least partially for opposition to technical changes in manufacturing on the part of people who derive most of their income from land rather than from their labor. Similarly, changes in the value of the resource used in nonagricultural production, in terms of nonagricultural output, can be expressed as $\hat{p}_S = \hat{c} - [\gamma n_A/(1-n_A)]\hat{N}_A + [\gamma/(1-n_A)]\hat{N} - \gamma\hat{S}$. The change in this value induced by a small improvement in nonagricultural production technology is $\hat{p}_S/\hat{c} = 1 - [\gamma n_A/(1-n_A)]\hat{N}_A/\hat{c} = 1.475$. Even in terms of the weighted price index, the change is positive and proportionally greater than the technological improvement: $(\hat{p}_S - \psi\hat{P})/\hat{c} = 1.04$.

How does the income or well-being of the entire economy fare? Previously, I used the indirect utility function to express the change in real well-being of an individual receiving labor income. Now, consider an aggregate indirect utility function that uses total income in the economy rather than the wage of a single individual. We can represent economy-wide income as the sum of incomes from productive resources; in rate-of-change form, this is $\hat{Y} = [\theta_A\alpha + (1 - \theta_A)\gamma]\hat{w} + \theta_A\beta\hat{r} + (1 - \theta_A)\delta\hat{p}_S$. Then, for the entire economy, $\hat{V}/\hat{c} = \hat{Y}/\hat{c} - \psi\hat{P}/\hat{c} = 0.075$. Overall, the members of the economy would judge the economy better off from the technical improvement in manufacturing, although a reduction in real income going to rentiers might complicate that perception.

A MODEL OF PRODUCTION AND EXTERNAL TRADE

Many stories could be developed for trading situations: different goods could be imported or exported, differences between competing foreign and local products could be greater or lesser, larger or smaller shares of outputs could be traded, etc. Within these parameters, a number of reasonable, but different, stories could be constructed for Dark Age Greek trade and even for Dark Age Cretan trade. The story I explore for the case of Dark Age Crete is as follows. The general structure of the economy remains the same as that explored in the previous models, but this "model Crete" exports agricultural products and imports nonagricultural, or manufactured, products. Trade plays a small part in the economy: 5 percent of agricultural output is exported to an unspecified "rest of the world." Given the remaining structural characteristics of this economy, this export share implies that 95 percent of Cretan consumption of nonagricultural output would be imported. Cretan agricultural products are distinct from those produced in the rest of the world, but foreign buyers consider them modest complements to their own agricultural products. This model Dark Age Crete imports manufactured goods that are perfect substitutes for local manufactured goods. Consequently, the production cost, or price, of the Cretan nonagricultural output in terms of the foreign nonagricultural output is 1 plus the transportation cost on a unit of that output.[14]

Clearly, other foreign trade stories are obvious. The nonagricultural products could be differentiated by place of origin, either in addition to or instead of the agricultural output. Attic and Corinthian fine pottery come immediately to mind. The focus could be shifted from an exporter of agricultural products to an exporter of manufactures, although the archaeological record suggests that Dark Age Crete exported agricultural products. Some of the Cretan agricultural exports, however, could be considered manufactured goods made from materials supplied by agriculture, for example, textiles. Another slight shift of emphasis could make Cretan exports substitutes for products in foreign lands rather than complements to them. All of these stories are worth exploring, if not for Crete, then for other regions of Dark Age Greece, and the present series of models can do no more than initiate a dialogue generating hypotheses about trade that might yield some implications that could be compared with archaeological evi-

dence or historical record.

This model of trade uses the production equations for agricultural and nonagricultural output used in the previous model. Now, however, in equating the supply of agricultural output with the demand for it, we must include foreign demand for Cretan agricultural output: $Q^d_{A_{total}} = Q^d_{A_{local}} + Q^d_{A_{foreign}}$. The local component of demand remains the same as in the previous model, while the foreign component can be described as $Q^d_{A_{foreign}} = b_2[P(1 + t_A)]^{\epsilon_F} P_F^{\sigma_F} (1+t_M)^{\omega_F} Y_F^{\eta_F}$. The first term in brackets is the c.i.f. (cost, insurance, and freight charges included) price of the Cretan agricultural output in the foreign land, in terms of the nonagricultural output; t_A is the transportation cost on the agricultural output expressed as a fraction of the f.o.b. (freight on board, or excluding transportation costs) cost of the nonagricultural product in the foreign country. Subscripts F on the price and income elasticities refer to the foreign land as opposed to Cretan elasticities. The second term in brackets, including its exponent, expresses the relationship between the price of the foreign land's agricultural output and that land's demand for the Cretan agricultural output; P_F is the price (cost) of the foreign agricultural product in terms of the Cretan manufactured good. The exponent is called the cross-price elasticity between the Cretan and foreign agricultural products; I assume that they are modest complements to one another, represented by $\sigma_F < 0$ (I use a value of -0.2 in the calculations below). The third term in parentheses, $1 + t_M$, is the relative price (cost) of the foreign manufactured good in terms of the Cretan manufactured good, and the exponent represents the responsiveness of foreign demand for the Cretan agricultural good to the relative price of the foreign manufactured good; $\omega_F > 0$ represents a substitute relationship.[15] This relative price derives from my assumption that the cost of producing the manufactured good in Crete is the foreign cost plus

---

[14] While the parameter values selected to represent many Dark Age Greek regions might be similar to those I have chosen for the study of Crete, they certainly would differ for a model tailored to represent Early Iron Age Phoenicia. Even some structural features of the model might be modified to capture Phoenician characteristics.

[15] I choose a complementary relationship between the foreign and Cretan agricultural products on the grounds that trade in the face of very high transport costs may be more likely when the traded goods are complements to one another; the substitute relationship between the Cretan agricultural good and the foreign manufactured good is chosen simply for balance. These relationships could be reversed without major changes in the results.

transportation costs, that is, the Cretan price is $1 + t_M$ times the "world" price, P_M^W. While this clearly is not the case for many simpler items such as pottery, it may capture well the cost relations for more complicated items.

The local demand has the same form as in the previous models, but the greater detail of the accounting requires some variation on the earlier notation: $Q^d_{A_{local}} = b_1 P^{\varepsilon_A} Y^{\eta_A}$. The subscripts A on the exponential parameters in the equation identify price and income elasticities of demand for the agricultural output.

Casting a contemporary accounting framework on these external exchanges, the absence of

a capital account implies a balanced merchandise account; that is, the value of imports equals the value of exports. The foreign component of demand for local agricultural production combined with the definition of total income in the economy, $Y = P_A Q_A + M_{local}$, implies this trade balance. Table B.4 reports the new and old symbols used in this model.

As in the previous model, labor is allocated across agricultural and nonagricultural activities so as to equalize labor's productivity in the alternative activities. The condition is identical to that in the last model, and I do not repeat the equation here. However, I do present the rate-of-

TABLE B.4. Symbols Used in the Model of Production and External Trade

Symbol	Definition/Interpretation
$Y, P, \varepsilon, \eta,$	Same as in previous models (Tables B.1–3)
$\theta_A, a, c, \alpha,$	
$\beta, \gamma, \delta, N_A,$	
$N_M, L, S,$	
θ_A, n_A	
$Q^d_{A_{local}},$	
$Q^d_{A_{foreign}}$	
$Q^d_{A_{total}},$	Local ("Cretan"), foreign, and total demands for the local agricultural product
M_{local}	Local production of the manufactured good
P_F	Cost (price) of the foreign agricultural good
Y_F	Total foreign income
t_A, t_M	Shipping costs of agricultural and manufactured goods, as share of base production costs
ε_F	foreign own-price elasticity of demand for local ("Cretan") agricultural good (responsiveness of foreign demand for Cretan agricultural good to changes in the delivered price—including transportation costs—of the Cretan agricultural good)
σ_F	Foreign cross-price elasticity of demand for local ("Cretan") agricultural good (responsiveness of foreign demand for Cretan agricultural good to changes in the price/cost of the foreign agricultural good)
ω_F	Foreign cross-price elasticity of demand for local ("Cretan") agricultural good (responsiveness of foreign demand for Cretan agricultural good to changes in the price/cost of the—foreign—manufactured good)
η_F	Foreign income elasticity of demand for local ("Cretan") agricultural good
ε_A	Local price elasticity of demand for the agricultural product (equivalent to ε in the previous models)
η_A	Local income elasticity of demand for the agricultural product (equivalent to η in the previous models)
b_1	Constant term in the local demand function for the agricultural product (equivalent to b in the previous models)
b_2	Constant term in the foreign demand function for the "Cretan" agricultural product (represents foreign tastes for that product)
b_3	Constant term in the local demand function for the manufactured good (represents tastes for the

change equations in matrix form:

$$\begin{bmatrix} -(1-\lambda)(e_A+\eta_A\theta_A)-\lambda e_F & \alpha-(1-\lambda)\eta_A\left[\theta_A\alpha-\dfrac{(1-\theta_A)\gamma\,n_A}{1-n_A}\right] \\[2mm] 1 & -(1-\alpha)-\dfrac{(1-\gamma)\,n_A}{1-n_A} \end{bmatrix}\begin{bmatrix} \hat{P} \\[1mm] \hat{N}_A \end{bmatrix} = \begin{bmatrix} \beta\,[(1-\lambda)\eta_A\theta_A-1] \\[1mm] -\beta \end{bmatrix}\hat{L}$$

$$+\begin{bmatrix} (1-\lambda)\eta_A(1-\theta_A)\delta \\[1mm] \delta \end{bmatrix}\hat{S} +\begin{bmatrix} \dfrac{(1-\lambda)\eta_A(1-\theta_A)\gamma}{1-n_A} \\[2mm] \dfrac{-(1-\gamma)n_A}{1-n_A} \end{bmatrix}\hat{N} +\begin{bmatrix} (1-\lambda)\eta_A\theta_A-1 \\[1mm] -1 \end{bmatrix}\hat{a} +\begin{bmatrix} 1-\lambda \\[1mm] 0 \end{bmatrix}\hat{b}_1 +\begin{bmatrix} \lambda \\[1mm] 0 \end{bmatrix}\hat{b}_2$$

$$+\begin{bmatrix} (1-\lambda)\eta_A(1-\theta_A) \\[1mm] 1 \end{bmatrix}\hat{c} +\begin{bmatrix} \lambda\sigma_F \\[1mm] 0 \end{bmatrix}\hat{P}_F +\begin{bmatrix} \dfrac{\lambda\omega_F t_M}{1+t_M} \\[1mm] 0 \end{bmatrix}\hat{t}_M +\begin{bmatrix} \dfrac{\lambda e_F t_A}{1+t_A} \\[1mm] 0 \end{bmatrix}\hat{t}_A +\begin{bmatrix} \lambda\eta_F \\[1mm] 0 \end{bmatrix}\hat{Y}^F$$

We need solve only for percent changes in the price of the Cretan agricultural output and in the allocation of labor to agriculture in Crete. The foreign and Cretan prices (which equal production costs) of the nonagricultural output are exogenous, and changes in the price of the Cretan agricultural output are implicitly in terms of the nonagricultural output. The remaining new parameters in this model are λ, the percentage of Cretan agricultural output exported, and Y_F, total income of the foreign land. I use these two equations to solve for percent changes in the two endogenous variables caused by changes in the exogenous variables on the right-hand side of the matrix expression. In addition, I use the expression for total Cretan income, Y, to calculate changes in total income and thereafter use the expression for indirect utility to calculate the change in real income associated with the exogenous changes specified on the right-hand side of the expression below.

Changes in several of the exogenous variables represent changes in the circumstances of external economic relations: P_F (the relative price of agricultural output in the foreign land), t_M and t_A (the transportation costs on nonagricultural and agricultural outputs), and Y_F (total income in the foreign land). To assist the discussion of how changes in these conditions affect the Dark Age Crete modeled here, I present the numerical values of these relationships in Table B.5. Each number is the percent change in an endogenous variable caused by a 1 percent change in the exogenous circumstance. The numerical values of the parameters remain the same for those parameters used in the previous models. The parameter values for the foreign land's demand for Cretan agricultural output are slightly more elastic than the corresponding parameters in the Cretan demand for its own agricultural output, reflecting greater price and income sensitivity in the demand for imported products than in the demand for domestic ones. Those values are $\varepsilon_F = -0.3$, $\sigma_F = -0.2$, and $\eta_F = 0.5$.

The first observation from Table B.5 is that the sensitivities of all the Cretan economic indicators to changes in foreign, or external, circumstances are small. The effects of changes in overseas agricultural production costs and transportation costs would be virtually imperceptible at the scale of the entire economy, although individual shippers might find reductions in transportation costs quite beneficial. Changes in foreign overall income, Y_F, and the foreign preference for the Cretan agricultural good, b_2, have the strongest effects and are most likely to be noticeable on the relative price of the Cretan agricultural good. Nevertheless, in terms of real well-being, the effect on indirect utility, V, would be practically unnoticeable.

Table B.6 offers a review of comparable effects of domestic economic changes. It is intuitively reasonable that the magnitudes of most of the responses are larger to domestic changes than to foreign changes operating through the 5 percent of the economy associated directly with foreign trade. The measure of aggregate income in terms of the manufactured good, Y, is not on

TABLE B.5. Responses of Agricultural Production Costs, Labor Allocations, and Nominal and Real Income to Changes in External Trading Circumstances

	$\hat{P}_F$	C	$\hat{t}_A$	$\hat{Y}_F$	$\hat{b}_2$
$\hat{P}$	-0.051	0.026	-0.039	0.129	0.257
$\hat{N}_A$	-0.005	0.003	0.004	0.013	0.027
$\hat{Y}$	-0.050	0.025	-0.036	0.126	0.252
$\hat{V}$	-0.002	-0.001	0.001	0.003	0.008

Note: $\hat{P}$ is the percent change in price (cost) of agricultural product in terms of the nonagricultural product resulting from a 1 percent change in one of the exogenous parameters listed across the top row of the table; $\hat{N}_A$ is the percent change in labor time used in agriculture; $\hat{Y}$ is the percent change in value of total income; $\hat{V}$ is the percent change in index of individual well-being (indirect utility). These four variables are endogenous. The exogenous parameters are defined as follows: $\hat{P}_F$ is a 1 percent change in the price (cost) of agricultural product in terms of nonagricultural (manufactured) products in "foreign lands"; $\hat{P}_F$ is a 1 percent change in the transportation rate on manufactured goods (imports to the model country), measured as a fraction of the relative price (cost) of the item without shipping charges; $\hat{t}_A$ is a 1 percent change in the corresponding transportation rate on agricultural products (exports from the model country); $\hat{Y}_F$ is a 1 percent change in total income in the "foreign lands," measured in terms of the nonagricultural product; $\hat{b}_2$ is a 1 percent change in the strength of preference for the "Cretan" agricultural product in the "foreign lands," i.e, how badly foreigners want the "Cretan" product.

TABLE B.6. Responses of Agricultural Production Costs, Labor Allocations, and Nominal and Real Income to Changes in Domestic Economic Circumstances

	$\hat{L}$	$\hat{N}$	$\hat{S}$	$\hat{a}$	$\hat{b}_1$	$\hat{b}_3$	$\hat{c}$
$\hat{P}$	-1.018	-3.649	0.217	-5.089	4.886	0.086	0.434
$\hat{N}_A$	-0.084	-0.603	-0.029	-0.422	0.504	-0.094	0.058
$\hat{Y}$	-0.801	-2.795	0.223	-4.004	4.785	-0.024	0.446
$\hat{V}$	0.166	-0.328[a]	0.017	0.831	0.144	-0.137	0.034

[a]Per capita and total changes diverge; per capita change is reported.

NOTE: Definitions of the four variables in the left-hand row are the same as in Table B.1. Parameters listed across the top row are exogenous: $\hat{L}$ is a 1 percent change in land available for agriculture; $\hat{N}$ is a 1 percent change in total population; $\hat{S}$ is a 1 percent change in the natural resource used in production of the nonagricultural (manufactured) good; $\hat{a}$ is a 1 percent change in the level of technology in agriculture in the model economy, i.e., technological or natural progress, or the same effect as a short-term disturbance in weather; $\hat{b}_1$ is a 1 percent change in the strength of preference of residents of "model Crete" for the agricultural good, i.e., how badly they want it; $\hat{b}_3$ is a 1 percent change in the strength of preference for the nonagricultural (manufactured) good, which also is the imported good; $\hat{c}$ is a 1 percent change in technology in production of the nonagricultural good, or technological change in "manufacturing."

a per capita basis, although this only becomes important in the case of a change in population, in Table B.6. Indirect utility is measured on an individual basis, but I have used only labor income as an approximation to total income. The response of aggregate income to a change in population (the third row of the second column in Table B.6) is the sum of the responses of everyone's income on our model "Crete"; to obtain the change in per capita income, we can subtract 1,

obtaining $\hat{Y}/\hat{N}$ = -3.795. The small responses to a change in the amount of the resource used in the nonagricultural output, S, also are intuitively reasonable in view of the small share of income produced in that activity.

The column of Table B.6 headed $\hat{b}_3$, second from the right in that table, represents a hypothesis that has appeared not infrequently in the literature about the Greek Dark Age: that Greek aristocrats developed a taste for foreign goods and, to acquire them, required their communities to export more, generating a kind of export-led economic growth. An increase in parameter $\hat{b}_3$ represents a shift in tastes—actually of everyone, not just of aristocrats, but that is an even more stringent form of the hypothesis—toward the manufactured good, which is exported, although a small amount of it is produced locally. What happens to this economy under these circumstances? Very little, and most of that is undesirable: the relative price of the manufactured product rises slightly, and a small bit of labor is reallocated from agriculture to production of that product, but total income (measured in terms of the manufactured good) falls a very small bit, and the index of well-being, $\hat{V}$, falls by an amount that could have been noticeable to contemporaries, if not in the archaeological evidence facing us three thousand years later. Turning ahead to Table B.8, the only really strong effect of this shift in preferences is a redistribution of income to people who own the resource that is used in the production of the manufactured good. There is a more important principle on display here than the relative unimportance of a shift in preferences to a product, very little of which is produced. The productive capacity of the economy has not been altered at all by the simple change in preferences. People with a heightened taste for the import have only one means to satisfy their demand for it: pay more. That, of course, reduces the quantity of the agricultural product that they have left to consume themselves, and by an amount greater than the equivalent valuation they place on the import. This may seem perverse, but its explanation is quite simple. If a society loses some of its taste for the product that they make relatively more easily (cheaply), and gains a taste for a good that it cannot produce as easily, it will be worse off than it would be if it liked better what it could produce more easily. Rather than export-led growth, we have an export-led decline. The economic boom of the eighth-century Greek renaissance probably is not attributable to an aristocratic rage to deposit foreign artwork in their graves. This exercise cannot disprove the possibility that Greek aristocrats at some time late in the Dark Age developed a heightened taste for

foreign items, only that such a change in tastes could not have led to an export boom that sparked the generalized economic resurgence. Something more substantial would have been required.

Is there any way out of this conclusion? Could the aristocrats not have gotten more work out of agricultural producers, say, by whipping or starving? The labor supply in the model is fixed, ruling out such a simple maneuver. Acquire more slaves? That would require real resources, and all resources in the model are fully used; further retrenchment of current consumption would be required to acquire more slaves, either by purchase, by raid, or by local breeding. What about exhorting labor to be more diligent or resourceful? More diligent means working harder, and full employment implies that everyone is working, on average, to the maximum of his or her capacity. More resourceful implies technological change—a change in the feasible ways of combining a given set of inputs to produce more output. Technical change could be represented by raising the value of **a** (the technology level in agriculture) or **c** (the technology level in manufacturing), but those changes are separate and distinct from the preference change.

Turning to the subject of the distribution of income, by that term I refer to the sources from which individuals' income would have derived: from their own labor, from the ownership of land and rights to residual income from it, and from ownership of the raw material, or "resource," as I call it, used in production of nonagricultural output. Some individuals, of course, would receive income from both land and their labor, and I make no attempt to characterize the individual or family concentration of income from land. An aggregate income share is defined as, say, rL/Y, for the land share, where **r** is the rent on a unit of land, in terms of nonagricultural output, **L** is the fixed area under cultivation, and **Y** is aggregate income. Similarly, labor's share is wN/Y, and the resource share is $p_S S/Y$, where **w** and p_S are the wage and the imputed value of a unit of the resource. The weighted sum of these percent changes must equal 0.[16] Table B.7 presents numerical values of

---

[16] The shares sum to 1: $s_L + s_N + s_S = 1$, where subscripts **L**, **N**, and **S** represent land, labor, and resources. In rate-of-change form, $s_L \hat{s}_L + s_N \hat{s}_N + s_S \hat{s}_S = 0$.

TABLE B.7. Changes in Aggregate Income Shares Caused by Changes in External Economic Circumstances

Income share	$\hat{P}_F$	$\hat{t}_M$	$\hat{t}_A$	$\hat{Y}_F$	$\hat{b}_2$
Land	-0.01	0.01	-0.00	0.01	0.03
Labor	0.01	0.00	-0.01	0.00	0.00
Resource	-0.01	0.00	0.07	-0.00	-0.50

the percent changes in each of these income shares caused by a 1 percent change in each of the circumstances that characterize the external economic environment. In Table B.8, I show numerical values of percent changes in Cretan income shares caused by changes in the domestic economic environment.

Changes in domestic economic circumstances on average have more prominent effects on income distribution than do changes in foreign circumstances. Table B.8 summarizes these relationships. The change in the share of labor income is particularly inert, with the single exception of its response to an increase in population, which reduces that share sharply. An increase in the level of technical productivity in agriculture, **a**, decisively benefits owners of the natural resource, **S**, and actually reduces the income share of land, which is used exclusively in agriculture. This result occurs because the increase in agricultural productivity sharply reduces the relative price of the agricultural good. If this model's structure is a fair representation of an economy of the early first millennium, this result may go some way toward explaining the slow growth of productivity in agriculture: neither landowners nor agricultural workers themselves stood to gain a lot as groups from greater agricultural productivity; but this comment must be balanced against the strong benefit to individuals depending on labor income derived from this increase: see Table B.6, row 4, column 4.

The production processes in the model so far have relied on a particular, mathematical functional form, known as the Cobb-Douglas form. That form imposes a particular degree of substitutability between inputs in production (e.g.,

between labor and land in agricultural production). Specifically, the Cobb-Douglas form imposes the relationship that a 1 percent change in the ratio of input costs (prices) causes a 1 percent change in the ratio of those inputs used in production, in the opposite direction. More concretely, a 1 percent increase in ratio of the cost of labor (the wage) to the cost of land (the land rental rate) would be followed by a 1 percent increase in the land/labor ratio in agricultural production. This parameter measuring this degree of substitutability is called the elasticity of substitution. The Cobb-Douglas function imposes a unitary elasticity of substitution. This degree of substitutability sometimes is considered restrictive, for the very practical reason that it is known that in some circumstances, the degree of substitutability between inputs in production is greater than or less than 1. One of the reasons to be interested in the value of the elasticity of substitution is that it can affect the distribution of income between suppliers of different inputs when relative input prices change. For instance, if the elasticity of substitution is greater than 1 and the wage rises (assuming only labor and land are used in some production process), the total costs accruing to labor will fall relative to the total costs accruing to land: that is, the distribution of income going to the owners of the inputs in this production process is tilted toward land—the share of land income rises and the share of labor income falls. With a unitary elasticity of substitution, the distribution of income going to the owners of inputs to a production process is invariant to changes in the relative price of the inputs. In the model above, which uses Cobb-Douglas forms for both production functions, as well as for the demand functions,

TABLE B.8. Changes in Aggregate Income Shares Caused by Changes in Domestic Economic Circumstances

Income share	$\hat{L}$	$\hat{N}$	$\hat{S}$	$\hat{a}$	$\hat{b}_1$	$\hat{b}_3$	$\hat{c}$
Land	-0.08	-0.37	-0.03	-8.43	0.50	0.01	-0.06
Labor	0.80	0.03	0.00	0.00	0.00	-0.06	-0.01
Resource	1.61	7.06	0.55	8.01	-0.78	0.92	0.61

the changes in income distribution throughout the economy are attributable to changes in the relative price of the outputs and in the relative quantities of the outputs; the Cobb-Douglas form puts a ceiling, so to speak, on the changes in income distribution that the model yields. A natural question is, "Is the Cobb-Douglas specification 'true' in some sense for the Dark Age Cretan economy?" but that question also is largely unanswerable. Consequently, a more relevant question is, "How much difference would different production functions, with different elasticities of substitution between inputs, make in the results?" In other words, does the technical restrictiveness of the Cobb-Douglas form bias the results in any fundamentally important way? The simplest way to address this question is to substitute other production functions for agriculture and manufactures and see the results. The mathematical structure of the analysis is very similar to that already presented, so I do not subject the reader to more of it, but I have substituted what are called "constant-elasticity-of-substitution" (CES) production functions for the Cobb-Douglas forms in the last model and recalculated the results. The CES functional form permits the elasticity of substitution to take any value between 0 and positive infinity (the elasticity of substitution is measured positively, by convention), although it imposes the same elasticity of substitution between every pair of inputs in the production function. Since both of the production functions I use in the model have only two inputs, this restriction does not affect the results. I have examined the case in which agricultural production is more flexible than in the Cobb-Douglas case (elasticity of substitution greater than 1) and nonagricultural production is less flexible (elasticity of substitution less than 1). The values I chose are 2.0 and 0.5. Empirically, these values represent what would be considered a good deal of substitutability in agriculture (2.0), which is a reasonable correspondence to contemporary traditional agriculture, and a noticeable degree of restriction on substitution possibilities, which intuitively corresponds to contemporary, traditional manufacturing in

developing countries.[17] The results of this examination do not vary substantially from the results with the Cobb-Douglas form. In most cases, the responsiveness of the relative production cost and of the labor allocation is less sensitive to the initial disturbances, and consequently, the changes in aggregate income and real well-being (indirect utility) are correspondingly smaller than with the Cobb-Douglas production functions. This general similarity (but not exact identity) of results is particularly gratifying, because the empirical material with which to discriminate between the two cases would be difficult, if not impossible, to obtain for this time period and region. The comparative results say that such a difference would not matter a lot to the conclusions we draw from the analysis at the level of generality and abstraction at which the models remain.

A MODEL OF EXTERNAL TRADE WITH IMPORTED KNOWLEDGE

The trade model so far shows very little influence of foreign events on local events in Crete because the share of traded goods is small. Nevertheless, the literature stresses the importance of the reception of foreign ideas on thinking in Dark Age Greece, and via that route, to greater influences on the Greek renaissance of the eighth century. The model as currently formulated indicates that technological changes in the local manufacturing sector, represented by $\hat{c}$, can have a fairly strong effect on the relative price of the agricultural good in Crete relative to the manufactured good, although the small size of the manufacturing sector limits the effect on overall well-being. Suppose that the ability to examine imported manufactured goods can give Cretan craftsmen new ideas about how to produce manufactured goods themselves—this corresponds roughly to the notion of new ideas penetrating Dark Age Greece.[18] We can represent this process by making the parameter representing the level of technology in manufacturing, C, a function of the quantity of imports in addition

---

[17] Cf. the values of the elasticity of substitution chosen to represent traditional agriculture and traditional manufacturing, with empirical reference to mid-twentieth-century a.c. developing countries in general, in the simulation model of Kelley, Williamson, and Cheetham 1972: 340–41.

[18] This idea is parallel to Arrow's concept of "learning by doing," in which productivity in a production process is a function of previous production levels: Arrow 1962: 155–73.

TABLE B.9. Responses of Agricultural Production Costs, Labor Allocations, and Nominal and Real Income to Changes in External Trading Circumstances (Endogenous Technical Change Model)

	$\hat{P}_F$	$\hat{t}_M$	$\hat{t}_A$	$\hat{Y}_F$	$\hat{b}_2$
$\hat{P}$	0.033	0.087	-0.131	0.437	1.169
$\hat{N}_A$	-0.015	0.005	-0.008	-0.038	-0.067
$\hat{Y}$	0.018	0.089	-0.134	0.445	1.183
$\hat{V}$	-0.013	0.006	-0.009	0.029	0.072

TABLE B.10. Responses of Agricultural Production Costs, Labor Allocations, and Nominal and Real Income to Changes in Domestic Economic Circumstances (Endogenous Technical Change Model)

	$\hat{L}$	$\hat{N}$	$\hat{S}$	$\hat{a}$	$\hat{b}_1$	$\hat{c}$
$\hat{P}$	-1.288	-4.617	0.275	-6.439	6.183	0.549
$\hat{N}_A$	-0.019	1.906	-0.043	-0.096	-0.191	-0.086
$\hat{Y}$	-1.084	3.505	0.283	-5.420	6.035	0.567
$\hat{V}$	0.139	-0.118[a]	0.022	0.919	0.162	0.045

[a]Per capita and total changes diverge; per capita change is reported.

to some completely exogenous source of change, c: $C = C(c, M^{imp})$. With this specification, any event that causes the level of imports to increase also will bring about some technological improvement in local manufacturing in Crete.

The equation structure of this model is quite similar to that of the previous model, so I do not report it, but I do report the numerical sensitivities of the model with imported knowledge, calculated with the same parameter values used in the earlier model.[19] Tables B.9–10 report the sensitivities of the production costs, labor allocations, and nominal and real income, and Tables B.11–12 report the sensitivities of the model Cretan income distribution in the revised model. In Table B.9, the effects of changes in the foreign parameters—that is, of events overseas—are much larger than they were in the previous model, sometimes by an order of magnitude. The impacts of changes in foreign income and tastes on Cretan relative prices are substantial, but their effects on labor allocations—and consequently on real outputs—are much smaller, and

as a result, the foreign impacts on real well-being are still small, both absolutely and relative to the impacts of domestic events. The foreign parameter with the largest impact on Cretan activities is b_2, the foreign taste for the Cretan agricultural product. A change in foreign income has a smaller impact on Cretan activities because I have assigned a foreign income elasticity of demand for the Cretan import to be less than 1; if it were in fact greater than 1, changes in foreign income would have greater impacts than changes in foreign tastes. Changes in the foreign relative agricultural price and in shipping costs still have small impacts, and if reductions in shipping costs affected both Cretan imports and exports similarly, the offsetting net result would be even smaller: a 1 percent reduction in overall shipping costs would cause roughly a 0.03 percent improvement in Cretan well-being. The importance of a 200-year period of such improvements should not be overlooked, however: an annual 1 percent productivity improvement in ocean shipping compounded over two centuries

[19] I briefly describe my procedure for implementing the **C** function. In the first equation, the **C** function goes in the formulation for Cretan aggregate income in the Cretan demand for agricultural products; in the second equation it is in the equation for labor productivity in manufacturing. Rather than use M^{imp} directly in the function, I rely on the relationship that the value of imports equals the value of exports: $M^{imp} = PQ_A^{exp}$, where $Q_A^{exp} = Q_A^{dforeign}$, which is defined in the text above. In the differentiations, I use the expression for foreign demand for the Cretan agricultural product in the **C** function.

Table B.11. Changes in Aggregate Income Shares Caused by Changes in External Economic Circumstances (Endogenous Technical Change Model)

Income share	$\hat{P}_F$	$\hat{t}_M$	$\hat{t}_A$	$\hat{Y}_F$	$\hat{b}_2$
Land	0.01	0.01	0.01	-0.03	-0.07
Labor	0.02	0.00	0.00	-0.01	0.00
Resource	-0.05	0.14	-0.22	0.73	-1.27

Table B.12. Changes in Aggregate Income Shares Caused by Changes in Domestic Economic Circumstances (Endogenous Technical Change Model)

Income share	$\hat{L}$	$\hat{N}$	$\hat{S}$	$\hat{a}$	$\hat{b}_1$	$\hat{c}$
Land	-0.01	0.41	-0.04	-0.10	-0.01	-0.09
Labor	0.20	-0.29	0.00	-1.00	0.18	0.00
Resource	0.36	7.83	0.88	1.83	-0.21	1.64

would, other things remaining equal, raise Cretan well-being in this model by 82 percent. In actual application, this calculation should be tempered by beginning with a smaller export share than 5 percent, possibly growing from around 1 percent to around 5 percent during such a two-century period; and sustaining a 1 percent improvement annually for two centuries could be optimistic. Still, whether the impacts of improvements in shipping raised well-being 80 percent or 40 percent—or even 20 percent, if we think that such improvements were more errat-ic—the calculations say that technological changes in shipping would have been important for the overall economies of Dark Age Greek regions.

In Table B.11, foreign events have stronger impacts on Cretan income distribution than they did in the previous model, although their effects are restricted for the most part to the "resource" income share, which, by virtue of its small size, can experience proportionally large changes that the other two shares absorb without major effect. Again, foreign tastes and foreign aggregate income have the greatest effects.

The story told by the simpler model emerges largely intact with this modification, although the modified model makes an important qualifi-cation. Foreign events have small impacts on Crete because of the small share of foreign trade in total economic activity, but the transfer of ideas along with a small share of trade substan-tially magnifies trade's impacts. The potency of this effect of foreign ideas suggests that other mechanisms for bringing foreign influences into Greece could widen the scope for foreign influ-

ence even further. Additionally, the small imme-diate impacts of improvements in shipping could be substantial if continued over a period of several centuries.

Modeling Issues: Level of Detail and Omitted Topics

The Cretan artifacts overseas look like man-ufactured goods, or at least crafts, and all the transport amphorae at Kommos suggest that at least some of them carried agricultural products to Crete. Should we study a model in which Crete exports and imports both agricultural and manufactured goods? I do not think that is nec-essary, or even particularly desirable. First, all models being abstractions, they are all wrong—even exclusively verbal ones—and their net virtues should be assessed by the insights they yield about a subset of the observational world. More importantly, I think little further insight is to be gained from such an expansion, and there are some real losses to be faced in terms of the proliferation of parameters and the necessity to assign values to them to obtain results about magnitudes. In choosing parameter values with which to analyze the model, the relative values of pairs of parameters frequently are important, in the sense that relative values can determine major elements of behavior in the model. With another product (a fourth product only makes the problem worse), we must decide, for several parameters, which product's (or sector's) value is in the middle—intermediate in value. The choice may affect the qualitative behavior of the system, and our empirical grounds for making the "middle" assignment are likely to be weak, or even completely arbitrary. With two sectors, the empirical guidance from contemporary or recent historical evidence is reasonably robust. As the number of sectors expands, we need to know more and more about the sectors, but our knowledge base is slender and inelastic. In a larger-sector model, switching around parameter values (e.g., changing the "middle assignment") could produce opposite behavioral responses to a single cause. For example, suppose that ratios of two productive inputs, land and labor, must be assigned to three goods or production sectors; let the ratios 1.5, 1.0, and 0.75 be assigned to sectors **a**, **b**, and **c**. With this assignment of parameter values, when (if) a particular price rises, the production volume of sector **b** may rise and that of sector **c** fall. If we let sector **c** take the middle parameter value (1.0) and sector **b** take the smallest value (0.75), the same price change could cause the output of sector **c** to rise and that of sector **b** to fall. The same phenomenon occurs with only two sectors, but there are more substantial grounds for making the relative parameter-value assignment; in the three-sector case, we may be less certain about the relative values of two of the sectors. In the example, I have used only one parameter—from the production side of the problem; there are other parameters whose relative values could be reversed between sectors, multiplying the possibilities for less-clearly guided parameter-value choices and the variability (= uncertainty) in the behavioral responses. Thus, we may be able to say what probably happened to aggregates of, say, plowshares and jewelry on the one hand, and olives and wheat on the other, but we may be much more limited in what we can say about the behavior of olives and wheat separately than we could as an agricultural aggregate. This is not to say that the two-sector model is the final degree of disaggregation that can be conducted usefully in analysis of an economy such as that of Dark Age Crete, for which the detail of available—or comparable—empirical evidence is thin. Some alternative concepts are available, such as the nontraded good, and some of these might repay further study. But the limits on prof-

itable expansion of detail I still believe are relatively tight. A Dark Age Greek input-output model is out of the question, and we must accept the limitations on the knowledge we may derive from social modeling of activity in this period, just as we have learned in other instances of the applications of physical-sciences techniques to archaeological problems.

In these models I have focused on the *consequences* of trade but have avoided addressing its *causes*. Causal questions can have answers at various levels, and it is worth discussing for a moment pieces I have left out. Let's start with a very general question: Why did the Greeks trade? Answers could run from, "Dimitri had some pots left over and this guy came along in a boat and he had some neat do-dads . . .," to "Dimitri was down on his luck and to get some jingle[20] was reduced to peddling a couple of his favorite knives, his wife's earrings, and a bag of lentils, which he couldn't stand anyway . . . none of his neighbors would buy this junk, so off he went (or he foisted them off on Hiram, who was passing through, for a couple of bottles of wine). . ." Clearly I am not attempting to answer questions at this level of chance—and essentially not at all the question of "why" people traded, although motivations are embedded in the models. Economic models of trade account for volumes of trade, directions of trade (which "countries" or regions sell which goods and buy which others), the effects of these exchanges on the earnings of the resources involved in the production, and the level of satisfaction trading partners achieve with these trades. By fixing the values of parameters θ_A and λ, I have assumed answers to the questions of (initial—"predisturbance") volumes and directions of trade—although the assumptions were carefully selected and the consequences of variations noted. To explain volume and direction, economic models would rely primarily on the relative quantities of factors of production ("inputs"—resources—e.g., labor and land) available in different trading regions and on production technologies—and, of course, on transportation costs. Quantification of the factor availability and technology concepts can be elusive for the early first millennium b.c., and the consequences questions

---

[20] Of course, coinage was not begun in the Greek world until probably sometime in the 630s, in East Greece, so some gold or silver (or even some base metal) dumps would do nicely for the example.

seem more interesting. I offer a brief justification of my omission of two topics under consequences, which some readers may miss and question. As for the concept of factor-price equalization (equalizing the levels, or ratios, of returns to production inputs like labor and land) accomplished by trade, I consider the volumes of trade small enough, and the transportation costs high enough, to make the issue of little practical importance in this period, and I do not address it here. The notion of "export-led growth" has been prominent in contemporary discussions of economic development, and at this moment it is implicit even in public debates about trade and industrial policies in the United States and many of its major trading partners. According to this concept, foreign trade somehow fuels growth— of total production, of incomes, of individual well-being and satisfaction. Why does not foreign trade have such an effect in these models of Dark Age Greece? First, there is such an effect, but it is limited by the initial volume of exports, the height of the shipping-cost wall, and the structure of production. I have addressed the first two of these limitations previously, but the third one only implicitly. If the export industry had increasing returns to scale,[21] a larger export volume would lower the production cost of the export good, raising income correspondingly. In the models here, agriculture is the export good, and increasing returns to scale do not characterize the agricultural sector as a whole (although

some products may be produced with increasing-returns technologies). However, the use of export profits from agriculture for investment in an increasing-returns manufacturing sector[22] could foster export-led growth. However, most manufacturing technologies in the first millennium b.c. do not seem to have been of the sort in which increasing returns or scale economies were particularly important, so the limitations of export-led growth imposed by the models developed here seem reasonable.

Correspondences between Economic Reasoning and Archaeological Records

How might the economic reasoning be joined supportively to archaeological evidence? Suppose we observe, say, an increase in wealth in burials and conclude that either a general increase in wealth or a concentration of wealth in a particular social group occurred.[23] The model of trade indicates that either event—increase or concentration in wealth—most likely would find its causes domestically rather than externally, with due regard to idea transmission via external transactions. Appeal to a concentration of wealth caused by elites' competition for prestige goods (frequently the manufactured or imported goods), which they deposited in graves according to hypothesis, begs the issue of where the

---

[21] Returns to scale refer to the relationship between increases in all inputs in a production process and the outputs derived from the inputs. If a 1% increase in all inputs (not just one or some, but all) yields a 1% increase in output, we have constant returns to scale, which characterize a wide array of production conditions empirically. If a 1% increase in all inputs brings forth an increase in output greater than 1%, increasing returns to scale characterize the production technology. If a 1% increase in all inputs yields an increase in output less than 1% (but still positive), the technology is characterized by decreasing returns to scale. The term "scale economies" is slightly different and focuses on production costs rather than output quantities. If some minimum quantity of one particular input or resource is required to produce any amount of a good, but more of it is not needed to produce greater quantities, producing a larger quantity of this good produced will reduce its average cost, because not all inputs must be increased (and paid for) as production volume is increased. Depending on the size (and cost) of the fixed input, these economies of scale dwindle as output increases, because a fixed cost is being divided by a larger output number. Economies of scale, in this sense, are more common than are genuinely increasing returns to scale deriving from the variable inputs to a production process. They also are more subject to "disappearing" beyond a certain range of output, which varies, of course, with the production process.

[22] At this point, some readers may be objecting to the concepts of profit, investment, and manufacturing "sectors" as inappropriate for a discussion of the early first millennium b.c. While these concepts may elicit images of towering oil refineries, 300-acre assembly-line factories, robber barons in top hats, etc., they are applicable to the humblest resource-allocation acts—the storage of a coconut to be used at a time of greater need, the exchange of a coconut for a tempered iron scraper, etc.

[23] Alternative explanations for a change in burial wealth include cultural and political changes, as suggested by Morris (1987), but that leaves open the explanation of that change itself.

additional goods came from: increased production or beggaring their neighbors. The trade model indicates that a shift in preferences toward the nonagricultural good, which corresponds to such a competition in consumption, reduces aggregate income but increases the share of the smaller aggregate income going to landowners and owners of the "resource" used in manufacturing, at the expense of income going to labor. Stated alternatively, if burial wealth increased because of such a competitive consumption game played by elites, with no other change increasing the productivity of the society, people possessing only labor—peasants or whatever the corresponding group would be called—would suffer a reduction in their well-being while people who owned things—land and other valued natural resources—would benefit. Whether this effect would have been large enough to be revealed by archaeological evidence, such as health conditions revealed by bones, rural household wealth, etc., is an open question, however, depending heavily on just how strong the consumption competition (change in preference) was.[24]

Several results stand out clearly in the economic reasoning, and these may suggest questions to pose to physical evidence as well as to the historical records where they exist. First, manufacturing is capable of propagating some effects that would look large to a proximate observer simply because the direct effect on manufacturing (or whatever one wants to call the nonagricultural activity) is large, but effects on the overall economy would be small (see Tables B.6 and B.8). For instance, the appearance of large quantities of gold in a few locations—graves or hoards of one sort or another—might have little implication for the well-being of the larger society. Evidence of population increase probably is a more secure indicator of aggregate prosperity than are a few localized accumulations of wealth. Second, the distribution of aggregate income among owners of productive resources is subject to greater change from disturbances in agriculture than from disturbances either in nonagriculture or from overseas (I am

speaking, of course, of "routine" economic disturbances, not extensive, physical disruptions such as revolutions and war). Tables B.7 and B.8 contain these results. Most of the political consequences of these agriculturally induced income-distribution changes would be fought out between owners of land and other resources; people owning little but their own labor would find their places in the pecking order little disturbed. Third, population growth may be an exception to the second result, inasmuch as the interests of pure labor owners are aligned with those of landowners against owners of the other resource; see Table B.8. In a society with serfdom and slavery, the definition of a labor owner must be expanded from a member of the landless peasantry to a landowner who also has a stake in the fate of income produced by labor, since such landowners control a good bit more labor than their own, personal efforts. Fourth, population carries with it the capacity for considerable social disruption by upsetting what may have been a long-standing distribution of societal income. These potential sources of economic and ensuing social change could be traced in an effort to gain insights to the determinants of the apparent renaissance of Crete during the Late Geometric and Orientalizing periods and its subsequent social and economic eclipse and somnolence in the Archaic and Classical periods.[25] These results are "speculative" only in the sense that we do not know exactly what the model "ought to be," in terms of structure and parameters. They are, in fact, the exact outcomes of a precise model; if it is believed that some features of the model should be explored in alternative specifications, those changes are possible, but whether the results would change much is another matter.

Finally, I must emphasize that the sequence of models I have developed here to study some characteristics of an economy that might be similar to that of Dark Age Crete is only a sampling of models that might be constructed to study issues about this economy. A model of trade in which variety of manufactured products is valued for itself could illuminate the workings of a

---

[24] Elsewhere I have examined the relative magnitudes of changes in burial wealth that would occur from various exogenous changes, and they can be small or large relative to the initiating causes: Jones forthcoming a and b.

[25] Cf. Morris's alternative interpretation (1992a: 118, 131–32, 136, 140–41), which ties Crete's rise and decline from roughly the tenth through the sixth century to its external commercial activities.

society reawakening after a period of material retrenchment and relative isolation.[26] The models I have developed here characterize an aggregate economy, although they are based on principles of individual behavior. This is not the only scale of interest. Models of household behavior and of the spatial structure of agricultural activity in a small region the size of, say, the Mesara or Lasithi could address issues that aggregate models must, by their nature, omit from consideration. In the latter type of problem, the Thünen model might prove more insightful than central-place theory, which has seriously weak theoretical underpinnings at critical points.[27] Household models could examine resource-allocation tendencies under various types of intra-unit decision-making and income-distribution systems, which would be of interest when it is believed that social structures may depart seriously from the model of the individual decision-maker.[28] As I noted above, the present examination can do little more than open a dialogue on the use of these techniques to assist archaeological inquiry.

---

[26] On the valuation of variety itself and the use of the concept in the study of trade, basic references are Dixit and Stiglitz 1977: 297–308; Lancaster 1979: chs. 2–3; and Helpman and Krugman 1985: chs. 6–9.

[27] On the Thünen model, see Samuelson 1983: 1468–88; and Jones 1991: 35–70. A major trade-off farmers face during a period of population expansion is longer trips to more distant fields versus limitations on intensification of production near home sites (either village or dispersed). Establishment of new settlements is a mechanism for resolving this problem. In "The Conundrum of Greek Population Growth in the 8th Century B.C." (Jones forthcoming b), I develop a Thünen-type model of this problem of agricultural expansion.

[28] For approaches to modeling the economic decisions of households with limited integration into markets, see Nakajima 1986; Bliss and Stern 1982; and Strauss 1986: 71–91.

Appendix C

THE CATALOGUES

The catalogues of artifacts produced overseas but found at Cretan sites (C.1-5) compile reports in the published literature, pruned to the extent possible by consideration of subsequent opinions. In these catalogues I cite the recommended provenance of each artifact, with reservations and alternatives noted, as well as the proposed dating, which is usually a range expressed in terms of ceramic period, though occasionally I give absolute dates. The source reporting the artifact is identified, as are subsequent endorsements and occasional reservations. The context in which the artifact was found is reported when that information is available. Thirty-eight different locations are represented, but the artifacts found at Knossos are divided into four sites or groups of sites: Fortetsa (C.1.1), the North Cemetery (C.1.2), the town (C.1.3), and a miscellaneous group (C.1.4).

Another catalogue (C.6) contains apparent Cretan artifacts found at sites outside Crete. Its structure is the same as that of the previous catalogues, with the addition of an entry noting any proposed provenance within Crete. Since compiling this catalogue involved canvassing a large number of excavation reports for sites outside Crete, it is likely to be less inclusive than the catalogues of foreign artifacts found in Crete.

All of these catalogues are unwieldy, so I have summarized provenance, date, and find site in a series of catalogue tables, which themselves are rather lengthy. **Table Cat. 1** summarizes the foreign artifacts in Crete by provenance and period. For example, the first column of that table identifies the Attic, or suspected Attic, artifacts found at each Cretan site and orders them by half-century periods. This switch from a combination of absolute and ceramic-period ranges of dates to what may appear to be a more exact chronological proposal requires explanation. The catalogue identification number of each artifact is accompanied by a range of absolute dates that corresponds to the range of dates described in the catalogue. I have converted ceramic periods to ranges of absolute dates, and I generally follow the Brock-Coldstream-Snodgrass absolute chronology.[1] However, the beginning of the Subminoan period is not dated as clearly as the later Cretan ceramic periods. Although it generally is agreed that it falls sometime in the eleventh century,[2] Brock's date of c. 1020 probably is too low.[3] Brock lowered Furumark's beginning of Subminoan from c.

---

[1] P. James (in James et al. 1991: 103–10) challenges the current absolute chronology of Greek ceramics, but the discussion this work has prompted has not yet produced clear directions for revision. Cf. Ray 1992: 213–14; Ward 1994: 362–63. On the important Stratum III at Tell Abu Hawam, see Balensi and Herrera 1985: 103–4; and Balensi 1985: 68–69.

[2] Betancourt 1985: 185.

[3] Brock 1957: 214–15. However, Mountjoy (1988: 26–27, table II) proposes lowering the beginning of Attic PG by thirty to fifty years, from c. 1050 to 1020/1000. Hankey (1988: 36–37) reviews how such a change could affect the interrelationships of chronologies for various regions in the eastern Mediterranean.

1075,[4] but offered little reasoning behind the change other than allowing half a century to each phase. His equation of Cretan EPG with Attic LPG at 970 yielded 1020 B.C. for the beginning of the Subminoan. Yet Brock's own reasoning regarding the slower development in the Cretan PG period[5] could be extended to the apparently even more conservative Subminoan period. Desborough subsequently placed the Cretan Type II bird vases in the Subminoan period and assigned an absolute dating to them of c. 1125–1050.[6] Desborough takes 1100 as the beginning of Subminoan, some twenty-five years after the transition to Submycenaean in Attica.[7] LM IIIC and Subminoan styles overlapped considerably during at least the first half of the eleventh century, and surely between 1100, the beginning

of my period of study, and 1075, LM IIIC probably would have been more common than Subminoan. I retain the round date for the period of study as an alternative to false chronological precision, but I have not included foreign objects found in late LM IIIC contexts unmixed with Subminoan artifacts.[8] Snodgrass recommends c. 925 as the transition from Subminoan to Cretan Protogeometric, compared with Brock's date of 970,[9] but I retain Brock's date. Coldstream's transition from Cretan MPG to LPG at c. 870 agrees with Brock's, but thereafter Coldstream's chronology produces later dates than does Brock's,[10] and I accept Coldstream's reasoning.[11] Coldstream's chronology ends with the terminal point of his period of study, around the juncture of the fourth and third quarters of the seventh century, while

---

[4] Furumark 1944: 262.

[5] Brock 1957: 213.

[6] Desborough 1972a: 61; 1972b.

[7] Desborough 1972a: 115.

[8] Manning and Weninger (1992: 654–55) find that the pattern of radiocarbon evidence as a whole around the Aegean supports the conventional LM IIIB–C chronology (c. 1350–1100/1060). They further infer that the conventional Egyptian chronology for this period also must be approximately correct.

[9] Snodgrass 1971: 131, 135. Snodgrass's dating leaves only thirty-five years for Early and Mature Geometric, according to Coldstream's and Brock's agreed dating of the transition from Mature Geometric to Late Geometric. That length of time seems short for the developments between Cretan EPG and LPG, and I retain Brock's transition at c. 970. I prefer a combination of a 130-year Subminoan and a longer developmental period for Cretan PG to a Subminoan of 175 years for central Crete and a 100-year Protogeometric period, which encroaches on Coldstream's detailed ceramic reasoning for transition dates between subsequent periods.

[10] Coldstream 1968: 330.

[11] Coldstream's divergence from Brock begins with a ten-year down-dating of the transition from Cretan LPG to PGB to put the end of Cretan LPG just inside the beginning of Attic MG I to accommodate an Attic MG I import found in a Cretan LPG context at Knossos (Coldstream 1968: 238–39). Coldstream and Brock assign the same number of years to PGB and Cretan EG, which in Brock's chronology ends c. 800 and in Coldstream's c. 790. Where Brock allowed thirty years to Cretan MG, Coldstream allows it forty-five years to get it into the first five years of Attic LG Ia to accommodate the slight acquaintance in later MG pithoi ornamentation at Knossos with the earliest Attic LG I styles (Coldstream 1968: 244). Coldstream's transition from Cretan MG to LG is twenty-five years later than Brock's. Both assign thirty-five years to Cretan LG, but Coldstream adds a ten-year transitional period between Late Geometric and Early Orientalizing. Brock allowed a long fifty-five years to the EO period, which he began with the appearance of freehand curvilinear ornament on the polychrome pithoi at Knossos. Coldstream points to the continued architectural discipline of the geometric ornament in the earlier of these vases and develops a separate category to accommodate the period of overlap when curvilinear ornament had not completely ousted the rectilinear motifs of the Geometric period (ibid.: 246). Coldstream dates the end of Cretan LG with the stratified appearance in the Knossos Road Deposit of well-dated Corinthian material with local pottery of late LG–EO; he concludes that Cretan EO should not have begun later than the end of Early Protocorinthian, and he reserves a decade within EPC for the Cretan transitional stage (ibid.: 254). Coldstream's absolute chronology, based on the appearance of Attic MG II in historically dated Near Eastern deposits (ibid.: 304–13) and Corinthian LG and EPC material in western sites (ibid.: 322–27), has found acceptance and corroboration: Benson 1970: 303–5; Cook 1969: 15. After the divergence in the dating of the SM–PG transition, Snodgrass's absolute chronology corresponds progressively more closely with Coldstream's from the LPG–EG transition through the transition from LG to EO. More recently, however, contrary to concurrent cases for down-dating, Cross (1986: 125–26 n. 12) has suggested that progress in dating Near Eastern sites may require raising the date of the transition from Attic Protogeometric to Early Geometric by a half-century. On cross-dating with Corinthian absolute chronology, see most recently Amyx 1988: 428.

Brock's chronology continues through the end of the Late Orientalizing period at c. 630. I use Brock's dating for the end of the Late Orientalizing period, but using Coldstream's date of c. 700 for the beginning of the Early Orientalizing, Brock's date of c. 680 for the beginning of the Late Orientalizing is early. Assuming a roughly similar pace of development for the two periods, I divide the period 700–630 in half at c. 665 for the transition from Early to Late Orientalizing. From 630 through the remainder of the seventh century are the early years of the Archaic period.[12]

I have omitted circa from the dates in these tables simply for reasons of space in already crowded tables, but the term is implicit. An additional feature of my presentational device is that the range of possible dates for an artifact almost invariably extends beyond the half-century in which it appears. Thus the appearance of an item in a half-century block is interpreted as a terminus post quem. An empty period box does not imply a period with no foreign artifacts, although a series of empty, adjacent half-century boxes will suggest a relative scarcity of artifacts from the later part of the series. I can think of no other presentational scheme that will convey the chronological uncertainty inherent in the artifacts with less visual clutter and possible confusion.

A structurally analogous catalogue table (**Table Cat. 2**) corresponds to the catalogue of Cretan artifacts found overseas. A catalogue table (**Table Cat. 3**) disaggregates the all-Crete table summarizing the foreign artifacts found in Crete to a series of major sites and regions. Within this table, I develop separate listings for each of the four Knossos site groupings, one for Kommos, and one each for the remaining sites in northern and eastern Crete, central and southern Crete, and western Crete.

---

[12] Brock's chronology ends the Late Orientalizing period, c. 630. Schäfer (1992: xxii) calls the period from c. 710 to 680 Early Orientalizing and Proto-Daedalic, the period 680 to 620 Orientalizing and Daedalic, and 620 to 580 Archaic. On the other hand, Coldstream (1992: 87) extends Late Orientalizing to c. 600, and calls the sixth century Early Archaic. When I use the term "Archaic," I use the Brock/Schäfer periodization, with possibilities of overlap into the early sixth century noted.

C.1. Catalogue of Overseas Artifacts Found at Knossos and Kommos

C.1.1. Overseas Artifacts Found At Knossos–Fortetsa

FROM	ITEM	DATE	SOURCE	FIND SITE/ CIRCUMSTANCES
1. Hittite region	lead lion w/ heart-shaped ears	EPG	Brock 1957: 22, 197, no. 201, pl. 13	Tomb XI, under bell krater no. 166
2. Egypt	faience ring	EPG, unlikely to be earlier than 20th or 21st Dynasty (1192–1075 or 1075–940)	Brock 1957: 15, 208, no. 106, pl. 173; Payne 1933a: 288–90; Skon-Jedele 1994: 1866, no. 2914	Tomb VI
3 Egypt (?)	5 spherical carnelian beads	EPG	Brock 1957: 22, 208, no. 194b	Tomb XI
4. Cyprus	iron spits	Cretan EPG	Brock 1957: 22, 202, no. 203; Karageorghis 1974; Boardman 1980: 37	Tomb XI; previously believed to be spears
5. Near East	ivory pendant in form of bull's head	EPG	Brock 1957: 22, 209, no. 199, pl. 13	Tomb XI
6. Near East	frag. of ivory pin head (?)	EPG	Brock 1957: 27, 209, no. 204, pl. 13	Tomb XI
7. Near East/ Cyprus/Egypt	necklace; over 50 small, flat beads of blue paste	EPG	Brock 1957: 22, 208, no. 194a; Skon-Jedele 1994: 1825–26, 1832, 1867, no. 2917	Tomb XI
8. Near East/ Cyprus/Egypt	large collection of tiny, flat, white paste beads	EPG	Brock 1957: 14, 208, no. 102; Skon-Jedele 1994: 1825–26, 1832, 1869, no. 2919	Tomb VI
9. Near East/ Cyprus/Egypt	faience bead frag.	EPG	Brock 1957: 15, 208, no. 107; Skon-Jedele 1994: 1832, 1870, no. 2929	Tomb VI
10. Cyclades, perhaps Naxos	amphora	"Attic PG and G type" (EPG context)	Brock 1957: 20, 189, no. 154, pl. 13; Snodgrass 1971: 125 n. 21	Tomb XI, found in EPG context
11. Cyclades, probably Melos	amphora	"Attic PG and G type" (EPG context)	Brock 1957: 32, 189, no. 269, pl. 19; Coldstream 1968: 165; Coldstream 1987a: 338 n. 18	Tomb L, found in LPG context
12. Cyclades (?)	amphora	"Attic PG and G type" (EPG context)	Brock 1957: 34, 189, no. 311, pl. 143	Tomb L, found in LPG context
13. Cyclades (?)	amphora	"Attic PG and G type"	Brock 1957: 59, 189, no. 629	Tomb VIII, uncertain context
14. Cyclades (?)	oinochoe	"Attic PG and G type" (EPG? context)	Brock 1957: 126, 190, no. 1446, pl. 109	Tomb P, found in PGB? context

C.1.1. Overseas Artifacts Found At Knossos–Fortetsa *continued*

FROM	ITEM	DATE	SOURCE	FIND SITE/ CIRCUMSTANCES
15. Cyclades (?)	oinochoe	"Attic PG and G type" (EPG? context)	Brock 1957: 130, 190, no. 1506, pl. 109	Tomb P, found in PGB? context
16. Attica (?)	skyphos on foot	Attic PG	Brock 1957: 13, 189, no. 58, pl. 7	Tomb VI, found in EPG context
17. Attica (?)	skyphos on foot	Attic PG	Brock 1957: 21, 189, no. 187, pl. 12	Tomb XI, found in EPG context
18. Attica (?)	lekythos	Attic PG	Brock 1957: 14, 189, no. 76, pl. 7	Tomb VI, found in EPG context
19. Cyprus (?)	bronze tripod stand	probably 2nd half 10th C.; not later than 1st half 9th C.	Brock 1957: 22, no. 188, pls. 13, 138; Payne 1933a: 167; Gjerstad 1948: 403; Catling 1964: 198, no. 19; Matthäus 1985: 305, 308, no. e, pl. 134.1; Matthäus 1987: 115, no. 23	Tomb XI (= Tomb E from Payne 1933a); if not Cypriot, closely related to examples found in Cyprus; Gjerstad (1948) considered it Cypriot
20. Attica (?)	4 bronze pins	Cretan PG	Brock 1957: 28, 195, nos. 250–251, pl. 18; Müller-Karpe 1962: 77, 77 n. 55	Tomb III; 2 each found in 2 PG pithoi
21. Egypt/ Phoenicia	frag. of faience figurine of Sekhmet (?)	PG	Brock 1957: 30, 208, no. 264, pl. 21; Coldstream 1977: 49 n. 61; Skon-Jedele 1994: 1827–28, 1832, 1859–60, no. 2899	Tomb IX, mixed grave context
22. Cyclades (?)	pedestal krater	"Attic PG and G type" (LPG? context)	Brock 1957: 128, 190, no. 1481, pl. 109; Hood and Boardman 1961: 77 n. 13	Tomb P, found in LPG? context
23. Cyclades	amphora	found in LPG–PGB context	Brock 1957: 129, 190, no. 1492, pl. 109	Tomb P, found in LPG–PGB? context
24. Corinth	aryballos	Corinthian G	Brock 1957: 63, 190, no. 668, pl. 45; Coldstream 1968: 244; Neeft 1987: no. 1002	Tomb TFT, found in MG context
25. Cyprus	gold diadem	mid-9th C., LPG	Brock 1957: 34, 197, no. 336, pl. 21; Coldstream 1977: 49 n. 61; Coldstream 1982: 267	Tomb L
26. Near East	faience bead or pin head, top side petals, underside flat	LPG	Brock 1957: 97, 208, no. 1113; Skon-Jedele 1994: 1827, 1870, no. 2928	Pithos X, Tomb II
27. Near East	cylindrical glass bead, decorated w/ wavy line	LPG	Brock 1957: 97, 208, no. 1117	Pithos X, Tomb II

C.1.1. Overseas Artifacts Found At Knossos–Fortetsa *continued*

FROM	ITEM	DATE	SOURCE	FIND SITE/ CIRCUMSTANCES
28. Luristan (possibly western Iran, Caucasus)	bronze pendant of naked female figure, Luristan type	mid-9th to mid-8th C.	Payne 1933a: 295, fig. 19; Brock 1957: 136, 197, 199, no. 1570, pl. 114; Herrmann 1968: 26, fig. 20; Muscarella 1977: 33 n. 4, 49, fig. 1; Moorey 1971: 26 nn. 4–6; Böhm 1990: 68–69, B15–I, pl. 20f	Tomb P; found between LPG bell krater and LG pithos; cf. Godard 1931: 67–68, pls. 31.111–114, 32.115–118, 36.153
29. Attica/ Boeotia (?)	bronze fibula, Sapouna-Sakellarakis Type IXa	mid-9th to mid-8th C.	Brock 1957: 97, 196, no. 1114, pl. 167; Ruckert 1976: 13 n. 33; Sapouna-Sakellarakis 1978: 106, no. 1481, pl. 42	Tomb II, "context doubtful"
30. Attica/ Boeotia (?)	bronze fibula, Sapouna-Sakellarakis Type IXa	mid-9th to mid-8th C.	Brock 1957: 97, 196, no. 1115, pl. 167; Sapouna-Sakellarakis 1978: 106, no. 1483, pl. 42	Tomb II, "context doubtful"
31. Cyclades (?)	4 black skyphoi	"Attic PG and G type" (PGB context)	Brock 1957: 38, 190, nos. 364–67, pl. 24	Tomb OD, found in PGB context
32. Cyclades (?)	black skyphos	"Attic PG and G type" (PGB? context)	Brock 1957: 48, 190, no. 462; Coldstream 1968: 167, 169	Tomb X, found in PGB? context
33. Cyclades (?)	black skyphos	"Attic PG and G type" (PGB? context)	Brock 1957: 49, 190, no. 478, pl. 35	Tomb X, found in PGB? context
34. Cyclades (?)	meander skyphos	"Attic PG and G type" (PGB? context)	Brock 1957: 50, 190, no. 494, pl. 35	Tomb X, found in PGB? context; perhaps Cretan
35. Cyclades (?)	black cup	"Attic PG and G type" (PGB? context)	Brock 1957: 48, 190, no. 467, pl. 35	Tomb X, found in PGB? context
36. Cyclades (?)	2-handled pithos	Attic MG I	Brock 1957: 47, 190, no. 454, pl. 31; Coldstream 1987a: 338 n. 20	Tomb X, found in PGB–MG context
37. Attica	oinochoe	"Attic PG and G type" (MG context)	Brock 1957: 46, 190, no. 441, pl. 35; Coldstream 1968: 244 n. 12	Tomb X, found in MG context; Brock suggested Cyclades
38. Cyclades (?)	black skyphos	"Attic PG and G type" (MG context)	Brock 1957: 51, 190, no. 520	Tomb X, found in PGB? context
39. Cyclades (?)	pedestal krater, base only	"Attic PG and G type" (MG context)	Brock 1957: 50, 190, no. 490; Hood and Boardman 1961: 77 n. 13	Tomb X, found in MG context
40. Cyclades (?)	pedestal krater	"Attic PG and G type" (MG context)	Brock 1957: 63, 190, no. 671, pl. 44; Coldstream 1968: 167, 169	Tomb TFT, found in MG context

C.1.1. Overseas Artifacts Found At Knossos–Fortetsa *continued*

FROM	ITEM	DATE	SOURCE	FIND SITE/ CIRCUMSTANCES
41. Italy	bronze spectacle fibula	c. 800	Brock 1957: 54, no. 558, pl. 37; Coldstream 1977: 102, 103; Sapouna-Sakellarakis 1978: 111, no. 1532, pl. 47	Tomb X, in 4-handled bucchero pithos of Cretan MG shape; similar to Alexander Type Ib: 1965: 69, 9, ill. 2
42. Cyprus	aryballos	Cretan MG context	Brock 1957: 63, 190, no. 669, pl. 45	Tomb TFT
43. Cyprus	aryballos	Cretan MG context	Brock 1957: 64, 190, no. 694, pl. 45	Tomb TFT
44. Cyprus	aryballos, frags.	Cretan MG context	Brock 1957: 75, 190, no. 842	Tomb VII
45. Near East, probably Egypt	necklace of blue paste beads, c. 8500 disk beads, fine quality	MG	Brock 1957: 66, 208, no. 726, pl. 44; Skon-Jedele 1994: 1836–37, 1866–67, no. 2915+	Tomb TFT
46. Baltic	c. 70 small amber beads, rough cylinders or oblate spheroids	Cretan MG context	Brock 1957: 54, 209, no. 564	Tomb X
47. Phoenicia	bronze bowl	c. 800 to mid-7th C.	Payne 1933a: 240; Brock 1957: 133–34, 200, no. 1559, pl. 114; Falsone 1987; Falsone 1988: 236; Markoe 1985: 116, 162–63, no. C1	Tomb P; served as lid to LO pithos
48. Cyprus	B-o-R lekythos	1st half 8th C.	Brock 1957: 47, no. 453, pl. 34; Markoe 1985: 117; Coldstream 1968: 357	Tomb X
49. Cyprus	aryballos, frags.	Cretan MG–LG context	Brock 1957: 49–50, 190, no. 489	Tomb X
50. Naxos (?)	amphora	LG	Brock 1957: 62, no. 652; Kourou 1984: 111 n. 47; Bocci 1962: 10, no. 2	Tomb TFT. Brock undecided between Naxian export and Cretan imitation; Kourou calls it export
51. Naxos (?)	amphora	LG	Brock 1957: 63, no. 673; Kourou 1984: 111 n. 47; Bocci 1962: 10, no. 2	Tomb TFT. Brock undecided between Naxian export and Cretan imitation; Kourou calls it export
52. Naxos (?)	amphora	LG	Brock 1957: 63, no. 680; Kourou 1984: 111 n. 47; Bocci 1962: 10, no. 2	Tomb TFT. Brock undecided between Naxian export and Cretan imitation; Kourou calls it export
53. Naxos (?)	amphora	LG	Brock 1957: 63, no. 681; Kourou 1984: 111 n. 47; Bocci 1962: 10, no. 2	Tomb TFT. Brock undecided between Naxian export and Cretan imitation; Kourou calls it export

C.1.1. Overseas Artifacts Found At Knossos–Fortetsa *continued*

FROM	ITEM	DATE	SOURCE	FIND SITE/ CIRCUMSTANCES
54. N. Syria	lyre-player seal, "jasper"	c. 730–700	Brock 1957: 96, no. 1074, pl. 174; Buchner and Boardman 1966: 30, no. 74; Boardman 1990b: 10–11	Tomb II; found w/ burial no later than mid-7th C.
55. Cyprus	aryballos	Cretan LG? context	Brock 1957: 126–7, 190, no. 1448, pl. 109	Tomb P
56. Cyprus	2-handled aryballos	Cretan LG? context	Brock 1957: 122, 190, no. 1411, pl. 109	Tomb P
57. Cyprus	alabastron-aryballos	Cretan LG? context	Brock 1957: 127, 190, no. 1458, pl. 109	Tomb P
58. Cyprus	small trefoil jug, frags.	Cretan LG? context	Brock 1957: 45, 190, no. 425	Tomb X
59. Cyprus	pyxis, B-o-R II(iv)?	Cretan LG? context	Brock 1957: 127, 190, no. 1451, pl. 103	Tomb P
60. Corinth	aryballos	PC	Brock 1957: 102, 190, no. 1174, pl. 109; Neeft 1987: no. 1003	Tomb P, found in LO context
61. Corinth	2 aryballoi	PC	Brock 1957: 131, 190, no. 1516–17, pl. 109; Neeft 1987: nos. 1004–1005	Tomb P, found by villager
62. Corinth	aryballos frag.	PC	Brock 1957: 96, 190, no. 1065	Tomb II, dromos, found in LO? context
63. Corinth	kotyle	PC	Brock 1957: 91, 190, no. 970, pl. 74	Tomb II, found in LO context
64. Corinth	kotyle frag.	PC	Brock 1957: 90, 190, no. 959	Tomb II, found in LO context
65. Corinth	kotyle	PC	Brock 1957: 102, 190, no. 1181, pl. 109	Tomb P, found in LO context
66. Corinth	concave pyxis frag., silhouette style	PC	Brock 1957: 100, 190, no. 1065	Tomb II, dromos, found in LO? context
67. Corinth	aryballos, unusually large	PC, 2nd qtr 7th C. (?)	Payne 1931a: 59–60, no. 11, pl. I, upper left	in Ashmolean Museum 1926, 233, gift of A. J. Evans
68. Cyprus	alabastron-aryballos	Cretan EO? context	Brock 1957: 69, 190, no. 754, pl. 49	Tomb F
69. Cyprus	small trefoil jug	Cretan EO? context	Brock 1957: 79, 190, no. 876, pl. 58	Tomb P2
70. Cyprus (?)	miniature neck-amphora, white-on-red fabric	Cretan EO? context	Brock 1957: 121, 190, no. 1403, pl. 109	Tomb P

C.1.1. Overseas Artifacts Found At Knossos–Fortetsa *continued*

FROM	ITEM	DATE	SOURCE	FIND SITE/ CIRCUMSTANCES
71. Phoenicia	blue faience alabastron	Cretan EO context	Brock 1957: 83, 208, no. 923, pls. 59, 173; cf. Hill 1976: 421, fig. 2 for Rhodian proposal; Skon-Jedele 1994: 1838–39, 1870–71, no. 2930	Tomb P2
72. Phoenicia	upper part of blue faience figurine, badly worn	Cretan EO context	Brock 1957: 83, 208, no. 924, pls. 59, 173; Skon-Jedele 1994: 1838–39, 1859, no. 2897	Tomb P2, from same pithos as no. 923
73. Babylonia or Assyria (?)/ Italy	small glass jug	probably O	Brock 1957: 139, 207, no. 1650, pl. 76; Barag 1970: 167 no. 9, fig. 73, 194–95	unassigned; in box w/ Tomb II frags.
74. Asia, not Egypt	molded glass bowl, green	O (?)	Brock 1957: 134, 208, no. 1567, pl. 112; Fossing 1940: 36, fig. 23; Harden 1956: 321; von Saldern 1959: 31, no. 11; von Saldern 1970: 225, no. 43	Tomb P
75. Near East or East Greece	necklace of flat faience beads	O (?); could be as early as LPG	Brock 1957: 100, 208, no. 1166; Skon-Jedele 1994: 1842, 1868, no. 2920+	below stones in dromos of Tomb P
76. Egypt	blue faience figurine, flute player	O	Brock 1957: 100, 208, no. 1149, pl. 173; Skon-Jedele 1994: 1841–42, 1860, no. 2900	Tomb I
77. Egypt	2 bronze bowls w/ lotus-bud handles	O (possibly much earlier: LPG–LO)	Brock 1957: 136, 200–201, no. 1571, pl. 113; 1980: 249, pl. 243a–c; Skon-Jedele 1994: 1842–43, 1857, nos. 2892–2893	Tomb P
78. Attica/ Boeotia (?)	bronze fibula, Sapouna-Sakellarakis Type IXc	O	Brock 1957: 99, 196, no. 1147, pls. 76, 167; Sapouna-Sakellarakis 1978: 108, no. 1516, pl. 46	Tomb I
79. Cyprus	aryballos	apparent Cretan LO context	Brock 1957: 109, 190, no. 1262, pl. 109	Tomb P
80. Cyprus (?)	tall-necked aryballos, white-on-red fabric	Cretan LO context	Brock 1957: 108, 190, no. 1251, pl. 109	Tomb P
81. Egypt	2 scarabs, "faintly lustrous" white glaze; 1 inscribed w/ name of Amenhotep	O, probably 26th Dynasty (664–525 B.C.)	Brock 1957: 97, 208 n. 2, nos. 1076–77, pls. 75, 173; Skon-Jedele 1994: 1839–40, 1862, 1864–65 nos. 2904, 2908	Tomb II had LPG to LO burials; majority Orientalizing

C.1.1. Overseas Artifacts Found At Knossos–Fortetsa *continued*

FROM	ITEM	DATE	SOURCE	FIND SITE/ CIRCUMSTANCES
82. East Greece	biconical bead, no glaze remaining, decorated w/ cut-out triangles	O	Brock 1957: 100, 208, no. 1161, pl. 173; Skon-Jedele 1994: 1842, 1868–69, no. 2923	Tomb I (dromos of Tomb P)
83. East Greece	cylindrical bead, traces of blue glaze, incised zigzag decoration	O	Brock 1957: 100, 208, no. 1164, pl. 174; Skon-Jedele 1994: 1842, 1869, no. 2924	Tomb I
84. East Greece	2 cylindrical beads, traces of pale blue glaze, incised cross-hatching	O	Brock 1957: 100, 208, nos. 1162–63, pl. 173; Skon-Jedele 1994: 1842, 1869, nos. 2925–2926	Tomb I
85. East Greece	bead, possibly representing animal's head, glazed composition	O	Brock 1957: 100, 208, no. 1165, pl. 174; Skon-Jedele 1994: 1842, 1869–70, no. 2927	Tomb I
86. Rhodes	scarab, pale green glaze	LO	Brock 1957: 97, 208, no. 1078, pls. 75, 173; Skon-Jedele 1994: 1839–40, 1861–62, no. 2903	Tomb II
87. Rhodes	juglet, aqua glaze	LO	Brock 1957: 133, 208, no. 1557, pls. 112, 173; Webb 1978: 63, no. 214; Skon-Jedele 1994: 1840–41, 1871–72, no. 2931	Tomb P
88. Rhodes	juglet, traces of aqua glaze	LO	Brock 1957: 133, 208, no. 1558, pl. 112; Webb 1978: 63, no. 215; Skon-Jedele 1994: 1840–41, 1872, no. 2937	Tomb P
89. East Greece (?) or North Syria	cocoon-shaped alabastron	LO	Brock 1957: 132, 190, no. 1527, pl. 109; Peltenberg 1969: 81 n. 47; cf. Jacopi 1932–33: fig. 43	Tomb P, uncertain context

C.1.2. Overseas Artifacts Found at Knossos–North Cemetery

FROM	ITEM	DATE	SOURCE	FIND SITE/ CIRCUMSTANCES
1. Italy	pin head of Italian type	SM	Catling 1978–79: 46	Tomb 200
2. N. Syria/Levant	ivory comb	SM	Catling 1978–79: 46	Tomb 200
3. Levant/Egypt	beads of glass, frit, & faience	SM	Catling 1978–79: 46	Tomb 200
4. Cyprus	80 gold globular beads; set of gold finger rings; gold rosettes for dress ornament	SM	Catling 1978–79: 46, figs. 1, 11; Coldstream 1989: 90	Tomb 200, woman's burial
5. Cyprus?	frags. of open-work 4-sided stand	SM	Catling 1978–79: 46; Catling 1984: 86–87, fig. 15.1–3,5–6; Matthäus 1988: 290	Tomb 201; Matthäus considers it Cretan
6. Cyprus?	frags. of rod tripod	SM or PG?	Catling 1984: 87, pl. 15.1–3,5–6; Matthäus 1988: 290; Coldstream 1989: 90	Tomb 100 (disturbed); Matthäus considers it Cretan
7. Phoenicia	bronze bowl, incised w/ lettering	earlier than 1000	Catling 1976–77: 12–13, figs. 27, 28; Cross 1980: 17; Puech 1983: 374–89	Tekke Tomb J
8. Attica	several belly-handled amphorae	late 10th C.– early 8th C.	Coldstream 1991: 293	several tombs from North Cemetery
9. Attica	2 kalathoi	Attic LPG	Catling 1982–83: 52; Coldstream 1991: 293, fig. 7	Tomb 207, no. 42
10. Attica	small krater	Attic LPG	Catling 1982–83: 52	Tomb 207
11. Attica	large frags. of krater	Attic LPG	Catling 1983: 39	Tomb 207
12. Attica	skyphos	Attic LPG	Catling 1982–83: 52; Catling 1983: 39	Tomb 207
13. Attica	3 low-based cups	Attic LPG	Catling 1982–83: 52	Tomb 207
14. Attica	3 large skyphoi	Attic LPG	Catling, AR 1976–77: 13–14, figs. 29, 30; Coldstream 1994b: 110	Tekke Tomb J
15. Attica	oinochoe	Attic LPG	Catling 1976–77: 13–14, figs. 29, 30; Coldstream 1994b: 110	Tekke Tomb J

C.1.2. Overseas Artifacts Found at Knossos–North Cemetery *continued*

FROM	ITEM	DATE	SOURCE	FIND SITE/ CIRCUMSTANCES
16. Attica	shoulder-handled amphora	Attic LPG	Catling 1976–77: 13–14, figs. 29, 30; Coldstream 1994b: 110	Tekke Tomb J
17. Attica	22 cups	Attic LPG	Catling 1976–77: 13–14, figs. 29, 30; Coldstream 1994b: 110	Tekke Tomb J
18. Attica	more than 30 clay beads	Attic LPG	Catling 1976–77: 13–14, figs. 29, 30	Tekke Tomb J
19. Attica	kantharos	Attic LPG	Coldstream 1991: 291, fig. 2	Tomb 285, no. 121
20. Euboea (Lelantine Plain)	amphoriskos	Euboean LPG	Popham et al. 1983: 283, 288, pl. 33e right; Coldstream 1991: 291, fig. 3	Tomb 285, no. 124
21. Euboea (Lelantine Plain)	amphoriskos	Euboean LG	Popham et al. 1983: 283, 288	KAM Tomb 12,8
22. Corinth	pyxis and lid	Corinthian LPG	Coldstream 1991: 291–93, fig. 4	Tomb 285, nos. 134, 138
23. Thessaly	amphora	LPG	Coldstream 1991: 293, fig. 6	Tomb 30, no. 4
24. East Greece, possibly Miletus	krater	LPG/SubPG	Coldstream 1991: 293, fig. 5	Tomb 285, no. 89
25. Euboea	skyphos	Euboean SubPG III–end 9th C.-early 8th C.	Kearsley 1989: 40–41, 95, 97, no. 103, fig. 21a	Tekke Tomb G, vase no. 123; Kearsley's Type 4a
26. Euboea	skyphos	Euboean SubPG III–end 9th C.-early 8th C.	Kearsley 1989: 41, 95, 97, no. 104, fig. 21b	Tekke Tomb G, vase no. 124; Kearsley's Type 4a
27. Euboea	frags. of 4 skyphoi	Euboean SubPG III–end 9th C.-early 8th C.	Kearsley 1989: 41	Tekke Tomb G; Kearsley's Type 4a
28. Attica	belly-handled amphora	Attic EG I	Catling 1982–83: 51–52, fig. 90; Catling 1983: 39; Liddy 1988: 30, fig. 18; Coldstream 1991: 293 n. 30, fig. 8	Tomb 207, no. 52; subjected to AAS

C.1.2. Overseas Artifacts Found at Knossos–North Cemetery *continued*

FROM	ITEM	DATE	SOURCE	FIND SITE/ CIRCUMSTANCES
29. Athens	high-footed skyphos	Attic LPG & EG I--just before & after 900	Catling 1978–79: 47	Tomb 285
30. Athens	neck amphora	Attic LPG & EG I--just before & after 900	Catling 1978–79: 47	Tomb 285
31. Athens	pyxis	Attic LPG & EG I--just before & after 900	Catling 1978–79: 46–47	Tomb 285
32. Athens	oinochoe	Attic LPG & EG I--just before & after 900	Catling 1978–79: 46–47	Tomb 285
33. Cyclades (Melos?)	amphora	EG	Kontoleon 1945–47: 1; Coldstream 1980a: 408, pl. 191; Coldstream 1987a: 338 n. 18	Tekke Tomb Q, vase no. 63
34. Cyprus?	bronze tripod	PG	Catling 1982–83: 51; Matthäus 1988: 287	Tomb 201; Matthäus considers it Cretan
35. Levant	ivory hilts on 2 short swords	PG	Catling 1982–83: 51	Tomb 201
36. North Syria	ivory poppyhead pin	PG	Catling 1982–83: 51	Tomb 201
37. Levant/Egypt	necklace of faience beads	PG	Catling 1982–83: 51	Tomb 201
38. Phoenicia	red-slip trefoil-lipped jug	mid-9th C.	Coldstream 1984a: 123, 126, no. 4, fig. 1, pl. 23	Tomb 292
39. Phoenicia	bichrome round-mouth jug	later 9th C.	Coldstream 1984a: 123, no. 1, fig. 1, pl. 23	Tomb 107
40. Cyprus, possibly Phoenicia	juglet, B-o-R I	late 9th C.	Coldstream 1984a: 129, 131, no. 30, fig. 2, pl. 25	Tomb 292, in late 9th century pyxis; similar to juglet from Akhziv
41. Cyprus	juglet, B-o-R	late 9th C. (?)	Coldstream 1984a: 131, no. 35	Tomb 285
42. Attica	9 cups	Attic MG I	Coldstream 1994b: 118	Tekke Tomb G
43. Attica	large belly-handled amphora	Attic MG I	Coldstream 1987a: 337 n. 13	Tomb 104 (Platon's Tekke Tomb G), no. G3

C.1.2. Overseas Artifacts Found at Knossos–North Cemetery *continued*

FROM	ITEM	DATE	SOURCE	FIND SITE/ CIRCUMSTANCES
44. Attica	large belly-handled amphora	Attic MG I	Coldstream 1987a: 337 n. 13	Tomb 104 (Platon's Tekke Tomb G), no. G83
45. Attica	pedestalled krater	Attic MG	Catling 1983: 37	Tomb 75
46. Cyprus	juglet, B-o-R I	850–750	Coldstream 1984a: 129, no. 31, pl. 25	Tomb 219; similar to CG III examples from Amathus
47. Cyprus	juglet, B-o-R I	850–750	Coldstream 1984a: 129, no. 32	Tomb 134; similar to CG III examples from Amathus
48. Cyprus or Phoenicia	2-handled juglet, B-o-R I	850–750	Coldstream 1984a: 128, no. 16, fig. 1, pl. 24	Tomb 104; similar to examples from Akhziv
49. Cyprus or Phoenicia	2-handled juglet, B-o-R I	850–750	Coldstream 1984a: 128, no. 17	Tomb H; similar to examples from Akhziv
50. Attica	large neck amphora	Attic MG II– LG I	Catling 1983: 39; Coldstream 1983: 204, fig. 5; Coldstream 1994b: 116	Tomb 219
51. Attica	footless krater w/ bucranium handles & lid surmounted by miniature oinochoe	Attic MG–LG I	Catling 1983: 39; Coldstream 1983: 203–4, figs. 3–4	Tomb 219
52. Attica	large horse-lid pyxis	Attic MG–LG I	Catling 1983: 39; Coldstream 1983: 202, figs. 1–2	Tomb 219
53. Egypt	large faience figure of recumbent lion	contemporane ous w/ Attic MG–LG I	Catling 1983: 39; Skon-Jedele 1994: 1861, no. 2902	Tomb 219
54. Syria	fragmentary ivory figurine of 2 naked females (goddesses?) back to back	9th–8th C.; LG–EO context	Böhm 1990: 42–43, 158, no. E7-I, fig. 6, pl. 16d	Tomb 219
55. Phoenicia	round-mouth jug, red-slip	c. 800–early 8th C.	Coldstream 1984a: 123, no. 2, fig. 1, pl. 23; Liddy 1988: 30	Tomb 283; subjected to AAS
56. Cyprus	trefoil-lipped jug, B-o-R II	beginning of B-o-R II, early 8th C.	Coldstream 1984a: 128, no. 14, pl. 24	Tomb 107
57. Cyprus	amphoriskos, B-o-R II	beginning of B-o-R II, early 8th C.	Coldstream 1984a: 125, 127, no. 7, fig. 1, pl. 23	Tomb 219

C.1.2. Overseas Artifacts Found at Knossos–North Cemetery *continued*

FROM	ITEM	DATE	SOURCE	FIND SITE/ CIRCUMSTANCES
58. Cyprus	trefoil-lipped jug, B-o-R II	beginning of B-o-R II, early 8th C.	Coldstream 1984a: 127–28, no. 12, fig. 1, pl. 24	Tomb 292
59. Cyprus	trefoil-lipped jug, B-o-R II	beginning of B-o-R II, early 8th C.	Coldstream 1984a: 128, no. 13, pl. 24	Tomb 175
60. Cyprus	2-handled juglet, B-o-R II	early B-o-R II, early 8th C.	Coldstream 1984a: 128–29, no. 18, fig. 1, pl. 24	Tomb 292
61. Cyprus	2-handled juglet, B-o-R II	early B-o-R II, early 8th C.	Coldstream 1984a: 129, no. 19	Tomb 292
62. Cyprus	juglet, B-o-R II	early B-o-R II, early 8th C.	Coldstream 1984a: 129, 131, no. 20, fig. 2, pl. 25	Tomb 285
63. Cyprus	juglet, B-o-R II	early B-o-R II, early 8th C.	Coldstream 1984a: 129, 131, no. 21, fig. 2, pl. 25	Tomb 285
64. Cyprus	juglet, B-o-R II, frags.	early B-o-R II, early 8th C.	Coldstream 1984a: 129, 131, no. 22	Tomb 285
65. Cyprus	juglet, B-o-R II	early B-o-R II, early 8th C.	Coldstream 1984a: 129, no. 23, pl. 25	Tomb 285
66. Cyprus	juglet, B-o-R II	early B-o-R II, early 8th C.	Coldstream 1984a: 129, no. 24, pl. 25	Tomb 285
67. Cyprus	juglet, B-o-R II	early B-o-R II, early 8th C.	Coldstream 1984a: 129, no. 25, pl. 25	Tomb 292
68. Cyprus	juglet, B-o-R II	early B-o-R II, early 8th C.	Coldstream 1984a: 129, no. 26, fig. 2, pl. 25	Tomb 292
69. Cyprus	juglet, B-o-R II	early B-o-R II, early 8th C.	Coldstream 1984a: 129, no. 27, pl. 25	Tomb 292
70. Cyprus	juglet, B-o-R II	early B-o-R II, early 8th C.	Coldstream 1984a: 129, no. 28, fig. 2, pl. 25	Tomb 292
71. Cyprus	juglet, B-o-R II	early B-o-R II, early 8th C.	Coldstream 1984a: 129, no. 29, pl. 25	Tomb 292
72. Cyprus	juglet, B-o-R II	early B-o-R II, early 8th C.	Coldstream 1984a: 129, no. 33	Tomb 104
73. Cyprus	juglet, B-o-R II	early B-o-R II, early 8th C.	Coldstream 1984a: 131, no. 34	Tomb 219
74. Cyprus	juglet, B-o-R II	early B-o-R II, early 8th C.	Coldstream 1984a: 131, no. 36	Tomb 107
75. Cyprus	juglet, B-o-R II	early B-o-R II, early 8th C.	Coldstream 1984a: 131, no. 37	Tomb 292

C.1.2. Overseas Artifacts Found at Knossos–North Cemetery *continued*

FROM	ITEM	DATE	SOURCE	FIND SITE/ CIRCUMSTANCES
76. Phoenicia	juglet, red-slip	8th C.	Coldstream 1984a: 123, no. 3, pl. 23	Tomb 293
77. Cyprus	juglet, Bichrome III	8th C.–early 7th C.	Coldstream 1979: 261; Coldstream 1984a: 127, no. 8, pl. 24	Tekke Tomb A
78. Cyprus	juglet, Bichrome III	8th C.	Coldstream 1984a: 127, no. 9, pl. 24	Tomb 106
79. Corinth	oinochoe & frags. of another	Corinthian LG or EPC	Catling 1978–79: 53, fig. 34; Catling 1983: 40, fig. 35	Tomb 34, 56, or 57
80. Kos, possibly Miletus	trefoil-lipped jug, bichrome red	late 8th C.	Coldstream 1984a: 123, 126, no. 5, pl. 23	Tomb 219
81. Kos, possibly Miletus	trefoil-lipped jug, bichrome red	late 8th C.	Coldstream 1984a: 123, 126, no. 6, pl. 23	Tomb 219
82. Cyprus	4 or 5 vases	Cypriot Archaic	Catling 1978–79: 55	Tomb 34, 56, or 57
83. East Greece	Bird bowl frag.	7th C.	Catling 1978–79: 52–55, figs. 36–38; Catling 1983: 40	Tomb 34, 56, or 57
84. East Greece	2 Wild Goat vases • large oinochoe • very large dinos	c. 630	Catling 1978–79: 52–55, fig. 35; Catling 1983: 40; Liddy 1988: 30	Tomb 34, 56, or 57; subjected to AAS
85. East Greece	jug w/ browsing stags	7th C.	Catling 1978–79: 52–55, fig. 39; Catling 1983: 40	Tomb 34, 56, or 57
86. Northwest	amber beads	O	Catling 1978–79: 50	Tomb 112
87. Chios	remains of phiale	7th C.	Catling 1978–79: 52–53	Tomb 34 or 56
88. Corinth	2 olpai	PC to Transitional	Catling 1978–79: 53, fig. 34; Catling 1983: 40, fig. 35	Tomb 34, 56, or 57

C.1.2. Overseas Artifacts Found at Knossos–North Cemetery *continued*

FROM	ITEM	DATE	SOURCE	FIND SITE/ CIRCUMSTANCES
89. East (Egypt?)	3 faience objects: • Ptah-shaped pendant or amulet • figure of Bes • figure of male wearing lofty crown	O	Catling 1978–79: 50; Catling 1983: 36; Leclant 1982: 120; Skon-Jedele 1994: 1858, nos. 2895–2896, 2898	Tomb 112
90. Levant/Egypt	beads, glazed composition, large quantity	O	Catling 1978–79: 50; Catling 1983: 36; Skon-Jedele 1994: 1868, no. 2922+	Tomb 112
91. Levant/Egypt	4 tiny frit scarabs	O	Catling 1978–79: 50; Catling 1983: 36; Leclant 1982: 120; Skon-Jedele 1994: 1865–66, nos. 2910–2913	Tomb 112
92. East	glass beads	O	Catling 1978–79: 50	Tomb 112

C.1.3. Overseas Artifacts Found at Knossos–The Town

FROM	ITEM	DATE	SOURCE	FIND SITE/ CIRCUMSTANCES
1. Attica	oinochoe	Attic PG, c. 1050–980	Coldstream 1972: 75, A30	excavations s of Royal Road
2. Euboea	amphora shoulder	Euboean PG	Coldstream 1972: 76	from poorly stratified deposit; recalls PG and SubPG from Lefkandi
3. Attica	2 frags. of a krater	Attic LPG, 2nd half 10th C.	Coldstream 1972: 75	Deposit B, Royal Road
4. Argos	skyphos	Argive EG	Coldstream 1972: 76	
5. Attica	tripod stand	Attic EG II	Coldstream 1972: 75	Deposit B, Royal Road
6. Cyclades (probably Melos)	small mug, rim and base	Cycladic MG	Coldstream 1972: 77	
7. Cyclades (probably Melos)	skyphos, rim and body	Cycladic MG	Coldstream 1972: 77	
8. Cyclades (probably Melos)	cup, rim to base	Cycladic MG	Coldstream 1972: 77	
9. Corinth	small pedestalled krater, foot	Corinthian MG	Coldstream 1972: 77	
10. Attica	krater frag.	Attic MG, c. 800–775	Coldstream 1972: 77	included in mud-brick wall
11. Attica (?)	vase	Attic MG	Coldstream 1972: 77	possible excellent local imitation
12. Corinth	skyphos	end of Corinthian MG or LG	Coldstream 1972: 77	
13. Corinth	kotyle rim	early Corinthian LG	Coldstream 1972: 77	
14. Corinth	kotyle	Corinthian LG	Coldstream 1972: 77	
15. Attica	1 vase frag.	mid- to 3rd qtr. 8th C.	Coldstream 1972: 77	Deposits D–F
16. Thera	large amphora neck	Theran LG or SubG, late 8th or early 7th C.	Coldstream 1972: 77	
17. Thera	large amphora neck	Theran LG or SubG	Coldstream 1972: 77	
18. Corinth	several vase frags.	Corinthian LG, late 8th C.	Coldstream 1972: 77	from road trials of 1960
19. Corinth	kotyle rim	end 8th C.	Coldstream 1973a: 41, K.21	from Well LA
20. Corinth	kotyle	end 8th C. or early 7th C.	Coldstream 1973a: 41, J.36	from Well LA
21. Corinth	kotyle	c. 700–650	Coldstream 1973a: 41, H.67	from Well H

C.1.3. Overseas Artifacts Found at Knossos–The Town *continued*

FROM	ITEM	DATE	SOURCE	FIND SITE/ CIRCUMSTANCES
22. Rhodes	krater rim	Rhodian LG, early 7th C.	Coldstream 1973a: 45, K.15	from poorly stratified deposit
23. Thera	large amphora shoulder	Theran SubG, mid-7th C.	Coldstream 1972: 77	
24. Corinth	kotyle rim, 2nd Black Figure style	MPC, c. 660–650	Coldstream 1973a: 41, K.22	from Well LA
25. Corinth	kotyle	mid-7th C.	Coldstream 1973a: 41, H.71	from Well H
26. Corinth	oinochoe or olpe	c. 650–620	Coldstream 1973a: 41, H.64	from Well H
27. Corinth	kotyle	2nd half 7th C.	Coldstream 1973a: 41, H.69	from Well H
28. Corinth	kotyle	2nd half 7th C.	Coldstream 1973a: 41, H.70	from Well H
29. Corinth	painted aryballos	c. 630–610	Coldstream 1973a: 41, H.61	from Well H
30. Corinth	oinochoe	late 7th C.	Coldstream 1973a: 41, H.65	from Well H
31. Corinth	powder pyxis	EC, late 7th C.	Coldstream 1973a: 41, H.66	from Well H
32. Corinth	kotyle	late 7th C.	Coldstream 1973a: 41, H.68	from Well H

C.1.4. Overseas Artifacts Found at Other Knossos Locations

FROM	ITEM	DATE	SOURCE	FIND SITE/ CIRCUMSTANCES
1. Argos	3 dress pins	SM	Hood et al. 1958–59: 257, fig. 34 VII 13 and 14; Desborough 1972b: 308	Gypsades tomb VII
2. Cyprus	pin w/ conical ivory head	SM	Hood and Coldstream 1968: 212–13, 214–18, fig. 4,B5; Hood 1973: 44–45, pl. 8.4; Desborough 1973: 82	tomb at Ayios Ioannis; reused LM II chamber tomb
3. E. Mediterranean	iron knife	1100–900 B.C.	Hood et al. 1958–59: 225, fig. 32, VII 12; Desborough 1972b: 308; Desborough 1973: 81–82	Gypsades tomb VII
4. Attica	skyphos, rim, wall and handle frags.	Attic EPG	Coldstream and Macdonald 1997: 204, no. A31, pl. 34f	reoccupied LM II house, west of SW House, Trench S VII 8, Deposit A
5. Attica	skyphos (?), lower body frag.	Attic EPG	Coldstream and Macdonald 1997: 204, no. A32, pl. 34f	reoccupied LM II house, west of SW House, Trench S VII 8, Deposit A
6. Attica	shoulder-handled amphora (?), rim frag.	Attic EPG	Coldstream and Macdonald 1997: 208, no. B42, fig. 8, pl. 36b	reoccupied LM II house, west of SW House, Trench S VII 8, Deposit B
7. Attica	krater, wall frag.	Attic EPG	Coldstream and Macdonald 1997: 208, no. B43, pl. 36b	reoccupied LM II house, west of SW House, Trench S VII 8, Deposit B
8. Attica	skyphos, wall frag.	Attic EPG	Coldstream and Macdonald 1997: 208, no. B44, pl. 36b	reoccupied LM II house, west of SW House, Trench S VII 8, Deposit B
9. Attica	skyphos, wall frag.	Attic EPG	Coldstream and Macdonald 1997: 208, no. B45, pl. 36b	reoccupied LM II house, west of SW House, Trench S VII 8, Deposit B
10. Attica	skyphos, wall frag.	Attic EPG	Coldstream and Macdonald 1997: 208, no. B46, pl. 36b	reoccupied LM II house, west of SW House, Trench S VII 8, Deposit B
11. Attica	skyphos, wall frag.	Attic EPG	Coldstream and Macdonald 1997: 208, no. B47, pl. 36b	reoccupied LM II house, west of SW House, Trench S VII 8, Deposit B
12. Attica	skyphos, rim frag.	Attic EPG	Coldstream and Macdonald 1997: 208, no. C20, pl. 36f	reoccupied LM II house, west of SW House, Trench S VII 3, Deposit C
13. Attica	globular pyxis frag.	Attic PG	Coldstream 1963: 34, 37, no. 17	Tekke Tomb II
14. Attica	2 skyphoi	Attic PG	Desborough 1952: 82, pl. 33	Tombs VI and VII

C.1.4. Overseas Artifacts Found at Other Knossos Locations *continued*

FROM	ITEM	DATE	SOURCE	FIND SITE/ CIRCUMSTANCES
15. Euboea	neck-handled amphora, neck to belly frag.	Euboean EPG	Coldstream and Macdonald 1997: 208, no. B41, pl. 36b	reoccupied LM II house, west of SW House, Trench S VII 8, Deposit B
16. Euboea	amphora (?), base frag.	Euboean EPG	Coldstream and Macdonald 1997: 208, no. C21, fig. 8, pl. 36f	reoccupied LM II house, west of SW House, Trench S VII 3, Deposit C
17. Egypt	faience beads	PG	Boardman 1960: 138, 148, no. 37; Skon-Jedele 1994: 1826, 1867, no. 2918+	Agios Ioannis Tomb V
18. Egypt	"hundreds" of flat, circular, blue paste beads	PG	Hogarth 1899–1900: 84; Boardman 1960: 148 n. 20; Skon-Jedele 1994: 1867, no. 2916+	Kephala Ridge, Hogarth's Tomb 6
19. Near East (Afghanistan)	round bead, lapis lazuli	PG	Hogarth 1899–1900: 84	Kephala Ridge, Hogarth's Tomb 6
20. Cyprus	pithos, possibly an unguent container	EPG–LG	Coldstream 1984	
21. Levant	scarab, pale blue paste, inscribed AMUN	PG to O	Coldstream 1963: 43, no. 4, fig. 15, pl. 14c; Skon-Jedele 1994: 1863, no. 2905	Tomb V (disturbed), Kephala Ridge (great mass of material is EO)
22. Euboea or Cyclades	skyphos w/ pendant semi-circles	PG	Payne 1927–28: 261, no. 147, pl. 6.12; Desborough 1952: 185–86; Hood and Boardman 1961: 77 n. 9; Coldstream 1968: 237 n. 2; Kearsley 1989: 40, 86, no. 102	Zapher Papoura tomb; from Evans's excavation of 1907
23. Euboea or Cyclades	stemmed krater w/ pendant semicircles	PG	Payne 1927–28: 247, no. 63, pl. 6.8; Coldstream 1968: 237 n. 2	Zapher Papoura; from 1927 excavation
24. Attica	skyphos	Attic LPG	Coldstream 1992: 69, GB no. 43, pl. 61.43	Room 3 of Unexplored Mansion, Deposit GB
25. Attica (?)	skyphos, rim frag.	Attic LPG	Coldstream 1992: 69, GB no. 44, pl. 61.44	Room 3 of Unexplored Mansion, Deposit GB; misfired
26. Attica	high-footed cup, rim frag.	Attic LPG	Coldstream and Macdonald 1997: 233, no. Z7, pl. 48b	unstratified
27. Euboea	amphora, shoulder frag.	Euboean LPG	Coldstream and Macdonald 1997: 220, no. X13, pl. 47d	Evans's 1930 sounding below West Court, Test Pit 3: w of W. Court, area s of Ramp

C.1.4. Overseas Artifacts Found at Other Knossos Locations *continued*

FROM	ITEM	DATE	SOURCE	FIND SITE/ CIRCUMSTANCES
28. Attica	skyphos frag.	late 10th C.	Coldstream 1992: 70, no. 6, pl. 25d.6	Unexplored Mansion, from a strip along edge of Little Palace
29. East Greece	amphora shoulder frag.	PG or EG	Coldstream 1992: 76, pl. 68	Unexplored Mansion, room/trench IV NS
30. Cyprus	small bronze rod tripod	LPG–EG (c. 800)	Hogarth 1899–1900: 83; Benton 1934–35: 125; Lamb 1929: 33; Brock 1957: 22; Gjerstad 1948: 403; Catling 1964: 198, no. 18; Matthäus 1985: 305, 308, no. f, pl. 134.2; Matthäus 1987: 115, no. 24	Tomb III; Gjerstad considered it Cretan
31. Euboea	skyphos rim sherd	PG	Hartley 1930–31: 80, 92, fig. 20.22; Kearsley 1989: 40	K03 Little Palace
32. Attica	krater wall frag.	Attic LPG or EG	Coldstream 1992: 76, GH no. 16, pl. 68	Unexplored Mansion, room/trench III E12
33. Attica	krater wall frag.	Attic LPG–EG I	Coldstream 1992: 69, GB no. 41, pl. 61.41	Room 3 of Unexplored Mansion, Deposit GB; identified by atomic absorption
34. Attica	several ceramic pieces	9th C.--Attic LPG–MG I	Sackett 1972–73: 63	near Unexplored Mansion
35. Attica	oinochoe shoulder frag.	Attic MG I	Coldstream 1992: 70, GC no. 15, pl. 62.15	nw corner of Unexplored Mansion, Deposit GC
36. Euboea	amphora body frag.	Euboean SPG	Coldstream 1992: GB no. 41, pl. 61.41	Room 3 of Unexplored Mansion; identified by atomic absorption
37. Attica	oinochoe strap handle	Attic EG II–MG I	Coldstream 1992: 69, GB no. 40, pl. 61.40	Room 3 of Unexplored Mansion
38. Attica	2 bowl sherds	Attic G	Hartley 1930–31: 88–89	K03 west of theatral area
39. Cyclades	skyphos	no earlier than Attic MG and probably not later than last of the 9th C.	Coldstream 1960: 161, no. 20, fig. 4; Coldstream 1968: 167, 169	Geometric well at Knossos, lower deposit; recalls beginning of Attic Geometric
40. Sardinia	askos	PGB–EO	Vagnetti 1989: 354–60; Ferrarese Ceruti 1991: 587–91, figs. 1–3; Ridgway 1992: 148	Tholos tomb 2, Khaniale Tekke ("goldsmith's tomb"), no. 111

C.1.4. Overseas Artifacts Found at Other Knossos Locations *continued*

FROM	ITEM	DATE	SOURCE	FIND SITE/ CIRCUMSTANCES
41. Near East	faience frags.	PGB–EO	Hutchinson and Boardman 1954: 216; Skon-Jedele 1994: 1873, no. 2937+	Khaniale Tekke, Tomb II (goldsmith's tomb), chamber
42. Near East	ivory crescent, possibly an inlay	c. 800	Dunbabin 1944: pl. 8, top; Hutchinson and Boardman 1954: 217, 226, no. 6; Boardman 1967: 69, no. 6	Khaniale Tekke Tomb II, from vase 57
43. Near East or Egypt	2 scarabs: • brown paste w/ hieroglyphic design • white paste w/ stylized beetle design	c. 800	Hutchinson and Boardman 1954: nos. 22, 23, figs. 3–4, 218–19, pl. 29,22–23; Boardman 1967: 64; Skon-Jedele 1994: 1834, 1863–65, nos. 2906, 2909	Tholos tomb II , Khaniale Tekke, in vase no. 104
44. Italy	amber inlay on penannular gold pendant	c. 800	Hutchinson and Boardman 1954: 217; Boardman 1967: 64, 68, no. 1	Tholos tomb 2, Khaniale Tekke, vase 57
45. Phoenicia?	silver dump, 7.25 grams; possibly half of silver Phoenician shekel (Sela system)	c. 800	Hutchinson and Boardman 1954: 219; Boardman 1967: 61–62, 69, no. 28; Skinner 1967: 38	Tholos tomb 2, Khaniale Tekke, vase 104; Hutchinson attributed quasi-monetary status under belief of mid-7th C. date
46. Egypt?	3 gold dumps: 19.00 (18.99), 18.95, and 18.10 grams (Egyptian Qedet system; 2-Qedet dumps?)	c. 800	Hutchinson and Boardman 1954: 219; Boardman 1967: 61–62, 69, nos. 11, 12, 27; Balmuth 1971: 4 n. 19, 5, pl. 1c; Skinner 1967: 38	Tholos tomb 2, Khaniale Tekke, vases 57 and 104; Hutchinson attributed quasi-monetary status under belief of mid-7th C. date
47. Euboea or Babylonia?	2 rectangular gold nuggets: 16.90 and 16.65 grams; agree w/ Euboean stater and gold Babylonian shekel standard (Daric system; 2-shekel dumps?)	c. 800	Hutchinson and Boardman, 1954: 219; Boardman 1967: 61–62, 69, nos. 10, 25; Skinner 1967: 38	Tholos tomb 2, Khaniale Tekke, vases 57 and 104; Hutchinson attributed quasi-monetary status under belief of mid-7th C. date
48. Egypt	2 scarabs	G	Helck 1979: 208, 321 n. 283; Herakleion Museum, case 153, nos. 1664–65	from Geometric graves

C.1.4. Overseas Artifacts Found at Other Knossos Locations *continued*

FROM	ITEM	DATE	SOURCE	FIND SITE/ CIRCUMSTANCES
49. Cyprus	• 6 clay toilet bottles • 2 lekythoi • small amphora • stamnos • jug w/ trefoil mouth w/o neck • flat spheroidal flask	G	Levi 1945a: 17 n. 37	from recently (in 1945) excavated tombs near Fortetsa, Tomb I. Possibly 2 little-described tombs noted by Woodward 1927: 245
50. Cyprus	2 toilet bottles	G	Levi 1945a: 17 n. 37	from recently (in 1945) excavated tombs near Fortetsa, Tomb II. Possibly two little-described tombs noted by Woodward 1927: 245
51. East	circular beads in blue paste, hundreds	G	Hogarth 1899–1900: 84	Kephala Ridge, Hogarth's Tomb 6
52. Attica	skyphos	Attic MG I	Coldstream 1992: 69, GB no. 45, pls. 51, 61.45	Room 3 of Unexplored Mansion, Deposit GB
53. Attica	krater rim	Attic MG II	Coldstream 1973: 21, no. 32	Sanctuary of Demeter, Stratified Votive Deposit A
54. Attica	amphora wall	Attic MG II	Coldstream 1973: 21, no. 33	Sanctuary of Demeter, Stratified Votive Deposit A
55. Attica	krater rim frag.	Attic MG II	Coldstream 1992: 72, no. 38, pl. 64	Pit 27, on hillside above Unexplored Mansion
56. Attica	skyphos rim frag.	Attic MG II	Coldstream 1992: 77, no. 59, pl. 71	Unexplored Mansion, Pit 51
57. Attica	krater wall frag.	Attic MG II	Coldstream 1992: 77, no. 60, pl. 71	Unexplored Mansion, room/trench VII 28
58. Attica	kantharos	Attic MG II	Coldstream 1992: 77, no. 66, pl. 71	Unexplored Mansion, room/trench XI 34; identified by atomic absorption
59. Attica	belly-handled amphora, body frag.	Attic MG II	Hartley 1930–31: 96, fig. 27.3; Coldstream and Macdonald 1997: 230, no. X14, pl. 47d	Evans's 1930 sounding below West Court, Test Pit 3: w of W. Court, area s of Ramp
60. Attica	belly-handled amphora, body frag.	Attic MG II	Coldstream and Macdonald 1997: 230, no. X15, pl. 47d	Evans's 1930 sounding below West Court, Test Pit 4: w of W. Court, area s of Ramp

C.1.4. Overseas Artifacts Found at Other Knossos Locations *continued*

FROM	ITEM	DATE	SOURCE	FIND SITE/ CIRCUMSTANCES
61. Attica	krater, rim frag.	Attic MG II	Coldstream and Macdonald 1997: 230–32, no. X16, fig. 20, pl. 47d	Evans's 1930 sounding below West Court, Test Pit 3: w of W. Court, area s of Ramp
62. Attica	krater, rim frag.	Attic MG II	Hartley 1930–31: 94, fig. 24.6; Coldstream and Macdonald 1997: 232, no. X17, fig. 20, pl. 47d	Evans's 1930 sounding below West Court, Test Pit 3: w of W. Court, area s of Ramp
63. Attica	skyphos rim	Attic MG	Coldstream 1973: 52	Sanctuary of Demeter, not from stratified deposit
64. Attica	amphora wall frag.	Attic MG	Coldstream 1992: 77, no. 65, pl. 71	Unexplored Mansion, room/trench XII 1; identified by atomic absorption
65. Attica	belly-handled amphora wall frag.	Attic MG	Coldstream 1992: 72, no. 39, pl. 64	Unexplored Mansion, Pit 27
66. Attica	krater, frag. of high foot	Attic MG	Coldstream 1992: 82, no. 9	Unexplored Mansion, from domestic context
67. Mainland?	krater rim frag.	MG	Coldstream 1992: 71, no. 8	Pit 27 (rubbish pit), on hillside above Unexplored Mansion; "possibly imported"--a few particles of silver mica
68. Levant— not Egypt	Egyptianizing blue paste scarab	MG (790–745)	British School 1975: 343; Coldstream et al. 1981: 143, 157, 162, no. 122, fig. 8; Skon-Jedele 1994: 1836, 1864, no. 2907	bulldozed tomb on lower Gypsadhes Hill-- Ephraimoglou Plot; found in urn 62; closed context
69. Attica	oinochoe strap handle frag.	Attic MG	Coldstream 1992: 70, GC no. 14, pl. 62.14	nw corner of Unexplored Mansion, Deposit GC
70. Attica or Cyclades	belly-handled amphora wall	Attic/Cyc. MG	Coldstream 1973: 52	Sanctuary of Demeter, not from stratified deposit
71. Corinth	skyphos wall and rim	Corinthian MG II	Coldstream 1973: 52, no. 3; Neeft 1975: 121 n. 234; Dehl 1984: 51, no. G28	Sanctuary of Demeter, not from stratified deposit
72. Corinth	protokotyle, rim frag.	Corinthian MG II	Coldstream and Macdonald 1997: 232, no. Y10, fig. 20, pl. 47f	possibly from Evans's "area s of West Court," Test Pit 5, s of West Court, area of Great West Wall
73. Eretria	pedestalled krater, frags. of body and ribbed stem	Euboean MG II (?)	Coldstream 1992: 72, no. 36, pl. 64	Pit 27, on hillside above Unexplored Mansion

C.1.4. Overseas Artifacts Found at Other Knossos Locations *continued*

FROM	ITEM	DATE	SOURCE	FIND SITE/ CIRCUMSTANCES
74. Eretria	krater wall frag.	Euboean MG II	Coldstream 1992: 72, no. 37, pl. 64	Pit 27, on hillside above Unexplored Mansion; like no. 36 but from different vessel
75. Cyclades ?	pedestalled krater	MG?	Hood and Boardman 1961: 73, 77, Tomb A, no. 7	from tombs near Sanitorium; from Cyclades if imported; could be local
76. Cyclades	2 pedestalled kraters	Cretan MG context	Hutchinson and Boardman 1954: 222, nos. 5, 19 and 20, pls. 21, 25	Khaniale Tekke Tomb II; Hood and Boardman 1961: 77 n. 13, particularly recommends no. 19
77. Cyclades (?)	pyxis	MG	Hutchinson and Boardman 1954: 222, no. 55, pl. 25	Khaniale Tekke Tomb II; import or good local imitation
78. Cyclades	skyphos	MG	Hutchinson and Boardman 1954: 226, no. 71, pl. 26; Coldstream 1968: 167	Khaniale Tekke Tomb II
79. Cyclades	cup	MG	Hutchinson and Boardman 1954: 226, no. 79, pl. 26; Coldstream 1968: 167	Khaniale Tekke Tomb II
80. Cyclades	cup	MG	Hutchinson and Boardman 1954: 226, no. 81, pl. 26; Coldstream 1968: 167	Khaniale Tekke Tomb II
81. Phoenicia	ivory frags. of a handle w/ palm-leaf finial	8th–7th C.	Boardman, BSA 62, 64, 70, no. 70	Tholos tomb 2, Khaniale Tekke
82. Cyprus	B-o-R I (iii) jug	MG–LG	Hood and Boardman 1961: 74, no. 15	similar ones in MG–LG at Fortetsa; from Tomb A, group of tombs at western edge of Roman cemetery, now occupied by Sanitorium
83. Cyprus	B-o-R I jug	MG–LG	Hood and Boardman 1961: 74, no. 15, pl. 10	from Tomb A, group of tombs at western edge of Roman cemetery, now occupied by Sanitorium
84. Baltic (?)	gold and amber bead	Cretan MG–LG	Hood and Boardman 1961: 70, 75, no. 33, fig. 11	from Tomb A, group of tombs at western edge of Roman cemetery, now occupied by Sanitorium
85. Paros	skyphos, rim to near base, w/ handle stump	Cycladic MG II–LG I	Coldstream 1992: 77, no. 67, pl. 71	Unexplored Mansion, room/trench XII 48; identified by atomic absorption

C.1.4. Overseas Artifacts Found at Other Knossos Locations *continued*

FROM	ITEM	DATE	SOURCE	FIND SITE/ CIRCUMSTANCES
86. Rhodes	rim frag. from large dinos	Cretan G	Hartley 1930–31: 95, fig. 26.2, pl. 17.5; Boardman 1961: 152 n. 9	K30 west of theatral area, trench north of road
87. Corinth	proto-kotyle rim frag.	Corinthian MG II	Coldstream 1992: 77, no. 70, pl. 71	Unexplored Mansion, room/trench VIII 30
88. Corinth	proto-kotyle body frag.	Corinthian MG II	Coldstream 1992: 77–78, no. 71, pl. 71	Unexplored Mansion, room/trench XII 28
89. Cyprus	oinochoe	B-o-R (early)	Coldstream et al. 1981: 153–54, 161, no. 77, pl. 26.77	tomb on lower Gypsadhes Hill
90. Attica	neck amphora	not before close of Attic MG; to "well into Attic LG"	Coldstream 1960: no. 79	Geometric well at Knossos, upper deposit
91. Attica	lid frag.	LG	Hartley 1930–31: 94, fig. 22.2	K30 west of theatral area, trench north of road
92. Attica	2 bowl sherds	LG	Hartley 1930–31: 92, fig. 22.1,3	K03 Little Palace
93. Argos (?)	krater wall frag.	Argive LG	Coldstream 1992: 77, no. 64, pl. 71	Unexplored Mansion, room/trench VII 28; possibly local imitation
94. Cyprus	Red Slip II lekythos	c. 750	Coldstream et al. 1981: 150–151, 161, no. 54, fig. 5, pl. 21	bulldozed tomb on lower Gypsadhes Hill-- Ephraimoglou Plot; found in urn 64
95. Euboea	skyphos, rim frag.	Euboean LG II	Coldstream and Macdonald 1997: 232, no. X18, pl. 47d	Evans's 1930 sounding below West Court, Test Pit 3: w of West Court, Great West Wall, area s of Ramp
96. Euboea	skyphos, rim frag.	Euboean LG II	Coldstream and Macdonald 1997: 232, no. Y7, pl. 47f	possibly from Evans's "area s of West Court," Test Pit 5, s of West Court, area of Great West Wall
97. Euboea	skyphos, wall frag.	Euboean LG II	Coldstream and Macdonald 1997: 232, no. Y8, pl. 47f	possibly from Evans's "area s of West Court," Test Pit 5, s of West Court, area of Great West Wall
98. Euboea	skyphos, wall frag.	Euboean LG II	Coldstream and Macdonald 1997: 232, no. Y9, fig. 20, pl. 47f	possibly from Evans' "area s of West Court," Test Pit 5, s of West Court, area of Great West Wall

C.1.4. Overseas Artifacts Found at Other Knossos Locations *continued*

FROM	ITEM	DATE	SOURCE	FIND SITE/ CIRCUMSTANCES
99. Argos	sherd	Argive LG	Alexiou 1950a: 310, pl. 16, 2nd row, no. 5; Courbin 1966: 552	
100. Paros	skyphos wall frag.	Parian LG	Coldstream 1992: 77, no. 69, pl. 71	Unexplored Mansion, room/trench VII 23; fabric like no. 68; identified by atomic absorption
101. Paros	amphora (?), wall frag.	Parian LG	Coldstream and Macdonald 1997: 232, no. X19, pl. 47d	Evans's 1930 sounding below West Court, Test Pit 3: w of West Court, area s of Ramp
102. Paros	skyphos, 2 rim and 1 base frags.	Parian LG	Coldstream and Macdonald 1997: 233, no. Z8, pl. 48b	unstratified
103. Paros	skyphos rim and body frag.	Parian LG or SubG	Coldstream 1992: 77, no. 68, pl. 71	Unexplored Mansion, from road, trench VI 7A; identified by atomic absorption
104. Euboea (?)	2 frags. of amphora (?) wall	8th C.	Coldstream 1992: 77, nos. 62–63, pl. 71	Unexplored Mansion, rooms/trenches XI 23, I 46; possibly local imitation
105. Cyprus	Red Slip II juglet	mid-8th C.?	Catling 1976–77: 17	Gypsadhes, Ephraimoglou Tomb 54 (nos. 18–20 unpublished)
106. Cyprus	cremation pithos--Cretan Bird Style	c. 750	Catling 1976–77: 17, fig. 41	Chamber tomb on Lower Gypsadhes, bulldozed during residential construction
107. Cyclades	pyxis	Cycladic LG?	Hutchinson and Boardman 1954: 225, no. 55, pl. 25	Khaniale Tekke Tomb II
108. Rhodes	bird bowl	1st half 7th C.	Payne 1927–28: 265, no. 175, pl. 11,6; Rumpf 1933: 59 n. 6; Boardman 1961: 152 n. 9	Zafer Papoura tombs, 1927 excavation
109. Cyprus (?)	2-handled aryballos B-o-R	LG–O?	Davaras 1968a: A.56	Atsalenio Tomb A; inside pithos A.12, dated to EO; alternatively described as Creto-Cypriot accompanying pithos A.2, dated to LG (p. 143)
110. Cyprus	frag. of BoR II juglet	c. 725–700	Popham et al. 1984: H124; Coldstream 1979: 261 n. 31	Unexplored Mansion, floor deposit

C.1.4. Overseas Artifacts Found at Other Knossos Locations *continued*

FROM	ITEM	DATE	SOURCE	FIND SITE/ CIRCUMSTANCES
111. Cyprus	oinochoe, wall frag.	B-o-R II	Coldstream and Macdonald 1997: 232, no. X20, pl. 47d	Evans's 1930 sounding below West Court, Test Pit 3: w of West Court, Great West Wall, area s of Ramp
112. Cyprus (?)	Lekythos, base and body frag.	B-o-R II	Coldstream and Macdonald 1997: 232, no. Y11, pl. 47f	possibly from Evans's "area s of West Court," Test Pit 5, s of West Court, area of Great West Wall; possibly "close local imitation"
113. Sparta (or Cyclades or East Greece)	bone or ivory fibula in form of bird w/ 2 smaller birds on its back	early 7th C. for comparanda from Naxos, Ephesus, and Sparta	Hood 1960–61: 26, fig. 28; Boardman 1963: 153 n. 1; Coldstream 1973: 169, no. 304, pl. 98	Sanctuary of Demeter, Deposit E; votive strew northwest of temple, w/ material from 5th to 3rd C.
114. East Greece— Dodecanese	wall of closed vessel-- large oinochoe or lekythos	late 8th C. – early 7th C.	Coldstream 1973: 21, no. 31	Sanctuary of Demeter, Stratified Votive Deposit A
115. Rhodes	oinochoe	"early Rhodian;" in Cretan EO deposit	Payne 1927–28: 265, no. 176*, pl. 10,7; Rumpf 1933: 59 n. 6, 72, no. IIIc7; Boardman 1961: 152 n. 9	Zafer Papoura tombs, 1927 excavation
116. Corinth	deep kotyle, 2 rims	EPC	Coldstream 1992: 78, nos. 72–75	Unexplored Mansion, room/trench XI 22; Room 1, floor 5 of Unexplored Mansion; XI 23, XI 25
117. Corinth	kotyle rim	EPC	Hartley 1930–31: 88–89, pl. 18.6; Weinberg 1943: 27; Neeft 1975: 122, Table 7, no. 4; Dehl 1984: 30, no. A11	K03 west of theatral area
118. Egypt or Phoenicia?	frags. of ostrich egg, perhaps from rhyton	late 8th–7th C.?	Hutchinson and Boardman 1954: 216, 228, no. 80; Boardman 1967: 70, no. 80; Skon-Jedele 1994: 1873, no. 2936+	Khaniale Tekke Tomb II
119. East Mediterannean -Phoenicia, Egypt?	frags. of green faience bottle w/ scale pattern outlined in brown	late 8th–7th C.?	Hutchinson and Boardman 1954: 228, no. 79; Boardman 1967: 70, no. 79; Skon-Jedele 1994: 1872, no. 2933	Khaniale Tekke tombs
120. Levant/Egypt	miniature faience segmented beads, Egyptian type	late 8th–7th C.	Hutchinson and Boardman 1954: 223, 228; Boardman 1967: 70, no. 78; Skon-Jedele 1994: 1837, 1868, no. 2921+	Khaniale TekkeTomb II; in dromos, w of doorway in upper burnt stratum

C.1.4. Overseas Artifacts Found at Other Knossos Locations *continued*

FROM	ITEM	DATE	SOURCE	FIND SITE/ CIRCUMSTANCES
121. Rhodes (Kameiros)	foot of vase	LGI to EO	Hartley 1930–31: 88–89	K03 w of theatral area
122. Cyprus	oinochoe B-o-R II (iv)	EO?	Davaras 1968a: 138, A.45, fig. 1	Atsalenio Tomb A, under pithos A.4--dated to EO
123. Euboea	SOS amphora, 3 wall frags.	EO–LO	Coldstream and Macdonald 1997: 220, 239, no. H38, pl. 42b	reoccupied LM II house, w of SW House, Trench S VII 3 or 7, Deposit G
124. Italy-Balkans	spectacle fibula	SubG to O	Lebessi 1970: 291, pl. 403b	grave at Mastabas, south of Herakleion
125. Corinth	aryballos	2nd qtr. 7th C.	Payne 1927–28: 265, no. 176 (w/o asterisk), pl. 11,2; Neeft 1987: no. 987	Zafer Papoura tombs, from Evans's 1907 excavation
126. Corinth	oinochoe base frag.	O	Coldstream and Sackett 1978: 56, no. 52, fig. 10, pl. 13	Unexplored Mansion, well 12, upper fill
127. Miletus (?)	wine amphora rim frag.	O	Coldstream and Sackett 1978: 56, no. 54; Johnston 1993: 376 n. 42	Unexplored Mansion, well 12, upper fill
128. Cyprus	B-o-R juglets (spherical flasks of Cypriot shape)	7th C.	Hutchinson and Boardman 1954: 225, nos. 59, 60, pl. 26	Khaniale Tekke Tomb II
129. Cyprus ?	frags. of bronze openwork stand w/ pomegranate pendant	7th C.	Hutchinson and Boardman 1954: 227, nos. 56–58, 60–61, 66, pls. 29, 30; Boardman 1967: 69–70	Khaniale Tekke Tomb II; in burnt deposit in dromos
130. Phoenicia/N. Syria	3 ivory pieces: disc head of bronze pin; studs w/ concave edges; eyes	7th C.	Hutchinson and Boardman 1954: 227, pl. 29; Boardman 1967: 64, 70, nos. 71–73	Khaniale Tekke Tomb II; in dromos
131. Cyprus	B-o-R juglet, shoulder frag.	7th C.	Coldstream 1992: 79, no. 124, pl. 73	Unexplored Mansion, V 4 room 10; identified by atomic absorption
132. Euboea	pottery	7th C.	Coldstream 1992: 79, no. 765, pl. 73	Unexplored Mansion, identified by atomic absorption
133. Corinth	pyxis lid, knob	7th C.	Coldstream 1992: 79, no. 137, pl. 73	Unexplored Mansion

C.1.4. Overseas Artifacts Found at Other Knossos Locations *continued*

FROM	ITEM	DATE	SOURCE	FIND SITE/ CIRCUMSTANCES
134. Corinth	kotyle frags.	MPC–LPC	Payne 1927–28: 265, no. 177	Zafer Papoura tombs, 1927 excavation
135. Corinth	kotyle frags.	MPC	Payne 1927–28: 265, no. 178	Zafer Papoura tombs, 1927 excavation
136. Corinth	oinochoe (?), lower body frag.	MPC	Coldstream and Macdonald 1997: 217, 239, no. G45, pl. 40f	reoccupied LM II house, w of SW House, Trench S VII 3 or 7, Deposit G
137. Mesopotamia?	biconical crystal beads	LO?	Hutchinson and Boardman 1954: 223	Khaniale Tekke Tomb II; found w of doorway in upper burnt stratum
138. Egypt (?)	frags. of faience	Cretan LO	Hutchinson and Boardman 1954: 216	Tholos tomb 2, Khaniale Tekke; possible imitation of Egyptian
139. Corinth	olpe, Chigi Group (?)	mid-7th C.	Payne 1927–28: 266–67, no. 179, pl. 25; Payne 1931: 20, 186, 272, no. 42, pl. 8,1–6; Payne 1933b: 24, pl. 32.3; Dunbabin and Robertson 1953: 178, no. 9; Benson 1953: 131, no. 1134, 138; Amyx 1988: 38, 285; Neeft 1991: 17	Herakleion Museum no. 10786. Zafer Papoura tombs, 1927 excavation; Amyx: "not securely attributable" to the Chigi Group--assigns to new group: "Gruppe der Sphingen mit mehrfach umbundenen Haar, " no. 4
140. Corinth	scraps of vases	PC—mid-7th C.	Hood 1959–60: 26	from Geometric well
141. Rhodes (?)	aryballos shoulder frag.	7th–6th C.	Coldstream 1992: 79, no. 125	Unexplored Mansion, room/trench VII 41
142. Corinth	oinochoe shoulder frag.	EC–7th C.	Coldstream 1992: 79, no. 126, pl. 73	Unexplored Mansion, room/trench XI 19
143. Corinth	oinochoe shoulder frag.	EC–7th C.	Coldstream 1992: 79, no. 127, pl. 73	Unexplored Mansion, D1a
144. Corinth	oinochoe shoulder frag.	EC–7th C.	Coldstream 1992: 79, no. 128, pl. 73	Unexplored Mansion, room/trench VIII 31
145. Corinth	alabastron wall frag.	EC–7th C.	Coldstream 1992: 79, no. 129, pl. 73	Unexplored Mansion, Pit 57
146. Corinth	alabastron wall frag.	EC–7th C.	Coldstream 1992: 79, no. 130, pl. 73	Unexplored Mansion, Pit 38
147. Corinth	alabastron wall frag.	EC–7th C.	Coldstream 1992: 79, no. 131, pl. 73	Unexplored Mansion, SW 29
148. Corinth	alabastron wall frag.	EC–7th C.	Coldstream 1992: 79, no. 132, pl. 73	Unexplored Mansion, Pit 57

C.1.4. Overseas Artifacts Found at Other Knossos Locations *continued*

FROM	ITEM	DATE	SOURCE	FIND SITE/ CIRCUMSTANCES
149. Corinth	alabastron, round base	EC–7th C.	Coldstream 1992: 79, no. 133, pl. 73	Unexplored Mansion, Pit 38
150. Corinth	pyxis lid, rim frag.	EC–7th C.	Coldstream 1992: 79, no. 134, pl. 73	Unexplored Mansion, Pit 57
151. Corinth	pyxis lid	EC–7th C.	Coldstream 1992: 79, no. 135, pls. 59, 73	Unexplored Mansion, SW 9; Pit 57; identified by atomic absorption
152. Corinth	powder pyxis	EC–7th C.	Coldstream 1992: 79, no. 136, pls. 59, 73	Unexplored Mansion, SW 29
153. Corinth	alabastron, w/ seated panther to left, by the Painter of Candia 7789 (influenced by the Duel Painter, of the Warrior Group)	Transitional/E C, c. 600	Banti 1965: 32; Amyx 1969: 18, pl. 6.1; Amyx 1988: 82; G. Rethemiotakis, pers. comm, 1/24/95; Neeft 1986: 14, 21, no. 18, fig. 1; Neeft 1991: 31	Herakleion Museum no. 7789; found at Phoinicia, sw of Knossos; purchased
154. East Greece	"Ionian" cup, body frag. w/ handle root	O–c. 600	Coldstream and Sackett 1978: 56, no. 53, pl. 13	Unexplored Mansion, well 12, upper fill
155. Corinth	sherds from several vases	A	Sackett 1972–73: 63	From well near Unexplored Mansion
156. Egypt	ivory plaque, column w/ Hathor-head capital incised on front	A	Boardman 1962: 30–31, no. 4, fig. 2; Skon-Jedele 1994: 1844, 1857, no. 2894	found in the Knossos storeroom
157. East or East Greece	faience vase frags., blue glaze, composition core; unspecified number of miniature vases decorated w/ floral motifs in black glaze	A	Levi 1927–29: 460; Skon-Jedele 1994: 1872–73, no. 2934+	from tombs on Kephala Ridge excavated by Hogarth
158. East or East Greece	frags. of a number of miniature vases, glazed composition	A	Levi 1927–29: 460; Skon-Jedele 1994: 1874, no. 2934	tomb at north end of Kephala Ridge excavated by Payne in 1927

C.1.5. Overseas Artifacts Found at Kommos

FROM	ITEM	DATE	SOURCE	FIND SITE/ CIRCUMSTANCES
1. Phoenicia	amphora frags.	10th–9th C.	Shaw 1986: 224	in temple dumps, lowest Iron Age levels
2. Levant, perhaps Phoenicia	coarseware, amphora frag.	9th C.–8th C.	Shaw 1981: 240, 250–51 n. 130, C3270	in Temple A
3. Cyprus	amphora frags., small number	9th–8th C. (?)	Shaw 1984: 278–79	Temple B (?)
4. Cyclades	skyphos	Atticizing MG, associated w/ PGB deposit	Shaw 1982: 188, C4420	
5. Phoenicia	amphora frags.	later 9th to early 8th C.	Shaw 1982: 188	from a dump
6. Phoenicia	transport amphora frags., type in use from c. 850 to c. 300	late 9th to 8th C.	Shaw 1984: 278–79, n. 52, pl. 60:a	in late Temple A/early Temple B (Temple A may date from as early as c. 925; Temple B succeeded A in 8th C. and continued in use until c. 600: Shaw 1982: 185. Catling 1981–82: 56 offers dates c. 825–750 for beginning of Temple B)
7. Phoenicia	jug frag.	late 9th to early 8th C.	Johnston 1993: 371	65A3/2:86, S of Bldg Q; possibly intrusive in 7th C. context
8. Egypt	faience figurine, lion-headed goddess (prob. Sekhmet) w/ small cat (prob. Bastet) at side	late 8th C. to c. 700	Shaw 1980: 229, F5, pl. 62:d,e; Skon-Jedele 1994: 1878–79, 1886–87, no. 2941	beneath floor slabs in Temple B, Phase 2; wedged between south and central uprights of tripillar shrine, facing west
9. Egypt	faience figurine, perhaps Nefertum (son of Sekhmet)	late 8th C. to c. 700	Shaw 1980: 229 n. 50, 235, F10, pl. 65:e; Skon-Jedele 1994: 1878–79, 1886, no. 2940	Temple B, between north and central pillars of tripillar shrine in Temple B
10. Levant, perhaps Phoenicia	coarseware, amphora frags.	8th C.	Shaw 1981: 240, 250–51 n. 130, C3134, C3294	floor of Temple B
11. Levant, perhaps Phoenicia	coarseware, amphora frag.	8th C.	Shaw 1981: 240, 250–51 n. 130, C3245	Geometric deposit far s of Temples, Walls P and Q
12. Egypt	6 faience bowl frags., 2 faience bowls, intact, glazed composition and Egyptian blue	8th–7th C.	Shaw 1981: 241 n. 96; Shaw 1984: 278; Skon-Jedele 1994: 1882, 1990–91, nos. 2951–2958	within Temple B and dumps to s and w; intact bowl from earliest hearth of Temple B

C.1.5. Overseas Artifacts Found at Kommos *continued*

FROM	ITEM	DATE	SOURCE	FIND SITE/ CIRCUMSTANCES
13. Egypt	7 faience single beads or bead groups	7th C.	Shaw 1981: 241 n. 96; Skon-Jedele 1994: 1882, 1989–90, nos. 2944–2950	upper levels of Temple B
14. Levant, perhaps Phoenicia	frags.of coarseware: chalice stem and amphora frags.	8th–7th C.	Shaw 1981: 240, 250–51 n. 130, C3078, I16	dump to s of Temple B, at level corresponding to 2 lower floors of Temple B
15. Levant, perhaps Phoenicia	coarseware, amphora frags.	8th–7th C.	Shaw 1981: 240, 250–51 n. 130, C3130, C3528	1st floor level of Temple B
16. Corinth	kotylai and skyphoi	later 8th C. (after construction of Temple B)	Shaw 1982: 189	from campfire near triangular hearth ne of Bldg. J.
17. Corinth	kotyle frag.	PC	Shaw 1979: 164, C973	lowest level of Altar H
18. Phoenicia	amphora frags.	7th C.	Shaw 1984: 281	below Bldg. Q (probably built in 7th C.; Shaw 1984: 281)
19. Corinth	22 frags.of kotylai and jugs	7th C.	Shaw 1982: 190	altar of Temple B
20. Corinth	ovoid aryballos	MPC IB, c. 675–660	Shaw 1981: 240–41 n. 94, C2988, fig. 7, pls. 59:c,d, 61c; Benson 1989: 49, pl. 17.5–6	thought to be work of "Corneto" painter or, Benson suggests (1989: n. 94), of his workshop; Benson (1989: 49) changed the painter's identification to "The Kommos Painter"
21. Corinth	ovoid aryballos	c 640–630	Shaw 1981: C3053, pl. 61c; Neeft 1987: 229, no. 1117, 379, fig. 186	from Temple B
22. Attica	SOS amphora, 3 frags. of neck, lip, and shoulder, both handles	mid-7th C.	Johnston 1993: 358, no. 78, C8406	s of Bldg. Q; not associated w/ Bldg. Q?
23. Corinth (?)	aryballos, badly burned, w/o decoration	2nd half 7th C.	Shaw 1980: 231, pl. 62:h	w of hearth in Greek temple; possibly Cretan
24. Rhodes	2 faience scarabs	late 7th C.	Shaw 1981: 241 n. 96; Skon-Jedele 1994: 1888–89, nos. 2942–2943	within Temple B
25. Levant	1 glass scarab	late 7th C.	Skon-Jedele 1994: 1882	within Temple B
26. Chios (and related)	transport amphoras, frags. of at least 5 jars; body sherds point to more	last qtr. 7th C.	Shaw 1986: 229–31; Johnston 1993: 364, nos. 105–109, fig. 8:A, pl. 78	floor of Bldg. Q; Rooms 30, 37, 40; nos. 106, 107 not certainly Chian

C.1.5. Overseas Artifacts Found at Kommos *continued*

FROM	ITEM	DATE	SOURCE	FIND SITE/ CIRCUMSTANCES
27. Lesbos	transport amphoras, frags. of at least 8 vessels	last qtr. 7th C.	Shaw 1986: 229–31; Johnston 1993: 363, nos. 101–104, fig. 8:A, pl. 78	floor of Bldg. Q; Rooms 30, 31, 37 rubble fill
28. East Greece	transport amphora frags.	last qtr. 7th C.	Shaw 1986: 229–31	floor of Bldg. Q
29. Attica	transport amphoras, frags. indicate 8–10 vessels, possibly fewer	last qtr. 7th C.	Shaw 1986: 229–31; Johnston 1993: 357–58, nos. 71–77, fig. 6:D, pls. 77–78	floor of Bldg. Q; Rooms 30, 31, 37
30. Egypt	faience bowl, "Egyptian Blue," broken	Iron Age	Shaw 1984: 278, F35	in area s and sw of Greek temples
31. Corinth	aryballos or alabastron, lip frag.	late 7th C.	Johnston 1993: 350, no. 50, C8153, pl. 76	Bldg. Q, Room 37
32. Corinth	aryballos, upper part, probably EC	late 7th C.	Johnston 1993: 350–51, no. 51, C8195	Bldg. Q, Room 37
33. Corinth	part of decorated pottery handle	late 7th C.	Johnston 1993: 351, no. 52, C8287	Bldg. Q, Room 37
34. Laconia (?)	amphora, frag. of neck and lip	late 7th C.	Johnston 1993: 351, no. 53, C8229, fig. 5:A	Bldg. Q, Room 37
35. East Greece	Wild Goat oinochoe, over 30 frags.	c. 620–610	Shaw 1986: 229, pl. 47 i; Johnston 1993: 351–52, 355, no. 54, C7516, pl. 77	Bldg. Q, Rooms 30, 31, 37
36. East Greece	oinochoe, duck decoration, 22 frags.	late 7th C.	Johnston 1993: 352, no. 55, C7655, pl. 77	Bldg. Q, Room 31
37. East Greece	oinochoe or similar vessel, base	late 7th C.	Johnston 1993: 352, no. 56, C8772, fig. 5:B	Bldg. Q, Room 31
38. East Greece	oinochoe or similar vessel, foot frag.	late 7th C.	Johnston 1993: 352, no. 57, C8794, fig. 5:C, pl. 77	Bldg. Q, Room 31
39. East Greece	strap handle of decorated vessel, 2 frags.	late 7th C.	Johnston 1993: 352–53, no. 58, C8303, pl. 77	Bldg. Q, Room 31
40. Samos/East Greece	cup, 22 frags.	late 7th C.	Johnston 1993: 354, no. 60, C7610, fig. 5:F	Bldg. Q, Room 31; clay appears Samian
41. East Greece	cup, lip and body frags.	late 7th C.	Johnston 1993: 354, no. 61, C8773, fig. 5:D	Bldg. Q, Room 31
42. East Greece	cup, 3 frags. of lip, shoulder, and wall	late 7th C.	Johnston 1993: 354, no. 62, C8318, fig. 5:G	Bldg. Q, Room 37

C.1.5. Overseas Artifacts Found at Kommos *continued*

FROM	ITEM	DATE	SOURCE	FIND SITE/ CIRCUMSTANCES
43. East Greece	cup, 8 frags.	late 7th C.	Johnston 1993: 354, no. 63, C8319, fig. 5:H	Bldg. Q, Room 37
44. East Greece	cup, foot frag.	late 7th C.	Johnston 1993: 354, no. 64, C8918, fig. 5:L	Bldg. Q, Room 37
45. East Greece	olpe, wall and foot frag.	late 7th C.	Johnston 1993: 355, no. 65, C8921, fig. 5:J	Bldg. Q, Room 31
46. East Greece	cup, lip frag.	late 7th C.	Johnston 1993: 355	Bldg. Q, Room 31, 60B/2:77
47. East Greece or the islands	jug(?), 4 rim and body frags.	late 7th C.	Johnston 1993: 355, no. 66, C8347, fig. 5:K	Bldg. Q, Room 37
48. East Greece or the islands	cup, foot	late 7th C.	Johnston 1993: 355, no. 67, uncat., fig. 5:N	Bldg. Q, Room 37
49. East Greece or the islands	small cup, foot frag.	late 7th C.	Johnston 1993: 355, no. 68, uncat., fig. 5:M	Bldg. Q, Room 31
50. East Greece or the islands	lid (?), 3 frags.	late 7th C.	Johnston 1993: 355, no. 69, C8285, fig. 5:O, pl. 77	Bldg. Q, Room 37
51. East Greece or the islands (?)	8 frags. of closed, decorated vase of moderate size	late 7th C.	Johnston 1993: 355, no. 70, uncat.	Bldg. Q, Room 37
52. Laconia (?)	transport amphoras, Black-painted Types A and B, frags. of at least 6, possibly more; body sherds suggest more	late 7th C.	Johnston 1993: 358–62, nos. 81–99, fig. 7, pl. 78	Bldg. Q, Rooms 30, 31, 37, 38
53. Samos	transport amphoras, frags. of unspecified number of vessels	late 7th C.	Johnston 1993: 365–66, 368–69, nos. 110–119, fig. 9, pl. 79; possibly no. 131, fig. 11:B, pl. 80	Bldg. Q, Rooms 31, 37, 38, area s of Bldg. Q
54. Miletus	transport amphoras, frags. of unspecified number of vessels	late 7th C.	Johnston 1993: 367–68, 369, nos. 120–127, fig.10, pl. 79; probably nos. 133, 134,	Bldg. Q, Rooms 31, 37, 38; dump on e side of Bldg. Q
55. Corinth	Corinthian-A transport amphora	late 7th C.	Johnston 1993: 370, no. 137, C8865, fig. 12:A	s of Bldg. Q; possibly many other vessels, but fabric is difficult to distinguish from other Mediterranean locations
56. Cyprus	handles of loop-handled jar	late 7th C.	Johnston 1993: 370, no. 138, C8847, pl. 80	Bldg. Q, Room 38

C.1.5. Overseas Artifacts Found at Kommos *continued*

FROM	ITEM	DATE	SOURCE	FIND SITE/ CIRCUMSTANCES
57. Cyprus	loop-handled jar, frag.	late 7th C.	Johnston 1993: 370	
58. Phoenicia	transport amphora, Levantine type	7th C.	Johnston 1993: 370–71, C8413	s of Bldg. Q, 64A2/3:84; identical to sherds found in levels earlier than Bldg. Q
59. Phoenicia	red-slipped jug frag.	7th C.	Johnston 1993: 371	s of Bldg. Q, 64A/3:84
60. Phoenicia/ North Africa	storage amphora frags., 33 sherds	7th C.	Johnston 1993: 371	31 sherds from Bldg. Q, Rooms 37, 39, 40; 2 sherds from s of Bldg. Q
61. Klazomene	transport amphora frag., lower part of a handle	late 7th to early 6th C.	Johnston 1993: 369, no. 136, I46, pl. 80	Bldg Q. Room 31
62. Rhodes/ East Greece	rosette bowl	late 7th C. to c. 550	Johnston 1993: 353–54, no. 59, C7487, fig. 5:E, pl. 77	Bldg. Q, upper rubble fill

C.2. Sites in North-Central and Eastern Crete

C.2.1. Overseas Artifacts Found at Aghios Georghios

FROM	ITEM	DATE	SOURCE	FIND SITE/ CIRCUMSTANCES
1. Peloponnesus (Corinth or Argos?)	aryballos, "Argive Monochrome" ware	late 8th to early 7th C.	Tsipopoulou 1987: 266–67, fig. 3, pl. I'; Tsipopoulou 1990: 141; Kourou 1988: 315, fig. 1	from grave; Sitea Mus. no. 3968; chemical analysis assigns clay to Peloponnese

C.2.2. Overseas Artifacts Found at Amnisos

FROM	ITEM	DATE	SOURCE	FIND SITE/ CIRCUMSTANCES
1. Cyprus (?)	bronze rod tripod frag.	9th C.	Marinatos 1935:198; Matthäus 1985: 306, 308, no. m, 328; Schäfer 1992: 224, no. D,1.b10	Sanctuary of Zeus Thenatos, Area D
2. Syria	bronze figurine	9th–7th C.	Dunbabin 1957: 36, pl. 8.1	Herakleion inv. 2316
3. North Syria (probably made locally by foreign craftsmen)	limestone head of a warrior, half life-size	2nd half 8th C.	Marinatos 1936b: 83, fig. 2; Marinatos 1937: 222, fig. l; Davaras 1972: 40, 51, figs. 42–43; Adams 1978: 5–8, pls. 1–2; Boardman 1978: 11, fig. 14; Schäfer 1992: 233, no. D,1.d.1, pl. 81.1–3	Sanctuary of Zeus Thenatos, Area D; found in lower part of the Roman stratum; disturbed stratigraphy
4. Egypt	handle of bronze vessel; ends in lotus-blossom design	SG, 745–710	Marinatos 1933: 99; Matthäus 1985: 251 n. 3; Schäfer 1992: 229, no. D,1.b12, pls. 75.3–4, 103.2; Skon-Jedele 1994: 1682, 1689, no. 2744	Sanctuary of Zeus Thenatos
5. Near East	ivory eye	2nd half 8th C. to A	Marinatos 1936b: 84, fig. 3, lower right; Marinatos 1937: fig. 6 upper right; Adams 1978: 5, fig. 1; Schäfer 1992: 233, no. D,1.d.1, pl. 81.4	Sanctuary of Zeus Thenatos; one of the eyes fits the empty socket in the limestone head of the warrior
6. Corinth	PC kotyle	c. 710–680	Schäfer 1992: 245, no. D,3.a4, pl. 98.5	Sanctuary of Zeus Thenatos, Area D
7. Corinth	skyphos	PC	Marinatos 1929: 98, fig. 3	from Cave of Eileithyia
8. Egypt or East Greece	faience figurine of Bês	A (could be later or earlier), 7th–6th C.	Marinatos 1933: 98, fig. 4.1; Shaw 1980: 247 n. 102; Schäfer 1992: 232–33, no. D,1.c13, pls. 79.3,6, 105.4; Skon-Jedele 1994: 1689, no. 2745	Sanctuary of Zeus Thenatos, Area D, Archaic level 4
9. Egypt	faience head of Nefertum	A	Marinatos 1933: 98, fig. 4.4; Skon-Jedele 1994: 1690, no. 2747	Sanctuary of Zeus Thenatos

C.2.2. Overseas Artifacts Found at Amnisos *continued*

FROM	ITEM	DATE	SOURCE	FIND SITE/ CIRCUMSTANCES
10. Egypt	faience lid and vase frag.	A	Schäfer 1992: 232, no. D,1.c2, pls. 78.4–5, 105.2	Sanctuary of Zeus Thenatos, Area D, Archaic level 4
11. Egypt	faience bowl w/ wicker appearance and lotus flower	A	Marinatos 1933: 99, fig. 5; Schäfer 1992: 231, no. D,1.c1, pls. 78.1–3, 105.1; Skon-Jedele 1994: 1683, 1692, no. 2761	Sanctuary of Zeus Thenatos, Area D, Archaic level 4
12. Rhodes (?)	frag. of faience perfume bottle (?) shaped like fish (tail only)	A	Marinatos 1935:198; Schäfer 1992: 232, 251, no. D,1.c3, pls. 78.6, 105.3; Skon-Jedele 1994: 1695, no. 2760	Sanctuary of Zeus Thenatos, Area D, Archaic level 4
13. Egypt	faience standing figure of Ptah or Nefertum	A	Marinatos 1934: 130, fig. 2.1; Schäfer 1992: 232, no. D,1.c4, pl. 78.7; Skon-Jedele 1994: 1691–92, no. 2751	Sanctuary of Zeus Thenatos, Area D, Archaic level 4
14. Egypt/ Cyprus	faience male figurine frag., Nefertum	A	Marinatos 1934: 130, fig. 2.2; Schäfer 1992: 232, no. D,1.c12, pl. 78.16; Skon-Jedele 1994: 1691, no. 2750	Sanctuary of Zeus Thenatos, Area D, Archaic level 4
15. Egypt or East Greece	faience Sekhmet figurine	A	Marinatos 1934: 130, fig. 2.3; Schäfer 1992: 232, no. D,1.c9, pl. 78.12,17; Skon-Jedele 1994: 1694, no. 2756	Sanctuary of Zeus Thenatos, Area D, Archaic level 4
16. Egypt or East Greece	faience Hathor head, from figurine or amulet, reddish-brown	A	Marinatos 1933: 98, figs. 4.4; Marinatos 1934: 130, fig. 2.4; Schäfer 1992: 232, no. D,1.c11, pl. 78.15; Skon-Jedele 1994: 1690, no. 2747	Sanctuary of Zeus Thenatos, Area D, Archaic level 4; Marinatos (1933) assigned fig. 4.4 with the head, fig. 4.3
17. Egypt	faience sitting figures, 2 frags. of Isis and Horus amulet	A	Marinatos 1934: 130, fig. 2.6,8; Lemerle 1935: 304, fig. 55; Schäfer 1992: 232, no. D,1.c7, pl. 78.11; Skon-Jedele 1994: 1692–93, nos. 2754–2755	Sanctuary of Zeus Thenatos, Area D, Archaic level 4
18. Egypt	faience amulet, head of Nefertum	A	Marinatos 1934: 131, fig. 2.5; Skon-Jedele 1994: 1691, no. 2749	Sanctuary of Zeus Thenatos
19. Egypt	faience amulet, lower body and base, dwarf-god	A	Marinatos 1934: 130, fig. 2.7; Skon-Jedele 1994: 1692, no. 2752	Sanctuary of Zeus Thenatos
20. Egypt	faience base of standing figurine	A	Schäfer 1992: 232, no. D,1.c5, pl. 78.8	Sanctuary of Zeus Thenatos, Area D, Archaic level 4

C.2.2. Overseas Artifacts Found at Amnisos *continued*

FROM	ITEM	DATE	SOURCE	FIND SITE/ CIRCUMSTANCES
21. Cyprus/ Phoenicia	faience Astarte figurine	A	Marinatos 1933: 98, fig. 4.2; Schäfer 1992: 232, 251, no. D,1.c8, pl. 79.1–2; Skon-Jedele 1994: 1695, no. 2759	Sanctuary of Zeus Thenatos, Area D, Archaic level 4
22. Egypt or East Greece	faience Bês figurine	A	Marinatos 1935:198; Schäfer 1992: 232, no. D,1.c10, pl. 78.13–14; Skon-Jedele 1994: 1689–90, no. 2746	Sanctuary of Zeus Thenatos, Area D, Archaic level 4
23. Egypt	faience female figurine	A	Marinatos 1935:198; Schäfer 1992: 233, no. D,1.c14, pls. 79.4–5, 105.5	Sanctuary of Zeus Thenatos, Area D, Archaic level 4
24. Phoenicia/ North Syria	small bone carving of human leg	A	Marinatos 1938: 134; Schäfer 1992: 234, no. D,1.e1, pls. 80.1–2, 110.1	Sanctuary of Zeus Thenatos, Area D, Archaic level 2; Marinatos considered it ivory
25. Egypt or East Greece	Sekhmet protome, glazed composition	A	Skon-Jedele 1994: 1694–95, no. 2758, unpublished	Sanctuary of Zeus Thenatos
26. Egypt or East Greece	faience figurine frag. of goddess seated on throne, probably Isis or Sekhmet, broken at waist	A	Marinatos 1933: 98, fig. 4.3; Schäfer 1992: 232, no. D,1.c6, pl. 78.9–10; Skon-Jedele 1994: 1694, no. 2757	Sanctuary of Zeus Thenatos

C.2.3. Overseas Artifacts Found at Anavlochos

FROM	ITEM	DATE	SOURCE	FIND SITE/ CIRCUMSTANCES
1. Cyclades	pottery?	MG–LG	Hood and Boardman 1961: 77 nn. 8, 13; Marinatos 1931–32: 5, 6–7, no. 16, fig. 5, right	grave
2. Corinth	kotyle frag. with meander band	Corinthian LG	Dehl 1984: 149 n. 707	in Aghios Nikolaos Museum, unpublished
3. Corinth	several small vase frags.	PC, mid-7th C.	Demargne 1931: 382, fig. 18; Tsipopoulou 1987: 263	from possible small sanctuary on hillside
4. Egypt	terracotta statuette	A	Demargne 1931: 401, no. 58, pl. 16,2	from possible small sanctuary on hillside

C.2.4. Overseas Artifacts Found at Arkades

FROM	ITEM	DATE	SOURCE	FIND SITE/ CIRCUMSTANCES
1. Egypt	brown scarab, no glaze remaining	c. 1250–850	Levi 1925: 7; Levi 1927–29: 478, pl. 12; Pendlebury 1930a: 11, no. 12, pl. 1,11; Skon-Jedele 1994: 1702–3, 1714, no. 2769	Tholos L
2. Egypt	white steatite scarab w/ Egyptian hieroglyphics	9th–mid-8th C.	Levi 1925: pl. 2b; Levi 1927–29: 57, 477–78 n. 6, fig. 41, pl. 12; Pendlebury 1930a: 11, no. 13, pl. 1,12; Skon-Jedele 1994: 1704–6, 1713–14, no. 2768	inhabited area, Great House; context contained decadent LM III pottery, Cretan Geometric pottery, and Protocorinthian pottery
3. Attica	amphora neck frag.	Attic MG I	Levi 1927–29: 435, fig. 582, upper center, TR140; Coldstream 1968: 256 n. 8; Snodgrass 1971: 84 n. 58	sporadic finds
4. Phrygia	iron fibula	8th C.	Levi 1927–29: 469 n. 1, pl. 9; Sapouna-Sakellarakis 1978: 20, 128, no. 1680	
5. Cyclades	pottery, various frags.	MG–LG	Hood and Boardman 1961: 77 nn. 8, 13	Pithos Graves 81, 104
6. Cyprus	hemispherical bronze bowl w/ lotus flower on handle	8th–7th C.	Levi 1927–29: 305, 472, fig. 590a–b, TM 20; Gjerstad 1948: 407	Tomb M
7. Baltic	amber seal	late 8th to early 7th C.	Levi 1927–29: 305, 477; Levi 1945b: 314, 316, fig. 24B; Strong 1966: 23	found in dumped earth from the excavation; bought by Herakleion Museum
8. Attica/ Boeotia (?)	bronze fibula frag.	7th C.	Levi 1927–29: 158, pl. 6; Sapouna-Sakellarakis 1978: 106, no. 1482, pl. 42	Pithos Grave 106
9. Corinth	oinochoe, Cumae Group (Central)	EPC/MPC I, c. 690–670	Levi 1927–29: 368, fig. 485; Payne 1931b: 8; Weinberg 1941: 37; Weinberg 1943: 41; Amyx 1988: 19; Benson 1986: 12, fig. 35; Benson 1989: 29, pl. 8.4	Tomb L
10. Corinth	aryballos	PC to late 8th C.	Levi 1927–29: 416, fig. 548; Dunbabin 1962: 19, no. 55	sporadic find
11. Corinth	lekythos ("orange quarter"); whitish clay, cream slip, black and violet paint	PC	Levi 1927–29: 121–22, fig. 102; Ure 1934: 90; Neeft 1987: no. 1000	Pithos Grave 41
12. Corinth	black polychrome jug	PC?	Hopper 1949: 171 n. 39	Pithos Grave 110; Levi (1945a: 16, pl.13,4) considers it Cretan

C.2.4. Overseas Artifacts Found at Arkades *continued*

FROM	ITEM	DATE	SOURCE	FIND SITE/ CIRCUMSTANCES
13. Corinth (?)	alabastron ("bombylios"); greenish clay, yellowish slip, black paint	PC	Levi 1927–29: 145, pl. 15	Pithos Grave 66
14. Corinth (?)	alabastron ("bombylios"); bright yellow clay, rosy-cream slip, smudged black paint	PC	Levi 1927–29: 121, fig. 101, pl. 15	Pithos Grave 40
15. Corinth (?)	alabastron ("bombylios"); greenish clay, brown paint (and also possibly violet)	PC	Levi 1927–29: 158–59, fig. 169, pl. 15	Pithos Grave 109
16. Cyprus or Levant	faience bead necklace, c. 400 flat beads	late 8th C.	Levi 1927–29: 222, 476, pl. 13; Boardman 1960: 148 n. 40; Skon-Jedele 1994: 1701–2, no. 2770+	from Tomb R, Pithos 40
17. Corinth	conical aryballos	c. 680–665	Levi 1927–29: 154, fig. 158; Rizzo 1984: 259, fig. 498; Neeft 1987: no. 988, fig. 186	Pithos 93, in bronze lebetes
18. Corinth	conical aryballos	c. 670–665	Levi 1927–29: 131, fig. 115; Neeft 1987: no. 1001, 358, 379	Pithos 55
19. Corinth	conical aryballos	c. 670–655	Levi 1927–29: 416, fig. 548; Neeft 1987: no. 997, 358, 379	stray
20. Corinth	ovoid aryballos	c. 660–655	Levi 1927–29: 346, no. 71, fig. 451; Neeft 1987: no. 991, fig. 186	Tomb L
21. Corinth	ovoid aryballos	c. 655–650	Levi 1927–29: 355, no. 88, fig. 463; Neeft 1987: no. 993, fig. 186	Tomb L
22. Corinth	ovoid aryballos	c. 655–640	Levi 1927–29: 346, no. 72, fig. 452; Neeft 1987: no. 992, fig. 186	Tomb L
23. Corinth	ovoid aryballos	c. 665–620	Levi 1927–29: 306, fig. 406; Neeft 1987: no. 998, fig. 186	Tomb M
24. Corinth	conical aryballos	c. 665–620	Levi 1927–29: 355, no. 89, fig. 464; Neeft 1987: no. 989, fig. 186	Tomb L

C.2.4. Overseas Artifacts Found at Arkades *continued*

FROM	ITEM	DATE	SOURCE	FIND SITE/ CIRCUMSTANCES
25. Corinth	ovoid aryballos	c. 640–625	Levi 1927–29: 331, no. 41, fig. 430; Neeft 1987: no. 990, fig. 186	Tomb L
26. Corinth	ovoid aryballos	c. 660–625	Levi 1927–29: 238, fig. 279; Neeft 1987: no. 994, fig. 186	Tomb R
27. Corinth	ovoid aryballos	c. 630–620	Levi 1927–29: 155, fig. 160; Neeft 1987: no. 995, fig. 186	Pithos 98
28. Corinth	aryballos w/ dots and bands	c. 630–620	Levi 1927–29: 417, fig. 550; Neeft 1987: no. 996, 358, 379	stray find
29. Corinth	aryballos w/ dots and bands	c. 630–620	Levi 1927–29: 114, fig. 92; Neeft 1987: no. 999, 358, 379	Tomb M
30. Corinth	football aryballos	c. 610–600	Levi 1927–29: 121, fig. 102; Neeft 1987: no. 1000, 358	Pithos 41
31. East Greece	faience bitch or small lion	mid-7th C.	Levi 1927–29: 337, fig. 442; Skon-Jedele 1994: 1704, 1713, no. 2767	Tomb L
32. Rhodes	oinochoe	mid-7th C	Levi 1927–29: 111, fig. 89a–b; Shefton 1979: 35	Pithos Grave 33; clay similar to that of Levi 1927–29: 353, fig. 462
33. Rhodes	oinochoe, Wild Goat style	mid-7th C.	Levi 1925: 8, pl. 6d; Droop 1925: 12; Levi 1927–29: 353–54, fig. 462, pl. 24; Payne 1933a: 122; Rumpf 1933: 59 n. 16, 70, no. IIIbB5; Boardman 1961: 152 n. 9	from Tomb L, no. 86
34. Rhodes, Kameiros	oinochoe, Wild Goat style	mid-7th C.	Levi 1927–29: 125, fig. 107, pl. 27; Levi 1925: 8, pl. 6e; Droop 1925: 12; Rumpf 1933: 59 n. 16, 71, no. IIIbB4; Boardman 1961: 152 n. 9	from Pithos 48
35. Local copy of Egyptian work	faience crouching lion	mid-7th C.	Levi 1927–29: 240, 461, fig. 281, pl. 19; von Bissing 1941: 61; Boardman 1961: 62 n. 4; Boardman 1980: 113–14, fig. 132; Skon-Jedele 1994: 1700	from Tomb R

C.2.4. Overseas Artifacts Found at Arkades *continued*

FROM	ITEM	DATE	SOURCE	FIND SITE/ CIRCUMSTANCES
36. Egypt or Rhodes	faience bowl, yellowish (Webb calls it off-white with brown touches; Pendlebury called it blue)	mid-7th C.?	Levi 1927–29: 317, N.15a, fig. 414, pl. 21; Levi 1925: 7, pl. 2b; Pendlebury 1930a: 11, no. 11; von Bissing 1941: 81–82, pls. 5.3, 6.1–2; Helck 1979: 209 n. 316; Webb 1978: 39, no. 150; Skon-Jedele 1994: 1703, 1716–1717, no. 2776	from Tomb L
37. Levant	disk beads, composition cores, glazed white and blue; unspecified number	7th C.?	Levi 1927–29: 143–44, pl. 13; Skon-Jedele 1994: 1702, 1715, nos. 2771+, 2772+, 2773+	Pyre F2, ne corner of cemetery; from various urns (unspecified) from the cemetery; chance finds
38. Levant	2 tapering cylindrical beads, glazed composition	7th C.?	Levi 1927–29: 144, pl. 13; Skon-Jedele 1994: 1702, 1716, nos. 2774–2775	chance finds from the cemetery
39. Levant or East Greece	frags. of 2 glazed-composition, flat-bottomed vases	7th C.?	Levi 1927–29: 440; Skon-Jedele 1994: 1718–19, nos. 2777–2778	sporadic finds
40. Corinth	alabastron, w/ male and female sphinxes	EC	Levi 1925: pl. 3 (third on top right); Payne 1931b: 186, 282, no. 326A	
41. Corinth	alabastron, w/ horse protome	EC	Levi 1925: pl. 3; Payne 1931b: 283, no. 354A	
42. Corinth	"football" (orange quarter) aryballos; fine, light yellow clay, all painted in dark brown, divided into incised slices w/ milky white lines superimposed on the brown paint	EC, c. 620–600	Levi 1927–29: 193. fig. 214, pl. 18; Ure 1934: 90; Hopper 1949: 171 n. 39	Tomb D, Pithos 110; Levi (1945a) considered it Cretan
43. Corinth	alabastron ("bombylios"), band and dot decoration; greenish clay, greenish slip, rosette on bottom	EC	Levi 1927–29: 137, fig. 126; Ure 1934: 91; Hopper 1949: 171 n. 39	Pithos Grave 60; Levi (1945a) considered it Cretan

C.2.4. Overseas Artifacts Found at Arkades *continued*

FROM	ITEM	DATE	SOURCE	FIND SITE/ CIRCUMSTANCES
44. Corinth (?)	alabastron ("bombylios"), band and dot decoration; very fine, light yellow clay, cream and dark brown slip	EC	Levi 1927–29: 149, fig. 148; Ure 1934: 91	Pithos Grave 74
45. Corinth (?)	trefoil jug	EC/MC	Levi 1927–29: 103, fig. 78, pl. 14; Hopper 1949: 171 n. 39	Pithos Grave 24
46. Corinth (?)	ball aryballos; whitish-greenish clay, bright yellow slip, black and violet paint, rosette on bottom, no foot	EC–MC	Levi 1927–29: 140, fig. 131; Ure 1934: 92	Pithos Grave 64
47. Corinth (?)	ball aryballos; whitish-greenish clay, greenish slip, black paint; flattened bottom, rosette on shoulder	EC–MC	Levi 1927–29: 163, fig. 175; Ure 1934: 92	Pithos Grave 131
48. Corinth	quatrefoil aryballos; whitish clay tending to greenish, cream slip, dark brown paint with some violet touches	MC?	Levi 1927–29: 151–52, fig. 153, pl. 18; Ure 1934: 102; Hopper 1949: 171 n. 39	Pithos Grave 81
49. Corinth	quatrefoil aryballos	MC?	Levi 1927–29: 157, fig. 164; Ure 1934: 102; Hopper 1949: 171 n. 39	Pithos Grave 104

C.2.5. Overseas Artifacts Found at Avli

FROM	ITEM	DATE	SOURCE	FIND SITE/ CIRCUMSTANCES
1. Phoenicia/ Egypt	large scarab w/ hieroglyphic decoration	7th C.	Hood 1957: 20	at Mingilisi, near Avli Pedhiados, nw of Arkades

C.2.6. Overseas Artifacts Found at the Diktaean Cave

FROM	ITEM	DATE	SOURCE	FIND SITE/ CIRCUMSTANCES
1. Egypt	bronze statue of Amon-Ra	before 1200 or after 800; 18th-19th Dynasty, possibly later	Hogarth 1899–1900: 107, pl. 10.1–2; Pendlebury 1939: 323; Shaw 1986: 247 n. 102; Herakleion inv. no. 422; Verlinden 1984: 228, no. IV.1, pl. 101; Phillips 1991: 774–75, no. 382; Skon-Jedele 1994: 1917–19	found in Lower Grotto of cave; probably Bronze Age according to Boardman (1961: 74); Hogarth suggested deposit date of c. 900; Phillips considers LBA date more likely than EIA, but uncertain
2. Egypt	bronze calf filled w/ lead	18th–19th Dynasty (?), possibly later	Boardman 1961: 74, no. 228 (AE.773), pl. 16; Phillips 1991: 770–71, no. 379; Skon-Jedele 1994: 1917	unclear; probably Upper Grotto
3. Egypt	carnelian ("cornflower") bead	no earlier than 18th Dynasty, possibly later	Boardman 1961: 72, no. 332 (AE.717), fig. 32, pl. 23; Phillips 1991: 770, no. 378; Skon-Jedele 1994: 1917–18	probably Upper Grotto
4. Egypt	amethyst scarab seal	12th Dynasty (?)	Boardman 1961: 69, 74, pl. 24; Phillips 1991: 771–73, no. 380	probably Upper Grotto
5. Near East (Syria-Phoenicia)	bronze leg, possibly from a figure of Reshef	G, possibly Bronze Age	Boardman 1961: 75, no. 16 (AE.626), pl. 3	probably Upper Grotto
6. Mainland Greece	bronze figurine of Venus, solid, cast	G	Boardman 1961: 12, 75, no. 33 (G.392; 1894.132), pl. 6	probably Upper Grotto
7. Mainland Greece	bronze bird, solid, cast	G	Boardman 1961: 75, no. 48 (AE.36), pl. 9	probably Upper Grotto
8. Mainland Greece	amber beads, barrel-shaped	G, possibly Bronze Age	Boardman 1961: 73, 75, no. 352 (AE.1515), fig. 32, pl. 23	probably Upper Grotto; Strong (1966: 19, 21 n. 6) suggests Bronze Age
9. North Italy	"Peschiera" daggers or knives	G	Boardman 1961: 75, no. 56, fig. 3A–D	probably Upper Grotto
10. Italy	bronze swivel pin of 2-piece fibula	G	Boardman 1961: 36–37, 75, no. 162, (AE.1525), fig. 16, pl. 13	probably Upper Grotto
11. Italy/ Sicily	bronze swivel pin of 2-piece fibula	G	Hogarth 1899–1900: 109, fig. 45, 4th on lower row; Pendlebury et al. 1937–38: 115 n. 4	Lower Grotto
12. North Italy (or Greece)	bronze biconical bead	G (probably)	Boardman 1961: 71, 75, no. 325, (AE.702), fig. 32	probably Upper Grotto
13. North Italy	spiral bead	G	Boardman 1961: 75, no. 229, (AE.1719), fig. 24, pl. 27	probably Upper Grotto

C.2.6. Overseas Artifacts Found at the Diktaean Cave *continued*

FROM	ITEM	DATE	SOURCE	FIND SITE/ CIRCUMSTANCES
14. Near East (?)	ivory spiral fibula, incised concentric circles, w/ some oxidized iron adhering to back	G	Hogarth 1899–1900: 113, no. 82, fig. 49 bottom; Blinkenberg 1926: 270, XV6c, fig. 315; Boardman 1961: 36 n. 3	Lower Grotto; Hogarth cites Bosnian parallels for shape
15. Near East	ivory disc fibula, w/ 2 rosettes; traces of iron	G	Hogarth 1899–1900: 113, nos. 79, 80, fig. 49 center; Blinkenberg 1926: 266–67, XV3a, fig. 312; Benton 1938–39: 59 n. 2, fig. 2	Lower Grotto
16. Near East	ivory disc fibula, w/ 2 rosette discs and 2 smaller spiral discs	G	Hogarth 1899–1900: 113, fig. 49 top; Blinkenberg 1926: 267, XV3b	Lower Grotto
17. East Greece (?)	disk bead, "buff faience"	late 8th–7th C.	Boardman 1961: 73, no. 348, fig. 32; Skon-Jedele 1994: 1919, 1923, no. 2964	probably Upper Grotto; Ashmolean Museum no. AE.1747
18. East Greece (?)	tiny biconical bead, blue glaze	late 8th–7th C.	Boardman 1961: 73, no. 349, fig. 32; Skon-Jedele 1994: 1919, 1923, no. 2965	probably Upper Grotto; Ashmolean Museum no. AE.1746
19. East Greece (?)	spherical bead, blue compound	late 8th–7th C.	Boardman 1961: 73, no. 351, fig. 32; Skon-Jedele 1994: 1919, 1923, no. 2966	probably Upper Grotto; Ashmolean Museum no. AE.1742
20. East Greece or Cyclades	frag. of fibula	c. 700	Boardman 1961: 36–37, fig. 16D	probably Upper Grotto; Herakleion Museum, no inv. number
21. East Greece	vase frags., glazed composition, unspecified number of miniature vases	7th C.	Levi 1927–29: 460;; Skon-Jedele 1994: 1919, 1923–24, no. 2967+	Lower Grotto
22. Near East (Syria-Phoenicia)	ivory figurine	7th C.	Hogarth 1899–1900: 113; Boardman 1961: 75	Lower Grotto
23. Corinth	PC aryballos	7th C.	Hogarth 1899–1900: 99.	in temenos, near surface; context not disturbed in modern times
24. Corinth	2 PC aryballoi	7th C.	Hogarth 1899–1900: 105; Johansen 1923: 88	from surface of temenos
25. Corinth	Middle or Late PC painted aryballos	7th C.	Boardman 1961: 56, 75	probably Upper Grotto; Herakleion no. 2163
26. Corinth	plain PC aryballos	7th C.	Evans 1897: 356	near mouth of cave, in a superficial layer near later discovery of temenos

C.2.6. Overseas Artifacts Found at the Diktaean Cave *continued*

FROM	ITEM	DATE	SOURCE	FIND SITE/ CIRCUMSTANCES
27. Egypt (possibly Phoenicia or Palestine; possibly local copy of import)	frag. of figure vase in shape of recumbent lion holding a vessel between its forelegs	O	Boardman 1961: 62, pl. 22	probably Upper Grotto
28. Corinth	Middle Corinthian aryballos with swan	c. 600–580	Boardman 1961: 56	probably Upper Grotto; Herakleion no. 2162

C.2.7. Overseas Artifacts Found at Dreros

FROM	ITEM	DATE	SOURCE	FIND SITE/ CIRCUMSTANCES
1. Attica	fibula	Attic G	Lemerle 1936: 487, fig. 29	from tomb
2. Rhodes	lid	G	Effenterre 1948: 37, pl. 18,6	
3. Egypt/ Phoenicia	beads, blue paste	G	Effenterre 1948: 40, 64, D42	Tomb 10
4. Attica/ Boeotia	bronze pin	G	Demargne and Effenterre 1937: 23–24, fig. 15.3	around walls near temple
5. Attica	krater sherd, Dipylon style	Attic LG	Effenterre 1948: 37, pl. 20,4; Lemerle 1936: 487; Coldstream 1968: 257 n. 8	from tomb
6. Corinth	oinochoe	PC	Marinatos 1936a: 266–67, fig. 32; Tsipopoulou 1987: 263, fig. 1, pl. H'	
7. Attica or Boeotia	bronze fibula	last qtr. 8th C.	Effenterre 1948: 42, 65, D53, pl. 47; Sapouna-Sakellarakis 1978: 107, no. 1494A, pl. 43	Tomb 13

C.2.8. Overseas Artifacts Found at Gouves (18 km east of Herakleion)

FROM	ITEM	DATE	SOURCE	FIND SITE/ CIRCUMSTANCES
1. Corinth	kotyle	c. 680–630	Lembesi 1971: 388, fig. 7, left	partially destroyed pit grave at site of Profitis Elias

C.2.9. Overseas Artifacts Found at Itanos

FROM	ITEM	DATE	SOURCE	FIND SITE/ CIRCUMSTANCES
1. Paros	rim of bowl	Parian G	Deshayes 1951: 208	like one found at Delos; found in wall foundations at summit of acropolis and elsewhere
2. Boeotia/ Rhodes (?)	oinochoe frag. (bird bowl?)	Boeotian LG	Deshayes 1951: 208, pl. 25.2; Boardman 1961: 152–53 n. 9	found in wall foundations at summit of acropolis and elsewhere
3. Corinth	kotyle frag.	EPC	Deshayes 1951: 208, fig. 3.3, pl. 25.3; Tsipopolou 1987: 275	found in wall foundations at summit of acropolis and elsewhere
4. Corinth	pyxis frag. (Thapsos Class krater?)	PC	Deshayes 1951: 208, fig. 3.2, pl. 25.4; Tsipopolou 1987: 275; Dehl 1984: 59, no. I13	found in wall foundations at summit of acropolis and elsewhere

C.2.10. Overseas Artifacts Found at Karphi

FROM	ITEM	DATE	SOURCE	FIND SITE/ CIRCUMSTANCES
1. Cyprus	bronze pendant, pear-shaped (pomegranate?)	LM IIIC–PG	Pendlebury et al. 1937–38: 113, 119, no. 539, pl. 29:1; Catling 1964: 211, no. 47; Matthäus 1985: 325, no. b, pl. 138.4	from Room 106, Western Quarter; Pendlebury considered it an earring
2. Italy or Sicily	swivel pin of 2-piece fibula	SM	Pendlebury et al. 1937–38: 102, 115, no. 171, pl. 28.1; Milojčić 1955: 163; Desborough 1964: 174 n. 2; Desborough 1972b: 126–27, pl. 23.	Ta Mnemata Tomb 4
3. Anatolia (?)	bronze arrowhead	SM to not later than 900	Pendlebury et al. 1937–38: 117, 121, no. 672, pl. 29; Snodgrass 1964: 147	from the Peak Sanctuary
4. Near East	frag. of greenish-blue faience; too small to identify purpose	SM	Pendlebury et al. 1937–38: 72, 132, no. 637	from Room 136, Eastern Quarter
5. Near East	biconical faience bead	SM	Pendlebury et al. 1937–38: 78, 133, no. 246; Desborough 1964: 175	Great House, Room 12

C.2.11. Overseas Artifacts Found at Kavousi

FROM	ITEM	DATE	SOURCE	FIND SITE/ CIRCUMSTANCES
1. Sicily/ Italy	horse fibula	SM–G	Hall 1904: 17; Blinkenberg 1926: 57, fig. 29; Milojčić 1955: 163, fig. 3.20; Boardman 1961: 36 n. 5; Sapouna-Sakellarakis 1978: 17, 41, pl. 3, no. 50; Gesell et al. 1983: 410–11	from an Aloni tomb (Tomb I?)
2. Cyprus (?)	4 firedog frags. in shape of warships	SM/EPG– LG/EO	Boardman 1971: 6–7, no. 12D, pl. ; Karageorghis 1974: 172; Gesell et al. 1983: 412	purchased by Arthur Evans; probably from tomb at Plai Tou Kastrou; Argive examples dated by pottery to c. 710: Coldstream 1977: 146
3. Euboea	hydria	LPG	Tsipopoulou 1990: 140, fig. 4, H696	
4. Cyprus	hemispherical bronze bowl w/ lotus flowers on handle	G	Levi 1927–29: 472 n. 5; Gjerstad 1948: 407 n. 10	in Herakleion Museum; Geometric vases reported in tombs of cemetery where bowl was found; contents of tomb where bowl was found are unknown
5. Egypt	various faience frags.	G	Boyd 1901: 145–46; Pendlebury 1930a: 19, no. 21; Demargne 1947: 112 n. 5; Skon-Jedele 1994: 1810– 11, 1813, no. 2889+	tholos tomb at Rusty Ridge, half a mile se of Kastro
6. Near East	blue glass bead, translucent; 6 others whole and 1 broken, of same style, more or less translucent	G	Boyd 1901: 145–46	tholos tomb at Rusty Ridge
7. Near East	2 pieces of thin, translucent blue glass	G	Boyd 1901: 145–46	tholos tomb at Rusty Ridge
8. Corinth	aryballos	G	Boyd 1901: 154–55; Johansen 1923: 88; Tsipopoulou 1987: 263, fig. 2, pl. T'	shaft grave at Chondrovolakes, midway between Vronda and Azoria Hill; Herakleion Museum no. 1977
9. Cyprus	aryballos	EO to Cypriot A I	Tsipopoulou 1990: 141, fig. 19.	

C.2.12. Overseas Artifacts Found in Lasithi Plain

FROM	ITEM	DATE	SOURCE	FIND SITE/ CIRCUMSTANCES
1. Corinth	juglet or aryballos	PC	Watrous 1982: 55, pl. 20:d, C	found at Augousti

C.2.13. Overseas Artifacts Found at Liliano

FROM	ITEM	DATE	SOURCE	FIND SITE/ CIRCUMSTANCES
1. Egypt, Delta, near Bubastis (?)	head of (Egyptianizing ?) faience female figurine (Astarte?)	7th C.	Kanta 1991: 438, pl. OH'.7,8; Kanta 1980: 71–73; Webb 1978: 102, 166 n. 39, no. 629; Skon-Jedele 1994: 1892–93, 1894, no. 2959	from cave sanctuary of Liliano; LM IIIB, Orientalizing, and 4th C. material found; Kanta considered it Phoenician

C.2.14. Overseas Artifacts Found at Mochlos

FROM	ITEM	DATE	SOURCE	FIND SITE/ CIRCUMSTANCES
1. Corinth	oinochoe; probably product of Amyx's "Early Monumentalist Artists"	MPC	Soles and Davaras 1995: 313; J. Soles, pers. comm., Jan. 12, 1995	beneath Hellenistic fort on top of the island

C.2.15. Overseas Artifacts Found at Olous

FROM	ITEM	DATE	SOURCE	FIND SITE/ CIRCUMSTANCES
1. Mainland Greece (?)	2 stirrup jars	SM (?)	Effenterre 1948: 29, O61 and O62, pl. 38	Tombs 27 and 23
2. Phoenicia/ Levant	parts of a necklace, possibly faience	G	Effenterre 1948: 40, 58, O117	Tomb 16

C.2.16. Overseas Artifacts Found at Palaikastro

FROM	ITEM	DATE	SOURCE	FIND SITE/ CIRCUMSTANCES
1. Attica/ Cyprus (?)	3 frags.of bronze tripod legs (1 of mainland contour and design; 1 of mainland decoration and Cretan contour; end of leg of tripod stand like the one from Vrokastro Karakovilia Chamber Tomb 1)	PG to end of 8th C.	Benton 1939–40: 51–52, nos. 6, 11, pls. 22,6A, B, 29.11; Maaß 1977: 38, 53, no. 9, pl. 15.5–7; Matthäus 1985: 308, no. g, pl. 134.3; Matthäus 1987: 115, no. 25	found in front of temple precinct

C.2.17. Overseas Artifacts Found at Patela (in Siteia Region)

FROM	ITEM	DATE	SOURCE	FIND SITE/ CIRCUMSTANCES
1. Near East	beads of glass paste	PG	Hood and Boardman 1955: 31; Platon 1956: 239–40	tholos tomb at spot called Patela, near ruined village of Sfaka

C.2.18. Overseas Artifacts Found at Praesos

FROM	ITEM	DATE	SOURCE	FIND SITE/ CIRCUMSTANCES
1. Attica or Corinth (?)	krater rim frag. (possibly several other Attic vases as well)	G	Bosanquet 1901–2: 235; Rutkowski and Nowicki 1985: 121; Papadakis and Rutkowski 1985: 136, no. 12, SMus.SK12	from burial in Skales Cave (cult grotto), Trench C, near Praesos: "not far from the quarries at the north end of the Praisos plateau and immediately above the gorge formed by the western arm of the Sitia River"
2. Corinth	globular aryballos	EG–MG	Bosanquet 1901–2: 243; Payne 1931b: 186	chamber of Tholos Tomb A
3. Phoenicia (?)	13 small blue and yellow beads	EG–MG	Bosanquet 1901–2: 244	chamber of Tholos Tomb A
4. Phoenicia (?)	small disc of striped, blue and yellow glass	EG–MG	Bosanquet 1901–2: 244	chamber of Tholos Tomb A
5. Attica (?)	rim base frag.	G	Papadakis and Rutkowski 1985: 137, no. 44, SMus.SK44	from cult Grottoto at Skales Cave, near Praesos, Trench D
6. Cyprus (?)	hemispherical bronze bowl w/ caprine protome on handle	G	Levi 1927–29: 472 n. 6; Gjerstad 1948: 407	Herakleion Museum no. 206
7. Paros	amphora	LG	Tsipopoulou 1990: 141, fig. 25	
8. Corinth	small aryballos	3rd qtr. 8th C. (or PC to 3rd qtr. 7th C.?)	Bosanquet 1901–2: 248–51; Droop 1905–6: 26, fig. 1, no. 2016; Johansen 1923: 18; Tsipopoulou 1987: 268, fig. 4, pl. IA'	Tomb C; dated by parallel at Perachora: Dunbabin 1962: 12, no. 7
9. Egypt (Naukratis?)	blue faience oinochoe or trefoil juglet	Late 7th C.	Bosanquet 1901–2: 244; Skon-Jedele 1994: 1910–11, 1915, no. 2962	Tholos A
10. Italy (?)	black bucchero oinochoe	LG to EO (?)	Bosanquet 1901–2: 244	
11. Corinth	cothon	early PC	Tsipopoulou 1987: 272, fig. 9, pl. IE'	Herakleion Mus. no. 2067
12. Corinth	cothon	early PC	Tsipopoulou 1987: 272–73, fig. 10, pl. I(T'	Herakleion Mus. no. 2068
13. Corinth	cothon	early PC	Tsipopoulou 1987: 272–73, fig. 11, pl. I(T'	Herakleion Mus. no. 6641
14. Corinth	kotyle	early PC	Tsipopoulou 1987: 273–274, fig. 12, pl. IZ'	Aghios Nikolaos Mus. no. 1418
15. Corinth	cothon	early PC	Tsipopoulou 1987: 275, fig. 13	Aghios Nikolaos Mus. no. 1319

C.2.18. Overseas Artifacts Found at Praesos *continued*

FROM	ITEM	DATE	SOURCE	FIND SITE/ CIRCUMSTANCES
16. Corinth	aryballos	end 8th C.	Tsipopoulou 1987: 269, fig. 5, pl. IB'	Herakleion Mus. no. 6247
17. Near East	frag. of ivory w/ incised rosette, traces of red and yellow coloring	G to 7th C.	Bosanquet 1901–2: 244; Jacobsthal 1956: 89	Tomb A
18. Cyprus	terracotta goddess figure	O or later	Forster 1901–2: 279	shrine at Mesavyrysis; Barnett (1948: 17, fig. 16a, b) claims Lydian origin, which Boardman (1961: 145 n. 5) disputes
19. Corinth	aryballos w/ elongated, pear-shaped body	PC, 7th C.	Bosanquet 1901–2: 243	vestibule of Tholos Tomb A
20. Corinth	pyxis lid	late PC	Tsipopoulou 1987: 272, fig. 8, pl. IE'	in Herakleion Mus.
21. Corinth	aryballos	7th C.	Tsipopoulou 1987: 270, fig. 6, pl. IΓ'	Herakleion Mus. no. 6248
22. Corinth	alabastron	7th C.	Tsipopoulou 1987: 271, fig. 7, pl. IΔ'	Herakleion Mus. no. 6246
23. East Greece	aryballos frags., "yellow-blue" glazed composition	O	Levi 1927–29: 460; Skon-Jedele 1994: 1911–1912, 1915, no. 2963	
24. Eastern Mediterranean (Rhodes, Syria, Phoenicia, Egypt)	gold sphinx	2nd half 7th C.	Marshall 1905–6: 65	Tomb 28

C.2.19. Overseas Artifacts Found at Rhiza/Kanli Kastelli

FROM	ITEM	DATE	SOURCE	FIND SITE/ CIRCUMSTANCES
1. Attica	skyphos	PG	Desborough 1952: 259	Rhiza, near Kanli Kastelli
2. Attica	skyphos	PG	Desborough 1952: 83	Kanli Kastelli, Herakleion no. 7431

C.2.20. Overseas Artifacts Found around Sitea

FROM	ITEM	DATE	SOURCE	FIND SITE/ CIRCUMSTANCES
1. Egypt	shawabti, 26th Dynasty	0–A (2nd half of 7th C.)	Pendlebury 1939: 344; Pendlebury et al. 1932–33: 97	surface find; reported from a dealer

C.2.21. Overseas Artifacts Found at the Trapeza Cave

FROM	ITEM	DATE	SOURCE	FIND SITE/ CIRCUMSTANCES
1. Egypt or Phoenicia	faience figurine of Bês	O–A	Pendlebury et al. 1935–36: 13; Boardman 1961: 152 n. 2; Phillips 1991: 189, 782–83, no. 386; Skon-Jedele 1994: 1928–29, 1931, no. 2969	found by Arthur Evans in 1896; context not reported. Bês figure more likely Orientalizing-Archaic than LBA

C.2.22. Overseas Artifacts Found at Vrokastro

FROM	ITEM	DATE	SOURCE	FIND SITE/ CIRCUMSTANCES
1. Egypt	7 faience seals and c. 250 blue faience beads: disk, barrel-shaped (2), spherical (3), tapering cylindrical (45)	20th–22nd Dynasty (1200–1085; 945–715)	Hall 1914: 135–36, 148, fig. 81, pl. 35; Pendlebury 1930a: 39, nos 58–65; Pendlebury 1939: 313; Desborough 1952: 266; Skon-Jedele 1994: 1933–37, 1944, nos. 2970–2976	6 seals from Chamber Tomb 1 on Karakovilia, 1 from Tomb 4 on Amygdhali; beads from Chamber Tomb 1; PG materials found w/ these
2. Cyprus	iron knife w/ bronze rivets	SM (?)	Hall 1914: 151, pl. 21A; Desborough 1964: 70	from Chamber Tomb 5
3. Cyprus	large bronze rod tripod	SM–EG (PGB?)	Hall 1914: 132, fig. 80, pl. 34,1; Catling 1964: 199, no. 20; Canciani 1970: 192; Matthäus 1985: 306, 308, no. 1 (el), pl. 136.1; Matthäus 1987: 116, no. 30	from Chamber Tomb 1, on Karakovilia
4. Attica	bronze fibula, Blinkenberg type II	SM	Hall 1914: 153, pl. 19.H; Blinkenberg 1926: 72, no. 15a, fig. 54; Müller-Karpe 1962: 76, fig. 40.1	from Chamber Tomb 6; cf. Kraiker and Kübler 1939: 83, fig. 2, from Grave 42
5. Attica (?)	6 bronze pins	SM–EG	Hall 1914: 144, fig. 85K; Jacobsthal 1956: 16, no. 46	from Chamber Tomb 3
6. Attica	2 horses of chariot teams, pyxis lids	Attic PG–G	Hall 1914: 102, fig. 56, nos. B, C; Hayden 1991: 132, nos. 32, 33	Room H, settlement on summit

C.2.22. Overseas Artifacts Found at Vrokastro *continued*

FROM	ITEM	DATE	SOURCE	FIND SITE/ CIRCUMSTANCES
7. Egypt	7 faience seals and blue faience beads	20th–22nd Dynasty (1200–1085; 945–715)	Pendlebury 1930a: 39, nos 58–65; Desborough 1952: 266; Hall 1914: 135–36; Pendlebury 1939: 313	from Chamber Tomb 1, on Karakovilia; PG materials found w/ these; said by Desborough to be unsafe for dating purposes
8. Naxos	krater	Cycladic MG	Hall 1914: 171–73, fig. 106; Kontoleontos 1945–47: 19; Coldstream 1968: 167, 169, 258 n. 3; Hood and Boardman 1961: 77 n. 13	from house adjacent to the bone enclosures
9. Euboea or Naxos	8 sherds from a single vase, possibly from workshop of the Cesnola Painter	LG	Hall 1914: 98, fig. 53a–d, f,g; Coldstream 1968: 172, 258 n. 4; Hood and Boardman 1961: 77 n. 12; Coldstream 1971: 6–8, pl. 2b.1–8	from the town, 3 different rooms; fabric consistent with Euboea
10. Attica/ Boeotia	bronze fibula, Blinkenberg type VIII	LG	Hall 1914: 157, no. 2, pl. 20,H; Blinkenberg 1926: 159, no. 1a; Sapouna-Sakellarakis 1978: 107, no. 1495, pl. 43	from Bone Enclosure 2
11. Attica/ Boeotia	bronze fibula, Blinkenberg type VIII	LG	Hall 1914: 158, no. 3, pl. 20,E; Blinkenberg 1926: 159–60, no. 1b; Sapouna-Sakellarakis 1978: 106, no. 1478, pl. 42	from Bone Enclosure 2
12. Attica/ Boeotia	iron fibula, Blinkenberg type VIII	LG	Hall 1914: 158, no. 4, pl. 20,I; Blinkenberg 1926: 160, fig. 140, no. 2a; Sapouna-Sakellarakis 1978: 106, no. 1487, pl. 43	from Bone Enclosure 2 (listed by Sapouna-Sakellarakis as Hall pl. 20J)
13. Attica/ Boeotia	bronze fibula, Blinkenberg type VIII	LG	Blinkenberg 1926: 160, no. 2b	not published in Hall 1914; in Herakleion Museum
14. Cyprus (?)	small jug	G	Hall 1914: 103, fig. 57E	from Room 11
15. Cyprus (?)	flask	G	Hall 1914: 166	from Bone Enclosure 7
16. Cyclades (?)	pyxis	Cycladic LG	Hall 1914: pl. 26; Hood and Boardman 1961: 77 n. 13	from Room 22

C.2.23. Overseas Artifacts Found at Zakro

FROM	ITEM	DATE	SOURCE	FIND SITE/ CIRCUMSTANCES
1. Egypt	parts of necklace of blue paste beads	LG	Hogarth 1899–1900: 145	at Hellenika

C.3.   Sites in Central and Southern Crete

C.3.1. Overseas Artifacts Found at Aghia Triada

FROM	ITEM	DATE	SOURCE	FIND SITE/ CIRCUMSTANCES
1. Syria	bronze winged horse	9th–7th C.	Dunbanin 1957: 36, pl. 8.3; Herrmann 1966: 155, no. 33; Kourou 1989: 115	Herakleion inv. unnumbered; Boardman (1961: 119) uncertain of origin

C.3.2. Overseas Artifacts Found at Gortyn

FROM	ITEM	DATE	SOURCE	FIND SITE/ CIRCUMSTANCES
1. Cyprus (?)	iron spits	Cretan PG	Alexiou 1966: 190; Coldstream 1977: 49; DiVita 1991: 317, figs. 6–7	tholos tomb
2. Euboea	pendant semicircle skyphos rim frag.	G	Rizza and Santa Maria Scrinari 1968: 140, no. 252, fig. 236:7; Kearsley 1989: 31, no. 75	area of Protoarchaic altar, in mixed deposit including LM III, PG, and G material
3. Euboea	possible pendant semicircle skyphos: 2 shoulder frags.	G	Rizza and Santa Maria Scrinari 1968: 141, nos. 274–275, fig. 239:6–7; Kearsley 1989: 31	
4. Rhodes	frags. of 2 bird cups	LG to no later than mid-7th C.	Levi 1955–56: 227; Boardman 1961: 152 n. 9	altar at top of hill
5. Egypt or Levant or East Greece	fragmentary faience figurine of Bês, broken at hips	7th C.	Levi 1955–56: 240, fig. 36; Skon–Jedele 1994: 1732, 1737, no. 2781	votive deposit around altar at top of hill
6. Egypt or Levant or East Greece	frag. of faience feather crown, possibly part of Bês figure, no. GRT.3	7th C.	Levi 1955–56: 229, fig. 36; Skon-Jedele 1994: 1732, 1737, no. 2781	votive deposit around altar at top of hill
7. Rhodes	faience flower umbel, or biconical whorl	7th C.	Levi 1955–56: 229, fig. 36	votive deposit around altar at top of hill
8. Corinth	oinochoe	LPC	Levi 1955–56: 227	acropolis

C.3.3. Overseas Artifacts Found at the Idaean Cave

FROM	ITEM	DATE	SOURCE	FIND SITE/ CIRCUMSTANCES
1. Egypt	3 frags. of incised ivory slab; reverse of Kunze's no. 8b has hieroglyphics, part of an ivory-covered chest?	after end of New Kingdom, 11th C.	Halbherr 1888: 755, no. 6, drawing; von Bissing 1923–24: 212–13; Kunze 1935–36: 219, 231, no. 8a–c, pl. 84A; Sakellarakis 1984: pl. 245a; Skon-Jedele 1994: 1745–47, 1764–65, no. 2793, fig. 44	
2. N. Syria	bronze bowl w/ pairs of bulls	9th C.	Matthäus, pers. comm. 1994	comparable to bowl from Athens, Kerameikos Grave 42
3. Egypt	c. a dozen small bronze jugs	9th–8th C.	Matthäus, pers. comm. 1994	
4. N. Syria	frags. of bronze bowls w/ figural decoration	9th–8th C.	Matthäus, pers. comm. 1994	
5. N. Syria	ivory head	9th–8th C.	Sakellarakis 1983: 457, fig. 4 a, b, g; Catling 1985–86: 91	Central Hall, Mound IV
6. N. Syria	frags. of pyxis lid, running spirals around edge	9th–8th C.	Sakellarakis 1983: 457, fig. 4 d	Central Hall, Mound IV
7. Syria	frag. of ivory phiale	9th–8th C.	Sakellarakis 1983: 461	Central Hall, Mound V
8. N. Syria	frag. of ivory lion's feet	9th–8th C.	Sakellarakis 1983: 461, fig. 4 e	Central Hall, Mound IV
9. N. Syria	rim frag. of ivory pyxis lid, fish-scale pattern (sphinx wing?)	9th–8th C.	Sakellarakis 1983: 461, fig. 4 st	Central Hall, Mound IV
10. N. Syria	frag. of ivory plaque w/ running spirals	9th–8th C.	Sakellarakis 1983: 466, fig. 5 b; Catling 1984–85: 61	Central Hall, Mound V; cf. Barnett 1957: pl. 68, S157 from SE Palace at Nimrud (Loftus Group)
11. N. Syria	ivory animal foreleg, carved in round	9th–8th C.	Sakellarakis 1983: 462, fig. 5 g	Central Hall, Mound IV
12. S. Syria (Damascus?) locally carved (?)	ivory pin head, double woman's head, back to back, wearing high polos w/ rhomboid design; on broken stem	9th–8th C.	Sakellarakis 1983: 468, fig. 6; Sakellarakis 1992: 116, pl. 19	Central Hall, Mound V; cf. Crowfoot and Crowfoot 1938: pl. 12.2; Sakellarakis, 1992, calls it Cretan carving

C.3.3. Overseas Artifacts Found at the Idaean Cave *continued*

FROM	ITEM	DATE	SOURCE	FIND SITE/ CIRCUMSTANCES
13. Syria	flat relief rim of ivory vessel	9th–8th C.	Sakellarakis 1983: 470	Central Hall, Mound V, middle level
14. Syria	frag. of ivory plaque, slightly curved	9th–8th C.	Sakellarakis 1983: 470	Central Hall, Mound V
15. Syria	frag. of ivory relief plaque w/ incised sphinx	9th–8th C.	Sakellarakis 1983: 470	Central Hall, Mound V
16. N. Syria	large frag. of incised ivory pyxis lid w/ interlaced circles	9th–8th C.	Sakellarakis 1983: 470, 477, fig. 7; Sakellarakis 1984: 548, fig. 3	Central Hall, Mounds IV–V; cf. Barnett 1957: pl. 31, 536a–c; and Muscarella 1980: 126–27, no. 246A, pl. 246A
17. Syria	4 frags. of ivory pyxis w/ relief of bull and incised leaf	9th–8th C.	Sakellarakis 1983: 470	Central Hall, Mound V
18. Syria	edge frag. of ivory pyxis wall, incised tree branches	9th–8th C.	Sakellarakis 1983: 470	Central Hall, Mound V
19. Near East	several triangular and square ivory inlays	9th–8th C.	Sakellarakis 1983: 470, 472, fig. 8 d, e, st	South Recess, Mound I
20. Near East	3 ivory eye inlays	9th–8th C.	Sakellarakis 1983: 470, 472, fig. 8 a–g	Central Hall, Mounds IV–V
21. Syria	frag. of ivory pyxis body w/ lines in relief	9th–8th C.	Sakellarakis 1983: 477	Central Hall, Mounds IV–V
22. Syria	frag. of ivory pyxis rim w/ incised leaves	9th–8th C.	Sakellarakis 1983: 477	Central Hall, Mounds IV–V
23. Syria	frag. of ivory pyxis body, traces of incised decoration	9th–8th C.	Sakellarakis 1983: 477	Central Hall, Mounds IV–V
24. Syria	frag. of ivory pyxis body	9th–8th C.	Sakellarakis 1983: 477	Central Hall, Mounds IV–V
25. N. Syria	ivory relief head of bull	9th–8th C.	Sakellarakis 1983: 477, fig. 8 e	Central Hall, Mounds IV–V
26. N. Syria	segment of ivory whisk handle	9th–8th C.	Sakellarakis 1983: 477, fig. 8 q	Central Hall, Mounds IV–V; cf. Barnett 1957: pl. 85, S290m

C.3.3. Overseas Artifacts Found at the Idaean Cave *continued*

FROM	ITEM	DATE	SOURCE	FIND SITE/ CIRCUMSTANCES
27. N. Syria	frag. of incised ivory pyxis lid, overlapping circles; leaf design on edge; ring decoration along obverse edge	9th–8th C.	Sakellarakis 1983: 481, fig. 9	Central Hall, level under Mounds IV and V; cf. Barnett 1957: pl. 31, S34d, S38a–c, from SE Palace at Nimrud (Loftus Group)
28. N. Syria	4-sided ivory handle, transverse hole through center, incised lines	9th–8th C.	Sakellarakis 1983: 483, fig. 10 a, r; Sakellarakis 1992: 117, pls. 6–7	Central Hall, Mound IV
29. N. Syria	frag. of ivory round carving of woman; breasts and necklace	9th–8th C.	Sakellarakis 1983: 481, fig. 10 b; Sakellarakis 1990: 351, fig. 15; Sakellarakis 1992: 115, pl. 14	Central Hall, Mound IV
30. N. Syria	frag. of capital with naked feet; piece of back	9th–8th C.	Kunze 1935–36: 221, 227, 231, no. 12, pl. 86; Sakellarakis 1992: 112, pl. 3	
31. N. Syria	recumbent ivory calf; attachment to a pyxis lid	9th–8th C.	Sakellarakis 1984: pl. 243 g; Sakellarakis 1990: 355, fig. 21; Sakellarakis 1992: 115, pl. 12	Central Hall, Mound IV; cf. Mallowan 1952: 256, fig. 25
32. Syria	frag. of ivory plaque; incised bull's body, lotus blossom	9th–8th C.	Sakellarakis 1984: 552	Central Hall, Mounds IV–V, level g
33. Syria	3 border frags. of ivory plaque	9th–8th C.	Sakellarakis 1984: 558	Central Hall, Mounds IV–V, level e
34. N. Syria	frags. of ivory sphinx, head and wings, carved in round	9th–8th C.	Sakellarakis 1984: 558–59, pl. 246 a	Central Hall, Mounds IV–V, level e
35. Syria	2 frags. of carved ivory plaque with incised wing	9th–8th C.	Sakellarakis 1984: 559	Central Hall, Mounds IV–V, level e
36. Syria	3 frags. of ivory pyxis lid	9th–8th C.	Sakellarakis 1984: 559	Central Hall, Mounds IV–V, level e
37. N. Syria	ivory pin head, carved double woman's head, low plain polos, protuberant eyes	9th–8th C.	Sakellarakis 1984: 543, pl. 249 g; Sakellarakis 1992: 116, pl. 18 b–d	turned in by area resident

C.3.3. Overseas Artifacts Found at the Idaean Cave *continued*

FROM	ITEM	DATE	SOURCE	FIND SITE/ CIRCUMSTANCES
38. N. Syria	ivory stave knob; stylized lotus decoration	9th–8th C.	Sakellarakis 1984: 524, pl. 240 g	from Southern Recess; cf. Barnett 1957: 213, S292, pl. 86,S292 from Loftus Group
39. N. Syria	frags. of ivory plaque with sphinxes	9th–8th C.	Sakellarakis 1987: 251, fig. 10	
40. N. Syria	frag. of naked feet on umbel-shaped ivory base	9th–8th C.	Halbherr 1888: 753–54, no. 3; Kunze 1935–36: 221–22, 227, 231, no. 13, pl. 84A; Barnett 1957: 51 n. 2; Sakellarakis 1983: 461, pl. 271 b; Sakellarakis 1990: 353, figs. 13–14	Sakellarakis's find (part of left foot) from Mounds IV–V; Kunze's piece from 1885 excavation
41. N. Syria	half of hollow naked female ivory figurine (pregnant?), perfume bottle? swimmer?	9th–8th C.	Halbherr 1888: 753–54, no. 2; von Bissing 1923–24: 212; Kunze 1935–36: 221, 227, 232, no. 14, pl. 84; Barnett 1957: 44 n. 9, 50; Sakellarakis 1990: 353, fig. 27	not Egyptian, as von Bissing originally thought; similar to Loftus Group; Barnett thought it was a naked female swimmer w/ outstretched arms holding bowl; Sakellarakis concurs with Barnett
42. N. Syria	ivory lion figure, w/ foreleg and paw holding bowl	9th–8th C.	Halbherr 1888: 743–54, no. 4; Kunze 1935–36: 223, 232, no. 16, pl. 86; Sakellarakis 1984: 560, fig. 6, pl. 246 b; Sakellarakis 1992: pl. 1	Central Hall, Mounds IV–V, level e; similar to pieces from Nimrud (Loftus Group)
43. N. Syria	ivory lion protome	9th–8th C.	Kunze 1935–36: 223, 227, 232, no. 17, pls. 84A, 86	"typical of Syrian realm"
44. N. Syria	rectangular posts of small ivory box or piece of furniture	9th–8th C.	Kunze 1935–36: 223 n.4, 232, no. 18, pl. 87	writing on reverse side; 2d-millennium Cretan script; this aspect is similar to several pieces from Arslan Tash containing Aramaic writing on reverse side: Thureau-Dangin et al. 1931: 91, 135–38, pl. 47
45. N. Syria	horn rhyton or perfume flask	9th–8th C.	Halbherr 1888: 755; Kunze 1935–36: 223, 232, no. 20, pl. 87	
46. Near East	ivory spindle	9th–8th C.	Kunze 1935–36: 223, 232, no. 21, pl. 86	"missing marks of origin"
47. Near East	small ivory spoon, handle broken	9th–8th C.	Kunze 1935–36: 223, 232, no. 22	"missing marks of origin"
48. Near East	small ivory spoon	9th–8th C.	Kunze 1935–36: 223, 232, no. 23, pl. 86	"missing marks of origin"
49. Near East	ivory handle, both ends broken	9th–8th C.	Kunze 1935–36: 232, no. 24, pl. 86	"missing marks of origin"

C.3.3. Overseas Artifacts Found at the Idaean Cave *continued*

FROM	ITEM	DATE	SOURCE	FIND SITE/ CIRCUMSTANCES
50. Near East	undecorated ivory disc, semicircle	9th–8th C.	Kunze 1935–36: 224, 233, no. 25, pl. 85	"missing marks of origin"
51. Near East	undecorated ivory disc, circular, w/ 3 holes	9th–8th C.	Kunze 1935–36: 224, 233, no. 26, pl. 85	"missing marks of origin"
52. Egypt	13 thick ivory plaques w/ incised decoration on both sides	9th–8th C.	Sakellarakis 1990: 353	
53. Near East	bronze bowl w/ spike omphalos	9th–8th C.?	Matthäus, pers. comm. 1994	
54. Near East	bronze bowls w/ moveable swing handles	9th–8th C.?	Matthäus, pers. comm. 1994	some may be local imitations
55. Near East	bronze bowls w/ ribbed decoration	9th–8th C.?	Matthäus, pers. comm. 1994	some may be local imitations
56. Egypt	bronze situla	9th–8th C.?	Matthäus, pers. comm. 1994	
57. Cyprus	several bronze bowls w/ lotus handles	9th–8th C.?	Matthäus, pers. comm. 1994	
58. Cyprus	several small bronze bowls	9th–8th C.?	Matthäus, pers. comm. 1994	
59. Near East	small bronze jug	9th–8th C.?	Matthäus, pers. comm. 1994	has close parallels at Megiddo
60. S. Syria (Damascus ?)	frag. of capital w/ back-to-back feet; speculated to have been originally figurine of naked woman	late 9th to early 8th C.	Kunze 1935–36: 221–22, 227, 231, no. 11, pl. 84; Barnett 1957: 50 n. 4; Sakellarakis 1990: 350–51, figs. 11–12; Böhm 1990: 42, 158, no. E8–I, pl. 17c	double feet known from Loftus Group; similar to example from Arslan Tash; Syrian art, but with some Egyptian connections; cf. Winter 1981: pl. 15.c,d
61. Phoenicia	small bronze piriform jug	early 8th C.?	Matthäus, pers. comm. 1994	type of jug well known in western Mediterranean at slightly later date
62. Italy	bronze fibula, Sapouna-Sakellarakis type XIb	800–700	Galanaki 1990: 174, pl. 21 b; MH 3049	from 1956 excavation
63. Assyria, N.W. Iran (?)	segments of gold necklace w/ quadruple wire spirals and pomegranate pendants	8th C.	Halbherr 1888: 752, drawing; Sakellarakis 1983: 465, pl. 272 g; Sakellarakis 1984: 563, 567, pl. 247 g; Sakellarakis 1988: 182, 184, figs. 18–19	Central Hall, Mound IV; cf. Maxwell-Hyslop 1971: 206–7, pl. 165, from Ziwiye

C.3.3. Overseas Artifacts Found at the Idaean Cave *continued*

FROM	ITEM	DATE	SOURCE	FIND SITE/ CIRCUMSTANCES
64. Phoenicia/ Egypt (?)	faience scarab, blue-green	8th C.	Sakellarakis 1983: 478, fig 8 i	Central Hall, Mound V
65. Phoenicia/ Egypt (?)	faience cylinder seal w/ parallel transverse lines	8th C.	Sakellarakis 1983: 478	Central Hall, Mound V
66. Near East	c. 125 pieces of faience, some from vessels	8th C. (?)	Sakellarakis 1984: 563, 566, 569, 571, 574, 576, 577, 578, 580, 581, 582, 583	Central Hall, Mounds IV and V, various levels
67. Phoenicia/ Cyprus (?)	ivory papyrus umbel, cut relief	8th C.	Kunze 1935–36: 221, 230, no. 4, pl. 85	similar to example from Enkomi
68. Phoenicia/ N. Syria	ivory male head, protuberant ears, hollow eyes	9th–8th C.	Sakellarakis 1984: 562, pl. 247 b; Sakellarakis 1987: 251, fig. 9; Catling 1985–86: 91	Central Hall, Mounds IV–V, level e. Cf. Barnett 1957: pl. 6 nos. C39 and C41, and pl. 96 no. 342; and Herrmann 1986: 238, no. 1286, pl. 337
69. Phoenicia	ivory sphinx, cut relief	8th C.	Kunze 1935–36: 219, 227, 230, no. 1; Barnett 1957: 51 n. 3, 128 n. 6, pl. 84	similar to examples from Layard Group and from Arslan Tash
70. Phoenicia	ivory grazing animal, cut relief	8th C.	Halbherr 1888: 753–54, no. 1; von Bissing 1923–24: 187–88 n. 2; Kunze 1935–36: 220, 230, no. 2; Barnett 1957: 128 n. 7	
71. Phoenicia	vertical ivory volutes, cut relief	8th C.	Kunze 1935–36: 220, 227, 230, no. 3, pl. 85	similar to example from Arslan Tash
72. Phoenicia	incised ivory relief, leaves of leafy plant	8th C.	Kunze 1935–36: 221, 227, 231, no. 5, pl. 85	carving style similar to that of Kunze no. 1
73. Phoenicia	ivory incised relief, palmette calyx	8th C.	Kunze 1935–36: 220, 227, 231, no. 6, pl. 85	similar to examples from Arslan Tash
74. Phoenicia	frags. of round ivory pyxis, inscribed herringbone pattern	8th C.	Kunze 1935–36: 220, 227, 231, no. 7, pl. 85	similar to examples from Nimrud
75. Phoenicia	inscribed plaited ivory band	8th C.	Halbherr 1888: 755, no. 5, drawing; Kunze 1935–36: 219, 227, 231, no. 9, pl. 85	similar to examples from Arslan Tash
76. Phoenicia	frag. of ivory lotus flower tube	8th C.	Kunze 1935–36: 221, 227, 232, no. 19, pl. 86	
77. Phoenicia (?)	frags. of plaque, sphinx	8th C.	Sakellarakis 1983: 435, pl. 259 g; Sakellarakis 1987: 151, fig. 10	similar to Layard Group

C.3.3. Overseas Artifacts Found at the Idaean Cave *continued*

FROM	ITEM	DATE	SOURCE	FIND SITE/ CIRCUMSTANCES
78. Phoenicia	ivory figure of grazing stag (?)	8th C.	Barnett 1948: 4, fig. 1; Barnett 1982: 56 n. 10	
79. Phoenicia	frags. of bronze bowl with pseudo-hieroglyphs	8th C.?	Matthäus, pers. comm. 1994	
80. Phoenicia	2 bronze bowls w/ decoration of sphinxes in Egyptianizing style	8th C.	Matthäus, pers. comm. 1994	1 is closely related to comparable finds at Nimrud
81. Phoenicia	frags. of bronze bull bowls	8th C.?	Matthäus, pers. comm. 1994	
82. Phoenicia	frags. of bronze bowl w/ scarabs and falcons	8th C.?	Matthäus, pers. comm. 1994	
83. N. Syria	bronze bowl w/ animal friezes	8th C.	Matthäus, pers. comm. 1994	comparable to shields from Idaean Cave
84. Italy	bronze spectacle fibula (Alexander type IVai)	8th C.	Blinkenberg 1926: 261, type XIV.8a; Alexander 1965: 22; Boardman 1961: 36 n. 3; Sapouna-Sakellarakis 1978: 113, no. 1542, pl. 47	from 1884 excavation; in Herakleion Museum
85. Mesopotamia	ivory bull's head	8th C. (9th/8th?)	Kunze 1935–36: 221, 232, no. 15, pl. 84A	may have belonged to piece of furniture; similarities to Layard Group?
86. Near East	ivory seal, square, horseman	c. 725	Sakellarakis 1983: 481; Sakellarakis 1984: 571, pl. 249 a, no. 6183; Sakellarakis 1988: 174, no. 3; Sakellarakis 1992: 124	Central Hall, Mounds IV–V, level q; carved locally
87. Near East	ivory seal; flat, rectangular, 2 stamped surfaces, w/ hole; horseman and standing quadriped (dog?)	c. 725	Sakellarakis 1983: 478, pl. 275 b, seal no. 4/83; Sakellarakis 1987: 151, fig. 11; Sakellarakis 1988: 174 n. 17 no. 2; Sakellarakis 1992: 124	Central Hall, Mound V, level e; carved locally
88. Near East	ivory seal; flat, rectangular, horseman	c. 725	Sakellarakis 1983: 478, seal no. 8/83; Sakellarakis 1984: 571, pl. 249 a; Sakellarakis 1987: 151, fig. 11; Sakellarakis 1988: 174 n. 17 no. 4; Sakellarakis 1992: 124	Central Hall, Mound V; carved locally
89. Near East	ivory seal	c. 725	Sakellarakis 1983: 485, seal no. 3/83; Sakellarakis 1988: 174 n. 17 no. 1; Sakellarakis 1992: 124	South Recess, level 1; carved locally

C.3.3. Overseas Artifacts Found at the Idaean Cave *continued*

FROM	ITEM	DATE	SOURCE	FIND SITE/ CIRCUMSTANCES
90. Near East	ivory seal	c. 725	Sakellarakis 1988: 174 n. 17 no. 5, seal no. 11–9–84; Sakellarakis 1993: 124	Central Hall, Mound V, level 3; carved locally
91. Mainland (?)/ Baltic	necklace of at least 13 spherical amber beads, w/ gold cylinders in string holes	LG	Sakellarakis 1988: 184–87 n. 91, figs. 21–23	Central Hall, North Recess, West Niche; Sakellarakis supposes Baltic source of amber; place of workmanship not known; Eretria cited as location where gold and amber are found together; Isis Grave and Grave A at Eleusis also have gold and amber; cf. Strong 1966: 22, 48, 54
92. Baltic	amber beads: 7 elliptical, 6 triangular, 6 discoid, 18 of varying shapes	LG	Sakellarakis 1988: 184	
93. Baltic	amber lentoid object	LG	Sakellarakis 1988: 187 n. 104, amber no. 9/83	
94. Baltic/ Italy (?)	sculpted amber head	LG	Halbherr 1888: 753, pl. 12, fig. 6; Sakellarakis 1988: 197 n. 105	Herakleion Mus. no. 1221; Sakellarakis suggests Italian workmanship; cf. Strong 1966: 67, pl. 20
95. Egypt	faience crouching lion	G–O	Halbherr 1888: 758, no. 1, 2 drawings; Levi 1927–29: 460–61, fig. 588; Boardman 1980: 113; Skon-Jedele 1994: 1747, 1765–66, no. 2794	
96. Egypt (?)	various frags. of faience, including frags. of faience utensils	G–O	Marinatos 1956: 224; Hood 1957: 23; École Française 1957: 632	a second small cave, c. 8 m above the level of the main cave
97. Phoenicia	shallow, flat-bottomed bronze patera	740/30–680	Halbherr 1888: Atlas, pl. 6.1; Demargne 1947: fig. 34; Markoe 1985: 113–14, 116, 163–64, no. C2	inclined platform of the outer cave
98. Phoenicia	shallow, flat-bottomed bronze patera	740/30–680	Halbherr 1888: Atlas, pl. 6.2; Demargne 1947: fig. 35; Markoe 1985: 116, 164, no. C3	
99. Attica/ Boeotia	fibula w/ etched plaque; common Boeotian style; Sapouna-Sakellarakis type IXb	c. 700	Blinkenberg 1926: 163–69, figs. 195–197, no. 4c; Boardman 1985: 29, fig. 19; Sapouna-Sakellarakis 1978: 107, no. 1497, pl. 44; Galanaki 1990: 174, pls. 22 a–b, 23; Athens Museum no. 11765	

C.3.3. Overseas Artifacts Found at the Idaean Cave *continued*

FROM	ITEM	DATE	SOURCE	FIND SITE/ CIRCUMSTANCES
100. Attica/ Boeotia	bronze fibula, Sapouna-Sakellarakis type IXb	c. 700	Sakellarakis 1984: 566, pl. 248 g; Galanaki 1990: 174, pl. 21 a; A.E. 553/84	
101. Phoenicia	round pendant, bronze	c. 700	Higgins 1969: 152, fig. 1; Helck 1979: 203 n. 224	
102. Corinth	2 kotylai	EO context	Sakellarakis 1988: 191	
103. Phoenicia/ Egypt	faience male figurine (Nefertum); decorative hieroglyphs on dorsal column	7th C.?	Halbherr 1888: 758–69, drawing 759–60; von Bissing 1923–24: 213, no. 1110; von Bissing 1941: 95 n. 178; Demargne 1947: 123; Skon-Jedele 1994: 1747, 1761–63, no. 2789, fig. 44	
104. Near East	ivory daedalic female figurine, half-round; locally carved from imported material	mid-7th C.	Sakellarakis 1984: 562, fig. 7, pl. 247 a; Sakellarakis 1992: 117, pls. 20–21	Central Hall, NW section, Mounds IV–V; locally carved
105. W. Phoenician locations	a few ivory objects	7th C. or later?	Sakellarakis 1990: 348	
106. Egypt	5 bronze jugs	mid-7th C. or appreciably earlier (?)	Halbherr 1888: 725, pl. 12, no. 9; von Bissing 1923–24: 213; Roeder 1956: 418–19; Boardman 1961: 152; Boardman 1980: 113; Skon-Jedele 1994: 1743–44, 1761, nos. 2783–2787, fig. 43	cf. IC.3
107. Egypt/ Phoenicia	faience statuette of Bês	late 7th C.	Halbherr 1888: 757–58, no. 4; Demargne 1947: 124; Shaw 1980: 247 n. 102; Skon-Jedele 1994: 1761, no. 2788	
108. Phoenicia/ Egypt	2 sphinx heads w/ Egyptian hairstyle	late 7th C.	Halbherr 1888: 757–58, nos. 2–3; von Bissing 1923–24: 213; Skon-Jedele 1994: 1764, nos. 2791–2792	
109. Egypt	faience figurine of flute player	late 7th C.	von Bissing 1923–24: 213; Demargne 1947: 124	early Naucratite product?

C.3.4. Overseas Artifacts Found at Inatos

FROM	ITEM	DATE	SOURCE	FIND SITE/ CIRCUMSTANCES
1. Egypt	oriental goddess figurine in bone (or ivory?)	8th–7th C., 25th Dynasty	Alexiou 1963: 311; Faure 1964: 91 n. 2; Skon-Jedele 1994: 1777, 1789–90, no. 2813; Böhm 1990: 37–38, 158, no. E9–I, pl. 15c	Eileithyia cave sanctuary near Tsoutsouros
2. Egypt or Phoenicia or East Greece	other faience scarabs and figurines	late 8th–7th C.	Megaw 1962–63: 30; Davaras 1968b: 85, 150; Shaw 1986: 247 n. 102; Alexiou 1963: 311; Helck 1979: 208, 321 n. 281	Eileithyia cave sanctuary near Tsoutsouros; 30 unitemized scarabs reported to be in Metaxas Collection
3. Rhodes	faience scarab, no glaze remaining	c. 735–630	Skon-Jedele 1994: 1776, 1784, 1796–97, no. 2833, fig. 45	Perachora-Rhodes (P-R) Hallmark Group, Type B variant: dated by parallels at Perachora
4. Rhodes	faience scarab, trace of blue glaze	c. 735–590	Skon-Jedele 1994: 1776, 1783, 1785, no. 2830, fig. 45	P-R Hallmark Group, Type A variant
5. Rhodes	faience scarab, no glaze remaining	c. 735–590	Skon-Jedele 1994: 1776, 1784, 1797–98, no. 2834, fig. 45	P-R Hallmark Group, Type B variant
6. Rhodes	faience scarab, traces of bluish-green glaze	c. 700–630	Skon-Jedele 1994: 1776, 1783, 1796, no. 2831, fig. 45	P-R Hallmark Group, Type A variant
7. Egypt or Rhodes	faience scarab, no glaze remaining	c. 700–630	Skon-Jedele 1994: 1776, 1783, 1796, no. 2832, fig. 45	dated by parallels at Perachora
8. Rhodes	faience scarab, no glaze remaining	c. 700–590	Skon-Jedele 1994: 1776, 1784, 1798, no. 2836, fig. 45	P-R Hallmark Group, Type B variant
9. Egypt or Rhodes	faience scarab, no glaze remaining	late 8th–7th C.	Skon-Jedele 1994: 1776, 1799, no. 2840	
10. Egypt or Rhodes	faience scarab, traces of bluish-green glaze	late 8th–7th C.	Skon-Jedele 1994: 1776, 1798, no. 2835, fig. 45	
11. Egypt or Rhodes	faience scarab, white glaze	late 8th–7th C.	Skon-Jedele 1994: 1776, 1801, no. 2844	
12. Egypt or Rhodes	faience scarab, blue compound	late 8th–7th C.	Skon-Jedele 1994: 1776, 1801, no. 2845	
13. Egypt (?)	faience scarab, no glaze remaining	late 8th–7th C.	Skon-Jedele 1994: 1776–77, 1800, no. 2841, fig. 45	
14. Egypt (?)	faience scarab, no glaze remaining	late 8th–7th C.	Skon-Jedele 1994: 1776–77, 1800, no. 2842	
15. Rhodes	faience cat amulet, no glaze remaining	late 8th–7th C.	Skon-Jedele 1994: 1777, 1794, no. 2824	

C.3.4. Overseas Artifacts Found at Inatos *continued*

FROM	ITEM	DATE	SOURCE	FIND SITE/ CIRCUMSTANCES
16. Rhodes	faience cat amulet, no glaze remaining	late 8th–7th C.	Skon-Jedele 1994: 1777, 1794, no. 2825	
17. Rhodes	faience cat amulet	late 8th–7th C.	Skon-Jedele 1994: 1777, 1794, no. 2826	in Metaxas Collection
18. Rhodes (?)	faience lion amulet, aqua glaze, black glaze on tail	late 8th–7th C.	Skon-Jedele 1994: 1777, 1794–95, no. 2827	
19. Rhodes	faience falcon, no glaze remaining	late 8th–7th C.	Skon-Jedele 1994: 1777, 1995, no. 2829	
20. Rhodes	faience trefoil juglet frag., aqua glaze	late 8th–7th C.	Skon-Jedele 1994: 1777, 1803–4, no. 2887	
21. Rhodes	flat faience disk beads, c. 160, glazed cream, yellow, aqua, and pale green	late 8th–7th C.	Skon-Jedele 1994: 1777, 1802–3, no. 2883+	
22. Rhodes	barrel-shaped bead, blue compound	late 8th–7th C.	Skon-Jedele 1994: 1777, 1803, no. 2884	
23. Egypt or Rhodes	faience Bês amulet, no glaze remaining	late 8th–7th C.	Skon-Jedele 1994: 1778, 1785, no. 2800	
24. Egypt or Rhodes	faience Bês amulet, blue compound	late 8th–7th C.	Skon-Jedele 1994: 1778, 1785, no. 2801	
25. Egypt or Rhodes	faience Bês amulet, no glaze remaining	late 8th–7th C.	Skon-Jedele 1994: 1778, 1785, no. 2802	
26. Egypt or Rhodes	faience Bês amulet, no glaze remaining	late 8th–7th C.	Skon-Jedele 1994: 1778, 1785–86, no. 2803	
27. Egypt or Rhodes	faience Bês amulet, traces of greenish-aqua glaze	late 8th–7th C.	Skon-Jedele 1994: 1778, 1786, no. 2804	
28. Egypt or Rhodes	faience Bês figure	late 8th–7th C.	Skon-Jedele 1994: 1778, 1786, no. 2805	in Metaxas Collection
29. Egypt or Rhodes	faience Bês (?) figure, light green glaze	late 8th–7th C.	Skon-Jedele 1994: 1778, 1786, no. 2806	
30. Egypt or Rhodes	faience Nefertum figure; glossy, pale green glaze	late 8th–7th C.	Skon-Jedele 1994: 1778, 1787–88, no. 2808	

C.3.4. Overseas Artifacts Found at Inatos *continued*

FROM	ITEM	DATE	SOURCE	FIND SITE/ CIRCUMSTANCES
31. Egypt or Rhodes	faience Nefertum figure, head and upper torso	late 8th–7th C.	Skon-Jedele 1994: 1778, 1788, no. 2809	
32. Egypt or Rhodes	faience frag. of male figure (Nefertum?), lower body only	late 8th–7th C.	Skon-Jedele 1994: 1778, 1788, no. 2810	
33. Egypt or Rhodes	faience male figure frag. (Nefertum?); lower body only, traces of aqua glaze	late 8th–7th C.	Skon-Jedele 1994: 1778, 1788–89, no. 2811	
34. Egypt or Rhodes	faience Nefertum (?) frag.; head and torso frags. of large male figure; glossy aqua glaze	late 8th–7th C.	Skon-Jedele 1994: 1778, 1789, no. 2812	
35. Egypt or Rhodes	faience Isis and Horus figure, no glaze remaining	late 8th–7th C.	Skon-Jedele 1994: 1778, 1790–91, no. 2814	
36. Egypt or Rhodes	faience Isis and Horus figure, no glaze remaining	late 8th–7th C.	Skon-Jedele 1994: 1778, 1791, no. 2815	
37. Egypt or Rhodes	faience Isis and Horus figure, pale greenish-aqua glaze	late 8th–7th C.	Skon-Jedele 1994: 1778, 1791–92, no. 2816	
38. Egypt or Rhodes	faience Isis and Horus figure, no glaze remaining	late 8th–7th C.	Skon-Jedele 1994: 1778, 1792, no. 2817	
39. Egypt or Rhodes	Sekhmet protome amulet, light blue glaze	late 8th–7th C.	Skon-Jedele 1994: 1778, 1792, no. 2818	
40. Egypt or Rhodes	faience amulet: pair of tiny male figures wearing high crowns, standing side by side; no glaze remaining	late 8th–7th C.	Skon-Jedele 1994: 1792–93, no. 2819	

C.3.4. Overseas Artifacts Found at Inatos *continued*

FROM	ITEM	DATE	SOURCE	FIND SITE/ CIRCUMSTANCES
41. Egypt or Rhodes	faience male figurine, core of Type II (coarse-grained) composition	late 8th–7th C.	Skon-Jedele 1994: 1793, no. 2820	
42. Egypt or Rhodes	faience male figure, head frag., black glaze on hair	late 8th–7th C.	Skon-Jedele 1994: 1793, no. 2821	
43. Egypt or Rhodes	faience male figure, body frag., no glaze remaining	late 8th–7th C.	Skon-Jedele 1994: 1793, no. 2822	
44. Egypt or Rhodes	faience cat amulet, white glaze	late 8th–7th C.	Skon-Jedele 1994: 1778–79, 1793–94, no. 2823	
45. Egypt or Rhodes	faience scarab, traces of green glaze	late 8th–7th C.	Skon-Jedele 1994: 1799, no. 2837, fig. 45	
46. Egypt or Rhodes	faience scarab, no glaze remaining	late 8th–7th C.	Skon-Jedele 1994: 1799, no. 2838, fig. 45	
47. Egypt or Rhodes	faience scarab	late 8th–7th C.	Skon-Jedele 1994: 1799, no. 2839, fig. 45	
48. Egypt or Rhodes	faience scarab, white glaze	late 8th–7th C.	Skon-Jedele 1994: 1800–1801, no. 2843	
49. Egypt or Rhodes	faience oblong seal, geometric decoration, no glaze remaining	late 8th–7th C.	Skon-Jedele 1994: 1801, no. 2846	
50. Egypt or Rhodes	ivory (or ivory-colored steatite) scaraboid	late 8th–7th C.	Skon-Jedele 1994: 1801–2, no. 2847	
51. Egypt or Rhodes	4 scarabs, glazed composition	late 8th–7th C.	Skon-Jedele 1994: 1802, nos. 2848–2851	
52. Egypt or Rhodes	scarab, blue compound	late 8th–7th C.	Skon-Jedele 1994: 1802, no. 2852	
53. East	2 faience plaques or beads; traces of aqua glaze, diagonal bands of black glaze; pierced twice for suspension	late 8th–7th C.	Skon-Jedele 1994: 1777, 1803, nos. 2885–2886	
54. Egypt	faience amulet of Horus-Re; no glaze remaining on body, wig glazed black, crown contains yellow-glazed sun-disk	7th C.	Skon-Jedele 1994: 1777, 1786–87, no. 2807	

C.3.5. Overseas Artifacts Found at Kato Syme

FROM	ITEM	DATE	SOURCE	FIND SITE/ CIRCUMSTANCES
1. Phoenicia, Syria, possibly Cyprus	frag. of cast bronze sistrum with Hathor head	late 8th–7th C.	Lembesi 1973: 108; Böhm 1990: 38–39, 154, no. B19–I, pl. 15d	Sanctuary of Hermes and Aphrodite
2. East Greece or Egypt	faience scarab	7th C.	Aupert 1975: 687; Leclant 1977: 293; Skon-Jedele 1994: 1806, 1808, no. 2888	Sanctuary of Hermes and Aphrodite

C.3.6. Overseas Artifacts Found at Kourtes

FROM	ITEM	DATE	SOURCE	FIND SITE/ CIRCUMSTANCES
1. North Syria (?)	top half of trefoil oinochoe	end of 9th to early 8th C.	Rocchetti 1988–89: 199, no. 66, fig. 66	from the early Italian excavations

C.3.7. Overseas Artifacts Found at Lasaia

FROM	ITEM	DATE	SOURCE	FIND SITE/ CIRCUMSTANCES
1. Attica (?)	skyphos	mid-8th C.	Tsipopoulou 1978: 163, P 25, fig. 8, pl. 43 a–b	from Mitsotakis collection; said to come from Kaloi Limena
2. Attica	skyphos, from Bird and Birdseed workshop	3rd qtr. 8th C.	Tsipopoulou 1978: 159–60, P 57, fig. 5, pl. 41 a–b	from Mitsotakis collection; said to come from Kaloi Limena
3. Corinth (?)	1-handled cup, Corinthian atticizing (?)	last qtr. 8th C.	Tsipopoulou 1978: 165–66, P 60, fig. 10, pl. 44 a	from Mitsotakis collection; said to come from Kaloi Limena
4. Attica	1-handled cup	last qtr. 8th C.	Tsipopoulou 1978: 162, P 26, fig. 7, pl. 42 b–g	from Mitsotakis collection; said to come from Kaloi Limena
5. Attica	oinochoe	late 8th C.	Tsipopoulou 1978: 158–59, P 59, pl. 40 g, e	from Mitsotakis collection; said to come from Kaloi Limena
6. Attica	1-handled cup	late 8th C.	Tsipopoulou 1978: 163–65, P 56, fig. 9, pl. 43 g	probably Attic; from Mitsotakis collection; said to come from Kaloi Limena
7. Attica	kantharos	late 8th to early 7th C.	Tsipopoulou 1978: 161, P 35, fig. 6, pl. 42 a	from Mitsotakis collection; said to come from Kaloi Limena

C.3.7. Overseas Artifacts Found at Lasaia *continued*

FROM	ITEM	DATE	SOURCE	FIND SITE/ CIRCUMSTANCES
8. Attica	olpe	1st half 7th C.	Tsipopoulou 1978: 157–58, P 34, fig. 4, pl. 40 b	from Mitsotakis collection; said to come from Kaloi Limena
9. Attica	skyphos	1st half 7th C.	Tsipopoulou 1978: 160–61, P 58, fig. 6, pl. 41 a	from Mitsotakis collection; said to come from Kaloi Limena

C.3.8. Overseas Artifacts Found at Phaistos

FROM	ITEM	DATE	SOURCE	FIND SITE/ CIRCUMSTANCES
1. Cyprus or Argos (more likely)	2 arched fibulae	SM	Levi 1955: 159, fig. 30; Desborough 1972b: 119	from tomb at foot of north slope of hill with Convent of St. George at Falandra; tomb cut by new road in 1954
2. Attica	skyphos w/o foot	Attic PG	Levi, 1961–62: F.2570, 408–9, fig. 51c; Snodgrass 1971: 84 n. 58	Room P
3. Euboea (?)	skyphos rim frag.	PG/G	Levi 1957–58: 283, 287, fig. 125B.d; Kearsley 1989: 57	from brickwork in Early Greek Houses A and H, built over Bastion II
4. Corinth	globular aryballos	G	Rocchetti 1974–75: 265, G25, fig. 133	Room G
5. Rhodes (possibly local imitation)	vase frag.	G	Rocchetti 1974–75: 249 CC46, fig. 110	Room CC
6. Rhodes	cup frag.	G	Rocchetti 1974–75: 284, st.84, fig. 164	surface finds
7. Euboea	2 skyphos frags.— shoulder and wall	G	Rochetti 1974–75: 287, fig. 167 top row, 3rd and 4th from left; Kearsley 1989: 57	surface finds
8. Cyclades	skyphos	Cyc. MG or Cretan PG-- 840–810 B.C.	Rocchetti 1974–75: 201, P9, fig. 45; Coldstream 1968: 239 n. 3	Room P
9. Euboea or Cyclades	vase	Eub/Cyc MG	Levi 1961–62: 408, fig. 51c; Coldstream 1968: 239 n. 3	
10. Attica or Cyclades	frag. of amphora neck	Attic MG II– LG I	Rocchetti 1974–75: 248, CC42, fig. 107	Room CC
11. Attica or Cyclades	skyphos frag.	Attic LG	Rocchetti 1974–75: 277, st.25, fig. 156b	surface finds

C.3.8. Overseas Artifacts Found at Phaistos *continued*

FROM	ITEM	DATE	SOURCE	FIND SITE/ CIRCUMSTANCES
12. Corinth	Pyxis lid frag.	PC	Rocchetti 1974–75: 248, CC41, fig. 106	Room CC
13. Samos	skyphos	710–640 (LG)	Rocchetti 1974–75: 202, P11, fig. 47	Room P
14. Euboea (or Tessaglia)	skyphos	no later than mid-7th C.	Rocchetti 1974–75: 263, G11, fig. 127	Room G
15. Corinth	aryballos	Late PC	Rocchetti 1974–75: 239, ra.29, fig. 97	stairway

C.3.9. Overseas Artifacts Found at Priansos

FROM	ITEM	DATE	SOURCE	FIND SITE/ CIRCUMSTANCES
1. Cyprus	bronze wall bracket for torch; bull's head at top; ladle-shaped	PG–O	Stucky 1981: 431 n. 3, figs. 1–4	in a Swiss private collection; found w/ Cretan PG, G, and Early Archaic pottery

C.3.10. Overseas Artifacts Found at Prinias

FROM	ITEM	DATE	SOURCE	FIND SITE/ CIRCUMSTANCES
1. Egypt	scarab	G	Helck 1979: 208, 321, n. 282; Herakleion Museum case 151	found in Geometric context
2. Attica/Boeotia (?)	fibula	mid-9th to mid-8th C.	Sapouna-Sakellarakis 1978: 106, no. 1479, pl. 42	Prinias find no. 73; in Herakleion Museum, unpublished
3. Attica/Boeotia (?)	fibula	mid-9th to mid-8th C.	Sapouna-Sakellarakis 1978: 106, no. 1480, pl. 42	Prinias find no. P.205; in Herakleion Museum, unpublished
4. Attica/Boeotia (?)	fibula	mid-9th to mid-8th C.	Sapouna-Sakellarakis 1978: 107, no. 1496, pl. 43	in Herakleion Museum, unpublished

C.3.11. Overseas Artifacts Found at Tylissos

FROM	ITEM	DATE	SOURCE	FIND SITE/ CIRCUMSTANCES
1. Syria or Cyprus	bronze man and bull on a base	c. 1000	Hazzidakis 1934: 68–69, 109, pl. 31.3; Pilali-Papasteriou 1985: 98–99, no. 246, pl. 24.246	mixed context: found near the Greek altar, ne of houses; 5th C. inscription found nearby
2. Sparta	small ivory figurine, seated female	c. 650–620	Levi 1927–29: 701, 704 n. 2, fig. 663; Lane 1933–34: 178 n. 12; Kunze 1935–36: 218 n. 1; Boardman 1961: 154 n. 1; Boardman 1963b: 153 n. 1; Marangou 1969: 194; Fitzhardinge 1980: 59	much like figurine in Dawkins 1929: 220–21, pls. 122.5–7, 123.1; uncertain find circumstance—seized by authorities (?)

C.4. Sites in Western Crete

C.4.1. Overseas Artifacts Found at Chania

FROM	ITEM	DATE	SOURCE	FIND SITE/ CIRCUMSTANCES
1. "Aegean region"	pyxis & lid	PG	Andreadhaki Vlasaki 1991: 414	pithos burial at Pelepakina, outside Chania, c. 2.5 km from the Kastelli
2. Euboea (?) or Parian	krater	LG	Coldstream 1971: 8, pl. 3e	under the Kastelli
3. Euboea/ Chalkis	neck frag. of SOS amphora	c. 725–700	Johnston and Jones 1978: 114, no. 70P216	from Kastelli site
4. Assyria (probably made locally by immigrant craftsmen)	limestone frieze slab, figures of standing female, horse, and archers in relief	last qtr. 8th to early 7th C.	Jantzen 1951: 80, pl. 56.5; Theophanides 1956: 218–19, fig. 1; Boardman 1961: 137–38, fig. 53; Boardman 1967: 66; Boardman 1978: 11, fig. 15; Boardman 1980: 57, 74, fig. 60; Davaras 1972: 12, fig. 12, 53, no. 9; Ridgway 1977: 257–58; Adams 1978: 11–13, pls. 3–4	thought to have come from a spot where the foundations of an archaic naos was destroyed during modern construction
5. Phoenicia/ North Syria	2 mold-made terracotta figurines of Astarte	700–650	Stewart 1990: 106, pl. 20	

C.4.2. Overseas Artifacts Found at Eleutherna

FROM	ITEM	DATE	SOURCE	FIND SITE/ CIRCUMSTANCES
1. Egypt	faience seal, 20th–22nd Dynasty	SM–PG	Xanthoudides 1907: 163–64, pl. 6 no. 42; Hall 1914: 136 n. 1; Pendlebury 1930a: xix, n. 3; Skon-Jedele 1994: 1719–22, 1724, no. 2779	purchased by Archaeologicaal Receipts Fund; probably found in ruins of ancient Eleutherna
2. Cyprus/ Syria	pieces of large bronze bowl with lotus handles	G–A	Stampolidis 1990a: 393 n. 40, fig. 23; Stampolidis 1990b: 294–95, pl. 60a	possibly 11th–10th C. production; heirloom?
3. Athens	larger pottery, kraters and amphorae	Attic MG–LG	Stampolidis 1990a: 388 n. 31	in cemetery
4. Corinth	larger pottery, kraters and amphorae	Corinthian MG/LG	Stampolidis 1990a: 388 n. 31	in cemetery
5. Phoenicia/ Egypt	hundreds of multicolored faience beads	G–A	Stampolidis 1990a: 388; Stampolidis 1990b: 293, pl. 59 g	female grave

C.4.2. Overseas Artifacts Found at Eleutherna *continued*

FROM	ITEM	DATE	SOURCE	FIND SITE/ CIRCUMSTANCES
6. Phoenicia/ Egypt	molded glass phiale frs.	G–A	Stampolidis 1990b: 294, pl. 60 a	male grave
7. Cyclades, Thera (?)	sherd decorated w/ circles connected w/ running tangents	Cycladic LG	Hartley 1930–31: 109–10, fig. 34.5; Drerup 1951: 105 n. 2	west side of acropolis (cemetery?)
8. Cyclades, Naxos (?)	sherds	Cycladic LG	Hartley 1930–31: 109–10, fig. 34.3–4, 35; Hood and Boardman 1961: 77 n. 8	west side of acropolis (cemetery?)
9. Corinth	larger pottery: kraters, oinochoai, and amphorae	PC, EC, C	Stampolidis 1990a: 388 n. 31; Stampolidis 1992: 141	in cemetery
10. Corinth	ovoid aryballos	PC	Stampolidis 1990a: fig. 18; Stampolidis 1990b: 295, pl. 61 g	
11. Corinth	pieces of a cothon	LO	Hartley 1930–31: 111, figs. 34,3–4, 35	1929 grave excavations
12. Corinth	pieces of a plate rim	LO	Hartley 1930–31: 111, figs. 34,3–4, 35; Hood and Boardman 1961: 77 n. 8	1929 grave excavations
13. Corinth	upper part of an aryballos, unpainted	LO	Hartley 1930–31: 111, figs. 34,3–4, 35; Hood and Boardman 1961: 77 n. 8	1929 grave excavations
14. Corinth	3 kotyle frags.	LO	Hartley 1930–31: 111, figs. 34,3–4, 35; Hood and Boardman 1961: 77 n. 8	1929 grave excavations
15. Near East	4 ivory heads, possibly from a piece of furniture	620–580	Stampolidis 1992: 141–61	funerary pyre in stratum with EC oinochoai; locally carved from imported material
16. Laconia	krater, early Laconian III	c. 600 to mid-6th C.	Hartley 1930–31: 111, figs. 34.6–7, 35; Droop 1931–32: 247–48; Hartley 1931–32: 251–53; Lane 1933–34: 178; Hood and Boardman 1961: 77 n. 8; Marangou 1969: 281 n. 1094a	1929 grave excavations; from unstratified context

C.4.3. Overseas Artifacts Found at Kissamo and Sites Nearby

SITE	ITEM	DATE	SOURCE	FIND SITE/ CIRCUMSTANCES
1. Attica/ Boeotia (?)	fibula	mid-9th to mid-8th C.	Sapouna-Sakellarakis 1978: 106, no. 1484, pl. 42	in Chania Museum, unpublished
2. Cyprus (?)	bronze pomegranate pendant (from bronze stand?)	8th C.	Payne 1931a: 54; Boardman 1961: 90–91, 93, no. 388, fig. 37, pl. 30	Ashmolean Museum AE.123c; purchased by A. J. Evans; said to come from a chamber tomb at Kissamo; placed in figure vase in recent times
3. East Greece or Egypt	biconical bead, pale green glaze, core of "buff-yellow" composition	8th–7th C.?	Boardman 1961: 94, no. 424, fig. 39; Skon-Jedele 1994: 1814, 1817, no. 2890	Ashmolean Museum no. AE.126b
4. East Greece or Egypt	unidentifiable frag., "scrap of blue frit"	8th–7th C.?	Boardman 1961: 94, no. 428; Skon-Jedele 1994: 1814, 1817, no. 2891	Ashmolean Museum no. AE.141a
5. Corinth	round aryballos, The Bead Painter	late EC to early 6th C.	Tzedakis 1964: 434, pl. 440a; Amyx 1988: 81	from Phalasarna, Pithos Grave 12
6. Corinth	several vases	late 7th to early 6th C.(?)	Johansen 1923: 88; Payne 1931b: 186	from Polyrhenia, c. 5 km south of Kissamo; in Herakleion Museum

C.4.4. Overseas Artifacts Found at Gavalomouri

FROM	ITEM	DATE	SOURCE	FIND SITE/ CIRCUMSTANCES
1. Attica	kantharos w/ high handles	Attic MG II/1st qtr. 8th C.	Andreadaki-Vlasaki 1985: 26, pl. IZ', photo 16; Andreadaki-Vlasaki 1990: 98 n. 51, pl. 4 , Chania Mus. No. 4071	Gavalomouri, Grave I; clay analyzed at Fitch Laboratory; same workshop as skyphos below
2. Attica	shallow cup	Attic MG II/1st qtr. 8th C.	Andreadaki-Vlasaki 1990: 98	Gavalomouri, Grave I
4. Attica	skyphos	Attic MG II/1st qtr. 8th C.	Andreadaki-Vlasaki, 1985: 26; Andreadaki-Vlasaki 1990: 98 n. 51, pl. 4 , Chania Mus. No. 4076	Gavalomouri, Grave I; clay analyzed at Fitch Laboratory; same workshop as skyphos below
5. Cyclades	skyphos	early Cycladic MG, end 9th C.-early 8th C.	Andreadaki-Vlasaki 1985: 26	Gavalomouri, Grave I

C.4.5. Overseas Artifacts Found at Patso

SITE	ITEM	DATE	SOURCE	FIND SITE/ CIRCUMSTANCES
1. Levant	Bronze statuette of Reshef	11th C.	Evans 1901: 125, fig. 15; Lamb 1929: 28, 35; Boardman 1961: 76; Bouzek 1972: 159–60, 161 no. 8; Negbi 1976: 37, no. 1406, pl. 28; Negbi 1982: 180; Helck 1979: 180 n. 44; Verlinden 1984: 228, no. IV.2, pl. 101; Naumann 1976: 70–71 n. 99; Seeden 1980: 125–26, 131, no. 1809, pl. 113; Renfrew and Cherry 1985: 306, no. 5, 308; Hoffman 1990: 26–27, 91–95; Kourou and Karetsou 1994: 118 no. 79, 144	Cave of Hermes Kronaios; in Ashmolean Museum
2. Attica	frag. of ceramic stand, Attic clay	Attic LPG	Kourou and Karetsou 1994: 116, no. 74, drawings 32–33, fig. 90; 141–42, 161	
3. East	unspecified number of frags. of miniature faience vases	LG–O	Levi 1927–29: 460; Skon-Jedele 1994: 1904, 1908, no. 2961+	

C.4.6. Overseas Artifacts Found at Tarra

FROM	ITEM	DATE	SOURCE	FIND SITE/ CIRCUMSTANCES
1. Egypt (?)	small scarab	O	Tzedakis 1971: 511; Aupert 1976: 738; Leclant 1977: 293; Skon-Jedele 1994: 1925, 1927, no. 2968	cemetery at Gialos, probably from burial of Orientalizing date

C.5. Overseas Artifacts with Uncertain Provenance in Crete

FROM	ITEM	DATE	SOURCE	FIND SITE/ CIRCUMSTANCES
1. Syria	bronze lyre player	9th–7th C.	Dunbabin 1957: 36, pl. 8.2	Herakleion inv. 2064; Boardman 1961: 119, uncertain of origin
2. Attica/ Boeotia (?)	fibula	mid-9th to mid-8th C.	Sapouna-Sakellarakis 1978: 107, no. 1494, pl. 43	in Herakleion Museum, no number, unpublished
3. Cyprus (?)	scarab seal, dark red-brown to black-brown soft stone	2nd half 8th C.	Kleiner and Ohly 1951: 14, 21, no. A1260, fig. 22, pl. 2.8; Boardman 1963b: 133, no. H1; Boardman 1970b: 264; Brandt 1968: 33, no. 106; Reyes 1939: 150 n. 208	from Crete; formerly in Arndt Collection
4. N. Syria (Aramaean)	lyre-player seal, red serpentine	c. 730–700	Porada 1956: 201, 210, fig. 16, pl. 17.16; Boardman 1961: 122, 124, no. 534 (Ashmolean no. 1938.1158), pl. 46; Buchner and Boardman 1966: 29, no. 71	uncertain; in Ashmolean Museum
5. N. Syria (Aramaean)	lyre-player seal, red serpentine	c. 730–700	Buchner and Boardman 1966: 29, no. 72; Copenhagen 3273	
6. N. Syria (Aramaean)	lyre-player seal, red steatite	c. 730–700	Porada 1956: 205, 211, fig. 42; Buchner and Boardman 1966: 29, no. 73; Louvre C24	
7. N. Syria (Aramaean)	lyre-player seal, green stone	c. 730–700	Buchner and Boardman 1966: 29, no. 75	once in Giamalakis Collection
8. N. Syria (Aramaean)	lyre-player seal, red serpentine	c. 730–700	Buchner and Boardman 1966: 29, no. 76, fig. 38; Munich A1258	
9. Rhodes	ceramic jug	Rhodian LG	Sieveking and Hackl 1912: 24, no. 455, fig. 57; Boardman 1961: 152–53 n. 9	allegedly from Crete
10. Attica (?)	hemispherical ivory seal, quadruped, apparently horned	late 8th C.	Boardman 1961: 124, no. 535, fig. 44, pl. 46; Boardman 1963b: 118, no. B26[*], pl. 14; Boardman and Vollenweider 1978: 3, no. 6, pl. 2	AE.1807; bought on Crete; gift of A. J. Evans to Ashmolean Museum
11. Egypt	scarab seal, blue frit	25th–26th Dynasty (c. 750–525)	Boardman 1961: 123–24, no. 536, AE.1808, fig. 44, pl. 46; Skon-Jedele 1994: 1953, no. 2987	bought on Crete

C.5. Overseas Artifacts with Uncertain Provenance in Crete *continued*

FROM	ITEM	DATE	SOURCE	FIND SITE/ CIRCUMSTANCES
12. Egypt	scarab seal, glazed steatite	25th–26th Dynasty (c. 750–525)	Boardman 1961: 123–24, no. 537, AE.1809, fig. 44, pl. 46; Skon-Jedele 1994: 1952–53, no. 2986	bought on Crete
13. Egypt	scarab, green faience	26th Dynasty	Pendlebury 1930a: 40, no. 69, pl. 1; Skon-Jedele 1994: 1952, no. 2985	
14. Egypt	ivory plaque: Hathor-head column	Cretan A	Boardman 1962: 30–31, fig. 2	found in the Knossos store-room
15. Peloponnese	oval plaque, pale green-gray serpentine; carved on both sides	early 7th C.	Boardman and Vollenweider 1978: 6, no. 24, pl. 5	Oxford 1938.758; bought on Crete (?); gift of A. J. Evans to Ashmolean Museum
16. Melos (?)	oval seal, red serpentine; running horse and dog; cup-spiral w/ palmette	mid-7th C.	Boardman 1961: 124, no. 539, pl. 46; Boardman 1963b: 128, G3; Boardman and Vollenweider: 1978: 4, no. 15	Oxford 1941.96; bought on Crete; gift of A. J. Evans to Ashmolean Museum
17. Corinth	globular aryballos, frieze: 4 warriors w/ round shields, helmets and lances	Transitional/EC	Sieveking and Hackl 1912: 24, no. 311	

C.6. Cretan Artifacts Found Overseas

FOUND AT	ITEM	DATE	CRETAN PROVENANCE	SOURCE	FIND SITE/ CIRCUMSTANCES
1. Latium? (local production)	• house models • house urns	LM IIIC or SM		Hencken 1968: 463, 467	from graves at Rome, in Alban Hills, at Grottaferrata, Castel Gandolfo, Marino, et al.; precolonization Cretan immigrants?
2. Kition	frag. of large vase	early SM?		Karageorghis 1960: 579–80, no. 29, figs. 129–30; Desborough 1964: 27; Desborough 1972b: 63	in a well in Chamber Tomb I, w/ stratified LH IIIC:2 pottery
3. Mycenae	stirrup jar	SM (LH IIIC late)		Wace 1921–22: 407, pl. 62.1b; Furumark 1944: 200; Desborough 1964: 36; Mountjoy 1986: 186 nn. 11–12, 188	pithos burial on terrace of Cyclopean Terrace House
4. Mycenae	relief pithos	SM (LH IIIC late)		Wace 1921–22: 407, pl. 62.2	pithos burial on terrace of Cyclopean Terrace House
5. Athens (?)	bronze fibula	SubMycenaean		Kraiker and Kübler 1939: 21, 83, fig. 2 left; Benton 1950: 20 n. 54; Müller-Karpe 1962: 119, fig. 3.10	Kerameikos, SM grave 42
6. Athens (?)	bronze fibula	SubMycenaean		Kraiker and Kübler 1939: 19, 83 n. 4; Benton 1950: 20 n. 54	Kerameikos, SM grave 33
7. Athens (?)	bronze fibula	SubMycenaean		Kraiker and Kübler 1939: 48, 83, fig. 2 left; Benton 1950: 20 n. 54; Müller-Karpe 1962: 120, fig. 5.12	Kerameikos, SM grave 108
8. Salamis (Cyprus)	3-legged cooking pot, coarseware	11th C.	like SM vase at Karphi	Yon 1971: 28–29, no. 55, pl. 19; Seiradaki 1960: 7, fig. 4:3	inv. no. 1393

C.6. Cretan Artifacts Found Overseas *continued*

FOUND AT	ITEM	DATE	CRETAN PROVENANCE	SOURCE	FIND SITE/ CIRCUMSTANCES
9. Salamis (Cyprus)	incised pitcher	SM--11th C.	similar to c. 12 from Karphi	Yon 1971: 41, no. 79, pl. 25; Yon 1979: 243, fig. 1	inv. no. 1524
10. Enkomi	vase	SM--11th C.	like 1 from Karphi	Dikaios 1969a: 316–17; Dikaios 1971: 492–93; Dikaios 1969b: pl. 95, no. 26; cf. pl. 106, no. 5; Kanta 1980: 313; Betancourt 1985: 186	Area I: Ashlar Building, central sector, 2 reconstructions of the megaron, Levels IIIB–C, Floor I
11. Kition	• terracotta figurine of goddess w/ upraised arms & polos • 3 fragmentary clay models of sanctuaries	SM type; 9th C. deposit		Karageorghis 1976: 91	temple area; from Minoan refugees? Heirloom?
12. Etruria; Coste del Marano, near Allumiere, northeast of Tarquinia (local production)	pre-Villanovan bronze cups w/ bulls' heads	LM to PG	probably based on survival of Minoan bulls' heads from chamber tomb at Mouliana (LM–PG)	Hencken 1968: 470	hoard; probably influence rather than import
13. Tarquinia? (local production?)	house urns	Villanovan IA, 930–800		Hencken 1968: 532, figs. 26b, 45g, 48e, f	Monterozzi, pozzo w/ house urn no. 3; Selcietello, gr. 45; Impiccato, gr. 51; influence may have come from Crete through Latium; probably not imports
14. Tarquinia (local production?)	leech-shaped fibulae w/ thickened bow & short catches	Villanovan IA–Villanovan IC (930/800–750)	may reflect Cretan examples from SM to PG at Vrokastro	Hencken 1968: 534–35	various graves at Selcietello, Selcietello Sopra, Impiccato
15. Tarquinia	2 "candelabra"	Villanovan I	only known parallel is Fortetsa no. 46--ceramic bird stand w/ birds	Hencken 1968: 538	1 from grave on Monterozzi; other has no history; "some connection may be suspected"

C.6. Cretan Artifacts Found Overseas *continued*

FOUND AT	ITEM	DATE	CRETAN PROVENANCE	SOURCE	FIND SITE/ CIRCUMSTANCES
16. Andros, Zagora	pot (at least 1)	G (?)		Cambitoglou et al. 1971: 58; Cambitoglou and Green 1970: 229	the town
17. Samos	skyphos or pyxis frag.	G		Technau 1929: 13, Beil. II.3; Eilmann 1933: 53; Roebuck 1959: 75 n. 16; Snodgrass 1971: 84 n. 58; Kilian-Dirlmeier 1985: 248	Heraion
18. Aigina	aryballoi	G		Johansen 1923: 19; Payne 1931b: 5 n. 1	
19. Corinth	aryballoi	G		Johansen 1923: 19; Payne 1931b: 5 n. 1	
20. Argolid	aryballoi	G		Johansen 1923: 19; Payne 1931b: 5 n. 1	
21. Delos	pomegranate vase	G		Dugas and Rhomaios 1934: pl. 52A; Courbin 1966: 535	
22. Rhodes-- Kameiros	pithos	c. 800	Cretan but not Knossian	Jacopi 1932–33: 123, fig. 135 *bis*; Brock 1957: 217 n. 2; Coldstream 1968: 274, 282; Snodgrass 1971: 127 n. 23	Patelle grave 39
23. Kasos?	large krater rim	MG–LG	east Cretan or local Kasian	Melas 1995: 161, no. 3, fig. 5	
24. Terni (Latium/ Etruria): in Apennines, c. 80 km ne of ancient Tarquinia	oinochoe; local copy of Cretan import	8th C.	similar to south Cretan vases	Stefani 1916: 217, fig. 26; Payne 1931b: 4 n. 2; Blakeway 1935: 130 n. 4; LoPorto 1974: 178, 187	Tomb 36

C.6. Cretan Artifacts Found Overseas *continued*

FOUND AT	ITEM	DATE	CRETAN PROVENANCE	SOURCE	FIND SITE/ CIRCUMSTANCES
25. Vulci (?)	2 pedestal-footed amphorae w/ lids and shoulder handles	2nd half 8th C.		Montelius 1895–1910: I.2, "Description Provisiore des Planches," 16, V, pl. 260, nos. 5 & 6; Blakeway 1935: 130 n. 9	tomb at Polledrara
26. Cerveteri (Latium/Etruria): 35 km wnw of Rome, near coast	jug	LG(?)		Blakeway 1932–33: 198, no. 12; Blakeway 1935: 130 n. 10; Åkerström 1943: 54, no. 16	in Cerveteri Room of Louvre, unnumbered at the time
27. Vetralla (Latium/Etruria): 15 km ne of ancient Tarquinia	tall-necked jug; local copy of Cretan import	8th C.	similar to south Cretan vases	Rossi-Danielli 1914: 333, fig. 24; Payne 1931b: 4 n. 2; Blakeway 1935: 130 n. 5, pl. 21, no. A3; LoPorto 1974: 178, 187	Tomb 9
28. Veii: 20 km n of Rome	bronze lion's head; local copy of Cretan work	8th C.		Brown 1960: 12–14; LoPorto 1974: 187	looks more Greek than Near East; reminiscent of Cretan shields
29. Gela	vase sherd	8th C.		Orsi 1906: 596, fig. 405; Payne 1931b: 5 n. 1; Blakeway 1932–33: 183, no. 33, pl. 24	Bitalemi; Payne: "perhaps Cretan"
30. Praeneste (40 km e of Rome)	bronze cauldron stands	8th C.–7th C.	probably made in same workshop as bronze tympanon from Idaean Cave	Boardman 1961: 158	from tombs
31. Capena (35 km n of Rome)	bronze bowl	8th C.–7th C.	probably made in same workshop as bronze tympanon from Idaean Cave	Boardman 1961: 158	

C.6. Cretan Artifacts Found Overseas *continued*

FOUND AT	ITEM	DATE	CRETAN PROVENANCE	SOURCE	FIND SITE/ CIRCUMSTANCES
32. Thera--Sellada (re-export?)	bronze rod tripod	G (last qtr. 8th C.)		Zapheiropoulos 1974: 199–200, pl. 140γ; Aupert 1975: 684, fig. 203; Catling 1975: 23, fig. 43; Catling 1984: 89; Matthäus 1985: 305 no. i; Matthäus 1988: 288	grave; Catling considers it Cypriot, transported to Thera via Knossos; Matthäus 1988 considers it possibly Cretan
33. Thera--Sellada (re-export?)	bronze tripod	G (last qtr. 8th C.)		Zapheiropoulos 1976: 332, pls. 209β, 210α; Touchais 1979: 605, fig. 172; Catling 1984: 85 n. 106, 89; Matthäus 1985: 305 no. j; Matthäus 1988: 288	grave; Catling considers it Cypriot, transported to Thera via Knossos
34. Thera--Sellada	pithos	G (EG?)		Zapheiropoulos 1973: 124, pl. 148β; Aupert 1976: 683	grave
35. Athens	bronze tripod	LG		Morgan 1990: 143	
36. Lindos	2 bronze tripod frags.	LG		Blinkenberg 1931: pl. 31.742; Willemsen 1957: 48; Morgan 1990: 143	
37. Samos	hemicylindrical "ivory" seal; linear incisions on back; centaur w/ branches	LG?	resembles seals from Idaean Cave	Karo 1933: 254, fig. 13; Boardman 1963b: 155, no. 16	under the great altar
38. Kasos	small krater, belly frag.	LG		Melas 1995: 161, no. 5, fig. 5	
39. Kasos	small belly frag.; micaceous clay	LG		Melas 1995: 161, no. 6, fig. 5	

C.6. Cretan Artifacts Found Overseas *continued*

FOUND AT	ITEM	DATE	CRETAN PROVENANCE	SOURCE	FIND SITE/ CIRCUMSTANCES
40. Chalkis	bronze bull figurine	LG	similar to figurines from sanctuary at Kato Syme Viannou	Papavasiliou 1912: 151, fig. 6; Schürmann 1996: 185	rural sanctuary, possibly of the Dioskouroi/Kabeiro i; about an hour's walk outside of Chalkis (in 1906), at a place called Peï, near the small town of Doukos
41. Olympia	large cauldron-handle: horse on open-work garland handle	8th C.		Willemsen 1957: 47, 59, 163, no. 913a, fig. 9, pl. 44	found at northeast corner of Temple of Zeus
42. Olympia	bronze open-work handle frag. w/ steerhead protome	8th C.		Willemsen 1957: 48, 57, nos. 13504+13518	
43. Olympia	bronze bull figurine	2nd half 8th C.		Neugebauer 1931: 38–39, no. 82, pl. 11; Zimmerman 1989: 299 n. 9	Olympia no. 7444; similar to example from Diktaean Cave
44. Olympia	2 bronze bovine figurines	LG		Zimmerman 1989: 299 n. 9	Olympia no. 8890, Athens MN 6242; similar to example from Cave of Hermes Kronaios at Patso
45. Olympia?	several bronze horse figurines	2nd half 8th C.		Zimmerman 1989: 299–306	Giamalakis group; at least some likely made by Cretan craftsmen at Olympia
46. Delphi?	bronze bull figurine	3rd qtr. 8th C.	similar to figurines from sanctuary at Kato Syme Viannou	Amandry 1944–45: 36, 41–42, no. 5, pl. 2.1; Rolley 1969: 99–100, no. 163, pl. 25; Schürmann 1996: 6, 185	beneath paving slabs of the Sacred Way (excavation from base of Boeotian Treasury to the small exedra south of the bouleteriod, on the other side of the Sacred Way); found around the level of the Bouleterion

C.6. Cretan Artifacts Found Overseas *continued*

FOUND AT	ITEM	DATE	CRETAN PROVENANCE	SOURCE	FIND SITE/ CIRCUMSTANCES
47. Delos	bronze horse figurine	3rd qtr. 8th C.		Deonna 1938: 211; Rolley 1973: 519–20, fig. 27; Zimmerman 1989: 294, no. CRE 5, 295 n. 16	from Sanctuary of Apollo; Rolley suggests end of 8th C.
48. Olympia	bronze pin, broken	Cretan LG	similar to pins at Arkades, Idaean Cave, and Knossos (Khaniale Tekke and Fortetsa)	Philipp 1981: 51, no. 71, Br. 12204, pls. 2, 28	east of east vestibule of Gymnasium
49. Taranto	terracotta relief, Theseus and Ariadne	3rd qtr. 7th C.		Langlotz 1928: 114–15, fig. 1; Jenkins 1932–33: 66 n. 7; Dunbabin 1948: 267 n. 3	in private collection
50. Tarquinia-- Monterozzi	several vases w/ Cretan influence	Villanovan IIB (Villanovan II c. 750– 700)		Blakeway 1932– 33: 197, nos. 80, 84; Hencken 1968: 573; LoPorto 1974: 178	La Tomba del Guerrero
51. Attica: Kerameikos, Koropi, Menidi	gold band work	c. 725	similar to locally carved ivory seals at Idaean Cave; Sakellarakis suggests same craftsmen	Cook 1951: 45– 49, pl. 10; Ohly 1953: 40–45, nos. A20a, A20, A22, figs. 19–20, photo after 40, pls. 10.1–3, 12.4; Sakellarakis 1992: 116	A20 from Kerameikos; A20a, Stathatos Collection, from grave near Koropi; A22 from grave near Menidi; Ohly (1953: 153 n. 10) cites steatite seal from Idaean Cave as possible parallel: Halbherr 1888: 757
52. Sparta	ivory seal	c. 725	similar to locally carved ivory seals at Idaean cave	Dawkins 1929: 240, pl. 168.4; Sakellarakis 1992: 115	Sanctuary of Artemis Orthia
53. Corinth	gold relief band	c. 725		Furtwängler 1884: 42, 99, 107, pl. 8.8; Payne 1931b: 222; Ohly 1953: 11–12, no. A21; Sakellarakis 1992: 116	"allegedly" from a grave

C.6. Cretan Artifacts Found Overseas *continued*

FOUND AT	ITEM	DATE	CRETAN PROVENANCE	SOURCE	FIND SITE/ CIRCUMSTANCES
54. Delos	5 vases	after c. 725		Coldstream 1968: 382 n. 3; Dugas 1928: 59–60, pl. 55, nos. 660, 662, 663; Dugas and Rhomaios 1934: pls. 50,13 & 52,15; Payne 1928: 274; Payne 1931b: 5 n. 1	Jones (1986b: 645, 651–52) questions Cretan provenances for 4 amphorae from Dugas and Rhomaios 1934: pls 49 and 50A; recommends Parian and possibly Naxian origins
55. Melos	3 vases	after c. 725		Coldstream 1968: 382	
56. Athens	frags. of large vase	after c. 725		Coldstream 1968: 382	acropolis
57. Delphi	bronze openwork stand	after c. 725		Amandry 1944–45: 56–61, inv. no. 6928, fig. 17, pl. 4.1; Coldstream 1968: 382; Rolley 1977: 115, no. 503, pl. 52	west of the Treasury of the Athenians
58. Delphi	bronze open-work stand	after c. 725		Filippakis et al. 1983: 119, 132, no. 32, R507	
59. Delphi	bronze open-work stand	after c. 725		Filippakis et al. 1983: 119, 132, no. 33, R509	
60. Delphi	bronze open-work stand	after c. 725		Filippakis et al. 1983: 119, 132, no. 84, R504	
61. Delphi	bronze open-work stand	after c. 725		Filippakis et al. 1983: 119, 132, no. 83	
62. Delphi	frags. of bronze votive shield, decorated w/ sphinxes and stags in repoussé	after c. 725		Amandry 1944–45: 45–49, figs. 8–9, pl. 3.1, inv. 6948; Coldstream 1968: 382; Filippakis et al. 1983: 119, 130, no. 35; Magou et al. 1986: 132; Rolley 1986: 28, fig. 5	found under the Sacred Way

C.6. Cretan Artifacts Found Overseas *continued*

FOUND AT	ITEM	DATE	CRETAN PROVENANCE	SOURCE	FIND SITE/ CIRCUMSTANCES
63. Delphi	bronze shield, decorated w/ animals in repoussé	after c. 725		Filippakis et al. 1983: 119, 130, no. 36, inv. no. P531	probably Cretan
64. Delphi	bronze shield, decorated w/ animals in repoussé	after c. 725		Filippakis et al. 1983: 119, 130, no. 85, inv. no. 1932	probably Cretan
65. Delphi	bronze mitra	after c. 725	similar to mitrai from Axos and Praisos	Perdrizet 1908: 102–3, no. 514; fig. 353; Boardman 1961: 156 n. 13; Hoffmann 1972: 27	found behind base of Gelon; inv. no. 1929
66. Delphi	bronze kouros statuette	after c. 640	similar to terracotta figurine from Gortyn and head vase from Arkades	Perdrizet 1897: 169, pls. 10–11; Perdrizet 1908: 34, pl. 3; Lamb1929: 75, pl. 216; Jenkins 1936: 4, 46, 64; Charbonneaux 1958: 140, pl. 6.1; Boardman 1961: 156 n. 14; Rizza and Santa Maria Scrinari 1968: 231, fig. 315a–b; Rolley 1969: 8, 14, 16; Wallenstein 1971: 34–35; Davaras 1972: 54–55, no. 21	Delphi Museum no. 2527
67. Delphi	bronze statuette	LG	parallel at Aghia Triada	Montelius 1924: 177, 180, figs. 631–632; Rolley 1969: no. 16; Rolley 1977: 146, no. I16	
68. Delphi	bronze statuette	LG		Rolley 1969: no. 174; Rolley 1977: 146, no. I174	Rolley less certain of Cretan origin than for statuette no. I16

C.6. Cretan Artifacts Found Overseas *continued*

FOUND AT	ITEM	DATE	CRETAN PROVENANCE	SOURCE	FIND SITE/ CIRCUMSTANCES
69. Dodona	bronze votive shield	after c. 725		Carapanos 1878: 298, no. 54; Kunze 1931: pl. 51d; Coldstream 1968: 382	
70. Miletus	bronze votive shield	after c. 725		Kunze 1931: 281; Coldstream 1968: 382	
71. Olympia	bronze bull figurine	LG/SubG		Neugebauer 1931: 55, no. 143, pl. 17; Zimmerman 1989: 299 n. 9	Olympia inv. no. 10002; by same hand as Athens MN 6242
72. Rhodes-- Ialysos	stamnos, small plates	end 8th–early 7th C.		Maiuri 1923–24: 304, fig. 200, 309, fig. 205; Blinkenberg 1931: 304–6; Levi 1927–29: 662–63	Grave 53
73. Perachora	terracotta relief plaque: Theseus and Ariadne; made from Cretan matrix	end 8th C.		Jenkins 1940: 230, no. 179, pl. 102	Temenos of Hera Limenia
74. Mylai (?) (Sicily)	three aryballoi (two miniature, c. 5 cm high)	8th C.–early 7th C.		Bernabò Brea and Cavalier 1959: 61, pl. 53.6; 77; 81, pl. 41.6; Coldstream 1969: 4 n. 33; LoPorto 1974: 176 n. 24, 177 n. 61; Dehl 1984: 223	graves 65, 77, 142; and 1 stray find; LoPorto calls these Rhodio-Cretan, but they are not Friis Johansen's <u>Kreis und Wellenband</u> style
75. Cumae	basin frag.	Cretan SubG– EO (end of 8th–early 7th C.)	resembles pithos lids at Arkades & Knossos	Payne 1931b: 5 n. 1; Blakeway 1932–33: 201, fig. 18; LoPorto 1974: 177, fig. 5	from necropolis; in Stevens Collection
76. Gela	globular small cup frag.	precolonizati on; end 8th C. to c. 640		Fiorentini and DeMiro 1983: 61, no. 4, fig. 8,m; 62	from acropolis, stratigraphic trials under Bldg. I, Room 1
77. Gela	pithos lid frag.	precolonizati on; end 8th C. to c. 640	like frag. found at Arkades	Fiorentini and DeMiro 1983: 61, no. 6, fig. 8,l(el)	from acropolis, stratigraphic trials under Bldg. I

C.6. Cretan Artifacts Found Overseas *continued*

FOUND AT	ITEM	DATE	CRETAN PROVENANCE	SOURCE	FIND SITE/ CIRCUMSTANCES
78. Gela	pyxis	1st years of colony to c. 650	similar to LG urn from Kavousi & another from Arkades	Orsi 1906: 596, fig. 404; Payne 1931b: 5 n. 1; Blakeway 1932–33: 183, no. 32, pl. 24; Dunbabin 1949: 139; LoPorto 1974: 179, pl. 19.4; Fiorentini and DeMiro 1983: 92–93, fig. 86	from Sanctuary of Bitalemi; PG motif, which persisted in Crete during 7th C.; Dunbabin revised Blakeway's dating from 8th C. to early 7th C.
79. Gela	pithos w/ lid	early years of colonization	south Cretan-- Arkades?	Orsi 1906: 124, pl. 5.2; Payne 1931b: 5 n. 1; Blakeway 1932–33: 183 n. 2; Dunbabin 1948: 230 n. 1; Coldstream, 1968: 375 n. 10; LoPorto 1974: 179, pl. 19.1; Fiorentini and De Miro 1983: 81, fig. 46 center	Borgo Cemetery, Tomb 211, infant burial, c. 630; "probably brought by 1st colonists"
80. Gela (?)	pithos	early years of colonization	south Cretan-- Arkades?	Orlandini and Adamesteanu 1956: 307–8, fig. 23.a–b; Coldstream 1968: 375 n. 10; LoPorto 1974: 181–82, pl. 19.5	Villa Garibaldi Cemetery, grave 32. Orlandini and LoPorto considered it Rhodio-Cretan; Coldstream called it Cretan
81. Cyrene?	7 figurines	as early as 2nd qtr. 7th C.		White 1984: 23 n. 10; Schaus 1985: 98 n. 44	Sanctuary of Demeter and Persephone; may have arrived via Thera
82. Kasos?	krater belly frag.; fabric "rather Cretan"; panther decoration of Cycladic type	1st half 7th C.		Melas 1995: 161, no. 4, fig. 5	
83. Thera	2 crude stone statuettes, female figures	beginning 7th C.	similar to one found at Lato	Dragendorff 1903: 305, figs. 492a & b; Demargne 1929: 386–87	from Schiff's grave

C.6. Cretan Artifacts Found Overseas *continued*

FOUND AT	ITEM	DATE	CRETAN PROVENANCE	SOURCE	FIND SITE/ CIRCUMSTANCES
84. Thera	gold plaques (1 certainly, 2 others likely)	early 7th C.	similar to ones at Idaean Cave	Pfuhl 1903: 228, pl. v:15; Boardman 1961: 139	grave 89:109
85. Thera	vases (upwards of 20)	late 8th C.– early 7th C.		Pfuhl 1903: 140–65, Beil. 19.2, 38.7–8; Dragendorff 1903: figs. 193, 212 (amphorae), 368, 369a–b, 499a–b, 499d–g (aryballoi, oinochoe, var. jugs); Weinberg 1943: 18; Boardman 1961: 156 n. 3	Messavouno; Sellada graves 80, 84, 93, Schiff's grave, private collection
86. Thera	several bronze pins; 1 bone pin	early 7th C.		Dragendorff 1903: 302, fig. 490b, 320, E2; Pfuhl 1903: 231, figs. 73–74; Jacobsthal 1956: 17, no. 55a; Boardman 1961: 156 n. 4; Kilian-Dirlmeier 1984: 219 n. 16	from Schiff's grave
87. Rhodes-Ialysos	silver finger ring	early 7th C.	similar in shape to gold one from Praisos	Jacopi 1929: 51, fig. 44; Higgins 1969: 152	from cremation tomb 23, item no. 4; inv. no. 10697; Higgins reported it as gold
88. Ithaka-Aetos	gold finial	early 7th C.; possibly as early as c. 725	like gold ornament from Khaniale Tekke tomb, Hutchinson and Boardman 1954	Robinson 1955: 37; Coldstream 1968: 382	
89. Gela	bronze patera (or phiale)	early 7th C.	reminiscent of paterae from Idaean Cave	Orsi 1906: 224–27, 226 n. 1, fig. 178; LoPorto 1974: 187 n. 185; Fiorentini and DeMiro 1983: 101–3, figs. 113–114	
90. Gela	cup frag.	1st years of colonization		Fiorentini and DeMiro 1983: 80, fig. 44	from oldest stratum of acropolis; in Gela Museum

C.6. Cretan Artifacts Found Overseas *continued*

FOUND AT	ITEM	DATE	CRETAN PROVENANCE	SOURCE	FIND SITE/ CIRCUMSTANCES
91. Gela	plate frag.	1st years of colonization		Fiorentini and DeMiro 1983: 81, fig. 45	from oldest stratum of acropolis; in Gela Museum
92. Satyrion	vase frag.	2nd qtr. 7th C.		LoPorto 1964: 230, fig. 47.10; LoPorto 1974: 186	
93. Taranto	vase frag., possibly mid-size amphora	G–O: 1st half 7th C.	north-central Crete	LoPorto 1974: 184–85, pl. 20.6; LoPorto 1959–60: 36, fig. 25c	from necropolis, tomb 15
94. Praeneste & Cerveteri	ivory lions; local copy of Cretan work	1st half 7th C.		Brown 1960: 2–3; LoPorto 1974: 187	Praeneste: Tomba Barberine & Tomba Castellani; Cerveteri: Tomba di Montetesto. In tradition w/ Nimrud ivories & projecting bronze lion head on Cretan shield Kunze no. 10, pls. 26–27
95. Gela	lip & handle of trefoil jug	1st half 7th C.		Fiorentini and DeMiro 1983: 67, fig. 13	
96. Gela	stamnos; local copy of a Cretan original	not later than mid-7th C.	similar decoration to vase from Arkades	Orsi 1906: 194, fig. 151; LoPorto 1974: 179–80, fig. 6; Fiorentini and DeMiro 1983: 92	Borgo Cemetery, Tomb 459
97. Perachora	terracotta relief plaque, running winged demon, made from Cretan matrix	mid-7th C.		Payne 1932: 242; Jenkins 1936: pl. 4.7; Jenkins 1940: 230–31, no. 180, pl. 102; Wallenstein 1971: 35, 105	Sanctuary of Hera Limenia; made from Corinthian clay; probably same matrix used to make Waldstein 1905: 47–49, pl. 49.1
98. Olympia	frags. of bronze reliefs	mid-7th C.	closely allied to tympanon from Idaean Cave	Boardman 1961: 156 n. 7	
99. Olympia	2 plain mitrai	mid-7th C.		Boardman 1961: 156 n. 8	
100. Olympia	bronze bull figurine	SubG		Zimmerman 1989: 299 n. 9	

C.6. Cretan Artifacts Found Overseas *continued*

FOUND AT	ITEM	DATE	CRETAN PROVENANCE	SOURCE	FIND SITE/ CIRCUMSTANCES
101. Athens	bronze bull figurine	SubG		Zimmerman 1989: 299 n. 9	Athens inv. no. MN 6242
102. Gela (not an import)	krater frag.; local clay	O	similar to vase at Arkades	Orsi 1906: 149, fig. 111; Dunbabin 1948: 230 n. 1; LoPorto 1974: 180–81, fig. 7	tomb 305 of Borgo necropolis; local clay; LoPorto suggests it may be from a local workshop of Cretan immigrants; Dunbabin (1948) thought it was a Cretan import
103. Delos	2 vases: amphora and amphora or krater base frag.	O		Brock 1935: 249; Poulson & Dugas 1911: 399, no. 66, fig. 59; Dugas 1935: 11, no. 5, fig. 1, pls. 3–4; 14, no. 14, pl. 67B	no. 14 from the Artemision
104. Etruria (?)	stone sphinx (local product made under Cretan influence)	7th C.		Loewy 1930: 99–100, pls. 7, 8.1	(formerly?) in private collection in Vienna
105. Gela	pithos	7th C.	south Cretan	Fiorentini and DeMiro 1983: 80–81, fig. 47	from necropolis of Borgo
106. Gela	oinochoe	7th C.		Fiorentini and DeMiro 1983: 81, fig. 48	from a grave; in Syracuse Museum
107. Gela	pot-bellied vase frag.	7th C.		Fiorentini and DeMiro 1983: 67, fig. 14,a	acropolis, Room 3, Stratum $5b_1$
108. Tocra (ancient Taucheira, North African coast w of Cyrene)	2 jug frags.	LO	no. 923 similar to jug from Fortetsa	Boardman & Hayes 1966: nos. 923, 925, pl. 56	
109. Tocra	mug	LO		Boardman & Hayes 1966: no. 927, pl. 56	
110. Tocra (?)	miniature hydra	LO		Boardman & Hayes 1966: no. 929	"perhaps Cretan"

C.6. Cretan Artifacts Found Overseas *continued*

FOUND AT	ITEM	DATE	CRETAN PROVENANCE	SOURCE	FIND SITE/ CIRCUMSTANCES
111. Tocra	dish w/ 3 vertical handles	LO		Boardman & Hayes 1966: no. 930, fig. 39, pl. 56	
112. Tocra	small bowl	LO		Boardman & Hayes 1966: no. 931, fig. 39, pl. 56	possibly East Greek
113. Tocra	neck-handled amphora	LO		Megaw 1963–64: 32, fig. 3	
114. Tocra	bowl	620–590		Boardman & Hayes, 1973: 37, no. 2105, fig. 16	Deposit I, Level 9
115. Tocra	mug	620–590		Boardman & Hayes 1966: 24, 34, no. 264, fig. 17, pl. 18; Boardman & Hayes 1973: 37	originally identified as Corinthian
116. Tocra	2 hydriae	LO (or 1st third of 6th C.)	no. 921 similar to hydria from Gortyn; clay similar to pots from Tylissos, Gornia, & Aghia Triada	Boardman & Hayes 1966: nos. 921, 923, pl. 56; Boardman & Schweizer 1973: 275 Diagram XX, 280	
117. Tocra	jug frag.	LO (or 1st third of 6th C.)	clay similar to pots from Tylissos, Gornia, & Aghia Triada	Boardman & Hayes 1966: no. 924, pl. 56; Boardman & Schweizer 1973: 275 Diagram XX, 280	from Deposit II
118. Tocra	pyxis	LO (or 1st third of 6th C.)		Boardman & Hayes 1966: no. 926, pl. 56	from Deposit II
119. Tocra	vase rim & handle	LO (or 1st third of 6th C.)		Boardman & Hayes 1966: no. 928	from Deposit II
120. Taranto	pyxis	2nd qtr. of 7th C. or later	similar to Fortetsa no. 1299	LoPorto 1959–60: 32, figs. 23–24; LoPorto 1974: 184–85, pl. 20.3–5	from Treasury District, pit grave, tomb 15; vase no. 52913 in Taranto Museum

C.6. Cretan Artifacts Found Overseas *continued*

FOUND AT	ITEM	DATE	CRETAN PROVENANCE	SOURCE	FIND SITE/ CIRCUMSTANCES
121. Brindisi	pyxis	c. 660		LoPorto 1974: 183–84, pl. 20.1–2	in pit grave w/ PC aryballos
122. Bassae	miniature armor • 2 miniature cuirasses • 1 miniature helmet • 1 set of greaves	mid-7th C.	cuirasses resemble Praisos & Gortyn miniatures; greaves similar to ones at Kavousi & Praisos	Snodgrass 1974: 196, pls. 23,1–2	thought to be dedications by soldiers from Lyttos & Aptera in 2nd Messenian War; possibly local manufacture of miniatures
123. Gela	clay head-- female figure w/ high headdress	mid-7th C.		Meola 1971: 65, 75, cass. 268, pl. 2d; LoPorto 1974: 183 n. 134, 187 n. 185; Fiorentini and DeMiro 1983: 100, fig. 109	
124. Olympia	bronze mitra	mid-7th C.		Yalouris 1960: 59; Schefold 1966: 42, pl. 26; Kunze 1968: 196–97, pls. ΛZ.1–2, ΛH.1–3; Bartels 1967a: 198, 203, pls. 102–105; Hoffmann 1972: 26, 39, pls. 46.2, 47.2; Ol. Mus. no. B4900	from north wall of stadium
125. Olympia	bronze head	LO		Studniczka 1928: pl. 20; Jenkins 1936: 38–39, 56, 63, pl. 4.6; Davaras 1972: 54, no. 19	
126. Kythera	alabastron	LO—mid-7th C.		Coldstream and Huxley 1973: 267, Q5, 306, pl. 86	from Palaiokastro
127. Kythera	aryballos	LO	parallels from Fortetsa and Arkades	Coldstream and Huxley 1973: 268, Q9, 306, pl. 87	

C.6. Cretan Artifacts Found Overseas *continued*

FOUND AT	ITEM	DATE	CRETAN PROVENANCE	SOURCE	FIND SITE/ CIRCUMSTANCES
128. Argos	terracotta relief plaque: running, winged demon; made from Cretan mold	mid-7th C.		Waldstein 1905: 47–49, pl. 49.1; Payne 1932: 242; Jenkins 1940: 230–31; Wallenstein 1971: 35, 105	Argive Heraeum
129. Samos	wooden figurine: Daedalic kore	late 8th C. – mid-7th C.	similar to artifacts from Gortyn and Arkades	Kyrieleis 1980: 94–103, inv. H.100; Kyrieleis 1983: 298–99, figs. 6–7; Shipley 1987: 51 n. 16, 56	Kyrieleis (1980: 100–101) suggests it may have been made by a traveling Cretan sculptor in Samos
130. Samos	ivory figurine of young male, part of kithara	mid- to last qtr. 7th C.	compare male figures from Praisos and Gortyn	Walter 1959; Walter 1963: 290–91, fig. 4; Ohly 1959: 54–55, figs. 7–8, Beil. 87–93, 96.1; Lebessi 1983; Stampolidis 1992: 148	
131. Samos	wooden figurine of Hera	c. 640	cf. skirt decoration w/ locally carved ivory figurine from Idaean Cave, Sakellarakis 1984: pl. 247α	Ohly 1967: figs. 1–2, pls. 43–47; Köpcke 1967: no. 1, 100–107; Kyrieleis 1980: 98–99; Kyrieleis 1983: 299–300	
132. Samos (?)	wooden woman's-head aryballos, Daedalic style	c. 640		Köpcke 1967: 115–16, no. 6, fig. 3, Beil. 58	Köpcke calls it local Samian work
133. Ithaka	black-figure dinos and other vases	3rd qtr. 7th C.	dinos matches items found at Afrati	Boardman 1961: 157 n. 4	
134. Magna Graecia	lower half of terracotta low relief of goddess (?), broken at waist; skirt and hands only	3rd qtr. 7th C.		Levi 1926: 170–71, no. 766, fig. 130; Dohan 1931: 214 n. 14	Italian provenance unknown; in Naples Museum

C.6. Cretan Artifacts Found Overseas *continued*

FOUND AT	ITEM	DATE	CRETAN PROVENANCE	SOURCE	FIND SITE/ CIRCUMSTANCES
135. Magna Graecia (?)	upper half of terracotta low relief of goddess (?); possible complement to <u>Terracotte figurate</u>, no. 766	3rd qtr. 7th C.		Studniczka 1891: 253–54; Levi 1926: 171; Jenkins 1932–33: 66 n. 7; Jenkins 1936: 54; Dunbabin 1948: 267 n. 3	in Santongelo Collection, Naples; Levi considered it a modern forgery
136. Cyprus?	bronze head vase, Daedalic style	2nd half 7th C.		Studniczka 1928: 247–48, figs. 3–4; Charbonneaux 1958: 140, pl. 62; Boardman 1961: 80	in Louvre
137. Olympia	bronze cuirass	c. 640–630		Hoffmann 1972: 22–23	
138. Aziris (North African coast, e of Derna)	spherical flask of Cypriot type	LG–EO (637–631)		Boardman 1966: 11, no. 13, pl. 29	
139. Delphi	bronze helmet	c. 630/620	like one found at Axos	Marcadé 1949; Snodgrass 1964: 28; Hoffmann 1972: 22, 46, pls. 18.1–2,4	
140. Delphi	bronze helmet, undecorated	last qtr. 7th C.		Kunze 1961: 59–61, 74, no. 11; Snodgrass 1964: 28–29; Hoffmann 1972: 27	
141. Olympia	bronze helmet, undecorated	last qtr. 7th C.		Kunze 1961: 59–61, 74, no. 1; Snodgrass 1964: 28–29; Hoffmann 1972: 27	
142. Taranto	terracotta head	c. 625		Jenkins 1932–33: 66; Jenkins 1936: 54, pl. 7.5; Dunbabin 1948: 267 n. 3; LoPorto 1974: 188 n. 189	in Berlin (formerly?)
143. Taranto	spheroid olpe	last qtr. 7th C.		LoPorto 1959–60: 90–91	tomb 46; possibly 7th C. Cycladic; definitely not local

C.6. Cretan Artifacts Found Overseas *continued*

FOUND AT	ITEM	DATE	CRETAN PROVENANCE	SOURCE	FIND SITE/ CIRCUMSTANCES
144. Sparta	straight-sided shallow pyxis	last qtr. 7th C.		Droop 1926–27: 58, pl. 6; Droop 1931–32: 249; Hartley 1930–31: 61 nn. 5–6; Hartley 1931–32: 254; Payne 1931b: 5 n. 1, 342 (XII); Lane 1933–34: 119	from Acropolis; Droop and Lane favored Laconian origin; Hartley and Payne favored Cretan
145. Sparta	terracotta head	late 7th C.		Woodward 1927–28: 85, 89–90, no. 5, fig. 5; Jenkins 1932–33: 66–67 n. 11; Carter 1985: 191 n. 141	acropolis
146. Olympia	bronze mitra	late 7th C.	reminiscent of mitra from Arkades	Bartels 1967b: 264; Hoffmann 1972: 26; Ol. Mus. no. 6999 unpublished	
147. Olympia	bronze mitra, fragmentary, undecorated	late 7th C.	reminiscent of mitra from Arkades	Bartels 1967a: 197, no. 1, pl. 100.1; Hoffmann 1972: 26; Ol. Mus. no. B1798	
148. Olympia	bronze mitra, fragmentary, undecorated	late 7th C.		Bartels 1967a: 197, no. 2, pl. 100.2; Hoffmann 1972: 26; Ol. Mus. nos. B2475 & B2735	
149. Olympia	bronze mitra, fragmentary, undecorated	late 7th C.	reminiscent of mitra from Arkades	Bartels 1967a: 197, no. 3, pl. 100.3; Hoffmann 1972: 27; Ol. Mus. no. B4923	
150. Olympia	bronze mitra, fragmentary, undecorated, border ornament of lotus-palmette chain	late 7th C.	reminiscent of mitra from Arkades	Bartels 1967a: 197, no. 4, pl. 100.1; Hoffmann 1972: 27	
151. Olympia	2 bronze mitrai	late 7th C.		Hoffmann 1972: 27	possibly Cretan

C.6. Cretan Artifacts Found Overseas *continued*

FOUND AT	ITEM	DATE	CRETAN PROVENANCE	SOURCE	FIND SITE/ CIRCUMSTANCES
152. Olympia	bronze pin head	late 7th C.	similar to two pins from Knossos, Sanctuary of Demeter, among earliest votives there	Philipp 1981: 52, no. 74, pl. 29	from southeastern section, western P40, archaic/classical stratum; parallels conform w/ Jacobsthal's SubG and O types; Coldstream, 1973b: 146–47, fig. 34, nos. 121, 124
153. Kythera	askos in form of a siren	c. 600	parallels in reserving techniques of the arms from Arkades	Coldstream and Huxley 1973: 270, R2, 306, pl. 88; Higgins 1959: 44, no. 1677, pl. 30; Maximova 1927: 147–48, pl. XXIX, no. 111	bequeathed to British Museum in 1869 by James Woodhouse, to whom it was given on Kythera by Sig. Legislatore

Table Cat.1. Origins and Dates of Overseas Artifacts Found at Cretan Sites, by Period (artifacts from Attica, Corinth, Cyprus and Egypt)

Period	Attica	Corinth	Cyprus	Egypt
1100-1050	**1100-970** VR.4 **1100-850** VR.5		**1100-970** VR.2; FS.1[1]; KNC.4-5; KN.2 **1100-900** EL.2 **1100-840** KRF.1; KNC.6 **1100-790** VR.3 **1100-680** KV.2	**c. 1250-850** ARK.1 **1100-1075(?)** VR.1 **1100-970** EL.1 **1075-920** KF.2 **1050-1000** IC.1
1050-1000	**1050-980** Ktwn.1			
1000-950	**1000-900** KF.16- 18; KN.13-14 **1000-950** FS.2; KN.4-12 **1000-850** VR.6 **970-850** KF.20 **970-700** PLK.1		**c. 1000** TYL.1[5] **970-920** KF.4 **970-710** KN.20 **970-840** GRT.1; KNC.30	**970-840** KF.21[2]; KN.17-18; KNC.37[1]
950-900	**950-900** Ktwn.3; KNC.8-19; KN.24- 25 **950-875** KN.33 **950-850** KN.32 **950-800** KN.34 **925-900** KN.28 **925-875** KNC.29- 32	**950-900** KNC.22	**950-800** KF.19[3]	**945-715(?)** VR.7
900-850	**900-875** KNC.28 **900-800** RZ.1 **900-700** DR.1; KN.38; PR.1[1] **900-700** PR.5 **875-850** Ktwn.5 **875-800** KN.37 **870-840** KN.26	**900-700** PR.1[1]	**900-800** AMN.1 **900-700** KM.3 **900-630** PRS.1 **870-840** KN.30	**900-750** KM.29; ARK.2
850-800	**850-800** ARK.3; KN.35,52; KNC.42-44 **850-760** KNC.45; KN.63-66,69 **850-750** KF.29- 30[3]; PRN.2-4[3]; KSM.1[3]; PU.2[3] **850-735** KNC.48- 50 **850-700** EL.3 **840-810** FS.8[4] **810-710** VR.10- 13[3]; DR.4[3]	**835-750** Ktwn.9 **830-720** EL.4 **820-745** PR.2 **810-720** FS.4 **810-710** KV.8	**c. 850** KF.25 **850-800** KN.89 **850-750** KNC.46- 47, 48-49[3] **850-700** IC.57-58 **820-800** KNC.40,[4] 41 **810-710** KN.50-51; VR.14-15; KV.4; PR.6	**850-700** IC.3, 52, 56 **850-735** KNC.53 **810-710** DR.3; KV.5; KN.48; PRN.1 **810-630** IC.95-96 **810-600** EL.5-6[2]

Table Cat.1. Origins and Dates of Overseas Artifacts Found at Cretan Sites, by Period *continued* (artifacts from Attica, Corinth, Cyprus and Egypt)

Period	Attica	Corinth	Cyprus	Egypt
800-750	**800-775** Ktwn.10, 11[2]; GVM.1-3 **800-760** KN.53-62 **800-750** KN.70[4] **800-735** FS.9[4] **790-760** KN.111-112 **790-745** KF.36-37 **760-720** KN.104 **760-700** DR.5; KN.91-92	**800-750** KN.71-72, 87-88 **790-745** KF.24 **770-735** Ktwn.12 **760-735** Ktwn.13 **760-700** Ktwn.14	**800-775** KNC.56-75 **800-750** KF.48 **800-700** KNC.77-78; KSM.2; IC.67[3] **800-650** ARK.6 **790-745** KF.42-44 **790-710** KF.49 **790-710** KN.82-83	**c. 800** KN.46 **800-700** IC.64-65[2] **800-600** KM.12-13; AMN.8[9] **790-745** KF.45[8] **770-680** DC.1[3]
750-700	**c. 750** LS.1 **750-725** Ktwn.15; LS.2 **725-700** DR.7[3]; LS.4-6 **720-700** PU.10 **720-650** ANV.3 **715-685** LS.7	**750-725** PR.8 **750-720** ANV.2 **750-690** KNC.79 **735-700** Ktwn.18 **725-700** KM.16 **720-700** Ktwn.19; ARK.10 **720-690** IT.3; KN.116-117; PR.11-16 **720-680** Ktwn.20 **720-630** DR.6; KM.17; EL.10; FS.12; IT.4; AMN.7; LSP.1; ARK.11-15 **720-600** KNC.88 **720-590** EL.9 **710-680** AMN.6	**c. 750** KN.94,105-106 **750-700** PU.3 **750-600** KNC.82 **745-710** KF.55-59 **745-630** KN.109 **725-700** KN.110 **720-690** ARK.16[6] **720-650** KTS.1[3,5]	**750-650** INT.1 **750-525** PU.11-12 **745-710** ZKR.1; AMN.4 **730-700** KM.8-9 **720-650** KN.120; INT.2[6] **720-600** KN.118-119[2]; KSM.3-4[9]; INT.10-12[6], 13-14[11], 23-52[6]
700-650	**c. 700** IC.99-100[3] **700-650** ML.1; LS.8-9 **700-630** KF.78[3] **700-600** ARK.8[3]	**700-680** KF.67; IC.102 **700-650** PR.19; Ktwn.21 **700-630** KN.126 **700-600** KM.19; KF.60-66; KN.133; DC.23-26; PR.21-22 **690-** KN.134-135 **690-670** ARK.9 **690-650** KN.136 **680-630** GV.1 **675-650** KN.125 **670-655** ARK.19 **665-630** EL.11-14 **665-620** ARK.23-24 **660-620** ARK.26 **660-655** ARK.20 **675-600** KM.20 **660-650** Ktwn.24 **655-650** ARK.21 **655-640** ARK.22	**700-630** KV.9 **680-665** KF.68-69, 70[3] **680-665** KN.122 **665-630** KF.79, 80 **700-600** KN.128-129,131 **680-600** PR.18	**700-630** KF.77; KNC.89-91[8]; INT.7[6]; TRA.1 **700-600** IC.103[2]; AVL.1[2]; ART.6[1,9]; LNO.1[2]; INT.54; KSY.1; KTS.2[9] **700-580** TRC.1[2] **680-630** KF.76; DC.27[4] **665-630** KN.137[5] **-650** IC.106 **664-525** KF.81; PU.13

Table Cat.1. Origins and Dates of Overseas Artifacts Found at Cretan Sites, by Period *continued* (artifacts from Attica, Corinth, Cyprus and Egypt)

Period	Attica	Corinth	Cyprus	Egypt
650-600	**c. 650** KM.22 **625-600** KM.29	**c. 650** Ktwn.25; KN.139-140 **650-640** GRT.8 **650-630** PR.20 **650-620** Ktwn.26 **650-600** Ktwn.27-28; KM.23; KN.142-153 **640-630** KM.21 **640-625** ARK.25 **640-600** PU.17 **630-620** ARK.27-29 **630-610** Ktwn.29; FS.15 **630-600** Ktwn.30-32; KN.155 **620-600** KM.31-33, 54; KSM.5; ARK.40-44 **610-600** ARK.30 **620-580** ARK.45-47 **c. 600-580** ARK.48-49; KSM.6 **c.600-580** DC.28	**620-600** KM.56-57 **630-580** AMN.14,[4] 21[3]	**c. 650** ARK.35[10], 36[6] **650-600** S.1 **630-580** AMN.9-10,11[6],13,14,[7] 15-16[9],17-20, 22[7], 23, 25-26[9]; PU.14; ANV.4; KN.156 **625-600** IC.107-108,[2] 109; PR.9
Other				**undated** DC.2-4
Notes	[1]or Corinth? [2]probably [3]or Boeotia [4]or Cyclades	[1] or Attica?	[1]less likely than Argos [2]question on provenance [3]possibly Phoenician [4]or Egypt [5]or Syria [6]or Levant	[1]or Levant [2]or Phoenicia [3]possibly Bronze Age [4]possibly Phoenicia or Palestine [5]question on provenance [6]or Rhodes [7]or Cyprus [8]or Near East [9]or East Greece [10]local copy [11]probably

Table Cat.1. Origins and Dates of Overseas Artifacts Found at Cretan Sites, by Period *continued*
(artifacts from Phoenicia, Cyclades, Rhodes and East Greece)

Period	Phoenicia	Cyclades	Rhodes	East Greece
1100-1050	**1100-1000** KNC.7			
1050-1000				
1000-950	**1000-800** KM.1 **970-840** KF.21[2]	**1000-920** KF.10-15 **970-840** KN.22-23[1]		**970-790** KN.29
950-900				**950-875** KNC.24[4]
900-850	**900-700** KM.2[1]	**870-840** KF.22; KNC.33 **870-810** KF.23; KM.4		
850-800	**c. 850** KNC.38 **850-800** KN.81 **850-700** KNC.47-48[3] **825-775** KM.5 **825-700** KM.6 **820-800** KNC.39 **820-780** KM.7 **810-745** PR.3-4 **810-600** EL.5-6[2]	**850-800** KN.39 **850-750** KN.75, 77-80; FS.9[1] **850-700** KN.70[2]; ARK.5 **840-810** KF.31-35[3]; FS.8 **810-790** GVM.4	**810-710** DR.2; FS.4[1,6]; KN.68	
800-750	**c. 800** KN.45 **800-780** KNC.55 **800-775** IC.61 **800-700** KM.10-11[1]; KNC.76; IC.67[3]; IC.64-65,[2] IC.69-82 **800-650** KF.47 **800-600** KM.14-15	**790-745** KN.76; KF.38-40 **800-735** FS.10[2] **790-710** ANV.1 **760-700** FS.11[2]	**745-680** PU.9	
750-700	**740-680** IC.97-98 **720-650** KN.118-119[2]; KTS.1[3,4]	**750-700** VR.16; KN.107	**735-630** INT.3 **735-590** INT4-5 **730-680** KN.121 **720-600** INT.10-12, 23-52[2] **720-600** INT.8,15-17,19-22 **720-600** INT.18[4]	**725-690** KN.114[1] **720-700** KNC.80-81[2] **720-650** DC.17-19 **720-600** KSM.3-4[10]
700-650	**c. 700** IC.101 **700-680** KF.71-72 **700-650** CHN.3[4] **700-600** KM.18; KN.130;[4] LNO.1,[2] IC.103[2]; AVL.1[2]; GRT.5-6[2] **700-580** TRC.1[2] **680-630** DC.27[2]	**c. 700** DC.17[5] **700-670** KN.113[4]	**700-680** KN.115 **700-650** KN.108 **700-630** INT.6, 7[2] **700-600** GRT.7 **700-580** INT.8 **700-575** KN.141 **690-670** Ktwn.22 **680-650** GRT.4 **680-630** KF.86-88	**c. 700** DC.20[8] **700-670** KN.113[7] **700-630** KN.127[4]; KF.82-85 **700-600** KNC.83,85; KN.154; DC.21; ARK.39[9]; PR.23; KTS.2[10] **680-630** KF.75[9]

Table Cat.1. Origins and Dates of Overseas Artifacts Found at Cretan Sites, by Period *continued* (artifacts from Phoenicia, Cyclades, Rhodes and East Greece)

Period	Phoenicia	Cyclades	Rhodes	East Greece
650-600	**630-580** AMN.21[2], 24[4] **625-600** IC.107-108[2] **620-600** KM.58-59, 60[5]		**c. 650** ARK.32-34, 36[2] **650-600** INT.2[2] **630-580** AMN.11[2], 12 **625-600** KM.24 **620-600** KM.62[3]	**c. 630** KNC.84 **630-580** AMN.15-16, 22, 25-26[10] **625-600** KM.28 **620-600** KM.36-39, 41-46, 47-51,[5] 54,[4]61[6] **620-610** KM.35 **620-580** KN.157-158[9]
Other				undated KF.89[3]
Notes	[1] Levant, perhaps Phoenicia [2] or Egypt [3] or Cyprus [4] or North Syria [5] or North Africa [6] ? (uncertain)	[1]or Euboea [2]or Attica [3]perhaps [4]or Sparta or East Greece [5]or East Greece	[1]possibly local imitation [2]or Egypt [3]or East Greece [4]probably	[1]Dodecanese [2]Kos or Miletus [3]possibly North Syria [4]Miletus [5]or Islands [6]Klazomene [7]or Sparta or Cyclades [8]or Cyclades [9]or Near East [10]or Egypt

Table Cat.1. Origins and Dates of Overseas Artifacts Found at Cretan Sites, by Period *continued* (artifacts from Argos, Melos, Paros, and Naxos)

Period	Argos	Melos	Paros	Naxos
1100-1050	**1100-970** KN.1; FS.1[1]			
1050-1000				
1000-950				
950-900				
900-850	**900-835** Ktwn.4			
850-800		**850-750** Ktwn.6-8[1]	**850-700** IT.1	**850-750** VR.8
800-750			**800-720** KN.85	
750-700	**750-690** KN.93, 99		**750-700** CHN.1[1] **750-700** KN.100-103 **745-710** PR.7	**750-700** EL.8; VR.9[1] **745-710** KF.50-53
700-650		**c. 650** PU.16[2]		
650-600				
Other				
Notes	[1]more likely than Cyprus	[1] probably; definitely Cycladic [2] ? (uncertain)	[1]or Euboean	[1]or Euboean

Table Cat.1. Origins and Dates of Overseas Artifacts Found at Cretan Sites, by Period *continued* (artifacts from Thera, Lesbos, Samos, and Chios)

Period	Thera	Lesbos	Samos	Chios
1100-1050				
1050-1000				
1000-950				
950-900				
900-850				
850-800				
800-750				
750-700	**750-700** EL.7 **745-670** Ktwn.16-17		**710-640** FS.12	
700-650	**700-650** Ktwn.23			**700-600** KNC.873
650-600		**625-600** KM.27	**620-600** KM.40[1], 53	**625-600** KM.26
Other				
Notes			[1] or East Greece	

Table Cat.1. Origins and Dates of Overseas Artifacts Found at Cretan Sites, by Period *continued* (artifacts from Assyria, Babylonia, Mesopotamia, Luristan)

Period	Assyria	Babylonia	Mesopotamia	Luristan
1100-1050				
1050-1000				
1000-950				
950-900				
900-850				
850-800			**850-700** IC.85	**850-750** KF.28[1]
800-750	**800-700** IC.63[1]	**c. 800** KN.47[1]		
750-700	**725-680** CHN.2			
700-650	**680-630** KF.73[2]		**665-630** KN.137	
650-600				
Other				
Notes	[1] or northwest Iran [2] or Babylonia	[1] or Euboea		[1] possible provenance

Table Cat.1. Origins and Dates of Overseas Artifacts Found at Cretan Sites, by Period *continued*
(artifacts from Euboea, Mainland Greece, Italy, and Sardinia)

Period	Euboea	Mainland Greece	Italy	Sardinia
1100-1050		**1100-970** OL.1	**1100-970** KRF.2; KNC.1 **1100-710** KV.1[1]	
1050-1000	**1050-900** Ktwn.2			
1000-950	**970-920** KN.15-16 **970-840** KN.22-23[1] **950-900** KNC.20			
950-900	**925-875** KN.31 **910-890** KNC.25-27 **-900** KN.27			
900-850	**900-850** KN.36 **900-800** FS.3 **870-840** KV.3			
850-800	**850-750** FS.7[1]	**850-760** KN.67[1]		**840-665** KN.40
800-750	**c. 800** KN.47[3] **800-750** KN.73-74[4] **800-700** KN.104	**790-710** DC.6-8[2]	**c. 800** KF.41 **c. 800** KN.44 **800-700** IC.62, 84 **790-710** DC.9-13[3]	
750-700	**750-700** VR.9[5] **725-700** CHN.2 **720-700** KN.95-98 **710-630** KN.123	**745-710** IC.91[3] **720-680** AGG.1[4,6]	**745-665** PR.10 **745-710** IC.94[4] **710-630** KN.124[5]	
700-650	**-650** FS.14[2] **700-600** KN.123	**700-675** PU.15[4]	**-c. 650** FS.12[2,7] **680-630** KNC.86[6]	
650-600				
Other				
Notes	[1]or Cyclades [2]or Tessaglia [3]or Babylonia [4]Eretria [5]or Naxos	[1]possibly Attica? [2]DC.8 possibly Bronze Age [3]or Baltic [4]Peloponnese [5]possibly Corinth [6]Argos or Corinth	[1]Possibly Sicily [2]Tessaglia [3]DC.12 possibly mainland Greece [4]or Baltic [5]or Balkans [6]possibly mainland Greece, northwest [7]or Euboea	

Table Cat.1. Origins and Dates of Overseas Artifacts Found at Cretan Sites, by Period *continued*
(artifacts from Eastern Mediterranean, North Syria or Syria, Levant, and Near East)

Period	Eastern Mediterranean	North Syria or Syria	Levant (otherwise unspecified)	Near East (otherwise unspecified)
1100-1050	**1100-900** KN.3	**1100-970** KNC.2,[1,3] **1100-900** EL.2[7]	**1100-1000** PTS.1	**1100-970** KRF.4-5 **1100-900** KRF.3[5]
1050-1000				
1000-950		**c. 1000** TYL.1 **970-840** KNC.36	**970-840** KNC.37[1] **970-630** KN.21	**970-920** KF.1[1], 5-9 **970-840** KNC.35; KN.19[4]; PTL.1
950-900				
900-850		**900-800** IC.2 **900-600** AMN.2; AGT.1; PU.1		**870-840** KF.26-27
850-800		**850-710** IC.4-11,12-18, 21-45 **850-700** IC.11[2], 46-51 **825-775** IC.60[2] **820-780** KRT.1		**850-700** IC.19-20, 46-51, 53-55, 59 **830-680** KN.41 **810-710** DC.5,[2,3] 14-16 **810-710** KV.6-7
800-750	**800-700** ARK.4[1]	**800-700** IC.83	**790-745** KN.68	**c. 800** KN.42-43 **790-745** KF.46 **800-700** IC.66 **800-600** PR.17
750-700		**750-700** AMN.3[6] **730-700** KF.54; PU.4-8 **720-650** KTS.1[3,7]	**720-650** KN.120[1]	**750-600** AMN.5 **745-630** PTS.2 **c. 725** IC.86-90 **720-600** INT.53
700-650		**700-650** CHN.3[3] **700-600** KN.130[3] **680-630** KF.74[4]	**700-600** ARK.25[2]	**700-630** KNC.89[8], 90[6]; KF.75[7] **700-600** DC.22[2]; GRT.5-6[7,8]
650-600	**650-600** PR.24	**630-580** AMN.23[3]		**c. 650** IC.104 **620-580** EL.15; KN.157-158[7]
Other		**undated** KF.82[5]		
Notes	[1]Phrygia	[1]or Levant otherwise [2]South Syria [3]or Phoenicia [4]Asia other than Egypt [5]possibly East Greece [6]local product of N. Syrian craftsmen [7]or Cyprus	[1]possibly from Egypt [2]or East Greece	[1]Hittite region [2]possibly Bronze Age [3]Syria or Phoenicia [4]Afghanistan [5]Anatolia [6]likely Egypt [7]or East Greece [8]possibly Egypt

Table Cat.1. Origins and Dates of Overseas Artifacts Found at Cretan Sites, by Period *continued*
(artifacts from Boeotia, Laconia, Baltic, and Western Poenician Sites)

Period	Boeotia	Laconia	Baltic	Western Phoenician Sites
1100-1050				
1050-1000				
1000-950				
950-900				
900-850				
850-800	**850-750** KF.29-30[1]; PRN.2-4[1]; KSM.1[1]; PU.2[1] **810-710** VR.10-13[1]; DR.4[1]			
800-750			**790-745** KF.46 **790-710** KN.84	
750-700	**740-690** IT.2 **725-700** DR.7[1]		**745-710** IC.91[1], 92-93, 94[2] **720-680** ARK.7	
700-650	**c. 700** IC.99-100[1] **700-630** KF.78[1] **700-600** ARK.8	**700-670** KN.113[1]		**700-(?)** IC.105
650-600		**650-620** TYL.2 **620-600** KM.34, 52 **c.600-550** EL.16		**650-600** KM.60[1]
Notes	[1]or Attica	[1]or Cyclades or East Greece	[1]or mainland Greece [2]or Italy	[1]possibly Phoenician

Key to Site Symbols

AGG	Aghios Georghios		KSM	Kissamo
AGT	Aghia Triada		KSY	Kato Symi
ANV	Anavlochos		Ktwn	Knossos, the town
ARK	Arkades		KV	Kavousi
AVL	Avlí		LNO	Liliano
CHN	Chania		ML	Mochlos
DC	Diktaean Cave		OL	Olontes
DR	Dreros		PLK	Palaikastro
EL	Eleutherna		PR	Praisos
FS	Phaistos		PRN	Prinias
GRT	Gortyn		PTK	Patéla
GVM	Gavalomouri		PTS	Patso
IC	Idaean Cave		PU	Provenance unknown
INT	Inatos		RZ	Rhiza
IT	Itanos		S	Sitea
KF	Knossos-Fortetsa		TRA	Tarra
KM	Kommos		TRC	Trapeza Cave
KN	Knossos, otherwise unspecified		TYL	Tylissos
KNC	Knossos, North Cemetery		VR	Vrokastro
KRF	Karphi		ZKR	Zakro
KRT	Kourtes			

Table Cat.2. Origins and Dates of Overseas Artifacts Found in Crete, by Period and Site

Table Cat.2.1. Origins and Dates of Artifacts Found at Knossos-Fortetsa (KF)

Period	Period frequency	Attica	Corinth	Cyprus	Egypt	Phoenicia
1100–1050	1/89				**2** (1075–920)	
1050–1000	0/89					
1000–950	19/89	**16–18** (1000–900) **20** (970–850)		**4** (970–920) **7–9** (970–920)[1]	**3** (970–920) **7–9** (970–920)[2] **21** (970–840)[1]	**21** (970–850)[1]
950–900	1/89			**19** (950–800)		
900–850	4/89					
850–800	10/89	**36** (850–800) **29–30** (850–750)[1]		**25** (c.850)		
800–750	14/89	**37** (790–745)	**24** (790–745)	**48** (800–750) **42–44** (790–745) **49** (790–710)	**45** (790–745)[3]	**47** (800–650)
750–700	10/89			**55–59** (745–710)		
700–650	29/89	**78** (700–630)[1]	**60–66** (700–600) **67** (700–650)	**68–70** (700–665) **79–80** (665–630)	**77** (700–630)[1] **76** (680–630) **81** (664–525)	**71–72** (700–680)
650–600	0/89					
Undated	1/89					
Site frequency		9/89	9/89	19.5/89	7/89	3.5/89
Notes		[1]or Boeotia		[1]or Egypt	[1]or Phoenicia [2]or Cyprus [3]possibly other Near East	[1]or Egypt [2]or Rhodes?

Table Cat.2.1. Origins and Dates of Artifacts Found at Knossos-Fortetsa (KF) *continued*

Cyclades	Near East	East Greece and Rhodes	Europe	Period
				1100–1050
				1050–1000
10–15 (970–840)	**1** (970–920)[1] **5–6** (970–920)			1000–950
				950–900
22 (870–840) **23** (870–810)	**26–27** (870–840)			900–850
31–35 (840–810)	**28** (850–750)[2]			850–800
38–40 (790–745)	**45** (790–745)[7]		**41** (c. 800)[1] **46** (790–745)[2]	800–750
50–53 (745–710)	**54** (730–700)[3]			750–700
	73 (680–630)[4] **74** (680–630) **75** (680–630)[8]	**82–85** (700–630) **75** (680–630)[3] **86–88** (680–630)[4]		700–650
				650–600
	89[6]	**89**[2]		Undated
20/89	10.5/89	8/89	2/89	Site frequency
	[1]Hittite region [2]Luristan [3]North Syria or Syria [4]Assyria or Babylonia [5]not Egypt [6]North Syria or East Greece [7]likely Egypt [8]or East Greece	[1]or Phoenicia [2]or North Syria [3]or Near East [4]Rhodes	[1]Italy [2]Baltic	Notes

Table Cat.2.2. Origins and Dates of Artifacts Found at Knossos-North Cemetery (KNC)

Period	Period frequency	Attica	Corinth	Cyprus	Egypt	Phoenicia
1100–1050	7/92			**4–5** (1100–970) **6** (1100–840)		**7** (1100–1000)
1050–1000	0/92					
1000–950	4/92			**34** (970–840)	**37** (970–840)[1]	
950–900	20/92	**8–19** (950–900) **29–32** (925–875)	**22** (950–900)			
900–850	5/92	**28** (900–875)				
850–800	16/92	**42–44** (850–800) **45** (850–760) **50–52** (850–735)		**42–41, 48–49**[1] (850–750) **40,**[1] **45** (820–800)	**53** (850–735)	**38** (c. 850) **48–49**[1] (850–750) **39** (825–800) **40**[1] (825–800)
800–750	24/92			**56–75** (800–775) **77–78** (800–700)		**55** (800–780) **76** (800–700)
750–700	7/92		**79** (750–690) **88** (720–600)	**83** (750–600)		
700–650	8/92				**90–91** (700–630)[1] **89** (680–630)[2]	
650–600	1/92					
Site frequency		24/92	3/92	32/92	3/92	6/92
Notes				[1]or Phoenician	[1]or Levant [2]or other Near East	[1]or Cyprus

Table Cat.2.2. Origins and Dates of Artifacts Found at Knossos-North Cemetery (KNC) *continued*

Cyclades	Near East	East Greece and Rhodes	Mainland Greece	Euboea	Italy and Sardinia	Period
	2–3 (1100–970)[1]				**1** (1100–970)	1100–1050
						1050–1000
	35 (970–840) **36** (970–840)[2] **37** (970–840)[3]					1000–950
		24 (950–875)	**23** (950–800)[1]	**20–21** (950–900)		950–900
33 (870–840)				**25–27** (910–890)		900–850
						850–800
						800–750
	54 (745–680)[2]	**80–81**[1] (720–700)				750–700
	90–91 (700–630)[1,3] **92** (700–630) **89** (680–630)[3]	**83, 85** (700–600) **88** (700–600)[2]	**86** (700–630)[2]		**82** (680–630)[1]	700–650
		84 (c. 630)				650–600
0/92	8/92	7/92	1.5/92	2/92	1.5/92	Site frequency
	[1]North Syria or Levant [2]North Syria [3]or Egypt	[1]Cos, possibly Miletus [2]Chios	[1]Thessaly [2]possibly Italy		[1]possibly mainland Greece	Notes

Table Cat.2.3. Origins and Dates of Artifacts Found at Knossos Town (Ktwn)

Period	Period frequency	Attica	Corinth	Cyprus	Egypt	Phoenicia
1100–1050	0/32					
1050–1000	2/32	**1** (1050–980)				
1000–950	0/32					
950–900	1/32	**3** (950–900)				
900–850	2/32	**5** (875–850)				
850–800	4/32		**9** (835–750)			
800–750	5/32	**10–11** (800–775)	**12** (770–735) **13** (760–735) **14** (760–700)			
750–700	6/32	**15** (750–725)	**18** (735–700) **19** (720–700) **20** (720–680)			
700–650	4/32		**21** (700–650) **24** (660–650)			
650–600	8/32		**25** (c. 650) **26** (650–620) **27–28** (650–600) **29** (630–610) **30–32** (630–600)			
Site frequency		6/32	17/32	0/32	0/32	0/32
Notes						

Table Cat.2.3. Origins and Dates of Artifacts Found at Knossos Town (Ktwn) *continued*

Cyclades	Near East	East Greece and Rhodes	Argos	Euboea	Italy and Sardinia	Period
						1100–1050
				2 (1050–900)		1050–1000
						1000–950
						950–900
			4 (900–835)			900–850
6–8 (850–750)[1]						850–800
						800–750
16–17 (745–670)[2]						750–700
23 (690–650)[2]		22 (690–670)[1]				700–650
						650–600
6/32	0/32	1/32	1/32	1/32	0/32	Site frequency
[1]probably Melos [2]Thera		[1]Rhodes				Notes

Table Cat.2.4. Origins and Dates of Artifacts Found at Knossos, Other Locations (KN)

Period	Period frequency	Attica	Corinth	Cyprus	Egypt	Phoenicia
1100–1050	3/158			**2** (1100–900)		
1050–1000	2/158					
1000–950	19/158	**13, 14** (1000–900) **4–12** (1000–950)		**20** (970–710)	**17–18** (970–840)	
950–900	8/158	**24, 25** (950–900) **33** (950–875) **32** (950–850) **34** (950–800) **28** (925–900)				
900–850	5/158	**38** (900–700) **37** (875–800) **26** (870–840)		**30** (870–840)		
850–800	23/158	**35, 52** (850–800) **63–66, 69** (850–760) **67**[1] (850–760) **70**[2] (850–750)		**49–50** (810–710) **89** (850–800)	**48** (810–710)	
800–750	35/158	**53–62** (800–760) **90** (760–720) **91–92** (760–700)	**71–72, 87–88** (800–750)	**82–83** (790–710) **111–112** (790–760)	**46** (c. 800)	**45** (c. 800) **81** (800–600)
750–700	25/158		**116–117** (720–690)	**94, 105–106** (c. 750) **109** (745–630) **110** (725–700)	**120** (720–650)[2] **118–119** (720–600)[1]	**120** (720–650)[2] **118–119** (720–600)[2]
700–650	20/158		**126** (700–630) **133** (700–600) **134–135** (690–) **136** (690–650) **125** (675–650)	**122** (680–665) **128–129, 131** (700–600)	**138** (665–630)[1]	**130** (700–600)[1]
650–600	18/158		**139–140** (c. 650) **142–153** (650–600) **155** (630–600)		**156** (630–580)	
Site frequency		41.5/158	27/158	19/158	7/158	4/158
Notes		[1]mainland, possibly Attica [2]or Cyclades			[1]or Phoenicia [2]or Levant	[1]or North Syria [2]or Egypt

Table Cat.2.4. Origins and Dates of Artifacts Found at Knossos, Other Locations (KN) *continued*

Cyclades	Near East	East Greece and Rhodes	Argos	Euboea	Italy and Sardinia	Period
	3 (1100–900)		**1** (1100–970)			1100–1050
				15–16 (1050–1000)		1050–1000
22–23 (970–840)[1]	**21** (970–630) **19** (970–840)[5]	**29** (970–790)		**22–23** (970– 840)[1]		1000–950
				27 (–900) **31** (925–875)		950–900
			36 (900–850)			900–850
39 (850–800) **70**[2] (850–700) **75, 77–80** (850–750)	**41** (835–810) **51** (810–710)	**86** (810–710)[2]			**40** (840–665)[1]	850–800
76 (790–745) **85** (800–720)[3]	**42–43** (c. 800) **47** (c. 800)[1] **68** (790–745)			**47** (c. 800)[2] **73–74** (800–750)[3] **104** (800–700)	**44** (c. 800) **84** (710–630)[3]	800–750
107 (750–700) **100–103** (750–700)[3]		**114** (725–690) **121** (730–680)[2]	**93, 99** (750–690)	**95–98** (720–700) **123** (710–630)	**124** (710–630)[2]	750–700
113 (700–670)[2]	**130** (700–600)[4] **137** (665–630)[3] **138** (665–630)[2]	**115** (700–680)[2] **108** (700–650)[2] **127** (700–630)[1] **141** (700– 600)[2] **154** (700–600)		**132** (700–600)		700–650
	157–158 (630–580)[6]	**157–158** (630–580)[3]				650–600
15.5/158	11.5/158	10/158	4/158	14.5/158	4/158	Site frequency
[1]or Euboea [2]or Sparta or East Greece [3]Paros [4]or Attica	[1]Babylonia; may be from Euboea [2]possibly from Egypt [3]Mesopotamia [4]possibly from N. Syria or Phoenicia [5]Afghanistan [6]or East Greece	[1]Miletus [2]Rhodes [3]or Near East		[1]or Cyclades [2]may be from Babylonia [3]Eretria	[1]Sardinia [2]Italy or Balkans [3]Baltic	Notes

Table Cat.2.5. Origins and Dates of Artifacts Found at Kommos (KM)

Period	Period frequency	Attica	Corinth	Cyprus	Egypt	Phoenicia
1100–1050	0/62					
1050–1000	0/62					
1000–950	1/62					**1** (1000–800)
950–900	0/62					
900–850	4/62			**3** (900–700)	**28** (900–750)	**2** (900–700)
850–800	5/62				**12–13** (800–600)	**5** (825–775) **6** (825–700) **7** (820–780)
800–750	4/62					**10–11** (800–700) **14–15** (800–600)
750–700	4/62		**16** (725–700) **17** (720–630)		**8–9** (730–700)	
700–650	3/62		**19** (700–600) **20** (675–600)			**18** (700–600)
650–600	41/62	**22** (c. 650) **29** (625–600)	**23** (650–600) **21** (640–630) **31–33, 55** (620–600)	**56–57** (620–600)	**24** (625–600)	**25** (625–600)[2] **58–59** (620–600) **60** (620–600)[1]
Site frequency		2/62	10/62	3/62	6/62	14/62
Notes					[1]"Iron Age"	[1]possibly North Africa [2]Levant

Table Cat.2.5. Origins and Dates of Artifacts Found at Kommos (KM) *continued*

Cyclades	East Greece and Rhodes	Laconia	Euboea	Italy and Sardinia	Period
					1100–1050
					1050–1000
					1000–950
					950–900
4 (870–810)					900–850
					850–800
					800–750
					750–700
					700–650
	26 (625–600)[1] **27** (625–600)[2] **28** (625–600) **35** (620–610) **36–51** (620–600)[3] **53** (620–600)[4] **54** (620–600)[5] **61** (620–600)[6] **62** (620–600)[7]	**34** (620–600) **52** (620–600)			650–600
1/62	24/62	2/62	0/62	0/62	Site frequency
	[1]Chios [2]Lesbos [3]**38** may be from Samos; nos. **45–49** may be from the Islands [4]Samos [5]Miletus [6]Klazomene [7]possibly Rhodes				Notes

Table Cat.2.6. Origins and Dates of Artifacts Found at Sites in Northern and Eastern Crete: Aghios Georghios (AGG), Amnisos (AMN), Anavlochos (ANV), Arkades (ARK), Avlí (AVL), Diktaean Cave (DC), Dreros (DR), Gouves (GV), Itanos (IT), Karphi (KRF), Kavousi (KV), Lasithi Plain (LSP), Liliano (LNO), Mochlos (ML), Olous (OL), Palaikastro (PLK), Patela (PTL), Praesos (PR), Rhiza (RZ), Sitea (S), Trapeza Cave (TRC), Vrokastro (VR), Zakro (ZKR)

Period	Period frequency	Attica	Corinth	Cyprus	Egypt	Cyclades
1100–1050	14/187	**OL 1** (1100–970)[1] **VR 4** (1100–970) **VR 5** (1100–850)		**VR 2** (1100–970) **KRF 1** (1100–840) **VR 3** (1100–790) **KV 2** (1100–680)	**ARK 1** (c.1250–850) **VR 1** (1100–1075?)	
1050–1000	0/187					
1000–950	3/187	**VR 6** (1000–850) **PLK 1** (970–700)				
950–900	1/187				**VR 7** (945–715?)	
900–850	8/187	**RZ 1–2** (900–800) **DR 1** (900–700) **PR 1,**[2] **5** (900–700)	**PR 1** (900–700)[1]	**AMN 1** (900–800)	**ARK 2** (900–750)	
850–800	27/187	**ARK 3** (850–800) **VR 10–13** (810–710)[3] **DR 4** (810–710)[3]	**PR 2** (820–745) **KV 8** (810–710)	**VR 14–15** (810–710) **KV 4** (810–710) **PR 6** (810–710)	**DR 3** (810–710)[2] **KV 5** (810–710)	**ARK 5** (850–700) **IT 1** (850–700)[1] **VR 8** (850–750)[2]
800–750	15/187	**DR 5** (760–700)		**ARK 6** (800–600)	**AMN 8** (800–600)[5] **DC 1** (770–680)[1]	**ANV 1** (790–710)
750–700	38/187	**DR 7** (725–700)[3]	**PR 8** (750–725) **ANV 2** (750–720) **ARK 10** (720–700) **PR 16** (720–700) **IT 3** (720–690) **PR 11–15** (720–690) **IT 4** (720–600) **ARK 11–15** (720–630) **AMN 7** (720–630) **LSP 1** (720–630) **DR 6** (720–630) **ANV 3** (720–650) **AMN 6** (710–680)	**ARK 16** (720–690)[3]	**ZKR 1; AMN 9** (745–710) **PR 9** (745–680)	**VR 9,**[4] **16** (750–700) **PR 7** (745–710)[1]

Table Cat.2.6. Origins and Dates of Artifacts Found at Sites in Northern and Eastern Crete: Aghios Georghios (AGG), Amnisos (AMN), Anavlochos (ANV), Arkades (ARK), Avlí (AVL), Diktaean Cave (DC), Dreros (DR), Gouves (GV), Itanos (IT), Karphi (KRF), Kavousi (KV), Lasithi Plain (LSP), Liliano (LNO), Mochlos (ML), Olous (OL), Palaikastro (PLK), Patela (PTL), Praesos (PR), Rhiza (RZ), Sitea (S), Trapeza Cave (TRC), Vrokastro (VR), Zakro (ZKR)
continued

Near East	East Greece and Rhodes	Italy and Other Europe	Mainland Greece	Boeotia	Period
KRF 4–5 (1100–970) **KRF 3** (1100–900)[9]		**KRF 2** (1100–970) **KV 1** (1100–710)[1]	**OL 1** (1100–970)[6]		1100–1050
					1050–1000
PTL 1 (970–840)					1000–950
					950–900
AMN 2 (900–600)[1]					900–850
PR 3–4 (810–745)[4] **DR 3, OL 2** (810–710)[4] **DC 5** (810–710)[3] **DC 14–16** (810–710) **KV 6–7** (810–710)	**DR 2** (810–710)[1]		**VR 8** (850–750)[1] **KV 3** (810–710)[1]	**VR 10–13** (810–710)[1] **DR 4** (810–710)[1]	850–800
PR 17 (800–600) **ARK 4** (800–700)[8]	**AMN 8** (800–600)[3]	**DC 9–13** (800–710)[2]	**DC 12** (800–710)[5] **DC 6–8** (790–710)		800–750
AMN 3–5 (750–600) **ARK 16** (720–690)[10]	**IT 2** (740–690)[2] **DC 17–19** (720–650)	**PR 10** (745–665) **ARK 7** (720–680)[3]	**VR 9** (750–700)[1,7] **AGG 1** (720–680)[3]	**IT 2** (740–690)[2] **DR 7** (725–700)[1]	750–700

Table Cat.2.6. Origins and Dates of Artifacts Found at Sites in Northern and Eastern Crete: Aghios Georghios (AGG), Amnisos (AMN), Anavlochos (ANV), Arkades (ARK), Avlí (AVL), Diktaean Cave (DC), Dreros (DR), Gouves (GV), Itanos (IT), Karphi (KRF), Kavousi (KV), Lasithi Plain (LSP), Liliano (LNO), Mochlos (ML), Olous (OL), Palaikastro (PLK), Patela (PTL), Praesos (PR), Rhiza (RZ), Sitea (S), Trapeza Cave (TRC), Vrokastro (VR), Zakro (ZKR)
continued

Period	Period frequency	Attica	Corinth	Cyprus	Egypt	Cyclades
700–650	33/187	ARK 8 (700–600)[3]	DC 23–26 (700–600) PR 21–22 (700–600) PR 19 (700–650) ARK 9 (690–670) ARK 17 (680–665) GV 1 (680–630) ARK 18 (670–665) ARK 19 (670–655) ARK 20 (660–655) ARK 21 (655–650) ARK 22 (655–640) ARK 23–24 (665–620) ARK 26 (660–625)	KV 9 (700–630) PR 18 (700–600)	AVL 1 (700–600)[2] LNO 1 (700–600) PR 23 (700–630)[5] TRC 1 (700–580)[2]	DC 20 (c. 700)[3]
650–600	45/187		PR 20 (650–630) ARK 25 (640–625) ARK 27 (630–620) ARK 40–44 (620–600) ARK 30 (610–600) ARK 45–47 (620–580) ARK 48–49; DC 28 (600–580)	AMN 14 (630–580)[1] AMN 21 (630–580)[2]	ARK 35,[6] 36[3] (c. 650) S 1 (650–600) AMN 9–10, 11[3] (630–580) AMN 13–14, 15–16[3], 17–20 (630–580)[4] AMN 22,[3] 23 (630–580) ANV 4 (630–580)	
Undated	3/187				DC 2–4	
Site frequency		14.5/187	58.5/187	13.5/187	30.5/187	6.5/187
Notes		[1]mainland Greece, possibly Attica [2]possibly Corinth [3]or Boeotia	[1]possibly Attica	[1]possibly Egypt [2]possibly Phoenicia [3]or Levant	[1]or before 1200 [2]possibly Phoenicia or Palestine [3]or Rhodes [4]no. 13 possibly from Cyprus [5]or East Greece [6]local copy	[1]Paros [2]Naxos [3]or East Greece [4]or Euboea

Table Cat.2.6. Origins and Dates of Artifacts Found at Sites in Northern and Eastern Crete: Aghios Georghios (AGG), Amnisos (AMN), Anavlochos (ANV), Arkades (ARK), Avlí (AVL), Diktaean Cave (DC), Dreros (DR), Gouves (GV), Itanos (IT), Karphi (KRF), Kavousi (KV), Lasithi Plain (LSP), Liliano (LNO), Mochlos (ML), Olous (OL), Palaikastro (PLK), Patela (PTL), Praesos (PR), Rhiza (RZ), Sitea (S), Trapeza Cave (TRC), Vrokastro (VR), Zakro (ZKR)

continued

Near East	East Greece and Rhodes	Italy and Other Europe	Mainland Greece	Boeotia	Period
DC 22 (700–600)[5] **ARK 37–38, 39**[8] (700–600) **TRC 1** (700–580)[5,7] **DC 27** (680–630)[5] **AVL 1** (700–600)[6]	**DC 20** (c. 700)[4] **DC 21** (700–600) **PR 23** (700–630)[3] **ARK 39** (700–600)[7]			**ARK 8** (700–600)[1]	700–650
PR 24 (650–600) **AMN 21** (630–580)[2] **AMN 24** (630–580)[5]	**ARK 31** (c. 650) **ARK 30–34** (c. 650)[1] **ARK 36** (c.650)[3] **AMN 12** (630–580) **AMN 11, 15–16, 22**[6]**, 25–26** (630–580)[3]		**TYL 2** (650–620)[4]		650–600
					Undated
27/187	16.5/187	8.5/187	7.5/187	4/187	Site frequency
[1]North Syria or Syria [2]Phoenicia or Cyprus [3]possibly Bronze Age [4]Phoenicia [5]Syria or Phoenicia [6]or Egypt [7]or East Greece [8]Phrygia [9]Anatolia [10]Levant or Cyprus	[1]Rhodes [2]or Boeotia [3]or Egypt [4]or Cyclades [5]or North Syria [6]Rhodes or Egypt [7]or Levant	[1]possibly Sicily [2]DC 12 possibly from mainland Greece [3]Baltic	[1]Euboea [2]DC 8 possibly Bronze Age [3]Peloponnese, probably Argos or Corinth [4]Laconia [5]possibly Italy [6]possibly Attica [7]or Naxos	[1]or Attica [2]or Rhodes	Notes

Table Cat.2.7. Origins and Dates of Artifacts Found at Sites in South and Central Crete: Aghia Triada (AGT), Gortyn (GRT), Idaean Cave (IC), Inatos (INT), Kato Symi (KTS), Kourtes (KRT), Lasala (LS), Phaistos (FS), Priansos (PRS), Prinias (PRN), Tylissos (TYL)

Period	Period frequency	Attica	Corinth	Cyprus	Egypt	Phoenicia
1100–1050	1/207			FS 1 (1100–970)[1]		
1050–1000	1/207				IC 1 (1050–1000)	
1000–950	2/207	FS 2 (1000–950)		TYL 1 (c. 1000)[3]		
950–900	1/207			GRT 1 (970–840)		
900–850	4/207			PRS 1 (900–630)		
850–800	75/207	PRN 2–4 (850– 750)[1]	FS 4 (810–720)	IC 57–58 (850–700)	IC3, 52, 56 (850–700) PRN 1 (810–700) IC 95–96 (810–630)	IC 68 (850–700)[4]
800–750	25/207	FS 8 (800–735)[2] FS 9 (760–700)[2]		IC 67 (800–700)[2]	IC 64–65 (800–700)[1]	IC 61 (800–775) IC 64–65 (800–700)[1] IC 67 (800–700)[2] IC 69–82 (800–700)
750–700	70/207	LS 1 (c. 750) LS 2 (750–725) LS 4–6 (725–700) LS 7 (715–685)	LS 3 (725–700) FS 12 (720–600)	KTS 1 (720–650)[2,3]	INT 1 (750–600) INT 2, 10–12, 23–52 (720–650)[4] INT 13–14 (720–650)	IC 97–98 (740–680) INT 1 (750–600) KTS 1 (720–650)[2,4]
700–650	20/207	IC 99–100 (c. 700)1 LS 8–9 (700–650)	IC 102 (700–680)		INT 7,[4] 54 (700–630) GRT 6 (700–600)[2,3] KSY 1 (700–600)[3] IC 103 (700–600)[1] IC 106 (–650) KTS 2 (700–600)[3]	IC 101 (c. 700) IC 103 (700–600)[1] GRT 5–6 (700–600)[1] IC 105 (700–)[3]

Table Cat.2.7. Origins and Dates of Artifacts Found at Sites in South and Central Crete: Aghia Triada (AGT), Gortyn (GRT), Idaean Cave (IC), Inatos (INT), Kato Symi (KTS), Kourtes (KRT), Lasala (LS), Phaistos (FS), Priansos (PRS), Prinias (PRN), Tylissos (TYL) *continued*

Cyclades	Near East	East Greece and Rhodes	Argos	Euboea/Boeotia	Period
			FS 1 (1100–970)[1]		1100–1050
					1050–1000
	TYL 1 (c. 1000)[7]				1000–950
					950–900
	IC 2 (900–800)[1] **AGT 1** (900–600)[2]			**FS 3** (900–800)	900–850
FS 9 (850–750)[1] **FS 8** (840–810)	**IC 4–6, 8–11, 16, 25–31, 34, 37–45** (850–700)[1] **IC 12** (850–700)[4] **IC 7, 13–15, 17–18, 21–24, 32–33, 35–36** (850–700)[2] **IC 19–20, 46–51, 53–55, 59** (850–710) **IC 68** (850–700)[6] **IC 85** (850–700)[3] **IC 60** (825–775)[4] **KRT 1** (820–780)[1]	**FS 5** (810–710)[1,2] **FS 6** (810–710)[1]		**FS 7,9** (850–750)[1] **PRN 2–4** (850–750)[2] **GRT 2–3** (850–750)	850–800
FS 10 (800–735)[2] **FS 11** (760–700)[2]	**IC 63** (800–700)[5] **IC 66** (800–700) **IC 83** (800–700)[1]				800–750
	IC 86–90 (c. 725) **INT 53** (720–650)	**INT 3** (735–630)[1] **INT 4–5** (735–590)[1] **INT 2, 9–12, 23–52** (720–650)[1,4] **INT15–22** (720–650)[1] **FS 10** (710–640)[3]			750–700
	GRT 5–6 (700–600)[6,8,9]	**INT 6** (700–630)[1] **INT 7** (700–630)[1,4] **GRT 7** (700–600) **KSY 1** (700–600)[4] **INT 8** (700–590)[1] **GRT 4** (680–650)[1] **KTS 2** (700–600)[4]		**IC 99–100** (c. 700)[2] **FS 14** (–650)[3]	700–650

Table Cat.2.7. Origins and Dates of Artifacts Found at Sites in South and Central Crete:
Aghia Triada (AGT), Gortyn (GRT), Idaean Cave (IC), Inatos (INT), Kato Symi (KTS), Kourtes
(KRT), Lasala (LS), Phaistos (FS), Priansos (PRS), Prinias (PRN), Tylissos (TYL) *continued*

Period	Period frequency	Attica	Corinth	Cyprus	Egypt	Phoenicia
650–600	8/207		**FS 15** (630–610) **GRT 8** (650–640)		**IC 107–108** (625–600)[1] **IC 109** (625–600)	**IC 107–108** (625–600)[1]
Site frequency		12.5/207	6/207	6.5/207	35.5/207	24.5/207
Notes		[1]or Boeotia [2]possibly Cyclades		[1]less likely than Argos [2]or Phoenicia [3]or Syria	[1]or Phoenicia [2]or Levant [3]or East Greece [4]or Rhodes	[1]or Egypt [2]or Cyprus [3]Western Phoenician sites [4]or North Syria

Table Cat.2.7. Origins and Dates of Artifacts Found at Sites in South and Central Crete:
Aghia Triada (AGT), Gortyn (GRT), Idaean Cave (IC), Inatos (INT), Kato Symi (KTS), Kourtes
(KRT), Lasala (LS), Phaistos (FS), Priansos (PRS), Prinias (PRN), Tylissos (TYL) *continued*

Cyclades	Near East	East Greece and Rhodes	Argos	Euboea/Boeotia	Period
	IC 104 (c. 650)				650–600
2.5/207	70/207	35.5/207	0.5/207	8/207	Site frequency
[1]or Euboea [2]or Attica	[1]North Syria [2]Syria [3]Mesopotamia [4]South Syria [5]Assyria or nw Iran [6]Phoenicia or North Syria [7]or Cyprus [8]or Egypt [9]or East Greece	[1]Rhodes [2]possibly local imitation [3]Samos [4]or Egypt	[1]more likely than Cyprus	[1]Cyclades or Euboea [2]Boeotia or Attica [3]Euboea or Tessaglia	Notes

Table Cat.2.8. Origins and Dates of Artifacts Found at Sites in West Crete:
Chania (CHN), Eleutherna (EL), Gavalomouri (GVM), Kissamo (KSM), Patso (PTS), Tarra
(TRA)

Period	Period frequency	Attica	Corinth	Cyprus	Egypt	Phoenicia
1100–1050	3/35			**EL 2** (1100–900)[1]	**EL 1** (1100–970)	
1050–1000	0/35					
1000–950	1/35	**CHN 1** (1000–870)[1]				
950–900	1/35	**PTS 2** (950–900)				
900–850	0/35					
850–800	6/35	**KSM 1** (850–750)[2] **EL 3** (850–700)	**EL 4** (830–720)		**EL 5–6** (810–600)[1]	**EL 5–6** (810–600)[1]
800–750	4/35	**GVM 1–3** (800–775)		**KSM 2** (800–700)		
750–700	10/35		**EL 10** (720–630) **EL 9** (720–590)		**KSM 3–4** (750–625)[2]	
700–650	6/35		**EL 11–14** (665–630)		**TRA 1** (700–630)	**CHN 5** (700–650)[2]
650–600	4/35		**KSM 5** (610–600)[1] **KSM 6** (c. 600)[2]			
Site frequency		7/35	9/35	1.5/35	5/35	1.5/35
Notes		[1]"Aegean region" [2]or Boeotia	[1]at Phalasarna [2]at Polyrhenia	[1]or Syria	[1]or Phoenicia [2]or East Greece	[1]or Egypt [2]or North Syria

Table Cat.2.8. Origins and Dates of Artifacts Found at Sites in West Crete:
Chania (CHN), Eleutherna (EL), Gavalomouri (GVM), Kissamo (KSM), Patso (PTS), Tarra
(TRA) *continued*

Levant	Cyclades	Euboea	Laconia	Laconia	Italy	Baltic	Period
PTS 1 (1100–1000) **EL 2** (1100–900)[1]							1100–1050
							1050–1000
							1000–950
							950–900
							900–850
	GVM 4 (810–790)						850–800
					IC 62 (800–700) **IC 84** (800–700)[1]		800–750
PTS 3 (745–710) **CHN 4** (725–680)	**CHN 2** (750–700)[3] **EL 7** (750–700)[1] **EL 8** (750–700)[2]	**CHN 2** (750–700)[1] **CHN 3** (725–700)			**IC 94** (745–710)[2]	**IC 91** (745–710)[1] **IC 92–93** (745–710) **IC 94** (745–710)[2]	750–700
CHN 5 (700–650)[2]							700–650
EL 15 (620–585)			**EL 16** (c. 600–550)	**TYL 2** (650–620)[1]			650–600
5/35	3.5/35	1.5/35	1/35	1/207	2.5/207	3.5/207	Site frequency
[1]or Cyprus [2]North Syria or Phoenicia	[1]Thera? [2]Naxos? [3]Paros or Euboea	[1]or Paros		[1]possibly East Greece or Cyclades	[1]Balkans [2]or Baltic	[1]or mainland Greece [2]or Italy	Notes

Table Cat.3. Locations of Cretan Artifacts Found at Sites Overseas, by Period and Region

Period	Period Frequency	Italy	Cyprus	Sicily	Western Greece
1100–1050	10/153	**SM–1000** 1.LAT[a] **LM–840** 12.ETR[a]	**1100–1000** 2.KTN **1100–1000** 8.SLM **1100–1000** 9.SLM **1100–1000** 10.ENK **1100–1000** 11.KTN[b]		
1050–1000	2/153				
1000–950	1/153			**970–630** 78.BLM	
950–900	3/153	**930–800** 13.TRQ[a] **930–750** 14–15.TRQ[a]			
900–850	0/153				
850–800	7/153				
800–750	9/153	**c. 800** 24.TRN **c. 800** 25.VUL **c. 800** 26.CRV **c. 800** 27.VTR **800–700** 28.VEI **800–650** 30.PRN; 31.CPN			
750–700	43/153	**750–700** 50.TRQ **710–675** 75.CUM		**710–640** 76–77.GEL	**725–?** 69.DDN
700–650	31/153	**700–650** 93.TRNT **700–650** 94.PRN & CRV **700–600** 104.ETR **675–650** 92.STR **675–600** 120.TRNT **c. 660** 121.BRN		**700–650** 95.GEL **700–615** 74.MYL **680–650** 78–80, 89–91.GEL **c. 675** 29.GEL **680–630** 96,102.GEL[c] **700–600** 105–106.GEL	**700–675** 88.ITH
650–600	45/153	**650–625** 134–135.MG **650–625** 49.TRNT **c. 625** 142.TRNT **625–600** 143.TRNT	**650–600** 136.CYP	**c. 650** 123.GEL	**650–625** 133.ITH
Period frequency		25/153	6/153	18/153	3/153
Notes		[a]Cretan influence on local artifacts	[b]SM type, found in 9th-century deposit	[c]local clay; may be from local workshop of Cretans	

Table Cat.3. Locations of Cretan Artifacts Found at Sites Overseas, by Period and Region *continued*

Central Mainland Greece	Aegean Islands	East Greece	North Africa	Period
1100–950 5–7.ATH				1100–1050
1050–950 3–4.MYC				1050–1000
				1000–950
				950–900
				900–850
810–710 19.COR; 20.ARG	**810–790** 34.THR **810–710** 16.AND; 17.SAM; 18.AGN; 21.DEL			850–800
	790–710 23.KAS	**c. 800** 22.KAM		800–750
750–725 40.DLF **750–700** 41–45.OLY **745–710** 35.ATH; 48.OLY; 46.CHL; 66–68.DLF **c. 725** 51.ATH; 52.SPR; 53.COR **725–?** 56.ATH; 57–66.DLF **715–700** 73.PER **710–680** 71.OLY	**750–725** 47.DEL **745–710** 37.SAM; 38–39.KAS **c. 725** 32–33.THR **725–?** 54.DEL; 55.MEL **720–680** 85.THR	**745–710** 36.LND **725–?** 70.MLT **720–680** 72.IAL		750–700
700– 100.OLY; 101.ATH **665–630** 125.OLY	**c. 700** 83–84, 86.THR **700–650** 82.KAS **680–630** 103.DEL	**c. 700–675** 87.IAL	**675–600** 81.CYR	700–650
c. 650 122.BSA; 98–99,124.OLY; 97.PER; 128.ARG **640–** 66.DLF **630–620** 139.DLF **640–630** 137.OLY **625–600** 144–145.SPR; 141. DLF; 135.OLY **620–600** 146–152.OLY	**c. 650** 129–132.SAM; 126–127.KTQ **c. 600** 153.KTQ		**637–631** 138.AZR **c. 630** 108–113.TOC **620–575** 114–115.TOC **600–570** 116–119.TOC	650–600
56/153	26/153	5/153	14/153	Period frequency
				Notes

Legend to Locations of Cretan Artifacts Found at Sites Overseas, by Period

AGN	Aigina		KAM	Kameiros (Rhodes)
AND	Andros		KAS	Kasos
ARG	Argos		KTN	Kition (Cyprus)
ATH	Athens		KYQ	Kythera
AZR	Aziris (North Africa)		LAT	Latium
BLM	Bitalemi (Gela)		MEL	Melos
BSA	Bassae		MG	Magna Graecia
CHL	Chalkis		MLT	Miletus
COR	Corinth		MYL	Mylai
CRV	Cerveteri (Latium/Etruria)		OLY	Olympia
CPN	Capena		PER	Perachora
CUM	Cumae		PRN	Praeneste
CYP	Cyprus (unspecified)		SAM	Samos
CYR	Cyrene		SLM	Salamis (Cyprus)
DEL	Delos		SPR	Sparta
DDN	Dodona		STR	Satyrion
DLF	Delphi		THR	Thera
ENK	Enkomi (Cyprus)		TOC	Tocra (North Africa)
ETR	Etruria		TRN	Terni (Latium/Etruria)
GEL	Gela		TRNT	Taranto
IAL	Ialysos (Rhodes)		VEI	Veii
ITH	Ithaka		VTR	Vetralla (Latium/Etruria)
TRQ	Tarquinia		VUL	Vulci (Latium/Etruria)

BIBLIOGRAPHY

Adams, L. 1978. *Orientalizing Sculpture in Soft Limestone from Crete and Mainland Greece*. BAR suppl. 42. Oxford: British Archaeological Reports.

Adams, R. M. 1974. "Anthropological Perspectives on Ancient Trade." *CurrAnthr* 15: 239–49.

—. 1990. "Introduction." In A. C. Gunter, ed., *Investigating Artistic Environments in the Ancient Near East*, 3–7. Washington, D.C.: Smithsonian Institution.

Akerlof, G. 1982. "Labor Contracts as Partial Gift Exchange." *Quarterly Journal of Economics* 97: 543-69.

Åkerström, Å. 1943. *Der geometrische Stil in Italien: Archäologische Grundlagen der frühesten historischen Zeit italiens*. SkrRom 9. Lund: C.W.K. Gleerup.

Albright, W. F. 1942. "The Role of the Canaanites in the History of Civilization." In *Studies in the History of Culture: The Disciplines of the Humanities*, 11–50. Menasha, Wis.: George Banta.

Alexander, J. 1965. "The Spectacle Fibulae of Southern Europe." *AJA* 69: 7–23.

Alexiou, S. 1950a. "Παραστάσεις πολύ ποδος ἐπὶ πρωτο ελληθικῶν ἐκ Κρήτης." *CretChron* 4: 294–318.

—. 1950b. "Πρωτογεωμετρικὸς ναΐσκος τῆς Συλλογῆς Γιαμαλάκη." *CretChron* 4: 441–62.

—. 1963. "Ἀρχαιότητες καὶ μνημεῖα Κρήτης." *ArchDelt* 18 B, pt. 2: 309–14.

—. 1966. "Μικραὶ ἀνασκαφαὶ καὶ περισυλλογὴ ἀρχαίων εἰς Κρήτην." *Prakt* 189–93.

Allbaugh, L. G. 1953. *Crete: A Case Study of an Underdeveloped Area*. Princeton: Princeton University Press.

Amandry, P. 1944–45. "Petits objects de Delphes." *BCH* 68–69: 36–74.

Amyx, D. A. 1969. "Observations on the Warrior Group." *CSCA* 2: 1–25.

—. 1988. *Corinthian Vase-Painting of the Archaic Period*. 2 vols. Berkeley: University of California Press.

Amyx, D. A., and P. Lawrence. 1975. *Corinth*. Vol. 7:2, *Archaic Corinthian Pottery and the Anaploga Well*. Princeton: American School of Classical Studies at Athens.

Anderson, G. M. 1988. "Mr. Smith and the Preachers: The Economics of Religion." *Wealth of Nations, Journal of Political Economy* 96: 1066–88.

André, J.-M., and M.-F. Baslez. 1993. *Voyager dans l'antiquité*. Paris: Fayard.

Andreadaki-Vlasaki, M. 1991. "The Khania Area, ca. 1200–700 B.C." In D. Musti et al., eds., *La transizione dal miceneo all'alto arcaismo: Al palazzo alla città. Atti del convegno internazionale, Roma 14–19 marzo, 1988*, 403–23. Rome: Istituto per gli studi micenei ed egeoanatolici, Monografie scientifiche, Serie Scienze umane e sociali.

—. 1985. "Γεωμετρικά νεκροταφεία στο νομό Χανίων." In *Πεπραγμένα τοῦ Ε' Διεθνοῦς Κρητολογικοῦ Συνεδρίου, Τομος, Α1: Τμημα Αρχαιολογικο*, 93–104. Chania: Φιλολογικὸς Σύλλογος Ὁ Χρυσόστομος.

—. 1990. "Παρατηρήσεις την Πρωτογεωμετρική ΣΤ' κεραμεική της Κρήτης." In *Πεπραγμένα τοῦ Ε' Διεθνοῦς Κρητολογικοῦ Συνεδρίου, Τομος Α1: Τμημα Αρχαιολογικο*, 10–35. Herakleion: Φιλολογικὸς Σύλλογος Ὁ Χρυσόστομος.

Angle, M., A. M. Conti, R. Dottarelli, A. Gianni, C. Persiani, L. Vagnetti, R. E. Jones, and L. Costantini. 1993. "Prime testimonianze micenei nel Latium Vetus." *PP* 48: 190–217.

Arafat, K., and C. Morgan. 1989. "Pots and Potters in Athens and Corinth: A Review." *OJA* 8: 311–46.

Arrow, K. J. 1962. "The Economic Implications of Learning by Doing." *Review of Economic Studies* 29: 155–73.

Artzy, M. 1990. "Nami Land and Sea Project, 1985–1988." *IEJ* 40: 73–76.

—. 1991. "Conical Cups and Pumice, Aegean Cult at Tel Nami, Israel." In R. Laffineur and L. Basch, eds., *Thalassa: L'Égée préhistorique et la mer*, Aegaeum 7, 203–6. Liège: Université de Liège.

—. 1994. "Incense, Camels and Collared Rim Jars: Desert Trade Routes and Maritime Outlets in the Second Millennium." *OJA* 13: 121–47.

Asaro, F., and I. Perlman. 1973. "Provenience Studies of Mycenaean Pottery Employing Neutron Activation Analysis." In *Acts of the International Archaeological Symposium "The Mycenaeans in the Eastern Mediterranean,"* 213–24. Nicosia: Department of Antiquities, Cyprus.

Åström, P. 1972. *The Swedish Cyprus Expedition*. Vol. 4:1C, *The Late Cypriote Bronze Age, Architecture and Pottery*. Lund: Swedish Cyprus Expedition.

—. 1973. "Discussion." In *Acts of the International Archaeological Symposium "The Mycenaeans in the Eastern Mediterranean,"* 359. Nicosia: Department of Antiquities, Cyprus.

Aubet, M. E. 1993. *The Phoenicians and the West: Politics, Colonies and Trade*. Translated by M. Turton. Cambridge: Cambridge University Press.

Aupert, P. 1975. "Chroniques des fouilles et découvertes archéologiques en Grèce en 1974." *BCH* 99: 589–694.

—. 1976. "Chroniques des fouilles et découvertes archéologiques en Grèce en 1975." *BCH* 100: 591–745.

Austin, M. M. 1970. *Greece and Egypt in the Archaic Age*. Cambridge: Cambridge Philological Society.

Austin, M. M., and P. Vidal-Naquet. 1977. *Economic and Social History of Ancient Greece*. Berkeley: University of California Press.

Avigad, N. 1982. "A Hebrew Seal Depicting a Sailing Ship." *BASOR* 246: 59–63.

Badian, E. 1970. "Piracy." In *OCD*, 2d ed.: 834.

Baines, J., and J. Málek. 1980. *Atlas of Ancient Egypt*. New York: Facts on File, 1980.

Bakir, G. 1981. *Sophilos: Ein Beitrag zu seinem Stil*. Mainz am Rhein: Philipp von Zabern.

Balensi, J. 1985. "Revising Tell Abu Hawam." *BASOR* 257: 65–74.

Balensi, J., and M.-D. Herrera. 1985. "Tell Abou Hawam 1983–1984, rapport préliminaire." *RBibl* 92: 82–128.

Balmuth, M. S. 1971. "Remarks on the Appearance of the Earliest Coins." In D. G. Mitten et al., eds., *Studies Presented to George M. A. Hanfmann*, 1–7. Mainz: Philipp von Zabern.

Banti, L. 1965 "Perachora, Pittore di.-2o." *EEA* 6: 32.

Barag, D. 1970. "Mesopotamian Core-Formed Glass Vessels (1500–600 B.C.)." In A. von Saldern et al., eds., *Glass and Glassmaking in Ancient Mesopotamia*, 131–200. London: Associated University Presses.

Barber, E.J.W. 1991. *Prehistoric Textiles: The Development of Cloth in the Neolithic and Bronze Ages, with Special Reference to the Aegean*. Princeton: Princeton University Press.

Barkay, G. 1992. "The Iron Age II–III." In A. Ben-Tor, ed., *The Archaeology of Ancient Israel*, 131–200. New Haven: Yale University Press.

Barnett, R. D. 1939. "Explorations in Cilicia: The Neilson Expedition: Fifth Interim Report, III: The Greek Pottery." *AnnLiv* 26: 98–130.

—. 1948. "Early Greek and Oriental Ivories." *JHS* 68: 1–25.

—. 1950. "The Excavations of the British Museum at Toprak Kale near Van." *Iraq* 12: 1–43.

—. 1957. *A Catalogue of the Nimrud Ivories in the British Museum*. London: Trustees of the British Museum.

—. 1982. *Ancient Ivories in the Middle East and Adjacent Countries*. Qedem 14. Jerusalem: Israel Exploration Society.

Bartels, H. 1967a. "Mitren." In E. Kunze, ed., *Bericht über die Ausgrabungen in Olympia, Herbst 1958 bis Sommer 1962*, OlBer 8, 196–207. Berlin: Walter de Gruyter.

—. 1967b. "Nachtrag." In E. Kunze, ed., *Bericht über die Ausgrabungen in Olympia, Herbst 1958 bis Sommer 1962*, OlBer 8, 263–64. Berlin: Walter de Gruyter.

Basch, L. 1969a. "Phoenician Oared Ships, Part I." *Mariner's Mirror* 55: 139–62.

—. 1969b. "Phoenician Oared Ships, Part II." *Mariner's Mirror* 55: 227–45.

—. 1983a. "When Is a Ram Not a Ram: The Case of the Punic Ship." *Mariner's Mirror* 69: 129–42.

—. 1983b. "Bow and Stern Appendages in the Ancient Mediterranean." *Mariner's Mirror* 69: 395–412.

—. 1986. "The Aegina Pirate Ships of c. B.C. 1700." *Mariner's Mirror* 72: 415–37.

—. 1987. *Le musée imaginaire de la marine antique*. Athens: Institut Hellénique pour la Préservation de la Tradition Nautique.

—. 1991. "Carènes égéennes à l'âge du bronze." In R. Laffineur and L. Basch, eds., *Thalassa, l'Égée préhistorique et la mer*, Aegaeum 7, 43–54. Liège: Université de Liège.

Bass, G. F. 1963. "Mycenaean and Protogeometric Tombs in the Halicarnassus Peninsula." *AJA* 67: 353–61.

—. 1967. *Cape Gelidonya: A Bronze Age Shipwreck*. TAPS 57, pt. 8. Philadelphia: American Philosophical Society.

—. 1973. "Cape Gelidonya and Bronze Age Maritime Trade." In H. A. Hoffner, ed., *Orient and Occident*, 29–38. Neukirchen-Vluyn: Neukirchener.

—. 1986. "A Bronze Age Shipwreck at Ulu Burun (Kaş): 1984 Campaign." *AJA* 90: 269–96.

Bass, G. F., and C. Pulak. 1989. "Excavations at Ulu Burun in 1986." In G. F. Bass et al., "The Bronze Age Shipwreck at Ulu Burun: 1986 Campaign," *AJA* 93: 1–12.

Becker, G. S. 1962. "Irrational Behavior and Economic Theory." *Journal of Political Economy* 70: 1–13.

—. 1965. "A Theory of the Allocation of Time." *Economic Journal* 75: 493–517.

Beidelman, T. O. 1989. "Agonistic Exchange: Homeric Reciprocity and the Heritage of Simmel and Mauss." *Cultural Anthropology* 4: 227–59.

Bell, M. R. 1982. "Preliminary Report on the Mycenaean Pottery from Deir el-Medina (1979–1980)." *ASAE* 68: 143–63.

—. 1983. "'Egyptian Imitations of Aegean Vases': Some Additional Notes." *Göttingen Miszellen* 63: 13–24.

Bennathan, E., and A. A. Walters. 1979. *Port Pricing and Investment Policy for Developing Countries*. New York: Oxford University Press.

Benson, J. L. 1953. *Die Geschichte der korinthischen Vasen*. Basel: Benno Schwabe.

—. 1961. "A Problem in Orientalizing Cretan Birds: Mycenaean or Philistine Prototypes?" *JNES* 20: 73–84.

—. 1970. Review of *Greek Geometric Pottery*, by J. N. Coldstream. *AJA* 74: 303–5.

—. 1986. "An Early Protocorinthian Workshop and the Source of Its Motifs." *BABesch* 61: 1–20.

—. 1989. *Earlier Corinthian Workshops: A Study of Corinthian Geometric and Protocorinthian Stylistic Groups*. Scripta Minora 1. Amsterdam: Allard Pierson Museum.

Benton, S. 1934–35. "The Evolution of the Tripod Lebes." *BSA* 35: 74–130.

—. 1938–39. "The Date of the Cretan Shields." *BSA* 39: 52–64.

—. 1939–40. "Unpublished Objects from Palaikastro and Praisos II:8: Bronzes from Palaikastro and Praisos." *BSA* 40: 51–59.

—. 1950. "The Dating of Horses on Stands and Spectacle Fibulae in Greece." *JHS* 70: 16–22.

Benveniste, E. 1948–49. "Don et échange dans le vocabulaire indo-européen." *L'Année sociologique*, 3d ser.: 7–20.

—. 1971. "Don et échange dans le vocabulaire indo-européen." In E. Benveniste, *Problems in General Linguistics*, ch. 26. Translated by M. E. Meek. Coral Gables, Fla.: University of Miami Press.

Benzi, M. 1988a. "Mycenaean Rhodes: A Summary." In S. Dietz and I. Papachristodoulou, eds., *Archaeology in the Dodecanese*, 59–72. Copenhagen: National Museum of Denmark, Department of Near Eastern and Classical Antiquities.

—. 1988b. "Rhodes in the LH IIIC Period." In E. B. French and K. A. Wardle, eds., *Problems in Greek Prehistory*, 253–62. Bristol: Bristol Classical Press.

—. 1992. *Rodi e la civiltà micenea*. Incunabula Graeca 94. Rome: Gruppo Editoriale Internazionale.

Benzi, M., and G. Graziado. 1996. "Late Mycenaean Pottery from Punta Meliso (Santa Maria di Leuca)." In E. deMiro, L. Godart, and A. Sacconi, eds., *Atti e memorie del secondo congresso internazionale di micenologia*, 3: 1523–29. *Archeologia*. Incunabula Graeca 98.3. Rome: Gruppo Editoriale Internazionale.

Bergoffen, C. J. 1991. "Overland Trade in Northern Sinai: The Evidence of Late Cypriot Pottery." *BASOR* 284: 59–76.

Bergonzi, G., and A. M. Bietti Sestieri. 1980. "Periodi I e IIA." In "La formazione della città nel Lazio," *DialArch*, n.s. 1–2: 47–64.

Bernabò Brea, L., and M. Cavalier. 1959. *Mylai.* Catania: Istituto Geografico de Novarra.

Betancourt, P. P. 1985. *The History of Minoan Pottery.* Princeton: Princeton University Press.

Biebl, R., and C. P. McRoy. 1971. "Plasmatic Resistance and Rate of Respiration and Photosynthesis of *Zostera marina* at Different Salinities and Temperature." *Marine Biology* 8: 48–56.

Bielman, A. 1994. *Retour à la liberté; Libération et sauvetage des prisonniers en Grèce ancienne. Recueil d'inscriptions honorant des sauveteurs et analyse critique.* Études Epigraphiques 1. Lausanne: École française d'Athènes and Université Lausanne.Bietak, M. 1993. "The Sea Peoples and the End of the Egyptian Administration in Canaan." In *Biblical Archaeology Today, 1990,* 298–302. Jerusalem: Israel Exploration Society.

—. 1994. "Neue Grabungsergebnisse aus Tell el-Dab`a und `Ezbet Helmi im östlichen Nildelta (1989–1991). VI: Die Wandmalereien aus Tell el-Dab`a/`Ezbet Helmi. Erste Eindrücke." *Ägypten und Levante* 4: 44–80.

—. 1996. *Avaris: The Capital of the Hyksos. Recent Excavations at Tell el Dab`a.* London: British Museum Press.

Bietak, M., and N. Marinatos. 1995. "The Minoan Wall Paintings from Avaris." *Ägypten und Levante* 5: 49–62.

Bietti Sestieri, A. M. 1973. "The Metal Industry of Continental Italy, 13th to the 11th Century B.C., and Its Connections with the Aegean." *PPS* 39: 383–424.

—. 1980. "Aggiornamento per i periodi I e IIA." In "La formazione della città nel Lazio," *DialArch*, n.s. 1–2: 65–78.

—. 1982. "Frattesina (Fratta Polesine, Rovigo)." In L. Vagnetti, ed., *Magna Grecia e mondo miceneo: Nuovi documenti,* 201–7. Taranto: Istituto per la storia e l'archeologia della Magna Grecia.

—. 1984. "Central and Southern Italy in the Late Bronze Age." In T. Hackens, N. D. Holloway, and R. R. Holloway, eds., *Crossroads of the Mediterranean,* Archaeologica Transatlantica 2, 55–122. Louvain-la-Neuve: Art and Archaeology Publications, College Erasme.

—. 1988. "The 'Mycenaean Connection' and Its Impact on the Central Mediterranean." *DialArch* 6: 23–51.

—. 1992. *The Iron Age Community of Osteria dell'Osa.* Cambridge: Cambridge University Press.

Bikai, P. M. 1979. *The Pottery of Tyre.* Warminster: Aris and Phillips.

—. 1987. "Trade Networks in the Early Iron Age: The Phoenicians at Palaepaphos." In D. W. Rupp, ed., *Western Cyprus: Connections, An Archaeological Symposium,* 125–28. Göteborg: Paul Åström.

Birmingham, J. M. 1961. "The Overland Route across Anatolia in the Eighth and Seventh Centuries B.C." *AnatSt* 11: 185–95.

Bisi, A. M. 1987. "Ateliers phéniciens dans le monde égéen." In E. Lipiński, ed., *Phoenicia and the East Mediterranean in the First Millennium B.C.*, Orientalia Lovaniensia Analecta 22, Studia Phoenicia 5, 225–37. Leuven: Peeters.

Bissing, F. W. von. 1923–24. "Untersuchungen über die 'phoinikischen' Metallschalen." *JdI* 38–39: 180–241.

—. 1941. *Zeit und Herkunft der in Cerveteri gefundenen Gefäße aus ägyptischer Fayence und glasiertem Ton.* SBMünch 7. Munich: Bayerischen Akademie der Wissenschaften.

Blackman, D. J. 1973. "Evidence of Sea Level Change in Ancient Harbors and Coastal Installations." In D. J. Blackman, ed., *Marine Archaeology,* Colston Papers 23, 115–37. London: Butterworths.

—. 1982. "Ancient Harbours in the Mediterranean, Part 1." *IJNA* 11: 79–104.

Blackman, D. J., and K. Branigan. 1975. "An Archaeological Survey on the South Coast of Crete, between the Ayiofarango and Christostomos." *BSA* 70: 17–36.

Blakeway, A. 1932–33. "Prolegomena to the Study of Greek Commerce with Italy, Sicily and France in the Eighth and Seventh Centuries B.C." *BSA* 33: 170–208.

—. 1935. "Demaratus: A Study in Some Aspects of the Earliest Hellenization of Latium and Etruria." *JRS* 25: 127–49.

Blegen, C. W., H. Palmer, and R. S. Young. 1964. *Corinth.* Vol. 13, *The North Cemetery.* Princeton: American School of Classical Studies at Athens.

Bleiberg, E. L. 1984. "The King's Privy Purse during the New Kingdom." *JARCE* 21: 155–67.

—. 1996. *The Official Gift in Ancient Egypt*. Norman: University of Oklahoma Press.

Blinkenberg, C. 1926. *Fibules grecques et orientales*. Det Kgl. Denske Videnskabernes Selskab, Historisk-filologiske Meddelelser. 13,1; Lindiaka 5. Copenhagen: Andr. Fred. Høst and Son.

—. 1931. *Lindos: Fouilles de l'acropole 1902–1914*. Vol. 1, *Les petits objets*. Berlin: Walter de Gruyter.

Bliss, C. J., and N. H. Stern. 1982. *Palanpur: The Economy of an Indian Village*. Oxford: Clarendon.

Bloch, M., and J. Parry. 1989. "Introduction: Money and the Morality of Exchange." In J. Parry and M. Bloch, eds., *Money and the Morality of Exchange*, 1–32. Cambridge: Cambridge University Press.

Blome, P. 1982. *Die figürliche Bildwelt Kretas in der geometrischen und früharchaischen Periode*. Mainz: Philipp von Zabern.

Boardman, J. 1954. "Catalogue of Finds." *BSA* 49: 224–28.

—. 1956. "Chian and Naucratite." *BSA* 51: 55–62.

—. 1960. "Protogeometric Graves at Agios Ioannis near Knossos." *BSA* 55: 128–48.

—. 1961. *The Cretan Collection in Oxford: The Dictaean Cave and Iron Age Crete*. Oxford: Clarendon.

—. 1962. "Archaic Finds at Knossos." *BSA* 57: 28–34.

—. 1963a. "Artemis Orthia and Chronology." *BSA* 58: 1–7.

—. 1963b. *Island Gems: A Study of Greek Seals in the Geometric and Early Archaic Periods*. Society for the Promotion of Hellenic Studies, suppl. 10. London: Society for the Promotion of Hellenic Studies.

—. 1965. "Tarsus, Al Mina, and Chronology." *JHS* 85: 5–15.

—. 1966. "Evidence for the Dating of Greek Settlements in Cyrenaica." *BSA* 61: 149–56.

—. 1967. "The Khaniale Tekke Tombs, II." *BSA* 62: 57–75.

—. 1968. "Crete and Libya in the Archaic Period." In Πεπραγμένα τοῦ Β᾿ Διεθνοῦς Κρητολογικοῦ Συνεδρίου Τόμος Α᾿. Τμῆμα ᾿Αρχαολογικόν, 134–36. Athens: Φιλολογικὸς Σύλλογος Ὁ Χρυσόστομος.

—. 1970a. "Orientalen auf Kreta." In *Dädalische Kunst auf Kreta im 7. Jahrhundert v. Chr.*, 14–25. Mainz: Philipp von Zabern.

—. 1970b. Review of *Antike Gemmen in deutschen Sammlungen*, vol. 1, *Staatliche Münzsammlung München*, Teil 1, *Griechische Gemmen von minoischcer Zeit bis zum später Hellenismus*, by E. Brandt. *JHS* 90: 264–65.

—. 1971. "Ship Firedogs and Other Metalwork from Kavousi." *CretChron* 23: 5–8.

—. 1977. "The Olive in the Mediterranean: Its Culture and Use." In The Royal Society and The British Academy, *The Early History of Agriculture*, 187–94. Oxford: Oxford University Press.

—. 1978. *Greek Sculpture: The Archaic Period: A Handbook*. London: Oxford University Press.

—. 1979. "Crete and Cyprus in the Seventh Century B.C." In *Acts of the International Archaeological Symposium "The Relations between Cyprus and Crete, ca. 2000–500 B.C.,"* 264–68. Nicosia: Department of Antiquities, Cyprus.

—. 1980. *The Greeks Overseas: Their Early Colonies and Trade*. 3d ed. London: Thames and Hudson.

—. 1985. *Greek Art*. Rev. ed. London: Thames and Hudson.

—. 1988a. "Trade in Greek Decorated Pottery." *OJA* 7: 27–33.

—. 1988b. "The Trade Figures." *OJA* 7: 371–73.

—. 1990a. "Al Mina and History." *OJA* 9: 169–90.

—. 1990b. "The Lyre Player Group of Seals: An Encore." *AA* 1–17.

Boardman, J., and J. Hayes. 1966. *Excavations at Tocra, 1963–1965*. Vol. 1, *The Archaic Deposits I*. BSA suppl. 4. London: Thames and Hudson.

—. 1973. *Excavations at Tocra, 1963–1965*. Vol. 2, *The Archaic Deposits II and Later Deposits*. BSA suppl. 10. London: Thames and Hudson.

Boardman, J., and F. Schweizer. 1973. "Clay Analyses of Archaic Greek Pottery." *BSA* 68: 267–82.

Boardman, J., and M.-L. Vollenweider. 1978. *Catalogue of the Engraved Gems and Finger Rings in the Ashmolean Museum*. Vol. 1, *Greek and Etruscan*. Oxford: Clarendon.

Bocci, P. 1962. *Ricerche sulla ceramica cicladica*. Studi Miscellanei 2. Rome: L'Erma di Bretschneider.

Böhlau, J. 1887. "Frühattische Vasen." *JdI* 2: 33–66.

Böhm, S. 1990. *Die 'nackte Göttin': Zur Ikonographie und Deutung unbekleideter weiblicher Figuren in der frühgriechischen Kunst*. Mainz: Philipp von Zabern.

Bondi, S. P. 1988. "The Course of History." In S. Moscati, ed., *The Phoenicians*, 38–45. New York: Abbeville.

Borchardt, J. 1972. *Homerische Helme: Helmformen der Ägäis in ihren Beziehungen zu orientalischen und europäischen Helmen in der Bronze- und frühen Eisenzeit*. Mainz: Philipp von Zabern.

—. 1977. "Helme." In H.-G. Buchholz and J. Wiesner, eds., *Kriegswesen 1. Schutzwaffen und Wehrbauten*, ArchHom E.1, 57–74. Göttingen: Vandenhoeck and Ruprecht.

Bosanquet, R. C. 1901–2. "Excavations at Praisos. I." *BSA* 8: 231–70.

Bosanquet, R. C., and R. M. Dawkins. 1923. *The Unpublished Objects from the Palaikastro Excavations, 1902–1906*. BSA suppl. 1. London: Macmillan.

Bouzek, J. 1972. "Syrian and Anatolian Bronze Age Figurines in Greece." *PPS* 38: 156–64.

—. 1974. *The Attic Dark Age Incised Ware*. Sborník Národního muzea Praze A 28: 1. Prague: Národní Museum.

—. 1985. *The Aegean, Anatolia and Europe: Cultural Interactions in the Second Millennium B.C.* SIMA 29. Göteborg: Paul Åströms Förlag.

—. 1994. "Late Bronze Age Greece and the Balkans: A Review of the Present Picture." *BSA* 89: 217–34.

Boyd, H. J. 1901. "Excavations at Kavousi, Crete, in 1900." *AJA* 5: 125–57.

Braidwood, R. J. 1940. "Report on Two Sondages on the Coast of Syria, South of Tartous." *Syria* 21: 183–221.

Brandt, E., ed. 1968. *Antike Gemmen in deutschen Sammlungen*. Vol. 1, *Staatliche Münzsammlung München*. Teil 1, *Griechische Gemmen von minoischer Zeit bis zum später Hellenismus*. Munich: Pestel.

Branigan, K. 1970. *The Foundations of Palatial Crete*. New York: Praeger.

—. 1981. "Minoan Colonization." *BSA* 76: 23–33.

—. 1989. "Minoan Foreign Relations in Transition." In R. Laffineur, ed., *Transition: Le monde égéen du bronze moyen au bronze récent*, Aegaeum 3, 65–71. Liège: Université de l'Etat à Liège.

Brann, E.T.H. 1962. *The Athenian Agora*. Vol. 8, *Late Geometric and Protoattic Pottery: Mid-8th to Late 7th Century B.C.* Princeton: American School of Classical Studies at Athens.

Braudel, F. 1972. *The Mediterranean and the Mediterranean World in the Age of Philip II*. 2 vols. New York: Harper and Row.

Bravo, B. 1980. "Sulân: Représailles et justice privée contre des étrangers dan les cités grecques." *AnnPisa*, ser. 3, 10.3, 675–987.

—. 1983. "Le commerce des céréales chez les Grecs de l'époque archaïque." In P. Garnsey and C. R. Whittaker, eds., *Trade and Famine in Classical Antiquity*, 17–29. Cambridge: Cambridge Philological Society.

—. 1984. "Commerce et noblesse en Grèce archaïque: A propos d'un livre d'Alfonso Mele." *DHA* 10: 99–160.

Brink, E.C.M. van den, ed. 1988. *The Archaeology of the Nile Delta, Egypt: Problems and Priorities. Proceedings of the Seminar Held in Cairo, 19–22 October 1986, on the Occasion of the Fifteenth Anniversary of the Netherlands Institute of Archaeology and Arabic Studies in Cairo.* Amsterdam: Netherlands Foundation for Archaeological Research in Egypt.

—, ed. 1992. *The Nile Delta in Transition: 4th–3rd Millennium B.C. Proceedings of the Seminar held in Cairo, 21–24 October 1990, at the Netherlands Institute of Archaeology and Arabic Studies.* Tel Aviv: Israel Exploration Society.

Brinkman, J. A. 1988. "Textual Evidence for Bronze in Babylonia in the Early Iron Age, 1000–539 B.C." In J. Curtis, ed., *Bronzeworking Centres of Western Asia, c. 1000–539 B.C.*, 135–68. London: Kegan Paul.

British School at Athens. 1975. "Knossos." *ArchDelt* B 30, 2: 343–46.

Brock, J. K. 1935. Review of *Delos*, vol. 17, *Les vases orientalisants de style non mélien*, by C. Dugas. *JHS* 55: 248–49.

—. 1957. *Fortetsa: Early Greek Tombs near Knossos*. BSA suppl. 2. Cambridge: Cambridge University Press.

Brown, R. B. 1975. "A Provisional Catalogue of and Commentary on Egyptian and Egyptianizing Artifacts Found on Greek Sites." Ph.D. diss., Department of History, University of Minnesota.

Brown, W. L. 1960. *The Etruscan Lion*. Oxford: Clarendon.

Brulé, P. 1978. *La piraterie crétoise hellénistique*. Annales littéraires de l'Université de Besançon, 233, Centre de Recherches de Histoire Ancienne 27. Paris: Université de Besançon.

Buccellati, G. 1967. *Cities and Nations of Ancient Syria: An Essay on Political Institutions with Special Reference to the Israelite Kingdoms*. Studi Semitici 26. Rome: Istituto di Studi del Vicino Oriente, Università di Roma.

Buchner, G. 1964. "Il dibattito." In *Metropoli e colonie di Magna Grecia: Atti del terzo convegno di studi sulla Magna Grecia tenuto a Taranto dal 13 al 17 ottobre 1963*, 263–74. Naples: L'Arte Tipografica.

Buchner, G., and J. Boardman. 1966. "Seals from Ischia and the Lyre-Player Group." *JdI* 81: 1–62.

Buchner, G., and D. Ridgway. 1993. *Pithekoussai*. Vol. 1, *La Necropoli: Tombe 1–723, Scavate dal 1952 al 1961*. Rome: Georgio Bretschneider.

Burkert, W. 1985. *Greek Religion: Archaic and Classical*. Translated by J. Raffan. Cambridge, Mass.: Harvard University Press.

—. 1992. *The Orientalizing Revolution: Near Eastern Influence on Greek Culture in the Early Archaic Age*. Translated by M. E. Pinder and W. Burkert. Cambridge, Mass.: Harvard University Press.

Burn, A. R. 1937. *The World of Hesiod*. New York: E. P. Dutton.

—. 1960. *The Lyric Age of Greece*. New York: St. Martin's.

—. 1984. *Persia and the Greeks*. 2d ed. Stanford: Stanford University Press.

Burr, D. 1933. "A Geometric House and a Proto-Attic Votive Deposit." *Hesperia* 2: 542–640.

Burrell, C. C., and J. R. Schubel. 1977. "Seagrass Ecosystem Oceanography." In C. P. McRoy and C. Helfferich, eds., *Seagrass Ecosystems: A Scientific Perspective*, 195–232. New York: Marcel Dekker.

Cadogan, G. 1973. "Patterns in the Distribution of Mycenaean Pottery in the East Mediterranean." In *Acts of the International Archaeological Symposium "The Mycenaeans in the Eastern Mediterranean,"* 166–74. Nicosia: Department of Antiquities, Cyprus.

Calhoun, G. M. 1926. *The Business Life of Ancient Athens*. Chicago: University of Chicago Press. (Reprinted New York: Cooper Square, 1968.)

Calmeyer, P. 1969. *Datierbare Bronzen aus Luristan und Kirmanshah*. Berlin: Walter de Gruyter.

Cambitoglou, A., and J. R. Green. 1970. "Ἀνασκαφαὶ Ζαγορᾶς—Προκαταρκτικὴ ἔκθεσις I: 1967 καὶ 1968–1969." *ArchEph*: 154–233.

Cambitoglou, A., J. J. Coulton, J. Birmingham, and J. R. Green. 1971. *Zagora*. Vol. 1, *Excavation Season 1967: Study Season 1968–69*. Sydney: Sydney University Press.

Caminos, R. A. 1958. *The Chronicle of Prince Osorkon*. Analecta Orientalia 37. Rome: Pontificum Institutum Biblicum.

Campbell, D. E. 1987. *Resource Allocation Mechanisms*. Cambridge: Cambridge University Press.

Canciani, F. 1970. *Bronzi orientali e orientalizzanti a Creta nell' VIII e VII sec. A.C.* Studiá Archaeologica 12. Rome: L'Erma di Bretschneider.

Carapanos, C. 1878. *Dodone et ses ruines*. Paris: Hachette.

Carter, J. B. 1985. *Greek Ivory Carving in the Orientalizing and Archaic Periods*. New York: Garland.

—. 1987. "The Masks of Ortheia." *AJA* 91: 355–83.

—. 1995. "Prinias and Karkamish: Syro-Phoenician Iconography Re-Contextualized in the Sculptural Program at Prinias, Crete." Paper presented November 10 at the Colloquium on Post-Minoan Crete. London: British School at Athens and Institute of Archaeology, University College London.

Cary, E., trans. 1954. Dio Cassius, *Roman History*. Vol. 3: *Books XXXVI–XL*. Loeb Classical Library. Cambridge, Mass.: Harvard University Press.

Cary, M. 1970. "Syle." *OCD*, 2d ed.: 1026.

Casson, L. 1974. *Travel in the Ancient World*. London: George Allen and Unwin.

—. 1986. *Ships and Seamanship in the Ancient World*. Rev. ed. Princeton: Princeton University Press.

Casson, S. 1938. "The Modern Pottery Trade in the Aegean." *Antiquity* 12: 464–73.

Catling, H. W. 1964. *Cypriot Bronzework in the Mycenaean World*. Oxford: Clarendon.

—. 1975. "Archaeology in Greece, 1974–75." *AR* 21: 3–28.

—. 1977a. "Excavations at the Menelaion, Sparta, 1973–1976." *AR* 23: 24–42.

—. 1977b. "The Knossos Area, 1974–76." *AR* 23: 3–23.

—. 1979. "Knossos, 1978." *AR* 25: 43–58.

—. 1982. "Archaeology in Greece, 1981–82." *AR* 28: 3–62.

—. 1983a. "Archaeology in Greece, 1982–83." *AR* 29: 3–62.

—. 1983b. "New Light on Knossos in the 8th and 7th Centuries B.C." *ASAtene*, n.s. 61: 31–43.

—. 1984. "Workshop and Heirloom: Prehistoric Bronze Stands in the East Mediterranean." *RDAC* 69–91.

—. 1985. "Archaeology in Greece, 1984–85." *AR* 31: 3–69.

—. 1986. "Archaeology in Greece, 1985–86." *AR* 32: 3–101.

—. 1991. *The Ancient Mariners*. 2d ed. Princeton: Princeton University Press.

Catling, R.W.V., and I. S. Lemos. 1990. *Lefkandi II: The Protogeometric Building at Toumba*. Part 1, *The Pottery. BSA* suppl. vol. no. 22. London: Thames and Hudson.

Catling, H. W., and A. Millet. 1965. "A Study of the Incised Stirrup-Jars from Thebes." *Archaeometry* 8: 3–85.

Catling, H. W., E. E. Richards, and A. E. Blin-Stoyle. 1963. "Correlatons between Composition and Provenance of Mycenaean and Minoan Pottery." *BSA* 58: 93–115.

Caubet, A., and F. Poplin. 1992. "La place des ivoires d'Ougarit dans la production du Proche Orient ancien." In J. L. Fitton, ed., *Ivory in Greece and the Eastern Mediterranean from the Bronze Age to the Hellenistic Period*, British Museum Occasional Paper 85, 91–100. London: Trustees of the British Museum.

Cavanagh, W. G., and R. R. Laxton. 1984. "Lead Figurines from the Menelaion and Seriation." *BSA* 79: 23–36.

Černý, J. 1952. *Paper and Books in Ancient Egypt*. London: H. K. Lewis. (Reprinted Chicago: Ares, 1985.)

—. 1975. "Egypt: From the Death of Ramesses III to the End of the Twenty-First Dynasty." *CAH* 2, pt. 2, 3d ed.: 606–57.

Champion, T. C. 1986. Review of *Farms, Villages and Cities: Commerce and Urban Origins in Late Prehistoric Europe*, by P. S. Wells. *Man*, n.s. 21: 554.

Champion, T., C. Gamble, S. Shennan, and A. Whittle. 1984. *Prehistoric Europe*. New York: Academic Press.

Charbonneaux, J. 1958. *Les bronzes grecs*. Paris: Presses Universitaires de France.

Cherry, J. F. 1986. "Polities and Palaces: Some Problems in Minoan State Formation." In C. Renfrew and J. F. Cherry, eds., *Peer Polity Interaction and Socio-Political Change*, 19–45. Cambridge: Cambridge University Press.

Cherry, J. F., and J. L. Davis. 1982. "The Cyclades and the Greek Mainland in LC I: The Evidence of the Pottery." *AJA* 86: 333–41.

Choremis, A. 1973. "Μυκηναϊκοὶ καὶ πρωτο-γεωμετρικοὶ τάφοι εἰς Καρποφόραν Μεσσηνίας." *ArchEph* 112: 25–74.

Cifola, B. 1988. "Ramesses III and the Sea Peoples: A Structural Analysis of the Medinet Habu Inscriptions." *Orientalia* 57: 275–306.

Cita, M. B., and W.B.F. Ryan. 1978. "The Deep-Sea Record of the Eastern Mediterranean Sea in the Last 150,000 Years." In C. Doumas, ed., *Thera and the Aegean World*, 1: 45–60. London: Thera Foundation.

Clairmont, C. 1955. "Greek Pottery from the Near East." *Berytus* 11: 85–142.

Cline, E. 1987. "Amenhotep III and the Aegean: A Reassessment of Egypt-Aegean Relations in the 14th Century B.C." *Orientalia*, n.s. 56: 2–36.

—. 1990. "An Unpublished Amenhotep III Faience from Mycenae." *JAOS* 110: 200–212.

—. 1991. "Monkey Business in the Bronze Age Aegean: The Amenhotep II Faience Figurines at Mycenae and Tiryns." *BSA* 86: 29–42.

—. 1994. *Sailing the Wine-Dark Sea; International Trade and the Late Bronze Age Aegean*. BAR International Series 591. Oxford: Tempus Reparatum.

—. 1995a. "Tinker, Tailor, Soldier, Sailor: Minoans and Mycenaeans Abroad." In R. Laffineur and W.-D. Niemeier, eds., *Politeia: Society and State in the Aegean Bronze Age*, Aegaeum 12, 265–83. Liège: Université de Liège.

—. 1995b. "'My Brother, My Son': Rulership and Trade between the LBA Aegean, Egypt and the Near East." In P. Rehak, ed., *The Role of the Ruler in the Prehistoric Aegean*, Aegaeum 11, 143–50. Liège: Université de Liège.

Cogan, M. 1973. "Tyre and Tiglath-Pilesar III: Chronological Notes." *JCS* 25: 96–99.

Cohen, E. E. 1992. *Athenian Economy and Society: A Banking Perspective*. Princeton: Princeton University Press.

Coldstream, J. N. 1960. "A Geometric Well at Knossos." *BSA* 55: 159–71.

—. 1963. "Five Tombs at Knossos." *BSA* 58: 30–43.

—. 1968. *Greek Geometric Pottery*. London: Methuen.

—. 1969. "The Phoenicians of Ialysos." *BICS* 16: 1–8.

—. 1971. "The Cesnola Painter: A Change of Address." *BICS* 18: 1–15.

—. 1972. "Knossos 1951–61: Protogeometric and Geometric Pottery from the Town." *BSA* 67: 63–99.

—. 1973a. "Knossos 1951–61: Orientalizing and Archaic Pottery from the Town." *BSA* 68: 33–64.

—. 1973b. *Knossos: The Sanctuary of Demeter*. BSA suppl. 8. London: Thames and Hudson.

—. 1974. "Sphinxes and Griffins from Geometric Knossos." In *Antichità cretesi, studi in onore di Doro Levi*, 2: 161–64. Catania: Università di Catania, Istituto di Archeologia.

—. 1977. *Geometric Greece*. New York: St. Martin's.

—. 1979. "Some Cypriote Traits in Cretan Pottery, c. 950–700 B.C." In *Acts of the International Archaeological Symposium "The Relations between Cyprus and Crete, ca. 2000–500 B.C.,"* 257–63. Nicosia: Department of Antiquities, Cyprus.

—. 1980a. "Some New Tombs from Early Hellenic Knossos." In Στήλη. Τόμος είς μνήμην Ν. Κοντολεόντος, 408–12. Athens: Saomateio hoi Philoi tou Nikolaou Knotoleontos.

—. 1980b. "Geometric Imports." In M. R. Popham and L. H. Sackett, with P. G. Themelis, eds., *Lefkandi I: The Iron Age*, BSA suppl. 11, 350–54. London: Thames and Hudson.

—. 1982. "Greeks and Phoenicians in the Aegean." In H. G. Niemeyer, ed., *Phönizier im Westen*, 261–75. Mainz: Philipp von Zabern.

—. 1983. "Gift Exchange in the Eighth Century B.C." In R. Hägg, ed., *The Greek Renaissance of the Eighth Century B.C.*, Acta Instituti Atheniensis Regni Sueciae, Series in 4°, 30, 201–6. Stockholm: Paul Åströms Förlag.

—. 1984a. "Cypriaca and Cretocypriaca from the North Cemetery of Knossos." *RDAC* 122–37.

—. 1984b. "Dorian Knossos and Aristotle's Villages." In *Aux origines de l'hellénisme: La Crète et la Grèce: Homage à Henri van Effentere*, 311–22. Paris: Université de Paris.

—. 1986. "Kition and Amathus: Some Reflections on Their Westward Links during the Early Iron Age." In V. Karageorghis, ed., *Cyprus between the Orient and the Occident*, 321–29. Nicosia: Department of Antiquities, Cyprus.

—. 1987a. "'Bilingual' Geometric Amphorae from the North Cemetery of Knossos." In Ειλαπινη. Τόμος Τιμητικός για τον Καθηγητή Νικόλαο Πλάτωνα, 335–39. Herakleion: Bikelaia Dhimotiki Bibliothike.

—. 1987b. "The Greek Geometric and Archaic Imports." In V. Karageorghis and O. Picard, eds., *Études chypriotes*, vol. 8, *La nécropoles d'Amathonte tombes 113–167*, pt. 2, *Céramiques non chypriotes*, 21–31. Nicosia: A. G. Leventis.

—. 1989. "Early Greek Visitors to Cyprus and the Eastern Mediterranean." In V. Tatton-Brown, ed., *Cyprus and the East Mediterranean in the Iron Age*, 90–96. London: British Museum Publications.

—. 1991. "Knossos: An Urban Nucleus in the Dark Age?" In D. Musti et al., eds., *La transizione dal miceneo all'alto arcaismo: Al palazzo alla città: Atti del convegno internazionale, Roma 14–19 marzo, 1988*, 287–99. Rome: Istituto per gli studi micenei ed egeo-anatolici, Monografie scientifiche, Serie Scienze umane e sociali.

—. 1992. "Early Hellenic Pottery." In L. H. Sackett, ed., *Knossos: From Greek City to Roman Colony: Excavations at the Unexplored Mansion*, vol. 2, *Text*, BSA suppl. 21, 67–87. London: Thames and Hudson.

—. 1994a. "A Figured Attic Geometric Kantharos from Kition." *RDAC* 155–59.

—. 1994b. "Urns with Lids: The Visible Face of the Knossian 'Dark Age'." In D. Evely, H. Hughes-Brock, and N. Momigliano, eds., *Knossos: A Labyrinth of History: Papers Presented in Honour of Sinclair Hood*, 105–21. London: British School at Athens.

—. 1996. "The Protogeometric and Geometric Pottery." In J. N. Coldstream and H. W. Catling, eds., *Knossos North Cemetery: Early Greek Tombs*, 311–420. *BSA* suppl. vol. 28. London: British School at Athens.

Coldstream, J. N., and P. M. Bikai. 1988. "Early Greek Pottery in Tyre and Cyprus: Some Preliminary Comparisons." *RDAC*, part 2: 35–44.

Coldstream, J. N., P. Callaghan, and J. H. Musgrave. 1981. "Knossos: An Early Greek Tomb on Lower Gypsadhes Hill." *BSA* 76: 141–65.

Coldstream, J. N., and G. L. Huxley, eds. 1973. *Kythera: Excavations and Studies Conducted by the University of Pennsylvania Museum and the British School at Athens*. Park Ridge, N.J.: Noyes.

Coldstream, J. N., and C. F. Macdonald. 1997. "Knossos: Area of South-West Houses, Early Hellenic Occupation." *BSA* 92: 191–245.

Coldstream, J. N., and L. H. Sackett. 1978. "Knossos: Two Deposits of Orientalizing Pottery." *BSA* 73: 45–60.

Collon, D. 1977. "Ivory." *Iraq* 39: 219–22.

Cook, J. 1934–35. "Protoattic Pottery." *BSA* 35: 165–219.

—. 1951. "A Geometric Amphora and Gold Band." *BSA* 46: 45–49.

Cook, R. M. 1937. "Amasis and the Greeks in Egypt." *JHS* 57: 227–37.

—. 1959. "Die Bedeutung der bemalten Keramik für den griechischen Handel." *JdI* 74: 114–23.

—. 1969. "A Note on the Absolute Chronology of the Eighth and Seventh Centuries B.C." *BSA* 64: 13–15.

—. 1972. *Greek Painted Pottery*. 2d ed. London: Methuen.

—. 1979. "Archaic Greek Trade: Three Conjectures." *JHS* 99: 152–55.

Cook, V. 1988. "Cyprus and the Outside World during the Transition from the Bronze Age to the Iron Age." *OpAth* 17: 13–32.

Coulson, W.D.E. 1983a. "The Architecture, Area IV." In W. A. McDonald, W.D.E. Coulson, and J. Rosser, eds., *Excavations at Nichoria in Southwest Greece*, vol. 3, *Dark Age and Byzantine Occupation*, 18–56. Minneapolis: University of Minnesota Press.

—. 1983b. "The Pottery." In W. A. McDonald, W.D.E. Coulson, and J. Rosser, eds., *Excavations at Nichoria in Southwest Greece*, vol. 3, *Dark Age and Byzantine Occupation*, 61–259. Minneapolis: University of Minnesota Press.

—. 1985. "The Dark Age Pottery of Sparta." *BSA* 80: 29–84.

—. 1986. *The Dark Age Pottery of Messenia*. SIMA-PB 43. Göteborg: Paul Åströms Förlag.

Courbin, P. 1966. *La céramique géométrique de l'Argolide*. Paris: E. de Boccard.

—. 1977. "Une pyxis géométrique argienne (?) au Liban." *Berytus* 25: 147–57.

—. 1993. "Fragments d'amphores protogéométriques grecques à Bassit (Syrie)." *Hesperia* 62: 95–113.

Courtois, J.-C. 1971. "Le sanctuaire du dieu au l'ingot d'Enkomi-Alasia." In C. F.-A. Schaeffer, ed., *Mission archéologique d'Alasia. Alasia I: 20ᵉ campagne de fouilles à Enkomi-Alasia, 1969*, 151–362. Paris: Klincksieck.

—. 1973. "Sur divers groupes de vases myceniens en Mediterranee orientale (1250–1150 av. J-C.)." In *Acts of the International Archaeological Symposium "The Mycenaeans in the Eastern Mediterranean,"* 137–64. Nicosia: Department of Antiquities, Cyprus.

Cribb, R.L.D. 1987. "The Logic of the Herd: A Computer Simulation of Archaeological Herd Structure." *JAnthArch* 6: 376–415.

Cross, F. M. 1980. "Newly Found Inscriptions in Old Canaanite and Early Phoenician Scripts." *BASOR* 238: 1–20.

—. 1986. "Phoenicians in the West: The Early Epigraphic Evidence." In M. S. Balmuth, ed., *Studies in Sardinian Archaeology*, vol. 2, *Sardinia in the Mediterranean*, 117–30. Ann Arbor: University of Michigan Press.

Crouwell, J. H. 1981. *Chariots and Other Means of Land Transport in Bronze Age Greece*. Amsterdam: Allard Pierson Museum.

—. 1992. *Chariots and Other Wheeled Vehicles in Iron Age Greece*. Amsterdam: Allard Pierson Museum.

Crowfoot, J. W., and G. M. Crowfoot. 1938. *Early Ivories from Samaria*. Samaria-Sebaste, Reports of the Joint Expedition in 1931–1933 and of the British Expedition in 1935, no. 2. London: Palestine Exploration Fund.

Crowley, J. L. 1989. *The Aegean and the East: An Investigation into the Transference of Artistic Motifs between the Aegean, Egypt, and the Near East in the Bronze Age*. SIMA-PB 51. Jonsered: Paul Åströms Förlag.

Csapo, E. 1991. "An International Community of Traders in Late 8ᵗʰ–7ᵗʰ C. B.C. Kommos in Southern Crete." *ZPE* 88: 211–16.

—. 1993. "A Postscript to 'An International Community of Traders in Late 8ᵗʰ–7ᵗʰ C. B.C. Kommos.'" *ZPE* 96: 235–36.

Culican, W. 1970. "Almuñécar, Assur and Phoenician Penetration of the Western Mediterranean." *Levant* 2: 28–36.

Davaras, C. 1967. "Εἰς νεώσοικος παρὰ τὴν Σητείαν." *ArchEph*: 84–90.

—. 1968a. "Two Geometric Tombs at Atsalenio near Knossos." *BSA* 63: 133–46.

—. 1968b. *Guide to Cretan Antiquities*. Park Ridge, N.J.: Noyes.

—. 1972. *Die Statue aus Astritsi: Ein Beitrag zur dädalischen Kunst auf Kreta und zu den Anfängen der griechischen Plastik*. AntP Beiheft 8. Bern: Francke.

—. N.d. *Knossos and the Herakleion Museum*. Athens: Editions Hannibal.

Davies, J. K. 1984. "Cultural, Social and Economic Features of the Hellenistic World." *CAH* 7, pt. 1, 2d ed.: 257–320.

Davies, N. de G., and R. O. Faulkner. 1947. "A Syrian Trading Venture to Egypt." *JEA* 33: 40–46.

Davis, J. L., and H. B. Lewis. 1985. "Mechanization of Pottery Production: A Case Study from the Cycladic Islands." In A. B. Knapp and T. Stech, eds., *Prehistoric Production and Exchange: The Aegean and Eastern Mediterranean*, Institute of Archaeology Monograph 25, 79–92. Los Angeles: Institute of Archaeology, University of California.

Davis, L. E., R. A. Easterlin, W. N. Parker, D. S. Brady, A. Fishlow, R. E. Gallman, S. Lebergott, R. E. Lipsey, D. C. North, N. Rosenberg, E. Smolensky, and P. Temin. 1972. *American Economic Growth: An Economist's History of the United States*. New York: Harper and Row.

Davis, R. 1962. *The Rise of the English Shipping Industry in the Seventeenth and Eighteenth Centuries*. London: Macmillan.

Dawkins, R. M., ed. 1929. *The Sanctuary of Artemis Orthia at Sparta*. London: Macmillan.

Deger-Jalkotzy, S. 1991. "Diskontinuität und Kontinuität: Aspekte politischer und sozialer Organisation in mykenischer Zeit und in der Welt der Homerischen Epen." In D. Musti, A. Sacconi, L. Rochetti, M. Rocchi, E. Scafa, L. Sportello, and M. W. Giannotta, eds., *La transizione del miceneo all'alto arcaismo dal palazzo alla città: Atti del Convegno Internazionale Roma, 14–19 marzo 1988*, 53–66. Rome: Consiglio Nazionale delle Ricerche.

—. 1991a. "Mykenische Herrschaftsformen ohne Paläste und die griechischen Polis." In R. Laffineur and W.-D. Niemeier, eds., *Politeia: Society and State in the Aegean Bronze Age. Proceedings of the Fifth International Aegean Conference, University of Heidelberg, Archäologische Institut, 10–13 April 1994*, 2: 367–77. Liège: Université de Liège.

—. 1991b. "Die Erforschung des Zusammenbruchs der sogenannten mykenischen Kultur und der sogenannten dunklen Jahrhunderte." In J. Latacz, ed., *Zweihundert Jahre Homer-Forschung; Rückblick und Ausblick*, 126–54. Stuttgart and Leipzig: B. G. Teubner.

—. 1991c. "Zum Verlauf der Periode SH IIIC in Achaia." In A. D. Rizakis, ed., *Achaia und Elis in der Antike. Akten des 1. Internationalen Symposiums, Athen, 19.–21. Mai 1989*, 19–29. Μελετήματα 13. Paris: Boccard.

—. 1995. "Mykenische Herrschaftsformen ohne Paläste und die griechische Polis." In R. Laffineur and W.-D. Niemeier, eds., *Politeia: Society and State in the Aegean Bronze Age, Proceedings of the 5th International Aegean Conference, University of Heidelberg, Archäologisches Institut 10-13 April 1994*, 2: 367-77. Liège: Université de Liège.

DeGraeve, M.-C. 1981. *The Ships of the Ancient Near East (c. 2000–500 B.C.)*. Orientalia Lovaniensia Analecta 7. Leuven: Departement Oriëntalistiek.

Dehl, C. 1984. *Die korinthische Keramik des 8. und frühen 7. Jhs. v. Chr. in Italien: Untersuchungen zu ihrer Chronologie und Ausbreitung*. AM-BH 11. Berlin: Gebr. Mann.

Dell, H. J. 1967. "The Origin and Nature of Illyrian Piracy." *Historia* 16: 344–58.

Demangel, R. 1949. "Bibliographie: Itanos." *Syria* 26: 394–95.

Demargne, P. 1929. "Terres-cuites archaïques de Lato." *BCH* 53: 382–429.

—. 1931. "Recherches sur le site de l'Anavlochos." *BCH* 55: 365–412.

—. 1947. *La Crète dédalique: Études sur les origines d'une renaissanee*. Paris: E. de Boccard.

Demargne, P., and H. van Effenterre. 1937. "Recherches a Dreros." *BCH* 61: 5–32.

Demetriou, A. 1989. *Cypro-Aegean Relations in the Early Iron Age*. SIMA 83. Göteborg: Paul Åströms Förlag.

Deonna, W. 1938. "Notes d'archéologie délienne." *BCH* 62: 209–35.

Derrida, J. 1992. *Given Time*. Vol. 1, *Counterfeit Money*. Chicago: University of Chicago Press.

Desborough, V. R. d'A. 1952. *Protogeometric Pottery*. Oxford: Clarendon.

—. 1954. "Mycenae 1939–1953: Part V: Four Tombs." *BSA* 49: 258–66.

—. 1955. "Mycenae 1939–1954: Part VI: Three Geometric Tombs." *BSA* 50: 239–47.

—. 1957. "A Group of Vases from Amathus." *JHS* 77: 212–19.

—. 1964. *The Last Mycenaeans and Their Successors*. Oxford: Clarendon.

—. 1972a. "Bird Vases." *CretChron* 24: 245–77.

—. 1972b. *The Greek Dark Ages*. London: Ernest Benn.

—. 1973. "Mycenaeans in Cyprus in the 11th Century B.C." In *Acts of the International Archaeological Symposium "The Mycenaeans in the Eastern Mediterranean,"* 79–87. Nicosia: Department of Antiquities, Cyprus.

—. 1979. "A Postscript to an Appendix." In *Studies Presented in Memory of Porphyrios Dikaios*, 119–22. Nicosia: Lions Club of Nicosia (Cosmopolitan).

—. 1980. "The Dark Age Pottery (SM–SPG III) from the Settlement and the Cemeteries." In M. R. Popham, L. H. Sackett, and P. G. Themelis, eds., *Lefkandi* I, BSA suppl. 11, 281–354. London: Thames and Hudson.

Desborough, V. R. d'A., R. V. Nicholls, and M. Popham. 1970. "A Euboean Centaur." *BSA* 65: 21–30.

De Sélincourt, A., trans. 1972. Herodotus, *The Histories*. Harmondsworth: Penguin.

Deshayes, J. 1951. "Tessons géométrique et archaïques d'Itanos." *BCH* 75: 201–9.

de Souza, P. 1995. "Greek Piracy." In A. Powell, ed., *The Greek World*. London: Routledge.

Dickinson, O.T.P.K. 1986. "Homer, the Poet of the Dark Age." *GaR* 33: 20–37.

—. 1994. *The Aegean Bronze Age*. Cambridge: Cambridge University Press.

Diener, L. 1968. "Beobachtungen bei der Röntgenuntersuchung einiger ägyptischer Mumien." *Orientalia Suecana* 17: 3–10.

Dietler, M. 1989. "Greeks, Etruscans, and Thirsty Barbarians: Early Iron Age Interactions in the Rhône Basin of France." In T. C. Champion, ed., *Centre and Periphery: Comparative Studies in Archaeology*, 127–41. London: Unwin Hyman.

Dikaios, P. 1969a. *Enkomi: Excavations, 1948–1958*. Vol. 1, *The Architectural Remains, The Tombs*. Mainz: Philip von Zabern.

—. 1969b. *Enkomi: Excavations, 1948–1958*. Vol. 3a, *Plates 1–239*. Mainz: Philip von Zabern.

—. 1971. *Enkomi: Excavations, 1948–1958*. Vol. 2, *Chronology, Summary and Conclusions, Catalogue, Appendices*. Mainz: Philip von Zabern.

DiVita, A. 1991. "Gortina in età geometrica." In D. Musti, A. Sacconi, L. Rochetti, M. Rocchi, E. Scafa, L. Sportello, and M. W. Giannotta, eds., *La transizione del miceneo all'alto arcaismo dal palazzo alla città: Atti del Convegno Internazionale Roma, 14–19 marzo 1988*, 309–19. Rome: Consiglio Nazionale delle Ricerche.

Dixit, A., and J. E. Stiglitz. 1977. "Monopolistic Competition and Optimum Product Diversity." *American Economic Review* 67: 297–308.

Dohan, E. H. 1931. "Archaic Cretan Terracottas in America." *MMS* 3: 209–28.

Donlan, W. 1989. "The Unequal Exchange between Glaucus and Diomedes in Light of the Homeric Gift-Economy." *Phoenix* 43: 1–15.

Dothan, T. 1979. "Minoan Elements and Influence at Athienou, Cyprus." In *Acts of the International Archaeological Symposium "The Relations between Cyprus and Crete, ca. 2000–500 B.C.,"* 173–77. Nicosia: Department of Antiquities, Cyprus.

Dothan, T., and A. Ben-Tor. 1983. *Excavations at Athienou, Cyprus, 1971–1972*. Qedem 16. Jerusalem: Israel Exploration Society.

Dothan, T., and M. Dothan. 1992. *People of the Sea: The Search for the Philistines*. New York: Macmillan.

Douglas, M. 1990. "Foreword: No Free Gifts." In M. Mauss, *The Gift*, vii–xviii. Translated by W. D. Halls. London: Routledge.

Dragendorff, H., ed. 1903. *Thera*. Vol. 2, *Theraischer Gräber*. Berlin: Georg Reimer.

Drerup, H. 1951. "Zweizelliges Heiligtum in Aptera." In F. Matz, ed., *Forschungen auf Kreta 1942*, 99–105. Berlin: Walter de Gruyter.

Droop, J. P. 1905–6. "Some Geometric Pottery from Crete." *BSA* 12: 24–62.

—. 1925. "The Pottery from Arcadia, Crete." *AnnLiv* 12: 11–14.

—. 1926–27. "Excavations at Sparta: The Native Pottery from the Acropolis." *BSA* 28: 49–81.

—. 1931–32. "Facts or Fancies." *BSA* 32: 247–50.

Duff, J. D., trans. 1928. Lucan, *The Civil War (Pharsalia)*. Loeb Classical Library. London: William Heineman.

Dugas, C. 1928. *Exploration archéologique de Delos*. Vol. 10, *Les vases de l'Heraion*. Paris: Edouard de Boccard.

—. 1935. *Exploration archéologique de Delos*. Vol. 17, *Les vases orientalisants de style non mélien*. Paris: Edouard de Boccard.

Dugas, C., and C. Rhomaios. 1934. *Exploration archéologique de Delos*. Vol. 15, *Les vases préhélleniques et géométriques*. Paris: Edouard de Boccard.

Dunbabin, T. J. 1944. "Archaeology in Greece, 1939–45." *JHS* 64: 78–97.

—. 1947. "Antiquities of Amari." *BSA* 42: 184–93.

—. 1948. *The Western Greeks*. Oxford: Clarendon.

—. 1949. Review of *Der geometrische Stil in Italien: Archäologische Grundlagen der frühesten historischen Zeit italiens*, by Å. Åkerström. *JRS* 39: 137–41.

—. 1957. *The Greeks and Their Eastern Neighbors*. Edited by J. Boardman. London: Society for the Promotion of Hellenic Studies.

—. 1962. *Perachora: The Sanctuaries of Hera Akraia and Limenia: Excavations of the British School of Archaeology at Athens 1930–1933*. Vol. 2, *Pottery, Ivories, Scarabs, and Other Objects from the Votive Deposit of Hera Limenia*. Oxford: Clarendon.

Dunbabin, T. J., and M. Robertson. 1953. "Some Protocorinthian Vase Painters." *BSA* 48: 172–81.

Earle, T. K. 1980. "A Model of Subsistence Change." In T. K. Earle and A. L. Christenson, eds., *Modeling Change in Prehistoric Subsistence Economies*, 1–29. New York: Academic Press.

—. 1985. "Prehistoric Economics and the Evolution of Social Complexity: A Commentary." In A. B. Knapp and T. Stech, eds., *Prehistoric Production and Exchange: The Aegean and Eastern Mediterranean*, Institute of Archaeology Monograph 25, 106–11. Los Angeles: University of California at Los Angeles.

École Française d'Athene. 1957. "Chroniques de fouilles et découvertes archéologiques en Grèce en 1956." *BCH* 81: 496–713.

Effenterre, H. van 1948. *Nécropoles du Mírabello. EtCret* 8. Paris: Librairie Orientale Paul Geuthner.

Eilmann, R. 1933. "Frühe griechische Keramik im samischen Heraion." *AM* 58: 47–145.

Elat, M. 1978. "The Economic Relations of the Neo-Assyrian Empire with Egypt." *JAOS* 98: 20–34.

Elayi, J. 1983. "Les cités phéniciennes et l'empire assyrien a l'époque d'Assurbanipal." *RAssyr* 77: 45–58.

—. 1988. "L'exploitation des cèdres du Mont Liban par les rois assyriens et néo-babyloniens." *JESHO* 31: 14–41.

Empereur, J.-Y. 1995. "Rapport sur les travaux menés en collaboration avec l'École française en 1994: Alexandrie (Égypte)." *BCH* 119: 743–60.

—. 1996. "The Discovery of the Pharos of Alexandria." *Minerva* 7: 5–6.

Errington, R. M. 1989. "Rome against Philip and Antiochus." *CAH* 8, 2d ed.: 244–89.

Evans, A. J. 1897. "Further Discoveries of Cretan and Aegean Script: With Libyan and Proto-Egyptian Comparisons." *JHS* 17: 327–95.

—. 1901. "Mycenaean Tree and Pillar Cult and Its Mediterranean Relations." *JHS* 21: 99–204.

—. 1921. *The Palace of Minos*. Vol. 1. London: Macmillan.

—. 1927. *The Palace of Minos*. Vol. 2, 1. London: Macmillan.

Evelyn-White, H. G., trans. 1914. Hesiod, *Works and Days*. Cambridge, Mass.: Harvard University Press, Loeb Classical Library.

Fagerström, K. 1988. *Greek Iron Age Architecture*. SIMA 81. Göteborg: Paul Åströms Förlag.

Fales, F. M. 1984. "The Neo-Assyrian Period." In A. Archi, ed., *Circulation of Goods in Non-Palatial Context in the Ancient Near East*, 207–20. Rome: Edizioni dell'Ateneo.

Falsone, G. 1987. "La coupe phénicienne de Fortetsa en Crete: Une reconsideration." In E. Lipiński, ed., *Phoenicia and the East Mediterranean in the First Millennium B.C.*, Orientalia Lovaniensia Analecta 22, Studia Phoenicia 5, 181–94. Leuven: Peeters.

—. 1988. "Phoenicia as a Bronzeworking Centre in the Iron Age." In J. Curtis, ed., *Bronzeworking Centres of Western Asia, c. 1000–539 B.C.*, 227–50. London: Kegan Paul.

Faulkner, R. O. 1975 "Egypt: From the Inception of the Nineteenth Dynasty to the Death of Ramesses III." *CAH* II, pt. 2, 3d ed.: 217–51.

Faure, P. 1964. *Fonctions des cavernes crétoises*. École Française d'Athène, Travaux et Mémoires 14. Paris: E. de Boccard.

—. 1966. "Les minerais de la Crète antique." *RA* 45–78.

—. 1987. *Parfums et aromates de l'antiquité*. Paris: Fayard.

Ferrarese Ceruti, M. L. 1991. "Creta e Sardegna in età postmicenea: Una nota." In D. Musti et al., eds., *La transizione dal miceneo all'alto arcaismo: Al palazzo alla città: Atti del convegno internazionale, Roma 14–19 marzo, 1988*, 587–91. Rome: Istituto per gli studi micenei ed egeo-anatolici, Monografie scientifiche, Serie Scienze umane e sociali.

Filippakis, S., E. Photou, C. Rolley, and G. Varoufakis. 1983. "Bronzes grecs et orientaux: Influences et apprentissages." *BCH* 107: 111–32.

Finley, M. I. 1959. "Was Greek Civilization Based on Slave Labor?" *Historia* 8: 145–64.

—. 1979. *The World of Odysseus*. 2d rev. ed. London: Penguin.

Fiorentini, G., and E. DeMiro. 1983. "Gela proto-arcaica." *ASAtene*, n.s. 61: 53–106.

Firth, R. 1965. *Primitive Polynesian Economy*. 2d ed. New York: Norton.

Fisher, E. 1985. "The Trade Pattern of the Mycenaeans in Southern Italy." *AJA* 89: 330.

Fitzhardinge, L. F. 1980. *The Spartans*. London: Thames and Hudson.

Forbes, H. 1989. "Of Grandfathers and Grand Theories: The Hierarchized Ordering of Responses to Hazard in a Greek Rural Community." In P. Halstead and J. O'Shea, eds., *Bad Year Economics: Cultural Responses to Risk and Uncertainty*, 87–97. Cambridge: Cambridge University Press.

Forster, E. S. 1901–2. "Praesos: The Terra-Cottas." *BSA* 8: 271–81.

—, trans. 1929. Lucius Annaeus Florus, *Epitome of Roman History*. Loeb Classical Library. London: William Heinemann.

Fossing, P. 1940. *Glass Vessels before Glass-Blowing*. Copenhagen: Ejnar Munksgaard.

Foster, B. R. 1977. "Commercial Activity in Sargonic Mesopotamia." *Iraq* 39: 31–43.

—. 1981. "A New Look at the Sumerian Temple State." *JESHO* 24: 225–41.

—. 1987. "The Late Bronze Age Palace Economy: A View from the East." In R. Hägg and N. Marinatos, *The Function of the Minoan Palaces*, Acta Instituti Atheniensis Regni Sueciae, Series in 4°, 35, 11–16. Stockholm: Paul Åströms Förlag.

Foxhall, L. 1995. "Bronze to Iron: Agricultural Systems and Political Structures in Late Bronze Age and Early Iron Age Greece." *BSA* 90: 239–50.

Foxhall, L., and H. A. Forbes. 1982. "Σιτομετρεία: The Role of Grain as a Staple Food in Classical Antiquity." *Chiron* 12: 41–90.

Frankenstein, S. 1979. "The Phoenicians in the Far West: A Function of Neo-Assyrian Imperialism." In M. T. Larsen, ed., *Power and Propaganda: A Symposium on Ancient Empire*, 263–94. Copenhagen: Akademisk Forlag.

Frankfort, H. 1936–37. "Notes on the Cretan Griffin." *BSA* 37: 106–22.

French, A. 1964. *The Growth of the Athenian Economy*. New York: Barnes and Noble.

French, E. B. 1986. "Mycenaean Greece and the Mediterranean World in the LH III." In M. Marazzi, S. Tusa, and L. Vagnetti, eds., *Traffici micenei nel Mediterraneo: Problemi storici e documentazione archeologia*, Magna Graecia 3, 277–82. Taranto: Istituto per la Storica e l'Archeologia della Magna Grecia.

—. 1992. "Archaeology in Greece, 1991–92." *AR* 38: 3–70.

Frost, F. J., and E. Hadjidaki. 1990. "Excavations at the Harbor of Phalasarna in Crete: The 1988 Season." *Hesperia* 59: 513–27.

Frost, H. 1963. *Under the Mediterranean: Marine Antiquities*. Englewood Cliffs, N.J.: Prentice Hall.

—. 1964. "Rouad, ses récifs et mouillages. prospection sous-marine." *Les Annales archéologiques de Syrie* 14: 67–74.

—. 1966. "The Arwad Plans 1964: A Photogrammetric Survey of Marine Installations." *Les Annales archéologiques de Syrie* 16: 13–28.

—. 1969. "The Stone-Anchors of Ugarit." In C. Schaeffer, ed., *Ugaritica*, 6: 235–44. Paris: Librairie Orientaliste Paul Geuthner.

—. 1971. "Recent Observations on the Submerged Harbourworks at Tyre." *BMusBeyr* 24: 103–11.

—. 1973. "The Offshore Harbour at Sidon and Other Phoenician Sites in the Light of New Dating Evidence." *IJNA* 2: 75–94.

—. 1975. "The Pharos Site, Alexandria, Egypt." *IJNA* 4: 126–30.

—. 1982. "The Birth of the Stocked Anchor and the Maximum Size of Early Ships." *Mariner's Mirror* 68: 263–73.

—. 1995. "Harbours and Proto-Harbours; Early Levantine Engineering." In V. Karageorghis and D. Michaelides, eds., *Cyprus and the Sea*, 1–21. Nicosia: University of Cyprus.

Furtwängler, A. 1884. "Archaischer Goldschmuck." *AZ* 42: 99–114.

—. 1886. "Erwerbungen der königlichen Museen zu Berlin im Jahre 1885, II: Antiquarium." *JdI* 1: 132–57.

Furumark, A. 1944. "The Mycenaean III C Pottery and Its Relation to Cypriote Fabrics." *OpAth* 3: 194–265.

—. 1950. "The Settlement at Ialysos and Aegean History c. 1550-1400 B.C." *OpArch* 6: 150–271.

Fussell, G. E. 1967. "Farming Systems of the Classical Era." *Technology and Culture* 8: 16–44.

Gabrici, E. E. 1913. "Cumae." *MonAnt* 22: 8–572.

Galanaki, P. 1990. "Οἱ χάλινες τοῦ Ἰδαίου Ἄντρου." In *Πεπραγμένα τοῦ στ Διεθνοῦς Κρητολογικοῦ Συνεδρίου* (6th Cretological Congress), Τόμος: Τμῆμα Αρχαιολόγικο, 171–77. Chania.

Gale, N. H. 1980. "Some Aspects of Lead and Silver Mining in the Aegean." In *Thera and the Aegean World*, 2: 161–95. London: Thera Foundation.

Gale, N. H., and Z. A. Stos-Gale. 1989. "Bronze Age Archaeometallurgy of the Mediterranean: The Impact of Lead Isotope Studies." In R. O. Allen, ed., *Archaeological Chemistry*, 4: 159–98. Washington, D.C.: American Chemical Society.

Galili, E., U. Dahari, and J. Sharvit. 1993. "Underwater Surveys and Rescue Excavations along the Israeli Coast." *INJA* 22: 61–77.

Galili, E., and N. Shmueli. 1983. "News from Israel." *INJA* 12: 178.

Galili, E., N. Shmueli, and M. Artzy. 1986. "Bronze Age Ship's Cargo of Copper and Tin." *INJA* 15: 25–37.

Gallant, T. W. 1982. "Agricultural Systems, Land Tenure, and the Reforms of Solon." *BSA* 77: 111–24.

—. 1985. *A Fisherman's Tale*. Miscellanea Graeca 7. Ghent: Belgian Archaeological Mission in Greece and the Seminar for Greek Archaeology of the State University of Gent.

—. 1991. *Risk and Survival in Ancient Greece: Reconstructing the Rural Domestic Economy*. Stanford: Stanford University Press.

Garbini, G. 1993. "Sull'origine dei fenici." *PP* 48: 321–31.

Gardiner, A. 1961. *Egypt of the Pharaohs*. Oxford: Clarendon.

Garlan, Y. 1978. "Signification historique de la piraterie grecque." *DHA* 4: 1–16.

—. 1983. "Greek Amphorae and Trade." In P. Garnsey, K. Hopkins, and C. R. Whittaker, eds., *Trade in the Ancient Economy*, 27–35. Berkeley: University of California Press.

—. 1989. *Guerre et économie en grèce ancienne*. Paris: Éditions la découverte.

Garnsey, P. 1985. "Grain for Athens." In P. A. Cartledge and F. D. Harvey, eds., *Crux: Essays in Greek History Presented to G.E.M. de Ste. Croix on His 75th Birthday*, 62–75. London: Duckworth.

—. 1988. *Famine and Food Supply in the Graeco-Roman World: Responses to Risk and Crisis*. Cambridge: Cambridge University Press.

Garnsey, P., and I. Morris. 1989. "Risk and the *Polis*: The Evolution of Institutionalized Responses to Food Supply Problems in the Ancient Greek State." In P. Halstead and J. O'Shea, eds., *Bad Year Economics: Cultural Responses to Risk and Uncertainty*, 98–105. Cambridge: Cambridge University Press.

Garstang, J. 1953. *Prehistoric Mersin: Yümük Tepe in Southern Turkey*. Oxford: Clarendon.

Gates, C. 1989. "Iconography at the Crossroads: The Aegina Treasure." In R. Laffineur, ed., *Transition: Le monde égéen du Bronze moyen au Bronze*, 215–25. *Aegaeum* 3. Liège: Université de Liège.

Gates, M.-H. 1990. "Artisans and Art in Old Babylonia and Mari." In A. C. Gunter, ed., *Investigating Artistic Environments in the Ancient Near East*, 29–37. Washington, D.C.: Smithsonian Institution.

—. 1995. "Archaeology in Turkey." *AJA* 99: 207–55.

Georgiou, H. S. 1991. "Bronze Age Ships and Rigging." In R. Laffineur and L. Basch, eds.,

Thalassa, l'Égée préhistorique et la mer, Aegaeum 7, 61–71. Liège: Université de Liège.

Gesell, G. C., L. P. Day, and W.D.E. Coulson. 1983. "Excavations and Survey at Kavousi, 1978–1981." *Hesperia* 52: 389–420.

—. 1995. "Excavations at Kavousi, Crete, 1989 and 1990." *Hesperia* 64: 67–120.

Gilboa, A. 1989. "New Finds at Tel Dor and the Beginning of Cypro-Geometric Pottery Import to Palestine." *IEJ* 39: 204–18.

Gill, D.W.J. 1988a. "Silver Anchors and Cargoes of Oil: Some Observations on Phoenician Trade in the Western Mediterranean." *BSR* 56: 1–12.

—. 1988b. "'Trade in Greek Decorated Pottery': Some Corrections." *OJA* 7: 369–70.

—. 1992. "The Ivory Trade." In J. L. Fitton, ed., *Ivory in Greece and the Eastern Mediterranean from the Bronze Age to the Hellenistic Period*, British Museum Occasional Paper 85, 233–36. London: Trustees of the British Museum.

Gillis, C. 1995. "Trade in the Late Bronze Age." In C. Gillis, C. Risberg, and B. Sjöberg, eds., *Trade and Production in Premonetary Greece: Aspects of Trade. Proceedings of the Third International Workshop, Athens 1993*, 61–86. SIMAL PB-134. Jonsered: Paul Åströms Förlag.

—. 1996. "The Asine Chamber Tombs–Graves of Kings?" In E. deMiro, L. Godart, and A. Sacconi, eds., *Atti e memorie del secondo congresso internazionale di micenologia*, 3: 1193–1203. *Archeologia*. Incunabula Graeca 98.3. Rome: Gruppo Editoriale Internazionale.

Gilmour, G. 1992. "Mycenaean IIIA and IIIB Pottery in the Levant and Cyprus." *RDAC* 113–28.

Gittlin, B. M. 1981. "The Cultural and Chronological Implications of the Cypro-Palestinian Trade during the Late Bronze Age." *BASOR* 241: 49–59.

Gjerstad, E. 1948. *The Swedish Cyprus Expedition*. Vol. 4, 2, *The Cypro-Geometric, Cypro-Archaic and Cypro-Classical Periods*. Stockholm: Swedish Cyprus Expedition.

—. 1961. Review of *Vom Anfang Roms: Studien zu den prähistorischen Forums- und Palatingräbern*, by H. Müller-Karpe. *Gnomon* 33: 378–82.

—. 1977. *Greek Geometric and Archaic Pottery Found in Cyprus*. Acta Instituti Atheniensis Regni Sueciae, Series in 4°, 26. Stockholm: Paul Åströms.

—. 1979. "A Cypro-Greek Royal Marriage in the 8th Century B.C.?" In *Studies Presented in*

Memory of Porphyrios Dikaios, 89–93. Nicosia: Lions Club of Nicosia (Cosmopolitan).

Gledhill, J., and M. Larsen. 1982. "The Polanyi Paradigm and a Dynamic Analysis of Archaic States." In C. Renfrew, M. J. Rowlands, and B. A. Seagraves, eds., *Theory and Explanation in Archaeology*, 197–229. New York: Academic Press.

Glotz, G. 1926. *Ancient Greece at Work*. Translated by M. R. Dobie. New York: Knopf.

Godard, A. 1931. *Les Bronzes du Luristan*. Ars Asiatica 17. Paris: G. van Oest.

Gödecken, K. B. 1988. "A Contribution to the Early History of Miletus: The Settlement in Mycenaean Times and Its Connections Overseas." In E. B. French and K. A. Wardle, eds., *Problems in Greek Prehistory*, 307–18. Bristol: Bristol Classical Press.

Goedicke, H. 1975. *The Report of Wenamun*. Baltimore: The Johns Hopkins University Press.

Goelet, O., Jr. 1996. "A New `Robbery' Papyrus: Rochester MAG 51.346.1." *JEA* 82: 107–27.

Goldman, B. 1960. "The Development of the Lion-Griffin." *AJA* 64: 319–28.

Goldman, H. 1956. *Tarsus*. Vol. 2. Princeton: Princeton University Press.

Goldsmith, R. W. 1987. *Premodern Financial Systems*. Cambridge: Cambridge University Press.

Gondicas, D. 1988. *Recherches sur la Crete occidentale: De l'époque géométrique à la conquête romaine: Inventaire des sources archéologiques et textuelles, position du problème*. Amsterdam: Adolf M. Hakkert.

Gonen, R. 1984. "Urban Canaan in the Late Bronze Period." *BASOR* 253: 61–73.

—. 1992. "The Late Bronze Age." In A. Ben-Tor, ed., *The Archaeology of Ancient Israel*, 211–57. New Haven: Yale University Press.

Gordon, A. H. 1983. "The Context and Meaning of the Ancient Egyptian Word *inw* from the Proto-Dynastic Period to the End of the New Kingdom." Ph.D. dissertation, University of California, Berkeley.

Grace, V. R. 1979. *Amphoras and the Ancient Wine Trade*. Princeton: American School of Classical Studies at Athens.

Graham, A. J. 1986. "The Historical Interpretation of Al Mina." *DHA* 12: 51–65.

Gray, D. 1974. *Seewesen*. ArchHom Bd. I, Kap. G. Göttingen: Vandenhoek and Ruprecht.

Greif, A. 1994. "Cultural Beliefs and the Organization of Society: A Historical and Theoretical Reflection on Collectivist and Individualist Societies." *Journal of Political Economy* 102: 912–50.

Greig, J.R.A., and J. Turner. 1974. "Some Pollen Diagrams from Greece and Their Archaeological Significance." *JAS* 1: 177–94.

Guest-Papamanoli, A., and R. Treuil. 1979. "Rapports sur les travaux de l'École Français en Grèce en 1978: Malia: II. Bâtiment immergé." *BCH* 103: 668–69.

Gunneweg, J., I. Perlman, and F. Asaro. 1987. "A Canaanite Jar from Enkomi." *IEJ* 37: 168–72.

Gurney, O. R. 1990. *The Hittites*. 2d rev. ed. London: Penguin.

Güterbock, H. G. 1967. "The Hittite Conquest of Cyprus Reconsidered." *JNES* 26: 73–81.

Gwynn, A. 1918. "The Character of Greek Colonization." *JHS* 38: 88–123.

Habicht, C. 1989. "The Seleucids and Their Rivals." *CAH*, vol. 8, 2d ed.: 324–87.

Hadjidaki, E. 1988. "Preliminary Report of Excavations at the Harbor of Phalasarna in West Crete." *AJA* 92: 463–79.

—. 1996. "Excavation of a Classical Shipwreck at Alonnesos." *Enalia Annual 1994* 4: 37-45.

Hadjisavvas, S. 1992. *Oil Processing in Cyprus: From the Bronze Age to the Byzantine Period*. SIMA 99. Nicosia: Paul Åströms Förlag.

Hägg, R. 1990. "The Cretan Hut-Models." *OpAth* 18: 95–107.

Hägg, R., and N. Marinatos. 1991. "The Giamalakis Model from Archanes: Between the Minoan and the Greek Worlds." In D. Musti et al., eds., *La transizione dal miceneo all'alto arcaismo: Al palazzo alla città: Atti del convegno internazionale, Roma 14–19 marzo, 1988*, 301–8. Rome: Istituto per gli studi micenei ed egeoanatolici, Monografie scientifiche, Serie Scienze umane e sociali.

Haggis, D. C., and K. Nowicki. 1993. "Khalasmeno and Katalimata: Two Early Iron Age Settlements in Monastiraki, East Crete." *Hesperia* 62: 303–37.

Halbherr, F. 1888. "Scavi e trovamento nell'Antro di Zeus sul Monte Ida in Creta." *Museo italiano di antichità classica* 2: 689–766.

Haldane, C. W. 1990. "Shipwrecked Plant Remains." *Biblical Archaeologist* 53: 55–60.

—. 1993. "Direct Evidence for Organic Cargoes in the Late Bronze Age." *WorldArch* 24: 348–60.

Hall, E. H. 1904. *Transactions of the Department of Archaeology of the University of Pennsylvania*. Vol. 1, pts. 1 and 2. Philadelphia.

—. 1914. *Excavations in Eastern Crete: Vrokastro*. University of Pennsylvania, The Museum Anthropological Publications 3. Philadelphia: University Museum.

Hallager, B. P., and P.J.P. McGeorge. 1992. *Late Minoan III Burials at Khania: The Tombs, Finds and Deceased in Odos Palama*. SIMA 93. Göteborg: Paul Åströms Förlag.

Hallager, E., and Y. Tzedakis. 1984. "The Greek-Swedish Excavations at Kastelli, Khania, 1982–1983." *AAA* 17: 3–20.

—. 1985. "The Greek-Swedish Excavations at Kastelli, Khania, 1984." *AAA* 18: 9–28.

—. 1986. "The Greek-Swedish Excavations at Kastelli, Khania, 1985." *AAA* 19: 11–26.

—. 1988. "The Greek-Swedish Excavations at Kastelli, Khania, I: The 1989 Excavations; II: The 1987 Excavations." *AAA* 21: 15–55.

Hallo, W. W. 1990. "The Limits of Skepticism." *JAOS* 110: 187–99.

—. 1992. "From Bronze Age to Iron Age in Western Asia: Defining the Problem." In W. A. Ward and M. S. Joukowsky, eds., *The Crisis Years: The 12th Century B.C.: From beyond the Danube to the Tigris*, 1–9. Dubuque, Iowa: Kendall/Hunt.

Halstead, P. 1987. "Man and Other Animals in Later Greek Prehistory." *BSA* 82: 70–83.

—. 1990. "Waste Not, Want Not: Traditional Responses to Crop Failure in Greece." *Rural History* 1: 147–64.

Halstead, P., and G. Jones. 1989. "Agrarian Ecology in the Greek Islands: Time Stress, Scale and Risk." *JHS* 109: 41–55.

Hamilton, R. W. 1934. "Excavations at Tell Abu Hawām." *QDAP* 4: 1–69.

Hanfmann, G.M.A. 1963. "The Iron Age Pottery of Tarsus." In H. Goldman, ed., *Excavations at Gözlü Kulu, Tarsus*, vol. 3, *The Iron Age*, 18–332. Princeton: Princeton University Press.

Hankey, V. 1966. "Late Mycenaean Pottery at Beth-Shan." *AJA* 70: 169–71.

—. 1967. "Mycenaean Pottery in the Middle East: Notes on Finds since 1951." *BSA* 62: 107–47.

—. 1970. "Mycenaean Trade with the South-Eastern Mediterranean." *MélBeyrouth* 46: 11–30.

—. 1972. "Aegean Finds at Late Bronze Sites in the South-Eastern Mediterranean." *BICS* 19: 143–45.

—. 1973. "The Aegean Deposit at El Amarna." In *Acts of the International Archaeological Sympo-* sium "The Mycenaeans in the Eastern Mediterranean," 128–36. Nicosia: Department of Antiquities, Cyprus.

—. 1979. "Crete, Cyprus and the South-Eastern Mediterranean, 1400–1200 B.C." In *Acts of the International Archaeological Symposium "The Relations between Cyprus and Crete, ca. 2000–500 B.C.,"* 144–57. Nicosia: Department of Antiquities, Cyprus.

—. 1980. "The Aegean Interest in El Amarna." *Journal of Mediterranean Anthropology and Archaeology* 1: 38–49.

—. 1988. "Note on the Chronology of LH III C Late and Submycenaean." *JdI* 103: 33–37.

Harden, D. B. 1956. "Glass and Glazes." In C. Singer et al., eds., *A History of Technology*, vol. 2, *The Mediterranean Civilizations and the Middle Ages*, 311–46. Oxford: Oxford University Press.

Harding, A. F. 1984. *The Mycenaeans and Europe*. New York: Academic Press.

Harding, A. F., and H. Hughes-Brock. 1974. "Amber in the Mycenaean World." *BSA* 69: 145–73.

Hartley, M. 1930–31. "Early Greek Vases from Crete." *BSA* 31: 56–114.

—. 1931–32. "Facts." *BSA* 32: 251–54.

Hartog, C. den. 1970. *The Sea-Grasses of the World*. Verhandelingen der Koninklijke Nederlandse Akademia van Witenschappen, Afd. Naturkunde. Tweede Reeds, Deel 59, no. 1. Amsterdam: North-Holland.

Haskell, H. W. 1984. "Stirrup Jars and the International Oil Trade." In C. W. Shelmerdine and T. G. Palaima, eds., *Pylos Comes Alive*, 97–106. New York: Archaeological Institute of America.

—. 1989. "LM III Knossos: Evidence Beyond the Palace." *SMEA* 27: 81–110.

Hawkins, J. D. 1988. "Kuzi-Tesub and the 'Great Kings' of Karkamis." *AnatSt* 38: 99–108.

Hayden, B. J. 1991. "Terracotta Figures, Figurines, and Vase Attachments from Vrokastro, Crete." *Hesperia* 60: 103–44.

Hayden, B. J., J. A. Moody, and O. Rackham. 1992. "The Vrokastro Survey Project, 1986–1989: Research Design and Preliminary Results." *Hesperia* 61: 293–353.

Hazzidakis, J. 1934. *Les villas minoennes de Tylissos*. EtCret III. Translated by F. Chapouthier and R. Joly. Paris: Librairie Orientaliste Paul Guethner.

Heichelheim, F. M. 1957. *An Ancient Economic History, from the Palaeolithic Age to the Migra-*

tions of the Germanic, Slavic, and Arabic Nations. Vol. 1. Rev. ed. Translated by J. Stevens. Leyden: A.W. Sijthoff.

Helck, W. 1971. *Die Beziehungen Ägyptens zu Vorderasien im 3. Und 2. Jahrtausend v. Chr.* Ägyptologische Abhandlungen, Bd. 5. Wiesbaden: Otto Harrossowitz.

—. 1979. *Die Beziehungen Ägyptens und Vorderasiens zur Ägäis bis ins 7. Jahrhundert v. Chr.* Darmstadt: Wissenschaftliche Buchgesellschaft.

—. 1983. "Die Fahrt von Ägypten nach Kreta." *MDIK* 39: 81–94.

—. 1987. "The Dissolution of the Palace Economy in the Ramesside Period." In R. Hägg and N. Marinatos, eds., *The Function of the Minoan Palaces*, Acta Instituti Atheniensis Regni Sueciae, Series in 4°, 35, 17–19. Stockholm: Paul Åströms Förlag.

Hellbing, L. 1979. *Alasia Problems*. SIMA 57. Göteborg: Paul Åströms Förlag.

Helpman, E., and P. R. Krugman. 1985. *Market Structure and Foreign Trade*. Cambridge, Mass.: Massachusetts Institute of Technology Press.

Heltzer, M. 1976. *The Rural Community in Ugarit*. Wiesbaden: Reichert.

—. 1978. *Goods, Prices and the Organization of Trade in Ugarit*. Wiesbaden: Reichert.

—. 1982. *The Internal Organization of the Kingdom of Ugarit*. Wiesbaden: Reichert.

—. 1984. "Private Property in Ugarit." In A. Archi, ed., *Circulation of Goods in Non-Palatial Context in the Ancient Near East*, 161–93. Rome: Edizioni Dell'Ateneo.

—. 1988a. "Sinaranu, Son of Siginu, and the Trade Relations between Ugarit and Crete." *Minos* 23: 7–13.

—. 1988b. "The Late Bronze Age Service System and Its Decline." In M. Heltzer and E. Lipiński, eds., *Society and Economy in the Eastern Mediterranean (c. 1500–1000 B.C.)*, Orientalia Lovaniensia Analecta 23, 7–18. Leuven: Peeters.

Hencken, H. 1950a. "Hersprung Shields and Greek Trade." *AJA* 54: 295–309.

—. 1950b. "Shields of the Hersprung Type." *AJA* 54: 259.

—. 1968. *Tarquinia, Villanovans and Early Etruscans*. 2 vols. American School of Prehistoric Research Bulletin 23. Cambridge, Mass.: Peabody Museum, Harvard University.

—. 1971. *The Earliest European Helmets: Bronze Age and Early Iron Age*. Peabody Museum Bulletin 28. Cambridge, Mass.: American School of Prehistoric Research, Peabody Museum, Harvard University.

Herman, G. 1987. *Ritualized Friendship and the Greek City*. Cambridge: Cambridge University Press.

Hermary, A. 1987. "Amonthe de Chypre et les phéniciens." In E. Lipinski, ed., *Phoenicia and the East Mediterranean in the First Millennium B.C.*, Orientalia Lovaniensia Analecta 22, Studia Phoenicia 5, 375–88. Leuven: Peeters.

Herrmann, G. 1986. *Ivories from Room SW37 Fort Shalmaneser. Ivories from Nimrud (1949–1963)*. Fasc. 4, 1. London: British School of Archaeology in Iraq.

Herrmann, H.-V. 1966a. *Die Kessel der orientalisierenden Zeit*. OlForsch VI. Berlin: Walter de Gruyter.

—. 1966b. "Urartu und Griechenland." *JdI* 81: 79–141.

—. 1968. "Frühgriechischen Pferdeschmuck vom Luristantypen." *JdI* 83: 1–78.

Hesse, B. 1988. "Comment" [on H. J. Greenfield, "The Origins of Milk and Wool Production in the Old World"]. *CurrAnthr* 29: 590–91.

Heurtley, W. A. 1934. "II. "Note on Fragments of Two Thessalian Proto-Geometric Vases (Pl. LXXXVIII) Found at Tell Abu Hawam." *QDAP* 4: 181.

Higgins, R. A. 1959. *Catalogue of the Terracottas in the Department of Greek and Roman Antiquities, British Museum*. Vol. 2. London: Trustees of the British Museum.

—. 1969. "Early Greek Jewellery." *BSA* 64: 143–53.

Hill, D. K. 1976. "An Early Greek Faience Alabastron." *AJA* 80: 420–23.

Hind, J.G.F. 1994. "Mithridates." *CAH*, vol. 9, 2d ed.: 129–64.

Hirschman, A. O. 1977. *The Passions and the Interests: Political Arguments for Capitalism before Its Triumph*. Princeton: Princeton University Press.

Hodder, I. 1974. "Regression Analysis of Some Trade and Marketing Patterns." *WorldArch* 6: 172–89.

—. 1982. "Toward a Contextual Approach to Prehistoric Exchange." In J. E. Ericson and T. K. Earle, eds., *Contexts for Prehistoric Exchange*, 199–211. New York: Academic Press.

Hodge, H. G., trans. 1927. *Cicero, The Speeches.* Vol. 9, *Pro Lege Manilia, Pro Caecina, Pro Cluentia, Pro Rabirio, Perduellionis.* Loeb Classical Library. London: William Heineman.

Hoffman, G. L. 1990. "Immigrants, Imports, and Problems in the Study of Influence: Archaeological Evidence for Artistic Transmission from the Near East to Crete, ca. 1100–ca. 700 B.C.–with Special Reference to the Tekke Jewelry." Ph.D. diss., Department of Classical Art and Archaeology, University of Michigan.

Hoffman, P. E. 1980. *The Spanish Crown and the Defense of the Caribbean, 1535–1585: Precedent, Patrimonialism, and Royal Parsimony.* Baton Rouge: Louisiana State University Press.

Hoffmann, H. 1972. "Appendix II: The Corslets of the 'Olympia' Group." In H. Hoffmann, with A. E. Raubitschek, *Early Cretan Armorers*, 50–53. Mainz: Philipp von Zabern.

Hoffmann, H., with A. E. Raubitschek. 1972. *Early Cretan Armorers.* Fogg Art Museum Monographs in Art and Archaeology I. Mainz: Philipp von Zabern.

Hogarth, D. G. 1899–1900a. "Knossos: II: Early Town and Cemeteries." *BSA* 6: 70–85.

—. 1899–1900b. "The Dictaean Cave." *BSA* 6: 94–116.

—. 1900–1901. "Excavations at Zakro, Crete." *BSA* 7: 120–49.

Hölbl, G. 1979. *Beziehungen der ägyptischen Kultur zu Altitalien.* 2 vols. Leiden: E. J. Brill.

—. 1981. "Die Ausbreitung ägyptischen Kulturgutes in den ägäischen Raum vom 8. bis zum 6. Jh. v. Chr." *Orientalia*, n.s. 50: 186–92.

—. 1987. "Zur kulturellen Stellung der Aegyptiaca in der mykenischen und frühgriechischen Welt." In E. Thomas, ed., *Forschungen zur ägäischen Vorgeschichte Das Ende der mykenischen Welt*, 123–42. Berlin: Ernst Wasmuth.

—. 1989a. "Ägyptische Kunstelemente im phönikischen Kulturkreis des 1. Jahrtausends v. Chr.: Zur Methodik ihrer Verwendung." *Orientalia*, n.s. 58: 319–25.

—. 1989b. *Ägyptisches Kulturgut auf den Inseln Malta und Gozo in phönikischer und punischer Zeit.* Vienna: Österreichischen Akademie der Wissenschaften.

Holloway, R. R. 1981. *Italy and the Aegean, 3000–700 B.C.* Archaeologica Transatlantica 1. Louvain-la-Neuve: Institut Supérieur d'Archéologie et d'Histoire de l'Art, College Erasmus.

—. 1991. *The Archaeology of Ancient Sicily.* London: Routledge.

—. 1992. "Italy and the Central Mediterranean in the Crisis Years." In W. A. Ward and M. S. Joukowsky, eds., *The Crisis Years: The 12th Century B.C.: From beyond the Danube to the Tigris*, 40–45. Dubuque, Iowa: Kendall/Hunt.

Holmes, T. L. 1973. "Egypt and Cyprus: Late Bronze Age Trade and Diplomacy." In H. A. Hoffner, ed., *Orient and Occident*, 91–98. Neukirchen-Vluyn: Neukirchener.

—. 1975. "The Foreign Trade of Cyprus during the Late Bronze Age." In N. Robertson, ed., *The Archaeology of Cyprus: Recent Developments*, 90–110. Park Ridge, N.J.: Noyes.

Hood, M.S.F. 1956. "Archaeology in Greece, 1955–1956." *AR* 2: 3–23.

—. 1957. "Archaeology in Greece, 1956–1957." *AR* 3: 3–25.

—. 1958. "Archaeology in Greece, 1957–1958." *AR* 4: 3–25.

—. 1960. "Archaeology in Greece, 1959–1960." *AR* 6: 3–26.

—. 1961. "Archaeology in Greece, 1960–1961." *AR* 7: 3–35.

—. 1973. "Mycenaean Settlement in Cyprus and the Coming of the Greeks." In *Acts of the International Archaeological Symposium "The Mycenaeans in the Eastern Mediterranean,"* 40–50. Nicosia: Department of Antiquities, Cyprus.

Hood, M.S.F., and J. Boardman. 1955. "Archaeology in Greece, 1955." *AR* 1: 3–38.

—. 1961. "Early Iron Age Tombs at Knossos." *BSA* 56: 68–80.

Hood, M.S.F., and J. N. Coldstream. 1968. "A Late Minoan Tomb at Ayios Ioannis near Knossos." *BSA* 63: 205–18.

Hood, M.S.F., G. Huxley, and N. Sandars. 1958–59. "A Minoan Cemetery on Upper Gypsades." *BSA* 53–54: 194–262.

Hood, S., and D. Smyth. 1981. *Archaeological Survey of the Knossos Area.* 2d ed. BSA suppl. 14. London: Thames and Hudson.

Hooker, J. T. 1976. *Mycenaean Greece.* London: Routledge and Kegan Paul.

Hopper, R. J. 1949. "Addenda to *Necrocorinthia.*" *BSA* 44: 163–257.

Hue, M., and O. Pelon. 1991. "Malia et la Mer." In R. Laffineur and L. Basch, eds., *Thalassa, l'Égée préhistorique et la mer*, Aegaeum 7, 117–27. Liège: Université de Liège.

Hulin, L. 1989. "Marsa Matruh 1987, Preliminary Ceramic Report." *JARCE* 26: 115–26.

Hult, G. 1983. *Bronze Age Ashlar Masonry in the Eastern Mediterranean: Cyprus, Ugarit, and Neighboring Regions*. SIMA 64. Göteborg: Paul Åströms Förlag.

Humbert, J.-B. 1982. "Tell Keisan, 1979, 1980." *IEJ* 32: 61–64.

Humphreys, S. C. 1967. "Archaeology and the Economic and Social History of Classical Greece." *PP* 114: 374–400.

—. 1978. *Anthropology and the Greeks*. London: Routledge and Kegan Paul.

Hunt, R. C. 1987. "The Role of Bureaucracy in the Provisioning of Cities: A Framework for Analysis of the Ancient Near East." In M. Gibson and R. D. Biggs, eds., *The Organization of Power: Aspects of Bureaucracy in the Ancient Near East*, SAOC 46, 161–92. Chicago: Oriental Institute, University of Chicago.

Hutchinson, R. W. 1962. *Prehistoric Crete*. Baltimore: Penguin.

Hutchinson, R. W., and J. Boardman. 1954. "The Khaniale Tekke Tombs." *BSA* 49: 215–28.

Iacovou, M. 1988. *The Pictorial Pottery of Eleventh Century B.C. Cyprus*. SIMA 79. Göteborg: Paul Åströms Förlag.

Iakovides, S. 1980. *Excavations of the Necropolis at Perati*. Institute of Archaeology, Occasional Paper 8. Los Angeles: University of California at Los Angeles.

—. 1996. "Mycenae in the Light of Recent Discoveries." In E. deMiro, L. Godart, and A. Sacconi, eds., *Atti e memorie del secondo congresso internazionale di micenologia*, 3: 1039–49. *Archeologia*. Incunabula Graeca 98.3. Rome: Gruppo Editoriale Internazionale.

Isager, S., and J. E. Skydsgaard. 1992. *Ancient Greek Agriculture: An Introduction*. London: Routledge.

Jackson, A. H. 1973. "Privateers of the Ancient Greek World." In M.R.D. Foote, ed., *War and Society: Essays in Honour and Memory of J. R. Western, 1928–1971*, 241–53. London: Paul Elek.

—. 1985. Review of *Raub und Beute in der archaischen Zeit der Griechen*, by W. Nowag. *Gnomon* 57: 655–57.

Jacobsthal, P. 1956. *Greek Pins and Their Connexions with Europe and Asia*. Oxford: Clarendon.

Jacopi, G. 1929. *Scavi nella necropoli di Jalisso, 1924–1928*. ClRh 3. Bergamo: Istituto archeologico di Rodi.

—. 1932–33. *Esplorazione archeologia di Camiro-II*. ClRh 6–7. Bergamo: Istituto archeologico di Rodi.

James, P., with I. J. Thorpe, N. Kokkinos, R. Morkot, and J. Frankish. 1991. *Centuries of Darkness: A Challenge to the Conventional Chronology of Old World Archaeology*. London: Jonathan Cape.

James, T.G.H. 1979. *An Introduction to Ancient Egypt*. New York: Harper and Row.

Jameson, M. H., C. N. Runnels, and T. H. van Andel. 1994. *A Greek Countryside: The Southern Argolid from Prehistory to the Present Day*. Stanford: Stanford University Press.

Janssen, J. J. 1992. Review of *Ancient Egypt: Anatomy of a Civilization*, by B. J. Kemp. *JEA* 78: 313–17.

Jantzen, U. 1951. "Die spätminoische Nekropole von Kydonia." In F. Matz, ed., *Forschungen auf Kreta, 1942*, 72–81. Berlin: Walter de Gruyter.

—. 1964. "Protogeometrisches aus Westkreta." In E. Homan-Wedeking and B. Segall, eds., *Festschrift Eugen v. Mercklin*, 60–62. Waldsassen: Stiftland.

—. 1972. *Samos*. Vol. 8, *Die ägyptischen und orientalischen Bronzen aus dem Heraion von Samos*. Mainz: Philipp von Zabern.

Jarvis, L. S. 1974. "Cattle as Capital Goods and Ranchers as Portfolio Managers: An Application to the Argentine Cattle Sector." *Journal of Political Economy* 82: 489–520.

Jeffrey, L. H. 1961. *The Local Scripts of Archaic Greece*. Oxford: Clarendon.

—. 1976. *Archaic Greece*. London: Methuen.

Jenkins, R.J.H. 1932–33. "Laconian Terracottas of the Dadalic Style." *BSA* 33: 66–79.

—. 1936. *Dedalica: A Study of Dorian Plastic Art in the Seventh Century B.C.* Cambridge: Cambridge University Press.

—. 1940. "Terracottas." In H. Payne, *Perachora*, 1: 191–255. Oxford: Clarendon.

Johansen, K. F. 1923. *Les vases sicyoniens: Étude archéologique*. Paris: Edouard Champion.

—. 1958. *Exochi: Ein frührhodisches Gräberfeld*. Copenhagen: Ejnar Munksgaard.

Johnston, A. W. 1974. "Trademarks on Greek Vases." *GaR* 21: 138–52.

—. 1979. *Trademarks on Greek Vases*. Warminster: Aris and Phillips.

—. 1991. "The Vase Trade: A Point of View." In T. Fischer-Hansen et al., eds., *Recent Danish Research in Classical Archaeology: Tradition and*

Renewal, Acta Hyperborea 3, 403–9. Copenhagen: University of Copenhagen, Museum Tusculanum Press.

—. 1993. "Pottery from Archaic Building Q at Kommos." *Hesperia* 62: 339–82.

Johnston, A., and R. E. Jones. 1978. "The 'SOS' Amphora." *BSA* 73: 103–41.

Johnston, P. F. 1985. *Ship and Boat Models in Ancient Greece*. Annapolis, Md.: Naval Institute Press.

Jondet, G. 1912. "Les ports antiques de Pharos." *Bulletin de la Societé Archéologique d'Alexandrie* 14: 252–66.

—. 1916. *Les ports submergés de l'ancien île de Pharos*. Mémoires présentés à l'Institut Égyptien, Tome 9. Cairo: L'Institut Français d'Archéologie Orientale.

Jones, D. W. 1991. "An Introduction to the Thünen Location and Land Use Model." *Research in Marketing* 5: 35–70.

—. 1993. "Phoenician Unguent Factories in Dark Age Greece: Social Approaches to Evaluating the Archaeological Evidence." *OJA* 12: 293–303.

—. Forthcoming a. "The Archaeology and Economy of Homeric Gift Exchange." *OpAth* 23.

—. Forthcoming b. "The Conundrum of Greek Population Growth in the 8th Century B.C.: Burials, Settlements, and Wells." *OpAth* 23.

Jones, D. W., and C. Kaul. 1983. "Location and Agricultural Risk in India." In M. Chatterji et al., eds., *Spatial, Environmental and Resource Policy in the Developing Countries*, 373–84. Aldershot, Hampshire: Gower.

Jones, H. L., trans. 1928. *Strabo, Geography*. Vol. 5, *Books X–XII*. Loeb Classical Library. London: William Heinemann.

Jones, R. E. 1985. "Greek Potters' Clays: Questions of Selection, Availability and Adaptation." In H.A.G. Brijder, ed., *Ancient Greek and Related Pottery*, Allard-Pierson Series 5, 21–30. Amsterdam: Allard-Pierson.

—. 1986a. "Chemical Analysis of Aegean-Type Late Bronze Age Pottery Found in Italy." In M. Marazzi, S. Tusa, and L. Vagnetti, eds., *Traffici micenei nel Mediterraneo: Problemi storici e documentazione archeologia*, Magna Graecia 3, 205–14. Taranto: Istituto per la Storica e l'Archeologia della Magna Grecia.

—. 1986b. *Greek and Cypriot Pottery: A Review of Scientific Studies*. Fitch Laboratory Occasional Paper 1. Athens: British School of Archaeology at Athens.

Jones, R. E., and C. Mee. 1978. "Spectrographic Analyses of Mycenaean Pottery from Ialysos on Rhodes: Results and Implications." *JFA* 5: 439–521.

Jones, R .E., and L. Vagnetti. 1991. "Traders and Craftsmen in the Central Mediterranean: Archaeological Evidence and Archaeometric Research." In N. H. Gale, ed., *Bronze Age Trade in the Mediterranean*, SIMA 90, 127–47. Jonsered: Paul Åströms Förlag.

—. 1992. "Traders and Craftsmen in the Central Mediterranean: Archaeological Evidence and Archaeometric Research (An Addendum)." *BSA* 87: 231–35.

Jones, R. E., with C. B. Mee. 1986. "Provenance Studies of Aegean Late Bronze Age Aegean Pottery." In R. E. Jones, *Greek and Cypriot Pottery: A Review of Scientific Studies*, Fitch Laboratory Occasional Paper 1, 411–36. Athens: British School of Archaeology at Athens.

Jonkers, E. J. 1959. *Social and Economic Commentary on Cicero's De Imperio Cn. Pompei*. Leiden: E. J. Brill.

Kanta, A. 1971. "Τὸ σπήλαιο τοῦ Διλιαγοῦ." *CretChron* 23: 425–39.

—. 1980. *The Late Minoan III Period in Crete: A Survey of Sites, Pottery and Their Distribution*. SIMA 58. Göteborg: Paul Åströms Förlag.

Kantor, H. J. 1947. *The Aegean and the Orient in the Second Millennium B.C.* AIA Monograph 1. Bloomington, Ind.: Archaeological Institute of America.

Karageorghis, V. 1959. "Chronique des fouilles et découvertes archéologiques a Chypre en 1958." *BCH* 83: 336–61.

—. 1960. "Fouilles de Kition 1959 (Étude sur les origines de la ville)." *BCH* 84: 504–82.

—. 1965. "Notes on Some Centaurs from Crete." *CretChron* 19: 50–54.

—. 1968. "Αἱ σκέσεις μεταξὺ Κύπρου καὶ Κρήτης κατὰ τὸν 11ου αἱ π.Χ." In *Πεπραγμένα τοῦ Β' Διεθνοῦς Κρητολογικοῦ Συνεδρίου*, Τόμος Α'. Τμῆμα Ἀρχαολογικόν 180–85. Athens.

—. 1969. *Recent Discoveries in Cyprus*. Suffolk: McGraw-Hill.

—. 1974. "Pikes or Obeloi from Cyprus and Crete." In *Antichità cretesi: Studi in onore de Doro Levi*, 2: 168–72. Catania: Università di Catania, Instituto di Archeologia.

—. 1975. *Alaas: A Protogeometric Necropolis in Cyprus*. Nicosia: Department of Antiquities, Cyprus.

—. 1976. *Kition, Mycenaean and Phoenician Discoveries in Cyprus*. London: Thames and Hudson.

—. 1982. "Metallurgy in Cyprus during the 11th Century, B.C." In J. D. Muhly, R. Maddin, and V. Karageorghis, eds., *Early Metallurgy in Cyprus, 4000–500 B.C.*, 297–302. Nicosia: Pierides Foundation.

—. 1990. *The End of the Late Bronze Age in Cyprus*. Nicosia: Pierides Foundation.

Karageorghis, V., and M. Iacovou. 1990. "Amathus Tomb 521: A Cypro-Geometric Group." *RDAC* 75–100.

Karo, G. 1911. "Minoische Rhyte." *JdI* 26: 249–70.

—. 1930. "Schatz von Tiryns." *AM* 55: 119–40.

—. 1933. "Archäologische Funde von Mai 1932 bis Juli 1933 Griechenland und Dodekanes." *AA* 191–262.

Katzenstein, H. J. 1973. *The History of Tyre, from the Beginning of the Second Millennium B.C.E. until the Fall of the Neo-Babylonian Empire in 538 B.C.E.* Jerusalem: Schocken Institute for Jewish Research.

Kearsley, R. 1989. *The Pendant Semi-Circle Skyphos: A Study of Its Development and an Examination of It as Evidence for Euboean Activity at Al Mina*. Bulletin of the Institute of Classical Studies no. 44. London: University of London, Institute of Classical Studies.

Kelley, A. C., and J. G. Williamson. 1974. *Lessons from Japanese Development: An Analytical Economic History*. Chicago: University of Chicago Press.

Kelley, A. C., J. G. Williamson, and R. J. Cheetham. 1972. *Dualistic Economic Development: Theory and History*. Chicago: University of Chicago Press.

Kemp, B. J. 1972. "Temple and Town in Ancient Egypt." In P. J. Ucko, R. Tringham, and G. W. Dimbleby, eds., *Man, Settlement and Urbanism*, 657–80. London: Duckworth.

—. 1992. *Ancient Egypt: Anatomy of a Civilization*. London: Routledge.

Kemp, B. J., and R. S. Merrillees. 1980. *Minoan Pottery in Second Millennium Egypt*. Mainz: Philipp von Zabern.

Kilian, K. 1988. "Mycenaeans up to Date, Trends and Changes in Recent Research." In E. B. French and K. A. Wardle, eds., *Problems in Greek Prehistory*, 115–52. Bristol: Bristol Classical Press.

Kilian-Dirlmeier, I. 1984. *Nadeln der frühhelladischen bis archaischen Zeit von der Peloponnes*. Prähistorische Bronzefunde 13.8. Munich: C. H. Beck.

—. 1985. "Fremde Weihungen in griechischen Heiligtumern vom 8. bis zum Beginn des 7. Jahrhunderts v. Chr." *JRGZM* 32: 215–54.

Killen, J. T. 1964. "The Wool Industry of Crete in the Late Bronze Age." *BSA* 59: 1–15.

Kirk, G. S. 1949. "Ships on Geometric Vases." *BSA* 44: 93–153.

Kitchen, K. A. 1972. "Ramesses VII and the Twentieth Dynasty." *JEA* 58: 182–94.

—. 1973. *The Third Intermediate Period in Egypt (1100–650 B.C.)*. Warminster: Aris and Phillips.

Klein, J. J. 1971. "'SOS Amphorae' and the Ancient Oil Trade." *AJA* 75: 206.

Kleiner, G., and D. Ohly. 1951. "Gemmen der Sammlung Arndt." *MüJb* 3: 7–31.

Kling, B. 1989. *Mycenaean IIIC:1b and Related Pottery in Cyprus*. SIMA 87. Göteborg: Paul Åströms Förlag.

Klippel, W. E., and L. M. Snyder. 1991. "Dark-Age Fauna from Kavousi, Crete: The Vertebrates from the 1987 and 1988 Excavations." *Hesperia* 60: 179–86.

Knapp, A. B. 1983. "An Alashiyan Merchant at Ugarit." *Tel Aviv* 10: 38–45.

—. 1990. "Ethnicity, Entrepreneurship, and Exchange: Mediterranean Inter-Island Relationships in the Late Bronze Age." *BSA* 85: 115–53.

Knapp, A. B., J. D. Muhly, and P. M. Muhly. 1988. "To Hoard Is Human: Late Bronze Age Metal Deposits in Cyprus and the Aegean." *RDAC*, pt. 1: 233–62.

Knorringa, H. 1926. *Emporos: Data on Trade and Traders in Greek Literature from Homer to Aristotle*. Amsterdam: H. J. Paris.

Koehl, R. B. 1985. *Sarepta*. Vol. 3, *The Imported Bronze and Iron Age Wares from Area II,X*. Beirut: Publications de l'Université Libanese.

Kontoleontos, N. M. 1945–47. "Γεωμετρικὸς Ἀμφορεὺς ἐκ Νάξου." *ArchEph* 84–85: 1–21.

Köpcke, G. 1967. "Neue Holzfunde aus dem Heraion von Samos." *AM* 82: 100–149.

—. 1987. "The Cretan Palaces and Trade." In R. Hägg and N. Marinatos, eds., *The Function of the Minoan Palaces*, Acta Instituti Atheniensis Regni Sueciae, Series in 4°, 35, 255–60. Stockholm: Paul Åströms Förlag.

—. 1990. *Handel*. ArchHom, Kap. M. Göttingen: Vandenhoeck and Ruprecht.

—. 1992. "What Role for Phoenicians." In G. Köpcke and I. Tokumaru, eds., *Greece between East and West: 10ᵗʰ–8th Centuries B.C.*, 103–13. Mainz: Philipp von Zabern.

Kourou, N. 1984. "Local Naxian Workshops and the Import-Export Trade of the Island in the Geometric Period." In H.A.G. Brijder, ed., *Ancient Greek and Related Pottery: Proceedings of the International Vase Symposium in Amsterdam, 12–15 April 1984*, 107–12. Amsterdam: Allard Pierson Museum.

—. 1987. "À propos de quelques atelièrs de céramique fine non tournée du type 'Argien Monochrome.'" *BCH* 111: 31–53.

—. 1988. "Handmade Pottery and Trade: The Case of the 'Argive Monochrome' Ware." In J. Christensen and T. Melander, eds., *Proceedings of the Third Symposium on Ancient Greek and Related Pottery*, 314–24. Amsterdam: Allard Pierson Museum.

—. 1989. "Aegean Orientalizing versus Oriental Art: The Evidence of Monsters." In V. Karageorghis, ed., *The Civilizations of the Aegean and Their Diffusion in Cyprus and the Eastern Mediterranean, 2000–600 B.C.*, 111–23. Larnaca: Pierides Foundation.

Kourou, N., and A. Karetsou. 1994. "Τὸ ἱερὸ τοῦ Ἑρμοῦ στην Πατσό Αμαρίου." In L. Rocchetti, ed., *Sybrita, la valle di Amari: Fra bronzo e ferro*, Incunabula Graeca 96, Fasc. 1: 81–164. Rome: Gruppo Editoriale Internazionale.

Kraiker, W., and K. Kübler. 1939. *Kerameikos*. Vol. 1, *Nekropolen des 12. bis 10. Jahrhunderts*. Berlin: Walter de Gruyter.

Krugman, P. R. 1991a. *Geography and Trade*. Cambridge, Mass.: Massachusetts Institute of Technology Press.

—. 1991b. "History and Industry Location: The Case of the Manufacturing Belt." *American Economic Review* 81: 80–83.

—. 1991c. "History versus Expectations." *Quarterly Journal of Economics* 106: 651–67.

—. 1991d. "Increasing Returns and Economic Geography." *Journal of Political Economy* 99: 483–99.

Kübler, K. 1943. *Kerameikos*. Vol. 4, *Neufunde aus der Nekropole des 11. und 10. Jahrhunderts*. Berlin: Walter de Gruyter.

Kunze, E. 1931. *Kretische Bronzereliefs*. Stuttgart: Kohlhammer.

—. 1935–36. "Orientalische Schnitzereien aus Kreta." *AM* 60/61: 218–33.

—. 1961. *Bericht über die Ausgrabungen in Olympia, Frühjahre 1956 bis 1958*. OlForsch VII. Berlin: Walter de Gruyter.

—. 1968. "Ein kretisches Meisterwerk des 7. Jahrhunderts vor Chr. aus Olympia." In Πεπραγμένα τοῦ Β' Διεθνῦς Κρητολογικοῦ Συνεδπίου (2d Cretological Congress), Τόμος Α' Τμῆμα Αρχαιολόγικο, 196–97. Athens.

Kuznets, S. 1967. "Quantitative Aspects of the Economic Growth of Nations: X. Level and Structure of Foreign Trade: Long-Term Trends." *Economic Development and Cultural Change* 15:2, pt. 2.

Kyrieleis, H. 1980. "Archaische Holzfunde aus Samos." *AM* 95: 87–147.

—. 1983. "Neue Holzfunde aus dem Heraion von Samos." *ASAtene*, n.s. 61: 295–302.

La Genière, J. de. 1979. "The Iron Age in Southern Italy." In D. Ridgway and F. R. Ridgway, eds., *Italy Before the Romans: The Iron Age, Orientalizing and Etruscan Periods*, 59–93. New York: Academic Press.

Lamb, W. 1929. *Greek and Roman Bronzes*. London: Methuen.

Lambrou-Phillipson, C. 1990. *Hellenorientalia: The Near Eastern Presence in the Bronze Aegean, ca. 3000–1100 B.C.* SIMA-PB 95. Göteborg: Paul Åströms Förlag.

—. 1991. "Seafaring in the Bronze Age Mediterranean: The Parameters Involved in Maritime Travel." In R. Laffineur and L. Basch, eds., *Thalassa, l'Égée prehistorique et la mer*, Aegaeum 7, 11–20. Liège: Université de Liège.

Lancaster, K. J. 1979. *Variety, Equity, and Efficiency*. New York: Columbia University Press.

Lane, E. A. 1933–34. "Lakonian Vase Painting." *BSA* 34: 99–189.

Langdon, S. 1992. "The Pottery of the Early Iron Age and Geometric Periods." In C. Runnels, D. J. Pullen, and S. Langdon, eds., *Artifact and Assemblage: The Finds from a Regional Survey of the Southern Argolid, Greece*, vol. 1, *The Prehistoric and Early Iron Age Pottery and the Lithic Artifacts*, 57–73. Stanford: Stanford University Press.

Langlotz, E. 1928. "Ein Votiverelief aus Tarent." In *Antike Plastik: Walther Amelung zum sechzigsten Geburtstag*, 113–17. Berlin: Walter de Gruyter.

La Riche, W. 1996. *Alexandria: The Sunken City*. Photography by S. Compoint. London: Weidenfeld and Nicolson.

Larsen, J.A.O. 1938. "Roman Greece." In T. Frank, ed., *An Economic Survey of Ancient*

Rome, 4: 259–498. Baltimore: The Johns Hopkins University Press.

Larsen, M. T. 1967. *Old Assyrian Caravan Procedures*. Istanbul: Nederlands Historisch-Archaeologisch Instituut in het Nabije Oosten.

—. 1987. "Commercial Networks in the Ancient Near East." In M. Rowlands, M. Larsen, and K. Kristiansen, eds., *Centre and Periphery in the Ancient World*, 47–56. Cambridge: Cambridge University Press.

Laurent-Täckholm, V. 1940. "A Mummy Coffin in the Egyptian Museum, Stockholm, and Its Plant Remains." *Svensk Botanisk Tidskrift* 34: 141–61.

Leatham, J., and S. Hood. 1958–59. "Sub-marine Explorations in Crete." *BSA* 53–54: 263–80.

Leclant, J. 1977. "Fouilles et travaux en Égypte et au Suodan, 1975–1976." *Orientalia* 46: 233–95.

—. 1982. "Fouilles et travaux en Égypte et au Suodan, 1978–1980." *Orientalia* 51: 49–122.

Leclant, J. 1996. "L'Égypte et l'Egéen au second millénaire." In E. deMiro, L. Godart, and A. Sacconi, eds., *Atti e memorie del secondo congresso internazionale di micenologia*, vol. 2, *Storia*, 613–25. Incunabula Graeca 98.2. Rome: Gruppo Editoriale Internazionale.

Leemans, W. F. 1950. *The Old-Babylonian Merchant*. Leiden: Brill.

Lehmann-Hartleben, K. 1923. *Die antiken Hafenanlagen des Mittelmeeres*. Klio Beiheft 14. Leipzig.

Lembesi, A. 1970. "Ἀνασκαφικαὶ ἔρευναι εἰῆ Ἀνατολικὴν Κρήτην." *Prakt* 256–97.

—. 1971. "Εἶς τάφος τοῦ 7ου π.Χ. αιωνος." *AAA* 4: 384–92.

—. 1973. "Ἱερὸν Ἑρμοῦ καὶ Ἀφροδίης παρὰ τὴν ἄτω Σύμην Βιάννου." *AAA* 6: 104–13.

—. 1975a. "Ἱερὸν Ἑρμοῦ καὶ Ἀφροδίτης εις Σύμην Βιάννου." *Prakt* B': 322–29.

—. 1975b. "The Fortetsa Gold Rings." *BSA* 70: 169–76.

—. 1983. "Τὸ ἐλεφάντινο εἰδωλιο τοῦ νέου ἀπό τή Σάμο." *ASAtene*, n.s. 61: 303–21.

—. 1985. *Τὸ ἱε ὁ τοῦ Ἑρῆ καὶ τῆς Ἀφροδίτης οτὴ Σύμη Βιάννου*. Vol. 1.1, *Χάλκινα κρητικά τορεύματα*. Βιβλιοθήκη τῆς ἐν Ἀθήναις Ἀρχαιολογικῆς Ἑταιρείας 102. Athens.

Lemerle, P. 1935. "Chronique des fouilles et découvertes archéologiques." *BCH* 59: 234–309.

—. 1936. "Chronique des fouilles et découvertes archéologiques." *BCH* 60: 452–89.

Lemos, A. A. 1991. *Archaic Pottery of Chios: The Decorated Styles*. Vol. 1. Oxford University Committee for Archaeology Monograph 30. Oxford: Oxford University Committee for Archaeology.

Lenk, B. 1937. "Thesprotoi." *RE* 2: 6, 63–69.

Leonard, A. 1994. *An Index to the Late Bronze Age Aegean Pottery from Syria-Palestine*. SIMA 114. Jonsered: Paul Åströms Förlag.

Leonard, A., M. Hughes, A. Middleton, and L. Schofield. 1993. "The Making of Aegean Stirrup Jars: Technique, Tradition, and Trade." *BSA* 88: 105–23.

Lerat, L. 1980. "Trois boucliers archaïques de Delphes." *BCH* 104: 93–114.

Lesko, L. H. 1992. "Egypt in the 12th Century B.C." In W. A. Ward and M. S. Joukowsky, eds., *The Crisis Years: The 12th Century B.C.: From beyond the Danube to the Tigris*, 151–56. Dubuque, Iowa: Kendall/Hunt.

Levi, A. 1926. *Le terrecotte figurate del Museo Nazionale di Napoli*. Firenze: Vallecchi.

Levi, D. 1925. "Arcadia, An Early Greek Town: New Italian Excavations in Crete." *AnnLiv* 12: 3–10.

—. 1927–29. "Arkades: Uni città cretese all'alba della civiltà ellenica." *ASAtene* 10–12: 9–723.

—. 1945a. "Early Hellenic Pottery of Crete." *Hesperia* 14: 1–32.

—. 1945b. "Gleanings from Crete." *AJA* 49: 270–328.

—. 1955. "Attività della Scuola Archeologica Italiana di Atene nell'anno 1954." *BdA* 40: 141–64.

—. 1955–56. "Gli scavi del 1954 sull'acropoli di Gortina." *ASAtene*, n.s. 17–18: 207–88.

—. 1957–58. "Gli scavi a Festòs nel 1956 e 1957." *ASAtene*, n.s. 19–20: 193–361.

—. 1961–62. "Gli scavi a Festòs negli anni 1958–60." *ASAtene*, n.s. 23–24: 377–504.

Lichtheim, M. 1976. *Ancient Egyptian Literature*. Vol. 2, *The New Kingdom*. Berkeley: University of California Press.

Liddy, D. J. 1988. "A Chemical Study of Early Iron Age Pottery from the North Cemetery, Knossos." In R. E. Jones and H. W. Catling, eds., *New Aspects of Archaeological Science*, Fitch Laboratory Occasional Paper 3, 29–32. Athens: British School of Archaeology at Athens.

—. 1989. "A Provenance Study of Decorated Pottery from an Iron Age Cemetery at Knossos, Crete." In Y. Maniatis, ed., *Archaeometry: Proceedings of the 25th International Symposium*, 559–70. Amsterdam: Elsevier.

Linder, E. 1986. "The Khorsabad Wall Relief: A Mediterranean Seascape or River Transport of Timbers." *JAOS* 106: 273–81.

Lindsay, W. S. 1876. *History of Merchant Shipping and Ancient Commerce.* Vol. 3. London: S. Low, Marston, Low, and Searle.

Liverani, M. 1979. "'Irrational' Elements in the Amarna Trade." In *Three Amarna Essays,* Monographs in the Ancient Near East 1, fasc. 5, 21–33. Translated by M. L. Jaffe. Malibu, Calif.: Undene Publications.

—. 1986. "La ceramica e i testi: Commercio miceneo e politica orientale." In M. Marazzi, S. Tusa, and L. Vagnetti, eds., *Traffici micenei nel Mediterraneo: Problemi storici e documentazione archeologica,* Magna Graecia 3, 405–12. Taranto: Istituto per la Storica e l'Archeologia della Magna Grecia.

—. 1990. *Prestige and Interest: International Relations in the Near East ca. 1600–1100 B.C.* Padua: Sargon.

Lluch, C., A. A. Powell, and R. A. Williams. 1977. *Patterns in Household Demand and Saving.* New York: Oxford University Press.

Loewy, E. 1930. "Daedalica Etruriae." *StEtr* 4: 97–100.

Lolos, Y. G. 1995. "Late Cypro-Mycenaean Seafaring: New Evidence from Sites in the Saronic and the Argolic Gulfs." In V. Karageorghis and D. Michaelides, eds., *Proceedings of the International Symposium "Cyprus and the Sea,"* 65–85. Nicosia: University of Cyprus.

—. 1996a. "Point Iria Wreck (1992) II: The Pottery." *ENALIA Annual 1992,* 4: 4–5.

—. 1996b. "Point Iria Wreck (1993) III: The Pottery." *ENALIA Annual 1992,* 4: 21–31.

Loon, M. N. van. 1966. *Urartian Art.* Istanbul: Nederlands Historisch-Archaeologisch Institut.

—. 1977. "The Place of Urartu in First-Millennium B.C. Trade." *Iraq* 39: 229–31.

LoPorto, F. G. 1959–60. "Ceramica arcaica dalla necropoli di Taranto." *ASAtene,* n.s. 21–22: 7–230.

—. 1964. "Satyrion (Taranto): Scavi e ricerchi nel luogo del più antico insediamento laconico in Puglia." *NSc,* serie 8ª, 18: 177–279.

—. 1974. "Vasi cretesi e pseudocretesi in Italia." In *Antichità cretesi, studi in onore di Doro Levi,* 2: 173–88. Catania: Università di Catania, Instituto di Archeologia.

—. 1986. "Le importazioni micene in Puglia: Bilancio di un decennio di scavi." In M. Marazzi, S. Tusa, and L. Vagnetti, eds., *Traffici micenei nel Mediterraneo: Problemi storici e documentazione archeologia,* Magna Graecia 3, 13–20. Taranto: Istituto per la Storica e l'Archeologia della Magna Grecia.

Lorimer, H. L. 1950. *Homer and the Monuments.* London: Macmillan.

LoSchiavo, F., E. Macnamara, and L. Vagnetti. 1985. "Late Cypriot Imports to Italy and their Influence on Local Bronzework." *BSR* 53: 1–71.

Lucas, A. 1962. *Ancient Egyptian Material and Industries.* 4th ed. London: Edward Arnold.

Luckenbill, D. D. 1927. *Ancient Records of Assyria and Babylonia* II. *Historical Records of Assyria from Sargon to the End.* Chicago: University of Chicago Press.

Lukash, S. S. 1984. "Italy and the Apennine Culture." In T. Hackens, N. D. Holloway, and R. R. Holloway, eds., *Crossroads of the Mediterranean,* Archaeologica Transatlantica 2, 13–54. Louvain-la-Neuve: Art and Archaeology Publications, College Erasme.

Maaß, M. 1977. "Kretische Votivdreifüsse." *AM* 92: 33–59.

MacDonald, B. R. 1986. "The Diolkos." *JHS* 106: 191–95.

Macdonald, C. F. 1986. "Problems of the Twelfth Century B.C. in the Dodecanese." *BSA* 81: 125–51.

Maddin, R., T. S. Wheeler, and J. Muhly. 1977. "Tin in the Ancient Near East: Old Questions and New Finds." *Expedition* 19, no. 2: 35–47.

Magou, E., S. Philippakis, and C. Rolley. 1986. "Trépieds géométriques de bronze: Analyses complémentaires." *BCH* 110: 121–36.

Mainwaring, G. E., and W. G. Perrin, eds. 1922. *The Life and Works of Sir Henry Mainwaring.* Vol. 2. Publications of the Navy Records Society 56. London: Navy Records Society.

Maisler, B. 1946. "Canaan and the Canaanites." *BASOR* 102: 7–12.

Maiuri, A. 1923–24. "Jalisos–Scavi della Missione Archeologica Italiana a Rodi (Parte I e II)." *ASAtene* 6–7: 83–341.

Malaval, B. 1909. "Un ancien port à Dékhéla." *Bulletin de la Societé Archéologique d'Alexandrie* 11: 371–74.

Mallowan, M.E.L. 1939. "Phoenician Carrying Trade." *Antiquity* 13: 86–87.

—. 1952. "Ivories of Unsurpassed Magnificence–The Finest and Largest from the Ancient Near East–Discovered in this Season's Excavations at Nimrud." *ILN*, August 16, 254–56.

Manning, S. W., and B. Weninger. 1992. "A Light in the Dark: Archaeological Wiggle Matching and the Absolute Chronology of the Close of the Aegean Late Bronze Age." *Antiquity* 66: 636–63.

Marangou, E.-L.I. 1969. *Lakonische Elfenbein und Beinschnitzereien*. Tübingen: Ernst Wasmuth.

Marasco, G. 1987. "Roma e la pirateria cilicia." *RSI* 9: 122–46.

Marazzi, M. 1986. "Repertori archeologici sui traffici micenei nel Mediterraneo orientale: Egitto, Cipro, Vicino-Oriente." In M. Marazzi, S. Tusa, and L. Vagnetti, eds., *Traffici micenei nel Mediterraneo: Problemi storici e documentazione archeologia*, Magna Graecia 3, 323–26. Taranto: Istituto per la Storica e l'Archeologia della Magna Grecia.

Marazzi, M., and S. Tusa. 1979. "Die mykenische Penetration im westlichen Mittelmeerraum." *Klio* 61: 309–51.

Marcadé, J. 1949. "Un casque crétois trouvé a Delphes." *BCH* 73: 421–36.

Marinatos, N. 1993. *Minoan Religion: Ritual, Image, and Symbol*. Columbia: University of South Carolina Press.

Marinatos, S. 1925–26. "Ἀνασκαφαὶ Νίρου Χάνι Κρήτης." *Prakt* 141–47.

—. 1929. "Ἀνασκαφαὶ ἐν Κρήτης." *Prakt* 94–104.

—. 1931–32. "Πρωτογεωμετρικὰ καὶ γεωμετρικὰ εὑρήματα ἐκ Κεντρικης καὶ." *ArchDelt* 14: 1–11.

—. 1932. "Ἀνασκαφὴ Ἀμνισῦ Κρήτης." *Prakt* 76–94.

—. 1933. "Ἀνασκαφὴ Ἀμνισῦ Κρήτης." *Prakt* 93–100.

—. 1934. "Ἀνασκαφὴ Ἀμνισῦ Κρήτης." *Prakt* 128–33.

—. 1935. "Ἀνασκαφαὶ ἐν Κρήτης." *Prakt* 196–220.

—. 1936a. "Le temple géométrique de Dréros II." *BCH* 60: 257–85.

—. 1936b. "Ἀνασκαφαὶ ἐν Ἀμνισοῦ Κρήτης." *Prakt* 81–86.

—. 1937. "Ausgrabungen und Funde auf Kreta 1937–37." *AA* 222–34.

—. 1938. "Ἀνασκαφαὶ Ἀμνισοῦ (Κρήτης)." *Prakt* 130–38.

—. 1956. "Ἐργασίαι ἐν Βαθυπέτρω, Ἀρχάναις καὶ Ἰδαίῳ ἄντῳ." *Prakt* 223–25.

Markoe, G. E. 1985. *Phoenician Bronze and Silver Bowls from Cyprus and the Mediterranean*. Berkeley: University of California Press.

—. 1990. "The Emergence of Phoenician Art." *BASOR* 279: 13–26.

Marshall, A. 1920. *Principles of Economics*. 8th ed. London: Macmillan.

Marshall, F. H. 1905–6. "Tombs of Hellenic Date at Praesos." *BSA* 12: 63–70.

Masson, O. 1990–91. "Un vieux problème: Alasia = Chypre?" *REG* 103: 231–35.

Matthäus, H. 1985. *Metallgefäßuntersätze der Bronzezeit, der geometrischen und archaischen Periode auf Zypern*. Prähistorische Bronzefunde 2.8. Munich: C. H. Beck.

—. 1987. "Bronzene Stabdreifüsse in Zypern und Griechenland–zur Kontinuität ostmediterranen Metallhandwerks." In E. Thomas, ed., *Forschungen zur ägäischen Vorgeschichte: Das Ende der mykenischen Welt*, 93–121. Berlin: Wasmuth.

—. 1988. "Heirloom or Tradition? Bronze Stands of the Second and First Millennium B.C. in Cyprus, Greece and Italy." In E. B. French and K. A. Wardle, eds., *Problems in Greek Prehistory*, 285–300. Bristol: Bristol Classical Press.

Matz, F., ed. 1951. *Forschungen auf Kreta 1942*. Berlin: Walter de Gruyter.

Mauss, M. 1921. "Une forme ancienne de contrat chez les Thraces." *REG* 34: 388–97.

—. 1923–24. "Essai sur le don." *L'Année sociologique*, n.s. 1: 30–186.

—. 1954. *The Gift: Forms and Functions of Exchange in Archaic Societies*. Translated by I. Cunnison. Glencoe, Ill.: Free Press.

Mavriyannaki, C. 1972. "Modellini fittili di costruzioni circolari dalla Creta minoica." *SMEA* 15: 161–70.

Maximova, M. I. 1927. *Les vases plastiques dans l'antiquité (epoque archaïque)*. Translated by M. Carslow. Paris: Paul Geuthner.

Maxwell-Hyslop, K. R. 1956. "Urartian Bronzes in Etruscan Tombs." *Iraq* 18: 150–67.

—. 1971. *Western Asiatic Jewellery, c. 3000–612 B.C.* London: Methuen.

Mazar, A. 1988. "A Note on Canaanite Jars from Enkomi." *IEJ* 38: 224–26.

—. 1989. "Comments on the Nature of the Relations between Cyprus and Palestine during the 12th–11th Centuries." In V. Karageorghis, ed., *The Civilizations of the Aegean and Their*

Diffusion in Cyprus and the Eastern Mediterranean, 2000–600 B.C., 95–104. Larnaca: Pierides Foundation.

—. 1990. *Archaeology of the Land of the Bible, 10,000–586 B.C.E.* New York: Doubleday.

—. 1992. "The Iron Age I." In A. Ben-Tor, ed., *The Archaeology of Ancient Israel*, 258–301. New Haven: Yale University Press.

—. 1993. "Beth Shan in the Iron Age: Preliminary Report and Conclusions of the 1990–1991 Excavations." *IEJ* 43: 201–29.

McClellan, T. L. 1992. "Twelfth Century B.C. Syria: Comments on H. Sader's Paper." In W. A. Ward and M. S. Joukowsky, eds., *The Crisis Years: The 12th Century B.C.: From beyond the Danube to the Tigris*, 164–73. Dubuque, Iowa: Kendall/Hunt.

McCloskey, D. N. 1976. "English Open Fields as Behavior towards Risk." *Research in Economic History* 1: 124–70.

—. 1983. "The Rhetoric of Economics." *Journal of Economic Literature* 31: 481–517.

—. 1985. *The Rhetoric of Economics.* Madison: University of Wisconsin Press.

—. 1990. *If You're So Smart: The Narrative of Economic Expertise.* Chicago: University of Chicago Press.

McCloskey, D. N. and J. Nash. 1984. "Corn at Interest: The Extent and Cost of Grain Storage in Medieval England." *American Economic Review* 74: 174–87.

McConnaughey, B. H., and R. Zottoli. 1983. *Introduction to Marine Biology.* St. Louis: C. V. Mosby.

McCoy, F. W. 1978. "Climate Change in the Eastern Mediterranean Area during the Past 240,000 Years." In C. Doumas, ed., *Thera and the Aegean World*, 2: 79–100. London: Thera Foundation.

McDonald, W. A., and W.D.E. Coulson. 1983. "The Dark Age at Nichoria: A Perspective." In W. A. McDonald, W.D.E. Coulson, and J. Rosser, eds., *Excavations at Nichoria in Southwest Greece*, vol. 3, *Dark Age and Byzantine Occupation*, 316–29. Minneapolis: University of Minnesota Press.

McGuire, R. A. 1980. "A Portfolio Analysis of Crop Diversification and Risk in the Cotton South." *Explorations in Economic History* 17: 342–71.

McKechnie, P. 1989. *Outsiders in the Greek City in the Fourth Century B.C.* London: Routledge.

Mee, C. 1978. "Aegean Trade and Settlement in Anatolia in the Second Millennium B.C." *AnatSt* 28: 121–56.

—. 1982. *Rhodes in the Bronze Age: An Archaeological Survey.* Warminster: Aris and Phillips.

Megaw, A.H.S. 1962–63. "Archaeology in Greece, 1962–63." *AR* 9: 3–33.

—. 1963–64. "Excavations at Tocra in Libya, 1963–64." *AR* 10: 31–32.

Meiggs, R. 1982. *Trees and Timber in the Ancient Mediterranean World.* Oxford: Clarendon.

Meijer, F. 1986. *A History of Seafaring in the Classical World.* New York: St. Martin's.

Melas, M. 1988. "Minoans Overseas: Alternative Models of Interpretation." *Aegaeum* 2: 47–70. Liège: Université de l'Etat à Liège.

—. 1995. "Geometrika from Kasos." In C. Morris, ed., *Klados: Essays in Honour of J. N. Coldstream*, BICS suppl. 63, 157–62. London: University of London, Institute of Classical Studies.

Mele, A. 1979. *Il commercio greco arcaico: Prexis ed emporoi.* Cahiers du Centre Jean Bérard 4. Naples: Istitut Français de Naples.

—. 1986. "Pirateria, commercio e aristocrazia: Replica a Benedetto Bravo." *DHA* 12: 67–109.

Melena, J. L. 1974a. "Coriander on the Knossos Tablets." *Minos* 15: 133–63.

—. 1974b. "Ku-pa-ro en las Tabillas de Cnoso." *Emerita* 42: 307–36.

Meola, E. 1971. *Terracotte orientalizzante di Gela ("Daedalica" Siciliae III).* Rome: Accademia Nazionale die Lincei.

Mercereau, R. 1993. "Cretan Cylindrical Models." *AJA* 97: 1–53.

Merrillees, R. S. 1962. "Opium Trade in the Bronze Age Levant." *Antiquity* 36: 287–92.

—. 1968. *The Cypriote Bronze Age Pottery Found in Egypt.* SIMA 18. Lund: Carl Bloms.

—. 1973a. "Discussion." In *Acts of the International Archaeological Symposium "The Mycenaeans in the Eastern Mediterranean,"* 325–27. Nicosia: Department of Antiquities, Cyprus.

—. 1973b. "Mycenaean Pottery from the Time of Akhenaten in Egypt." In *Acts of the International Archaeological Symposium "The Mycenaeans in the Eastern Mediterranean,"* 175–86. Nicosia: Department of Antiquities, Cyprus.

—. 1987. *Alashia Revisited.* Cahiers de la Revue Biblique 22. Paris: J. Gabalda et Cie.

Michaelidou-Nicolaou, I. 1987. "Repercussions of the Phoenician Presence in Cyprus." In E. Lipiński, ed., *Phoenicia and the East Mediter-*

ranean in the First Millennium B.C., Orientalia Lovaniensia Analecta 22, Studia Phoenicia 5, 331–38. Leuven: Peeters.

Millard, A. R., and H. Tadmor. 1973. "Adad-Nirari III in Syria: Another Stele Fragment and the Dates of His Campaigns." *Iraq* 35: 57–64.

Millett, P. 1983. "Maritime Loans and the Structure of Credit in Fourth-Century Athens." In P. Garnsey, K. Hopkins, and C. R. Whittaker, eds., *Trade in the Ancient Economy*, 36–52. Berkeley: University of California Press.

—. 1984. "Hesiod and His World." *Proceedings of the Cambridge Philological Society* 220: 84–115.

—. 1991. *Lending and Borrowing in Ancient Athens.* Cambridge: Cambridge University Press.

Mills, J. S., and R. White. 1989. "The Identity of the Resins from the Late Bronze Age Shipwreck at Ulu Burun (Kaş)." *Archaeometry* 31: 37–44.

Milne, J. G. 1939. "Trade between Greece and Egypt before Alexander the Great." *JEA* 25: 177–83.

—. 1945. "The Economic Policy of Solon." *Hesperia* 14: 230–45.

Milne, L. J., and M. J. Milne. 1951. "The Eelgrass Catastrophe." *Scientific American* 184, no. 1: 52-55.

Milojčić, V. 1948–49. "Die dorische Wanderung im Licht der vorgeschichtlichen Funde." *AA* 11–36.

—. 1955. "Einige 'mitteleuropäische' Fremdlinge auf Kreta." *JRGZM* 2: 153–69.

Mitchell, H. 1940. *The Economics of Ancient Greece.* Cambridge: Cambridge University Press.

Mokhtar, G. 1993. "Pre-Alexandria: Keys to the Rise of an Immortal City." In G. L. Steen, ed., *Alexandria, The Site and the History*, 21–33. New York: New York University Press.

Mommsen, H., T. Beier, U. Diehl, and C. Podzuweit. 1992. "Provenance Determination of Mycenaean Sherds Found at Tell El Amarna by Neutron Activation Analysis." *JAS* 19: 293–302.

Montelius, O. 1924. *La Grèce préclassique.* Vol. 1. Stockholm: Ivaar Hæggströms.

—. 1969. *La civilisation primitive en Italie depuis l'introduction des métaux.* 5 vols. Rome: L'Erma di Bretschneider. (Originally published 1895–1910, Stockholm: Imprimerie Royale.)

Moorey, P.R.S. 1971. *Catalogue of the Ancient Persian Bronzes in the Ashmolean Museum.* Oxford: Clarendon.

—. 1974. *Ancient Persian Bronzes in the Adam Collection.* London: Faber and Faber.

—. 1988. "Bronzeworking Centres of Western Asia c. 1000–539 B.C.: Problems and Perspectives." In J. Curtis, ed., *Bronzeworking Centres of Western Asia, c. 1000–539 B.C.*, 23–32. London: Kegan Paul.

—. 1994. *Ancient Mesopotamian Materials and Industries: The Archaeological Evidence.* Oxford: Clarendon.

Moran, L. R., D. Larkins, and M. W. Webb. 1994. "The Business Situation." *Survey of Current Business* 74: 1–29.

Morgan, C. A. 1988. "Corinth, the Corinthian Gulf and Western Greece during the Eighth Century B.C." *BSA* 83: 313–38.

—. 1990. *Athletes and Oracles: The Transformation of Olympia and Delphi in the Eighth Century B.C.* Cambridge: Cambridge University Press.

Morris, I. 1986a. "Gift and Commodity in Archaic Greece." *Man*, n.s. 21: 1–17.

—. 1986b. "The Use and Abuse of Homer." *ClAnt* 5: 81–138.

—. 1987. *Burial and Ancient Society: The Rise of the Greek City State.* Cambridge: Cambridge University Press.

—. 1989. "Circulation, Deposition and the Formation of the Greek Iron Age." *Man*, n.s. 24: 502–19.

Morris, S. P. 1984. *The Black and White Style: Athens and Aigina in the Orientalizing Period.* Yale Classical Monograph 6. New Haven: Yale University Press.

—. 1992a. *Daidalos and the Origins of Greek Art.* Princeton: Princeton University Press.

—. 1992b. "Introduction." In G. Köpcke and I. Tokumaru, eds., *Greece between East and West: 10th–8th Centuries B.C.*, xiii–xviii. Mainz: Philipp von Zabern.

Morrison, J. S., and R. T. Williams. 1968. *Greek Oared Ships 900–322 B.C.* Cambridge: Cambridge University Press.

Moscati, S. 1968. *The World of the Phoenicians.* New York: Praeger.

—. 1988. "Ostrich Eggs." In S. Moscati, ed., *The Phoenicians*, 456–63. New York: Abbeville.

Mountjoy, P. A. 1986. *Mycenaean Decorated Pottery: A Guide to Identification.* SIMA 73. Göteborg: Paul Åströms Förlag.

—. 1988. "LH III C Late versus Submycenaean: The Kerameikos Pompeion Cemetery Revisited." *JdI* 103: 1–33.

Muckelroy, K. 1978. *Maritime Archaeology*. Cambridge: Cambridge University Press.

Muhly, J. D. 1970. "Homer and the Phoenicians: The Relations between Greece and the Near East in the Late Bronze and Early Iron Ages." *Berytus* 19: 19–64.

—. 1992. "The Crisis Years in the Mediterranean World: Transition or Cultural Disintegration." In W. A. Ward and M. S. Joukowsky, eds., *The Crisis Years: The 12th Century B.C.: From beyond the Danube to the Tigris*, 10–26. Dubuque, Iowa: Kendall/Hunt.

Muhly, J. D., T. Stech Wheeler, and R. Maddin. 1977. "The Gelidonya Shipwreck and the Bronze Age Metals Trade in the Eastern Mediterranean." *JFA* 4: 353–62.

Müller-Karpe, H. 1960. *Vom Anfang Roms. Studien zu den prähistorischen Forums- und Palatingräbern*. RM-EH 5. Heidelberg: Kerle.

—. 1962. "Metallbeigaben der Früheisenzeitlichen Kerameikos-Gräber." *JdI* 77: 59–129.

Murray, O. 1980. *Early Greece*. Stanford: Stanford University Press.

—. 1983. "Discussion" [of Coldstream, "Gift Exchange"]. In R. Hägg, ed., *The Greek Renaissance of the Eighth Century B.C.* Acta Instituti Atheniensis Regni Sueciae, Series in 4°, 30, 207. Stockholm: Paul Åströms Förlag.

Muscarella, O. W. 1962. "The Oriental Origin of Siren Cauldron Attachments." *Hesperia* 31: 317–29.

—. 1977. "The Archaeological Evidence for Relations between Greece and Iran in the First Millennium B.C." *JANES* 9: 31–57.

—. 1978. "Urartian Bells and Samos." *JANES* 10: 61–72.

—. 1980. *The Catalogue of Ivories from Hasanlu, Iran*. University Museum Monograph 40. Philadelphia: The University Museum, University of Pennsylvania.

—. 1988. "Background to the Luristan Bronzes." In J. Curtis, ed., *Bronzeworking Centres of Western Asia c. 1000–539 B.C.*, 33–44. London: Kegan Paul.

—. 1992. "Greek and Oriental Cauldron Attachments." In G. Köpcke and I. Tokumaru, eds., *Greece between East and West: 10th–8th Centuries B.C.*, 16–45. Mainz: Philipp von Zabern.

Nagy, G. 1990. *Greek Mythology and Poetics*. Ithaca, N.Y.: Cornell University Press.

Nakajima, C. 1986. *Subjective Equilibrium Theory of the Farm Household*. Amsterdam: Elsevier.

Naumann, U. 1976. *Subminoische und protogeometrische Bronzeplastik auf Kreta*. AM-BH 6. Berlin: Gebr. Mann.

Neeft, C. W. 1975. "Corinthian Fragments from Argos at Utrecht and the Corinthian Late Geometric Kotyle." *BABesch* 50: 97–129.

—. 1986. "The Painter of Candia 7789." In H.A.G. Brijder, A. A. Drukker, and C. W. Neeft, eds., *Enthousiasmos: Essays on Greek and Related Pottery Presented to J. M. Hemelrijk*, 13–22. Amsterdam: Allard Pierson Museum.

—. 1987. *Protocorinthian Subgeometric Aryballoi*. Amsterdam: Allard Pierson Museum.

—. 1991. *Addenda et Corrigenda to D. A. Amyx, Corinthian Vase-Painting in the Archaic Period*. Scripta minora 3. Amsterdam: Allard Pierson Museum.

Negbi, O. 1976. *Canaanite Gods in Metal: An Archaeological Study of Ancient Syro-Palestinian Figurines*. Tel Aviv: Institute of Archaeology, Tel Aviv University.

—. 1982. "Evidence for Early Phoenician Communities on the Eastern Mediterranean Islands." *Levant* 14: 179–82.

—. 1988. "Levantine Elements in the Sacred Architecture of the Aegean." *BSA* 83: 339–57.

—. 1992. "Early Phoenician Presence in the Mediterranean Islands: A Reappraisal." *AJA* 96: 599–615.

Neugebauer, K. A. 1931. *Katalog der statuarischen Bronzen im Antiquarium, Staatliche Museen zu Berlin*. Vol. 1, *Die minoischen und archaisch griechischen Bronzen*. Berlin: Walter de Gruyter.

Neumann, J., and S. Parpola. 1987. "Climatic Change and the Eleventh-Tenth Century Eclipse of Assyria and Babylonia." *JNES* 46: 161–82.

Nicholls, R. V. 1958–59. "Old Smyrna: The Iron Age Fortifications and Associated Remains on the City Perimeter." *BSA* 53–54: 35–137.

Nicolaou, K. 1976. *The Historical Topography of Kition*. SIMA 43. Göteborg: Paul Åströms Förlag.

—. 1979. "Minoan Survivals in Geometric and Archaic Cyprus." In *Acts of the International Archaeological Symposium "Relations between Cyprus and Crete, ca. 2000–500 B.C.,"* 249–56. Nicosia: Department of Antiquities, Cyprus.

Niemeier, W.-D. 1995. "Aegina–First Aegean 'State' outside of Crete?" In R. Laffineur and W.-D. Niemeier, eds., *Politeia; Society and State in the Aegean Bronze Age*, 73–79. *Proceedings of* the *Fifth International Aegean Conference, University of Heidelberg, Archäogisches Institut 10–13 April 1994*, vol. 1. *Aegaeum* 12. Liège: Université de Liège.

Niemeyer, H. G. 1984. "Die Phoenizier und die Mittelmeerwelt in Zeitalter Homers." *JRGZM* 31: 3–94.

—. 1993. "Trade before the Flag? On Principles of Phoenician Expansion in the Mediterranean." In *Biblical Archaeology Today, 1990*, 335–44. Jerusalem: Israel Exploration Society.

North, D. C. 1968. "Sources of Productivity Change in Ocean Shipping, 1600–1850." *Journal of Political Economy* 76: 953–70.

—. 1985. "Transactions Costs in History." *Journal of European Economic History* 14: 557–76.

Nougayrol, J. 1955. *Le palais royal d'Ugarit*. Vol. 3, *Textes accadiens et hourrites des archives est, oest et centrales*. Paris: Imprimerie Nationale.

Nowag, W. 1983. *Raub und Beute in der archaischen Zeit der Griechen*. Frankfurt: Haag and Hercher.

Nowicki, K. 1990. "The West Siteia Mountains at the Turn of the Bronze and Iron Ages." *Aegaeum* 6: 161–82. Liège: Université de Liège.

—. 1994. "A Dark Age Refuge Centre near Pefki, Crete." *BSA* 89: 235-68.

Oates, J. 1986. *Babylon*. Rev. ed. London: Thames and Hudson.

O'Connor, D. 1983. "New Kingdom and Third Intermediate Period, 1552–664 B.C." In B. Trigger et al., *Ancient Egypt: A Social History*, 183–278. Cambridge: Cambridge University Press.

Oded, B. 1974. "The Phoenician Cities and the Assyrian Empire in the Time of Tiglath-Pilesar III." *ZDPV* 90: 38–49.

—. 1979. *Mass Deportations and Deportees in the Neo-Assyrian Empire*. Wiesbaden: Dr. Ludwig Reichert.

Ohly, D. 1953. *Griechische Goldbleche des 8. Jahrhunderts v. Chr*. Berlin: Gebr. Mann.

—. 1959. "Zur Rekonstruktion des samischen Geräts mit dem Elfenbeinjüngling." *AM* 74: 48–56.

—. 1967. "Neue Holzfunde aus dem Heraion von Samos: Befund und Rekonstruktion der Herastatuette." *AM* 82: 89–99.

Oppenheim, A. L. 1967. "Essay on Overland Trade in the First Millennium B.C." *JCS* 21: 236–54.

—. 1977. *Ancient Mesopotamia*. Rev. ed. Chicago: University of Chicago Press.

Orlandini, P., and D. Adamesteanu. 1956. "Gela–Ritrovamenti vari." *NSc* 10, ser. 8: 203–401.

Ormerod, H. A. 1924. *Piracy in the Ancient World*. London: Hodder and Stoughton.

Ormerod, H. A., and M. Cary. 1932. "Rome and the East." *CAH*, vol. 9: 350–96.

Orsi, P. 1906. "Gela. Scavi del 1900–1905." *MonAnt* 17: 5–763.

Osborne, R. 1987. *Classical Landscape with Figures*. Dobbs Ferry, N.Y.: Sheridan House.

—. 1996. "Pots, Trade and the Archaic Greek Economy." *Antiquity* 70: 31–44.

Palaima, T. G. 1991. "Maritime Matters in the Linear B Tablets." In R. Laffineur and L. Basch, eds., *Thalassa, l'Égée préhistorique et la mer*, Aegaeum 7, 273–310. Liège: Université de Liège.

Palmer, R. 1989. "The Role of Direct Exchange in the Mycenaean Palace Economy." *AJA* 93: 272.

Pålsson Hallager, B. 1983. "A New Social Class in Late Bronze Age Crete: Foreign Merchants in Khania." In O. Krzyszkowska and L. Nixon, eds., *Minoan Society*, 111–19. Bristol: Bristol Classical Press.

—. 1985. "Crete and Italy in the Late Bronze III Period." *AJA* 93: 293–305.

Papadakis, N., and B. Rutkowski. 1985. "New Research at Skales Cave near Praisos." *BSA* 80: 129–37.

Papadopoulos, T. J. 1988. "The Dodecanese and the Western Peloponnese in the Late Bronze Age: Some Thoughts on the Problem of Their Relations." In S. Dietz and I. Papachristodoulou, eds., *Archaeology in the Dodecanese*, 73–75. Copenhagen: National Museum of Denmark, Department of Near Eastern and Classical Antiquities.

Papadoupoulos, T. J., and R. E. Jones. 1980. "Rodiaca in Achaea." *OpAth* 13: 225–35.

Papavasiliou, G. A. 1912. "Ἱερὸν Διοσκούρων Καβείρων παρὰ τὴν Χαλκίδα." *Prakt*: 145–53.

Pâris, J. 1916. "Contributions a l'étude des ports antiques du monde grec II: Les établissements maritimes de Délos." *BCH* 40: 5–73.

Parke, H. W. 1970. "Mercenaries (Greek and Hellenistic)." *OCD*, 2d ed.: 672–73.

Parker, A. J. 1992. *Ancient Shipwrecks of the Mediterranean and the Roman Provinces*. BAR-IS 580. Oxford: Tempus Reparatus.

Patton, W. R., trans. 1922, 1923. Polybius, *The Histories*. Vol. 2, *Books III–IV*, Vol. 3, *Books V–VIII*. Loeb Classical Library. Cambridge, Mass.: Harvard University Press.

Payne, H.G.G. 1927–28. "Early Greek Vases from Knossos." *BSA* 29: 224–98.

—. 1928. Review of *Exploration archéologique de Delos*, vol. 10, *Les vases de l'Heraion*, by C. Dugas. *JHS* 48: 274.

—. 1931a. "Hellenic Cretan" and "Protocorinthian, Corinthian and Italo-Corinthian." In J. D. Beazley, H.G.G. Payne, and E. R. Price, *CVA Great Britain 9: Oxford, Ashmolean Museum*, Fasc. 2 (Text): 53–57, 59–74. Oxford: Clarendon.

—. 1931b. *Necrocorinthia: A Study of Corinthian Art in the Archaic Period*. Oxford: Clarendon.

—. 1932. "Archaeology in Greece, 1931–32." *JHS* 52: 236–55.

—. 1933a. "Archaeology in Greece, 1932–33." *JHS* 53: 266–99.

—. 1933b. *Protokorinthische Vasenmalerei*. Berlin: Heinrich Keller.

Payne, H.G.G., et al. 1940. *Perachora: The Sanctuaries of Hera Akraia and Limenia: Excavations of the British School of Archaeology at Athens 1930–1933*. Vol. 1, *Architecture, Bronzes, Terracottas*. Oxford: Clarendon.

Payne, S. 1973. "Kill-Off Patterns in Sheep and Goats: The Mandibles from Aşvan Kale." *AnatSt* 23: 281–303.

Pearson, G. W., and M. Stuiver. 1986. "High-Precision Calibration of the Radiocarbon Time Scale, 500–2500 B.C." *Radiocarbon* 28: 839–62.

Pecorella, P. E., and L. Rocchetti. 1985. "The Italian Archaeological Mission at Ayia Irini." In V. Karageorghis, ed., *Archaeology in Cyprus 1960–1985*, 193–94. Nicosia: A. G. Leventis Foundation.

Pellegrini, G. 1903. "Tombe greche archaiche e tombe greco-sannitica a tholos della necropoli de Cuma." *MonAnt* 13: 201–94.

Peltenburg, E. J. 1969. "Al Mina Glazed Pottery and Its Relations." *Levant* 1: 73–96.

—. 1986. "Ramesside Egypt and Cyprus." In V. Karageorghis, ed., *Acts of the International Archaeological Symposium "Cyprus between Orient and Occident,"* 149–79. Nicosia: Department of Antiquities, Cyprus.

Pemberton, E. G. 1989. *Corinth*. Vol. 18:1, *The Sanctuary of Demeter and Kore: The Greek Pottery*. Princeton: American School of Classical Studies at Athens.

Pendlebury, H. W., J.D.S. Pendlebury, and M. B. Money-Coutts. 1935–36. "Excavations in the Plain of Lasithi, I: The Cave of Trapeza." *BSA* 36: 5–131.

—. 1937–38. "Excavations in the Plain of Lasithi, III: Karphi: A City of Refuge in the Early Iron Age of Crete." *BSA* 38: 57–145.

Pendlebury, J.D.S. 1930a. *Aegyptiaca: A Catalogue of Egyptian Objects Found in the Aegean Area*. Cambridge: Cambridge University Press.

—. 1930b. "Egypt and the Aegean in the Late Bronze Age." *JEA* 16: 75–92.

—. 1939. *The Archaeology of Crete*. London: Methuen.

Pendlebury, J.D.S., E. Eccles, and M. B. Money-Coutts. 1932–33. "Journeys in Crete, 1934." *BSA* 33: 80–100.

Pennas, H. 1992. "Point Iria Wreck." *ENALIA Annual 1990*, 2: 39–41.

Pennas, H., and Y. Vichos. 1996a. "Point Iria Wreck (1992) I: Exploratory Survey." *ENALIA Annual 1992*, 4: 4.

—. 1996b. "Point Iria Wreck (1993) I: Excavation and Results." *ENALIA Annual 1992*, 4: 6–16.

Perdrizet, P. 1897. "Sur la mitré homérique." *BCH* 21: 169–83.

—. 1908. *Monuments figurés: Petits bronzes, terres cuites, antiquités diverses*. FdD 5. Paris: Thorin et Fils.

Perlman, I. 1973. "Discussion." In *Acts of the International Archaeological Symposium "The Mycenaeans in the Eastern Mediterranean,"* 334. Nicosia: Department of Antiquities, Cyprus.

Perloff, H. S., E. S. Dunn, Jr., E. E. Lampard, and R. F. Muth. 1960. *Regions, Resources and Economic Growth*. Baltimore: The Johns Hopkins University Press.

Perrin, B., trans. 1917. Plutarch, *The Parallel Lives*. Vol. 5, *Agesilaus and Pompey, Pelopidas and Marcellus*. Loeb Classical Library. London: William Heinemann.

Persson, A. W. 1942. *New Tombs at Dendra Near Midea*. Skrifter Utgivna av Kungl. Humanistiska Vetenskopssamfundet i Lund 24. Lund: C.W.K. Gleerup.

Petruso, K. M. 1984. "Prolegomena to Late Cypriot Weight Metrology." *AJA* 88: 293–304.

—. 1992. *Keos*. Vol. 8, *Ayi Irini: The Balance Weights: An Analysis of Weight Measurement in Prehistoric Crete and the Cycladic Islands*. Mainz: Philipp von Zabern.

Pfuhl, E. 1903. "Der archaische Friedhof am Stadtberge von Thera." *AM* 28: 1–273.

—. 1923. *Malerei und Zeichnung der Griechen*. Vol. 1. Munich: F. Bruckmann.

Philipp, H. 1981. *Bronzeschmuck aus Olympia*. Ol-Forsch XIII. Berlin: Walter de Gruyter.

Phillips, J. S. 1991. "The Impact and Implications of the Egyptian and 'Egyptianizing' Material Found in Bronze Age Crete, ca. 3000–ca. 1100 B.C." Ph.D. diss., Department of Egyptian Archaeology, University of Toronto.

Phillips, R. C., and E. G. Meñez. 1988. *Seagrasses*. Smithsonian Contributions to the Marine Sciences 34. Washington, D.C.: Smithsonian Institution Press.

Pieridou, A. 1973. Ὁ Πρωτογεωμετρικὸς Ρυθμὸς ἐν Κύπρῳ. Athens: Athenais Archaiologikes Hetaireias.

Pilali-Papasteriou, A. 1985. *Die bronzenen Tierfiguren aus Kreta*. Prähistorische Bronzefunde 1.3. Munich: C. H. Beck.

Pini, I. 1990. "Some Considerations on the Use of Seals for Administrative Purposes in Mycenaean Greece." *SMEA* 28: 107–16.

Platon, N. 1956. "Ἀνασκαφὴ μινωικῆς ἀγροικίας εις Ζοῦ Σητείας." *Prakt* 232–40.

Ploug, G. 1973. *Sukas II: The Aegean, Corinthian and Eastern Greek Pottery and Terracottas*. Copenhagen: Munksgaard.

Pohl, H. 1993. *Die römische Politik und die Piraterie im östlichen Mittelmeer vom 3. bis zum 1. Jh. v. Chr.* Berlin: Walter de Gruyter.

Poidebard, A. 1939. *Un grand port disparu, Tyr: Recherches aériennes et sous-marines 1934–1936*. Paris: Paul Geuthner.

Poidebard, A., and J. Lauffray. 1951. *Sidon: Aménagements antiques du port de Saida. Étude aerienne au sol et sous-marine 1946–50*. Beirut: République Libanaise Ministère des Travaux Publics.

Pomerance, L. 1973. "The Possible Role of Tomb Robbers and Viziers of the 18th Dynasty in Confusing Minoan Chronology." In *Antichità cretesi: Studi in onore di Doro Levi*, 1: 21–30. Catania: Università di Catania, Istituto di Archeologia.

Popham, M. R. 1978. "An Early Euboean Ship." *OJA* 6: 353–59.

—. 1979a. "Connections between Crete and Cyprus between 1300–1100 B.C." In *Acts of the International Archaeological Symposium "The Relations between Cyprus and Crete, ca. 2000–500 B.C.,"* 178–91. Nicosia: Department of Antiquities, Cyprus.

—. 1979b. "Discussion" [following K. Nicolaou, "Minoan Survivals in Geometric and Archaic Cyprus]. In *Acts of the International Archaeological Symposium "The Relations between Cyprus and Crete, ca. 2000–500 B.C.,"* 318. Nicosia: Department of Antiquities, Cyprus.

—, ed. 1984. *The Minoan Unexplored Mansion at Knossos*. BSA suppl. 17. London: Thames and Hudson.

—. 1995. "An Engraved Near Eastern Bronze Bowl from Lefkandi." *OJA* 14: 103–7.

Popham, M. R., A. M. Pollard, and H. Hatcher. 1983. "Euboean Exports to Al Mina, Cyprus, and Crete: A Reassessment." *BSA* 78: 281–90.

Popham, M. R., and L. H. Sackett. 1968. *Excavations at Lefkandi, 1964–66: A Preliminary Report*. London: Thames and Hudson.

Popham, M. R., and L. H. Sackett, with P. G. Themelis, eds. 1979. *Lefkandi*. Vol. 1, *The Iron Age: Plates*. BSA suppl. 11. London: Thames and Hudson.

—. 1980. *Lefkandi*. Vol. 1, *The Iron Age: Text*. BSA suppl. 11. London: Thames and Hudson.

Popham, M. R., L. H. Sackett, and P. G. Themelis. 1980. "The Tombs, Pyres and Their Contents." In M. R. Popham and L. H. Sackett, with P. G. Themelis, eds., *Lefkandi*, vol. 1, *The Iron Age*, BSA suppl. 11, 109–96. London: Thames and Hudson.

Popham, M. R., E. Touloupa, and L. H. Sackett. 1982. "Further Excavation of the Toumba Cemetery at Lefkandi, 1981." *BSA* 77: 213–48.

Popham, M. R., L. H. Sackett, L. H. Jeffrey, H. W. Catling, and E. A. Catling. 1980. "The Other Finds." In M. R. Popham, and L. H. Sackett, with P. G. Themelis, eds., *Lefkandi*, vol. 1, *The Iron Age*, BSA suppl. 11, 81–97. London: Thames and Hudson.

Porada, E. 1956. "A Lyre Player from Tarsus and his Relations." In S. S. Weinberg, ed., *The Aegean and the Near East: Studies Presented to Hetty Goldman*, 185–211. Locust Valley, N.Y.: J. J. Augustin.

—. 1965. "Cylinder Seals from Thebes." *AJA* 69: 173.

—. 1966. "Further Notes on the Cylinders from Thebes." *AJA* 70: 194.

Posener, G. 1957. "Les asiatiques en Égypte sous les XIIe et XIIIe dynasties." *Syria* 34: 145–63.

Posner, R. A. 1980. "A Theory of Primitive Society, with Special Reference to Law." *Journal of Law and Economics* 23: 1–53.

Postgate, J. N. 1979. "The Economic Structure of

the Assyrian Empire." In M. T. Larsen, ed., *Power and Propaganda: A Symposium on Ancient Empire*, 193–221. Copenhagen: Akademisk Förlag.

—. 1992. *Early Mesopotamia: Society and Economy at the Dawn of History*. New York: Routledge.

Poulson, F., and C. Dugas. 1911. "Vases archaïques de Délos." *BCH* 35: 350–422.

Powell, M. A. 1977. "Sumerian Merchants and the Problem of Profit." *Iraq* 39: 23–29.

—. 1989. "Masse und Gewichte." *RLA* 7: 457–517.

Pritchett, W. K. 1956. "The Attic Stelai, Part II." *Hesperia* 25: 178–317.

—. 1980. *Studies in Ancient Greek Topography*. Vol. 3. University of California Publications in Classical Studies 22. Berkeley: University of California Press.

—. 1991. *The Greek State at War*. Vol. 5. Berkeley: University of California Press.

Puech, É. 1981. "L'ivoire inscrit d'Arslan-Tash et les rois de Damas." *RBibl* 88: 544–62.

—. 1983. "Présence phénicienne dans les îles à la fin du IIe millénaire." *RBibl* 90: 365–95.

Pulak, C. 1988. "The Bronze Age Shipwreck at Ulu Burun, Turkey: 1985 Campaign." *AJA* 92: 1–38.

Quilici, L. 1985. "La mission italienne a Ayia Irini (Kyrenia)." In V. Karageorghis, ed., *Archaeology in Cyprus 1960–1985*, 182–92. Nicosia: A. G. Leventis Foundation.

Quiller, B. 1981. "The Dynamics of the Homeric Society." *SymbOslo* 56: 109–55.

Raban, A. 1984. "The Thera Ships: Another Interpretation." *AJA* 88: 11–19.

—. 1987. "The Harbor of the Sea Peoples at Dor." *BiblArch* 50: 118–26.

—. 1988. "The Constructive Maritime Role of the Sea Peoples in the Levant." In M. Heltzer and E. Lipiński, eds., *Society and Economy in the Eastern Mediterranean (c. 1500–1000 B.C.)*, Orientalia Lovaniensia Analecta 23, 261–94. Leuven: Peeters.

—. 1990. "Man-Integrated Coastal Changes along the Israeli Shore of the Mediterranean in Ancient Times." In S. Bottema, G. Entjes-Nieborg, and W. van Zeist, eds., *Man's Role in the Shaping of the Eastern Mediterranean Landscape*, 101–11. Rotterdam: A. A. Balkema.

—. 1991. "Minoan and Canaanite Harbours." In R. Laffineur and L. Basch, eds., *Thalassa, l'Égée préhistorique et la mer*, Aegaeum 7, 129–47. Liège: Buteneers.

Raban, A., and E. Galili. 1985. "Recent Maritime Archaeological Research–A Preliminary Report." *IJNA* 14: 321–56.

Rasmussen, E. 1977. "The Wasting Disease of Eelgrass (*Zostera marina*) and Its Effects on Environmental Factors and Fauna." In C. P. McRoy and C. Helfferich, eds., *Seagrass Ecosystems: A Scientific Perspective*, 1–51. New York: Marcel Dekker.

Rathje, A. 1976. "A Group of 'Phoenician' Faience Anthropomorphic Perfume Flasks." *Levant* 8: 96–106.

Ray, D. J. 1992. Review of *Centuries of Darkness*, by P. James. *JHS* 112: 213–14.

Re, L. 1986. "Presenze micenee in Anatolia." In M. Marazzi, S. Tusa, and L. Vagnetti, eds., *Traffici micenei nel Mediterraneo: Problemi storici e documentazione archeologia*, Magna Graecia 3, 343–65. Taranto: Istituto per la Storica e l'Archeologia della Magna Grecia.

Reber, K. 1991. *Untersuchungen zur handgemachten Keramik Griechenlands in der submykenischen, protogeometrischen und der geometrischen Zeit*. SIMAL P-b 105. Jonsered: Paul Åströms Förlag.

Redfield, J. M. 1986. "The Development of the Market in Archaic Greece." In B. L. Anderson and A.J.H. Latham, eds., *The Market in History*, 29–58. London: Croom Helm.

Redford, D. B. 1992. *Egypt, Canaan and Israel in Ancient Times*. Princeton: Princeton University Press.

Reed, C. M. 1984. "Maritime Traders in the Archaic Greek World." *AncW* 10: 31–43.

Reed, N. B. 1976. "Griffins in Post-Minoan Cretan Art." *Hesperia* 45: 365–79.

Reese, D. S. 1982. "Recent and Fossil Shells from Tomb XVII, Gypsades Cemetery, Knossos, Crete." *BSA* 77: 249–50.

—. 1987. "Palaikastro Shells and Bronze Age Purple Dye Production in the Mediterranean Basin." *BSA* 82: 201–6.

Reheja, G. G. 1988. *The Poison in the Gift*. Chicago: University of Chicago Press.

Reisner, G. A., C. S. Fisher, and D. G. Lyon. 1924. *Harvard Excavations at Samaria, 1908–1910*. 2 vols. Cambridge, Mass.: Harvard University Press.

Renfrew, C. 1972. *The Emergence of Civilization: The Cyclades and the Aegean in the Third Millennium B.C.* London: Methuen.

—. 1975. "Trade as Action at a Distance: Questions of Integration and Communication." In

J. A. Sabloff and C. C. Lamberg-Karlovsky, eds., *Ancient Civilization and Trade*, 3–59. Santa Fe: University of New Mexico Press.

—. 1977. "Alternative Models for Exchange and Spatial Distribution." In T. K. Earle and J. E. Ericson, eds., *Exchange Systems in Prehistory*, 71–90. New York: Academic Press.

—. 1986a. "Varna and the Emergence of Wealth in Prehistoric Europe." In A. Appadurai, ed., *The Social Life of Things: Commodities in Cultural Perspective*, 141–68. Cambridge: Cambridge University Press.

—. 1986b. "Introduction: Peer Polity Interaction and Socio-Political Change." In C. Renfrew and J. F. Cherry, eds., *Peer Polity Interaction and Socio-Political Change*, 1–18. Cambridge: Cambridge University Press.

Renfrew, C., and J. F. Cherry. 1985. "The Other Finds." In C. Renfrew, ed., *The Archaeology of Cult: The Sanctuary at Phylakopi*, BSA suppl. 18, 299–359. London: Thames and Hudson.

Reyes, A. T. 1994. *Archaic Cyprus: A Study of the Textual and Archaeological Evidence*. Oxford: Clarendon.

Reynolds, L. G. 1985. *Economic Growth in the Third World, 1850-1950*. New Haven: Yale University Press.

Ridgway, B. 1977. *The Archaic Style in Greek Sculpture*. Princeton: Princeton University Press.

Ridgway, D. 1990. "The First Western Greeks and Their Neighbors, 1935–1985." In J.-P. Descoeudres, ed., *Greek Colonists and Native Populations*, 61–72. Oxford: Clarendon.

—. 1992a. "Demaratus and His Predecessors." In G. Köpcke and I. Tokumaru, eds., *Greece between East and West: 10th–8th Centuries B.C.*, 85–92. Mainz: Philipp von Zabern.

—. 1992b. *The First Western Greeks*. Cambridge: Cambridge University Press.

—. 1995. "Archaeology in Sardinia and South Italy, 1989–94." *AR* 41: 75–96.

Riis, P. J. 1969. "The First Greeks in Phoenicia and Their Settlement at Sukas." *Ugaritica* 6: 435–50. Paris: Librairie Orientaliste Paul Geuthner.

—. 1970. *Sukas I: The North-East Sanctuary and the First Settling of Greeks in Syria and Palestine*. Copenhagen: Munksgaard.

Rizza, G., and V. Santa Maria Scrinari. 1968. *Il santuario sull'acropoli di Gortina*. Monografie della Scuola Archeologia di Atene e della

Missioni Italina in Oriente 2. Rome: Istituto Poligrafico della Stato.

Rizzo, M. A. 1984. "Arkades." In *Creta Antica: Cento anni di archeologia italiana (1884–1984)*, 257–63. Rome: De Luca.

Robinson, M. 1955. "Gold Ornaments from Crete and Ithaca." *BSA* 50: 37.

Rocchetti, L. 1974–75. "La ceramica dell'abitato geometrico di Festòs a occidente del palasso minoico." *ASAtene*, n.s. 52–53: 169–300.

—. 1988–89. "La ceramica della necropoli di Curtes." *ASAtene*, n.s. 66–67: 173–257.

Roebuck, C. 1951. "The Organization of Naukratis." *CP* 46: 212–20.

—. 1959. *Ionian Trade and Colonization*. Archaeological Institute of America and the College Art Association of America, Monographs on Archaeology and Fine Arts 9. New York: Archaeological Institute of America.

Roeder, G. 1956. *Ägyptische Bronzefiguren: Staatliche Museum zu Berlin, Mitteilungen aus der ägyptischen Sammlung*. Vol. 6. Berlin: Staatliche Museum zu Berlin.

Rolley, C. 1969. *Les statuettes*. FdD V: 2. Paris: E. de Boccard.

—. 1973. "Bronzes géométrique et orientaux a Délos." In *Études Deliennes*, BCH suppl. 1, 491–524. Paris: E. de Boccard.

—. 1977. *Les trépieds à cuve clouée*. FdD V: 3. Paris: E. de Boccard.

—. 1986. *Greek Bronzes*. Translated by R. Howell. London: Sotheby's.

Röllig, W. 1983. "On the Origins of the Phoenicians." *Berytus* 31: 79–93.

—. 1992. "Asia Minor as a Bridge between East and West: The Role of the Phoenicians and Aramaeans in the Transfer of Culture." In G. Köpcke and I. Tokumoru, eds., *Greece between East and West: 10th–8th Centuries B.C.*, 93–102. Mainz: Philipp von Zabern.

Rosati, R., ed. 1989. *La ceramica attica nel Mediterraneo. Analisi computerizzata della diffusione le fasi iniziali (630–560 a.C.)*. Bologna: Cooperativa Libraria Universitaria Editrice Bologna.

Rosen, R. M. 1990. "Poetry and Sailing in Hesiod's Works and Days." *ClAnt* 9: 99–113.

Rosen, S. 1987. "Dynamic Animal Economics." *American Journal of Agricultural Economics* 69: 547–57.

Rosen, S., K. M. Murphy, and J. A. Scheinkman. 1994. "Cattle Cycles." *Journal of Political Economy* 102: 468–92.

Rossi-Danielli, L. 1914. "Vetralla–Necropoli di Poggio Montano." *NSc* 11: 298–352.

Rowlands, M. J. 1971. "The Archaeological Interpretation of Prehistoric Metalworking." *WorldArch* 3: 210–24.

Ruckert, A. 1976. *Frühe Keramik böotiens: Form und Dekoration der Vasen des späten 8. und frühen 7. Jahrhunderts v. Chr.* AntK-BH 10. Bern: Franke.

Rumpf, A. 1933. "Zu den klazomenenischen Denkmälern." *JdI* 48: 53–83.

Runnels, C. N. 1985. "Trade and the Demand for Millstones in Southern Greece in the Neolithic and the Early Bronze Age." In A. B. Knapp and T. Stech, eds., *Prehistoric Production and Exchange: The Aegean and Eastern Mediterranean*, Institute of Archaeology Monograph 25, 30–43. Los Angeles: University of California at Los Angeles.

Runnels, C. N., and T. H. van Andel. 1987. "The Evolution of Settlement in the Southern Argolid, Greece: An Economic Explanation." *Hesperia* 56: 303–34.

Rutkowski, B., and K. Nowicki. 1985. "Report on Investigations in Greece, III: Studies in 1984." *Archeologia* (Warsaw) 36: 119–29.

Rutter, J. 1992. "Cultural Novelties in the Post-Palatial Aegean World: Indices of Vitality or Decline?" In W. A. Ward and M. S. Joukowsky, eds., *The Crisis Years: The 12th Century B.C.: From beyond the Danube to the Tigris*, 61–78. Dubuque, Iowa: Kendall/Hunt.

Ryan, W.B.F. 1972. "Stratigraphy of Late Quaternary Sediments in the Eastern Mediterranean." In D. J. Stanley, ed., *The Mediterranean Sea: A Natural Sedimentation Laboratory*, 149–69. Stroudsburg, Pa.: Dowden, Hutchinson and Ross.

Sackett, L. H. 1972–73. "The Unexplored Mansion at Knossos: A Preliminary Report on the Excavations from 1967 to 1972. Part II: Post-Minoan Occupation above the Unexplored Mansion." *AR* 19: 62–71.

Sader, H. 1992. "The 12th Century B.C. in Syria: The Problem of the Rise of the Aramaeans." In W. A. Ward and M. S. Joukowsky, eds., *The Crisis Years: The 12th Century B.C.: From beyond the Danube to the Tigris*, 157–63. Dubuque, Iowa: Kendall/Hunt.

Sage, E. T., trans. 1958. Livy, *History of Rome (Ab Urbe Condita)*. Vol. 10, *Books XXI–XXXVI*. Loeb Classical Library. Cambridge, Mass.: Harvard University Press.

Saggs, H.W.F. 1955. "The Nimrud Letters, 1952, Part II." *Iraq* 17: 126–54.

—. 1967. "The Nimrud Letters, 1952, Part VI." *Iraq* 25: 70–80.

—. 1984. *The Might That Was Assyria*. London: Sidgwick and Jackson.

—. 1988. *The Greatness That Was Babylon*. Rev. ed. London: Sidgwick and Jackson.

Sahlins, M. D. 1960a. "Political Power and the Economy in Primitive Society." In G. E. Dole and R. L. Carneiro, eds., *Essays in the Science of Culture in Honor of Leslie A. White*, 390–415. New York: Crowell.

—. 1960b. "Production, Distribution and Power in a Primitive Society." In A.F.C. Wallace, ed., *Men and Cultures: Selected Papers of the Fifth International Congress of Anthropological and Ethnological Sciences*, 495–500. Philadelphia: University of Pennsylvania Press.

—. 1963. "Poor Man, Rich Man, Big-Man, Chief: Political Types in Melanesia and Polynesia." *Comparative Studies in History and Society* 5: 285–303.

—. 1968. *Tribesmen*. Englewood Cliffs, N.J.: Prentice-Hall.

—. 1972. *Stone Age Economics*. Chicago: Aldine.

Sakellarakis, J. 1974. "Le thème du pêcheur dans l'art préhistorique de l'Égée." *AAA* 7: 370–90.

—. 1983. "Ἀνασκαφὴ Ἰδαίου Ἄντρου." *Prakt* 415–500.

—. 1984. "Ἀνασκαφὴ Ἰδαίου Ἄντρου." *Prakt* 507–99.

—. 1987. "Ἑκατὸ χρόνια στὸ Ἰδαῖου Ἄντρου." *ArchEph* 126: 237–63.

—. 1988a. "Some Geometric and Archaic Votives from the Idaean Cave." In R. Hägg, N. Marinatos, and G. C. Nordquist, eds., "Early Greek Cult Practice," *SkrAth* 4, 38: 173–93. Stockholm: Paul Åströms Förlag.

—. 1988b. "The Idaean Cave: Minoan and Greek Worship." *Kernos* 1: 207–14.

—. 1992. "The Idaean Cave Ivories." In J. L. Fitton, ed., *Ivory in Greece and the Eastern Mediterranean from the Bronze Age to the Hellenistic Period*, British Museum Occasional Paper 85, 113–40. London: Trustees of the British Museum.

—. 1993. "Ivory Trade in the Aegean in the 8th Century B.C.E." In *Biblical Archaeology Today, 1990*, 345–66. Jerusalem: Israel Exploration Society.

Saldern, A. von. 1959. "Glass Finds at Gordion." *JGS* 1: 23–49.

—. 1970. "Other Mesopotamian Glass Vessels (1500–600 B.C.)." In A. von Saldern et al., *Glass and Glassmaking in Ancient Mesopotamia*, 201–29. London: Associated University Presses.

Sallares, R. 1991. *The Ecology of the Ancient Greek World*. Ithaca, N.Y.: Cornell University Press.

Salmon, J. B. 1984. *Wealthy Corinth*. Oxford: Clarendon.

Sams, G. K. 1974. "Phrygian Painted Animals: Anatolian Orientalizing Art." *AnatSt* 24: 169–96.

Samuelson, P. A. 1983. "Thünen at Two Hundred." *Journal of Economic Literature* 21: 1468–88.

Sandars, N. K. 1987. *The Sea Peoples*. Rev. ed. London: Thames and Hudson.

Sanders, G.D.R. 1984. "Reassessing Ancient Populations." *BSA* 79: 251–62.

Sanders, I. F. 1982. *Roman Crete*. Warminster: Aris and Phillips.

Sapouna-Sakellarakis, E. 1978. *Die Fibeln der griechischen Inseln*. Prähistorische Bronzefunde 14.4. Munich: C. H. Beck.

Sapouna-Sakellarakis, E., and J. Sakellarakis. 1984. "The Keftiu and the Minoan Thalassocracy." In R. Hägg and N. Marinatos, eds., *The Minoan Thalassocracy: Myth and Reality*, Acta Instituti Atheniensis Regni Sueciae, Series in 4°, 32, 197–203. Stockholm: Paul Åströms Förlag.

Sasson, J. M. 1966. "Canaanite Maritime Involvement in the Second Millennium B.C." *JAOS* 86: 126–37.

Säve-Söderbergh, T. 1946. *The Navy of the Eighteenth Egyptian Dynasty*. Uppsala Universitets Årsskrift 1946: 6. Uppsala: Almqvist and Wiksells.

Schachermeyr, F. 1979. *Die ägäische Frühzeit: Die Ausgrabungen und ihre Ergebnisse für unser Geschichtsbild*. Vol. 3, *Kreta zur Zeit der Wanderung, vom Ausgang der minoischen Ära bis zum Dorisierung der Insel*. Vienna: Österreichischen Akademie der Wissenschaften.

Schaeffer, C.F.A. 1973. "Discussion." In *Acts of the International Archaeological Symposium "The Mycenaeans in the Eastern Mediterranean,"* 327–29. Nicosia: Department of Antiquities, Cyprus.

Schäfer, J. 1991. "Amnisos–Harbor-town of Minos?" In R. Laffineur and L. Basch, eds., *Thalassa, l'Égée préhistorique et la mer*, Aegaeum 7, 111–16. Liège: Buteneers.

—, ed. 1992. *Amnisos: Nach den archäologischen, historischen und epigraphischen Zeugnissen des Altertums und der Neuzeit*. Berlin: Gebr. Mann.

Schaus, G. P. 1985. *The Extramural Sanctuary of Demeter and Persephone at Cyrene, Libya*. Vol. 2, *The East Greek, Island, and Laconian Pottery*. Philadelphia: The University Museum, University of Pennsylvania.

Schefold, K. 1966. *Myth and Legend in Early Greek Art*. Translated by A. Hicks. London: Thames and Hudson.

Schiering, W. 1968. "Landwirtschaftliche Geräte." In W. Richter, *Die Landwirtschaft im homerischen Zeitalter*, ArchHom Bd. II, Kap. H, 147–58. Göttingen: Vandenhoeck and Ruprecht.

Schofield, E. 1982. "The Western Cyclades and Crete: A 'Special Relationship.'" *OJA* 1: 9–25.

Schofield, L., and R. B. Parkinson. 1994. "Of Helmets and Heretics: A Possible Egyptian Representation of Mycenaean Warriors on a Papyrus from el-Amarna." *BSA* 89: 157–70.

Schürmann, W. 1996. *Die Tierstatuetten aus Metal. Das Heiligtum des Hermes und der Aphrodite in Syme Viannou*, vol. 2. Bibliotek der Archaologischen Gesellschaft zu Athen Bd. 159. Athens: Athenais Archailogiki Hetaireia.

Schweitzer, B. 1918. "Untersuchengen zur Chronologie und Geschichte der geometrischen Stile in Griechenland II." *AM* 43: 1–152.

—. 1971. *Greek Geometric Art*. Translated by P. and C. Usborne. London: Phaidon.

Seeden, H. 1980. *The Standing Armed Figurines in the Levant*. Prähistorische Bronzefunde 1.1. Munich: C. H. Beck.

Seidl, U. 1988. "Urartu as a Bronzeworking Centre." In J. Curtis, ed., *Bronzeworking Centres of Western Asia, c. 1000–539 B.C.*, 169–75. London: Kegan Paul.

Seiradaki, M. 1960. "Pottery from Karphi." *BSA* 55: 1–37.

Semple, E. C. 1916. "Pirate Coasts of the Mediterranean Sea." *Geographical Review* 2: 134–51.

Sen, A. K. 1981a. "Ingredients of Famine Analysis: Availability and Entitlements." *Quarterly Journal of Economics* 95: 433–64.

—. 1981b. *Poverty and Famines: An Essay on Entitlement and Deprivation*. Oxford: Clarendon.

Shaw, J. W. 1969. "A Foundation in the Inner Harbor at Lechaeum." *AJA* 73: 370–72.

—. 1979. "Excavations at Kommos (Crete) during 1978." *Hesperia* 48: 145–73.

—. 1980. "Excavations at Kommos (Crete) during 1979." *Hesperia* 49: 207–50.

—. 1981. "Excavations at Kommos (Crete) during 1980." *Hesperia* 50: 211–51.

—. 1982. "Excavations at Kommos (Crete) during 1981." *Hesperia* 51: 164–95.

—. 1984. "Excavations at Kommos (Crete) during 1982–1983." *Hesperia* 53: 251–87.

—. 1986. "Excavations at Kommos (Crete) during 1984–1985." *Hesperia* 55: 219–69.

—. 1989. "Phoenicians in Southern Crete." *AJA* 93: 165–83.

—. 1990. "Bronze Age Aegean Harbourworks." In D. A. Hardy et al., eds., *Thera and the Aegean World III*, 1: 420–36. London: Thera Foundation.

—. 1992. "Brief Summary of Excavations at Kommos, Crete, Season XVII (1992)." Mimeo. Pitsidia, Crete, August 20.

Shaw, J. W., and M. C. Shaw. 1993. "Excavations at Kommos (Crete) during 1986–1992." *Hesperia* 62: 129–90.

Shaw, M. C. 1985. "Late Minoan I Building J/T, and Late Minoan III Buildings N and P at Kommos: Their Nature and Possible Uses as Residences, Palaces, and/or Emporia." In *A Great Minoan Triangle in Southcentral Crete: Kommos, Hagia Triada, Phaistos*, Scripta Mediterranea 6: 19–30. Toronto: Society for Mediterranean Studies.

—. 1994. "Bull and Maze: A Minoan Fresco from Egypt." *AJA* 98: 331.

Shay, J. M., and T. Shay. 1978. "Modern Vegetation and Fossil Plant Remains." In G. Rapp and S. E. Aschenbrenner, eds., *Excavations at Nichoria in Southwest Greece*, vol. 1, *Site, Environs and Techniques*, 41–59. Minneapolis: University of Minnesota Press.

Shefton, B. B. 1979. *Die "rhodischen" Bronzekannen*. Marburger Studien zur Vor- und Frühgeschichte 2. Mainz: Philipp von Zabern.

Shelmerdine, C. W. 1985. *The Perfume Industry of Mycenaean Pylos*. SIMA-PB 34. Göteborg: Paul Åströms Förlag.

Shepherd, J. F., and G. M. Walton. 1972. *Shipping, Maritime Trade and the Economic Development of Colonial North America*. Cambridge: Cambridge University Press.

Sherratt, A., and S. Sherratt. 1991. "From Luxuries to Commodities: The Nature of Mediterranean Bronze Age Trading Systems." In N. H. Gale, ed., *Bronze Age Trade in the Mediterranean*, SIMA 90, 351–87. Jonsered: Paul Åströms Förlag.

Shipley, G. 1987. *A History of Samos, 800–188 B.C.* Oxford: Clarendon.

Sieveking, J., and R. Hackl, eds. 1912. *Die königliche Vasensammlung zu München*. Vol. 1, *Die älteren nichtattischen Vasen*. Munich: J. B. Obernetter.

Silberberg, E. 1987. *The Structure of Economics: A Mathematical Analysis*. New York: McGraw-Hill.

Singer, I. 1983. "Western Anatolia in the Thirteenth Century B.C. According to the Hittite Sources." *AnatSt* 33: 205–17.

—. 1988. "The Origin of the Sea People and Their Settlement on the Coast of Canaan." In M. Heltzer and E. Lipiński, eds., *Society and Economy in the Eastern Mediterranean (c. 1500–1000 B.C.)*, Orientalia Lovaniensia Analecta 23, 239–50. Leuven: Peeters.

Skia, A. N. 1898. "Παναρχαίας Ἐλευσινιακῆς νεκροπόλεως." *ArchEph* 29–122.

—. 1912. "Νεώτεραι ἀνασκαφαὶ ἐν τῇ παναρχαία Ἐλευσινιακῇ νεκροπόλει." *ArchEph* 1–39.

Skinner, F. G. 1967. *Weights and Measures: Their Ancient Origins and Their Development in Great Britain up to 1855*. London: Her Majesty's Stationery Office.

Skon-Jedele, N. J. 1994. "`Aigyptiaka': A Catalogue of Egyptian and Egyptianizing Objects Excavated from Greek Archaeological Sites, ca. 1100–525 B.C., with Historical Commentary." Ph.D. diss., Department of Ancient History, University of Pennsylvania.

Smith, A. 1937. *An Inquiry into the Nature and Causes of the Wealth of Nations*. New York: Random House. (Originally published 1776.)

Smith, T. R. 1987. *Mycenaean Trade and Interaction in the West Central Mediterranean 1600–1000 B.C.* BAR-IS 371. Oxford: British Archaeological Reports.

Smith, W., ed. 1873. *A Dictionary of Greek and Roman Geography*. Vol. 1. London: John Murray.

Smith, W. S. 1965. *Interconnections in the Ancient Near East*. New Haven: Yale University Press.

Smithson, E. L. 1961. "The Protogeometric Cemetery at Nea Ionia, 1949." *Hesperia* 30: 147–78.

—. 1968. "The Tomb of a Rich Athenian Lady, ca. 850 B.C." *Hesperia* 37: 77–116.

Snedecor, G. W., and W. G. Cochran. 1967. *Statistical Methods*. 6th ed. Ames: Iowa State University Press.

Snodgrass, A. M. 1964. *Early Greek Armour and Weapons from the End of the Bronze Age to 600 B.C.* Edinburgh: Edinburgh University Press.

—. 1965. "Barbarian Europe and Early Iron Age Greece." *PPS* 31: 229–40.

—. 1971. *The Dark Age of Greece.* Edinburgh: Edinburgh University Press.

—. 1974a. "An Historical Homeric Society?" *JHS* 94: 114–25.

—. 1974b. "Cretans in Arcadia." In *Antichità cretesi, studi in onore di Doro Levi*, 2: 196–201. Catania: Università di Catania, Instituto di Archeologia.

—. 1980. *Archaic Greece.* Berkeley: University of California Press.

—. 1982. "Cyprus and the Beginnings of Iron Technology in the Eastern Mediterranean." In J. D. Muhly, R. Maddin, and V. Karageorghis, eds., *Early Metallurgy in Cyprus, 4000–500 B.C.*, 285–95. Nicosia: Pierides Foundation.

—. 1983a. "Archaeology." In M. Crawford, ed., *Sources for Ancient History*, 137–84. Cambridge: Cambridge University Press.

—. 1983b. "Heavy Freight in Archaic Greece." In P. Garnsey, K. Hopkins, and C. R. Whittaker, eds., *Trade in the Ancient Economy*, 16–26. Berkeley: University of California Press.

—. 1983c. "The Greek Early Iron Age: A Reappraisal." *DHA* 9: 73–86.

—. 1987. *An Archaeology of Greece.* Berkeley: University of California Press.

—. 1991. "Bronze Age Exchange: A Minimalist Position." In N. H. Gale, ed., *Bronze Age Trade in the Mediterranean*, SIMA 90, 15–20. Jonsered: Paul Åströms Förlag.

Soles, J. S., and C. Davaras. 1995. "1994 Excavations at Mochlos, Crete." *AJA* 99: 312–13.

Stampoulidis, N. 1990a. "Eleutherna on Crete: An Interim Report on the Geometric-Archaic Cemetery." *BSA* 85: 375–403.

—. 1990b. "Γεωμετρική 'ομηρική ταφική πυρά στην Ελεύθερνα." In *Πεπραγμένα τοῦ στ᾽ Διεθνοῦς Κρητολογικοῦ Συνεδρίου (6th Cretological Congress), Τόμος* A2: *Τμῆμα 'Αρχαιολόγικο*, 289–98. Chania.

—. 1992. "Four Ivory Heads from the Geometric/Archaic Cemetery at Eleutherna." In J. L. Fitton, ed., *Ivory in Greece and the Eastern Mediterranean from the Bronze Age to the Hellenistic Period*, British Museum Occasional Paper 85, 141–61. London: Trustees of the British Museum.

Starr, C. G. 1977. *The Economic and Social Growth of Early Greece 800–500 B.C.* New York: Oxford University Press.

Stech-Wheeler, T., J. D. Muhly, K. R. Maxwell-Hyslop, and R. Maddin. 1981. "Iron at Taanach and Early Iron Metallurgy in the Eastern Mediterranean." *AJA* 85: 245–68.

Stefani, E. 1916. "Antichi sepoleri in Terni." *NSc* 13: 191–226.

Steffy, J. R. 1985. "The Kyrenia Ship: An Interim Report on Its Hull Construction." *AJA* 89: 71–101.

—. 1991. "The Ram and Bow Timbers: A Structural Interpretation." In L. Casson and J. R. Steffy, eds., *The Athlit Ram*, Nautical Archaeology Series 3, 6–39. College Station: Texas A & M University Press.

—. 1994. *Wooden Ship Building and the Interpretation of Shipwrecks.* College Station: Texas A & M University Press.

Stern, E. 1990. "New Evidence from Dor for the First Appearance of the Phoenicians along the North Coast of Israel." *BASOR* 279: 27–34.

—. 1993. "The Renewal of Trade in the Eastern Mediterranean in Iron Age I." In *Biblical Archaeology Today, 1990*, 325–34. Jerusalem: Israel Exploration Society.

Stewart, A. 1990. *Greek Sculpture.* New Haven: Yale University Press.

Stieglitz, R. R. 1984. "The Ugaritic Inscription from Hala Sultan Tekke." *OpAth* 15: 193.

—. 1990. "The Geopolitics of the Phoenician Littoral in the Early Iron Age." *BASOR* 279: 9–12.

Stillwell, A. N. 1948. *Corinth.* Vol. 15: 1, *The Potters' Quarter.* Princeton: American School of Classical Studies at Athens.

Stillwell, A. N., and J. L. Benson. 1984. *Corinth.* Vol. 15: 3, *The Potters' Quarter: The Pottery.* Princeton: American School of Classical Studies at Athens.

Stos-Gale, Z. A., and N. H. Gale. 1982. "The Sources of Mycenaean Silver and Lead." *JFA* 9: 467–85.

Strauss, J. 1986. "The Theory and Comparative Statics of Agricultural Household Models: A General Approach." In I. Singh, L. Squire, and J. Strauss, eds., *Agricultural Household Models: Extensions, Applications, and Policy*, 71–91. Baltimore: The Johns Hopkins University Press.

Strøm, I. 1992. "Evidence from the Sanctuaries." In G. Köpcke and I. Tokumaru, eds., *Greece between East and West: 10th–8th Centuries B.C.*, 46–60. Mainz: Philipp von Zabern.

Strong, D. E. 1966. *Catalogue of the Carved Amber in the Department of Greek and Roman Antiquities*. London: Trustees of the British Museum.

Stubbings, F. M. 1951. *Mycenaean Pottery from the Levant*. Cambridge: Cambridge University Press.

Stucchi, S. 1984a. "Die archaischen griechischen Vasen und die Kyrenaika: Importe, Imitationen und Einflüsse–ein Überblick." In H.A.G. Brijder, ed., *Ancient Greek and Related Pottery*, 139–43. Amsterdam: Allard Pierson Museum.

—. 1984b. "I vasi greci arcaici e la Cirenaica: importazioni, imitazione ed influenze." *RendLinc*, ser. 8, 39: 161–71.

Stucky, R. 1981. "Eine bronzene Wandapplike aus Kreta." *AA* 431–39.

Studniczka, F. 1891. "Archaisches Thonrelief der Sammlung Santangelo." *RM* 6: 253–57.

—. 1928. "Ein frühgriechischer Bronzekopf in Karlsruhe." In *Antike Plastik: Walther Amelung zum sechzigsten Geburtstag*, 245–54. Berlin: Walter de Gruyter.

Sundwall, J. 1943. *Die älteren italischen Fibeln*. Berlin: Walter de Gruyter.

Svennilson, I. 1954. *Growth and Stagnation in the European Economy*. Geneva: United Nations Commission for Europe.

Symenoglou, S. 1985. *The Topography of Thebes: From the Bronze Age to Modern Times*. Princeton: Princeton University Press.

Sznycer, M. 1979. "L'inscription phénicienne de Tekke près de Knossos." *Kadmos* 18: 89–94.

Täckholm, V. 1956. *Student's Flora of Egypt*. Cairo: Anglo-Egyptian Bookshop.

Tadmor, H. 1975. "Assyria and the West: The Ninth Century and Its Aftermath." In H. Goedicke and J.J.M. Roberts, eds., *Unity and Diversity: Essays in the History, Literature, and Religion of the Ancient Near East*, 36–48. Baltimore: The Johns Hopkins University Press.

Talbert, R.J.A., ed. 1985. *Atlas of Classical History*. London: Croom Helm.

Taylour, W. 1958. *Mycenaean Pottery in Italy and Adjacent Areas*. Cambridge: Cambridge University Press.

Technau, W. 1929. "Griechische Keramik im samischen Heraion." *AM* 54: 6–64.

Tenenti, A. 1959. *Naufrages, corsaires et assurances maritimes à Venise 1592–1609*. Paris: Service d'Edition et de Vente des Publications de l'Education Nationale.

Themelis, P. G. 1983. "Die Nekropolen von Lefkandi-Nord auf Euboea." In S. Deger-Jalkotzy, ed., *Griechenland, die Agäis und die Levant während der "Dark Ages" vom 12. bis zum 9. Jhn. v. Chr.*, 145–60. Vienna: Österreichischen Akademie der Wissenschaften.

Theophanides, B. A. 1956. "Ναὸς Ἥρας Σαμίας ἐν Κυδωνίᾳ Κρήτης." *ArchEph* 218–24.

Thureau-Dangin, F. 1931. "Vocabulaires de Ras-Shamra." *Syria* 12: 225–66.

Thureau-Dangin, F., A. Barrois, G. Dossin, and M. Dunand. 1931. *Arslan-Tash, Atlas*. Paris: Librairie Orientaliste Paul Guethner.

Touchais, G. 1979. "Chronique des fouilles et découvertes archéologiques en Grèce en 1978." *BCH* 103: 527–615.

Townsend, R. M. 1993. *The Medieval Village Economy*. Princeton: Princeton University Press.

—. 1994. "Risk and Insurance in Village India." *Econometrica* 62: 539–91.

Trigger, B. G. 1978. *Time and Tradition: Essays in Archaeological Interpretation*. New York: Columbia University Press.

Tsipopoulou, M. 1978. "Πρωτογεωμετρικά καὶ γεωμετρικά αγγεία από τή συλλογή Κ. καὶ Μ. Μητσοτάκη." *ArchDelt* A 33: 146–67.

—. 1987. "Κοριθική κεραμεική στην Ανατολική Κρήτη κατά τις φάσεις Υστερη Γεωμετρική καὶ Πρώιμι Ανατολίζουσα." *CretChron* 27: 262–82.

—. 1990. "Ceramica de periodo subminoico geometrici ad orientalizzante in Creta orientale." *Seminari, Consiglio Nazionale della Ricerche-Instituto per gli Studi Miceni ed Egeo-Anatolici* 138–44.

Tsipopoulou, M., and L. Vagnetti. 1995. *Achladia: Scavi e recerche della Missione Greco-Italiana in Creta orientale (1991–1993)*. Incunabula Graeca 97. Rome: Gruppo Editoriale Internazionale.

Tubb, J. N. 1988. "The Role of the Sea Peoples in the Bronze Industry of Palestine/Transjordan in the Late Bronze-Early Iron Age." In J. Curtis, ed., *Bronzeworking Centres of Western Asia, c. 1000–539 B.C.*, 251–70. London: Kegan Paul.

Tzedakis, Y. 1964. "Ἀρχαιοντητες καὶ μνῆμεια δυτικής Κρήτης." *ArchDelt* 24 B, pt. 2: 428–36.

—. 1971. "Ἀρχαιοντητες καὶ μνῆμεια δυτικής Κρήτης." *ArchDelt* 26 B, pt. 2: 508–17.

—. 1979. "Cypriot 'Influences' on the Geometric Pottery of Western Crete." In *Acts of the International Archaeological Symposium "Relations between Cyprus and Crete, ca. 2000–500 B.C.,"* 192–98. Nicosia: Department of Antiquities, Cyprus.

Tzedakis, Y., S. Chryssoulaki, Y. Venieri, and M. Avgouli. 1990. "Les routes minoennes: Le route de Coirovmamore" et la controlê des communications." *BCH* 114: 43–62.

Tzedakis, Y., S. Chryssoulaki, S. Voutsaki, and Y. Venieri. 1989. "Les routes minoennes: Rapport préliminaire, défense de la circulation ou circulation de la défense?" *BCH* 113: 43–75.

Tzedakis, Y., and A. Kanta. 1978. *Καστέλλι Χανιῶν: Ἀναλυτική μελέτη τῆς κερμεικῆς ἀπό τή στρωματογραφηένη ταφρο Β καί τό πεγάδι.* Incunabula Graeca 66. Rome: Edizione dell'Ateneo and Bizzarri.

Uphill, E. 1984. "User and his Place in Egypto-Minoan History." *BICS* 31: 213.

Ure, P. N. 1934. *Aryballoi and Figurines from Rhitsona in Boeotia.* Cambridge: Cambridge University Press.

—. 1946. "Ring Aryballoi." *Hesperia* 15: 38–50.

Vagnetti, L. 1970. "I Micenei in Italia: La documentazione archeologica." *PP* 25: 359–80.

—. 1980. "Appendix II: Mycenaean Imports in Central Italy." In E. Peruzzi, *Mycenaeans in Early Latium*, Incunabula Graeca 75, 151–67. Rome: Edizioni dell'Ateneo and Bizzarri.

—, ed. 1982. *Magna Grecia e mondo miceneo: Nuovi documenti.* Taranto: Istituto per la storia e l'archeologia della Magna Grecia.

—. 1985. "Late Minoan III Crete and Italy: Another View." *PP* 220: 29–33.

—. 1989. "A Sardinian Askos from Crete." *BSA* 84: 354–60.

Vagnetti, L., and R. E. Jones. 1988. "Towards the Identification of Local Mycenaean Pottery in Italy." In E. B. French and K. A. Wardle, eds., *Problems in Greek Prehistory*, 335–48. Bristol: Bristol Classical Press.

van Andel, T. H. 1987. "The Landscape." In T. H. van Andel and S. B. Sutton, *Landscape and People of the Franchthi Region. Excavations at Franchthi Cave, Greece*, fasc. 2: 3–62. Bloomington: Indiana University Press.

van Andel, T. H., and C. N. Runnels. 1987. *Beyond the Acropolis.* Stanford: Stanford University Press.

van Andel, T. H., C. N. Runnels, and K. O. Pope. 1986. "Five Thousand Years of Land Use and Abuse in the Southern Argolid, Greece." *Hesperia* 55: 103–28.

Van de Moortel, A. 1994. "Graffito de bateau de l'âge du bronze à Malià." *BCH* 118: 389–97.

Van Doorninck, F. H. 1982. "Protogeometric Longships and the Introduction of the Ram." *IJNA* 11: 277–86.

Vanschoonwinkel, J. 1991. *L'Égée et la Méditerranée Orientale à la fin du deuxième millénaire: Témoinages archéologiques et sources écrites.* Archaeologica Transatlantica 9. Louvain-la-Neuve, Belgium: Art and Archaeology Publications, Collège Érasme.

Varoufakis, G. J. 1982. "The Origin of Mycenaean and Geometric Iron on the Greek Mainland and in the Aegean Islands." In J. D. Muhly, R. Maddin, and V. Karageorghis, eds., *Early Metallurgy in Cyprus, 4000–500 B.C.,* 315–24. Nicosia: Pierides Foundation.

Veenhof, K. R. 1972. *Aspects of Old Assyrian Trade and Its Terminology.* Leiden: E. J. Brill.

Vegas, M. 1989. "Archaische und mittelpunische Keramik aus Karthago." *RM* 96: 209–65.

—. 1992. "Carthage: La ville archaïque. Céramique d'importation de la période du géométrique récent." In *Livras*, Collection de l'École française de Rome 166, 181–89. Rome: École française de Rome.

Vercoutter, J. 1954. *Essai sur les relations entre égyptiens et préhellènes.* L'Orient Ancien Illustré 6. Paris: Stanislas Lassalle.

—. 1956. *L'Egypte et le monde égéen préhellénique.* Cairo: L'Institut Français d'Archeologie Orientale.

Verdelis, N. M. 1958. *Ο Προτογεομετρικός Ρυθμός τῆς Θεσσαλίας.* Βιβλιοθήκη τῆς ἐν Ἀθήναις Ἀρχαιολογικῆς Ἑταιρείας 42. Athens: Ἀθήναις Ἀρχαιολογικὴ Ἑταιρεία.

Verlinden, C. 1984. *Les statuettes anthropomorphes crétoises en bronze et en plomb, du IIIe millénaire au VIIe siècle av. J.-C.* Archaeologica Transatlantica 4. Louvain-la-Neuve: Institut Supérieur d'Archéologie et d'Histoire de l'Art, Collège Érasme.

Vermeule, E. 1972. *Greece in the Bronze Age.* 2d ed. Chicago: University of Chicago Press.

—. 1985. Review of *Pyla-Kokkinokremos: A Late 13th Century B.C. Fortified Settlement in Cyprus*, by V. Karageorghis and M. Demas. *AJA* 89: 359–60.

Vermeule, E., and F. Z. Wolsky. 1990. *Toumba tou Skourou: A Bronze Age Potters' Quarter on Morphou Bay in Cyprus.* Cambridge, Mass.: Harvard University Press.

Vichos, Y. 1996. "Point Iria Wreck (1993) II: The Stone Anchors." *ENALIA Annual 1992,* 4: 17–20.

Vickery, K. F. 1936. *Food in Early Greece.* Illinois Studies in the Social Sciences 70. Urbana: University of Illinois.

Vincent, L. H. 1924a. "Chronique, l'année archéologique 1923 en Palestine: 3. Les fouilles américaines de Beisân." *RBibl* 33: 424–28.

—. 1924b. "Le nouvel hypogée de Byblos et l'hypogée royal de Gézer (suite 1): 1." *RBibl* 33: 161–85.

Vincentelli, L., and F. Tiradritti. 1986. "La Presenze egea in Egitto." In M. Marazzi, S. Tusa, and L. Vagnetti, eds., *Traffici micenei nel Mediterraneo: problemi storici e documentazione archeologia,* Magna Graecia 3, 327–34. Taranto: Istituto per la Storica e l'Archeologia della Magna Grecia.

Wace, A.J.B. 1921–22. "Excavations at Mycenae: X. The Cyclopean Terrace Building." *BSA* 25: 403–7.

Wachsmann, A. *Aegeans in the Theban Tombs.* OLA 20. Leuven: Peeters, 1987.

Wachsmann, S., and K. Raveh. 1981. "An Underwater Salvage Excavation near Kibbutz ha-Hotrim, Israel." *IJNA* 10: 160.

—. 1984. "Concerning a Lead Ingot Fragment from ha-Hotrim, Israel." *IJNA* 13: 169–76.

Walbank, F. W. 1967. *A Historical Commentary on Polybius II: Commentary on Books VII–XVIII.* Oxford: Clarendon.

Waldbaum, J. C. 1978. *From Bronze to Iron: The Transition from the Bronze Age to the Iron Age in the Eastern Mediterranean.* SIMA 54. Göteborg: Paul Åströms Förlag.

—. 1982. "Bimetallic Objects from the Eastern Mediterranean and the Question of the Dissemination of Iron." In J. D. Muhly, R. Maddin, and V. Karageorghis, eds., *Early Metallurgy in Cyprus, 4000–500 B.C.,* 325–50. Nicosia: Pierides Foundation and Department of Antiquities, Cyprus.

Waldstein, C. 1905. *The Argive Heraeum.* Vol. 2, *Terra-Cotta Figurines, Terra-Cotta Reliefs, Vases and Vase Fragments, Bronzes, Engraved Stones, Gems, and Ivories, Coins, Egyptian, or Graeco-Egyptian Objects.* Boston: Houghton Mifflin.

Walker, T. S., and N. S. Jodha. 1986. "How Small Farm Households Adapt to Risk." In P. Hazell, C. Pomareda, and A. Valdéz, eds., *Crop Insurance for Agricultural Development: Issues and Experience,* 17–34. Baltimore: The Johns Hopkins University Press.

Walker, T. S., and J. G. Ryan. 1990. *Village and Household Economies in India's Semi-Arid Tropics.* Baltimore: The Johns Hopkins University Press.

Wallace, M. B. 1970. "Early Greek Proxenoi." *Phoenix* 24: 189–208.

Wallenstein, K. 1971. *Korinthische Plastik der 7. und 6. Jahrhunderts vor Christus.* Bonn: Herbert Grundmann.

Wallinga, H. T. 1964. "Nautika (I): The Unit of Capacity for Ancient Ships." *Mnemosyne* 17: 1–40.

—. 1993. *Ships and Sea-Power before the Great Persian War: The Ancestry of the Ancient Trireme.* Mnemosyne suppl. 121. Leiden: E. J. Brill.

Walter, H. 1959. "Ein samischer Elfenbeinjüngling." *AM* 74: 43–47.

—. 1963. "Die Ausgrabung im Heraion von Samos (1952–1962)." *ArchDelt* 18 B, pt. 2: 286–96.

Walton, F. R., trans. 1957. Diodorus Siculus, *Library of History.* Vol. 11, *Fragments of Books XXI–XXXII.* Loeb Classical Library. Cambridge, Mass.: Harvard University Press.

Warburton, D. A. 1997. *State and Economy in Ancient Egypt: Fiscal Vocabulary of the New Kingdom.* Orbis Biblicus et Orientalis 151. Fribourg, Switzerland: University Press.

Ward, W. A. 1994. Review of *Centuries of Darkness,* by P. James. *AJA* 98: 362–63.

Warren, P. 1969. *Minoan Stone Vases.* Cambridge: Cambridge University Press.

—. 1991. "A Merchant Class in Bronze Age Crete? The Evidence of Egyptian Stone Vases from the City of Knossos." In N. H. Gale, ed., *Bronze Age Trade in the Mediterranean,* SIMA 90, 295–301. Jonsered: Paul Åströms Förlag.

Watrous, L. V. 1982. *Lasithi: A History of Settlement on a Highland Plain in Crete.* Hesperia suppl. 18. Princeton: American School of Classical Studies at Athens.

—. 1985. "Late Bronze Age Kommos: Imported Pottery as Evidence for Foreign Contact." In J. W. Shaw and M. C. Shaw, eds., *A Great Minoan Triangle in Southcentral Crete: Kommos, Hagia Triada, Phaistos,* Scripta Mediterranea 6: 7–18.

—. 1987. "The Role of the Near East in the Rise of the Cretan Palaces." In R. Hägg and N. Marinatos, eds., *The Function of the Minoan Palaces: Proceedings of the Fourth International Symposium at the Swedish Institute in Athens, 10–16 June 1984*, Skrifter Utgivna av Svenska Institutet i Athen, 4 , 35, pp. 65–70. Stockholm: Paul Åströms Förlag.

—. 1989. "A Preliminary Report on Imported 'Italian' Wares from the Late Bronze Age Site of Kommos on Crete." *SMEA* 27: 69–79.

—. 1992. *Kommos*. Vol. 3, *The Late Bronze Age Pottery*. Princeton: Princeton University Press.

—. 1995. "Crete and Egypt in the Seventh Century B.C.: Temple A at Prinias." Paper presented at the Colloquium on Post-Minoan Crete. London: British School at Athens and Institute of Archaeology, University College London, November 10–11.

Watrous, L. V., D. Xatzi-Villianou, K. Pope, N. Maurtzas, J. Shay, C. T. Shay, J. Bennet, D. Tsoungarakis, E. Angelomati-Tsoungarakis, C. Vallianos, and H. Blitzer. 1993. "A Survey of the Western Mesara Plain in Crete: Preliminary Report of the 1984, 1986, and 1987 Field Seasons." *Hesperia* 62: 191–248.

Webb, V. 1978. *Archaic Greek Faience*. Warminster: Aris and Phillips.

Wees, H. van. 1992. *Status Warriors: War, Violence and Society in Homer and History*. Amsterdam: J. C. Gieben.

Weill, R. 1980. *Phoenicia and Western Asia to the Macedonian Conquest*. Translated by E. F. Row. Chicago: Ares. (Originally published 1940, London: Harrap.)

Weinberg, S. S. 1941. "What Is Protocorinthian Geometric Ware?" *AJA* 45: 30–44.

—. 1943. *Corinth*. Vol. 7, 1: *The Geometric and Orientalizing Pottery*. Cambridge, Mass.: Harvard University Press.

Weiner, A. B. 1992. *Inalienable Possessions: The Paradox of Keeping-While-Giving*. Berkeley: University of California Press.

Weinstein, J. M. 1981. "The Egyptian Empire in Palestine: A Reassessment." *BASOR* 241: 1–28.

—. 1992. "The Collapse of the Egyptian Empire in the Southern Levant." In W. A. Ward and M. S. Joukowsky, eds., *The Crisis Years: The 12th Century B.C.: From beyond the Danube to the Tigris*, 146–47. Dubuque, Iowa: Kendall/Hunt.

Weiss, H. 1997. "Archaeology in Syria." *AJA* 101: 97–148.

Wells, B., C. Runnels, and E. Zangger. 1990. "The Berbati-Limnes Archaeological Survey. The 1988 Season." *OpAth* 18: 207–38.

—. 1993. "In the Shadow of Mycenae." *Archaeology* 46: 54–58, 63.

Wells, P. S. 1980. *Culture Contact and Culture Change: Early Iron Age Central Europe and the Mediterranean World*. Cambridge: Cambridge University Press.

—. 1983. *Rural Economy in the Early Iron Age: Excavations at Hascherkeller, 1978–1981*. American School of Prehistoric Research Bulletin 36. Cambridge, Mass.: Peabody Museum, Harvard University.

—. 1984. *Farms, Villages, and Cities: Commerce and Urban Origins in Late Prehistoric Europe*. Ithaca, N.Y.: Cornell University Press.

—. 1992. "Crisis Years? The 12th Century B.C. in Central and Southeastern Europe." In W. A. Ward and M. S. Joukowsky, eds., *The Crisis Years: The 12th B.C.: From beyond the Danube to the Tigris*, 31–39. Dubuque, Iowa: Kendall/Hunt.

Wente, E. F. 1973. "The Report of Wenamon." In W. K. Simpson, ed., *The Literature of Ancient Egypt*, 2d ed. 142–55. New Haven: Yale University Press.

Wente, E. F., and C. C. Van Siclen. 1976. "A Chronology of the New Kingdom." In *Studies in Honor of George R. Hughes*, SAOC 39, 217–61. Chicago: Oriental Institute, University of Chicago.

West, M. L., trans. 1988. Hesiod, *Works and Days*. Oxford: Oxford University Press.

Westerberg, K. 1983. *Cypriot Ships from the Bronze Age to c. 500 B.C.* SIMA-PB 22. Göteborg: Paul Åströms Förlag.

White, D. 1984. *The Extramural Sanctuary of Demeter and Persephone at Cyrene, Libya*. Vol. 1, *Background and Introduction to Excavations*. Philadelphia: The University Museum, University of Pennsylvania.

White, H., trans. 1912. Appian, *Roman History*. Vol. 2, *Books VIII.2–XII*. Loeb Classical Library. London: William Heinemann.

Whitley, J. 1991a. "Social Diversity in Dark Age Greece." *BSA* 86: 341–65.

—. 1991b. *Style and Society in Dark Age Greece: The Changing Face of a Pre-Literate Society 1100–700 B.C.* Cambridge: Cambridge University Press.

Whittlesey, J. H., J. W. Myers, and C. C. Allen. 1977. "The Whittlesey Foundation 1976 Field Season." *JFA* 4: 181–96.

Wide, S. 1899. "Geometrische Vasen aus Griechenland." *JdI* 14: 26–43.

Wiener, M. H. 1987. "Trade and Rule in Palatial Crete." In R. Hägg and N. Marinatos, eds., *The Function of the Minoan Palaces*, Acta Instituti Atheniensis Regni Sueciae, Series in 4°, 35, 261–67. Stockholm: Paul Åströms Förlag.

—. 1991. "The Nature and Control of Minoan Foreign Trade." In N. H. Gale, ed., *Bronze Age Trade in the Mediterranean*, SIMA 90, 325–50. Jonsered: Paul Åströms Förlag.

Wilford, J. N. 1993. "Ancient Greek Shipwreck Found: Cargo Was Fine Wine." *The New York Times*, April 11, C1.

Willemsen, F. 1957. *Dreifusskessel von Olympia: Alte und neue Funde*. OlForsch III. Berlin: Walter de Gruyter.

Willetts, R. F. 1965. *Ancient Crete: A Social History from Early Times until the Roman Occupation*. London: Routledge and Kegan Paul.

Williams, C. K. 1970. "Corinth, 1969: Forum Area." *Hesperia* 39: 1–39.

—. 1979. "Corinth, 1978: Forum Southwest." *Hesperia* 48: 105–44.

—. 1982. "The Early Urbanization of Corinth." *ASAtene*, n.s. 44: 9–19.

Williamson, J. G. 1974. *Late Nineteenth-Century American Development: A General Equilibrium History*. Cambridge: Cambridge University Press.

Wilson, J. A. 1958. "The Journey of Wen-Amon to Phoenicia." In J. B. Pritchard, ed., *The Ancient Near East*, 1: 16–24. Princeton: Princeton University Press. (Originally published 1955, in J. B. Prichard, ed., *Ancient Near Eastern Texts Relating to the Old Testament*, 2d ed., 25–29. Princeton: Princeton University Press.)

Winter, I. J. 1976. "Phoenician and North Syrian Ivory Carving in Historical Context." *Iraq* 38: 1–25.

—. 1981. "Is There a South Syrian Style of Ivory Carving in the Early First Millennium B.C.?" *Iraq* 43: 101–30.

—. 1983. "Carchemish Ša Kišad Puratti." *AnatSt* 33: 190–94.

—. 1988. "North Syria as a Bronzeworking Centre in the Early First Millennium: Luxury Commodities of Home and Abroad." In J. Curtis, ed., *Bronzeworking Centres of Western Asia, c. 1000–539 B.C.*, 193–225. London: Kegan Paul.

Wiseman, D. J. 1975 "Assyria and Babylonia c. 1200–1000 B.C." *CAH* II, pt. 2, 3d ed.: 443–81.

Wiseman, J. 1978. *The Land of the Ancient Corinthians*. SIMA 50. Göteborg: Paul Åströms Förlag.

Wood, E. M. 1989. *Peasant-Citizen and Slave: The Foundations of Athenian Democracy*. Corrrected paperback edition. New York: Verso.

Wood, J. W., G. R. Milner, H. C. Harpending, and K. M. Weiss. 1992. "The Osteological Paradox: Problems of Inferring Prehistoric Health from Skeletal Remains." *CurrAnth* 33: 343–58.

Woodward, A. M. 1927. "Archaeology in Greece, 1926–27." *JHS* 47: 234–63.

Woodward, J. M. 1927–28. "Excavations at Sparta, 1924–25. III. Terracottas, Plastic Vases, Reliefs." *BSA* 29: 75–107.

Wotzka, H.-P. 1990. "The Abuse of User." *BSA* 85: 449-53.

Wright, H. E. 1972. "Vegetation History." In W. A. McDonald and G. R. Rapp, eds., *The Minnesota Messenia Expedition: Reconstructing a Bronze Age Regional Environment*, 188–99. Minneapolis: University of Minnesota Press.

Xanthoudides, S. A. 1907. "Ἐκ Κρήτης." *ArchEph* 141–86.

Yakar, J. 1993. "Anatolian Civilization Following the Disintegration of the Hittite Empire: An Archaeological Appraisal." *TelAviv* 20: 3–28.

Yalouris, N. 1960. "Mykenische Bronzeschutzwaffen." *AM* 75: 42–67.

Yellin, J. 1989. "The Origin of Some Cypro-Geometric Pottery from Tel Dor." *IEJ* 39: 219–27.

Yoffee, N. 1993. "Too Many Chiefs? (or, Safe Texts for the '90s)." In N. Yoffee and A. Sherratt, eds., *Archaeological Theory: Who Sets the Agenda?* 60–78. Cambridge: Cambridge University Press.

Yon, M. 1970. "Sur une représentation figurée chypriote." *BCH* 94: 311–17.

—. 1971. *Salamine de Chypre II. La tombe T. I. du XIe s. av. J.-C.* Paris: E. de Boccard.

—. 1979. "Chypre et la Crète au XIe s." In *Acts of the International Archaeological Symposium "Relations Between Cyprus and Crete, ca. 2000–500 B.C.,"* 241–48. Nicosia: Department of Antiquities, Cyprus.

—. 1985. "Mission archéologique françoise de Salamine: La ville bilan 1964–1984." In V. Karageorghis, ed., *Archaeology in Cyprus 1960–1985*, 202–18. Nicosia: A. G. Leventis Foundation.

—. 1987. "Le royaume de Kition." In E. Lipiński, ed., *Phoenicia and the East Mediterranean in the*

First Millennium B.C., Orientalia Lovaniensia Analecta 22, Studia Phoenicia 5, 357–74. Leuven: Peeters.

—. 1992. "The End of Ugarit." In W. A. Ward and M. S. Joukowsky, eds., *The Crisis Years: The 12th Century B.C.: From beyond the Danube to the Tigris,* 111–22. Dubuque, Iowa: Kendall/Hunt.

Yon-Calvet, M. 1973. "La fin de l'epoque mycénienne a l'est de Chypre et son heritage géométrique." In *Acts of the International Archaeological Symposium "The Mycenaeans in the Eastern Mediterranean,"* 295–302. Nicosia: Department of Antiquities, Cyprus.

Young, D. 1965. "Some Puzzles about Minoan Woolgathering." *Kadmos* 4: 111–22.

Young, G. M. 1938. "Archaeology in Greece 1937–1938." *JHS* 58: 217–39.

Young, R. S. 1967. "A Bronze Bowl in Philadelphia." *JNES* 26: 145–54.

Zangger, E. 1994. "Landscape Changes around Tiryns during the Bronze Age." *AJA* 98: 189–212.

Zapheiropoulos, N. E. 1973. "'Ανασκαφὴ Σελλάδας Θήρας." *Prakt* 121–26.

—. 1974. "'Ανασκαφὴ Σελλάδας Θήρας." *Prakt* 194–200.

—. 1976. "'Ανασκαφὴ Σελλάδας Θήρας." *Prakt* 330–33.

Zettler, R. L. 1992. "Twelfth Century B.C. Babylonia: Continuity and Change." In W. A. Ward and M. S. Joukowsky, eds., *The Crisis Years: The 12th Century B.C.: From beyond the Danube to the Tigris,* 174–81. Dubuque, Iowa: Kendall/Hunt.

Ziebarth, E.G.L. 1929. *Beitrage zur Geschichte des Seeraubs und Seehandels im alten Griechenland.* Hamburg: Friederichsen, de Gruyter.

Zieman, H. C., and R. G. Wetzel. 1980. "Productivity in Seagrasses: Methods and Rates." In R. C. Phillips and C. P. McRoy, eds., *Handbook of Seagrass Biology: An Ecosystem Perspective,* 87–116. New York: Garland STPM.

Zimansky, P. E. 1985. *Ecology and Empire: The Structure of the Urartian State.* SAOC 41. Chicago: Oriental Institute, University of Chicago.

Zimmerman, J.-L. 1989. *Les chevaux de bronze dans l'art géométrique grec.* Mainz: Philipp von Zabern.

Zimmern, A. 1931. *The Greek Commonwealth.* 5th ed. New York: Oxford University Press.

INDEX